MW01128180

The assistance of the following is acknowledged. They were either formally interviewed for this book or contributed opinions, personal recollections or anecdotes.

Evelyn Aguilera (Cordisco), David Armour, John Barber, David Barnes, Peter Bakstansky, Peter Bartko, Geoff Bell, Nigel Bell, Peter Benjamin, Bill Best, Krishna Biltoo, Paul Blank, Teddy Boutrop, Andrew Brodie, Stephen Butcher, Norma Carter, Julian Childs, John Christopherson, Martin Church, Barry Clark, Michael Cooling, Rosemarie Corscadden, Andrew Delaney, Michael Dodgson, William Dunn, Nick Dyne, John Entwisle, Claude Erbsen, Bob Etherington, Jonathan 'Jonny' Fitzgerald, Sir Ian Fraser (deceased), Pam Friedberg, Anne Gable, Peter Gagan, John Gunn, Frank Hawkins, Roger Hawkins, Ian Hillier-Brook, Neil Hirsch, Julie Holland, Peter Howse, Ray Hubbard, JoAnn Hull, John Hull, Christopher Hume, Mary Patestas (Ivaliotis), Martha Jessop ("M"), Sir Peter Job, Harold Leblang, George Levine, Peter Lomax, Gerald Long (deceased), Anne Long, John Lowe, Greg Manning, Lauren Manning (Butler), Maureen Marlowe, Alex McCallum, Jack McConville, James Mullally, Michael Nelson, Robert Nagel, Andrew Nibley, Sheila Nicholls, Patrick O'Sullivan, Charles (Chuck) Palmer, David Palmer, Victor Peeke, John Ransom, Steven Rappaport, Professor Donald Read, Michael Reilly, Daphne Renfrew, John Roberts, Ann Rostow, Elizabeth Rumbold (Moss), Scott Rumbold, David Russell, Tony Sabatini, Jack Scantlin, Fran Schreiber, Phil Siegel, Herbie Skeete, Nick Slater, Tony Smith, Annette Snape, Rick Snape (deceased), John Stephens, Phil Taylor, John Terranova, Peter V. Thomas, Rhodri Thomas, Dorry Tompsett, David Ure, Robert Van Roten, Victor Vurpillat, Debra Walton, Elizabeth Wade, Peter Wade, Roger Webb, Sir Denis Weatherstone (deceased), Angela Wilbrahim, Rosalyn Wilton, Linda Wong, Esther Zimet (deceased).

Along with these acknowledgements, I extend my respects to those who exercised the right to withhold their cooperation. If it had been someone else's book, I might have been among them. My respects do not however include the lady in Reuters' public relations office who sniffily declined to provide photographs of past executives on the grounds that Reuters had neither sponsored nor approved the book. So much for the idea of a free press.

To Scott
From Alex McCallom
8.11.2010

# TALES FROM THE
# SOUTH PIER

# TALES FROM THE SOUTH PIER

John Jessop

ATHENA PRESS
LONDON

TALES FROM THE SOUTH PIER
Copyright © John Jessop 2008

All rights reserved

No part of this book may be reproduced in any form
by photocopying or by any electronic or mechanical means
including information storage or retrieval systems
without permission in writing from both the copyright
owner and the publisher of this book.

ISBN: 978 1 84748 167 2

First published 2008
ATHENA PRESS
Queen's House, 2 Holly Road
Twickenham TW1 4EG
United Kingdom

Printed for Athena Press

*To Martha my wife (and unpaid editor),*
*and*
*my daughter Sara—the 'Childperson'*

# Table of Contents

# Foreword

This book has been a long time coming, as those who urged me to write it kept reminding me. "You'd better get it out before half the people in it are dead," they admonished. I had a ready riposte: "What you really mean is I'd better get it out before *I'm* dead."

Here it is then, as requested, a personal recollection of events that announced the dawn of the era now universally recognized as the Information Age.

I like to think of it as an adventure story. Its heroes spring from a motley group of pioneering enterprises that helped to change the way we live by exploiting a revolution in the technology of communications. These companies, known rather prosaically as "market-data vendors," earned their living selling information about money to institutions that made their living trading money. They still do.

What follows—I should make clear from the start—is partly history but mostly memoir. A mighty useful word is memoir; it allows an author to blame errors of fact on fallible powers of recollection, a privilege not granted to historians. To underline the point, let me quote a line borrowed from a film I saw recently: "I'm not going to tell the story the way it happened. I'm going to tell it the way I remember it."

Seekers of *zeitgeist* need look no further than the underlying themes of the story—the sublime convergence in the second half of the twentieth century of information and money. Information provided the *zeit*, money the *geist*. Or maybe it was the other way around. These ancient and inseparable companions have enjoyed, throughout the ages of man, a close but unremarkable relation-ship, but some time in the early 1960s they ventured beyond mere companionship to embark on a torrid affair. It was a romance nurtured by a matchmaker of transcendental, almost mystical power: the brilliant new technology of communication.

The market-data industry's claim to fame—somewhat overshadowed, I feel, by New Age titans such as Bill Gates and Steve Jobs—is that it contributed in large measure to the electronic revolution that changed, as it continues to change, the way we live. The responsibility assumed by these so-called market-data vendors was to nurture the growth of a global financial trading community by providing a constant, life-sustaining drip-feed of essential up-to-the-second information—market quotes, statistics, analysis and news—into desktop computers programmed for the purpose. Such workstations now populate, indeed dominate, the offices of every banker, broker, speculator, arbitrageur, hedger, and professional investor on the planet.

So indispensable is this uninterrupted electronic infusion of intelligence that any break in the flow can bring global trading markets to a grinding halt (a fact demonstrated on those rare occasions when one of the key vendors suffers some kind of service breakdown). Such a level of reliance has resulted in a number of vendors making a great deal of money, more in fact than all but a handful of their well-heeled customers.

Some of the companies in question, such as Quotron, Telerate, and Bloomberg, were spawned by the technology revolution. Others, such as Reuters and Dow Jones, boasted origins dating back to the nineteenth century. We shall shortly make their acquaintance, for this is an account of how they, and a few others like them, came to shape, dominate and, in a much-favored modern term, globalize the markets they serve—or, in some sad cases, once served.

My chief qualification in writing it is that I'm ancient enough myself to have been present at the industry's creation. I spent over forty-odd years in the business, which embraces its childhood, adolescence, and adulthood.

My career in information began when I joined Reuters, then a famous news agency of colorful Victorian origins, though frankly one whose financial condition belied its fame. It had, in short, seen better days. I vaguely aspired to become—and for a short time became—a journalist. First, though, I had to "learn the trade" in time-honored fashion by fetching tea for the perpetually thirsty occupants of a wire-service newsroom.

What follows is based on that and subsequent experiences, including thousands of conversations held over the years with colleagues and customers. As for those events in which I did not personally participate, they have been researched to the best of my ability, including interviews with those who were willing to be quoted. (More than a few, surprisingly, were unwilling.)

I have tried to be fair to all concerned, lavishing praise where due, but applying a bit of stick where, in my opinion, deserved.

I should add in passing that the idea for the book emerged—aptly enough, you may think, after reading it—from a liberally liquefied lunch I shared with three friends, each a former executive with Reuters, at El Vino, a famous old Fleet Street watering hole once almost exclusively habituated by journalists, now almost entirely infested by lawyers. The only person present with an editorial background, I was duly "elected" to write it. My companions that day, as on innumerable occasions before and since, were John Lowe, Peter Thomas, and Herbie Skeete. Thanks a lot, fellas!

At the time of writing, the information business had traveled a long, long way from the first transmission, in 1844, of Samuel Finley Breese Morse, via his sensational electric telegraph and its eponymous code.

That signal event, if you'll pardon the pun, seems an appropriate way to open the story.

John Jessop
JessopJD@aol.com

# Prologue

To begin at the beginning, let's take a brief, whimsical excursion in time to the capital of the fledgling American republic of 1844.

We find ourselves, in this election year, aboard a Washington-bound train crammed with politicians and journalists making the 45-mile journey home from the Democratic Party's presidential nominating convention in Baltimore. An opinionated bunch at any time, our traveling companions on this occasion have a great deal about which to opine. Contrary to the widespread expectation of a routine convention and a preordained coronation of the favored candidate, they have instead witnessed a tumultuous affair, a display of party politics red in tooth and claw. It has delivered a presidential nominee of such obscurity that he lends his name to a new political coinage: the "dark horse."

The event opened quietly enough, the Democratic faithful showing up in confident anticipation of rubber-stamping the candidature of the popular front-runner, the former president, Martin Van Buren. But it didn't happen that way. Far from it. What Van Buren's supporters failed to appreciate was the extent to which "Little Van"—all five feet, five inches of him—had angered his party's most powerful faction, an unholy alliance of Dixiecrats and northern conservatives, by coming out against the annexation of Texas. The future of that territory is one of the burning political issues of the day.

In the event it is Van Buren who is burned. Arrogantly oblivious to the danger, he walks straight into an ambush—a last-minute motion tabled by his opponents mandating a two-thirds majority for victory on the first nominating ballot. The motion is easily adopted and, just as the dissidents have planned, Van Buren falls just short of the required votes for victory. The shock throws the convention into pandemonium, and the chaos persists as six more bruising rounds fail to produce a clear winner. As a result, exasperated convention managers are left with little choice but to throw the contest open to all-comers. From these largely anonymous and undistinguished ranks emerges a compromise candidate: one James K. Polk, a former governor of Tennessee, and a one-time speaker of the House of Representatives.

Some compromise! Polk is not only an ardent expansionist but also a slave-owning anti-abolitionist. He is, to boot, a dour and inscrutable fellow, hardly the kind of figure that proclaims a sure-fire election winner. But Polk is no political fool; in a conciliatory gesture to northern liberals, he promises to serve only one term (a pledge that he will keep) and wins the nomination by acclamation, in the process earning the distinction of becoming the first "dark horse" candidate in presidential history.

Polk's unexpected rise to prominence is the startling news our fellow passengers, the gentlemen of the press, are bursting to reveal to the expectant throng they know will be waiting at Washington station. A revelation there will certainly be, but it is the journalists who will be on the receiving end.

As our train squeals to a halt in Washington, a mob advances along the platform chanting "Hurrah for Polk" and waving improvised "Polk for President" banners. The reporters are astonished, as well they might be, for the message has mystifyingly arrived ahead of the messengers, an embarrassment known in the scribbling trade, then and ever since, as a scoop.

Nor is it the first scoop of its kind in this madcap election season. Two weeks earlier, during the Whig convention, also held in Baltimore, news of Henry Clay's nomination became the talk of Washington a full hour before the train came in. That episode, though as curious as its successor, attracted much less attention, probably because Clay had been a virtual shoo-in, and the report dismissed as nothing more than confident speculation put about by Clay's supporters.

But nobody could possibly have anticipated the Polk nomination. It is a genuine sensation, the biggest political upset in living memory. It is one that has consigned the bumptious, self-regarding Washington journalists to humiliating irrelevance.

The source is soon revealed. It is a sensational new medium of communication that uses electricity. Its inventor and promoter is a painter and arts professor of some renown, named Samuel Finley Breese Morse. His device is called an electro-magnetic telegraph, and he has just given a demonstration of it to an audience of bemused and skeptical congressmen in the basement of a federal building. They are stunned by news of Polk's nomination. Many are reluctant to believe it until the Baltimore train arrives with confirmation.

An instrument of almost mystical simplicity, Morse's telegraph allows the transmission of intelligence by interrupting an electric current flowing along a wire. Its significance is that it can deliver a signal almost instantaneously over distances measured in miles. The invention, if it works only half as effectively as Morse claims it will, can be nothing less than a sensation, for it is about to end centuries of reliance on horse and wheel, a means of communication essentially unaltered since Roman times.

Steam propulsion, it is true, has lately caused the wheels to turn faster— much faster—but not at unimaginable speeds. Consider, for example, the splendidly picturesque locomotive, with its high, pot-bellied smokestack, now puffing contentedly beside us at Washington station. A fine and unaccustomed sight it may be, but as an instrument for delivering information of a time-critical nature it has just been rendered obsolete. For somewhere back along the tracks over which we have just traveled at breakneck rates of up to forty miles per hour, we have been overtaken by an invisible impulse traveling close to the speed of light.

The human source of Professor Morse's news is a young business associate, Alfred Vail, who, prior to the convention, we now learn, had set up a transmitter a few miles outside Baltimore. As soon as runners from the convention hall informed him of Polk's nomination, Vail, using a code invented by Morse and himself, used a device resembling a horizontal door-knocker to tap out a series of short and long strokes—dots and dashes—to send a signal down the telegraph line to his mentor, Morse, in Washington.

What is immediately clear is that the electric telegraph will not merely change the habits of journalists but transform the communication dynamic of society at large. We have, in short, just witnessed what pundits in later years might call a Defining Moment.

And so it is hailed on this day, May 26, 1844.

"Unquestionably the greatest invention of the age," trumpets one New York newspaper, reflecting the unqualified enthusiasm of a profession which, despite having just suffered the embarrassment of becoming the telegraph's first victim, will soon embrace it as a grateful beneficiary. The public is no less captivated. Indeed, the expectation immediately takes root that the telegraph will serve as the catalyst to unite the scattered communities of the nascent American republic, already menaced by outbreaks of regionalism, most notably the growing threat of secession by the slave-owning southern states.

James Gordon Bennett, modern-thinking editor of the *New York Herald*, for one, has no doubt about the social and political potential of the new medium. The telegraph, he declares, will "blend into one homogeneous mass ... the whole population of the republic ... do more to guard against disunion than all the experienced, the most sagacious, and the most patriotic government, could accomplish."

High hopes indeed. And they reside for the time being entirely in the hands of the man responsible for administering today's electric shock: Samuel Morse.

Morse is no mystery man. He already enjoys a lofty reputation on both sides of the Atlantic as a portrait painter, as a member of the Royal Academy in Britain, and as the founder of its American equivalent, the National Academy of the Art of Design. Over the past decade, however, he has turned his attention exclusively and almost obsessively to science, and in particular to developing an electric telegraph. If obsession is as much a prerequisite for genius as talent, then Morse must be regarded as a genius. An admiring biographer, Carleton Mabee, a century later, entitles his book *The American Leonardo*.

This so-called Leonardo was born in Charlestown, Massachusetts, a suburb of Boston, in 1791, the first-born son of a Congregationalist minister whose family had been conspicuously well connected in New England society for several generations. Morse's paternal grandfather had been a president of Princeton University. His own father, Jedidiah, had also achieved fame, first as a map-maker—the so-called Father of American Geography—later as a staunch defender of Congregationalist orthodoxy against the liberalizing ravages of Unitarianism. Samuel inherited his father's religion, passion, and energy, and would greatly expand his proclivity for controversy.

Into one lifetime Morse packed four successful careers, as artist, teacher, inventor and businessman, not to mention a brief, unsuccessful foray into politics. In each vocation he contrived to generate bitter resentments. Even the founding of the National Academy represented a rebellion against the ruling artistic establishment of the day, presided over by the great painter John Trumbull. But it was Morse's venture into politics that was most inflammatory. As an attempt to exploit Morse's newly found fame, it failed dismally—most would say mercifully. Morse had been recruited by the Native American Party to run for mayor of New York City as an advocate of a number of extremist positions of the kind that might be embraced these days by the evangelistic Right. They included a demand for limits on immigration, blatantly aimed at Irish Catholics, and an enthusiastic endorsement of slavery. Morse was no sheep in wolf's clothing: he was every bit as radical as his party, perhaps more so. A devout Protestant upbringing no doubt explains the deep-seated animus against popery. As for slavery, Morse believed it to be ordained by God, a part of life's natural order.

After losing the election, Morse's political aspirations dissolved, and telegraphy began to consume his attention. This new interest emerged during the time he was living in Paris, earning a modest living by painting portraits of society figures. His evident inspiration was the published works of the French physicist, André-Marie Ampère.

Ampère's findings descended from a long line of experiments on the properties of electromagnetism, which had been all the rage in scientific circles since the turn of the century. Hans Christian Oersted, a Dane, had concluded in 1819, after deflecting a compass needle by running current through a wire, that electricity produced a magnetic field. William Sturgeon, in England, advanced the theory by discovering that an iron bar bent into the shape of a horseshoe and wrapped in wire would conduct electricity to form a powerful magnet. Joseph Henry, America's foremost practical scientist—and destined to become an important figure in Morse's ambitions—went further by using numerous small coils rather than a single large one and found a way of insulating them against loss of power. Henry even deduced in published papers that such a device could form the basis of a telegraphic device. A German mathematician, Karl Friedrich Gauss, had actually transmitted electric signals along a cable strung across the rooftops of the university town of Göttingen. The exercise may well have been witnessed by one of his young protégés, a bank clerk named Israel Beer Josaphat, later better known by his adopted name, Paul Julius Reuter. Of Mr. Reuter, more anon.

What Morse no doubt understood best from studying these experiments was that most of the scientists involved in them were more devoted to the cause of higher learning than to the generation of profit. This lack of business acumen was Morse's commercial opportunity. His destiny was resolved during a voyage from England to America in 1832 on the packet steamer *Sully*, during which Morse found himself among an erudite and social group of passengers anxious, or at least willing, to listen to his formative ideas about exploiting electricity. One in particular, a Dr. Charles Jackson of Boston, seemed eager to offer his own theories. One evening over dinner, so the story goes, the conversation turned to electromagnetism. Jackson discussed an experiment he himself had observed, noting that electricity could actually be seen along a wire whenever the circuit was broken. Morse's rejoinder to this became legendary: "If the presence of electricity can be made visible in any part of a circuit, I see no reason why intelligence may not be transmitted instantaneously by electricity."[1]

It was a significant remark, not so much in the scientific as in the legal sense. Morse would later claim, in filing for patents, that he had reached his conclusion independent of the many and varied experiments conducted by others. That dozens of scientists of renown had reached it before him is something of which Morse was either unaware, as he would later claim, or which he chose to ignore, which he would later deny. At any rate, so excited was he by his "discovery" that he spent the rest of the voyage locked in his cabin, feverishly scribbling ideas in notebooks that would later be produced to support his patent applications.

Morse's work found its commercial focus, and a derivative source, in the activities of a pair of British scientists-cum-businessmen, William Fothergill Cooke and Charles Wheatstone. Morse saw them as his principal rivals in a race to get his patents registered, and was disappointed to learn in 1837 that they had beaten him to it by receiving in London the world's first telegraphic patent. It was granted for a device called a needle galvanometer, in which electrical impulses passed through a coil caused five magnetized needles to point in directions indicating alphabetic codes. It was also the first device to market, being put to commercial use by the Great Western Railway between Paddington station and the village of West Drayton, a few miles to the west, for

[1] Carleton Mabee, *The American Leonardo*, Alfred A. Knopf Inc., 1943, p.149

sending messages about train arrivals. It was the earliest example of what would be an enduring symbiosis between the telegraph and the railroads.

The Cooke-Wheatstone triumph forced Morse to acknowledge his short-comings as a scientist. His response was to assemble a team of developers to form the basis of a business partnership. His first recruit was William Gale, a colleague of Morse's on the faculty of New York University. Gale's only contribution to the venture, but possibly its most important, was to introduce Morse to the great Joseph Henry.

Most of Morse's various partners came to regret their association with him, none more so than Henry. The practical aspects of Henry's pioneering work formed the essential basis of Morse's project, but Henry was a shining epitome of the rule that brilliant scientists usually make inept businessmen. His great mistake was to omit to file for patents covering his work, an oversight that Morse lost no time in correcting, though making sure to file them in his own name, with scant recognition of Henry's contribution. Only later, after the telegraph had become a commercial sensation, did Henry realize his naïveté and its financial consequences. For the rest of his life he nursed a deep resent-ment of his one-time protégé.

Morse seems to have been equally dismissive in his treatment of another associate, the previously encountered Alfred Vail, a brilliant engineering student at New York University, where he had become a devoted Morse disciple. Over time, his contribution to the telegraph, in practical terms, may have been as incalculable as Henry's. He perfected a compact transmission appliance—the familiar spring-loaded "door-knocker" transmitter—and took on much of the work devising Morse's eponymous dots-and-dashes user code. Vail also contributed to the venture considerable sums of money borrowed from his wealthy father. In time, like Henry, Vail would become disillusioned with Morse, and the lack of recognition of his role in the venture degenerated into a bitter legal dispute.

Among the more fortunate of Morse's partners may be counted Ezra Cornell, a plow designer and inventor, and a persuasive salesman for his own creations. Cornell was recruited to create a machine to excavate the trenches for telegraphic cables and to simultaneously lay the cables in them. His device worked well enough but trenching did not; electric current running through underground cables tended to leach out into the earth. As a result, trenching was replaced by an overhead system involving the stringing of wires along poles—another idea first put into practice by Cooke and Wheatstone—and insulated by glass "doorknobs," another brainwave from Cornell. Ezra Cornell used the fame from his work on the telegraph to make a fortune, much of which he donated to the founding of the university that bears his name.

By 1844, Morse had become a familiar, and derided, figure in the corridors of Congress as an energetic lobbyist for government funds for his telegraph. After a six-year campaign he was finally rewarded with a grant of $30,000 to build an experimental telegraphic line between Baltimore and Washington. Congress had originally favored a national semaphore system involving construction of hundreds of towers from which men would relay semaphore signals using flags or boards. The government had probably taken its cue from France, where such a system had been in official use since Napoleonic times. Skilled signalers could send short messages of up to twenty-five words about eighty miles in three minutes. The French semaphore was deployed mainly for military intelligence, but the government found other uses for it, notably the distribution of the winning number of the national lottery—perhaps the first known use of telegraphic communication for financial speculation.

Morse managed to wean Congress away from its odd devotion to semaphore. The argument, one of compelling logic even for myopic politicians, was that the communication needs for a country as vast as the United States could hardly be satisfied by armies of elevated flag-wavers strung across 3000 miles of hostile terrain. But to the very end, he had to fend off competing claims for Congressional funding, principally one for an exciting new science—or so many Congressmen believed it to be—called mesmerism. Morse's victory was later described by one political cynic as a triumph of magnetism over mesmerism.

One politician in particular, no stranger to cynicism himself, had made an essential contribution to Morse's success: F.O.J. Smith, the honorable senator from Maine, chairman of the Committee of Commerce, affectionately known to his colleagues as Fog, an ironical reflection of his intellectual vigor. Smith had long been an ardent advocate of the telegraph, and for good reason. Even as he was nudging his committee towards voting for the appropriation, he was securing a secret interest in Morse's company as a shareholder—a conflict of interest that evidently troubled neither him nor Morse. Later, having experienced the inevitable falling out with Morse, and having joined the ever-expanding list of litigants against him, Smith was bothered a great deal.

Morse may be dismissed, and has been, as no more than a scientific dabbler, a clever, self-serving promoter of the ideas of others. But there can be no doubting his qualities of imagination and persistence. However, such persistence always evolved into ruthlessness. The impulse to push aside those who had made crucial contributions to his success demeaned Morse while he was alive and undermined his reputation after his death.

Time now, however, to move on from the foibles of the man to the enduring consequences of his invention.

Sadly, the state of disunion of which James Gordon Bennett had spoken became the order of the day as tensions between the northern and southern states heightened rather than receded. If the telegraph could not bring harmony at home, perhaps it could abroad. Such hopes were raised in 1858— by which time America had installed some 50,000 miles of telegraph lines— with the laying of the first transatlantic cable. Exultant New Yorkers, not usually counted among the more gullible people on the planet, took to the streets in their thousands in riotous celebration, a response, one newspaper complained, that "displays all the extravagance of incipient delirium."

It was more, though, than merely an excuse for a party, and more than pride in an American technological triumph. It was a profound and almost desperate longing by Americans for more intimate contact with the Old World that so many of them had recently felt obliged to abandon. As a telegrapher in Halifax, Nova Scotia, the telegraph cable's North American landing point, plaintively wired an opposite number in Europe, "Please give some news for New York; they are mad for news." (New York would have to wait. For all the hoopla on both sides of the Atlantic, including a public exchange of messages between Queen Victoria and President Buchanan, the cable rarely worked properly, and within weeks of its completion failed altogether. Another eight years passed before a new and, this time, permanent link was established.)

If it did nothing else, the telegraph inevitably transformed both the character and economics of journalism. Long-winded pomposity, a hallmark of pre-telegraphic journalists, was rendered impractical for wired dispatches paid for by the word. What was now required was a crisp style with a frugal emphasis on facts: more stories, fewer words. Connectivity posed another problem: the expense of hiring far-flung correspondents, which proved beyond the means of even the well-heeled metropolitan newspapers, let alone the shoestring news sheets of one-horse towns. All of these new issues arose at a time when the public demand for news was rising fast. Major events, such as the 1846 war with Mexico, served to whet the appetite.

One solution to the problem of rising transmission costs was worked out by a group of six newspaper owners in New York. Although bitter rivals for circulation, they were drawn together by a common concern: the high cost of bringing European news into New York by telegraph from Halifax and Boston, the first two points of call for most transatlantic packet boats.

In May 1848, meeting in a back room on the premises of the *New York Sun*, they agreed to set aside their customary hostilities to form a syndicate "to procure foreign news by telegraph from Boston in common."[2] For the purposes of this document, they called themselves the Associated Press (AP). The AP found it expedient to sell this news to newspapers in Washington and Baltimore, and in time would be happy to distribute to any other newspaper wishing to be connected to the AP's expanding telegraphic network.

---

[2] Edwin Emery, *The Press and America*, Prentice-Hall Inc., 1962, p.255

In Europe, ancient barriers of language and custom offered less scope for such collaboration. Even so, the European telegraphic network, sponsored by governments as well as private interests, and less inhibited by distance, grew just as rapidly as its American counterpart. It did so despite political obstacles, including a less-than-ardent devotion among most European governments to the idea of a free press. Given that particular impediment, it is perhaps not surprising that the Continental telegraph owed its success not so much to a clamor for news among the reading public as to a growing demand in commercial circles for market news.

The continental European powers—which is to deliberately exclude the island nation sheltering behind its massive naval shield and a doctrine called Splendid Isolation—were scarcely less peaceable than the states of the Union, as the tumults of 1848, the so-called Year of Revolutions, demonstrated. But even authoritarian governments of a distinctly belligerent tendency managed for more than half a century to avoid waging war against each other, usually being too busy putting down domestic insurrections. As a result, they continued to trade with each other. This, the most significant consequence of the industrial revolution, may have been the most significant insurrection of all. As trade flourished, financial speculators proliferated, forming a new mercantile class. High-speed communication of commercial news by telegraph, in a volatile political climate, became their lifeline.

Banks and moneychangers opened shops in all the main European capitals, and trading markets sprang up everywhere. Arbitrageurs (the French spelling lent the term a degree of respectability) provided the vital market ingredient of liquidity. Cities vied with each other for the title of Entrepôt Capital of Europe. Ignoring formality and unrestrained by regulation, such markets were exchanges in name only. They were often no more than gentlemen's clubs convened on street corners or in ale houses and coffee shops.

In financial, as in political terms, Paris and Berlin soon dominated the continent, with Brussels acting as a useful bridge between the two. By 1850, the three cities were connected by the telegraph and formed a commercial axis. But even combined they were neither bigger nor more influential than the single, much reviled, much feared financial center across the Channel.

Trafalgar and Waterloo had made Britain the dominant world power, a position that was exploited in a brief imperial adventure that established dominion over a quarter of the world's population. The telegraph would be a further important adjunct to British imperialism, though in 1850 the line stopped at the English Channel, placing Britain at a temporary disadvantage in its access to European commercial intelligence.

But not for long.

In 1851, after several failed attempts, a cable was laid between Calais and

Dover. Its longevity was assured by the use of a new rubbery insulating material called gutta-percha, developed by the inventor Michael Faraday. Telegraphic news was about to become big business in Britain.

For one European institution, intelligence gathering and distribution, telegraph or no telegraph, was old hat. The merchant banking empire founded by Mayer Amschel Rothschild, a financial genius from the Jewish ghetto in Frankfurt, had formed itself into a ubiquitous network of agents, informers, and couriers scattered across Europe. It was, at its core, a discrete family business, and everywhere it was not so, it was defined instead by race. But over time, these Jewish connections opened up to those outside the faith, and the network became a less easily defined confederation of commercial interests, some partly created through Rothschild marriages, others by commercial expediency. However defined, the Rothschild network had become a formidable force in Europe, an intelligence network of immense influence derived from powerful personal connections in every capital.

Emperors, kings, princelings, electors, presidents, and prime ministers all had cause to seek the financial patronage of the Rothschilds. It was repaid with the utmost efficiency and discretion. There may be no better example of the confidence placed in the Rothschilds' ability to organize a complex financial deal in secret than that bestowed by the British government on Nathan Mayer Rothschild, founder of the London branch of the dynasty. Nathan, though he arrived in England speaking scarcely a word of English, was particularly adept as a communicator.

Somehow, through his network of correspondents, Nathan became the first man in England to receive news of Wellington's victory at Waterloo. He had a vested interest in the proceedings, having been the principal source of financing of Wellington's army in the campaigns against Napoleon in Spain and Portugal.

How Nathan came by the news twenty-four hours before anyone else became the subject of diverse and improbable legends, many patently absurd. One story, almost certainly fanciful, placed him at the very scene of the battle, his portly figure having supposedly been spotted astride a white charger on the fringes of the battlefield. Other tales had him in England, listening to messages from a clairvoyant, receiving a visit from a mysterious French envoy, and intercepting the news from an English yachtsman who had picked it up, serendipitously, before embarking from a French port. Take your pick.

The likeliest event is that he was in London, standing by to receive word from one of his couriers. Rothschild agents would certainly have been dispatched to Belgium to await developments and then to speed the news to London by any and all available means. What he did with the information is also a matter for conjecture. Tipping off the British government was one of them. As a biographer relates, "By whatever means he received the information, Nathan's first impulse was, naturally, to report the magnificent news to the Prime Minister and, despite the late hour, he hastened to Downing Street, only to be confronted by an imperious butler who informed him that Lord Liverpool had retired for the night and was not to be disturbed. Even in the morning, when the Rothschild message was delivered, His Lordship declined to believe something which ran counter to all his official intelligence. N.M., meanwhile, had obeyed his second impulse—to go down to the Exchange and invest heavily in government stock."[3]

So, another famous scoop—and what these days might be considered a blatant case of insider trading.

Mere mortals in the financial community, having no access to armies of agents or couriers or friends in high places, managed as best they could to stay in touch with the world. For them, the telegraph emerged as the great equalizer. What were largely missing were the messengers to exploit it—men who understood markets and the power of information to influence them.

Europe quickly fell under the dominion of three such men. The honor of being the first of his class fell to Charles-Louis Havas, a Frenchman, followed by Bernhard Wolff and Paul Julius Reuter, German Jews who—not coincidentally—had both worked briefly at the Havas agency in Paris. All three formed businesses motivated by profit, a distinction that separated them philosophically from their American counterpart, the Associated Press, which was a co-operative formed for reasons of economy and convenience. There would soon be another important difference. The European agencies quickly placed their emphasis on commercial news, to be sold to private clients as well as to newspapers.

Havas, a flamboyant, multilingual businessman, had a knack for cultivating government contacts. He claimed newspaper connections going back to Napoleonic times, when he had owned a stake in the leading national journal of its day, the *Gazette de France*. But his principal business interest—and the source of his early fortune—was the munitions industry: Havas had helped finance and equip Napoleon's army at Waterloo. Having picked the losing side, he was financially ruined. He reappeared, in a business context, two decades later, translating newspaper articles for a living.

Agence Havas opened for business in Paris in 1835, more than a decade before the telegraph, and in its early days it functioned as little more than a clipping service, a translator of foreign newspaper articles for the French press. Copy was conveyed to Paris by stagecoach or train. Carrier pigeons were also used occasionally, an idea Havas may have borrowed from Rothschild (although pigeons had been similarly used during and since Roman times). By

---

[3] Derek Wilson, *Rothschild: A Story of Wealth and Power*, Mandarin Press, 1988, p.58

the 1840s, Agence Havas had expanded from redistributing published copy to reporting original news, and with the arrival of the telegraph operated as a telegraphic news agency with a network of correspondents in the main European capitals. The benign early regime of Louis-Philippe tolerated a free press in France, and Havas enjoyed the patronage of several government departments as well as the enthusiasm of the flourishing Paris press.

Conditions being less liberal elsewhere on the continent, France became a magnet for Europe's political outcasts. Two of them, both refugees from Prussian authoritarianism, showed up at Havas looking for work. First came Bernhard Wolff, a physician by profession and market speculator by disposition. Shortly afterward he was joined by Paul Julius Reuter, a former bank clerk and bookseller. Neither could be described as radical. They, like thousands of others, had simply run afoul of excessive bureaucratic authority. Each was assigned to the Havas office near the Paris Bourse where they could hardly have failed to be impressed by the growing demand for commercial news. Before long, both headed back to Germany to strike out on their own. Reuter, back in the country of his birth, was the less successful of the two and shortly, on the advice of a friend, departed for London.

It is Reuter's story that we shall shortly take up.

# Parrots

"A Career in News with Opportunities for Overseas Travel."[1]

That eye-catching slogan—recalled as accurately as memory will allow—jumped out of the classified pages of a London evening newspaper in the late summer of 1959. Though typical of the hyperbole routinely deployed in a medium regarded by the capital's white-collared unemployed as their very own Last Chance Saloon, to an involuntary school dropout of seventeen, idling away his working days in a London bookshop notorious for paying breadline wages, it was a proposition too tantalizing to pass up.

The callow, book-peddling pauper was me.

Viewed from the perspective of the era now universally acknowledged as the Information Age, the year in question seems rooted in a time hardly less remote than the Iron Age.

In Britain, Prime Minister Harold Macmillan (himself a character who seemed to have wandered in from a bygone era) famously declared that we supposedly affluent Britons had "never had it so good"—a plausible enough premise to propel his rejuvenated Conservative Party to an impressive election victory. As if to confirm the now famous aphorism, news came out that the proportion of British households with television sets had soared in just four years from 40 percent to 70 percent. The telephone was a much less common appliance. My household, far from unique, shared a so-called party line with our next-door neighbors. As for the computer, it was then a sinister, room-sized monster attended by men in white coats, scarcely removed from the realm of science fiction.

In the wider world, Britain's post-war retreat from Empire had moved inexorably towards the sunset that was never supposed to occur, and for the most part in orderly fashion, the Union Jack being ceremoniously lowered with almost as palpable a sense of relief in London as in most of the newly liberated capitals. America, by way of contrast, was still constructing an empire—albeit with the consent of the governed—Alaska and Hawaii becoming that year, 1959, the 49th and 50th states of the Union. America's nemesis, Russia, meanwhile was busy creating its own Union, though of a very different kind, one in which the governed were not usually asked whether they consented or not.

---

[1] Harold Macmillan speech to Conservative Party rally, Bedford, 1957, July 20, BBC (also cited in Oxford Dictionary of Quotations)

Armed to the teeth with nuclear weapons, and ever more sophisticated means of launching them, the two superpowers confronted each other across a formidable European divide, memorialized by Winston Churchill as the Iron Curtain. Although the Cold War held an anxious world in its thrall, tensions eased temporarily in 1959 when the Soviet leader, Nikita Khrushchev, accepted an invitation by President Dwight D. Eisenhower to make a goodwill tour of the United States. The visit was adjudged to be an unexpected triumph until Khrushchev visited a Hollywood movie set, where he professed to being scandalized by the sight of scantily clad chorus girls—an emblem, if ever there was one, of Western decadence. (For the record, the movie was *Can-Can*, and one of the chorus girls in a state of *déshabillé* was Shirley MacLaine.) Khrushchev promptly laughed off the tirade as just one of his little jokes—and America heaved a sigh of relief.

Scandal of a different kind unfolded in America that year when Charles Van Doren, a professor of English at Columbia University (as was his famous and much-admired father) found himself talked into appearing as a contestant on a hit television quiz show called *Twenty-One*, on which he became a long-running and hugely popular winner. Fame turned to shame, though, when Charlie was talked into appearing before a Senate subcommittee convened to hear evidence of corruption in television quiz shows. There, cameras flashing, his dad watching from the public seats, he admitted that the program's producers had regularly and secretly given him the answers off camera in advance of the questions being asked on camera.

Senator John Fitzgerald Kennedy of Massachusetts prepared to declare himself a candidate for the presidency, thereby bidding to become the first Roman Catholic to occupy the Oval Office.

But back to that "career in news" mentioned earlier…

The invitation was posted by an enterprise called Comtelburo. It sounded suspiciously like one of Comrade Khrushchev's espionage agencies. What it claimed to be was a "leading international economic news service." The fine print described the jobs on offer as "entry-level clerical positions"—ill-disguised code for office-speak for dogsbodies.

My interest in the world of news was acute. It had long been stimulated by many a bone-chilling post-dawn spent delivering newspapers. The fascination lay in what to me was the ineffable process that spawned, virtually every day of the year, those millions of words and hundreds of pictures, now crammed into my distended satchel. My newsround, along with countless others like it, merely represented the final stage of a remarkable journey that conveyed the news, from all corners of the earth, to twenty million breakfast tables across Britain. How could such a thing be organized nearly every blessed day of the year? The process struck me as nothing short of miraculous.

On the remote chance Comtelburo might actually be what it claimed to be, I fired off a fulsome letter of application. It was written in the knowledge that one particular aspect of the advertisement rang encouragingly true: Comtelburo listed a business address on Fleet Street, then the physical heart of the British newspaper industry.

An appropriate moment, perhaps, to take a brief metaphorical walk along the infamous thoroughfare that now beckoned as my prospective working venue.

★

Thoroughfare may be a rather grandiose term for a narrow, nondescript street barely a quarter of a mile in length, but Fleet Street had once been designated a highway as one of the main entry points to the City of London from its westerly twin, the City of Westminster. No sooner has it penetrated the famous Square Mile than the Street comes to an abrupt halt on the western bank of the now subterranean River Fleet—an invisible line of demarcation—before reluctantly pushing on to the much older settlement, on the Fleet's eastern bank. There stood an enclave occupied since Roman times, and for centuries afterwards, by residents whose stock-in-trade was money. The names of many of its streets reveal its diverse mercantile history: Change Alley, Poultry, Cornhill, Old Jewry, Cheapside.

Fleet Street's traditional associations were with printing and news. They had a religious flavor and dated back to medieval times, the area having been settled by Carmelite friars, then the sole practitioners of the art of applying ink to paper. An adjoining, westerly compound known as the Temple, founded by the crusading Knights Templar, further testifies to the area's religious roots.

Hemmed in to the west by lawyers and to the east by money-changers—hardly the kind of people that journalists would choose as neighbors, one suspects, but undoubtedly useful as sources of news and gossip—Fleet Street began to develop its own peculiar, and rapidly mythologized, character.

The first commercial printing shop in the area was opened in 1500, by the aptly named Wynkin de Worde, a former apprentice of William Caxton, the inventor of England's first printing press. Others followed in steadily rising numbers and, before long, from the maze of alleys and squares around his establishment at the eastern end of the Street, at a decent distance from the lawyers congregated at the other end, emerged the world's first information ghetto.

The word "ghetto" is used in the accepted, as well as the original, sense. Fleet Street over the years has been demonized by many a nose-in-the-air critic. The poet Hilaire Belloc, for example, in *The Happy Journalist*, found it a place of "nasty lanes and corners foul." Nasty and foul it may have been, but it was cherished by its inhabitants as an intellectually and socially congenial village, blessed by a strategically ideal location astride the umbilicus that connects the twin enclaves of Britain's political and financial establishments. In early times, when Westminster and "the City" (as the financial community is always known) were separated by open country, politicians and bankers exchanging visits were more or less obliged to travel along Fleet Street. Apart from being the most direct route, it offered the added attraction of providing a convenient place to stop for refreshment. It was riddled with ale houses and coffee shops, many less than salubrious or even safe. In such establishments, information could be freely bartered with the journalists, publishers, pamphleteers, pundits, lobbyists, literary layabouts, and other purveyors of intelligence and gossip who had taken to hanging about the place. (The "hanging about" finally came to an abrupt and ignominious end only a few years before this book was written.)

Fleet Street was in decline even as this author arrived on the scene. By the end of the 1950s, the newspaper industry had lost much of its former swagger. It was crippled by a financial crisis largely of its own making, paralyzed by the worst relations between management and unions ever devised. In a country so beset by industrial chaos that it was known as the Sick Man of Europe, this ranked as quite an achievement.

Even so, Fleet Street clung to its status as the physical heart of the newspaper industry. It was known to its admirers as the Street of Ink. Its many implacable critics preferred Street of Shame, or Grub Street. To a newcomer like me, the place still seemed raffish enough. Not by accident did the Street boast one coffee shop for twenty taverns (a ratio since sadly reversed).

The working inhabitants had long been renowned no less for their affinity with booze than for their felicity with words. But sociable high spirits were being inexorably undermined by rising concern about the financial health, indeed the very survival, of newspapers. The ink on the news pages may have run black, but on virtually every Fleet Street profit statement it ran deepest red. The press corps tended to ignore their own battle for survival, to the point where they seemed to many outsiders to be taking an unwarranted holier-than-thou delight in chronicling the general air of gloom and introspection attending Britain's economic decline.

Palpable signs of the Street's own demise abounded. It was hard not to notice, in the dimmer corners of the Street's more popular saloons, ale- or claret-quaffing cabals of printers and journalists dolefully predicting their own inevitable, and possibly imminent, extinction. It is probably only fair to point out that journalists, for all their opinionated self-assuredness in print, tend to be a sensitive, introspective and pessimistic bunch in private, even during the best of times. And the 1950s were the worst of times. (In the event, the despondency was unwarranted. Newspapers would survive, even if Fleet Street itself could not, and prosper as never before. But nobody could have known that at the time, when virtually every newspaper appeared to be in mortal peril of closure.)

Some editors did venture to mention the Street's suffering in their papers, although not so daringly as to admit that the wounds were largely self-inflicted. Those who did risked little by incurring the wrath of their proprietors.

The press barons—as they were reverentially, but for the most part undeservedly, known—enjoyed waging war on politicians, but closer to home they showed considerably less aggression. All along Fleet Street they found themselves engaged in a commercial war waged on two fronts, and in disorderly retreat on both. Of the newspaper industry's twin nemeses, commercial television was the more feared by far. A hugely popular phenomenon from the start, it was famously depicted at the time—ironically by a prominent newspaper owner, Lord Thomson, who had perceptively acquired a franchise—as "a license to print money." And so it would prove. But elsewhere in the paperbound branch of the Fourth Estate, television loomed as nothing more than a license to steal readers and advertising income. The second foe of the barons was a more familiar one, and more insidious by virtue of the fact that it formed an integral part of the industry's own establishment: Fleet Street's unholy alliance of print unions. As rapacious and reactionary a gang of cut-throats as ever represented any industrial craft, ardent Luddites to a man, they seemed determined beyond all reason to contest to the death the owners' right to modernize Fleet Street's printing methods and working practices, many of which dated back to Victorian times. Fearful owners were usually more than willing to surrender to unreasonable union demands. Indeed, the impression was widespread that the more outrageous the union demands, the more inclined the owners were to capitulate to them. One archaic tradition that stood out as more blatantly reckless than all the rest was the printers' resolute insistence on retaining workers in huge numbers for jobs that no longer existed—in some cases, for jobs shamelessly invented for the sole purpose of securing employment for members' friends and relatives. Fleet Street thereby achieved the disagreeable status of a national joke—at least in matters of industrial relations.

But for all its problems, the Street retained, even in the 1950s, something of what Americans call a "buzz." It was stimulated every afternoon and evening by another sound, a deep subterranean roar, loud enough to shake the buildings from which it emanated. The din reassuringly announced that the printing presses were rolling for the early editions. There was further comfort in the sight of long lines of delivery vans, formed up, engines idling, clogging the surrounding streets as they waited for the first bundles to emerge. This was a welcome signal to journalists, their work largely done for the day, to "adjourn"—as it was quaintly expressed—to the saloon favored by their particular paper. The taproom, of course, was regarded as an extension of the newsroom—and, in many cases, vice versa.

To observe that Fleet Street's working inhabitants were fond of their grog is to indulge a platitude: journalists and booze were then, if not now, as synonymous as sailors and seas. As one veteran observer, columnist Alan Watkins, later described the scene, "The entire ship anchored beside the Thames between St. Paul's and the Law Courts floated on a sea of alcohol." Many of its lovingly recalled watering holes might be more accurately described as hellholes. Most were scruffy dives, crowded with noisy, ill-tempered literary louts. Social courtesies were strictly rationed. Fistfights were by no means rare. This was especially true of the fabled King and Keys, remembered by one journalist as Hogarthian, "a ghastly bearpit where wild-eyed savages swore and fought and extinguished their cigarettes in other people's glasses of whisky."

The epilogue is anticlimax. Fleet Street's days were numbered. Its association with news survives today only as a metonym for the British press. It managed to struggle on to the mid-1980s, until the much-reviled Australian media mogul, Rupert Murdoch, a newcomer to the Street, removed the few remaining titles, which he happened to own, a mile or so down river to a derelict former dockland area called Wapping. The Diaspora was expressly organized to destroy once and for all the stranglehold of the print unions. In that, it succeeded, although ironies abounded—among them the fact that the money came from a rejuvenated Reuters, of which more anon.

There were others. Newsmen found it hard to decide whether they should mourn or celebrate, being unable to determine which they hated more, Murdoch or the unions. And the Diaspora occurred just as the fortunes of newspapers were starting to revive.

No sooner had the last newsman decamped than Fleet Street was invaded, in a pincer movement from both ends, by neighboring tribes: investment bankers from the east, lawyers from the west, each profession as driven and humorless as the other. Between them they quickly achieved what would once have been derided as unthinkable: they turned Fleet Street into a virtually alcohol-free zone. That legendary fictional Fleet Street character, Lunchtime O'Booze (*Private Eye* magazine), must be turning in his grave as I write.

But before further nostalgic digressions undermine this whole enterprise, perhaps we should return to the plot.

★

The mysterious Comtelburo's response to my application letter was an invitation to attend an interview and what was laughingly called a literary test. For these purposes I found myself entering a solid, rather forbidding Portland stone building, No. 85, at the eastern end of Fleet Street. It was an imposing structure, decidedly non-modernistic, designed by Sir Edwin Lutyens, the foremost British architect of the period between the World Wars. The only clue to the identity of its occupants was a matching pair of copper plates at the entrance announcing them as the Press Association and Reuters, Britain's leading news agencies. The former was devoted to domestic affairs, the latter to international news. Of Comtelburo there was no trace.

It was a pinstriped "porter" in the vaulted vestibule who confirmed, with flagrant distaste, that I had come to the right place.

"Second floor," he snapped, with a thumb cocked skyward.

His look, one of pained incredulity, was evidently directed at my sartorial ensemble of drainpipe trousers and pointed winkle-picker shoes. Neither did he seem impressed by the Tony Curtis pompadour that cascaded over my forehead like a windswept weaverbird's nest.

The disapproving eyes followed me to the lift, and then a shout stopped me short. "Oi, you! Broke yer leg, 'ave yer? At your age you can take the stairs."

Upstairs I was greeted effusively by Dick Paine, Comtelburo's personnel manager—as directors of human resources were then called. An amiable man behind the excruciating name, he wore a perpetual smile, as if rehearsing for a toothpaste commercial. He was a lovely man, though, and altogether deserving of the cliché "unfailingly courteous." (Later, I learned that he had joined the company on the very day his father retired from it after fifty years of service. Dick Paine would put in forty-four years.)

"This won't take long," he promised, a pledge he more than fulfilled by ushering me out of his office fifteen minutes later.

But not before offering me a job.

Plainly, the sole purpose of the procedure had been to establish that I was neither a physical freak nor an obvious nutcase—or perhaps to establish that I was. The latter condition, I would argue later, should have been a prerequisite. As for the writing test, it would not have unduly challenged an intelligent twelve-year-old. An intelligent twelve-year-old would have turned down the pay offer that followed.

"We'll start you at four pounds fifteen shillings and sixpence a week," said a beaming Dicky Paine. "I trust that's satisfactory."

It was far from satisfactory, but the shock had reduced me to a speechless stupor.

An inner voice, unfamiliar and insistent, intervened, urging rejection: "You want at least another pound. Make it two. If he won't budge, tell him to stuff the fucking job. Go on, tell him!" A second voice, this one audible and bearing an uncanny resemblance to my own, spurned the advice: "Yes, that'll be fine."

Thus was concluded, in craven ignominy, my very first commercial negotiation.

By way of compensation, Paine imparted two spirit-lifting snippets of information. The first was that I would be working in Comtelburo's newsroom. The second was that the company was no outpost of the Soviet empire but the commercial news division of Reuters, a name revered in press circles throughout the world.

It was known even to me, courtesy of a 1940 film called *A Dispatch From Reuters*, the kind that Hollywood calls a biopic. Occasionally aired on television, it featured in the title role Edward G. Robinson, better known for playing gangsters, in one of the few parts in which he was not required to gun down most of the cast.

Comtelburo itself had no such dramatic history. Before Reuters bought it, the company had once flourished in its own right as a Liverpool-based telegraphic agency specializing in South American commodities, with a token outpost in New York. Comtelburo had been snapped up by Reuters in 1944 for only a few thousand pounds, after wartime disruptions to international trade had all but wrecked its business. Reuters' own commercial division, itself struggling to survive, was promptly, if inexplicably—Reuters being the better-known name—renamed for the newly acquired business. As markets that had been closed during the war gradually reopened, and national economies recovered, Comtelburo regained most of its customers. Recovery fell short of spectacular, but it was solid enough that the company, by the end of the 1950s, was able to turn in modest but rising annual profits. Controversially, the surplus was promptly spirited away to subsidize Reuters' money-losing general news division—a source of resentment in both camps—of which more later.

Working in a Fleet Street newsroom, even one as unusual as Comtelburo's, with its narrow focus on financial and commodities markets, was an adolescent fantasy fulfilled. Actually, it was the only one fulfilled. All the others—such as opening the batting for England and engaging, *ménage a trois*, with Grace Kelly and Ava Gardner—had proved beyond my ingenuity. It was a bubble all but pricked on my first day at work when, once again, I encountered the sullen attendant I had met on my initial visit.

"Got the job, eh?" was his astonished reaction. "Second floor—up the stairs."

So, once more, up the stairs I hopped, not for the last time, and not even for the last time that morning. Indeed, I was about to become intimately familiar with the stairways of 85 Fleet Street, as I will relate.

As Dicky Paine guided me towards the newsroom's swing doors, from behind them came a din suggesting a place of manic activity. For all the glamorous images propagated by Hollywood writers, a newsroom, reduced to its essence, is nothing more than a factory. A more interesting factory perhaps than, say, a ball-bearing plant, but still nothing more than a place in which raw materials are subjected to a manufacturing process before being turned into finished products. The raw material of the average newsroom is a mass of incoherent verbiage that must be refined into readable and informative copy. The trash-peddling Murdoch would doubtless add "entertaining" to the criteria.

At Comtelburo, with its fixation on news about obscure commodities from countries probably known only to stamp collectors, "readable and informative" would be difficult to achieve, "entertaining" almost impossible.

Comtelburo's newsroom in the physical sense was quintessential: a sweat-shop in which looms and sewing machines were replaced by typewriters and teleprinters, women by men. It covered an area equal to half a football field. Drab inadequately describes the décor. The walls were nicotine yellow, the furniture a military khaki, the linoleum flecked with cigarette burns and in places so worn that the concrete base peeked through. The room was hot and steamy, as bustling as a London street market, strident Cockney voices straining to be heard above the din. A permanent human procession of copy boys and helmeted messengers dashed in and out like the demented residents of a disturbed anthill.

It was, in a word, marvelous.

To a newcomer the tumult was incomprehensible, but the place soon conveyed a palpable sense of purpose and urgency, derived in part from the incessant racket from row upon row of teleprinters arrayed against walls and partitions. The printers were Comtelburo's principal information conduits, incoming and outgoing. They commanded attention by frequently sounding alert bells signaling stories of importance. In the argot of the newsroom these were called "snaps." Other cables were designated Priority, Urgent and Ordinary.

Only rarely were the snaps of an epochal nature; Comtelburo was mainly concerned with the arcana of company announcements, bank rate changes, official economic statistics and the like. But occasionally the newsroom had cause to hold its collective breath over something infinitely more dramatic. One such event, seared into my memory, was the final phase of the Cuba missile crisis of 1962, a week-long standoff between Khrushchev and Kennedy, during which American warships blockaded the island as Soviet cargo vessels, allegedly loaded with nuclear missiles, steamed towards them. It was a tense time. The confrontation could have erupted at any moment into outright hostilities announcing the opening of the Third World War, this one a nuclear conflict. The jangling of nerves was almost as audible as the alert bells that rang incessantly. Even so, the knowledge that an expectant and frightened world was hanging on every word in every Reuters dispatch invested in most of us a sense of awe, the feeling that we were not merely observing history in the making but participating in it.

But the abiding recollections of Comtelburo are inevitably more prosaic. One lingering impression, almost indescribable, but which I can conjure up in my mind forty-odd years later, was the newsroom's peculiar and pervasive miasma—an aromatic distillation of ink, sweat, oil, cigarettes, cold tea, and wet raincoats. This was reinforced on foggy autumn evenings by sulfurous vapors that seeped in through windows and doors like the mist that precedes vampires in horror films. Once inside, these fumes mingled with the fug generated internally by hundreds of cigarettes to create a permanent cirrus formation that swirled just below ceiling level. Visibility decreased with each ascending foot. Anyone much over six feet tall literally walked with his head in the clouds.

Nearer the ground, row upon row of etiolated faces hunched in intense concentration, fags dangling from lips, over ledgers, typewriters, or teleprinters. Just about everyone smoked—mainly roll-ups made from Old Holborn tobacco and Rizla papers, which were cheaper than packaged brands and less easily cadged.

The newsroom was laid out according to function and, naturally, in strict observance of Fleet Street's immutable laws of demarcation. The occupants fell into three distinct tribal units: journalists, teleprinter operators, and clerks. The latter, among which I would be counted, were known in Comtelburo's homegrown nomenclature as tabulators.

The journalists occupied two blocks of desks in the middle of the floor. Editors and reporters represented the aristocracy in Fleet Street's microcosmic class system. Many identified with the popular image of their profession by affecting a vaguely bohemian manner in dress and speech, favoring a sartorial mode of corduroys, bright waistcoats, and piss-speckled suede desert boots. Conversations were peppered with "old boys" and "my dear chaps." A few could actually claim to be pukka reporters, having once worked for regional or national newspapers. Most, though, had graduated from Comtelburo's clerical ranks—the route that I hoped to take. In general they were a pretty dreary bunch, hardly typical of the breed. Financial news then occupied a lowly place on the journalistic totem, somewhere below that of sports reporters. They rejoiced in membership of the National Union of Journalists, a friendly and rather benign body, especially in the context of Fleet Street's unhappy traditions in matters of labor relations.

Below the journalists in the pecking order, socially and economically, came the teleprinter operators. Their contribution to the enterprise was to punch copy—news stories from the journalists, lists of prices from the tabulators—a job of mind-numbing tedium that seemed to duly paralyze the mental faculties of those performing it. It must also have adversely affected their social attitudes, for while journalists and tabulators managed to work together in peaceful coexistence—to borrow a contemporary Cold War expression—the operators seemed doggedly intent on precisely the opposite.

To an underlying attitude almost invariably unhelpful, most operators added sullen and belligerent. The common response to an unreadable piece of copy was to throw it into the air with a dramatic flourish: "Can't read this crap." The operators insisted on being sequestered in areas marked out by three-foot-high partitions that served no other purpose than to recognize their absurdly inflated status as artisans. How punching copy could possibly be considered a craft was a mystery even to those acquainted with Fleet Street's ingrained eccentricities. The accolade came with all the other advantages derived from their affiliation with the National Graphical Association, the same union that represented the featherbedding militants who worked the Street's printing presses. The NGA's power at Comtelburo, no less than anywhere else on the Street, was alarming. An organization of entrenched and unwarranted privilege, its authority derived from its ability to bring the place to a grinding halt within minutes. Though rarely exercised—and never during my days on the Street—the threat alone was enough to send shudders down management spines, admittedly not the stiffest around.

Languishing at the bottom of the social hierarchy were the tabulators. We, too, worked inside our own bureaucratic stockades, an army of Bob Cratchits, whose main function was to record in battered ledgers endless lists of prices from stock and commodity markets around the world. These were then transcribed onto "flimsies"—carbon-paper sandwiches—for transmission to various other points around the world. Tabulators belonged to the National Society of Operative Printers and Assistants (NATSOPA), a title that made up in length what membership failed to confer in benefits.

Membership was compulsory in all three unions. My first mandated act at 85 Fleet Street was to join NATSOPA. Each union was represented at branch level, or chapel, by a shop steward known as Father of the Chapel, two more vestiges of the Street's monastic origins.

As for my role in Comtelburo's brittle mayhem, it was revealed in what was referred to as my introductory briefing. Lasting all of five minutes, it took the form of a comedy sketch performed by one of Comtelburo's resident stand-up comics, Albert Murray, my new boss.

Big Albert was the head of a clerical group called Day Markets Section, which processed prices from markets in the European time zone. There was also an Evening Markets Section for the American time zone. Much to my chagrin, I learned that I would have to work the evening shift every other week—a far cry from Dicky Paine's stipulation that "you might, should the occasion arise, occasionally be called on to work irregular hours."

Day Markets was mostly populated by south Londoners, a garrulous crew united in their suspicion of anyone hailing from north of the Thames—one of London's ingrained oddities—and in their apparent contempt of Comtelburo's management. It was hard to discern a management presence deserving of contempt—but that is probably what they meant. As one old lag put it, "In this asylum, mate, the lunatics have been in charge for years—and a bloody good job, too."

Albert was the head inmate, apparently one of several Murrays—all related—working in the building. (Reuters was then, like the rest of Fleet Street, an unashamedly dynastic employer.) Albert was a bear of a man with a bulbous, purpling nose reminiscent of W.C. Fields. He shared W.C.'s acute cynicism, too, expressed through an impressive repertoire of sarcastic one-liners. They were amusing unless you were on the receiving end. His party trick was to simulate the sounds of a cricket match—willow striking leather, raucous appeals for a wicket—complete with commentary. He had a memorable catchphrase, the one with which, at the end of each working day, he signed off his shift: "And that, ladies and gentlemen, concludes today's entertainment from the South Pier."

My formal designation on the South Pier was Traffic Clerk—actually code for copy boy. The job involved tracking down missing cables, incoming and outgoing, and if necessary ordering their retransmission. Incoming cables went astray for a broad variety of reasons, of which the most common was annihilation by sunspots. In those days, traffic was transmitted over radio circuits, for which sunspots posed a constant threat. I retain to this day an image of sunspots swooping down on Comtelburo's defenseless columns of cables like squadrons of dive-bombing Stukas. Inattentive operators added their own contribution to missing outgoing cables by punching the wrong destination addresses.

Whatever my official job description, it masked a truly critical function, one that Murray revealed with what struck me as unnecessary relish. Before attending to anything, he intoned gravely, no matter how important, I was to make sure that my colleagues were well provided with tea. For the second time in my brief career at 85 Fleet Street, I was rendered speechless with humiliation. Before responding—I just wasn't sure how to respond—I received another portentous admonition: "Make it strong, make it hot, make it sweet, and keep it coming."

"Just like our women," some eavesdropper inevitably chipped in. This gem was followed by a more strident interjection. "ROSIE!"

Rosie, for the benefit of readers not acquainted with cockney rhyming slang, is short for Gypsy Rose Lee, meaning tea. The anguished cry emanated from Tom Barclay, Albert Murray's deputy, a man with a hair-trigger temper and a serious drinking problem—in his case, tea. Count Dracula in search of blood-donating victims would have presented no more terrifying a sight than Tom Barclay with an empty mug.

Tom's anguished *cri de coeur* invariably set off a ritualistic chant: "ROSIE, ROSIE, ROSIE, ROSIE…"

An enamel pitcher materialized in my hand. Chipped, stained, and of great antiquity, it had evidently seen considerable action. Judging by the colorful kaleidoscope of growths flourishing inside, Alexander Fleming might have used it to nurture penicillin cultures. I was mortified by what I saw as a demeaning task. But outrage would have to be postponed, for I was already being waved away impatiently.

"Off yer go, son," cried Albert. "And mind you're back soon. No loitering. And don't use the lifts. You'll find the back stairs much quicker."

My destination, invariably, was Manzi's, an odious, grease-encrusted sandwich bar across the street. There, my pitcher was filled with foaming, mud-colored soup that might have been pumped in directly from the nearby Thames, laced with enough sugar to turn it into treacle.

The commercial arrangement under which I operated was dictated by time-honored custom. I had to pay for the tea out of my own pocket, but I could recover the cost by flogging it around the newsroom at fourpence a mug. Only to tabulators, mind. The operators had special dispensation to make their own tea in-house, and the journalists tended to drink coffee. Anyway, to cross demarcation lines, even for a mug of tea, might have risked bringing all Fleet Street out on strike.

Fourpence a go was more than enough to cover the cost. With care, a pitcher could produce a profit as high as a shilling. Margins could be enhanced—and often were—by observing the shameful tradition of "topping up" from the hot water tap in the washroom or, more indecently still, with slops from the dozens of mugs lying around the newsroom.

The Manzi tea-run may have been one of Comtelburo's more profitable ventures. Its proceeds allowed me to accompany my colleague, Barry Clark, to The Old Bell, once a week, for a decent lunch. The old waitress there was sufficiently moved by our emaciated appearance to give us extra custard with our desserts: "You boys look as if you could use a bit of fattening up."

She should see us now!

Between trips to Manzi's, there were occasional moments to spare for rounding up missing cables. The task was made easier by Comtelburo's practice, observed for reasons of economy and security, of giving them code-names. Economy was imposed by the post office practice of charging for cables by the word, a single-word title being cheaper than a longer descriptive one. Codes also deterred interception by information pirates. The names tended to reflect a cable's points of origin: bourse prices from Frankfurt might be designated Fritz, Ghana cocoa prices, Fudge. They lent a surreal quality to newsroom conversation.

"Parrot! Anyone 'ere seen my bloody Parrot?"

Parrot, I seem to recall, was a regular afternoon cable bearing opening coffee prices from Brazil. Evidently more susceptible to sunspots than most, Parrot was the bane of my working afternoons—as it was for Jim Vincent, the man responsible for handling it, one of Comtelburo's more irascible characters. His conviction was that, in Parrot's irregular appearances, a dastardly plot had been hatched to make his life difficult.

"Where's my bloody Parrot, then?"

"Sorry, Jim, everything from South America is delayed. Sunspots again."

"Sunspots my arse. Why is it always my Parrot that goes down?"

"Dunno, mate. But tell you what, why don't you have it sent by night, then there'll be no sunspots around."

"Yeah, and then you'll be tellin' me it's fuckin' moonspots."

Sunspots were nothing compared with the hazards that confronted copy once it had made it inside 85 Fleet Street. Cables intrepid enough to survive extra-terrestrial ambushes now had to navigate their way through an obstacle course of some of the most hilariously inefficient instruments of office communication ever assembled. It was as if Heath Robinson (or his American counterpart, Rube Goldberg) had been given the run of a well-stocked scrapyard.

My favorite was the Catapult, a spring-loaded device designed to carry copy across the newsroom in a small, flat container propelled along an overhead wire. It traveled at a velocity that must have represented some kind of indoor speed record. Having reached its destination, the container was supposed to thump into a rubber buffer, a jolt designed to deposit the cargo into a nylon stocking poised above a wire basket, while simultaneously returning the empty container to its point of origin. As often as not, the contents spilled out on the cursing heads of those seated in its flight path. I once saw the container overshoot the buffer and crash into a wall, missing a bystander, and a window, by inches. Its final act of devilry was to nearly scalp a very tall, visiting American—a hazard he must have supposed had been eradicated with the end of the Indian wars. Shortly after that, the Catapult was dismantled, considered a threat to public safety.

A hardly less incredible device was the Intestine, a pneumatic tube system designed to carry copy between floors. Running vertically through the building like a giant digestive tract, it differed from the biological version in one crucial respect: whatever was fed into it at one end rarely emerged at the other. What it did instead, almost unerringly, was to swallow the tubes placed into it with a lascivious slurp before consigning them to some black hole in the metaphysical bowels of the building. Sadly, the Intestine, too, found itself shut down— although because it could not physically be consigned anywhere, being imbedded in the building's infrastructure, it probably remains there to this day.

The catapult was replaced by an even loonier device called the Belt, a constantly moving conveyor belt partitioned into six tracks, designed to carry copy to six different stations, each manned by an operator. Like its predecessors, the Belt suffered from a conceptual flaw. Because it could run neither the entire length nor breadth of the newsroom without impeding pedestrian passageways, it had to be divided into sections. Interchanges were constructed to get over this problem, which simply rendered the system worthless. Needless to say, the Belt soon went the way of its illustrious forebears.

As I completed my first week at work, my father ventured to inquire about my progress. "I know you work for Reuters, but what is it exactly that you do?" My response was designed to disguise the menial nature of my job. "Well, when I'm not running around with Rosie, I get to go on safari, hunting for lost parrots."

"Ask a silly question, get a silly answer," was his only comment.

My mother, who managed the tiny Findlay's news kiosk on the platform at Blackfriars Undergound station, was no less bemused. When I told her I worked for a news agency, she initially took it into her head that I was in the same business as hers. "Though I'm sure your shop is much bigger than mine," she added admiringly.

I was soon relieved of my shame as a tea-boy by intervention from an unexpected quarter: Kit, one of Comtelburo's cleaning ladies. Kit was a woman possessed of a certain style, with an impeccable blue-rinse bouffant to prove it. She was also a woman with a commendable desire for self-improvement. She had a keen eye for a commercial opportunity and had quietly approached Dick Paine, seeking dispensation to operate a twice-daily tea wagon. From this she proposed to serve not only tea and coffee but buttered rolls and sticky buns as well.

On the grounds that it was daft to pay copy boys to spend most of the working day fetching tea, Paine gave his approval. I felt more relieved than Mafeking, doubtless as happy to ditch my enamel pitcher as Kit her broom and dustpan.

"Cha from the Char," she cleverly named the enterprise. And a resounding success it was, too. "One in the eye for those dreadful Manzi boys," she chortled. Amen to that, too.

Silly questions about the nature of Comtelburo's business were by no means unique to my father. Reuters' endorsement of the curious activities on the second floor was regarded in every other department of the agency as a disturbing symptom of management dementia. The attitude was endemic in the general news division up on the fourth floor, in defiance of all management attempts to quash it.

"You're just a bunch of pimps down there," a senior editor once went out of his way to tell me after I had committed some minor misdemeanor. "Worse still, you're all barking mad."

Derek Jameson, a former Reuters news editor, later to achieve fame as a tabloid editor and television personality, recalled the antagonism in his memoirs: "The numerologists who appeared to run [Comtelburo] were always trying to get their dispatches on to the newswires. They always got shoved to the back of the queue. 'Sorry, cock,' we would say, 'they've just formed their 29th postwar government in Italy. No room for your crap'."[2]

Even up in the seventh-floor executive suite, the attitude toward the so-called commercial services seemed hardly more than indulgent. Management ambivalence stemmed from the absence of anything remotely resembling a corporate strategy, other than to keep running news services at a loss, in the hope that the shareholders, several cooperative bodies representing the newspapers of Britain and the Commonwealth, would foot the bill through ever-rising subscriptions. That ignored the reality that most newspapers were financially even worse off than Reuters itself.

As for Comtelburo, its role was explained in stark terms in a 1947 management report to the board. Comtelburo existed, it said, "for the sole purpose of subsidizing the [general] news service." This implied that if Comtelburo failed to make enough money to that end, it would have no other reason to exist, which would no doubt have sent the general news division into paroxysms of glee. But how was the general news division otherwise supposed to be financed? Answer came there none.

The irrational prejudice of the general news division probably took root during the commercial division's tough times in and immediately after the Second World War. But it persisted even after Comtelburo started to turn in regular annual profits. Earnings from the commercial services actually doubled during the 1950s, allowing Reuters to reach, in the year in which I joined the company, a heady surplus of £143,197. It was a large enough sum to encourage Comtelburo's management to ask, with what the general news people no doubt viewed as unmitigated gall, that it be allowed to keep some money aside to invest in its own future.

It was in that context that a new breed of junior executive began to appear

---

[2] Derek Jameson, *Touched by Angels*, Ebury Press, 1988, p.154

on the second floor. Comtelburo's retained earnings were spent largely on a management recruitment scheme, designed to attract a "better class" of employee. Most were graduates from Oxford and Cambridge. Many came armed with impressive but irrelevant degrees in Oriental art, or geography, or European history. Many, though, had useful skills in two or three languages, which the company often exploited whimsically by sending German speakers to Madrid and Spanish speakers to Singapore.

Those of us deprived of the blessings of Oxbridge schooling regarded management trainees arriving on the second floor for "basic training" with amused contempt. Understandably bewildered by Comtelburo's lunacies, they were perfect victims for cruel practical jokes.

One chinless wonder, fresh down from Oxford, was sent on a "reporting assignment" to nearby Smithfield meat market with a mission to "take soundings" about trends in prices. "Your best bet is to talk to the porters," he was told. "They're the ones who really know what's going on, and they're only too happy to talk to reporters."

"Jolly good," trilled our intrepid correspondent, with unsuspecting enthusiasm. He returned, an hour or so later, a pitiful sight, and sadly disillusioned.

"I say, those chaps were not exactly cooperative," he complained. "Rude fellows, swore a lot. One of them actually had the nerve to tell me I belonged in a fucking asylum."

"Well, that's okay," was the predictable response, "because, in case you hadn't noticed, you're in one."

"I say, are you quite sure this is really the kind of thing I'm supposed to be doing?"

Another gullible victim was instructed to answer a telephone, over which he would shortly receive the day's closing prices from the "Dundee Marmalade Exchange." He had accumulated a list of quotes for such breakfast delights as "Dundee Rough Cut," "Bitter Lemon," and "Chunky Seville" before the barely stifled mirth of his colleagues became apparent.

"You rotten bastards," he hissed.

"Money for jam, this job," someone quipped.

Comtelburo's clients often seemed hardly less bewildered. A cable from Greece containing closing prices from the Athens bourse was routinely signed off by the Reuters correspondent there, whose surname was Modiano. For several weeks a leading financial newspaper published a daily list of Athens stocks that included "Modiano" along with a "price"—in reality, the cable's time-stamp. The error was uncovered only when a reader called in to say that he had been trying for some time, unsuccessfully, to trace a company of that name.

As part of their training program, management recruits were invited to cut their editorial teeth by writing about some of the more obscure commodities. Like gunnybags.

Many a journalistic molar, mine included, was sharpened on gunnybags (a hemp material used in industrial packaging). There rarely being anything remotely interesting to write about in gunnybags, it presented a true test of journalistic ingenuity. "The gunnybag market was largely unchanged today, with trade sources reporting little or no activity," was about as far as a trainee might go before succumbing to a severe case of writer's block. You could, at a pinch, improvise: "Gunnybag prices appeared to be unaffected by reports of renewed armed clashes on the India-Pakistan frontier." Or, for that matter, Arsenal's surprise victory over Manchester United the previous Saturday.

Of course they were unaffected. Gunnybag prices apparently had not changed significantly in living memory. If they had, nobody had noticed.

There must have been a real place where gunnybags were traded, perhaps in a tavern in a gas-lit alley in the City of London. I don't remember. It was typical of Comtelburo not only to contrive to discover such arcane markets, but somehow to persuade clients to pay for information about them.

Cables from far-off places carrying prices for gunnybags and other little-known commodities often failed to appear for months. During such intervals it was a common newsroom practice simply to record prices as unchanged, certainly a convenient alternative to spending futile hours hunting for material of such profound immateriality.

"Unchanged!" became as familiar a newsroom proclamation as "Rosie!"

If senior managers were aware of the custom—which constituted a firing offence in an enterprise founded on devotion to The Truth—they seemed ill disposed to intervene. But then, the paying customers hadn't noticed, either. Anyway, management on the newsroom floor was conspicuous by its absence. The exceptions were a couple of news editors, who sat side-by-side in a corner, comfortably ensconced behind a glass screen. From this enclave they occasionally emerged, usually to go to lunch—perhaps with gunnybag traders. The inmates stayed at their desks to run the asylum.

The time served in Comtelburo's barmy army left me with affectionate and abiding memories. We learned a great deal about the nature of markets—much of it admittedly worthless. We laughed a lot. In fact, we spent most of our time laughing. Forty years on, some of us chuckle still, over an occasional bottle of claret in El Vino.

What Paul Julius Reuter, the company's much-admired founder, would have made of it all is beyond speculation. He started his agency by gathering prices and news on markets, much as we were doing. And he would surely have recognized in Comtelburo much that was familiar in his own day.

To that formidable figure and his works, the next chapter is devoted.

And that, ladies and gentlemen, concludes today's entertainment from the South Pier.

# Paul Julius Reuter

Paul Julius Reuter was a swashbuckling pioneer of the first information revolution, the nineteenth-century version inspired by the invention of the electronic telegraph. As a master of the medium that helped to establish Britain's global hegemony, he deserves recognition as an eminent Victorian. Somehow, though, the honor seems to have eluded him. His name is relatively familiar, if frequently mispronounced, through the institution of the news agency that bears his name, but his achievements remain largely unknown to the general public. Historians tend to overlook him. In my own library there are a dozen history books covering the nineteenth century and not one sees fit to mention Julius Reuter or his agency. The man was by all accounts a modest and unassuming fellow, and in appearance far from the swashbuckler of popular image, so he probably would not have cared.

That Reuter was German by birth was no disqualification for status as a British hero. Queen Victoria had as much German blood as he (and perhaps shared his Jewish roots, too, if recent revelations about some of her father's affairs are true). And once settled in his adopted country, he took great delight in becoming in many respects more English than most Englishmen. His standing probably suffers less from the accident of his foreign birth than from his failure to qualify as a scientist, inventor, or explorer. He was not even a journalist, which might have been an advantage in matters of self-promotion. He was, rather, a man of business, which at times undoubtedly worked to his disadvantage; Britain reluctantly acknowledges only its industrial and commercial heroes, and never in quite the same way as its military leaders and empire-builders. Only from America, it seems, do men of commerce enter heaven.

To say that his personality was self-effacing is not to say that he was shy or retiring. His various portraits and caricatures, and the few surviving photographs, give the impression of a man of self-assured modesty. The bespectacled and generously bewhiskered face suggests a kindly, perhaps absent-minded uncle, but behind the posed benignity something steely lurks. He was said to be a sociable man, an enthusiast for dinner parties, musical evenings, and family gatherings. It was in business affairs that he demonstrated his serious side. His overriding quality was that of perseverance, and it was the one that he was most often called upon to demonstrate. He is described by a contemporary admirer as "short, vivacious, energetic, with bird-like piercing eyes, in conversation always succinct and to the point." Handy characteristics, it might be said, for someone intent on a career in news.

He did achieve fame during his time. *Vanity Fair* magazine printed his caricature in 1872 as one of its "Men of the Day" series and his name was favorably mentioned by the Monarch, who once observed, in a dig at her ministers, that Reuter seemed to know more about world affairs than they did. His dispatches at that time appeared in newspapers around the world, as they still do. At the peak of his powers he would not have been short of dinner invitations or requests for speaking engagements, but he seems by and large to have resisted the call to celebrity. Not a man about town, then, and certainly not one to make a great effort to be embraced by the British Establishment.

Imperial Britain's most prominent messenger he may have been, but Pax Britannica was not a cause he openly espoused. Whatever his views on that subject, as on most others, they seem to have been scrupulously withheld from public scrutiny. Like his agency's journalists, he felt bound by the necessary constraints of impartiality and anonymity—although many others of his kind were not quite so scrupulous.

What can, of course, be safely assumed is that he was by inclination a capitalist. He was staunchly in favor of the interests of free markets. His telegraphic services, largely focused on financial news, helped to propagate those markets, and the markets in turn nourished his company (a symbiotic relationship still intact a century and a half later).

It detracts nothing from his reputation as something of a business genius to say that he enjoyed his fair share of luck. It was Julius Reuter's particular good fortune to enter a commercial world about to be reshaped by a surge of remarkable scientific inventions, of which the telegraph was perhaps the most significant. Its impact was immediate and far-reaching. The telegraph astonished the public every bit as much as the Internet would a century and a half later, stimulating an insatiable public hunger for information about society itself.

Even more voracious was the appetite in commercial circles for information about markets. The telegraph and markets were made for each other, a fact that Reuter was quick to recognize, if at first slow to exploit. It created the first instance of the phenomenon we would in later times call globalization. Indeed, the nascent Industrial Age of Reuter's day had many facets almost uncannily redolent of the present, post-industrial, technology-obsessed era.

The boom in trade and markets spawned by the Industrial Revolution offered unprecedented opportunities to an emerging mercantile class of producers, merchants, shippers, and bankers, not to mention the army of speculators that floated in their wake. If it was not the first class in history to aspire to wealth through means other than heredity, it was the first to do so on an international scale. Reuter was prominent among its founding members.

He was in many ways in a class of his own. The man defies being pigeonholed. (Insiders will pardon the expression; others will be enlightened shortly.) Reuter has attracted the word "genius." Perhaps he was one, but he seems to have been clever rather than brilliant, an opportunist rather than an innovator, well-read without being an intellectual. He did have something of the intellectual's innate curiosity about the world, but it was always devoted to the tangible business of making money rather than the promotion of erudition.

He became in time eminently successful at making money, but first he stumbled, for his business instincts were not always sound and his timing was sometimes unfortunate. The year in which he chose to start his first solo venture, after leaving Havas, was 1848, Europe's so-called Year of Revolutions. Political upheaval was endemic throughout the Continent, but the turmoil was uneven, varying from one country to the next, as well as unpredictable, being subject to sudden changes in the national political climate. Obliged to abandon Germany for France, where tolerance for free speech seemed much healthier, a few years later Reuter found the situations unexpectedly reversed and was obliged to make the same journey in reverse. Britain, a land of relatively liberal values, stood aloof from continental chaos. It was thus in London that Reuter found welcome and permanent stability.

None of his three early business initiatives exploited the telegraph. The first, in Berlin, was in the long-established field of book publishing; the second, in Paris, no more than a postal clipping service. The third took him to Aachen and, for the first time, into the realm of market reporting. But his business there was reliant on the use of carrier pigeons, which even the Romans would not have described as cutting edge. And, ironically, although it was the telegraph that would one day make his fortune, it was also the telegraph that first put him out of business.

If innovation and invention were lacking in these early ventures, other attributes would rise to the surface. Opportunism and persistence have been mentioned. It was the ability to bounce back from adversity that became Reuter's trademark quality. It was reinforced by an intuitive flair for negotiation, which emphasized good humor and a disabling charm rather than dour, single-minded aggression. Once he had broken his string of early failures, he steadily pulled away from his early rivals. That he endured, while they fell by the wayside, may be attributed to various factors. Some of his competitors increasingly fell under government influence, reducing them to mere channels for official propaganda. Others dabbled in advertising or other profit-making chimera. Reuter, by contrast, stuck single-mindedly to the business of news, principally the news of business. In doing so, he ensured that his enterprise was invested with those qualities universally accepted as critical to any news organization: objectivity, accuracy, dependability, and a reputation for fair dealing. Those were also, of course, his personal qualities.

Let us briefly review the life and career of the gentleman in question.

The name that made Reuter famous was adopted relatively late in his life. He was born, in 1816, the year after Waterloo, Israel Beer Josaphat, the third son of Samuel Levi Josaphat, acting chief rabbi in Kassel, capital of the north German state of Hesse. Though far from wealthy, the Josaphats were respectable, middle class, well educated and pious in their observance of the Jewish faith and traditions of their race. One of his elder brothers became a university professor, the other a Talmudic scholar.

The rabbinate was a vocation into which Israel Beer might have been drawn had his father not died when Israel was only thirteen. As a result, he was sent away, evidently for economic reasons, to live with an uncle who owned a bank in the university town of Gottingen. The apparent intention was to prepare him for a career in finance, and to that end he worked at his uncle's establishment for several years, though apparently without enthusiasm or distinction. The city's academic life had, meanwhile, encouraged different aspirations.

At some point, the young Israel Beer met and was befriended by Karl Friedrich Gauss, a professor at Gottingen University, and sometimes called the father of modern mathematics. The boy ran errands for Gauss, attended his lectures and became fascinated by his experiments with the transmission of electrical signals by wire, an activity then all the rage in European scientific circles. At some point, Israel may have assisted Gauss in a famous project that involved running wires across the city rooftops as part of a demonstration of the emerging communications medium. If so, it is reasonable to assume that the event planted in his mind the seeds of recognition of the commercial potential of telegraphy.

Grateful for his uncle's patience, but bored by banking, Israel Beer left Gottingen and "disappeared" for several years before showing up, at the age of twenty-eight, in Berlin. Like many others, he may have been drawn to the city's lively social scene, or to the opportunity to become immersed in its commercial energy, or both. In each respect he seems to have been successful. It was in Berlin, a year after arriving, that Israel Beer met, courted, and married, in a civil ceremony, Ida Maria Magnus, daughter of a local government bureaucrat, and a Protestant. Aside from the happy longevity of their marriage and three children, its most significant consequence was his conversion to his wife's religion. From this, Israel Beer Josaphat emerged, after a second marriage ceremony in a London church, with the name by which he would become famous.

The motives behind Reuter's abandonment of his original faith have excited speculation, particularly by Reuters' own corporate historian, Professor

Donald Read. In his company-commissioned book, *The Power of News*, Read attributed the decision to commercial motives. Reuter, he wrote, "saw no reason why his career should be restricted by his Jewishness."[1]

It is true that such conversions were by no means unusual at the time. Many ambitious and progressive Jews, stifled by the exclusionary aspects of their own community, were persuaded to change religion or names, or both, to become assimilated into society at large. As Paul Johnson, in *A History of the Jews*, points out: "Conversion to Christianity was one way in which Jews reacted to the age of emancipation."[2] He adds that "many Jews were motivated more by self-interest than by self-preservation, as in the example of the poet Heinrich Heine, who frankly depicted his own conversion as an 'entrance ticket' to European society." But ascribing such motives to Reuter, as Read does, seems unfair, the charge being both unproved and unprovable. Since the two events coincided, marriage is as likely an explanation for his conversion as any; so why bother with others? (Read generally appears to have something of an obsession with supposed Jewish influences in news—comparable perhaps to the fear of those Americans, during the Cold War, who constantly imagined "reds under the bed." As one of Reuter's successors punned, the phobia seems to have been co-opted by Read as "Jews in the news.")

At least one commercial advantage accrued from the change of name. It meant that his famous dispatches would carry the byline "Reuter" rather than "Josaphat"—which despite the ring of biblical authenticity might not have caught on quite so readily. But why Reuter? The choice has never been explained. A common enough name in Germany, Reuter can be translated as "rider" or "messenger." Reuter did, apparently, have a friend of the same name, a wool merchant in London. Make of it what you will.

What engaged Reuter's professional attention during his early years of marriage, presumably living in Berlin, is obscure until 1847. In that year he became a partner in an established bookshop and publishing enterprise, apparently with the help of his wife's money. While the venture was profitable, Reuter suddenly pulled out after a few months. At the same time he also pulled out of Germany. The reasons are not documented. Professor Read recounts a story, unconfirmed, that Reuter may have made off with substantial funds, the proceeds of a book fair, belonging to the company, causing his partner, Joseph Stargardt, to suffer a nervous breakdown. If true, it certainly does not chime with Reuter's otherwise unblemished record of honesty—as Read, having raised the issue, then takes the trouble to point out. Anyway, why would Reuter, with affluent in-laws and no evident reason to resort to desperate measures, take up embezzlement?

---

[1] Donald Read, *The Power of News*, Oxford University Press, 1992, p.8
[2] Paul Johnson, *A History of the Jews*, Harper and Row, 1987, p.312

The political climate presents a more plausible reason. His firm, Reuter und Stargardt, may have attracted the attention of the authorities by printing articles espousing unpopular political opinions. This was, after all, 1848, and Germany, as in most other continental European countries, was going through a period of social and political turmoil to which the predictable response of an authoritarian government was to suppress dissent—published dissent in particular—with great severity. If such articles had been published, they were not likely to have been written by Reuter himself. He was no radical and there is no evidence of his having held any firm political views of any kind. Nor would any become evident in his later career, except through his enthusiastic devotion to markets. The only thing that is clear is that, whatever the reasons, Mr. and Mrs. Reuter appear to have left Germany in something of a hurry.

They resurfaced in Paris, where Julius took a job as a translator at Agence Havas.

Suppressing his personal business ambitions to gain experience, Reuter worked at Havas for about a year. He had followed in the footsteps of another refugee from German authoritarianism, Bernhard Wolff, a physician by profession but market speculator by disposition. As luck would have it, Havas assigned both men to handle financial news from an office near the Paris Bourse, a vantage from where they could hardly have failed to be impressed by the growing demand for financial and commercial news. In doing so, Havas had unwittingly trained his future competitors. Sure enough, as soon as they had learned the ropes, Reuter and Wolff each left to start his own agency. For that purpose Wolff returned to Germany. Reuter remained in Paris.

Reuter seems to have based his business on a reversal of the Havas model by translating copy from French newspapers for subscribers in Germany. Staffed only by Reuter and his wife Ida, the operation was run from the living room of their seedy Paris apartment. An obviously appalled friend described the place in terms that could have come from Dickens: "...curtains damp and mouldering; the fireplace filled with remnants of hastily eaten meals, ashes, half-burnt pieces of wood and pieces of paper; a cracked mirror over the damaged marble-covered fireplace; cobwebs on the plaster moldings on the ceiling; a rocky table under which a scarred dog used to sit with one leg perpetually out of action; and a dark background of heaps of paper and a press."[3] (Journalists at Comtelburo, a century later, would have recognized it as the prototype for their own newsroom.)

The company soon foundered, a victim of the proprietor's inexperience perhaps, or, just as likely, the growing censorship of newspapers by the illiberal government of Emperor Louis Napoleon III. The reasons were unimportant when the creditors came knocking, as they now did. The result was that the

---

[3] Graham Storey, *Reuters' Century*, Max Parrish & Co. 1951, p.7

Reuters were once again obliged to pack up and leave town. This time it was back to Germany where, in a role reversal with France typical of the vagaries of 19th-century European politics, a new regime had been installed, this one with a more relaxed attitude to free speech.

On the advice of a friend, Reuter opened up for business in Aachen, a railway junction on the Belgian border, occasionally also known as Aix-la-Chapelle, depending on whether the prevailing ownership was French or German. Berlin probably would have been Reuter's first choice, but his former colleague, Wolff, had already set up shop there. Aachen, however, did offer certain attractions: it was a lively commercial center in its own right, and connected to Berlin via the new Prussian state telegraph line. One drawback was that it was not yet connected in the other direction, to Brussels.

Brussels would soon be linked with Paris by telegraph, but that still left a 100-mile gap between Brussels and Aachen. This presented Reuter with an opportunity. The plan he devised was to have market prices and commercial news from various cities collected in Brussels and then taken to Aachen. There he had a fair number of local clients and more could be serviced by sending dispatches by telegraph to Berlin.

How to get the information to Aachen was the issue. By train, easily the fastest means of conventional transportation, the trip from Brussels took nearly ten hours—too slow for time-sensitive market information. Mail coaches took even longer.

The alternative, hardly an original idea, but one that Reuter had seen successfully employed at Havas, was to use pigeons. They could make the trip in two hours.

As it happened, Reuter's landlord, Heinrich Geller, a local baker and brewer, was also an avid pigeon breeder. Four dozen trained birds were "rented" from Geller. Reuter also repaid him for his kindness in befriending him and Ida on their arrival in the city by awarding him a stake in the new enterprise. It was called, somewhat inappropriately—but perhaps with premonition—the Institute for the Promotion of Telegraphic Dispatches.

For eight months the daily routine in Aachen was constant. Each afternoon, as soon as the stock markets closed, Reuter's agent in Brussels transcribed the day's closing prices from the local bourse, as well as prices from Paris and other cities, onto light tissue paper. These lists were placed in small silk bags and attached to the underside of the wings of Geller's pigeons. Three birds were dispatched for each flight as an insurance against casualties. In Aachen, Geller waited for the incoming birds at his pigeon loft and, from there, a messenger ran the copy around to Reuter's office. Legend has it that the Institute's clients were locked in to ensure that everyone received the information at the same time—an early manifestation of the news embargo.

The service was a brilliant triumph but inevitably short-lived. Reuter must have known all along that his agency would sooner or later be threatened by the ever-expanding telegraph, clearly destined to become an uninterrupted line linking Paris and Berlin, and, sure enough, construction of the line was soon underway from both ends. As the gap was closed to a mere five miles, Reuter replaced his pigeons with relays of horses. But this was merely buying time. Aachen, at least in communications terms, was being reduced to irrelevance. Reuter's institute was soon as redundant as its location, and effectively out of business.

Where next for the Reuters? Paris, where Havas ruled the roost, was hardly an option. Neither was Berlin, now dominated by Wolff. Sound advice now came from someone Reuter had met at a trade fair. His name was Werner Siemens, founder of the great German engineering dynasty. As Siemens recalled in his memoirs: "I met a Mr. Reuter ... whose lucrative business was being relentlessly destroyed by installation of the electric telegraph. When Mrs. Reuter, who accompanied her husband on the trip, complained to me about this destruction of their business, I advised the pair to go to London and to start there a cable agency..."[4] His advice was heeded.

Paul Julius Reuter's arrival in London in the summer of 1851 is unlikely to have been noticed. Capital of a mighty empire and the hub of the rapidly expanding wheel of world commerce, London that year was a magnet for the mobile elite of international society, courtesy of the Great Exhibition of the Works of Industry of All Nations. Conceived by Prince Albert, Queen Victoria's husband and consort, the displays were housed under Joseph Paxton's enormous glass canopy, later known as Crystal Palace, in Hyde Park. The exhibition opened amid royal pomp and ceremony to cheering, patriotic crowds. The event was billed as a showcase for international inventions, but its generally understood purpose was to celebrate Britain's industrial power.

Reuter may have been too busy to notice the commotion. His interests were better served by a more significant, if less publicized, event on the British calendar that year. After several failed attempts, a submarine cable had been successfully laid under the English Channel, connecting Britain's telegraphic network with those on the Continent. Britain's days of Splendid Isolation were nearing their end, and Reuter, with dozens of agents and contacts still in place across Europe, was probably better placed to exploit the opportunity than any man in London. Whether by accident or design, Siemens's advice had been prescient.

Reuter wasted no time before showing up at the London Stock Exchange with a proposal to provide its members with regular price lists and news bulletins from the continental Bourses. If he had expected objections of all

---

[4] Graham Storey, *Reuters' Century*, Max Parrish & Co. 1951, introductory quotes

kinds, not least the fact that he was virtually unknown in London, he must have been astonished when the Exchange promptly accepted his offer. With this first scalp attached to his belt, Reuter could afford to set up his telegraphic agency. It was located in a one-room office within walking distance to the Exchange (a spot now marked by a granite bust of Reuter, commissioned by the company). A twelve-year-old assistant was hired to handle the paperwork, leaving Reuter, the consummate salesman, time to secure additional clients.

The instinct to start the London business with financial rather than general news was sensible. Creating a newspaper service from scratch in a city well-served by a press with extensive international connections was never likely to be easy. Reuter would discover as much during an early visit to Mowbray Morris, editor of *The Times*, London's most influential newspaper. *The Times* operated its own network of foreign correspondents, which meant that Morris could afford to be loftily dismissive. "The proprietors of *The Times* are not prepared to enter into arrangements with you," he wrote to Reuter.

Mowbray's rejection was a blessing in disguise. It forced Reuter to concentrate on commercial services, which were much more lucrative and could be sold in a business field much less hidebound than the press. And should they prosper, there would be enough of a surplus to finance general news operations. That proved to be the case—establishing an operating pattern that would typify Reuters for much of its subsequent existence.

The first newspaper deal was seven long years in coming, and it emerged from an unlikely source: the *Morning Advertiser*, London's oldest daily paper, founded in 1794 by the Licensed Victuallers' Association. In 1858, its editor, James Grant, accepted an offer of a two-week free trial of Reuter's service, having extracted the promise of a substantial discount in exchange for a long-term agreement. As Grant recalled: "[Reuter] at once applied himself to the carrying out of his engagements; and most certainly the result of the comparison between his organization and that of the morning papers at the time proved the very great superiority of his. Not only did I at once give a permanent acceptance to Mr. Reuter's proposals, but the managers of the other journals did the same,"[5] including *The Times*.

Before long, the faith of the London press was justified by a famous scoop—one that testifies to the imagination that Reuter applied to promoting his business.

In February 1859, Emperor Louis Napoleon let it be known that he would deliver to the French legislature a speech that was expected to reveal the prospects for war between France and Austria. Reuter requested a journalistic privilege that is now customary but, at the time, was unprecedented: an advance copy of the text. Surprisingly, the French government agreed, with the

---

[5] Graham Storey, *Reuters' Century*, Max Parrish & Co. 1951, p.23

sole proviso that it would be delivered to Reuter's office in Paris in a sealed envelope under embargo—that is, it was not to be opened until the Emperor had stood up to speak. Reuter booked one hour of exclusive cable time between Paris and London. Bilingual employees stood by ready to translate the text, which would then be rushed to the London newspapers by messenger. The exercise went off exactly as planned and, within an hour of the speech, the papers hit the streets with special editions reporting Louis Napoleon's belligerent remarks. They caused a sensation, throwing the stock market into a panic. Two months later France and Austria were at war.

That scoop—and others that followed, including an over-mythologized scoop on the assassination of President Lincoln, the details of which seemed to change with each telling—established the agency's influence and authority, especially in government circles. Queen Victoria is said to have paid twenty pounds to subscribe to Reuter's telegram service for six months. Its quality was recognized in a note she wrote to her favorite Prime Minister, Benjamin Disraeli, complaining about the poor intelligence she received from some of her ministers and ambassadors, in which she referred to Reuter as "the one who generally knows."[6]

That same year, 1865, brought a change in the agency's status from privately owned business to public company. Reuter had been working on ambitious plans to operate his own cable across the North Sea into northern Europe with a landfall on the Frisian Island of Norderney. There it was supposed to link up with proposed new telegraph lines extending eastward to join a new overland line from Russia to India, Britain's most valuable dominion. The King of Hanover promised cooperation but offered no money. Bereft of royal largesse, the project required finance in an amount that only the City of London was equipped to raise. A public offering of stock was organized and Reuter's rights in the Norderney venture, along with his news agency, became part of a public enterprise called Reuter's Telegram Company.

Public or not, the company was structured to remain, at its core, a family business. Reuter was appointed managing director by a board of directors selected more for their dependence on him than their independence *from* him, and Reuter had no trouble extracting a mandate giving him virtually unimpaired authority right up to his retirement. He also retained the right to choose his successor.

The flotation marked the first of three occasions when the ownership of Reuters passed into public hands. It would be the least controversial.

One measure of Reuter's growing power in international news circles was his ability to negotiate news exchange agreements with his former rivals, Havas and Wolff, both almost entirely favoring Reuter's interests. Having once

---

[6] Graham Storey, *Reuters' Century*, Max Parrish & Co. 1951, p.61

challenged them for continental supremacy from a position of weakness, he could now offer them a world partnership from a position of strength, Britain having far more national interests around the world than their own countries. The arrangement amounted to a cartel, and as such it became known. As a carve-up typical of discredited European power politics, it was hated—especially by the Associated Press, a powerful new American agency, and the AP would spend nearly half a century working evangelically for its destruction.

Success came at a price. By 1878, Julius Reuter had worked himself into a state of poor health. At the age of sixty-one, he wasn't so much ill as worn out—but not by the business of news. He had long been distracted by a painful preoccupation with one of the wilder commercial ideas to spring from that fertile mind.

The project in question was an ambitious, and in retrospect improbable, scheme, devised by Reuter, to develop and industrialize the isolated, backward but strategically important kingdom of Persia. The Shah of the day, Nasir ed-Din, awarded an investment group, privately organized by Reuter outside the affairs of his agency, a huge and complex industrial development concession. Among the exclusive rights it offered were contracts to operate the national railway and central bank, to exploit the country's mineral and forestry resources, and to create highways, irrigation, and dozens of other public works. The Shah would personally receive 20 percent of the profits. The British government expressed a political interest in the project's success as a means of curbing the expansionist ambitions of Russia, then Britain's chief diplomatic rival. The British Foreign Office declined to offer Reuter financial backing, which he didn't need anyway, but indicated its willingness to give, in the event of failure, certain guarantees, which he did want, and generally offered discreet encouragement.

The concession created a sensation in Europe. Lord Curzon, a former British foreign secretary, characterized it in his memoirs as "the most complete and extraordinary surrender of the entire industrial resources of a kingdom into foreign hands that has probably ever been dreamed of, much less accomplished."[7]

Those, unfortunately, were also the views of the Persians who mattered most, which did not include the Shah and his entourage. The mullahs, the religious leaders of Persia's Shiite Muslims, reacted angrily. Protesters were exhorted to take to the streets of Tehran and the demonstrations turned violent. Russia tabled vigorous diplomatic objections and exploited the situation behind the scenes by intriguing with the mullahs. The pressure proved too much for the Shah. Fearing for his throne, not to mention his skin, he capitulated to the mullahs. Two years after he had signed the concession, he

---

[7] Dennis Wright, *The English Among the Persians*, William Heinemann, 1977, p.102

was forced to cancel it. Reuter was left high and dry. His response was to seek government help in securing compensation for his losses. In this he failed, too, largely because Foreign Office mandarins had acted in character—leading Reuter on with winks and nods and then leaving him in the lurch with denials and shakes of the head; and, in failing, he exhausted himself.

In retrospect, the "Persia caper" can be viewed either as a venture of great imagination and boldness, one that might have succeeded but for spineless British officialdom, or nothing more than a madcap scheme propelled by vanity and political naïveté. The only certainty is that it ended in spectacular failure and embarrassment.

Reuter took time off to recover. In fact, he would never fully redirect his attention to the neglected business of the news agency, with unfortunate consequences.

Baron de Reuter, as he now called himself (a title bestowed in his native Germany by the Duke of Saxe-Coburg-Gotha, Queen Victoria's brother-in-law) retired to the South of France in 1878. Professionally he was a spent man, privately a contented one. He died in 1899 at the age of eighty-two, at his villa on the Promenade des Anglais in Nice.

★

The agency stayed in the family. Reuter's eldest son, Herbert, had been running the day-to-day business for the previous twenty years, a period in which the agency had continued to thrive. But a new century announced a changing world, and it would confront Herbert with financial and management problems that he was temperamentally ill-equipped to handle.

Herbert's inevitable burden was to wear the dreadful label so often pinned to inheritors, that he was "not the man his father was." Herbert had in fact been a reluctant successor. Family connections aside, he was far from qualified, or suitable, for the job. He was a shy and scholarly man, not gregarious and straightforward as his father had been. He was retiring almost to the point of being reclusive, and in social intercourse unfathomable. In his youth he had refused to have anything to do with the business, preferring to indulge his preoccupations with music and mathematics. With a classical education from Harrow and Oxford, and time spent in France for graduate studies in music, he was cultured and well-read, but these attributes alone were of little help in the world of business. He rarely left the house. He disliked travel, hardly ever venturing into Europe, and never outside it.

He was persuaded to join the agency only when his father had become distracted by the unraveling Persia Concession. At the age of twenty-three, blond hair worn flamboyantly at shoulder length, he is said to have "sauntered" into the office with an air of calculated indifference. Once he had taken up the

Chief News Editor's chair, he seemed to settle into the job, even showed signs of enjoying it. Unfortunately, he would soon have to become a business manager rather than a journalist, and, in a troubled period for the agency, obliged to operate commercially with its principal line of business, general news, increasingly resistant to profitability. Famous scoops continued to enhance Reuters' reputation as a source of news, but they did little for the bottom line. Herbert often seemed overwhelmed.

Such problems never troubled the increasingly powerful and single-minded American news cooperative, the Associated Press. Basking in the growing industrial power of the United States, the AP was generously funded by its members and had them in sufficient numbers to cover its operating costs. As AP men liked to emphasize with smug nobility, the agency had no interest in profits; its sole objective was to reduce its members' expenses. This gave AP a purity of purpose. Reuters enjoyed no such advantages of scale and, as a public company, had shareholders to satisfy. Furthermore, it also faced expanding competition from an emerging group of domestic agencies, spawned by the abolition of newspaper taxes in 1855. In bringing news stand prices down to levels that attracted millions of fresh readers, its chief consequence was public demand for the kind of homegrown stories, mainly items of entertaining trivia, that Reuters was neither equipped nor inclined to cover. The new agencies were more than ready to supply them.

Worse was to come. Dissatisfied with the local news they received from the telegraph companies, in 1868 Britain's provincial newspapers formed a domestic cooperative, which they called, reversing the American nomenclature, the Press Association. While the PA was not formed for the specific purpose of competing with Reuters, its success encouraged the formation of several news agencies that did. Two years later, for example, the Exchange Telegraph appeared, specializing in financial news, traditionally Reuters' preserve, and made its mark by securing the right to report company news directly from the London Stock Exchange. Extel immediately became the service favored by stockbrokers. That Reuters had not been the natural choice for such an award suggested that its management was asleep at the switch.

Even so, the public impression of Reuters was that of a grand imperial institution of solid authority. That was also the American view. "Reuters Rex sat at the crossroads of the world of news and controlled the traffic," wrote Kent Cooper, a general manager at AP (and no friend of Reuters) in his gloating, evangelical memoir, *Barriers Down*.

Cooper's depiction of Reuters as "dignified, conservative and omniscient" may have reflected its popular image, but being long on prestige and short of cash was cold comfort to Reuters' shareholders. A complacent and inattentive bunch, they had not been unduly alarmed about the company's deteriorating financial condition. But then one day the board, facing up to financial difficulties, voted to eliminate the dividend. Herbert's response to the wave of complaints from shareholders, suddenly aroused from slumber, was to assure them that Reuters was considering lucrative alternative sources of revenue.

The first attempts at diversification were decidedly mixed. An advertising venture, Reuters Financial Publicity Department, was quickly brought down by inept management. Among its many other failings, it had incurred the hostility of the press by telling advertisers that advertisements placed through Reuters "would enable us to make representations for extended editorial reference to your interests." The man responsible for the unforgivable sin of confusing the interests of church and state was promptly fired—a disgrace to which he responded by committing suicide.

A financial remittance business, first started in 1891, proved more durable. By utilizing its extensive communications network to transmit private telegraphic money transfers—and to undercut the fees charged by banks and telegraph companies—the service proved popular among immigrants from empire as a means of sending money home to their families. But Herbert seemed oblivious to the inherent risk of competing with his own customers, particularly the banks, or to the idea that they might retaliate. When they did strike back with improved services of their own, Reuters could offer no response.

As bad as those experiences had been, Reuters' venture into banking was worse. It announced the beginning of Herbert's downfall. Known first as Reuters Bank, later as British Commercial Bank, it was funded by public subscription that increased the share capital of Reuter's Telegram Company five-fold. It was run as a separate business from the news agency, but it was Herbert, a neophyte in banking affairs, who personally ran the bank. And Herbert it was who decided that the bank's principal activity should be foreign exchange. In reaching this conclusion, he had fallen under the influence of one Arnold J. Hajduska, a decidedly odd fellow hired from an obscure institution called the Jewish Banking Corporation, apparently on the recommendation of Reuters' chief accountant. Hajduska's professed genius in currency trading and international lending was never demonstrated, but evidently Herbert's trust in him knew no bounds. Herbert's faith in his own powers was equally misplaced. He insisted on personally evaluating most of the bank's loan proposals, and inevitably got many of them wrong.

Reuters' Editor-in-Chief, Fredric W. Dickinson, in common with many of his colleagues, could only look on in fearful wonder. His assessment of Herbert was blunt. "He believed that he thoroughly understood finance and that he was a shrewd businessman. In both respects he was mistaken."

The bank headed relentlessly toward disaster, undermined not only by

Hajduska's bumbling and Herbert's dabbling but also by the onset of the First World War. The hapless Hajduska was stranded on the continent when war broke out. Presumably interned, he simply disappeared, never to be seen again.

With the share price sinking, Herbert was left to endure alone the humiliation of a public scolding from shareholders and private expressions of anger from his fellow directors. Both, it must be said, were long overdue. It seemed likely that he would be forced to resign. The issue was resolved in more tragic fashion.

One day in April 1915, the second year of the war, an increasingly distraught Herbert was informed in his office by telephone that his wife, who had long been handicapped, had died after suffering a brief illness. Herbert was inconsolable. Three days later, consumed with guilt that he had neglected her in favor of his business affairs, he locked himself in the summerhouse of his estate in Reigate, fifteen miles outside London, and shot himself.

Herbert's only son, Hubert, was the last male heir of the Reuter line. But he was even less qualified to run the company than his father had been. Hubert, like his father, was something of a dreamer and a romantic. He had also followed Herbert's example in declining to join the company, becoming instead a full-time schoolteacher and part-time poet. His fate, too, was resolved in tragic fashion. A year after Herbert's suicide, having resigned his officer's commission in a county regiment, Hubert enlisted as a private in the Black Watch. He was killed on the Somme while heroically attempting to rescue wounded comrades.

Reuters, both news agency and bank, survived the rest of the war, but no longer as a family business. That died with Hubert in Flanders.

Family-run concerns are always susceptible to the vagaries of inheritance. Some may have taken comfort from the fact that Reuters would no longer be exposed to that particular problem, and never again subjected to amiable incompetents such as Herbert. Nor would it be.

But what came next would be even worse, as we shall see.

# Fred

"Know what futures are, son?"

The significance of the question was that, after four years of tireless devotion to the cause of Comtelburo's missing parrots, I was about to get a promotion. Richly deserved and long overdue it was, too, or so I felt strongly at the time. Forty years on, I can admit that it was neither. None of the work I had done merited comparison with the Seven Labors of Hercules. To be honest, it barely rated a scout badge—unless they give one for creative tea-making.

Frank Taylor, who had just replaced Albert Murray as head of Day Markets, was asking the question. He didn't say why he was asking it, but I knew that something was up, and my guess was that it was connected with Albert's sudden disappearance. Murray had been transferred from his beloved South Pier to a sleepy Comtelburo outpost in the City of London called, with impeccable logic, the City Office. Exactly what went on there was something of a mystery. Though barely half a mile from 85 Fleet Street, it was as remote from the newsroom as one of those half-forgotten desert forts of the French Foreign Legion. It was staffed by a small band of market reporters assigned to cover the Baltic Exchange (shipping), and the London Metal Exchange, which ranked among the City's least known and least dynamic enterprises. According to popular belief, the occupants of City Office dutifully observed the traditions of the markets they covered by spending their mornings planning three-hour lunches, and their afternoons sleeping off the effects of three-hour lunches.

Yes, Frank confirmed, I was about to follow Albert into the City, but not to the City office. With a sigh of relief, I learned that I was bound instead for Plantation House, a sprawling City office building that then housed the markets in the so-called "soft" commodities: cocoa, sugar, coffee, rubber, and something unappealingly known as greasy wool. They were futures markets. (Plantation House fell to the wrecker's ball a few weeks before I wrote this.)

No, I was far from sure what futures were, I confessed to Frank Taylor. I did have a vague idea but found it impossible to articulate in plain English. "Er, they're commodities that are bought and sold, um, for hedging, without the buyers or sellers ever setting eyes on what's been bought or sold," was the best I could manage—or something like that. I wasn't entirely clear what "hedging" was either.

I might as well have quoted the well-known anonymous ditty:

*In the City they sell and buy*
*And nobody ever asks them why.*
*But since it contents them to buy and sell*
*God forgive them, they might as well.*

Despite the pathetic inadequacy of my response, Taylor was amiably tolerant. "That'll do for a start, son," he said. "But read up on the subject, and fast. You start on Monday morning, God 'elp 'em."

Plantation House bore no resemblance to the conventional image of an exchange. Never having been there, I had imagined a large, paper-strewn arena filled with booths and crowded with frantically gesticulating traders. The reality was a warren of rooms, alcoves, halls and connecting passageways, with no evident focal point. Sugar and cocoa, then the most active markets, enjoyed the privilege of having their own trading rooms. Coffee traders congregated at one end of a very large and dimly lit central hall, as if unable to afford a room of their own. In the same hall, some distance away, the rubber men gathered around a particular pillar. Somewhere to the rear of the building, greasy wool was traded in a chapel-like space overlooked by a public gallery. I rarely saw anyone doing business there, but visitors would pop in from time to time for quiet meditation.

As well as these major commodities, various minor ones were traded. Don't ask me to name them. Gunnybags may have been one. Business was conducted at various designated locations—a column here, a corner there—by furtive-looking men with notepads. Everyone surreptitiously watched everyone else, presumably for signs or gestures that might betray a trading secret. I found the ambience of Plantation House predatory, conspiratorial, clubby, and clique-ridden—a place more reflective of its street-corner origins than ideally suited to its purposes. I hated the place the moment I set foot in it.

If markets are supposed to function for the benefit of the investing public, it seemed an alien concept at Plantation House. Unlike the London Stock Exchange, which put out a price ticker, none of the commodities markets had any mechanism to provide public access to prices. Instead, they relied on Comtelburo to do the job for them. Comtelburo—or Reuters Economic Services, as it had been renamed—had been awarded exclusive rights to collect and distribute information from the trading floors, a privilege to which the company attached great importance, both for its financial value and for what it supposedly conferred in prestige. Reuters fulfilled its contract by placing price reporters at listening posts on the trading floors and assigning journalists to wander about the place to pick up trade gossip. Telephones were installed on each of the trading floors with direct lines to the newsroom at 85 Fleet Street.

There, the prices and gossip we called in were merged with "hard" news from other parts of the world and transmitted to clients over Reuters' various specialized teleprinter services (sometimes referred to as newswires or, confusingly, tickers).

As a tabulator and NATSOPA member I was confined to reporting prices, the reporting of news being a privilege reserved for journalists. Despite my aversion to Plantation House, and as it turned out to the job, being there represented a great career opportunity. By company tradition, clerks aspiring to become journalists first had to graduate by working as price reporters. I was about to take the first steps along that road—or so I thought.

Sugar was to be my beat—or, if you like, beet. The sugar trading "floor" was a rectangular room, perhaps half a tennis court in size, and marked out by a white perimeter line. At one end a desk was reserved for the presiding "chairman," a kind of ombudsman appointed by members to keep a supervisory eye on things and to resolve disputes between traders. The other three sides were defined by benches and behind them, against the walls, by ranks of telephone booths from which members received buy and sell orders and market intelligence from their offices, and vice versa. Reuters had been allocated an inconspicuous corner booth. This was furnished, as were all the others, with a high stool, a shelf, and a telephone; in our case, with a direct line to 85 Fleet Street. At the other end of the line a tabulator was permanently stationed to take down any prices I saw fit to call in.

Trading was conducted according to the rules of open outcry, which requires traders to announce bids and offers by shouting them out loud. This they did heatedly and often manically. Audible communication was supplemented by the kind of hand signals used by tic-tac men at racetracks.

Despite its designation as the official reporting agency, Reuters was resented by many traders, and our representatives were accordingly often treated as unwelcome interlopers and snoops. "Just don't get in the way, boy," was the condescending advice from the occupant of my neighboring booth. "And don't let me catch you listening in on my private calls." Both were reasonable requests, even if rudely expressed. My polite response was that I had no prurient interest in hearing what I was not supposed to hear (which was not entirely true then and would certainly change if ever I became a pukka reporter). A few of my colleagues had managed to endear themselves to the traders by running errands or exchanging gossip. As a new boy, all I could do was to hover at the fringes of the crowd like one of Fagin's pickpockets—which is no doubt how we were regarded.

A curious crowd it was too, a cross-section of post-war London society, with plummy-voiced graduates from the finest public schools mingling cheek-by-jowl with rougher diamonds from London's East End. It heralded a permanent change in the City's demography. There was no tension. The two factions got along perfectly, each deriving amusement from the other by exchanging good-natured impersonations of accents and mannerisms. The cultural divide surfaced only during lunch breaks, as the posh brigades from Surrey and Hertfordshire made for nearby restaurants or wine bars for oysters and Chablis, while the lively lads from less salubrious quarters charged down to the pub for pie and ale.

The traders might represent an emerging class-blind City, but the trading routines remained resolutely antiquated. Three times a day, at the opening, midday and the closing, a formal ritual took place, known as the Call. Presided over by the chairman, the Call's purpose was to establish the day's official prices, accomplished by taking traders through a roll call of each of the trading months. Between calls, trading was left to informal open outcry. Activity veered from torpor to frenzy and back, usually with no transition between. The lulls, which could be prolonged, I found stupefying. Relief from boredom came, in my case, by mastering the *Manchester Guardian* crossword, which I was soon regularly able to finish before the end of the day. Other crossword aficionados on the floor made a point of being unimpressed. For the most part readers of *The Times* or the *Daily Telegraph*, they found my affection for the liberal *Guardian* evidence of a subversive tendency.

They may have been right.

There were other popular pastimes. Analyses of the previous night's telly were endless. One trader, a budding Wordsworth, insisted on reading his awful poetry out loud (he did seem to spend considerable time wandering lonely as a cloud). Another, a former circus acrobat, entertained us by performing impressive somersaults and one-armed headstands. There was considerably more betting on horses than on markets. And of course there was much snoozing—a dangerous disposition given a time-honored custom of shoving lighted newspapers under the doors of booths occupied by dozing members. On festive occasions firecrackers might be tossed around. Such pranks were often the subject of posted notices threatening harsh disciplinary action (which might have pointed out, if only for dramatic effect, that Plantation House stood barely a hundred yards from the spot where the Great Fire of London had broken out in 1666).

The portent of a violent eruption in trading was usually a trader emerging lethargically from his booth to announce a bid or offer breaking a market deadlock. This sometimes provoked pandemonium, as traders spilled out of their booths like soldiers tumbling from bunks at reveille to form a seething, impenetrable scrum in the middle of the trading floor. When this happened, the poor reporter was rendered virtually impotent, because it was virtually impossible to make sense of what was going on inside the maul. "May at 50! …

Yours at 49! … Bollocks! … July 51 … Three done, two more wanted … May 51 … Christ! Who's got July? … Where's fucking July? … Will somebody tell me where the fuck July just traded?"

Trading would go on in that vein for several minutes. All a reporter could do, lurking ineffectually behind the white line like a linesman at a football match trying to spot infringements, was to pick up as many trades as possible. Sometimes it wasn't many. My habit was to jot them down on a notepad before dashing over to the telephone to call them in. Omissions were inevitable. Sequences often got reversed. Much of the time even the traders were confused. It was all splendidly archaic and unavoidably hit-or-miss.

Reuters' clients, however, were far from amused. Nor were they shy about conveying their displeasure to my superiors at 85 Fleet Street, who in turn appeared to take a positive delight in relaying the complaints to me. "We missed a key trade, old boy. How did you let that happen?" Or, "How come you reversed the order? We're showing the market going up when in fact it's heading down." There was no answering the charges; they were perfectly justified. During frantic periods, only someone with a photographic memory or the mind of an extraterrestrial of massively superior intelligence could have coped. Or so it seemed to me, being neither of those things. Self-doubt led me to believe I was the only reporter having trouble. I wasn't, but clearly some of us found the work more challenging than others, and obviously I wasn't one of the others. Later I would understand that customer dissatisfaction reflected less a fall in reporting efficiency than heightened expectations due to rising market activity.

The company's initial reaction was to reject any suggestion that its reporting methods were questionable. But the complaints persisted and management was finally forced to acknowledge that there might be something better than a practice as patently inadequate as eavesdropping. And that was before the teletype operators had a chance to mangle the figures.

From this period of self-evaluation emerged a strange device. Its brief and inglorious life is worth a digression, if only because it offers a vivid image of Reuters' first, child-like steps along the yellow-brick road to automation. It was known as the Magic Pen.

Arriving on the trading floor one morning, late as usual, I found two men squeezed into the booth on the sugar floor. One was Bernard Gagan, the Deputy Chief Financial News Editor (a manifestation of Fleet Street's weakness for convoluted editorial titles), the other a man I didn't recognize, speaking a form of English I didn't understand. The reason for their presence sat on the shelf inside the booth. It resembled a child's scribble pad, from which dangled a cord with an attachment that looked like a pen, exposing the device as something electronic.

"This is going to make everyone's life easier," Bernie declared breezily. "We're installing it on a test basis. I want you to use it to send prices to Fleet Street. It should be much faster than the telephone."

"How does it work?" I asked.

"It's an electronic notepad," Bernie explained, in the manner of a science professor outlining some complex theory to a first-year student. "Fascinating concept. It uses a, well, um, a kind of magic pen." Having coined the immortal term, and despite evincing a less than profound grasp of the technology, Bernie plowed on undaunted. "Here's how it works. You write prices onto this pad here, and they come out on a similar pad at the receiving end, exactly as you've written them." The receiving pad apparently had a proboscis-like arm, like the stylus on an electrocardiograph or lie-detection machine. Responding to impulses received over the telephone line, the stylus converted them into a perfect replica of what the sender had written—at least in theory.

The practice was something else.

The Magic Pen, it soon became clear, had a singular, fundamental, and fatal flaw: far from faithfully replicating the characters written by the sender, it reduced them to gibberish, the quality of reproduction varying between the barely legible and the kind of scrawls applied to nursery walls by infants with crayons. No matter how scrupulously the sender attempted to compensate for the system's peccadilloes by writing with p-a-i-n-s-t-a-k-i-n-g precision, virtually every transmission ended up as graffiti. All this emerged over the course of a two-week trial period, but, in truth, in the first seconds of that two-week trial.

There are no prizes for guessing who got blamed. At 85 Fleet Street the recipients of these fantastic hieroglyphics regarded them not so much as a manifestation of electronic epilepsy but as proof of the sender's incompetence or illiteracy; or worse, Luddism. Suspicions of sabotage were exacerbated by my ill-advised remark in a pub to the effect that if the company really intended to get serious about market reporting, it could do worse than revert to more traditional methods, like the Baron's pigeons. This throwaway line, overhead by my supervisor, made its way back to Fleet Street—and considerably faster and more accurately than the Magic Pen could have transmitted it—which, you might say, only proved my point.

After a couple of weeks of futile scribbling, the deficiencies of the Magic Pen became the subject of an investigation. If it had been a criminal investigation, I would have been a prime suspect. I certainly felt like one. At any rate, Bernie Gagan reappeared on the sugar floor one day to personally supervise a final, definitive test of the system. Presumably the intention was to show a slow-witted dolt like me how, with a little more care and attention, the device could be made to work effectively. Tests usually precede a project launch. This one had all the hallmarks of a post-mortem.

Bernie, it seemed, had been the project's sponsor. He had spent money on it that the company could ill afford and it was in danger of turning into yet another in a series of Heath Robinson-esque contraptions. Bernie was a nervous and indecisive man and, under pressure, tended to mumble while twiddling vigorously with his mustache, which often made it difficult to catch what he was saying. In that respect he was a human version of the Magic Pen.

"I suppose we'd better get on with it," he muttered.

Trading not having started yet, a circle of curious traders had formed around us. At the receiving end, I later learned, an even bigger crowd had gathered, creating a tableau that I imagine might have been reminiscent of Morse's first demonstration to Congress of his electric telegraph.

Bernie cracked his knuckles purposefully, but then hesitated. "Why am I doing this? It's your job. You write, I'll observe." He picked up the telephone. "All set at this end. You too? Good."

"What shall I write?" came my limp response, Magic Pen in hand.

"Whatever you think is appropriate."

As an opportunity to record a suitably memorable epitaph, this took some beating. With exaggerated care, and in neat block capitals, I wrote a single word: B-A-L-L-S.

Gagan smiled. Over the telephone, he heard an exultant cry of relief from Fleet Street. "Coming through now," said the voice. This was followed by a puzzled commentary. "It's a bit fuzzy...it looks like...no, I think it's...84115...or perhaps 84118...Which is it?"

It was a precious moment. Even Bernie managed a nervous chuckle. Some of us couldn't stop laughing for days. My pal, Barry Clark, then a price reporter on cocoa, shared my mirth over a pint, but offered a warning: "I'm afraid you may not be laughing when all this catches up with you. They'll be looking for a scapegoat."

By the time we got back from lunch that day, the Magic Pen had disappeared, never to be seen again, thereby performing its one and only successful trick. It was a fate I expected to share. Sure enough, a couple of weeks later I found myself back at 85 Fleet Street—if not in disgrace, then hardly in a state of grace. My reporting career, about ninety days of it all told, was apparently over.

Before my departure from Plantation House, Bernie's Magic Pen was replaced by another odd-looking device. This one resembled an old-fashioned calculating machine, with a sloping alphabetic keyboard topped by a display panel consisting of three round portholes. It was described as a stock quotation terminal. When a stock or commodity symbol was entered, the portholes displayed the price with a neon-like illumination provided by wire coils encased in bulbs called nixie tubes. There were inevitable references to piss-holes in the snow. In more polite circles it became known as Reuters' three-eyed monster. Its real name was Stockmaster. This device was a genuine breakthrough.

Although designed as a data retrieval product, Stockmaster could also be configured into a data insertion device, as the one in my booth had been. Any prices I entered into it went straight to a central database and from there, on request, directly to clients. I have to say it worked pretty well, but then anything would have after the Magic Pen. The response time was sometimes a little slow, causing problems when trading was exceptionally heavy, but it was a giant step forward from its predecessor.

Stockmaster was the product of an American firm called Ultronic. It had been highly successful as a stock quotation system in the United States. Thousands of them had been installed in stock brokerage offices across the country. Mike Nelson, the general manager of Reuters Economic Services, having seen the machine working while on a visit to New York, had negotiated an arrangement for Reuters to distribute the service in Europe. The deal was considered something of a risk: Europeans were then notoriously suspicious of automation of any kind, and Reuters was virtually broke. But Nelson's punt turned out to be something of a coup. In fact, Stockmaster was destined to save Reuters' bacon.

My immediate problem was how to save my own bacon. Back at Fleet Street, no new assignments came my way. Salaried idleness was no more an unusual phenomenon at Reuters than it was everywhere else on the Street, but after several weeks of wandering aimlessly around the newsroom in search of a project, I fully expected to get the chop.

Then, during one of my interminable walkabouts, I fell in with the most memorable of Cockney characters in a company that boasted a great many of them. His name was Fred Taylor. The younger brother of Frank Taylor, he had decided to make it his personal mission to revive my flagging career. He collared me in Kit's morning tea-trolley queue and we got chatting. After a while, he made a proposition. "Why don't you come and sit next to me, cocker? I'll teach you a thing or two about business, and about life." He was right about that, as he would be about many other things. I pulled up a chair, in my mind at least, and my career prospects brightened immediately.

Fred had grown up in the working-class south London suburb of Catford (as did my father, a telling coincidence, perhaps). He and his brother, like so many at Comtelburo, had joined Reuters straight out of school, starting as messengers. Fred's employment had been interrupted by war, in which he had served with the Royal Air Force as a radio operator in North Africa. "I was one of Monty's secret weapons," he used to say. I can well believe it. Military service was the only occasion on which he had ever set foot outside Britain. He hoped it would be the last. "Bloody glad I was to get back in one piece, I can tell yer, cocker, and 'ere I intend to stay. Y'can keep 'abroad,' as far as I'm concerned."

His most remarkable quality was high intelligence. It was supplemented by what we now call street-smarts. He claimed to have attended the best school in Britain: "the University of the Gutter." This he enunciated with an emphatic, almost violent glottal stop.

He was close to six feet tall but far from strapping. He had a pronounced stoop and a shuffling walk. His appearance was disheveled, the result of bad posture combined with a wardrobe handed down, or in his case up, by his teenage sons. A sallow, almost olive complexion gave him a distinctly unhealthy look. The sad truth, increasingly apparent over the years as his breathing became increasingly wheezy, was that he was not a well man. Even in the days before personal health took the form of a national obsession, any doctor would have taken him to task for his fat-laden working-man's diet—the liver sausage or cheese sandwich that he invariably ordered for lunch—and his aversion to any form of physical activity. Not that Fred would have voluntarily given any doctor a chance to examine him. Worse, he smoked more than nearby Bermondsey power station. Like so many others in the newsroom he rolled his own, but rarely bothered to, because it was easier to cadge from others. In this well-practiced facility for scrounging, he competed with his brother. It had earned them a shared nickname. They were universally known as Giss, derived from their trademark opener: "Giss a fag, cocker." The cry was as familiar around the newsroom as the previously encountered "Unchanged!"

Fred is perhaps best remembered for another distinctive physical characteristic: neglect or uncompromising British dentistry had deprived him of his natural teeth and he refused to wear dentures. Their absence created a facial void that served only to emphasize the general impression of gauntness.

His designated role in the newsroom was unclear. For as long as anyone could remember he had taken uncontested advantage of Comtelburo's benign chaos to avoid doing much of anything. He spent endless hours on the telephone, but to what purpose was obscure. When not on the phone he passed the day trolling the newsroom for conversation, tea, and fags.

He did, come to think of it, have one specific task: Fred was responsible for calculating the Reuters UK Stock Index, published each day and offered up as an alternative to the better-known *Financial Times Index*. Fred was supposed to add up the closing prices of the component stocks and perform some kind of calculation based on a simple mathematical formula, but he rarely remembered to do it and, after a while, couldn't be bothered to. He had, in any case, come up with a much easier method of calculating the index than the one formally prescribed: he made it up. He had noticed over time that the movement in the

Reuters index was usually about half that of the FT index. So that is what he'd make it each day, give or take a point or two for camouflage. If the FT index rose 4.2 points, Fred's index would go up, say, 2.3 points.

Unfortunately, this clever ruse was exposed when a client questioned the index. The man he complained to was Sydney Gampell, Reuters' resident economist and market guru. Gampell, who was supposedly well connected in the highest central banking circles or so he said, achieved a God-like status at Reuters. His principal claim to divinity was a weekly economic commentary, published as a newsletter under the title *Economic X-Ray*. It was his custom, every Wednesday, to dictate the piece to his secretary, in an inimitable stream-of-consciousness style, delivered in a deep-throated mumble. Few, including the poor secretary who typed it, dared to incur the wrath of the almighty by questioning his copy, grammatically or otherwise, which meant that it often emerged in print as gibberish. The punters didn't seem to notice.

Anyway, Gampell strolled over to Fred to mention that some technical analyst in the City had written in with a complaint. He'd been tracking the Reuters index for some months and discovered that somehow it didn't quite compute. Fred's color drained. I have never seen a man look so scared. He turned to me. "What are we goin' to do, cocker?"

We? "This is all your doing," I told him. "You broke it, you bloody well fix it."

But his misery was too pitiful to watch, especially when the index was calculated that day in the proper manner and showed Fred's figure to be substantially below the true one. John Roberts, a fellow tabulator, reluctantly volunteered to join me in coming up with a corrective plan of action. It was a simple scheme. Unable to issue the true index without revealing a sudden and inexplicable leap in the figure, we went with a figure based on the "Taylor formulation" but added a few inconspicuous points. This exercise we repeated each day for several weeks until we had caught up with the real number. Discovery would have cost us our jobs. Fortunately, the complainant, whose letter was ignored by us and evidently forgotten by Gampell, was never heard from again. Fred's gratitude was boundless. "I won't forget this in a hurry, cocker," he assured me.

And he was as good as his word, which was plainly more reliable than his numbers.

Fred's most endearing talent was a knack, best described in his own words, for "stirring the shit." He had apparently done a good deal of stirring during a stint as NATSOPA's Father of the Chapel. To this role, by all accounts, he had brought the same effortless flair for creating bedlam as Harpo contributed to many a Marx Brothers film. On one infamous occasion Fred protested noisily about the sanitary state of the newsroom after a cleaning lady claimed to have spotted a rat under a desk. There were even mutterings about downing tools.

But what the British, with somewhat twisted logic, call "industrial action" was averted when the offending rodent, after a long search, was located and identified as a mislaid fur glove. From then on management regarded Fred with suspicion, though this was tinged with amusement.

After that, he quickly graduated from union affairs. He fancied himself in the role of sage and philosopher. In these roles, he presented himself to the growing influx of management trainees passing through the newsroom on their way to exotic locations around the world. If training meant a stint working as a reporter in the newsroom, a long chat with Fred was also considered no less essential a part of the curriculum. It was, in any event, unavoidable. Any time spent with Fred was considered worthwhile, however, if only for its entertainment value.

One Oxford graduate is said to have received a piece of advice for which he was no doubt grateful at the time, but which he must now be glad he ignored. "You'll never make it far in this business, cocker," Fred told one trainee, a quiet, sandy-haired young man down from Oxford. "Yer just not cut out for it; much too quiet; far too polite; no killer instinct. In my opinion yer'd be much better off in some other line of business."

The recipient of this wisdom was one Michael Nelson, who would soon rise rapidly through the ranks to become Comtelburo's general manager, and keep going higher. I should note that, in the interests of accuracy, that several people have repeated this story over the years, placing it in the realm of legend. Nelson told me he had no recollection of it at all.

A similar story circulated involving the same two men. Fred liked to boast that he was one of Nelson's key advisors. When people looked skeptical, Fred would say, "It's the truth what I'm telling yer. As Nelson himself said to me one day, 'Fred, if ever I need your bloody advice I'll bloody well ask for it.' "

Fred had exactly the opposite advice for me than the tip he'd given to Nelson, which, considering his impact on that gentleman, could well have sent my career spiraling in exactly the opposite direction. "You could go a long way in this company, cocker," he told me. "Fancy yer chances as a journalist, do yer? Well, lookin' around at the competition, I fancy 'em too. Bloody 'opeless, all of 'em. Your mum could do a lot better than this lot. But first we'll 'ave to polish you up a bit. So giss a fag and let's start talkin' about it."

"Er, what exactly is it we're supposed to be doing?" It was something I wanted to understand if only to explain the curious phenomenon of Fred's desk, which, amid a landscape of devastation, was entirely unencumbered by paper, ledgers, typewriter, or anything else. Fred responded with a conspiratorial wink. "What we do around 'ere is strictly between you and me, cocker. Just remember this: the Lord 'elps them who 'elp themselves. And I've got a few ideas the Old Geezer 'upstairs' might 'elp us with."

With that fortifying invocation of divine help, he produced from his pocket a tattered clipping from *The Economist* magazine. *The Economist*! "Just take a butchers at this," he said, handing it to me.

The article was about a new trading market in dollar deposits, known as Eurodollars. It was a market that had quietly emerged to become one of the hot topics of conversation in the City. *The Economist* explained how the market had developed, and why it had caught the imagination of the investment community. It was going to be very big, the article concluded. Impressed, Fred had been trying without success to persuade the second-floor journalists to cover it.

"Those silly buggers don't understand any of it, cocker. All they're good for is tearin' copy off one printer, making a few scribbles, and shovin' it out on another. Most of 'em couldn't write a rude note on a lavatory wall." If I was then hardly in a position to pass judgment, my guess was that Fred wasn't far off the mark. And it did seem as if there was very little original reporting other than of commodities markets. The easier option was to edit ready-made copy supplied by the various outside agencies with which Reuters had news exchange agreements, notably the Press Association and Exchange Telegraph in Britain, and the AP and Dow Jones in the United States.

"We're gonna start shit-stirrin' around 'ere," said Fred, explaining his Grand Plan. "The place needs waking up, believe me."

At least one senior newsroom figure shared Fred's opinion of the second-floor journalists as unimaginative and lazy. Dave Armour, the Financial News Editor, was a laconic Canadian intellectual with a devil-may-care attitude to authority and a short fuse, especially when required to suffer fools gladly. He was one of the few journalists in the newsroom who understood international money markets. He was also an incisive and rapid writer. He and Fred were kindred spirits socially, Armour proving to be as adept at borrowing money and avoiding paying for drinks as Fred was for cadging fags and dodging work.

Armour would prove to be Fred's staunch ally in a battle for which he and Fred were already secretly preparing. The battleground was a new financial newswire called the International Financial Printer, edited in Brussels. The brainchild of Glen Renfrew, a hard-driving Australian said to be one of the company's potential management stars, the IFP was Reuters' first commercial newswire to be edited centrally and transmitted directly to international clients, for the first time bypassing local Reuters' offices and its various European agents. Armour helped Renfrew to set up the service before returning to London, Europe's biggest capital market and the greatest source of news, to initiate coverage of the emerging Eurodollar market. Impressed by Fred's knowledge and aware that Fred had been quietly developing his City contacts, Armour encouraged him to cultivate them. "Take 'em to lunch," he told Fred. "Don't worry about the bills: the company will pick up the tab. We need to get involved in this market." In a company in which expense accounts were frowned upon, this was shockingly subversive.

How Fred had made these City acquaintances, or why, was not something anyone bothered to ask or that he cared to explain. He needed no prompting from Armour to expand the process. What fascinates me now as much as then, is that Fred was talking to relatively senior figures who must have had precious little time for idle chit-chat and even less inclination to risk trading confidences by talking to a news organization. But Fred deployed a disarming manner and a well-camouflaged talent for eliciting information. He prodded away at his sources relentlessly, like a jabbing boxer probing for an opening. Whatever market intelligence he picked up he gleefully passed to Armour, who repaid the compliment by showering Fred with exaggerated flattery, so spurring him to ever greater efforts.

Whenever Armour was out of the office, Fred would type notes about his conversations. In doing so, he adopted a facsimile of the house editorial style. After a while, these short and occasional *billets doux* became extended to regular market commentaries. Very pithy some of them were, too. When it came to digging up dirt, and finding an explication for the inexplicable, Fred was what in sporting realms would be called a natural.

Before long, his phone was ringing incessantly. Half the time, with Fred busy on another line, it was left to me to pick up the calls. Fred welcomed someone to share the burden, and for that I was a natural. Soon I began to develop my own City sources and, with Fred's encouragement, writing my own commentaries. Our reports started to find their way directly on to the wires, especially if Armour was in the filing editor's seat, or "slot." "Great piece, Fred," Armour would yell over. "I'm running it just as is. Keep it up. You too, JJ. Liked your stuff on sterling, by the way."

We had a bit more trouble with the slot-men (copy editors). Peter Evans, a thoughtful and somewhat meticulous Welshman, was a particular bane. "I think we've got to work on this piece a little, boy-o." He was often right. Mike Topliss was a pest of a different kind, passing our copy through without complaint but only after heavy editing, usually eliminating the more interesting parts of a story, and sometimes the entire point of it. A third sub-editor, Frank Nunnay-Elam, was so terrified of running anything we wrote that he had to be browbeaten into using it.

They were all entitled to be nervous: as members of the NUJ they were knowingly acting as accessories to an illicit activity. Fred and I, by working as reporters without the endorsement of management, and without fulfilling the obligation to join the union, had crossed a sacred demarcation line. The news editors, Bill King and Bernie Gagan, were well aware of what was going on but chose to turn a blind eye. We were all inviting trouble, but carried on blithely, becoming less inhibited with each passing week.

Fred now considered himself something of a guru on the subject of Eurodollars. But for all his mellifluous guile on the telephone, he felt distinctly uncomfortable in physical encounters with his sources. The telephone offered Fred a comforting anonymity; face-to-face contact exposed his social insecurities, which stemmed from his south London accent, his scruffy appearance, and the absence of teeth. He was further embarrassed by a lack of affinity with alcohol. This, he felt, put him at a disadvantage in a community which then, much more than now, considered extended and liquid lunches an integral part of the City's fellowship, its ineffable numen. Fred was not a teetotaler in the strictest sense of the word, but I never saw him consume more than a glass of wine or a half-pint of beer at a single sitting. He preferred to take lunch at his desk with a sandwich, a mug of tea and the *Financial Times*, from which he extracted clippings until the paper—someone else's, of course—had been reduced to lace. In the evenings, usually no later than five o'clock, he was content to go home to his council house in south London for a quiet evening of telly.

Invitations to lunches and other social events in the City nonetheless arrived regularly and were received by Fred with some trepidation. But as much as Fred hated going to them, he was reluctant to turn them down, secretly coveting the attention. His quandaries were painful to watch. We did notice, however, and with some amusement, that his shoes began to shine more brightly and that his suits were being pressed once in a while, the evidence being the cleaning tags he invariably forgot to remove. But his ultimate concession to respectability arrived one Monday morning in the form of a new set of teeth. To say that they protruded was an understatement; the teeth showed up first that day, with Fred trailing some distance behind. Although they looked enormous, he appeared years younger. "Don't say a fuckin' word," he growled at Roberts and me. We couldn't even if we'd wanted to, being contorted in our effort to suppress hysterics. After that, the teeth reappeared only when Fred had a lunch appointment.

We enjoyed these lunchtime excursions even if Fred did not, because he always came back with an amusing account of them. One outing found him in some gilded bank's paneled dining room, seated between a brigadier and a rear admiral. Both had evidently enjoyed a "good war" and proceeded to talk about it at length. Fred was invited to represent the flying service, which he did with relish, and which I recall here as far as memory allows:

"I 'ad a good bleedin' war too, cocker," he told them. "I survived. And I would've earned meself a coupla stripes if it 'adn't been for my in'erited condition."

"And what inherited condition was that, Mr. Taylor?" the brigadier had felt obliged to ask.

"Cowardice," replied Fred, with a straight face.

"Yer should 'ave seen their silly bloody faces," he delighted in telling us later.

As a convenient alternative to turning down invitations, Fred began to offer them to me. I didn't mind standing in. In fact, I relished the chance. My *savoir-faire* was somewhat underdeveloped, too, but for me every City lunch was a foray into an adventurous unknown. One of the earliest was just that, although it is difficult to recall the details. The occasion was a formal luncheon in an impressive chandelier-bedecked dining room at Cater Ryder, one of London's discount houses. The problem was that I allowed myself to be over-served, as the ports and brandies circulated. Suddenly, the room started to spin alarmingly and the next I knew I was in the gents, my head between my knees, being dabbed with wet towels by a pinstriped butler. A partner of the firm kindly arranged to have me driven home in a company limousine. That turned a few heads on my street of council houses. I called the next day to apologize to my host. "Say nothing more about it, old boy," he replied graciously. "We were delighted you enjoyed yourself so much and hope to see you again."

Gradually I learned to hold my drink, a skill no less important in the City, and at Reuters, than that of holding a conversation. As my confidence grew I began to fancy myself a regular man-about-town, a dab hand with a French menu and wine list. My contacts list grew ever greater. While Fred was happy to go out to lunch occasionally, I was soon going out nearly every day. I invested in my first suit.

"We make a good team, cocker," he beamed at me one day, admiring my turnout. "One thing I know, it sure beats doin' whatever it is management thinks we're supposed to be doin'."

And so we proceeded on our forbidden quest, our output becoming imprudently prodigious. Some of it was sensational, market-moving stuff—if I say so myself. Our copy was regularly picked up in the *Evening Standard*, usually in the daily report on the trials of the pound sterling—without attribution of course. Fred kept a clipping file. "For evidence," he said, which suggested an impending trial.

In hindsight, it was a mistake to have celebrated our little triumphs so loudly. We were becoming noticed—and resented. And although most of the journalists were perfectly willing to leave us to cover markets they didn't pretend to understand, a few had started to fret about the illegality of it all. There were whispered suggestions that management would soon be forced to intervene, before the NUJ got wind of what was going on.

Fred and I thought we held a trump card. Reuters' subscribers had responded favorably to our market commentaries. Armour had been getting calls congratulating him on the improving coverage. Some callers admittedly had been encouraged to ring by Fred himself, but others were spontaneous. There were even a few calls inquiring about subscribing to the IFP. "See, cocker, we're makin' a big impact," Fred exulted. "We're movin' markets and sellin' printers. And that's what it's all about."

Watching markets move in response to our little commentaries was a little worrying. Some of the material we put out, especially on days when there was little definitive to report, was, frankly, plain nonsense. I have no doubt I would be embarrassed to read it today. We regularly breached one of the cardinal rules of journalism—never to put out uncorroborated hearsay from a single source. In doing so, we were not so much responding to market rumors as starting them. Fred's attitude, no less than mine if I'm honest, was that generating gossip was the whole idea of the exercise. Armour didn't seem to be bothered. Absurdity compounded irresponsibility. One day Fred wrote a piece about negative market rumors surrounding the French franc, citing a published report in an "authoritative financial magazine" called *l'Equipe*. On the foreign-exchange market, the franc responded with a short, sharp decline.

"*L'Equipe* is authoritative alright," I pointed out, "but mainly on cycling and football. It's a bloody sports magazine."

It said something about the slot man who had let the piece through. Fred was not in the least discomfited. "Just goes to show what some of these traders really know, dunnit? The markets are just a game."

On one occasion, I picked up a rumor that the prime minister of the day, Harold Wilson, was planning a televised address to the nation on the subject of the economy—and particularly on the status of the pound. Sterling had been exposed to unrelenting pressure in the foreign-exchange markets, and to rampant speculation about devaluation. In this highly charged atmosphere the "D" word was more or less taboo, especially at Reuters, which, as a news agency, enjoyed less of a license to indulge in conjecture than newspapers. The future of the pound occasionally vacated the front pages but it rarely faded as a topic of lunchtime conversation in the City. The Wilson rumor reached me from two foreign-exchange traders and, on a whim, I decided to call 10 Downing Street for a response. I got one in the form of an abusive earful from a deputy press officer, whose name I've forgotten. "You people [the press] are irresponsible," he ranted. "You're the cause of half the trouble in the markets. Don't you understand you're undermining the national currency every time you put out this kind of rumor? You print it and I'll be putting a call through to your boss. I happen to know your managing director Gerald Long very well and I know he wouldn't approve of Reuters being a party to this sort of thing…"

Somewhat shaken, I hustled over to tell Armour. "He threatened you, huh? Give me the guy's phone number. You just wait here and listen." He offered an encouraging wink.

Armour got through to him right away and the torrent now flowed in the reverse direction. "Reuters will print what it sees fit, not what Downing Street wants us to print. Don't think you can bully my reporters with threats when they're only doing their job. By all means call Gerry Long. I'll tell him to expect your call. Meanwhile, you do your bloody job as you see fit, and we'll get on with ours."

I found all this hugely entertaining. But when Armour hung up he turned to me with a disapproving scowl. "Very enterprising, calling Downing Street, but pull a stupid stunt like that again and I'll have your guts for garters. Next time you hear a rumor like that, you call me. Or pass it on to the general news desk upstairs. We've gotta follow procedures on stuff like this. We can't have junior reporters calling Downing Street. Hell, you're not even a junior fucking reporter. And by the way, as every journalist in Britain except you is aware, Wilson's on holiday this week in the Scilly Isles."

Soon the burgeoning Taylor-Jessop news agency reached the end of its unnatural life. Not surprisingly, Bernie Gagan had received a complaint from the NUJ's Father of the Chapel. Bernie's tacit consent now suddenly turned to shocked disapproval. He had no choice but to act. Armour was summoned to Gagan's office, emerging to give us the bad news himself. "Sorry, guys, I've gotta shut you down. You know how it is. We've had a good run, and I hope you'll keep feeding us good stuff. But nothing written, okay?"

Fred was livid. "Fuck 'em. I'm not makin' another phone call, ever." He was as good as his word. A prolonged and rather histrionic sulk followed, with Fred folding his arms in a conspicuous gesture of protest. And for the next three days he stayed home, struck down, his wife explained unconvincingly, by a severe head cold. I drifted off into other activities.

A few weeks later, I was invited to Gagan's office. Armour was there already. They both looked grave. This could only spell more trouble, I thought.

Gagan opened the conversation. "So, you want to be a reporter?" The mustache, I noticed, was getting a vigorous massage. "Look, if you'd like to try out for the NUJ, we'll back you. There'll be a test, of course. But if you do well, the company will be glad to sponsor you for membership. Fair enough?" I could only agree that it was more than fair.

I took the examination at a desk near the newsroom doors. I found it relatively easy. There was only one troublesome moment: I was asked to give an example of a split infinitive. Familiar with the term but unable to come up with a definition, I cheated by whispering the question to a nearby journalist.

He didn't know what it meant either. Other than that, I apparently passed with honors.

The day my temporary NUJ membership card arrived in the post, my parents took me down to our local for a celebratory drink. My father introduced me to a dozen people in the bar as "my son, the journalist." The other patrons seemed unimpressed. A few looked hostile.

So, too, the following morning, did Fred. He had not been invited to take the test. It was, in his view, a blatant example of discrimination. He had a point. "My face just don't fit around 'ere, cocker, I know that," he moaned. Fred was partly mollified when Armour got him a compensating salary increase. "Gimme the money any day," Fred chortled—less than convincingly, I thought.

Modesty compels me to disclaim unusual success in my official career in journalism. Modesty is largely justified. I could write adequately; my spelling was good; and I undoubtedly had a "nose" for a story. In that respect, Fred had taught me better than any journalism course could have done.

Diversifying from market reporting into company news gave me scope to indulge in the occasional scoop. Fred looked on admiringly as I broke my first one: a merger between two leading British brewers, Bass and Charrington. The methodology was classic Fred. I had picked up a hint of the story from a stockbroker half an hour before the stock market was to close. Charrington's shares, I noticed, had been moving up steadily, and suspiciously, for two days. I called Bass's public relations office. "No comment," came the standard response, but with a fatal afterthought: "Anyway, Charles Barker, our PR agency, handles all press inquiries." I phoned Barker's. "I understand you're handling the Bass-Charrington announcement. When do you plan to release it?"

"Not before the market closes, of course. By the way, how on earth did you find out about it?"

Gotcha!

Another small triumph was breaking news of a merger between two other drinks companies, International Distillers and Vintners, and Showerings.

"Trust you to specialize in the booze industry," said Fred.

For the most part, though, my days were spent, like those of a policeman, in a tedious routine of company shareholder meetings, turgid interviews with corporate executives, and writing stock-market reports. I began to understand, although without approving, why so many of my colleagues had opted for the quiet, easy life of the rewrite man.

Then, on a Friday afternoon in September 1967, less than three years into my journalistic career, Bernie Gagan telephoned to invite me for what he called "a little chat."

It was a call I'd half been expecting.

For two days I'd sat brooding at my desk watching at least a dozen of my colleagues file in and out of Bernie's office in a more or less constant procession. They had all looked fearful on the way in and relieved on the way out. Something was clearly afoot, and because there is no such thing as a newsroom secret, it didn't take a half-decent reporter more than a few minutes to discover what. What was afoot was America.

Faced with contractual demands it could not meet, Reuters had terminated its long-standing news exchange agreement with the Associated Press and, by extension, with Dow Jones. The two American agencies had formed an alliance and were now intent on competing with us rather than cooperating. Reuters would have to start collecting its own news in America and the company needed "volunteers" to go to New York to establish an expanded base there. Reuters even intended to launch an American financial newswire.

Astonishingly, Bernie had found no takers for the assignment. One candidate after another had pleaded disqualifying personal circumstances: a new mortgage, a new baby, or a recently acquired medical condition. It struck me as a sad symptom of the company's lack of editorial vigor. I felt no disappointment in not being among the first to be asked to go. Being relatively new to the job, I would not have been surprised not to be asked at all. It was far from clear in what esteem I was held by my newsroom peers, including Gagan, whose life I had made difficult on several occasions.

But now, as the lugubrious procession petered out, and my colleagues' collective response to the company's predicament became common knowledge, I could at least entertain the possibility of becoming a late substitute.

The question came out right away. "How would you feel about going to New York?" Bernie went on to explain the circumstances before reaching for the soft soap. "It'll just be for six months, I would think. Good experience, you know. We've been quite impressed with your contributions to the wire of late and we think you're an ideal candidate. Give it some thought over the weekend and let me know what you think on Monday. And please keep this under your hat."

"I can tell you right now," I said. "I'll go."

Bernie looked shocked. "Don't you have to talk it over with your wife?"

"I have already. She's up for it, too." Bernie looked puzzled, evidently blind to the possibility of a leak. "The word is out," I explained.

"Someone's been talking," he mumbled.

"No," I replied, "everyone's been talking. This is, after all, a Fleet Street newsroom."

After that, he got down to the details. "We'd like you there as soon as possible; how about Monday week? I apologize for the short notice, but you understand we have to react quickly."

Monday week would be just fine, I told him.

We were shaking hands when Bernie sprang a little surprise of his own.

"By the way, I'll be going over with you." Bernie planned to be in New York for a few weeks before moving down to Washington to supervise coverage of economic news from government agencies. "Now we'll find out what we're really made of as newsmen," he said with a wry grin. "America should be a lot of fun."

For six months it was.

And for another sixteen years after that…

# Roderick Jones

Every adventure story must have least one villain. In this book there are remarkably few, but even if there were dozens the diminutive Sir Roderick Jones would stand out from the rest, complete with black hat, waxed mustache, and curled lip. The temptation is great to consign him and his works to a footnote, but he is not so easily dismissed. Which, it has to be said, is entirely in keeping with his personality.

The fact is that Jones looms over Reuters' history as a figure of inescapable significance. The first man to run Reuters whose name was not Reuter, his impact on the agency's affairs in the period between the World Wars reverberated still, fifty years on. (His legacy, a Trust document designed to protect Reuters' editorial integrity, provided newspaper copy on the very day on which this sentence was written.) He owns the unique distinction of having both bought and sold the company, doing so on each occasion amid great controversy and suspicion of his motives. His rearguard action in preserving the European news cartel to block the inevitable emergence of the United States affected American attitudes to Reuters, and vice versa, decades after he had left the company. And he remains, as I write, the company's only chief executive to be forced to resign in disgrace.

One way or another he had a greater impact on Reuters in the first century of its existence than any man except Paul Julius himself. The company survived Jones, and perhaps emerged all the stronger for it—wiser anyway—which is why an account of what Jones meant to Reuters, perhaps better expressed as what Jones did to Reuters, commands as many pages as it does.

Herbert Reuter's suicide in April 1915 was the event that gave Jones his chance for the glory he so obviously craved. That he grasped his opportunity is entirely to his credit: he did no more than many others would have done in the circumstances, and most would have faltered. That he exploited it to line his own pocket, discarding in the process as many of the agency's sacred principles as stood in his way, is to his everlasting shame.

Herbert's death had pitched the company into a state of despondency and chaos. Its prestige lay in ruins, its finances in tatters. The other serious consequence of Herbert's amiable autocracy was that it left no obvious candidate for the succession. The company secretary, one Walter Bradshaw, reluctantly took the job on an interim basis, but his own misgivings about his qualifications for the position proved fully justified and the company continued to drift aimlessly. The public response was more emphatic: Reuters' share price plunged from £12 to a precarious £3.

Now, even the company's traditionally benign and malleable shareholders began to stir. At the annual general meeting, in previous years a brief, worshipful ceremony, animated only by the polite applause at the end of it, some shareholders were incited to a shocking state of belligerence. Reuters' directors, most of whom understood little of the company's business (a recurring theme, this) were exposed to withering fire from the floor. An acrimonious debate was crowned with the final indignity of a motion of no confidence, directed specifically at the acting chairman, Mark Napier. A director for nearly thirty years, his was a leonine and statesmanlike presence. He was, as politicians like to say of loyal but uninspired colleagues, a "safe pair of hands" and a man usually above the fray and beyond criticism. Not on this occasion. His boardroom colleagues had every right to be alarmed because if Napier fell they would almost certainly follow. The moment was as fraught as it was unprecedented. In the end, the board had the votes to win handily. But the message to Napier was clear: find someone to put the house in order or you and your friends will find yourselves evicted.

Six thousand miles away, in Cape Town, one man had no doubt that he, and he alone, was qualified to carry out the necessary repairs. Roderick Jones had been Reuters' general manager in South Africa for ten years. From that distance he could only watch the sorry spectacle in London with deepening concern and frustration. His concern was natural enough. The frustration sprang from an unnatural expectation that he would receive a summons to return to London to save the day. It was a typically bold presumption, for while Jones ran a "tight ship" in South Africa, he had no experience of running a large organization, let alone of rescuing one on the brink of insolvency. Even so, a campaign was launched to push Jones's claim to the succession. Largely orchestrated by Jones himself, it would pay off sooner than even he could have predicted.

In a company populated mainly by family retainers of advanced years, Jones offered the advantages of youth and energy. He was then thirty-seven, a bachelor, slight of build, and standing no more than five foot five inches in his customary platform shoes. He was dapper and fastidious, conveying in manner and dress the impression of a man-about-town, or, as circumstances sometimes dictated, a country gentleman. In neither respect was he to the manner born. In his memoirs, *A Life in Reuters*,[1] Jones hardly mentions his origins, presumably because they were out of kilter with his self-promoted image. Little is actually known about his early life except that he was born near Manchester, the son of a hat salesman, and seems to have experienced an

---

[1] Sir Roderick Jones, *A Life in Reuters*, Hodder & Stoughton, 1951, p.26

economically deprived and unaffectionate childhood. His education sprang mainly from the private tutelage provided by a Scottish grandfather, supposedly a cousin of a former Archbishop of Canterbury, which took, in his own words, "a strong literary and biblical direction." His book omits any reference to his compulsory schooling or the fact that he did not attend university.

Following the death of his father—Jones's sole reference to him in his memoirs—he left England at the age of sixteen to live with an aunt in Pretoria, capital of the independent Boer republic of the Transvaal. There he made his mark in news as a reporter with various local papers, sometimes acting as a "stringer," or part-time correspondent, for Reuters. Jones's reputation as a journalist of initiative was enhanced when he secured an interview with Dr. Leander Starr Jameson, vainglorious leader of the Jameson Raid, an ill-advised and ill-fated adventure to "liberate" the Transvaal from Boer rule. Captured by the Boers, Jameson was tried for treason and found guilty. Spared the death penalty, largely for reasons of political expediency, he was handed over to the British in the expectation that he would be shipped back to England to stand trial under British law, as indeed he was. Jones's scoop was to secure a brief interview with Jameson at Pretoria railway station. It wasn't much of a story, the prisoner being in no position to say anything controversial, but it provided the only eyewitness account of Jameson in captivity. Jameson will reappear in this story shortly, once more in the company of Jones, though under remarkably different circumstances.

For the Jameson scoop and for his various other editorial accomplishments, Jones was rewarded with an offer to join Reuters in London. There, too, he evidently made his presence felt, for within three years he was heading back to Cape Town, at the precocious age of twenty-eight, as Reuters' general manager in South Africa. He seethed with ambition, and not just to be a star reporter. Though a competent journalist, he was blessed with a far more practical talent: the ability to endear himself to powerful men. He longed to be one of them. For a time he even nursed an ambition to become prime minister of South Africa, and given the connections he had cultivated in high government circles, the notion may not have been as far-fetched as it sounds. Jones had already established friendships with each of the Boer leaders, Paul Kruger, Louis Botha, and Jan Smuts. He was soon enjoying the company of other men of influence, in English- as well as Dutch-speaking circles, gliding in and out of government offices by means of special passes and frequenting exclusive country clubs, membership of which, given his modest income, must have been beyond his reach.

During his assignment in London he liked to boast that he had captured the admiring attention of Herbert Reuter—for all the good it would do him now.

More importantly, he had also gained the respect of Frederic W. Dickinson, the company's senior editorial figure, whose opinions carried some weight in the company—which would do him a great deal of good. Jones was far from idle during the crisis of 1915. He busied himself lobbying Dickinson and other London contacts, and gathered an impressive portfolio of written testimonials from his friends in high places and from various well-known literary figures (including, it has been claimed, though not by Jones himself, that great imperial yarn-spinner, Rudyard Kipling). The most important endorsement was that of Lord Gladstone, a Liberal peer recently returned to London after a term as first governor general of the Union of South Africa. Evidently written with the encouragement of Dickinson, it praised Jones for having "steered his course in a very difficult and puzzling country with a fidelity to his many friends and to his official duties, and with an efficiency, that are equally remarkable."[2] As it happened, Gladstone was a close friend of Mark Napier, which, if nothing else, guaranteed Jones a hearing. It was just one of the many relationships in a web of connections within Britain's ruling Liberal Party establishment—a web in which Jones would make sure he, too, became comfortably entangled.

And so it came about, less than three months after Herbert's death, that the virtually unknown Jones was invited to sail to London to present his case for the succession. Unlikely as the candidacy had seemed at the start, it was now almost game, set, and match.

At head office, Jones found exactly what Dickinson had warned him about: a rudderless ship, low in efficiency, with morale at rock bottom. Company finances were deteriorating by the day as the Great War, bogged down in the mud on the Somme, steadily eliminated many of the company's continental sources of income. Reuters' employees may have felt a superficial kinship with the Tommies at the front: they were tired, dispirited, and desperate for a competent general to lead then out of stalemate. Jones wasted no time impressing anyone at Reuters who mattered that he was that general. He seems to have impressed Napier in particular.

Napier's political connections were impressive. As a young barrister he had once shared chambers with Herbert Asquith, now Prime Minister, and the two remained on friendly terms. He was equally well known in financial circles, and as well liked in the City as he was in Westminster. He himself was beyond personal ambition. What he offered Reuters, then, was the wisdom and guile of the elder statesman. In the event, he settled for becoming a willing, and some would say gullible, accomplice in Jones's intrigues.

In his appraisal of Jones, he seems to have fallen at the first fence. The two men appear to have hit it off immediately. Jones relates in his memoirs that,

---

[2] Sir Roderick Jones, *A Life in Reuters*, Hodder & Stoughton, 1951, p.114

soon after his arrival in London, he and Dickinson were invited to spend a weekend at Napier's country home in Kent, evidently to give the host a chance to evaluate this pretender to the top job. Jones obviously impressed, as Napier at some point told Dickinson, who in turn revealed the confidence to Jones: "I like your young friend—*looks* rather like a boy, but I think he's the man for our money."[3]

The latter part of the observation would turn out to be literally true.

If the manner and methods of Jones in his public life came under less scrutiny in his own time than they deserved to, the retrospective judgments of writers and historians have been comprehensive, and unusually harsh. It is hard to argue with them.

Even Professor Read, not a man given to blunt appraisals, could find little good to say about him, though he does take the precaution of falling back on Freudian mitigation. Jones's defects are attributed to his penurious childhood, his poor education and—mystifyingly, since Jones himself never admitted it—to embarrassment that his parents were married only a few weeks before his birth. "These insecure origins," Read explains, "marked Jones for life. He over-compensated by acting too emphatically as if he came from a 'good' family and had received a 'good' education. He dressed with excessive correctness. He never missed a chance to make money, much of which he spent while head of Reuters living in conspicuous style…"[4]

A boardroom contemporary, Malcolm Graham, a former Press Association chairman, remembered "an awkward little chap, very full of himself, and a snob who had to create a tremendously big impression."[5]

Another uncompromising critic was author and diarist James Lees-Milne, who spent an evidently miserable adolescent interlude at Reuters as Jones's "third and junior secretary." Recalling the experience in his memoirs, *Another Self*, Lees-Milne is scathingly personal. "He was in stature a little undersized. He was spruce, and dapper, and perky. I would describe his appearance as that of a sparrow were it not for his waist which, instead of being loose, was tight, pinched in by a conspicuous double-breasted waistcoat which he habitually wore like a corset. This constrictive garment gave him the shape of a wasp. His face too resembled that of a wasp seen under a microscope. It was long and the bulbous nose was proboscis-like. His small eyes darted rapidly in his head in the manner of that insect. They never rested on their victim, yet because of a feverish activity missed nothing. His mouth too was sharp and vespine. His sting was formidable and unlike the bee's could be repeated."[6]

[3] Sir Roderick Jones, *A Life in Reuters*, Hodder & Stoughton, 1951, p.140

[4] Donald Read, *The Power of News*, Oxford University Press, 1992, p.116

[5] John Lawrenson/Lionel Barber, *The Price of Truth*, Mainstream Publishing, 1985, p.41

[6] James Lees-Milne, *Another Self*, Hamish Hamilton, 1970, p.122

One might observe that it takes one to know one, but Lees-Milne wasn't finished: "When his Rolls Royce drove up each morning to the main entrance of Reuters, a bell rang violently in every passage of the building to announce the Chairman's arrival. There was a general scurry and flurry of alarm. When it drove off in the evening another bell rang more softly. There was a contrasting sigh of relief and relaxation of tension."

A more succinct verdict came from a Jones protégé, and his successor as Reuters' general manager, Sir Christopher Chancellor. Jones, he told a colleague, was an "awful man, a crook and a shit."

For all his faults, Jones did have demonstrable talents as an executive. He combined to good effect a shrewd business brain and the ability to think on his feet in difficult situations—a skill he would frequently be called on to exercise. It can even be said that he had vision, even if it was such that would not command universal acclaim. He could have used his talents to become a heroic figure in Reuters—a knight rescuing the damsel in distress—but most of his creative energy was diverted to supporting the craving for wealth and status. Having achieved both, he enjoyed them, as one critic put it, in the manner of "an imperial proconsul"[7]—a privileged world of chauffeured limousines, star-studded banquets, dinner parties in town, and weekends at country estates, including his own not inconsiderable spread in Sussex, fifty miles south of London. His marriage, in 1920, to the novelist Enid Bagnold, author of *National Velvet* and *The Chalk Garden*, was the society wedding of the year. Her friends, from literary and artistic circles, complemented his, drawn largely from the great and the good in the Liberal Party. As much as Jones enjoyed the company of Liberals, he himself was clearly an enthusiastic Conservative. A self-proclaimed patriot, he believed fervently in the idea of Britain as an imperial power and of Reuters as an instrument of that power. In the event, it would be a fatal attraction.

Jones claimed in his memoirs that he started out as head of Reuters with four objectives: to overhaul the internal organization; to rescue the company from "incipient insolvency;" to reconstitute the ownership; and to "deliver Reuters into the permanent keeping of the newspapers of the United Kingdom." The first two invite no quibbles, and Jones was successful in achieving them. Of the second two, more needs to be said.

Once Jones had been "enthroned in the Founder's chair"—his words, and surely a sign of regal delusions—he actually got away to an impressive start. Positive results were achieved through long-overdue measures to reduce operating expenses, and through ruthless efficiency campaigns, which he supervised personally and energetically. Even Reuters' bank, pulled back from the brink by the installation of a competent management, started to turn in a

---

[7] Jonathan Fenby, *The International News Services*, Schocken Books, 1986, p.44

creditable performance. As Reuters' financial position improved, so did the share price, which doubled from its all-time low to £6.

Part of the reason was that Jones had started buying shares on the open market for his own account, and in substantial enough quantities that he was soon listed among the largest shareholders. Where the money for these purchases came from is unclear. Jones claimed that he used savings from his South African years, which he described as "not unremunerative," and by borrowing "up to the full limit of my credit." It has been suggested that Jameson and other cronies may have advanced further loans. If the sources of his cash are obscure, his agenda was less so. His top priority, understandably, was to dispose of the troublesome bank. This he accomplished within a year or two and at a substantial profit. The second one—far more controversial and, he must have supposed, more difficult—was to dispose of the shareholders.

This part of the plan was nearly sabotaged by an unexpected and most unwelcome intervention. In September 1916, less than a year after Jones had taken office, the directors received an approach from Godfrey Isaacs, managing director of Marconi's Wireless Telegraph Company. There was no love lost between the companies. Marconi's was considered a rival and was resented for its well-established position in the exciting new business of wireless communication, which Reuters felt was unfairly enhanced by a government-sanctioned monopoly on all news received by radio for publication anywhere in the British Empire. There was also deep suspicion of Isaacs himself, who was known in the City as a shady character. Even so, a Reuters director, Gerald Williams, arranged to meet with Isaacs to hear what he had to say. One imagines that Isaacs wasted little time getting to the point, which was that Marconi was willing to pay £500,000 to purchase Reuters. This worked out at £10 a share, a premium of £3 over the market price. Such an offer, if publicly disclosed, was bound to appeal to shareholders. Jones confessed to being "gravely alarmed."

Jones had long felt that the free market in Reuters' shares represented "a constant peril" by exposing the company to a takeover through open-market purchases (an exercise with which he, of all people, was familiar). But most of all he had feared an American predator. As he later, and somewhat snootily, explained, "The United States was not yet in the war, and Americans, not all of whom were Anglophile, were as free to acquire Reuter shares as anybody else!" Marconi's was not an American company, but it might have been the next worst thing.

As the City considered Godfrey Isaacs a sharp practitioner, so Westminster viewed his brother Rufus. Four years earlier, when he was attorney general, Rufus had been implicated in an insider trading scandal involving David Lloyd George, the then chancellor of the exchequer. Although an official enquiry had cleared them both of wrongdoing, Rufus Isaacs's testimony had been regarded as suspect, and the affair had seriously embarrassed the Liberal government of the day. Overlaying his suspicion of Isaacs was Jones's personal concern that a deal with Marconi would "ruin completely all my plans for Reuters' future."

It was only natural, then, that Jones should now determine that Reuters' only means of survival, not to mention his own, was to forestall Marconi's by encouraging a bid from a "friendly" party. The trouble was that none came immediately to mind—at least none that would allow Jones the kind of freedom he currently enjoyed—which is what led Jones to what can be argued was the only other option, and one that he now reached: Jones himself would buy Reuters. Actually, he and Napier would buy it jointly. The chairman would be needed to line up his City contacts to finance the bid.

Napier, for once, balked, initially expressing himself "dumbfounded" by the idea. Not only did he consider it unrealistic, but he also seems to have been far from convinced that, in light of the war risks and the company's persistent losses over the years, Reuters actually represented a good investment. But Jones, pulling out all the stops, talked him around. They agreed on equal ownership. Napier would remain as chairman and Jones would retain his position as chief executive but with "enlarged powers." The board was persuaded to delay a response to Isaacs to give Napier time to prepare an alternative presentation. And to supplement belt with braces, Napier alerted the Foreign Office to Isaacs's approach with a view to a government veto of the Marconi bid as contrary to the national interest, under emergency wartime legislation known as the Defence of the Realm Act.

Official involvement might not have ended there. Jones and Napier had already secretly worked out a scheme to involve the government in Reuters' ownership. Asquith's administration had been responsive. Engaged in war on the propaganda as well as on the Western front, the government was bound to be concerned about the future of a company it considered vital to the cause of presenting Britain's case to the world. Jones had no qualms about replacing shareholders with civil servants: a government-sponsored rescue, in contrast to a Marconi takeover, would keep him in his job. And of course he and Napier were comforted by the knowledge that between them they had many friends in high places. The matter had gone so far as the distribution of a discussion paper to the board. But while the directors were not in principle opposed to the plan, they found themselves unable to agree on the financial terms. The document was shelved.

With or without government participation, the Jones-Napier plan to acquire Reuters involved a questionable subterfuge: only Napier's name would appear on the purchase document. Jones's participation was to be kept from directors and shareholders until after the deal had gone through. To reveal his own position, Jones wrote later, might have been regarded as a "provocation" because of his youth and inexperience. Besides, as Jones explained to his nervous partner, "the directors had participated in two previous negotiations. Their bargaining and procrastinating had, in my judgement, wrecked both." So, to bring them in at the start would "at least mean delay, and in the end perhaps shipwreck for a third time." What chief executive worth his salt allows himself to be thwarted by such a trivial body as his own board? The answer is that, even in an unregulated age, Jones was engaged in a highly irregular maneuver.

Napier had no trouble organizing the money. His first call was to his old friend at 10 Downing Street. Asquith in turn called his brother-in-law, Lord Glenconner, chairman of the Union Bank of Scotland. Glenconner had no hesitation in approving a three-year loan of £550,000—enough to acquire Reuters' entire equity at £11 a share, £1 above the Marconi bid. He invited two more gentlemen of commerce to join the scheme, supposedly to guarantee the loan. One was Lord Peel, a director of the London and Provincial Bank, and son of the former Prime Minister. The other was Jones's old friend Leander Starr Jameson, a late guest of His Majesty's prison service but, after an early release, now triumphantly refurbished as Sir Starr Jameson, chairman of the British South Africa Company, the corporate creation of his close friend and arch colonialist Cecil Rhodes. Also secretly invited along for this new Jameson Raid was yet another guardian of the Empire, John Buchan. The former *Times* war correspondent, and author of *The Thirty-Nine Steps* and other thrillers, was now attached to the Foreign Office as director of intelligence in a newly formed propaganda unit, the Department of Information.

Napier, Glenconner, Peel, and Jameson were publicly announced as the principals behind the bid. That they were fronting for Jones was a deceit in itself, of course, but it was compounded by the fact that they were also secretly acting as nominees for another entity. The Government would be involved after all. Glenconner's loan had actually been guaranteed by the Foreign Office, which in return would retain a single voting share carrying the right to nominate one director empowered to veto certain board appointments and any corporate actions defined as "contrary to public policy." The director proposed, almost needless to say, was John Buchan. (The veto was never revealed and never exercised. It expired when the loan was paid off three years later.)

The transaction had no trouble getting past the grateful shareholders, and a reconstructed Reuters Telegram Company emerged as Reuters (1916) Limited. Of the 999 new shares issued, Napier and Jones between them owned 498, the balance being held in the name of the Foreign Office as security against the loan. Three years later, when Napier died, another secret facet of the deal was revealed. By prior agreement, Napier's estate sold most of his shares to Jones, who emerged with the majority of Reuters' shares and with it unfettered control of the company.

By then Jones had achieved the social status to go with his wealth. In the last year of the war, he was made a Knight Commander of the British Empire. The honor was bestowed not for his part in resurrecting Reuters but for his contribution to the war effort on behalf of the British government. In yet another controversial act committed in the name of patriotism, Jones had taken up a position as Adviser of Cable and Wireless Propaganda, reporting to Lord Beaverbook, at the newly formed Ministry of Information. The controversy was that, in accepting the assignment, Jones had seen fit to retain his job as Reuters' chief executive. To him the interests of Reuters, His Majesty's Government and Roderick Jones were one and the same, especially in wartime. To critics the conflicts were clear-cut, war or no war. Although Jones worked for the government *pro bono*, as Reuters' major shareholder he stood to benefit from government contracts, such as those the ministry now saw fit to award to Reuters for distributing cables reflecting official policies. This material was given the attribution "Agence Reuter" to distinguish it from Reuters' regular copy. "Its object," Jones explained in a ministry memorandum, "is to secure that a certain class of news, of propaganda value, is cabled at greater length than would be possible in the normal Reuter service."

The issue went to Parliament. Even the politicians were uncomfortable. A House of Commons select committee, in its report on national expenditure, pointed out that because of the "considerable amounts" being spent on Reuters cables, Jones's position was "on principle open to objection." Under pressure to make a choice between government and Reuters, Jones chose the latter and resigned from the ministry, citing ill health as the reason. By then, with the end of the war only weeks away, it was little more than a gesture.

During the early inter-war years, Reuters' financial position once more began to give rise to concern. And once more Jones's behavior in the gathering crisis would prove to be debatable.

The source of the company's difficulties was a familiar one: the general news division kept losing money faster than the commercial services could make it. Jones's response, in the guise of public interest, was to transfer the problem to another organization. The best means of securing Reuters' future, he declared in 1925, was to turn ownership over to the press—or, as he later put it, to "deliver it into the safekeeping of the newspapers of the United Kingdom." It made a change from the "safe hands" of the government, but was just as open to objection, if only on practical grounds. Cooperative ownership could not work in Britain as effectively as it did in the United States. There the Associated Press had newspaper subscribers in such numbers that it could easily afford to fund a national news service—or for that matter an international service, should it choose to launch one.

That much could not have been lost on Jones, whose motives in handing Reuters to the press must therefore once again be queried. If cooperative ownership was the solution he had favored all along, as he would later claim, why had no attempt been made to implement it before?

There may have been practical reasons for not doing so, but the obvious conclusion is that Jones was acting yet again for reasons of personal gain. Reuters in 1925 was no longer the attractive commercial entity that it had been, or had seemed to be, in 1916. Jones had purchased the company then for his own profit and personal convenience in 1916. Why not get rid of it for the same reasons in 1925? The loans to purchase the company had long since been paid off, which meant that the proceeds of the sale—even at a discounted price—would accrue to Jones personally. And he would probably get to keep his job into the bargain. In that light, the sale can be viewed as an opportunity that any intelligent businessman would have jumped at. The difference, in Jones's case, is that he sought to disguise his true motives by wrapping them up in the Union Jack.

In any event, the Press Association, representing Britain's provincial newspapers, bought a 51 percent interest in Reuters directly from Jones for £160,000 with an option to buy the rest of his shares at the same price (which it exercised five years later). The Fleet Street nationals were invited to join the deal under the umbrella of their own organization, the Newspaper Proprietors Association (NPA, later called the Newspaper Publishers Association), but the press barons, reviving ancient rivalries, fell to bickering. Unable to agree on how the NPA shares should be distributed (an issue that would return to tax them half a century later) they also failed to reconcile NPA objectives with those of the detested Press Association, whose directors were scorned as country bumpkins.

Wearisome as Fleet Street politics could be, Jones now faced trouble in the international arena. The fuse had been smoldering quietly for some time.

The man with the matches was Kent Cooper, a general manager of the Associated Press. A man with an evangelical mission, he also had the bully pulpit from which to launch it. Cooper's avowed intent was to rid the world of the news cartel that had carved up the world into spheres of national influence since Victorian times. Fashioned by Reuters, Havas, and Wolff when the world was a vastly different place, it lingered as no more than an anachronism. But though outmoded in every sense, the cartel still effectively determined geographically which agencies did what and where, and in contract language replete with phrases such as "exclusive exploitation" that conveyed to American ears an unashamedly imperialistic tone.

The AP had reluctantly joined the alliance, but its status was that of a junior partner. The AP was virtually excluded from operating anywhere outside the United States, unlike its new rival, United Press, which was free to operate freely overseas. Reuters in effect had told the AP, "You Yanks stay home and take care of your own patch—it's quite big enough, old boy—and we'll continue to supply you with news from everywhere else." This humiliation, of being awarded a franchise in its own country by a gang of decadent Europeans with delusions of imperial grandeur, had stuck in AP craws for decades. Aside from anything else, it ignored the geopolitical reality of growing American power and influence.

Jones nevertheless resolved to preserve the cartel to the last. The combatants in the battle, if it can be reduced to personalities, were to be Jones and Cooper—Jones representing King, Empire, and the status quo, Cooper fighting for liberty, democracy, and the tide of history. The chapter titles in Cooper's account of the conflict, *Barriers Down*, written in 1941,[8] long after the dust had settled, give some idea of the evangelical fervor he brought to the battle. "A Crusade is Born," "A Great Moral Concept," "Isolating the Vanquished," "Reuters in Wrath" are just a few.

The AP landed the first blow. Of all places it was struck in Japan, a country that in the late twenties might be characterized as an emerging nation. Although Japan had been opened up to Western culture by the United States alone, and had developed into an industrial power under American rather than British sway, the country had always been Reuters' exclusive news domain under the rules of the cartel. But the leading Japanese news agency, Kokusai Tahushin-sha (International News Agency) had started to fret about its long-standing news exchange agreement with Reuters. The concern was not so much that Reuters was British but that the terms of the contract were onerous. Jones's aggrieved response was to make it abundantly clear to Kokusai that Reuters was senior partner in the relationship, and intended to remain so. The Japanese promptly turned to the AP for help.

A strong relationship with an American agency made sense because of the cultural ties, but the unspoken incentive was to replace a partner from a country trying to prop up a declining empire with one that represented a rising industrial superpower. Prodded by the AP, Kokusai continued to press Reuters for more lenient contract terms, including permission to sell Japanese news overseas and to take AP news, alongside Reuters copy, into Japan. When Reuters stood firm, Kokusai had no choice but to renew its contract for another three years, but from that point on it was clear that the AP was the preferred mentor. And as if in recognition of its new allegiance, the Japanese company reorganized as an AP-style press cooperative under the name Rengo.

---

[8] Kent Cooper, *Barriers Down*, Farrar & Rinehart, 1942, p.107

For the next five years, the skirmishing intensified. In 1933 it turned into open warfare.

The AP and Rengo signed a contract firmly establishing the AP as Rengo's principal partner, opening up the Asian market to the Americans. Jones was furious. Meeting with Cooper in London, he made it clear that he took a dim view of Cooper's constant intriguing. In Cooper's politely worded account, "Sir Roderick stated in most friendly terms that he felt I had rather got out of bounds in my operations of the past several years."[9] As indeed he had, that being the whole point of the exercise.

Jones's reaction was to expel the AP from the cartel while continuing to limit the AP's geographical scope for operating outside America. Welcoming the showdown, Cooper called Jones's bluff. He preemptively declared the AP's intention to leave the cartel and to establish operations wherever and with whatever partners it pleased.

In case his resolve might be doubted, Cooper opened an AP office in London, followed by offices in France and Germany. Cooper rubbed salt in the wound by making overtures to the Press Association, the AP's British counterpart, with a view to signing a contract separate from the one covered by Reuters. Jones counter-punched by proposing a new four-way treaty between the three European agencies and the AP, but one that would retain the insulting proviso that the AP stay out of Europe and Asia.

Even more objectionably, Jones demanded a sizable differential payment from the AP to Reuters. The differential had been removed just a few years earlier. Restoring it could only mean that Reuters considered news from overseas was still more important to the AP than American news was to Reuters. Jones knew this wasn't the case; in one last, desperate gamble he was simply trying to bully the AP back into line.

With the contest now in the final round, and Cooper way ahead on points, Jones's corner wisely threw in the towel. Reuters' board ordered Jones to sail to New York to sign a contract disavowing Reuters' historical privileges. The cartel was irrevocably abandoned.

The consequences of this humiliating defeat marked a watershed for Jones in his relations with his board. He had long treated his fellow directors with haughty arrogance, which had long been resented. There must have been more than a few gloating smiles when he was forced to submit in a fight he should never have picked in the first place. It was the first stage in a process that would peel away the remaining layers of Jones's credibility. He should have read up on his friend Kipling. Like Danny Dravot in *The Man Who Would Be King*, Jones convinced his subjects that he was a divinity until, when scratched, he bled and was then destroyed by the mob.

---

[9] Kent Cooper, *Barriers Down*, Farrar & Rinehart, 1942, p.122

The last layer was stripped off in 1941, two years into the Second World War, and in circumstances remarkably similar to those that had almost brought Jones down during the First World War. The issue was again his involvement with the government and his weakness for subterfuge.

The origin of Jones's fatal crisis can be dated to November 1937 when he met informally with Prime Minister Neville Chamberlain to discuss an increase in wireless transmissions overseas by Reuters to combat the flood of propaganda coming from Hitler's Reich. Jones's assertion was that Reuters should be paid for this service to the nation through heavily discounted tariffs, which would avoid the appearance of direct government subsidies and the public opprobrium they would attract. Chamberlain was interested but referred Jones to the Postmaster General, the minister responsible for wireless policy. To him Jones proposed a "special rate" for transmitting 12,000 words a day, five times Reuters' normal traffic. The minister favored the plan, but, because it involved aspects of international policy, passed Jones on to the Foreign Office. It would be Jones's undoing.

For all their elegant observance of protocol, the Foreign Office mandarins harbored deep suspicions about Jones's motives. An element of jealousy may have been involved. The Foreign Office operated its own information service and some officials, somewhat illogically, may have regarded Reuters as a rival. But issues of a personal nature, questioning Jones's motivations, loomed larger. An early Foreign Office memorandum indicated as much: "They [Reuters] have now decided to take full advantage of the present sympathetic atmosphere, and possibly to exploit Foreign Office anxieties about the news situation abroad, by laying claim to assistance on a much wider front..."[10]

Left to its own devices the Foreign Office might have sent Jones packing, but other government agencies had become involved. One was a special cabinet committee, under Sir Kingsley Wood, formed to examine "what steps should be taken to improve, enlarge and facilitate the distribution of news from this country ... with particular reference to the position of Reuters and their application to the GPO [General Post Office] for special facilities."[11] The Wood committee agreed that Reuters should be supported, despite Foreign Office protests that "no subsidy be given to Reuters or preferential telegraphic rates which could be represented as such" on the ground that these would be "foreign to British traditions."[12]

With their respective positions plainly stated, but with no sign of give or take by either side on crucial issues, Jones and the Government, through negotiation and correspondence, went at it for another two years. By then, the

---

[10] John Lawrence/Lionel Barber, *The Price of Truth*, Mainstream Publishing, 1985, pp.60-61
[11] Ibid., pp.64-65
[12] Ibid., pp.64-65

situation had developed into an open grudge match between Jones and the Foreign Office. The virulent views of the mandarins were demonstrated by their insistence that a condition of any agreement should be Jones's removal from office in favor of someone the government would have the right to approve. It was a wholly unreasonable demand for an official role in Reuters' affairs, which Jones, for reasons other than personal, was perfectly justified in resisting. But at no time does it seem to have occurred to him to refer the matter to his board. If the substance of the negotiations had been leaked to Reuters' directors it would have created a firestorm. Jones would insist that the board had been kept abreast of the negotiations, and so it had, but only in the vaguest terms. Jones had misinformed his colleagues, whom he considered an amiable group of duffers from the provincial press, that the situation was well under control.

By the summer of 1938, Jones and Sir Horace Wilson, a senior advisor to Chamberlain, were able to agree on basic principles. The services Reuters would provide to the government and on what commercial terms were laid out in a paper from the Foreign Office, characterized as a "Gentlemen's Agreement." It is an extraordinary document and anyone but Jones would have interpreted its terms as a blatant threat to Reuters' independence. Conceding that Jones couldn't be forced out immediately, the Foreign Office insisted that he nominate a "younger" man as his designated successor. The nominee, who would be subject to government approval, would take over as Reuters' chief executive within five years. Without referring to the board, Jones put forward the name of a candidate. So sensitive was this condition that he was referred to in the Gentlemen's Agreement only as "X". It was in fact the most senior of three general managers who reported to Jones, his own protégé, Christopher Chancellor.

The other terms of the deal were no less extraordinary, and were acutely specific, even down to mentioning the salary to be paid to "X". Jones had cut himself in, of course. He would relinquish the title of managing director and hand over most of his executive powers to "X", but remain as chairman. As compensation for being kicked upstairs, he would assume the additional title of governor, or president, and, as the document put it, "engage in the larger development of Reuters in the interests of the state." As for his own salary, the agreement merely mentioned that Wilson had been given "a certain explanation about this."

The schedule of disbursements to Reuters was laid out. They amounted to £39,500 a year, a tidy but not spectacular sum. There was no mention of reduced tariffs, only of direct payments for service rendered. At all times, Reuters was to bear in mind "suggestions made to them on behalf of the Government as to the development and orientation of their news service…" To ensure compliance, continuing payments would be contingent on "the

Government being satisfied with the progress achieved."

In September 1939, days after Britain declared war against Germany, Jones released to the board a Memorandum of Understanding covering the various agreements he had negotiated. It was a sanitized summary, with emphasis on the payments schedule. The key document, the Gentlemen's Agreement, and its various attachments were not circulated. The board approved the plan, subject to formal agreements. Only one director questioned it. William J. Haley, representing the *Manchester Evening News*, thought it might be going a bit too far in giving the Foreign Office a say in Reuters' affairs. Little did he know! Jones was smoothly reassuring and Haley, as disadvantaged in his ignorance as his colleagues, went along. The future editor of *The Times* and Director General of the British Broadcasting Corporation, Haley was a stern figure of unbending rectitude; it was said, apparently by J.B. Priestley, that he was a man with two glass eyes. Jones probably made a mental note to be wary of Haley.

One attachment—a letter—was definitely not circulated. Originally pinned to the main agreement, and regarded by the Government as integral to it, the letter had been detached by Jones. It became infamous as the "Perth Letter."

Lord Perth was senior minister at the Foreign Office. His letter to Jones was largely a recapitulation of the Gentlemen's Agreement, but it included a hand-written postscript referring to "X", the secret successor nominated by Jones. It read, "Since the above letter was drafted I learn that you propose Mr. Christopher Chancellor to the post referred in Paragraph A above. I have pleasure in informing you that Mr. Chancellor's appointment to the post will be acceptable to His Majesty's Government."[13]

Although Jones had the only copy of this letter sent to Reuters, the Government had one, too. Which was unfortunate, because it was the Government, accidentally or otherwise, that now spilled the beans.

Jones's duplicity was exposed at a time when he had few reliable allies on the board. Constant rotation of directors, under Press Association rules, meant that he was always dealing with newcomers who had little time to fall under his spell and who were inclined to a more critical view of his autocratic style than their longer-serving colleagues. Practical rather than worldly men, these "provincials" were more concerned with Reuters' financial affairs than with complex issues of state, and to some of them the company's finances were unfathomable. Some commented that they seemed to be arranged more with a view to paying huge commissions to Sir Roderick Jones than to paying reasonable dividends to the Press Association. As the deputy chairman, McLean Ewing had once expressed it: "I doubt if any director has ever had the temerity to ask what his 'commission' amounted to…"[14]

Jones must have found such remarks far from reassuring. Chickens were

---

[13] John Lawrence/Lionel Barber, *The Price of Truth*, Mainstream Publishing, 1985, p.83

[14] John Lawrence/Lionel Barber, *The Price of Truth*, Mainstream Publishing, 1985, p.76

coming home to roost in coop-loads. Early in 1940 he was told that his employment contract, due to expire in 1941, would not be renewed. Jones, never one to give up without a fight, may have been preparing to negotiate his way out of his predicament when a thunderbolt launched from Whitehall arrived at 85 Fleet Street.

Late in 1940, negotiations between Reuters and the Government had entered the final stages. The Government was represented at one of these meetings by Sir Walter Monckton, director general of the Ministry of Information, once a division of the Foreign Office and now a department in its own right. On Reuters' side of the table sat Jones, alongside two other board members and Christopher Chancellor. At some point, Monckton casually mentioned the Perth letter. Startled but composed, Jones denied knowledge of it. Haley and the others having given no indication that they had understood the significance of this exchange, Jones must have heaved a sigh of relief.

But a few days later, at a second meeting, Monckton again dropped a reference to the Perth letter. This time Jones admitted its existence but dismissed it as irrelevant; he hadn't agreed to the terms of the letter, he protested, nor had he even bothered to reply to it. The reaction of Haley and Samuel Storey, the other Reuters director present, has been described as "dumbfounded." They demanded to know more. Both of Haley's glass eyes were now on full alert. Jones continued to pretend that the letter was of little consequence. He wasn't sure he could even lay his hands on it.

Had Monckton been put up to opening Pandora's Box? Haley had no doubt of it. "The ministry deliberately betrayed him," he wrote later.[15] But on whose initiative? The hero-culprit is unknown, but the finger of suspicion has often pointed at "X". Chancellor may have been a Jones protégé, but they were not friends. Chancellor was a Haley protégé, too, and they had become very close friends.

Haley and Storey now had no choice but to break the news to the board. On February 3, 1941, the day before a board meeting that promised to be stormy, Haley and Storey, continuing their investigation into the affair, summoned Jones to a meeting. Let Jones's own account describe the exchange that followed.

> At one stage, after repeated reassertion of complaint by Haley and Storey, I said to Haley, in reply to an invidious remark he had made, "Do you suggest that I deliberately concealed this from the Board?"
>     Haley: "Yes I do."
>     Jones: "Then I can only say that I am very sorry for you. I did no such thing."[16]

[15] Donald Read, *The Power of News*, Oxford University Press, 1992, p.192
[16] Ibid., p.193

With that, Jones left the room to prepare the resignation he knew he would be asked to tender the next day.

The Government had little more to say about the Reuters affair, except to see the negotiations with Reuters through to a watered-down agreement, with all the controversial bits removed. As Brendan Bracken, the new Minister of Information, told the House of Commons in its debate on the sale of shares to the NPA: "…if a news agency was regarded throughout the world as being the property of the British government, its news value would be very small."[17] Common sense at last!

For Reuters there were two lasting consequences, both engineered by Haley. First, the national newspapers—the press barons—were finally brought into ownership alongside the provincial press. The Press Association gave up half its shares to accommodate them. Second, a special Trust was created to protect Reuters for all time from outside control or influence, official or otherwise.

The wording of the 1941 Trust is significant—or would be four decades on, when Reuters would once more confront the prospects of public ownership.

The Press Association and the Newspaper Proprietors Association hereby record their mutual agreement that they will regard their respective holdings of shares in Reuters as in the nature of a trust rather than as an investment and hereby undertake to use their best endeavours to ensure:

a) That Reuters shall at no time pass into the hands of any one interest group or faction.

b) That its integrity, independence and freedom from bias shall at all times be fully preserved.

c) That its business shall be so administered that it shall supply an unbiased and reliable news service to British Dominion Colonial Foreign and other newspapers and agencies with which it had or may hereafter have contracts.

d) That it shall pay due regard to the many interests which it serves in addition to those of the Press, and

e) That no effort shall be spared to expand, develop and adapt the business of Reuters in order to maintain in every event its position as the leading world news agency.[18]

No one gave the Trust a further thought until 1982 when, having gathered dust in a filing cabinet for forty years, it played a key part in a long-running front-page drama that even the glass-eyed Haley could not have foreseen.

---

[17] Read, *The Power of News*, p.193
[18] Ibid., p.244

My own final observation, from the perspective of time, is that there is something distinctly Nixonian about Sir Roderick Jones. Like Richard M. Nixon, the only president of the United States to resign, Jones was competent, durable and charismatic. If both had the potential for greatness, or at least a chance to be remembered as much for their good deeds as for their misdeeds, it was constantly stifled by controversy born of actions that could only be interpreted as self-serving. At the risk of my competing with Professor Read in Freudian analysis, both suffered from a persecution complex born of humble origins and both indulged in self-justifying denials of the wrongdoings that eventually brought them down. Both tried to stay in their jobs by keeping certain conversations secret from their peers—and in both cases it was the peers who became the prosecutors. Both of course became unique in resignations brought about by disgrace.

An aberration Jones might have been, but his ghost would haunt Reuters for years to come.

# Americans

It was Reuters' custom to impose on correspondents about to be "posted" abroad, a series of irksome corporate formalities. They would be better described as worthless informalities.

In my case, they included a cursory medical examination by the company doctor and something described as an "orientation briefing" by a representative of the staff department. Sound in body and mind was evidently the state in which Reuters intended its envoys to go forth into the world. Quite right too, soundness of body and mind not being the condition most readily associated with British journalists working abroad.

The medical was reassuringly uneventful—reassuring not just because it implied a clean bill of health, but because rumors concerning the company doctor were such as to induce in male patients a dread of that moment in the proceedings when they are asked to cough. My cough went off without a hitch, so to speak, which left me wondering how these lurid stories about the allegedly queer quack got started. They were, as far as I know, completely groundless. But then, as critics of Fleet Street would have pointed out, lack of foundation has not always stood in the way of a good story.

Even less eventful, though hardly reassuring, was the so-called orientation. It was, if anything, disorienting. The briefing officer was one Dominick Jones, who merits a mention here as yet another living embodiment of Reuters' endearing eccentricity. He is worth it for another reason. I had never met Jones—never heard of him, in fact—nor was there any reason to attach any significance to the name, Jones being as unremarkable a moniker outside Wales as it is inside. Only after the briefing did I learn that I'd just spent an hour with the progeny of the eponymous rascal encountered in the previous chapter. I would never have guessed it. On the basis of everything known about or attributed to Sir Roderick, his amiable offspring presented the perfect antithesis of the expression "like father like son." In short, Dominick Jones was hilariously indecisive, bumbling, and painfully shy. He was also, throughout my interview, an encyclopedic source of worthless enlightenment.

"New York can be very hot," was the first thing he felt obliged to tell me. "You'll be well advised to take some light clothing."

"Still hot there in October, is it?" I thought the question worth asking, as we were now in the last week of September.

"Oh no, it'll be pleasant there now, much cooler. But it does get very cold in winter, much colder than London."

"Then I suppose I should take some warm clothing?"

"Yes, you're absolutely right. Better to take both light and warm clothing, I suppose."

"Of course, I'm only going for six months. I'll be back before the summer."

"Well, that's a good point," he conceded, by now looking every bit as bewildered as I was.

The entire interview went on in the same surreal vein, Dominick Jones assiduously ticking off topics from a list that must have been compiled back in his father's day. "How about pith helmet and puttees?" I asked. "Ha, ha," responded Jones. There was some discussion about taking crockery and cutlery before we agreed that neither would be necessary. Not on the list was the more crucial question of my recently purchased house, specifically how the mortgage payments would be covered in my absence. Dominick Jones was adamant that the company was not prepared to help financially. "Rent it out for six months," he suggested. (I did just that—unfortunately to a group of jazz musicians who disappeared after three weeks, first having burned down most of the kitchen.)

I left the meeting with the feeling that I had just read for a role in a Harold Pinter play.

The Jones interview having proved uproariously pointless, my imminent departure had me thinking less about climate and clothing than about the reception Reuters could expect from its American rivals. We were, after all, preparing to compete with two home-grown enterprises with the same totemic status in the United States that Reuters enjoyed in Britain. The Associated Press and Dow Jones had both recently acted towards Reuters in an overtly hostile manner, and they would undoubtedly seek to exploit home-field advantage by eliciting the support of their many sympathetic associates and contacts in the American business and media communities.

Chilling confirmation of such fears came from an AP reporter of my acquaintance over a bottle of Muscadet in El Vino. "Expect no quarter," was the grave warning. "AP men don't hate Limeys, of course, but they despise Reuters. It's a deeply ingrained prejudice. Every man jack believes Reuters is in the British Government's pocket and always has been. They'll believe it no matter what. Hell, even I believe it. Knocking Reuters is a part of AP history, imbedded in the culture. We've all been brainwashed by *Barriers Down*."

I had not then read it. My companion offered an alternative cinematic analogy.

"You remember Gary Cooper in *High Noon*—the lone sheriff going out to do battle with crazy Frank Miller and his gang? Well, you get the idea. In this case the Cooper in question was Kent, the lone newsman of integrity going up against bully-boy Roderick Jones and his European sidekicks."

"That's romanticized bullshit," was my response. "For a start, the AP is much, much bigger and richer than Reuters. And that Jones-Cooper stuff is ancient history."

Anyway, as a financial journalist, I was not bothered as much by the traditional antagonism of the AP as by the new quarrel with Dow Jones. "Well, they won't put out the welcome mat, either. Stands to reason. You're invading their turf. They're bound to react, and it won't be gently."

I mentioned all these fraught observations to Bernie Gagan. He laughed them off. "I shouldn't let it worry you, old boy. The more the AP and Dow Jones respond to us, the more it means we're bothering them, and the better we're doing our jobs."

Although the main contest would be against Dow Jones, it had fallen to the Associated Press to fire the opening shots.

Late in 1966, Gerald Long, Reuters' general manager, received a visit from his AP counterpart, Wes Gallagher, ostensibly to discuss the terms of a renewed news exchange contract. The agencies had swapped news for as long as anyone could remember—had done so even during the Jones-Cooper skirmishes during the thirties. Such agreements had always been common practice throughout the industry, as we have seen, but they did not imply fraternity, as has also been made clear. In fact, contacts between the AP and Reuters on the personal level were irregular, and usually more businesslike than social. Hatchets may have been buried, but historical slights had not been entirely forgotten, and American suspicions lingered that Reuters, like Britain, still harbored delusions of imperial grandeur. As my drinking companion had pointed out, such anti-colonial attitudes were especially prevalent within the Associated Press.

Not surprisingly, then, a certain *froideur* was evident right from the start of the Gallagher-Long meeting. And as the discussion proved to be less about how to renew the existing agreement, which dated back about twenty years, than about how not to renew it, the atmosphere became progressively icier. The participants—contestants might be a better word—presented an interesting contrast in styles. The earthy, stone-faced Gallagher was an AP man to his fingertips and, in Long's words, "no friend of Reuters"—and possibly, given his Irish heritage, no natural Anglophile, either. Across the table the Cambridge-educated and almost obsessively cerebral Long returned the compliment by being neither respectful of the AP nor conspicuous in his admiration for the United States, his internationalism always finding a focus in Europe rather than in the New World.

Many years later, Long would describe Gallagher as a "sourpuss, intent on mischief." At the same time, Gallagher probably found it hard to warm to

Long's bristling belligerence. With the *pro forma* pleasantries out of the way, the meeting degenerated into a grim confrontation. The following account comes mainly from a 1994 interview with Long.

The AP was prepared to sign a new agreement, Gallagher told him. The only thing standing in the way was the relative worth of the news to be exchanged. Gallagher now reversed the ploy used by Roderick Jones on Kent Cooper three decades earlier. The AP, he said, believed it was getting less value from the Press Association wire of mainly British news, representing Reuters' half of the deal, than Reuters was receiving in return from the AP's so-called A-wire of American news. Gallagher, as quoted by Long, said, "We're exchanging elephants for apples. This can't go on."

In plain commercial terms it meant that, if the arrangement were to continue, the AP would require a substantial differential payment. Facing Long, Gallagher was coy about the figure, but it was later revealed as $200,000 a year. Though not in itself an enormous figure it was, as Long later observed, "a fortune for us at that time."

Long deadpanned in front of Gallagher. Reuters' board, he said, would obviously have to be consulted if the figure should prove to be of any magnitude, and he could not predict the response (which was no less than the truth). Gallagher nodded, but, as he rose to leave, Long came back with a question. Was there any room for maneuver? Could a deal be negotiated based on some reasonable percentage of whatever value the AP put on non-American news? Gallagher's response, again as quoted by Long, was blunt and derisive: "You can't have a percentage of fuck all!"

Long no doubt found the remark deeply offensive, but he was privately prepared to concede that American news did have more value to Reuters than foreign news to the AP, reflecting the geopolitical reality that the United States now enjoyed the superpower status that Britain had long since relinquished. He had in fact shared with the board his view that, in a free world increasingly dominated by the United States, dependence on the AP posed a long-term threat to Reuters' future. It meant that Reuters would one day have to go it alone in the United States—and, in Long's opinion, the sooner the better. "My view was simplistic: Reuters cannot work at second-hand in the country that is the greatest producer and the greatest consumer of news." Gallagher's bombshell thus presented to Long the excuse he had been waiting for to confront the Reuters' board with that reality.

As shocking as directors found the proposed differential payment, they found the prospect of a complete break with the AP even more alarming. Several were thrown into panic. Long played the statesman. Before making any response to Gallagher, he insisted that the company should at least obtain, for purposes of comparison, an elementary costing for an independent US operation. Stuart Underhill, one of Long's deputy general managers, was accordingly dispatched to New York to determine what Reuters would have to spend to produce a minimal but adequate American service.

A mild-mannered Canadian, and by common consent not one of life's innovators, Underhill at least seems to have understood what was required of him. After three months of "research" he duly returned to London with an estimate of $225,000—a figure only marginally higher than the AP differential. Underhill's arithmetic suited Long's purpose perfectly, so much so that it aroused suspicion. Thirty-odd years later I asked the question some directors surely asked at the time: had Underhill been told what figure he should present? Long's response was an enigmatic smile. "Let's just say that it was a very convenient number."

Business logic alone might have made the boardroom vote a toss-up, but Long felt the need to argue his case with considerable passion. A strong-willed man with an acute sense of history, he resented what he called "the AP's unshakeable belief in its inevitable supremacy" every bit as much as he scorned the imperialist pretensions of Roderick Jones that had created the animus between the two agencies in the first place.

Long had been wise not to underestimate his task in winning over the directors. The regional newspaper executives on the board were bound to oppose the break, mainly out of fear of the unknown, but also due to the dread of having to pay higher subscriptions for Reuters' news service. Their concerns were shared even by the more internationally minded directors, some of whom Long suspected had been influenced by Stan Swinton, head of the AP World Service. "Swinton was always getting at these people whenever they went to New York, saying, 'Long is mad.' This was a quite frequent contention at the time, you see. The AP attitude was that Reuters operating alone in the United States simply couldn't be done." Coming from the flamboyant, profane and hard-drinking Swinton, a legend in the AP, any assertion that Long was mad might be regarded as a classic case of the pot calling the kettle black.

Long's run-in with Gallagher was not an isolated portent of trouble between Reuters and its American partners. A few months earlier, a similar acerbic exchange had occurred between Michael Nelson and William F. Kerby, chief executive of Dow Jones & Company. In the course of investigating the potential for taking the Dow Jones famous "Broad Tape" financial newswire into the international market, Kerby was reportedly angered to "discover" that Dow Jones copy was being used prolifically in Reuters' news services. "Discover" gets quotation marks because this was something he should have known about and almost certainly did. Under a news exchange contract between the companies, Reuters was perfectly entitled to use Dow Jones material and had been doing so for years. Kerby's indignation stemmed, therefore, not from illicit use but from his belief, an echo of Gallagher's, that Reuters was getting something of a free ride at Dow Jones's expense—that the American economic and financial news put out by Dow Jones was over-whelmingly more significant than the foreign material received from Reuters in return.

With the existing agreement coming up for renewal, Kerby flew to London and invited Nelson to lunch to discuss an alternative proposal: instead of signing a new contract, why not consider some form of joint venture? Confident that he held all the best negotiating cards, Kerby had every reason to suppose that Nelson would find the offer tempting. And so he might have done if the terms Kerby contemplated had not been so heavily biased in favor of Dow Jones. Nelson played his only card. Guessing that Kerby would not want to be left without an international news partner, he unhesitatingly rejected the idea.

Kerby's indigestion that day had an unexpected but perhaps, in hindsight, inevitable result: Dow Jones set about finding an international ally closer to home. Kerby started by courting United Press International, an American agency with international connections, especially in South America, but when UPI dragged its feet Kerby turned to the AP.

To Reuters executives, it was becoming clearer by the day that both its American partners were prepared, were indeed preparing, to abandon their long-standing relationships with Reuters in order to compete with the British agency around the world. The gloves were coming off for what was shaping up to be another old fashioned, bare-knuckled Anglo-American prize fight.

Armed with Underhill's report, and an acute sense of destiny, Long decided to press the board for a decision. The choice, as he expressed it forcefully, was a simple one: appeasement or war. Negotiate new agreements on unfavorable and probably humiliating terms, or break off relations and fight. Long had been right to be wary about the reaction of the directors. Even those not panicked were distinctly uneasy. Into the latter camp fell certain Fleet Street representatives, of whom the most vocal was the loftily aristocratic Lord Drogheda, chairman of the Pearson Group, owner of the *Financial Times*. His principal ally, according to Long, was Sir Denis Hamilton, representing Times Newspapers. Both men were urbane, cultured, and well connected in London society. Drogheda was a prominent champion of the arts whose various extra-curricular roles included chairmanship of the Royal Opera House. Hamilton, a phlegmatic, self-made north-countryman, had risen through the ranks, first in the British Army, where he had served as a senior member of Field Marshal Montgomery's staff, and then in Fleet Street, as a protégé of Lord Thomson. He would shortly become Long's board chairman at Reuters. On the question of Reuters' relationships with the Americans, he was a dove, but seemed content to play second fiddle to the more vocal Drogheda. In both respects he attracted Long's undying scorn.

With a decision beckoning, there was considerable consternation in the boardroom.

"By God, they didn't like it one bit," Long recalled with a guffaw. Drogheda suggested postponing the AP discussion, evidently hoping that deferral would somehow cause the issue to disappear. Drogheda was privately aghast at the thought of a break with the AP, but his public posture, according to Long, was one of affected unconcern. "Surely this is not a terribly important matter. We're in no hurry. We should take time to think about it. Why don't we take a decision at the next meeting?" What he was really thinking, Long suspected, was that Swinton may well have been right: Long was indeed mad, utterly mad, to think that Reuters could survive in the world without the assistance of the mighty Associated Press.

Responding to Drogheda's prevarication, an exasperated Long sprang to his feet and, effectively putting his future on the line, declared, "I'm sorry, but I must have your decision now. This is one decision that cannot be postponed."

It was a moment seared deep into Long's memory. As he sat down he was convinced that the argument was lost, his job along with it. "I'll be lucky if I survive this," he whispered in the ear of Nigel Judah, Reuters' finance director, the only other executive present. Judah, he recalled, winked as a sign that he was not so pessimistic. Judah was right: Long's outburst had done the trick. Without further discussion, Reuters' directors reluctantly voted for the historic break with the Americans.

It may have been Gerry Long's finest hour.

So it came about, several months later, on a balmy Sunday evening in October 1967, that a Boeing 707 in the livery of Pan American World Airways deposited Bernie Gagan and me at New York's recently renamed John F. Kennedy (formerly Idlewild) airport. Gagan was relieved to be on terra firma. "Hate these big planes," he said. It was an extraordinary remark coming from a war hero, a man who had flown more than forty combat missions with the Royal Air Force, as waist gunner and radio operator, in the Second World War.

We were both booked into the Wentworth Hotel on 46th Street, conveniently located two blocks from Reuters' office on Avenue of the Americas, or what most New Yorkers still knew as Sixth Avenue. The Wentworth might be politely described as spartan. Grubby also comes to mind; there was more food imbedded in the carpet in my room than the hotel kitchen could serve in a week. A tan-colored cockroach the size of an armadillo, its picnic interrupted by my arrival, eyed me menacingly from atop the television set that did not work. You never forget your first New York City cockroach. The Wentworth was a stud farm for the damned things.

If the Wentworth was less than welcoming, at least it prepared me for my reception at the office the next morning. As instructed, I announced myself to the secretary sitting outside the office of Cyril Smith, Reuters' North America manager. Smith was something of a company legend. The portly figure and facial features were those of Alfred Hitchcock. So was the personality. Smith, exiled from London eleven years earlier after some minor and forgotten transgression, had "gone native." "I wouldn't go back to Fleet Street at gunpoint," he once told me. (It never came to that of course, but years later, on a voluntary visit to London, poor old Cyril provided Reuters' annual management luncheon with the only dramatic incident anyone could remember by dropping dead in the middle of cocktails—a touch of Hitchcock even in his final act.)

Given my welcome, I would have gladly gone back to London that day. Smith had been expecting Gagan but claimed not to have been told about me. Having observed the hapless Dominick Jones in action, I was prepared to believe him. Grumpily interrupting a meeting with his deputy, Des Maberley, a visiting Mike Nelson and an early-risen Bernie Gagan, Smith emerged to offer what I could only assume was the customary local greeting. The image still in my mind is that of a crimson-faced scowl and a foot-long cigar in a pudgy fist.

"I've only just heard about you. Is there anyone in this fucking company who knows what the hell's going on? If they do, they certainly don't bother to tell me. Well, if you're assigned to the newsroom, I suppose you'd better get in there right away. I'll catch up with you later. See Alex or David—they'll show you the ropes."

Alex was Alex McCallum, a mild-mannered Oxford graduate I had met briefly during his induction period in London. He had been in New York for six months, having been airlifted in from Brussels after a stint editing the IFP and teaching Belgians how to play rugby. David was my former mentor Dave Armour. He, too, had been in town just a few months, having mysteriously disappeared from the second-floor newsroom one day amid rumors that he had been fired. Like Smith, he had chosen American exile over bleaker alternatives.

"Don't go calling the White House just yet," he quipped, a reference to the Downing Street episode. "Hang around and I'll buy you lunch."

Predictably, I was the one who bought lunch, a stand-up affair at a dingy McCann's bar across the street—and lent Armour ten dollars into the bargain. Some things, at least, were reassuringly normal. McCallum, as a long-standing friend, won't mind my saying that he, too, never seemed to have any cash.

That same evening, at a meet-the-staff session he had organized, I was the one who paid for the drinks. At this rate, I faced a return to London in six months stony-broke.

Our Mission Impossible, Armour explained, borrowing the title of a popular new television series, was to start a financial newswire aimed at the American investment market. Reuters' first-ever news venture in North America would compete head-on with the Dow Jones Newswire, a printer service sometimes called the Dow Jones Ticker, also popularly known as the "Broad Tape." By whatever name it was known, the service was a fixture in every stockbroker's office and bank across the land. That, by contemporary estimates, amounted to some 5000 machines. We would be competing with more than a machine; if the Broad Tape was a national institution, the parent company was even more so. The stock-market's fluctuations had long been measured by the Dow Jones Industrial Average, and one million well-heeled Americans started each working day by scanning the *Wall Street Journal*, the business community's own newspaper, published of course by Dow Jones & Company. This was an outfit with an impressive pedigree, a legendary reputation, and considerable clout.

The Broad Tape, acknowledged as the sole and unimpeachable source of all corporate news announcements, had not faced serious competition since the previous century. How seriously would we be taken? An indication of what we could expect appeared in an internal Dow Jones memorandum from Joe Guilfoyle, the Broad Tape's managing editor, distributed to his reporters on the eve of battle. It was couched in terms redolent of the Revolutionary Wars. It derided Reuters as "our bumptious British cousins." Guilfoyle admonished his troops to ensure that we were kept in our place, which he made clear was back in London where we belonged. His sales manager, Albert Anastasia, supported the sentiment in the earthier vernacular of the Brooklyn waterfront. "I want these Limey bastards driven back into the sea," he is reported to have told his sales force.

Guilfoyle was a man of fierce demeanor and upright parade-ground bearing. By reputation he could have drunk Brendan Behan under the table. But if he was a tyrant inside the newsroom, he was a charmer outside it. To that I could personally testify. Guilfoyle lived in the same Long Island community as me, and in chance morning meetings at the train station unfailingly extended a friendly greeting before, an hour later, doing his damnedest to put Reuters, and me, out of commission.

Guilfoyle and Anastasia could count on the support of one senior colleague with an even more combative nature than their own, the redoubtable Bill Clabby. His precise role in the organization over the years was sometimes unclear, but his devotion to Dow Jones was absolute and he was the man often designated, at public events, as the company's tambourine-thumping evangelist. Next to Clabby, Guilfoyle and Anastasia came across as shy and retiring. Clabby thrived on confrontation. He seemed to possess little talent or appetite for much else (though anyone with ten children, as Clabby had, must have possessed certain talents best left to the imagination). The in-your-face style, though, was mostly bluster. Faced with a resolute opponent, prepared to stand his ground and trade insult for insult, Clabby usually backed down—the mark of the schoolyard bully.

Clabby and I were destined to clash frequently and sometimes bitterly. No particular incident comes to mind to explain our mutual dislike. Buffalo Bill (as we dubbed him) simply seemed pathologically incapable of getting on with anyone with a mandate to harm his beloved Dow Jones. For my own part, I confess to having made little effort to understand this overbearing loyalty, which was alien to my somewhat more benign view of professional rivalry.

Even Dow Jones's most senior executive figure, chairman and chief executive Warren Phillips, a courtly soft-spoken gentleman of the old school, seemed unusually fired up by Reuters' arrival. "Phillips bore into the [Reuters] problem relentlessly," wrote Edward E. Scharff, in *Worldly Power: The Making of the Wall Street Journal*. "Bureau chiefs and reporters were told to call major corporations on their beats and deliver a message: Dow Jones demanded at least an even break with Reuters on all news stories. At least that was the part of the message that was articulated. The unspoken part, reporters felt, was that Dow Jones was prepared to punish those who gave too much cooperation to Reuters."[1]

The implied threat—in many instances beyond implied—was that corporate public relations executives friendly to us would find it hard to get stories about their companies into the *Wall Street Journal*. The ploy did not sit well with the *Journal*'s reporters, who saw it as an assault on the paper's editorial integrity. Neither did Phillips's injunction that any potentially market-moving articles being prepared for the newspaper were first to be submitted to the ticker for distribution, which meant that rival papers would be tipped off to the story. *Journal* reporters learned to detest their own Broad Tape as much as they were being exhorted to destroy Reuters.

Reuters' first American-born newswire was launched without fanfare on the first working day of the new year, 1968. The service was named the Reuter-Ultronic Report, a less than eye-catching name which recognized that this was a joint venture between Reuters and Ultronic, maker of the three-eyed monster I had first encountered a few years earlier in the London Sugar Market. Ultronic's contributions to the project were a high-speed teleprinter—

---

[1] Edward E. Scharff, *Worldly Power: The Making of the Wall Street Journal*, Beaufort Books, 1986, p.192

high-speed being a relative term—and the management of the sales team. This left Reuters to concentrate on the editorial product. The venture was in part a grateful payback to Ultronic for having generously underwritten the Stockmaster deal in Europe, but once again the suspicion was that Ultronic had been called on to pay most of the bills. This was not an unduly harsh financial burden, as Ultronic's management had since sold the business to Sylvania Corporation, the electronics manufacturing division of the General Telephone and Electronics Corporation.

The RUR versus the Broad Tape was hardly an evenly matched contest. The great assault on Dow Jones's formidable American redoubt was to be undertaken by no greater force than a commando unit of imported Brits. A dozen of us had been drafted in to man the general and financial news desks in New York. A few others, like Bernie Gagan, had been posted to Washington to cover news emerging from the government agencies, particularly those responsible for the regular announcements of the national economic statistics carefully watched by Wall Street. We were supported by a handful of local hires. There was also a strategic reserve of long-serving Comtelburo employees, most of them concerned with commodities, located in New York and Chicago, and most frankly well past their prime; in the kind of offensive we were about to launch they would be about as useful as one-legged pacifists. Beyond the three cities mentioned, Reuters had no offices. Nor were there plans to open any. For coverage from other cities we would have to rely on part-time stringers. These were recruited randomly as we went along. Randomly was when we heard from most of them. Our opponents, in contrast, employed dozens of reporters in New York, and hundreds more worked from Dow Jones offices located in all the major cities. Guilfoyle also had access to the general news services of the AP and United Press International.

The Spartans were about to take on the might of Persia. Horatio had 300 men at his disposal. We fell well short of three dozen.

It went without saying that the RUR was expected to operate on a tight budget. Tight is an inadequate word. It was a shoestring, and a frayed one at that. But we were all up for a fight, as partisans in hopeless causes so often are, and on the day of reckoning, armed with broom handles for rifles, off we marched with a jaunty step to the sound of distant gunfire.

In combat for the first time we performed honorably. As military dispatches might have put it, early successes were achieved in the face of heavy enemy fire, and a small bridgehead was secured. There were times, though, when our gallant band was in danger of being overwhelmed by the volume of copy, a daily avalanche of corporate press releases—earnings, dividends, mergers, acquisitions, and product announcements—and the telephones rang incessantly. None of this was surprising since every corporate public relations department at every exchange-listed company in America had been invited to call us with announcements. And even if only half of them actually did so, it still amounted to several hundred calls a day. Naturally, no one had thought to install a switchboard capable of handling such volumes, but then there would not have been enough people to pick up the calls anyway. Every day we worked a shift of up to ten hours, most of them spent in a heightened state of tension punctuated by regular bouts of frenzy and despair. None of us had ever worked as hard before. I have never worked as hard since. The same, it must be said, applied to our drinking. By day we donated our hearts and minds to the cause, by night we offered our livers.

Our "recovery room" was the Pig and Whistle on 49th Street, around the corner from the office. The regular patrons, or patients, were McCallum and me and Bob Kearns, one of Reuters' early American recruits. A lumbering and amiable giant with hollow legs, Bob seemed to inhale Budweisers (which some would say at least had the merit of his not having to taste them). I can conjure him up even now, weaving his uncertain way home up Fifth Avenue after a therapeutic session at the Pig, towering over the crowds like Gulliver taking an evening stroll in Lilliput. McCallum and I lived on Long Island, which meant a train ride home. It was my good fortune to live at the end of a branch line, which meant I could never miss my stop. McCallum was not so lucky. At least twice a week he would sleep through his station, to wake up in a panic in some desolate island outpost with an unpronounceable Indian name.

In enduring several years of this punishing routine, over the course of which we became regular late-night patrons of some of the East Side's best-known singles bars, McCallum and I contrived to fire lethal torpedoes into our foundering marriages. It used to be said that if you could remember the sixties you couldn't have been there. Some of us felt that way about the seventies, too.

Paradoxically, the unmanageable daily avalanche of copy sometimes worked in our favor. Reuters possessed a secret weapon: Ultronic's printer, a conventional-looking device purchased off-the-shelf, ran three times faster than Dow Jones's ancient machine, an odd-looking column printer with an award-winning art deco design that dated back to the 1930s. While the RUR spat out copy at a feverish rate of 150 words a minute, the Broad Tape could only chug away at a sleep-inducing 50 wpm. And Ultronic could, if necessary, crank up to a mind-boggling 300 wpm! Even at half that rate, we had a considerable advantage, especially on unusually busy days. Whenever the flood of corporate news started to back up, as during the quarterly earnings "seasons" of the year, when most companies reported their results, we could shift copy much faster than Dow Jones.

And shift it we did—"like shit through a goose" in Dave Armour's memorable scatology—leaving our rival to suffer the discomfort of severe constipation.

Since very few companies saw fit to call us first with press releases—craven submission to the systematic bullying of Guilfoyle and Clabby had seen to that—we were grateful for any advantage, however slight. By pushing out a much greater volume of copy we greatly increased our quotient of scoops. Guilfoyle might get most stories *in* first, but he couldn't necessarily get them *out* first.

We worked hard to create other opportunities to level the playing fields. For instance, Des Maberley and Alex McCallum constantly lobbied the New York Stock Exchange to rewrite its disclosure rules. Its handbook of procedures made a point of mentioning Dow Jones as a public outlet for press releases. Reuters should be listed too, we insisted. The Exchange politely refused to budge. Of course it did: Dow Jones and the "Big Board" had been working together for a century or more and Reuters was merely a troublesome foreign interloper. The smaller American Stock Exchange was far more accommodating in every respect. The Amex agreed immediately to list Reuters in its handbook—a minor concession by the exchange and a major triumph for us that probably represented one underdog doing a favor for another.

The times were sympathetic to our cause. Full and immediate disclosure of potentially market-moving news had suddenly become a fear-inspired mantra in the corporate world.

A year earlier, in 1966, the Securities and Exchange Commission had brought an action against an executive at Morgan Guaranty for using privileged information to buy shares in a company of which he was a director. The case went on to become a landmark in the annals of "insider trading." It attracted more attention than it might have in ordinary circumstances, because the executive concerned had a famous name, Thomas S. Lamont, son of the renowned Thomas W. Lamont, a partner of JP Morgan himself in the 1920s and one of the most powerful men on Wall Street. The company was Texas Gulf Sulphur. The privileged information was a potentially lucrative ore strike the company had made in Timmins, Ontario two years earlier. Lamont's transgression was to pass this good news on to his bank colleagues, who promptly acted on it by buying shares in large numbers on behalf of their clients. Lamont compounded the offence by buying shares for himself and his family. The sins were inadvertent, Lamont having had every reason to believe when he committed them—and to the extent that he gave the matter any thought—that the news was public knowledge by virtue of a company press release.

By the time Lamont got round to buying shares for his own account, there actually had been a press release, but the SEC had a new interpretation of what constituted inside information. In this formulation, "insiders" were obliged not just to wait until public disclosure had been made before acting on it but to allow "a reasonable amount of time" to expire after that. The language was imprecise and the case against Lamont was considered flimsy. In the end, the charges were dropped but, as it turned out, posthumously. By then Lamont, who had resigned his job, had fallen into ill health and before long he died—a martyr, his friends maintained, to unwarranted persecution.

Little wonder then that corporate public relations executives had become paranoid about prompt disclosure. And of course we encouraged them to be so, with the admonition: "Remember Texas Gulf Sulphur'.

Each day, Dow Jones and Reuters religiously monitored each other's performance, as measured by the number of "beats" or scoops recorded. We stationed a clerk in a broker's office somewhere on Wall Street, watching the Broad Tape. Guilfoyle likewise had someone, somewhere else on Wall Street, keeping an eye on ours. This enabled both sides, whenever the other had a story out first, to chase the company or agency concerned for the news. Dow Jones invariably emerged as the day's clear winner, the margin of victory rarely varying from decisive. This prompted Guilfoyle to brag about it to the *Chicago Tribune*, which quoted him in an article about our rivalry. "Ever since the competition started there has never been a day when we haven't beaten them more than they've beaten us. The ratio runs about 60 to 70 percent in our favor." There was no disputing his figures—our own were actually worse—but Guilfoyle had unwittingly played into our hands. The claim was less a boast than an admission, the revelation being that we could beat Dow Jones up to 40 percent of the time, which tended to enhance, rather than diminish, our credibility. Our salesmen gratefully distributed the *Tribune* clipping to hundreds of prospective customers.

Meanwhile, Clabby had been busy, too. He had been going around various government agencies complaining that Reuters only beat Dow Jones as often as it did because we deliberately broke embargoes on important economic indicators. We did it, he claimed, by advancing our printer's "time-clock" by one minute, allowing us to jump the gun. Actually, there was no such thing as a clock on the RUR, the timestamp on a story being manually punched in by a teleprinter operator. No doubt he occasionally got it wrong, but to assert, as Clabby did, that we were deliberately flouting embargoes was nonsense and he, I suspect, knew it. In the event, his campaign to elicit punitive measures, such as having Reuters barred from official press conferences, failed, but from then on we did go out of our way to make sure that our time-stamps always reflected the exact release time. As a foreign company we were especially sensitive about relations with government agencies.

Dow Jones's retaliatory measures went so far as to spend money. A year or so after the RUR's appearance, a decision was made to replace the venerable Broad Tape column printer with a new model that matched ours in speed. To add insult to injury, Dow Jones went to the same manufacturer that Ultronic used. If nothing else, we had the satisfaction of knowing that it would take a considerable investment by Dow Jones to replace thousands of terminals. It also meant that for several years the Broad Tape was doomed to operate at a financial loss.

What really gave the RUR its early impetus, though, had nothing to do with faster transmission rates or alleged violations of embargoes. Reuters' excellent coverage of international news meant that we were always likely to spring a foreign surprise and, early in April, just three months after the RUR launch, we did just that.

A few weeks earlier, President Lyndon Johnson had announced on television his startling decision not to run for re-election. Barely less sensationally, Johnson had also disclosed that a peace overture had been made to North Vietnam: the United States would halt its bombing campaign if Hanoi would agree to talks. Tired of a war that appeared to be increasingly unwinnable, and brutalized every evening by televised images of GIs being shipped home in body bags (not to mention endless weekends of student protests), America breathlessly awaited a response. Many expert observers felt that Hanoi would reject the overture, especially as the North appeared to be gaining the upper hand in the fighting.

On April 3, 1968, ten minutes before the stock market opened, bells rang in the Reuters newsroom in New York proclaiming a sensational development. The story was datelined Singapore, where Reuters' office, monitoring Radio Hanoi, had picked up a statement from the North Vietnam government. The gist of it was that, subject to suspension of the American bombing campaign and other "acts of war against the North," Hanoi was prepared to engage in full-scale peace talks. We rushed the story out on the RUR, alert bells clanging, and waited for the market reaction.

Nothing happened.

The stock-market averages scarcely twitched. The lack of response was deafening. We were undoubtedly alone with the Hanoi story—our Broad Tape "spy" had confirmed as much. So why had the stock market failed to respond to it?

There were two reasons, two sides of the same coin. The first was that the RUR had too few subscribers to have a market-moving impact. The second was that Wall Street had been brainwashed into believing that until something appeared on the Broad Tape it had not actually happened.

Seven minutes after the market opening, and seventeen minutes after our story had appeared, Dow Jones finally ran a news flash. It was a desperate catch-up story from UPI, not nearly as definitive as ours, but the market response was immediate and dramatic. The Dow Jones Industrial Average, which had only inched ahead as our news slowly made the rounds, suddenly shot up ten points. (An insignificant fluctuation by today's standards, but a substantial market move back then.) "There's a piece on Dow Jones that peace talks may start," I remember a PR man telling me breathlessly over the phone. "The market's really going wild. Gee, I hope you guys have the story, too."

It was galling, to put it mildly.

Joe Daffin, the RUR sales manager, made us feel better. He was far from galled; he was cock-a-hoop. The telephones had been ringing off the hook, he reported. "Reckon we'll sell a hundred printers today."

We did, as I recall.

When memory fails, there is always the clipping file. One article I managed to retain from that truly momentous year—the Martin Luther King and Robert Kennedy assassinations were yet to come—was an article in *Institutional Investor* magazine headlined "The Battle of the Broad Tapes."

The Reuters-Dow Jones contest, the magazine reported, "has put fresh emphasis on the way news has an impact on prices. It has added a hard-nosed dimension to the competition between reporters, something the financial community hadn't seen in a long time."[2]

*Esquire* magazine jumped on the story, too. "Dow Jones, for years the only high-speed ticker in existence, is suffering, and Reuters, with an occasional twinge of growing pains, is jubilant."[3] The same article quoted a Dow Jones reporter as saying that Joe Guilfoyle had "become a maniac on the subject of Reuters" and would "sacrifice anything to beat Reuters on a story." *Business Week* was equally intrigued, particularly by the exploits of "Lightfoot" Leo Fasciocco, Reuters' Philadelphia stringer, who had beaten the Dow Jones reporter to the punch at several company meetings. "I outrun them for the fun of it," Leo says. The Dow Jones man was not impressed. "He usually does it by breaking release time," he complained.[4]

We were not above a few sacrifices of our own. One of our more enterprising New York reporters, Norma Walter, amused us one day by describing with relish how she had thwarted Dow Jones at some blue-chip company's annual shareholders meeting. "There happened to be two available phones outside the hall. I got to them first and, while I was dialing one, jammed my chewing gum hard into the coin slot of the other one. The Dow Jones guy went apeshit. I was laughing so hard I could hardly call the story in."

In another incident, an annual meeting was disrupted by an unseemly

---

[2] Peter Landau, *Institutional Investor*, July 1968
[3] *Esquire* magazine, April 1968
[4] *Business Week*, February 27, 1971

scuffle between rival reporters. In their frenzy to get to a telephone, they fell over chairs and started to wrestle with each other on the floor, much to the astonishment of a dozen directors and several hundred shareholders. We received a letter of complaint from the company, to which we naturally responded with a contrite letter of apology. Our pugilistic reporter had it laminated as if it were a college graduation certificate. In a sense, it was.

What did it amount to, this Battle of the Broad Tapes? What form of journalism were we and our rivals practicing—the highest or the lowest? In one sense—that we were engaged in a struggle to get news to our respective readers first—it was arguably the highest. On the other hand, our slavish commitment to speed produced services that fell considerably short of exemplary on any number of levels. Some of the reporters we hired struggled to master a basic English sentence. We used to laugh, or cry, at one Rich Bianco (by now I hope enjoying the fruits of some alternative profession) whose approach to the language may be compared to that of a band of Vandals contemplating a defenseless village. Nor did he have a compensating nose for news. And, as if suspect literacy and editorial incompetence were not enough to contend with, he was also partially deaf. All of which virtually guaranteed, under the immutable rules of Sod's Law, that it was always our Rich who picked up the telephone whenever a market-moving story was called in. If planet Mars had ever announced a takeover bid for planet Earth, it can be said with absolute certainty that Bianco would have been the one to take the call. "And how are you today, my friend? Now speak slowly and carefully…First, let me find some paper. I seem to have run out…By the way, did you happen to catch those crazy Mets last night…?"

We survived the hapless Bianco, of course, and various other impedimenta to good order.

We would soon be engaged in a far greater challenge than thwarting Dow Jones reporters, or even Rich Bianco.

Word reached us of an emerging newsroom technology—one that would sadly replace our beloved typewriters (but happily replace the teletype operators). It was called video editing, and it involved typing stories into desktop terminals known as CRTs—an acronym for cathode ray tubes—or alternatively as VDUs (for video display units).

Screen products had been quietly catching on. The airlines, it is true, had been using video terminals for many years, but few other industries had found a use for them, until the financial markets cottoned on to the benefits of screen technology—thanks largely to a product called the Quotron, a stock quotation retrieval device. Ultronic's funny old three-eyed monster, Stockmaster, was in Quotron's direct line of descent. Now the company had come out with a screen-based product called Videomaster. Designed to replace Stockmaster, it was capable of displaying an entire screen-full of data, which could moreover be compiled by the user. And, before long, Videomaster would pioneer an even more startling development: a version of the product that could process words as well as figures, which meant that it could display news alongside quotes. The days of the teleprinter were numbered.

Words on a screen! What would they think of next? We were all flabbergasted.

How childishly insignificant these breakthroughs seem now, especially as I reflect on the word processor in front of me, a device whose miraculously diverse functions I have hardly begun to explore, but which offers direct, instant and affordable access, via the Internet, to half the population of the planet; a device on which I can write a book, buy books and just about anything else, download photographs, open a bank account, and manage the household budget. But back in the seventies, a less credulous age, every barrier dismantled or record broken, in any field, used to leave us breathless in wonder. Consider the more sensational developments of my lifetime—the breaking of the sound barrier, the first four-minute mile, the scaling of Everest, the cordless telephone, the transistor radio; all now seem perfectly inconsequential. In the sixties, technological innovations had a shelf life of years, perhaps decades. Now, in a totally credulous age, their novelty wears thin within weeks.

The significance of this strangely unheralded moment—the arrival of words on a screen—was that it opened the miraculous age of the desktop computer.

The computer's arrival at hidebound Reuters coincided with the arrival of a new general manager for North America, Glen Renfrew. Fresh from his success leading the European marketing campaign for Stockmaster, and fired with ambition to take the top job at Reuters, he was determined to transform Cyril Smith's sleepy New York editorial outpost into a Glen Renfrew technology-led money-spinning powerhouse.

Alex McCallum, in what would be his last project for the company, was charged with the responsibility for designing Reuters' first video-editing system. McCallum was the ideal candidate: thoughtful, meticulous, intimately acquainted with all the issues involved in editing, storing, transferring, and transmitting copy. Reuters might have chosen to purchase any number of off-the-shelf solutions, but all had proved too expensive or too complex for our limited budget and relatively simple needs. We ended up buying the hardware from a garage-based operation on Long Island. Because there were likely to be relatively few problems with Reuters' single union, the Newspaper Guild of New York, a relatively benign organization, the New York office was the company's perfect guinea pig. It certainly could not have been London, where the NGA would have shut down Fleet Street and organized a campaign of sabotage at the merest whiff of automation.

McCallum's video-editing initiative was just one minor float in an ever-lasting parade of desktop information-handling products designed for the investment community. Thomas Edison had started a similar movement at the turn of the century with his revolutionary stock ticker, which, even going into the 1960s, had hardly changed in fundamental design. But the transistor, soon to become the ubiquitous silicon chip, was about to transform the electronics industry.

As far as the financial markets were concerned, the wave of innovation in desktop information devices had begun a decade earlier with the remarkable instrument device mentioned earlier—the Quotron. The product emerged from a Los Angeles-based firm called Scantlin Electronics, founded in 1957 by John R. Scantlin, a smart, mercurial twenty-seven-year-old with a degree in electrical engineering from Cal Tech. Scantlin had the southern Californian's obligatory taste for fast cars, surfing, and skiing, but his temper could be as short as his crewcut, and in business matters he was no mere California dreamer. He was a man with a mission to make money. After a brief but disillusioning career at General Dynamics, a California-based defense contractor, Jack Scantlin had emerged into the wider world with something of a chip on his shoulder. The defense industry, he felt strongly, had "ruined electronics" by wasting money on mediocre products of little or no utility. Recoiling from the grandiose commercial improbabilities all too prevalent in the defense industry, he set out to develop products that could be sold to the public—if not to the consumer public then to a specialized community with an obvious need—and above all with profit in mind. The community he soon targeted was the world of stockbrokers, the men and women who handled the money being made by the increasingly affluent post-war generation of stock-market investors.

As he told *Newsweek* magazine in 1960: "You're always hearing about pushing further the frontiers of science."[5] At Scantlin, he said, "We're an anchor on the state of the art. If we see an uphill battle … we might even duck it … Our interest is what we put out the door." It was this no-nonsense attitude that attracted his financial backers, most of whom knew little about the business. They included Peter Davis, a West Coast advertising executive, William R. Staats & Co., a Los Angeles investment firm, Elisha Walker, a New York City realtor, and Laurence Rockefeller, one of the scions of the great Standard Oil fortune. The company had made its early profits—$160,000 in 1959 on revenue of about £1 million—largely from radiotelephone products. Neither the figures nor the products were much to write home about. That was about to change with the introduction of Scantlin's new product, a device designed for stockbrokers called the Quotron System 7.

---

[5] *Newsweek Magazine*, February 13, 1960

It was a boon to the credibility of Scantlin Electronics (soon to be renamed Quotron Systems) that many of the users with first-hand knowledge of the product worked for the same brokerage firms that would soon be recommending the stock. They found it an odd-looking object. Someone described it as a wedge of cheese with buttons. Entering the alphabetic ticker symbol to call up a stock produced a short strip of tape with the information requested printed on it. What was revolutionary about the Quotron was that it was an interrogation device; that is, it allowed the user to specify the information to be extracted. Other machines, little changed either in function or appearance from Edison's 19th-century contraptions, simply spewed out ticker tape all day, forcing users to wade through yards of the stuff to locate the stocks they wanted. Quotron-7 became an instant success and something of a sensation. For stockbrokers constantly harassed by calls from clients asking for stock prices it was a godsend. If Quotron-7 had a price tag to match—a single machine cost $265 a month, additional units $15 a month—it was worth every last cent.

On the back of the Quotron's success, Scantlin Electronics went public in 1960 at $12 a share. As the company thrived in a market hitherto wary of electronics after a series of corporate failures in the field, within five months the price almost tripled to $33. By the end of the first year, Quotrons had been installed in 180 stock brokerage firms, and dozens of orders were backed up in the company's sales pipeline.

Inevitably, Quotron's brilliant success attracted competitors. One was Bunker Ramo, another electronic offshoot from a defense contractor. A third entrant was Ultronic, founded by a group of executives from Radio Corporation of America, yet another company with interests in the defense business. These three companies soon dominated the market, with Quotron out front but feeling the heat. Company executives soon started to wonder how much traffic the American market could bear, and whether Europe might offer opportunities for expansion. Bunker Ramo, for one, had started talking to Telekurs, an information company owned by the Swiss Banks, about a distribution deal.

Michael Nelson of Reuters shortly became aware of the proliferation of stock quotation devices. While on a visit to New York in 1963, he noticed that Cyril Smith had installed a pair of Ultronic's Stockmasters in Reuters' New York office. Partly motivated by the Bunker Ramo initiative in Switzerland, Nelson commissioned a survey to determine whether a significant market for stock quotation devices existed in Europe. The results were not particularly encouraging. The European bourses were less active than the American markets, interest in American stocks was marginal, and European stockbrokers, tradition-bound and habit-ridden, tended to view technology with more suspicion than their American counterparts. Europe did not seem to offer a compelling commercial opportunity.

Nelson disagreed—survey or no survey. Ignoring the survey's findings, he asked Smith to arrange a meeting with Jack Scantlin with a view to cutting a deal for the right to distribute Quotron, then the most popular product on the market, in Europe. Scantlin at first seemed intrigued by the idea, but Nelson and Smith found it hard to persuade him to discuss the commercial details.

" 'Oh yes, very interesting, very interesting,' " was how Nelson recalled Scantlin's response, "but we just couldn't pin him down." Nelson thought of Scantlin as "more a technical man than a businessman." After several more futile attempts to do a deal with Scantlin, Nelson turned to Ultronic.

Robert Sinn, Ultronic's president, a former RCA engineer, had none of the typical engineer's approach to business. He was an entrepreneur, a sociable fellow who liked to do deals. Right from the start, Sinn warmed to Nelson and to the idea of a deal with Reuters. Nelson's timing was fortuitous. A few months earlier, Ultronic had actually ventured into Europe on its own, with a view to servicing the European branches of its major American clients, but Sinn had found the cost of putting in an Atlantic communications line to service a limited number of customers prohibitive. He had also become frustrated dealing with Europe's bureaucracies, especially the state-owned telecommunications companies. Reuters, an international news organization with a global network and an office in every major financial center, offered attractions on several levels.

In February 1964 Sinn flew to London for talks with Nelson, Cyril Smith, and Don Ferguson, Reuters' communications director. Both sides quickly agreed that working together indeed offered mutual advantages. A lunch was arranged at the Waldorf Hotel for the purpose of outlining a formal agreement. Ferguson explained that Reuters had a voice circuit across the Atlantic ideally suited to carrying Ultronic's data.

Sinn got excited about this until Nelson stepped in to mention that the circuit was already pretty full.

"No problem," said Sinn, "we'll time-division multiplex it."

The Reuters men—Ferguson included—were baffled. TDM? How did it work? Was anyone else doing it?

Sinn explained the concept. He did not know if anyone was using it for long-line overseas communications, but splitting one big circuit into multiple circuits was a technique widely used in the United States. Sinn promised that Ultronic would supply Reuters with a specially designed "black box" to make it work.

With that problem out of the way, Nelson raised another, more formidable, issue. Reuters, he was obliged to explain somewhat sheepishly, had no cash.

Sinn suddenly looked crestfallen. The emollient Nelson, backed by an ebullient Smith, went to work on him. Sinn's enthusiasm for a deal, and the thought that Reuters might turn to Bunker Ramo, or even Quotron, if Ultronic failed to come through, gave them a head start they had not enjoyed with Jack Scantlin.

"Okay," said Sinn finally. "Here's the deal. Ultronic will put up the money and we'll start the joint venture on a marginal cost basis and split the profit fifty-fifty."

Worried about his competitors Sinn may have been, but his offer to Reuters was generous to a fault—certainly one that Nelson can hardly have imagined he could ever have negotiated. It earned Bob Sinn a special place in Reuters' pantheon of heroes.

To manage the project, Reuters formed a new operating unit, the Computer Services Division, and placed it under the control of a brash young Australian executive, Glen Renfrew, a former journalist with an aptitude for technology. It was a decision that, in light of Renfrew's outstanding performance in the job, Nelson would have reasons at first to cheer and later to regret.

The advent of the computer age started me thinking about my future. The proliferation of screen-based products portended a switch in emphasis from pure news products to broader, screen-based information services in which news would be reduced to merely a constituent. Printer services would soon be dead, replaced by desktop information retrieval devices. In this new auto-mated world the newsroom would become an annex.

The future, I decided, lay in marketing.

By this time, 1972, I had scaled the exalted height of editorship of the Reuter Financial Report (so renamed after Ultronic faded from the scene). I could, I suppose, have contemplated an editorial career of great promise. What price the agency's most senior editorial post, a position that then commanded a seat on the executive committee? A distinctly long shot, I decided, more for someone in sync with the political mainstream than an inveterate gadfly and controversialist like me. As for my current job, it was less that of a journalist than a teacher—and if I scarcely qualified for the former, I was certainly not up to the latter. Anyway, supervising unruly and disrespectful reporters was nowhere near as much fun as being an unruly and disrespectful reporter oneself. A change was also in order for the benefit of my health. The newsroom remained a harrowing, nerve-jangling place. A year or so earlier, that would have been part of its attraction. Now I was jaded. The magic of news, the power of words, and the thrill of the scoop had all steadily relinquished their grip on my imagination. The battle with Dow Jones could never be won or lost, at least not definitively, and it had already been reduced to skirmishing from the opposing trenches. Few cared anymore about the daily log of "beats." The clerk monitoring the Broad Tape had long been eliminated for economy reasons.

Most of my editorial pals, moreover, had already disappeared. Bernie Gagan still slaved away with undimmed enthusiasm in the Washington slot, but in New York Dave Armour and Alex McCallum had left the company—both as a result of "philosophical differences" with Maberley—and a number of other kindred spirits had drifted away. There was, too, a tailor-made replacement for me as editor, one Maggie Klein, a former AP reporter from North Carolina, a woman of talent and blatant ambition.

I took my preoccupations to Glen Renfrew. Reuters needed someone to design services for screen products, I told him. Client needs ought to be researched, a function for which the salesmen were not qualified. A bridge was required between product development and sales—call it marketing if you must. A home-grown candidate with a background in news and knowledge of the markets would be ideal. In short: me.

Renfrew, I must say, did not seem greatly impressed. He no doubt had preoccupations of his own. These probably included a grand scheme he had in mind, or so I had gathered, to deliver information to clients via the hot new medium of cable television. So-called CATV networks were spreading rapidly all over the United States, expanding the habits of millions of American viewers by spreading the gospel of unrestricted choice. Renfrew was obsessed with the idea of using it as a vehicle for delivering financial data. "I'll design the products," I offered.

A week later, I was doing just that.

# Troika

For a short period during the 1950s the Soviet Union was governed by a ruling triumvirate known as a troika, from the Russian word for a vehicle drawn by three horses abreast. For most of the 1970s Reuters was managed under a similar arrangement.

Reuters' three "horses" were each briefly encountered in the previous chapter: Gerald Long, Michael Nelson, and Glen Renfrew.

Abreast does not necessarily mean equal. As the agency's chief executive, Long formally outranked his colleagues. His role, to extend the Soviet analogy, may be compared to that of party secretary, a front man responsible for articulating strategy and for enforcing adherence to the sacred manifesto. Long often seemed ill at ease with the world. At Reuters, he was respected rather than admired. His manner was overbearing and perplexing, which soured his relations with his peers and frequently brought him into conflict with his directors. Fortunately for him, the board was as spineless as an earthworm, and about as visionary. Personality quirks aside, Long presented a figure of intimidating intelligence and bellicose authority and, in contrast to his boardroom colleagues, lacked nothing in courage.

While Long played master of ceremonies to the board, day-to-day responsibility for managing the business fell to Nelson, his prime minister. The ultimate apparatchik, the clever and understated Nelson brought to his office the virtues of cold efficiency and steely purpose. They served an ambition stoked by an emerging consensus that he was Long's heir apparent. Not that this was an expectation Long had ever encouraged. Indeed, having given Renfrew a place at the top table by promoting him to manage the North American division, and by publicly declaring the position to be on a par with Nelson's, it may be said that Long had effectively—and perhaps calculatedly—discouraged the notion.

Renfrew, the last to join the troika, was charismatic, energetic, straight talking, and full of ideas. He was sociable to a fault—a euphemism for an affinity with the bottle. It was this "sociability" that attracted the kind of proletarian adulation to which neither of his colleagues at the top table could ever hope to aspire, and which they silently resented. The New York assignment was widely perceived as Renfrew's ultimate test, a make-or-break opportunity that would either vault him into a position to challenge the growing assumption of Nelson's automatic accession, or destroy his career.

Much of the early betting **was** that Renfrew, indomitable and charismatic, might yet emerge triumphant.

The three men formed **a** formidable and fascinating management team: formidable because of the **extra**ordinary collective intellect; fascinating because in the three starkly contrasting personalities and competing egos there was ripe potential for conflict, especially between the two pretenders to the throne. A team it was for all that. Company insiders were uncomfortably aware of the lack of personal chemistry between the three—which endless taproom speculation reflected, and perhaps even stimulated—but outsiders were never allowed so much as a peek behind the public façade of unity and bonhomie. It was a performance worthy of the Old Vic.

This triumvirate had emerged from a curious sequence of events involving two other men who, for a time, had battled for supremacy at Reuters. One was a mercurial Austrian, representing the commercial services, the other an enigmatic Scot, a champion of the general news division. The contest culminated in the abrupt departure of the former and the untimely death of the latter. While neither of these gentlemen deserves a place in this narrative on the basis of their own accomplishments, a brief digression is worthwhile for two reasons. First, because their rivalry, which pitted the second floor against the fourth, marked the beginning of the end of the long-running battle for Reuters' corporate soul. Second, because, if it had not occurred, or at least if the outcome had been different, Reuters might have become a very different company from the one described in the next few chapters of this book.

Before Long's regime there had been no such thing as a troika—or anything else that smacked of shared responsibility. Reuters, as we have seen, had established a tradition of autocratic chief executives, sometimes to its advantage (as in the time of Julius Reuter) and sometimes to its disadvantage (as in the times of Herbert Reuter and Roderick Jones). Long's immediate predecessor, Walton A. "Tony" Cole, was another who hankered for absolute rule, a form of government which, if history is any guide—Reuters' own history in particular—tends to induce in the ruler a distinctly more nervous disposition than in the ruled. This was certainly true of Cole. A large and assertive man, his public displays of bombast impressed the lower orders, but tended to attract the scorn of many of his peers, who recognized that the gruff public persona was nothing but camouflage for private terrors of self-doubt and insecurity.

Of humble origins, and lacking in formal education, the portly and bespectacled Cole was a canny Scot with an uncanny resemblance to King Farouk of Egypt. In both heart and mind he considered himself first and foremost a journalist and, once ensconced in the top executive post at Reuters, he remained at all times an ardent defender of the general news service in which he had made his mark. Typical of his breed, he failed to appreciate fully the value of the commercial services, sometimes giving the impression that he resented them—another unfortunate company tradition perpetuated during the Jones regime. But even though he bled editorial ink, Cole spent most of his tenure in the role of salesman, chiefly for his beloved general news service, a cause for which he traveled the world ceaselessly, exhaustingly and, much of the time, unavailingly.

The global expeditions left Cole little time to spend on Comtelburo's affairs. That would not have troubled him. His negative view of trading markets was that they were unlikely to recover from wartime disruption for some considerable time, if ever. In which case, how could Comtelburo possibly be of any significant value to a great international news agency except, in the unlikely event that markets did rebound, as a useful milch cow for general news? The attitude was not entirely at variance with those of his immediate predecessors, Jones and Chancellor. Neither had displayed an overt animus to commercial services, but, as Chancellor once told the board, Comtelburo's ability to fund general news was the sole reason for its existence and would be shut down immediately if it should ever lose its capacity to make profits. As it happened—as it had always happened—the black ink regularly produced by the commercial services flowed in vivid contrast to the perpetual tides of red ink generated by the general news services. For this Cole ought to have been grateful. That he was not may be attributed not just to his dim view of market prospects but to his fear-induced reasoning that any second-floor executive who could exploit Comtelburo's achievements would need careful watching as a potential rival. This irrational attitude, of fearing commercial services even while dismissing them, may be regarded as one of the many symptoms of Cole's paranoia.

Sure enough, a perceived rival did emerge from the second floor—an egocentric Austrian-born firebrand named Alfred Geiringer. Alfie, as he was generally known, was ambitious, abrasive, self-assured, and opinionated—the very qualities that Cole most dreaded in a colleague. Geiringer was not a natural Comtelburo man. He had joined Reuters in 1937 as an assistant to Reuters' correspondent in Vienna, but was forced to decamp for London two years later when German troops entered his homeland to enforce the Anschluss. Driven by a fierce desire to succeed in his adopted country, Geiringer quickly made his presence felt on the general news desk at 85 Fleet Street as a man able to make things happen. This organizational flair was recognized when, towards the end of the war, Chancellor assigned him to help rebuild Reuters in central Europe, a job which involved assisting the Allied occupation authorities in restructuring the German press. It was in Berlin in this role that Geiringer came across Gerry Long, a serving British Army intelligence officer engaged in the same cause. Fellow linguists and men of strong opinions, they hit it off right away. Geiringer elicited from Long a promise that, as soon as he had completed his interrupted studies at Cambridge, he would apply for a job at Reuters. Long had been only too happy to keep the pledge.

In 1952, Geiringer was once more tapped by Chancellor for a difficult assignment, this time to restore the flagging commercial services to their pre-war profitability. To this task he applied fabled Teutonic single-mindedness and an energy to which the second floor had rarely been subjected. The irony was that Geiringer shared Cole's pessimistic view of the prospects for a renaissance in trading markets, his attitude nurtured in large part by the shocking scenes of physical devastation he had witnessed in post-war Germany. Those indelible images convinced him that industrial reconstruction rather than financial speculation would drive any post-war recovery, and that the best hope for Comtelburo's resurrection lay in producing in-depth corporate and industrial intelligence. Such services, he believed, would be in such huge demand that they could be sold at premium subscription prices.

On both counts he could not have been more wrong. The twin misjudgment was underlined by two spectacular commercial failures of his making. The first, a venture called the International Business Unit, folded within three years, having failed to attract sufficient clients to cover its operating costs. The second, a bulletin service called International Business Facts, had suffered from the same problem and met the same fate after little more than a year. Fortunately, Comtelburo had kept its other irons in the fire, and managed to retain some measure of continuity and profitability.

If Geiringer's commercial achievements were less than stellar, what then was his lasting contribution to Reuters? Ironically, it was for his knack for employing subordinates who came to understand the financial world far better than he ever had. For hiring Gerry Long, Geiringer can take only partial credit—and Long never actually worked for the commercial services—but for the other members of the troika, both recruited for Comtelburo, he deserves full marks.

The irony was that Geiringer initially hired them for his ill-fated business intelligence products. Because these services called less for journalistic flair than for sophisticated analytical skills, Geiringer, in 1952, had sought and received Chancellor's permission to break Comtelburo's rather whimsical hiring tradition by recruiting graduates from Oxford and Cambridge. Mike Nelson was among the first of the Oxbridge rookies to arrive that year. A quietly spoken and apparently shy graduate of Magdalen College, Oxford, Nelson returned to London armed with a degree in modern history, intent on a career in news. Actually, Reuters was only his third choice of employer. He first tried to join the AP, and then the British United Press, only to be told by both agencies that they preferred to hire reporters with previous experience on newspapers. Geiringer had no such prejudice. He was looking for strategic thinkers, not ambulance chasers, and in the former category Nelson seemed to fit the bill perfectly.

Renfrew was recruited rather more fortuitously. Just a few weeks before Nelson joined Comtelburo, Renfrew, fresh off the boat from Sydney, had strolled into 85 Fleet Street unannounced—wearing shorts, it has been reported—looking for work. A hall porter sent him up to see Geiringer, who granted him an interview. So taken was Geiringer by the Australian's combination of brass and intelligence that he hired him on the spot, even raising the salary he had first offered when Renfrew brazenly asked for more money.

If, talent-spotting skills aside, Geiringer is to be scorned for his business acumen, he takes the biscuit for at least one act of inspiration with lasting consequences. It was an event that some at Reuters, including Mike Nelson, often cited as having exercised a defining influence on the company's subsequent approach to commercial services. Nelson it was who recounted the incident for this story.

Comtelburo's City News Ticker one day made a serious mistake reporting British Petroleum's dividend. Trading on the London Stock Exchange was thrown into chaos. The shares of BP and many other blue-chip companies fell sharply, then recovered, as stockbrokers grappled with the conflicting versions of the story floating around the City. The market settled down only after Reuters issued a humiliating correction. The next day the London newspapers gleefully took the agency to task for the error. Arriving at the office that morning, Geiringer immediately called a staff meeting. The most positive expectation was that expletives would fly and the most negative that heads would roll. To the astonishment of all present, including an impressionable young Nelson, Geiringer's manner was uncharacteristically serene. He spoke with quiet conviction. "I have only one observation to make on yesterday's fiasco. If the financial community depends on Reuters so much that the market can gain or lose millions of pounds on the basis of such an error, then clearly we are not charging enough. Raise the price of the ticker by one-third immediately."

The Geiringer-Cole rivalry was bound to end in tears, and did. Geiringer's truculent swagger and his high-level connections on Fleet Street—acquired through his marriage to the daughter of a prominent newspaper executive, who also happened to be a close friend of Chancellor's—had brought him increasingly into conflict with Cole, and finally, in 1958, to the ultimate collision. The clash arose from Geiringer's bold proposal that Comtelburo be more or less spun off from the rest of the agency as a separate division, with its own management and its own independent communications network. The idea may have been controversial but it was hardly new. Comtelburo had always harbored an underground movement—more a debating society really—dedicated to throwing off the oppressive yoke of the general news division. It can be argued, therefore, that Geiringer's plan fell more into the category of a political statement than a serious business proposal. And as much as Cole must have resented it, he also had every reason to be confident that it would be rejected by the board. But instead of allowing nature to take its course he panicked. Marching indignantly into Chancellor's office, he delivered an ultimatum: "Geiringer or me!" Chancellor had become increasingly irritated with the troublesome Austrian and, anyway, had little choice but to go with his senior executive.

Geiringer promptly resigned.

A few years later, Cole suffered a more tragic fate. One January morning in 1963, a visitor to Reuters' executive suite was ushered into a waiting area by Cole's secretary, who then went off to find her boss. She returned in tears. She had found Cole sprawled on his office sofa, apparently asleep. In fact, he was dead, struck down by a massive heart attack.

Picking Cole's successor fell to a board of directors uniquely unqualified for the task. The Press Association representatives, for example, were blissfully unencumbered by knowledge of what Reuters did in the world. Their realm was confined to provincial Britain. As Long later acidly remarked, "Most of them had never traveled farther than Margate." To be fair, they had little incentive to get deeply involved in Reuters' affairs, being appointed strictly by rotation, largely on the principle of Buggins' turn, and restricted to terms of three years.

As a result, they shuffled in and out of the boardroom in an executive simulation of musical chairs. Not that serving on Reuters' board was an unwelcome chore. Their association with a famous international institution conferred a certain social status back home in the provinces—and the perks were attractive, too. For those reasons alone the PA directors could be relied on to show up dutifully for board meetings and luncheons, though they seldom opened their mouths except to eat.

Ostensibly more worldly-wise, their colleagues from the national press seemed hardly better informed about Reuters' business, or sufficiently motivated to learn. To them, the agency's constant pleas for higher subscription rates were a constant source of irritation, especially as there was usually little choice but to cough up. But even angry press barons regarded a Reuters board seat as a useful door-opener during overseas trips, which were additionally enhanced by the convenience of a rented car and driver, not to mention a free dinner or two. In general, though, the attitude to news agencies from the print side of the industry was largely one of patronizing indifference. Reuters' newswires provided a useful alert mechanism for the owners' papers, especially for coverage from the more remote parts of the world, but not much else. If agency journalists were any good, it was often argued, they would be working for newspapers. Agency men understandably resented this imputation of inferiority.

In short, the image of the good ship *Fleet Street* was that of white-shirted print men patrolling the bridge while bare-chested agency men toiled down in the boiler room. And Reuters' general manager—no longer, since the Roderick Jones affair, an automatic member of the board—was treated with no more respect than the chief stoker. The result of the board's collective ignorance, combined with the absence of a permanent chairman (yet another Jones legacy) was discontinuity, complacency, and a lack of strategic vision.

And so, after Cole's death, the board inevitably succumbed to confusion. A shortlist of candidates was quickly circulated. It contained the names of Cole's four deputy general managers. All were card-carrying journalists with impeccable news agency credentials. Three were considered "safe," which meant that they could be relied on to observe the courtesy of being seen rather than heard, and to keep a lid on newswire subscriptions.

The fourth candidate was written off as a rank outsider.

The front-runner, by common consent, at least outside the boardroom, was a veteran correspondent, Doon Campbell. Like Cole, he was a Scot and a graduate of the old school of wire service correspondents. Although born with one arm, which disqualified him from military service, he was never happier than when crouching in a trench, typewriter to hand, in the midst of a battle or street riot. In 1944, when he was twenty-four, Campbell had achieved heroic fame on D-Day by splashing on to a Normandy beach with the first wave of British troops. The "action" man was also considered a "nice" man, courteous, well-mannered and uncontroversial—fine qualities that helped to balance the derring-do image, though perhaps not the kind to suggest a shoo-in for the agency's top post. Campbell's only real rivals, or so it was thought, were a couple of amiably competent but distinctly unexciting "colonials." Patrick Crosse, an urbane South African whose management style stressed polite formality and scholarly memoranda, and the previously encountered Canadian, Stuart Underhill.

The fourth, dark-horse candidate was Gerald Long, a Yorkshireman by temperament as well as birth. He was the least known of the four, and, at thirty-nine, the youngest. He was, however, not altogether unknown. Some directors remembered a self-assured fellow, fluent in German and French, who, a year or two earlier, on the occasion of a board junket to celebrate Paul Julius Reuter's first successful business venture, had squired them around Aachen. Long's field experience included assignments in Germany and France, plus a brief posting in Ankara, before the Turkish government expelled him— a badge of honor in press circles. Intellectually, Long left the other candidates far behind, but "safe" was the last adjective anyone would apply to the owner of a famously complex and prickly personality.

His appearance and manner were those of an indignant major, the rank he had achieved after his four post-war years in the British Army. A full military mustache complemented a ridge of hair that dissected an otherwise close-cropped skull like a wayward hedge. He wore an almost perpetual baleful stare. The kindest interpretation of this hostility was that it was indiscriminant. If he gave the impression of a man forever on the verge of exploding into rage, it was because he often was. The mood could change without warning, but less often to one of affability than one of gloomy introspection.

Long, it was understood by the directors, would be difficult to handle: too difficult, perhaps.

But for once, Reuters' normally infallible grapevine had got it wrong. When the astonishing news came through that Reuters' chairman, John Burgess, had summoned the unfathomable Long rather than, say, the affable Campbell, the gasps of astonishment around 85 Fleet Street were audible.

Only the inquest remained. Who was this Long fellow, anyway? What was he about? And, since no one seemed to know for sure, how had the board arrived at such an unexpected and, as many thought, inexplicable decision? The answers to the first two questions would become clear soon enough. As for the third, most of the theories have long been forgotten, and whatever clues existed at the time have presumably disappeared with the deaths of most of those involved. Long himself remained forever convinced that he owed his job to the intervention, behind the scenes, of a secret admirer, Christopher Chancellor. Although he had retired in 1959, Chancellor was known to be in regular contact with several of the board's most powerful figures, including Cecil King, chairman of the Mirror Group, and Roy Thomson, the Canadian newspaper magnate, and soon to be proprietor of *The Times*. There may well have been others.

To back his belief, Long cited an incident that had occurred three years earlier when Chancellor, on the customary retirement tour of Reuters offices, had visited Bonn, where Long was then stationed as the Regency's chief representative in Germany.

After a formal company dinner, Chancellor made a point of inviting Long for a nightcap and, according to Long, told him: "I've been very pleased with your progress and I've told the board that, if any time they have to look for a successor to Mr. Cole, they should look to you." Long's unspoken reaction at the time was, "I bet you tell that to all the correspondents"—but the remark remained vivid in his mind.

Even so, Long was stunned by the board decision, perhaps for the first time in his life rendered speechless. Burgess, a fellow Yorkshireman with a similar forthright manner, in offering the position had to snap him out of his daze: "Come on, man, do you want the bloody job or not?" Bloody may have been the operative word.

If Reuters' owners expected the agency's business and the polite conventions of board meetings to be carried on pretty much as usual, they were in for a disagreeable surprise. If, on the other hand, he had been pitched into the job to shake the company up—and it must be assumed that someone had that in mind—then they would be far from disappointed. But first, Long had to take a long, hard look at his corporate inheritance.

His assessment of the company's condition could not have been less reassuring. Years later he recalled the experience with a grimace. "Reuters' future wasn't exactly secure. It was a bit of a rocky situation, in fact. I spent three years in what I would say was a very dangerous existence, and a very unpleasant one. I wouldn't care to do it again. We were working on the thinnest of margins. One major mistake would have been the end of us. It's easy to forget now the strain of those early years, when we knew how precarious the situation was."

The agency that year reported a loss of £51,000. Many a Fleet Street newspaper were in dire financial straits. Bankruptcy beckoned, for Reuters and them.

Though new to the job, Long decided early on that the board collectively would be of little help. Where, after all, had they been for the past several years? Long resolved instead to sound out some of the directors individually. He started with Cecil King, supposedly one of his backers for the job. King was a physical giant and, as befitted the name, a somewhat imperious figure. It was likely that his views would typify the press barons' lofty attitude towards the agency. His greeting was certainly baronial. Long was ushered into a vast office incongruously warmed by a roaring fire in an expansive grate. King had prepared a lecture.

Gathering world news was becoming ever more expensive, he pointed out, and Reuters would need a lot of cash. It would not be available from the owners, who had none to give. From where then? "There's only one thing you can do, Mr. Long, and that is to go to the Government and ask them for a great deal of money."

Long was taken aback but had little choice but to listen deferentially. As he put it, "I turned my Yorkshire cloth cap around in my hot little hands and said

'Yes sir, no sir' but I came out of Mr. Cecil King's office muttering 'Bugger that!' "

King and the other owners would be happy, Long was led to believe, if Reuters did nothing more, year after year, than financially keep its head above water. Long vehemently deplored such an approach: "The break-even idea was total balls. The board had this idea of finance called a 'working surplus.' They said, 'Reuters is not a profit-making organization, but we do need to have a little cash in hand.' They never defined any of this, of course, and it just seemed to me to be nonsense."

At that moment, Reuters' true cash position was something of a mystery, even inside the company. Cole, typically, had been excessively secretive about company finances. The only person he had trusted, and the only man alive acquainted with the complete picture, was Nigel Judah, the finance director. But Judah inadvertently now became Long's immediate problem. Less than a month after taking over, Long was informed that Judah had been taken ill and rushed to hospital. The diagnosis was diverticulitis. It meant the removal of Judah's colon and an extended post-operative recovery. The operation itself was successful, but the wound became infected. Peritonitis set in, giving serious cause for concern. Long visited Judah in hospital and found him sealed up in a glass compartment. His appearance was shocking. "Literally all skin and bone," Long recalled. "By God, I thought we'd lost him."

Judah pulled through, but for months remained too weak to be released from the hospital. In what must surely be among the most bizarre briefings in corporate history, Long and Judah spent hours poring over the company books at Judah's bedside, much to the evident displeasure of the hospital staff. When Judah was finally sent home to recuperate, the exercise was resumed at Judah's house, with "occasional trips to the Dorchester for tea and cucumber sandwiches."

Long found the experience "alarming"—not only Judah's condition but also the unfolding revelations about Reuters' financial state. He resolved then and there that the only way to keep Reuters going without government aid, which was anathema, and without help from the owners, which was out of the question, was to make money on a normal commercial business basis. "And the only way to do that was to develop the commercial services."

It was a bold and momentous decision, and not necessarily one that the owners wanted to hear. But then the unexpected was Gerry Long's forte.

It sprang from a unique and, to many, inexplicable personality that was stamped on Reuters from the moment he took office. Ruling the company with a perverse truculence, Long inspired fear and respect in more or less equal measure. Affection proved more elusive. Indifference was certainly not an option. Long's opinions came in only two forms: passion and grudge, and both were engaged only in absolute terms. He expected equally strong opinions in others. Moderation, to Long, was merely a refuge for life's nonentities.

Long may not have consciously ruled by terror, but whenever he roamed the executive floor at 85 Fleet Street the place became, in the words of a then junior and later senior manager, "electric with tension." Long gave off sparks whenever he entered a room. His mood was always evident from the expression. But, jovial or grim, it could change in seconds, and there was no sure formula for dealing with either condition. "Everyone dreaded business meetings and cocktail parties," the terrified manager recalled. "As for chance encounters in the corridor, they could be heart-stopping. It was like bumping into Dracula in a dark alley."

"Rudest man I ever met," Renfrew snorted years later, remembering some social slight involving Mrs. Renfrew. "Colleagues, juniors, directors, wives, it didn't matter—an impossible character, not at all normal. Brilliant, of course, but far too ethereal to live amongst us mortals." Nelson was said to be in awe of him.

After a while there were murmured complaints about Long's offensive manner. Certain directors were said to be regretting their choice. Was there ever any danger of Long being dismissed? The thought must have crossed more than one mind in the boardroom. Nothing happened, of course, and it may be imagined that, for all the hurt feelings, the board might have had trouble finding someone brave enough to deliver the message.

Long's relentless intellectualism often seemed as much a burden to its owner as it was to others, something to be dragged around like Jacob Marley's chains, and he often cut a withdrawn, preoccupied, and isolated figure. He could hardly complain. He had little tolerance for empty pleasantries, and even casual conversation could quickly turn into verbal combat. Harold Evans, editor of *The Times* and a colleague in later years, summed up the risk in his memoir, *Good Times, Bad Times*. "A conversation with Long is alarming. One might travel over great areas of human interest without provoking more than a polite raising of the eyebrow or a series of gloomy nods, but as soon as one strays into pretension, reckless in the desire to elicit a response, there is an ambush. French canals, dictionaries, poached eggs, the guillotine, Zen Buddhism, sea legs...the areas of danger are as unpredictable as his ferocity."[1]

I was once a witness to one of Long's "ambushes" at a business luncheon for clients in New York. Table-talk had turned to baseball and the respective merits of the local rivals, the Yankees and the Mets. Plainly bored, Long decided to switch the conversation to another sporting topic. "Sumo wrestling, now there's a fascinating business..." The guests could only listen in bemused wonder.

---

[1] Harold Evans, *Good Times, Bad Times*, Weidenfeld & Nicholson, p.170

Long's ferocious manner could hardly be ascribed to the arrogance of privilege. He himself laughingly blamed genetics—Yorkshire on his father's side, Irish on his mother's. Education may have been a factor. Courtesy of a scholarship, Long attended St. Peter's school in York, founded in 627 by Paulinus, a Roman scholar, making it Britain's second-oldest recorded educational establishment. St. Peter's most famous alumnus was Guy Fawkes, one of the conspirators in the 1605 plot to blow up the Houses of Parliament. Twenty years after Long had left, his headmaster, John Dromfield, remembered him as one of the school's most brilliant pupils. Long's Latin master, Kenneth Rhodes, had no less vivid a recollection: "Ah, he of the purple passages!" (The foregoing recollections are courtesy of Alex McCallum, another graduate of St. Peter's.) From York the purple passages transferred to Emmanuel College, Cambridge, where Long read modern languages—an academic vocation he turned into a lifelong preoccupation.

After languages, opera and cooking emerged as foremost among his many passions. His culinary pronouncements entered the realms of fable. After a business dinner in New York, Long was asked by the maître d' what he'd thought of the food. "Positively vile and almost inedible," was the unadorned response. He once stalked out of a four-star restaurant in Brussels after spotting, through the kitchen doors, a chef employing a utensil Long considered inappropriate, leaving behind a stunned assembly of clients and colleagues.

In retirement at his Normandy farmhouse near Bayeux (where he had a bust of Paul Julius Reuter installed in the garden), Long's recollection of his rough manner, mellowed by age, verged on contrition. "It may have led to some imperfect understandings, even perhaps to some material disadvantages to the company. I do regard it as a failing that I've often treated people rather roughly. I should have controlled this better. I mean, I wanted to frighten some people, but I certainly didn't want to frighten most people."

Long returned reassuringly to combative form when asked to respond to criticism of his performance as a manager, particularly in the context of Professor Read's comment in the company history that he was "not himself a businessman."[2]

"How the hell do you define a businessman, anyway? It's like saying Christopher Columbus wasn't a sailor. He couldn't do everything. His sailors did the work. He ran the ship." Long acknowledged his lack of specific expertise with a typical aphorism. He was, he maintained, "a specialist at being a generalist." The assertion will no doubt bring a snigger from his detractors. The verdicts on Long's place in Reuters' history can be harsh. My own, arrived at after acknowledging all his personal quirks and prejudices, are more benign.

---

[2] Donald Read, *The Power of News*, Oxford University Press, 1992, p.286

If Long did nothing else for Reuters, he introduced certainty, confidence, and a fine intuitive judgment at a time when the company desperately needed all three. The successful initiatives for new products came from minds other than his own, but it was Long who created the environment in which innovation and risk were allowed to prosper. And it was Long, and he alone, who managed to wheedle the necessary approvals out of a reluctant board. Like his three predecessors, he emerged from a general news background, but unlike them he always championed the commercial services. While he knew next to nothing about financial markets, he recognized that they held the key to a profitable future—a view by no means universally shared at the time. He had little grasp of technology, either, but did not allow his ignorance to stand in the way of progress or to stifle projects dependent on untried and financially risky methods of delivering information.

Self-confidence allowed him to defer to the decisions of subordinates such as Nelson and Renfrew, acknowledging that they knew more about running the business than he did. His particular role, which they surely recognized as well as he did, was to apply the considerable force of his personality to get decisions from the board on their behalf. In acting as a servant of the executive office and a master of the board, he reversed convention. It required a bloody-minded audacity, which he exercised in full measure.

Long was guided above all by a keen sense of Reuters' history and its role in a changing world. His first responsibility as chief executive, as he saw it, was to "restore Reuters' lost pride and authority." That meant reverting to the principles and methods of its founder, a man he held in great affection and considered a business genius. Paul Julius Reuter, he liked to point out, had been the only man in the agency's history to run the company successfully. Gerry Long was determined to become the second.

The troika's mandate, self-imposed in the absence of a directive from a hapless board, was to transform the company from struggling news cooperative to global information powerhouse. This meant emphasizing profitability and growth, neither of which had been conspicuously evident for the best part of half a century, and exploiting emerging information technologies, these, too, being something of a novelty—though no more to Reuters than to any other organization.

In the best Reuters tradition, all three men had reached the top by way of journalism and overseas postings. For all the fun poked at Reuters' ad hoc international management academy—not least by its own students—it probably turned out per capita as many graduates as any prestigious American business school. Doing so would contribute in no small measure to the company's startling apotheosis.

This academy, like the Almighty, often worked in mysterious ways, such as the peculiar penchant for sending Russian speakers to Buenos Aires and French speakers to Singapore. But if it was something of a joke, every college is entitled to its eccentricities. The essence, and principal achievement, of the Reuters academy was that it produced commercial jacks-of-all-trades. Journalists sent overseas were required, for economic reasons, to assume various responsibilities besides that of reporting. Between filing front-page stories from some of the world's trouble spots, they might also be obliged to punch their own copy, sell news printer services, personally install them, maintain office accounts, order office supplies, hire local staff, and entertain visiting dignitaries. It struck many of them at the time as absurdly utilitarian; hotshot correspondents were not supposed to be lumbered with housekeeping chores—to spend one day interviewing the country's prime minister and the next poring over the company's books. Many resented this boy-scout approach. But in retrospect it proved highly beneficial, producing not just competent journalists but managers who understood on several levels how Reuters' business functioned. As a by-product it also imposed a certain degree of humility. Some correspondents could take all of this in stride. Others chose to ride off on their high horses. Long, Nelson, and Renfrew had all graduated from this academy, and each man was profoundly and fondly grateful for the experience.

If there was one other matter in which the members of the management troika were in perfect step, it was the view that technology held the key to the company's future. By the start of the seventies it was clear that the days of printer services, and all the crazy attendant functions—of carbon "flimsies" and ham-fisted teleprinter operators, of five-level ticker tape and "climbing monkeys"—were numbered. Information technology (IT being just one component of the approaching vanguard of technological acronyms) would define not just the decade but the rest of the century, and woe betide any enterprise, especially one in the business of communicating knowledge, that failed to recognize its growing power. Many did, of course, and woe was usually the result. Others managed to stagger past the recognition stage, only to prove incapable of venturing further. Reuters would not be one of them.

The Information Age, heralded by Marshall McLuhan's post-war blathering about a global village, and the medium becoming the message, had been a long time coming, but the professor's facile prognostications finally seemed ready to become reality. The computer, though still in most commercial circles a mystifying and unloved novelty, was beginning to shed its public image as a destroyer of jobs and souls. Far from driving millions out of work, the electronics industry was responsible—or soon would be—for putting millions into work, largely on the back of a wondrous little device called the silicon chip. The ubiquitous chip, like some kind of emblematic pet always ready to learn new party-tricks, even started to inveigle its way into the public affection. Its most impressive trick had been to proliferate without generating the kind of public alarm that had greeted the first computers.

In 1960, just two years after Jack Kilby of Texas Instruments had become the first man to integrate circuits on a silicon chip, the American semi-conductor industry reported a "staggering" annual turnover of $10 million, earning the accolade of a *Business Week* cover story. "The World's Fastest Growing Business" was the theme. "The industry," gushed the magazine, "is an almost classical example of the particular kind of growth that technological innovation can fire up throughout the US economy."[3] A decade on, the business was growing even more rapidly, and civilization had so far neither been destroyed nor even undermined. Indeed, as each revelation of the chip's capabilities arrived in a friendly consumer form—hearing aids, pocket calculators, digital watches, and automatic cameras—it attracted an increasingly warm public response: "These damned things are just amazing!"

Apart from all the other possibilities, information technology was a great commercial leveler. Many well-heeled corporations in many fields were suddenly exposed to competitive pressure, and not only from traditional rivals but also from renegade technologists of eccentric genius operating out of garage shops. Suddenly they found themselves deprived of many of their supposed advantages of wealth and size. Quotron and Ultronic, both started by refugees from the corporate world, had seized on that fact. Reuters now had the same opportunity. Renfrew, for one, as Reuters' self-taught and, for a time, sole technology guru, recognized the opportunity. It was noticeable that he now spent less and less time in bars and more and more time in planes in search of potential applications and prospective business partners. Nelson, to be fair, had led the way with the Ultronic venture, and for this he had firmly staked his claim to be considered, when the time came, for the company's top job. All the more reason to suppose, then, that Renfrew was now anxious to find a project to match his rival's achievement.

At this point, Reuters' rise from the ashes was far from assured. Company finances had greatly improved since the back-to-back successes of Stockmaster and Videomaster, but Reuters was not yet out of the woods. By the start of the seventies, Ultronic Corporation could no longer be relied on for philanthropic generosity. Since its acquisition by GTE, the company had lost much of its entrepreneurial vigor. Many old friends of Reuters, such as Bob Sinn, had moved on. New ventures and directions beckoned Reuters—but were they the calls of angels or sirens? The troika knew the difference; or at least, in making the right choices, rode its luck.

---

[3] *Business Week* magazine, 1960

Luck! Long, in retirement, bristled at the suggestion that good fortune had anything to do with it. "There was nothing inevitable about any of our moves, even if certain of my colleagues now modestly claim that there was [a reference to a paper Nelson had written]. Management is paid to make decisions, and to take certain risks. On a collective and premeditated basis we did both."

Collective is the key word. In matters of technology and markets Long was, as has been mentioned, content to rely on subordinates. But he also had something of a fetish for hierarchy, insisting on orderly delegation. He liked to receive business reports in comprehensible rather than comprehensive form. In translating them for the board, he exploited his talent for language rather than his command of the subject.

As the principal source of such reports, the clinical and methodical Nelson was the perfect foil. Nelson, too, favored delegation, and for this purpose gathered around him a loyal entourage, mainly drawn from the ranks of Oxbridge graduate trainees. He controlled the group with a chilly formality and matched Long's slavish adherence to protocol. This earned him a reputation as a cold fish. And he did have an appetite for market research, competitive analysis, and business plans. The more facts and figures the better. Intuition, once the source of all Reuters' business initiatives, no longer sufficed. Nelson studied business reports and memoranda with a practiced and unforgiving eye. They were examined as much for grammatical precision and matters of form as for business logic. Many were returned with Nelson's marginal comments on inappropriate titles, misspellings, careless syntax, or missing apostrophes. One author was admonished to use surnames in listing the recipients of future memoranda. He had used initials. Initials, Nelson decreed, were only to be used for members of the executive committee. Another sender was upbraided for using paperclips. Staples were preferred, he was told, to avoid pages from one memo becoming accidentally attached to another.

The London-born son of a carpenter, Nelson was short, slight, and diffident, almost prim, in manner. Sitting on the train from the south London suburb of Beckenham, he could be taken for a bank manager or a clerk in an insurance company. In terms of chic, Beckenham stood at the opposite end of the spectrum from the north London "village" of Highgate where Long personally prepared lavish dinners for friends and clients. With his own friends, Nelson was said to be relaxed and jolly, which contrasted with his punctilious and haughty demeanor in the office, where he was respected for his intelligence and resolve, but was unable to command much more affection than Long. Unlike his troika colleagues, he provided little grist for the office gossip mill. Long, addicted to controversy, was constantly in the news for one outrageous pronouncement or another. Rumors abounded that he had a world-class collection of pornography. The press delighted in reporting the exploits of his delinquent son. Renfrew was renowned for his wild exploits during drinking sessions with cronies. Later he would be suspected of being involved in a plot to take over the company. There seemed to be no interesting skeletons in Nelson's closet. If there were, the closet doors were kept securely locked.

Nelson dominated meetings with menacing silence. He preferred to let others do the talking, intervening only what he felt was necessary to guide the discussion toward his own predetermined goals. His reticence on such occasions disconcerted some of his more outgoing colleagues.

At a European sales meeting, a regional country manager, having delivered a glowing report on the year's business performance, sat down amid loud applause and threw an expectant glance at the head of the table, obviously hoping for some kind of appreciative gesture. Nelson's response was devastatingly understated. "Thank you, that was most interesting." Afterwards, in the bar, the manager was reduced to asking, "What do you have to do around here to get some kudos, dance on the fucking table?" To which Nelson's response would have been, "I think perhaps that would be quite inappropriate."

Motivational enthusiasm simply fell outside his repertoire.

Renfrew was altogether a different personality. As one might expect of the youngest of ten children born to a New South Wales coal miner, he was ambitious, driven, robust, direct, affable, and short-fused. He could never be described as prim. He lacked Long's sense of hierarchy and detested Nelson's pinched public decorum. He disliked meetings, regarding them as occasions used for buck-passing and point-scoring. His preference was for the informality of a lunchtime discussion or a session in the pub. While Long and Nelson rarely mingled with the staff after hours, Renfrew's summons to evening drinks constituted an extension of the working day, and potentially the most productive part of it. A thousand diverse and radical ideas vied for primacy in Renfrew's febrile imagination, but he preferred to pursue them personally, mainly outside the office in situations where his instincts and enthusiasms could be more freely vented. Renfrew had formed his own band of internal disciples, of course, but it was a different gang from Nelson's, one in which rough humor and a tolerance for alcohol qualified more than cultivated boardroom manners and an aptitude for polite intrigue. Judging by his alleged involvement in many a bar-room altercation, he could be as forthright and aggressive socially as he was professionally. Some of these incidents have doubtless been embellished in accordance with that cardinal rule of legerdemain: "When the facts clash with the legend, print the legend." But too many incidents left little scope for plausible denials, and many were confirmed by unimpeachable sources.

In the earliest known Renfrew escapade, he was allegedly pulled out of Hong Kong after giving a senior colleague there a black eye. Another rumor given wide circulation was that he had once challenged Long to "come outside" to settle some dispute. The most famous incident occurred during an office party in a pub called The Cogers, conveniently if incongruously located on the ground floor of Reuters' building (which had been constructed around the saloon to preserve its long-term lease on the site). So many witnesses subsequently claimed to have attended the incident that they would fill the Albert Hall. Enough *were* actually there to testify to establish certain essential facts beyond dispute.

Some time towards the end of the evening, it seems, a burly barman took offence at remarks directed at an inebriated and emotional secretary by an equally inebriated and emotional Reuters executive—allegedly one Max Siebenmann, Reuters' manager in Switzerland. Renfrew's response was to offer the barman a piece of advice, namely to attend to matters behind the bar instead of in front of it. To this instruction the barman evidently took strong exception. Offence may have been caused by the informal terminology employed, which, according to several witnesses, may be roughly translated as, "Mind your own fucking business or I'll knock your fucking head off." Offence was taken in the opposite direction by the response, approximately recalled as, "Come outside and we'll see whose fucking head gets knocked off." The ensuing fracas, which started inside the Cogers, spilled out onto the street. Renfrew, no doubt disadvantaged by the fact that his glass had been copiously filled all evening by his protagonist, appears to have come off distinctly second best. Several accounts recall him adopting a supine position across the trunk of a parked car, like some British heavyweight contender, taking repeated blows to head and body. Eventually, a London marketing executive, John Albanie, acting as a referee, though not necessarily a neutral one, stepped in gallantly to absorb most of the punishment himself. By now matters had become serious enough to warrant the attention of the constabulary. In the finest tradition of the London bobby, official intervention was both benign and sensible. "You're all silly buggers and far too old for this," declared the constable, who had some advice to add. "Now all of you, just shove off home and sleep it off."

"Oh dear, oh dear, oh dear," muttered John Ransom, a Reuters executive of a more peaceful disposition, and on that evening one of the many reluctant bystanders. Ransom, a particular favorite of Nelson's, can still be induced to shake his head in disbelief decades later. "It was all true and all most unfortunate. Certainly not the sort of thing Mike Nelson would have approved of." Certainly not, indeed.

John Albanie appeared in the office the next day proudly sporting an oversized "shiner." "Dunno why you go to that place," Renfrew told him ungratefully. "It's a dump, always full of troublemakers. By the way, who won?" Some would say in later years that such ingratitude, on this occasion manifested over a minor incident, constituted one of Renfrew's failings on much larger issues.

On another occasion not so many years later, Renfrew was hustled out of a New York saloon after one of the patrons, taking offence at some remark Renfrew had made, pulled a knife on him. (The establishment in question, for those who like to keep tabs on such things, was Sam's Cordial Bar on Seventh Avenue, a scabrous, roach-infested establishment directly across the street from Reuters' office. The colleagues, also for the record, were Harvey Cooper and Peter Holland.)

Renfrew's rough ways and acid-tongued disdain for convention chimed with the popular image of the Wild Colonial. But Renfrew was no thick-necked larrikin. He conceded nothing to his colleagues in erudition. He had left the University of New South Wales with a fine degree and in his travels around Europe had developed a talent for languages, claiming to be fluent in at least three of them (an assertion that drew skeptical harrumphs from Long). He also evinced a keen interest in literature and, when personal finances permitted, fancied himself as an art collector (more derisive grunts from Long). In short, there was more, much more, to Renfrew than met the eye.

It was often said that Renfrew despised Britain, or at least what he saw as its effete establishment. Some were convinced that he had little time for Poms in general. If so, it represented an attitude deeply, if subconsciously, ingrained in certain fiercely competitive Australians. (And one that echoed, for example, the alleged opinion of his compatriot, Rupert Murdoch, whose father had once infamously heaped abuse on the British for sacrificing Australian manhood in the Gallipolli disaster.) "Get rid of him, he's trouble," a senior executive is said to have advised the company after the Hong Kong incident. Similar sentiments were often heard over the years. Renfrew himself once confessed to an interviewer that he might have retained some of the "rough manners" of the Australian mining construction camp in which he had once worked as a student to pay for tuition fees. But if Renfrew's excesses were deprecated by Long he chose to ignore them. And if they were anathema to Nelson, he, too, turned a blind eye worthy of his namesake.

The fact is that Renfrew was simply too valuable a corporate asset to be discarded, which both Long and Nelson in turn had recognized by promoting him. He in turn had repaid their faith with interest. Renfrew's contribution to revenue growth and corporate profits through his marketing management of Stockmaster and Videomaster had become part of corporate folklore. Perhaps more to the point, Renfrew, alone of the senior management group, under-stood and was capable of exploiting the emerging technologies. Or such was the expectation at the time.

From the moment they joined the troika, Nelson and Renfrew were inevitably regarded by corporate celebrity-watchers as young Turks locked in a battle for the succession. Long was years away from retirement age and unlikely to leave before reaching it, but succession politics had always been something of an obsession at 85 Fleet Street.

Accordingly, the company divided into distinct and highly partisan Nelson and Renfrew factions. The lines were drawn even more clearly after Long offered Renfrew a power base in North America. It was tantamount to announcing the opening of an election campaign.

Some power base. American operating losses were persistent and growing, a condition unlikely to change unless new electronic products could be developed for the American market and sold in large quantities. Profitability was a tall order, some said an implausible one; Nelson for one, who considered it "out of the question."

There would be no election, of course. Universal suffrage was no more the authorized method of appointing leaders at Reuters than it was in any other company. Not that the contestants were deterred from acting as if it actually was—though to give both the benefit of the doubt, they were both tainted by the presumably unauthorized antics of their more ardent supporters, who often behaved less like corporate managers than idealistic young campaign workers.

It may strike the reader now—as it naïvely struck many of us at the time—that the outcome ought to be related to business performance, by what Americans call a track record, and nothing else. On that narrow basis, a clear and unchallenged "winner" would indeed emerge. But would the "winner" also be the one elected?

As American chat-show hosts like to say, "Stay tuned."

# Monitor

On Sunday, August 15, 1971, millions of television viewers in the United States were disappointed to learn that *Bonanza*, America's favorite weekend television show, a western, had been bumped off the prime-time schedule that evening by President Nixon. The President, the White House let it be known, would be addressing the nation on the subject of the economy. Few Americans could figure out what kind of emergency could have arisen to warrant such a disruption to their summer evening viewing routine. Nixon was about to tell them, though many would be none the wiser for it even when he had.

The American economy was in crisis, he said, beset by manifold problems that included widening payments and trade deficits, rising unemployment, low growth, and persistent inflation. The last two combined to create a relatively uncommon condition known as stagflation. Nixon proceeded to announce a series of radical corrective measures. The most sensational of them, or at least the best remembered, were a ninety-day freeze on prices and wages and a temporary 10 percent surcharge on imports. Each was as unexpected as it was controversial—all the more so coming from a conservative Republican president. But Nixon had just been warming up for the main event. The real problem, he explained, was the underlying threat to the soundness of the once almighty dollar and, by extension, to world financial stability. It was in that context, toward the end of his broadcast, that Nixon baffled an already astonished audience with a reference to some kind of "window." The window was made of gold, apparently, and Nixon was "suspending" it—whatever that meant.

*Bonanza*-deprived viewers were by no means alone in their bemusement. Two days earlier, Nixon's favorite speechwriter, William Safire, had been summoned to Camp David, the weekend presidential retreat in Maryland, to prepare for what Herb Stein, a senior White House adviser, had told him "could be the most important weekend in the history of economics since March 4, 1933."

"We closing the banks?" Safire asked flippantly.

"Hardly," came the response. "But I wouldn't be surprised if the President were to close the gold window."[1]

Safire, a self-confessed ignoramus in economic matters, had no idea what a

---

[1] Tom Wicker, *One of Us*, Random House, 1991, p.542

"gold window" was. Which was ironic, since Nixon was about to ask him to explain it to their 240 million fellow Americans. When Safire, aboard the presidential helicopter en route to Camp David, casually mentioned Stein's comment to a fellow passenger, a man from the Treasury Department, the man "leaned forward, put his face in his hands, and whispered, 'My God.' "

The "gold window," Safire now learned, was a euphemism for a unique and vital international banking mechanism: the obligation of the United States to convert dollars into gold, on demand, at an officially agreed price of $35 per ounce. "Suspending" the window, translated, meant terminating the obligation. Even to sophisticated Americans this was so much gobbledygook. But to erudite non-Americans it was tantamount to the leader of the Free World unilaterally taking a wrecker's ball to the granite edifice of global capitalism.

The Government, anticipating the immediate aftershocks, decreed that American financial markets would not open the next day. Most other countries followed suit.

In fact, world markets stayed closed for the entire week. When, finally, they did reopen they succumbed to panic and confusion. Order would not be restored for many months. Even now, thirty years on, the consequences of Nixon's dimly remembered address reverberate still, like a prolonged seismic tremor.

What, the reader may well ask, has any of this to do with the subject of this narrative? A great deal, as it happens, and to Reuters in particular. A brief review of the events that preceded and followed the August 15 broadcast, one of the more obscure of Nixon's many memorable television moments, may be in order.

Consumed by the traumatizing events of the 1960s—Vietnam, assassinations, the civil rights campaign, the endless marches and street protests associated with all three—many Americans overlooked the fact that the United States had also been battered and bloodied in economic terms. Nixon alluded to the reasons in his broadcast. Taken alone, not one of the problems heralded a crisis, but collectively their impact was alarming. If America did not recognize it, Wall Street did, and the stock market opened the new decade by recording its biggest fall since 1929, ending the longest running bull market in history and delivering yet another blow to American prestige and confidence. Nixon might have chosen to ride out the storm, but the 1970 market crash and its underlying causes had significant political as well as economic dimensions. By threatening the financial well-being of Nixon's blue-collar army of "forgotten" Americans, many of them first-time investors—and therefore potentially first-time Republican voters—stagflation jeopardized the re-election prospects of scores of Republican candidates in the

1972 congressional elections. Given the political pressure to turn the economy around, it is perhaps not so surprising that Nixon pulled from his hat whatever rabbits came to hand. That one of those rabbits would be a change in America's pledge to uphold the value and convertibility of the dollar simply had not occurred to anyone inside the United States. But if it was pretty much a non-event to Americans, it came as a shocking revelation to foreigners, especially to those governments and other institutions holding dollars in large amounts.

It was a promise that successive American administrations, Republican and Democrat alike, had solemnly upheld. It had been the cornerstone of the world monetary order since 1944 under an agreement thrashed out by the western allies at an acrimonious conference in the mountain resort of Bretton Woods, New Hampshire. Under the 1944 rules, only the US dollar was officially convertible into gold; all other currencies were valued against the dollar, but were permitted to fluctuate only within a trading range limited to 1 percent of their agreed parity values. The only exceptions allowed were officially sanctioned devaluations, but, since governments tended to regard the defense of their currencies as a matter of national honor, to be abandoned only as a matter of last resort, these were bound to be infrequent. Central bankers referred to this system as one of fixed exchange rates (fixed meaning inflexible, not rigged, though some speculators would argue that they were one and the same).

Bretton Woods had been devised to create a sufficiently stable international monetary system to encourage the post-war economic recovery, and by common consent it had worked reasonably well for a generation. The problem that emerged during the 1960s was that the dollar stockpiles around the world, accumulated as the result of America's expanding payments deficit, had become worth considerably more than the gold held in the vaults at Fort Knox. The gap was sometimes referred to as the "dollar overhang."

Currency speculators worried about it and, in the foreign-exchange market, selling pressure on the dollar began to build intolerably. Even so, governments and corporations refused to panic, in the belief that an American government's pledge was ironclad. If the United States dollar could no longer be considered a bulwark against financial chaos, then nothing was. But the decade that had nurtured so many iconoclasms now produced another: the questioning of faith in exchange rates maintained by governments at what many perceived to be artificial and unsustainable levels.

Speculative raids against the dollar, and other currencies in their turn, became ever more frequent and increasingly severe. Whenever bad news about the American economy hit the newswires ("bad" being defined as anything that fell short of market expectations), dollars were dumped in growing quantities. Each attack was a fire alarm summoning the Fed, the Bank of England and other central banks to tackle the blaze. But bucket chains were hardly adequate in the face of an inferno. Official intervention to support the dollar usually sent the speculators packing, but only for as long as it took them to prepare for the next attack.

The dollar had become, in a word much beloved by financial journalists, "beleaguered."

Any study of the British government's long and costly battle to prop up the pound, ending in the humiliating devaluation of 1967, ought to have convinced the monetary authorities that market sentiment could not be denied for long, and certainly not forever. Something had to give and, as every trader knew, when push came to shove it would not be governments that represented the market's natural impulses but speculators, no matter how negatively they might be portrayed.

Which brings us to that fateful Sunday evening of August 15, 1971.

Nixon's closing of the gold window effectively terminated Bretton Woods. What might replace it was anyone's guess, including the central bankers representing the ten leading industrial powers. The so-called Group of Ten hurriedly convened at the Smithsonian Institute in Washington to work out an alternative plan. The prospects were considered slim. "The best that can be hoped for," the *Wall Street Journal* opined, "is that the US and other nations will now work together towards a new arrangement without the inflexibility that helped doom the old system."[2]

So, when financial markets reopened a week later, currencies were allowed to "float," which meant that they could fluctuate freely in response to supply and demand, but still only within prescribed narrow trading bands. The arrangement was described as a "managed" or "dirty" float, since central banks would still find it necessary to intervene to maintain parities and some semblance of order. And intervene they did, though for the most part no more effectively than before. Thus, a second Smithsonian Agreement emerged before the end of the year, representing yet another valiant attempt to preserve, albeit in more flexible form, the essence of Bretton Woods. The dollar was devalued by raising the official gold price to $38 an ounce and trading bands were widened, currencies now being allowed to fluctuate 2.25 percent around their new fixed values.

Smithsonian II, like its predecessor, proved to be a valiant but futile effort. Speculators returned to the market in growing numbers, turning 1972 into another year of perpetual market turmoil. The response was a further dollar devaluation. When that, too, failed to work, it finally dawned on the central bankers that market forces had prevailed over governments. In February 1973, eighteen months after Nixon's Sunday-night thunderbolt, fixed exchange rates were finally and irrevocably abandoned. Citibank's chairman, Walter Wriston,

---

[2] *Wall Street Journal*, August 16, 1971

memorialized the event, in the title of his book, as *The Twilight of Sovereignty*.

The international capital market had one more upheaval to endure. In October of that year, the Arab states declared war on Israel, simultaneously imposing an oil embargo on countries perceived to be friendly to their enemy. For American motorists, the experience of lining up for hours at gasoline pumps for the privilege of paying twice the normal price was a staggering humiliation—as if the previous decade had not done enough to undermine America's supposedly immutable sense of well-being.

The consequences of August 15 were profound and permanent. Freed from government controls, the currency and related markets entered a period of unprecedented volatility. Traders cherish volatility, of course, and, for financial institutions everywhere, the world of floating rates offered sparkling new opportunities to generate income. It meant a re-examination of the fundamental purpose of the trading room. While many leading international banks had always considered trading a useful, if risky, source of income, the great majority had never regarded it as more than a facility to service the needs of their corporate clients; in short, a necessary encumbrance rather than a desirable source of profit. Trading rooms, often located figuratively if not literally in the basement, had seldom fallen under the scrutiny of senior executives. Now they began to migrate to a higher floor, there to be equipped with the latest technology and showcased to visitors as proof of the institution's global capabilities. Before long, the trading room would provide an ideal launching pad for management careers, as opposed to functioning merely as a convenient place to park executives entering their professional dotage.

Naturally, rising market volatility underscored the importance of access to breaking news and up-to-date market quotes. Sensational, market-moving stories had been relatively unchallenging when markets were not permitted to move. Now that markets could fluctuate without bounds, traders could vent their creative talents to the full, as indeed they did. Headline writers could slip the leash, too, since sterling now really could "plunge" and the dollar "soar."

For information-providers this new order, or disorder, presented unprecedented opportunities—a chance to introduce brand-new products to a brand-new audience, actually to create a marketplace. For Reuters, the only market-data vendor with a global presence, it offered an opportunity to provide fresh momentum to the company's faltering recovery.

★

"I've heard some bloody silly ideas in my time," the head currency trader growled at the Reuters salesman over a lunchtime pint in London, "but this one takes the cake. Now let me get this straight: you want me to put my dealing prices up on your bloody screens for every Tom, Dick, and Harry to look at all day and, what's more, pay a premium for the privilege. What genius came up with this little scam?"

He was right: it *was* a bloody silly idea.

Anyone who knew how the foreign-exchange market worked understood that the trading price was the joker in the trader's pack in a game for two players. Traders at the bigger banks tweaked it subtly to compete effectively with their peers and manipulated it shamelessly to exploit those toiling in relative ignorance at smaller institutions. The already narrow spread between the bid and the offer represented the profit margin on each transaction. Reuters, using its high-speed network to connect hundreds, perhaps thousands, of traders around the world, at big and small institutions alike, threatened to reduce those spreads even further. The knowledge gap would disappear, trading profits would shrink to nothing, and thousands of jobs would be lost. Such, at any rate, was the widely held belief among foreign-exchange and money traders.

Naturally, the Reuters man had a different view. "Just think of all the extra business you could attract by displaying your quotes to a much wider audience." (The providers of quotes would be known in Reuters parlance as "contributors" and non-contributing viewers as "recipients"—a commercial variation of the biblical injunction that it is more blessed to give than to receive.)

"Extra business! That's a very questionable proposition, my friend. What isn't in doubt is that my margins will disappear because right now I'm one of the few who know what's going on—and I know what's going on because I make it my business to. With your service, everyone in the whole fucking world will know what's going on. I make the best two-way prices in the business. Why should I be picked off all day long by tinpot outfits that don't even bother to make a market? Do you people have the faintest idea how this business actually works?"

The Reuters man offered rather limply that a great deal of research had gone into the matter—which, by Reuters' admittedly modest standards, was true.

"Well, you tell the bloody fools in your research department they've got it all wrong. It's a load of balls—unless, of course, you're about to tell me that Reuters will pay me a great deal of money for my trouble."

The Reuters man developed a sudden avid interest in his shoelaces. "Well, actually, the idea is that you pay us for the service, and additionally for contributing. Think of it as a form of advertising."

The trader looked dumbfounded. "Advertising! I'm not running a bloody ad agency. All I see is that I'm supposed to do all the work, take my clothes off in public until I'm stark-bollock naked, and pay Reuters for doing it. You must be barmy. How many chumps have you managed to talk into signing up for this fiddle?"

"There's been quite a lot of interest," the Reuters man said brightly, before delivering a flattering contradiction. "Actually, because of the importance of your bank as a market leader, you're one of the first we've really talked to. Naturally your opinion is important to us."

"Well, when you've signed up at least twenty of my competitors, you can come back and talk to me. Meanwhile, here's a friendly tip: start looking for alternative employment."

The foregoing, I hasten to point out, is a composite conversation—fictional but by no means far-fetched. Dozens of such encounters, with minor variations, occurred in the City of London and other European centers during the course of 1972 and 1973—and in New York a year later, to which I can personally testify, having been involved in dozens of them.

The proposed Reuters service, I recall someone saying, could only have been dreamed up by someone with just enough knowledge of trading to be dangerous or someone so far removed from the market that reality never inconveniently intruded. Actually, it was a combination of the two: in the first instance, my old comrade-in-arms Fred Taylor; in the second, a promising young executive and Nelson protégé named André Villeneuve.

Physically and otherwise, they made an odd couple. Villeneuve was plump, pink and owlish, a self-confessed gastronome with an accent of cut crystal and an awkward manner, in each respect the perfect counterpoint to Fred. The walrus and the carpenter.

I had seen little of Fred for several years. During my absence in New York he had been promoted, in recognition of his market knowledge and his extensive City contacts, and was now working in the sales department as a customer-relations assistant. He was the proud owner of a business card. He wore his dentures to the office every day. "You look ten years younger," I told him during a visit to London. "Well, I wish I was twenty years younger, "he growled. He was then in his early fifties and in very good form, all piss and vinegar, as usual bursting with ideas. Most were, as ever, boldly imaginative, some downright batty.

In the latter category, a particular notion had taken his fancy. He had been peddling it around the City for some time. The idea had grown out of conversations with one of his market contacts, Norman Lawrence, a Eurodollar trader at Strauss Turnbull, a leading bond trading house. Lawrence, one of Fred's favorite sources, had a Videomaster on his desk. He was happy with the service, but it had its deficiencies, as he often mentioned to Fred. "This thing is great for stocks and commodities," he would say, "but why can't I get other markets, like foreign exchange and deposits? That's where all the action is these days, Fred, as you well know."

Both men knew exactly why not. Trading in stocks and commodities usually took place in a single physical location, an exchange. Pricing information was readily available to the public, being broadcast throughout the trading day by means of a ticker. By contrast, deals in currencies and deposits were done through bilateral conversations between traders, locally by telephone—sometimes with a broker in the middle, sometimes directly—internationally by telex. Information was hard to come by, traders being under no obligation to publicly disclose details of transactions that were considered private treaties between the parties. Far from being anxious to "advertise" their bids and offers, most money traders nursed an almost obsessive secrecy about what they did and how they did it, an attitude which, in their minds, helped to preserve the mystique of their profession.

Fred, undeterred by such objections, was intrigued by Lawrence's complaint. But how could this information be obtained? "The dealers, of course," Lawrence told him. "Go talk to them about providing quotes. Tell them that if people like me can see their rates on Videomaster, we'll do business with them."

Fred spent months talking to currency and money-market traders without finding anyone even remotely interested in the idea. And inevitably, with not a solitary prospect in sight, he was unable to find anyone at Reuters willing to sponsor the project. "Interesting idea, Fred. Let us know when you get a nibble." Fred was nothing if not dogged—and persistence, our parents teach us, brings its own reward. Accordingly, midway through 1973, just as things looked terminally futile, Fred suddenly discovered both prospects and a sponsor.

André Villeneuve was one of Reuters' bright young management trainees. Fresh from a three-year assignment in Brazil, he found himself temporarily at a loose end in London. Nelson interrupted Villeneuve's siesta by giving him a project. Sales of Stockmaster and Videomaster were fading rapidly, Nelson confided, with the market approaching saturation point. Reuters needed something to replace them, or at least enhance them, but the company had nothing, absolutely nothing, in the pipeline. Outwardly confident, Nelson was inwardly a deeply worried man.

True to form, he commissioned a market survey. Its focus, he told Villeneuve, should be the European banks—the Swiss banks in particular. Switzerland was vital to Reuters. As a source of income it ranked second only to Britain itself. In the business context, it is one of those countries that British companies often describe as "difficult"—a charge usually backed by British allegations of Swiss xenophobia and countered in return by Swiss complaints of the shabby practices of British companies when operating abroad. Although there was some truth in both allegations, they were motivated largely by rivalry. Zurich in the 1960s aspired to replace London as Europe's key financial center. The ambition was fired by the view—widely shared, incidentally, in Frankfurt and even in New York—that the City of London, like the British economy and the pound sterling, was in irreversible decline. Anglo-Swiss relations were put under additional strain in mid-decade when a British cabinet minister, seeking scapegoats for repeated speculative attacks on the pound, famously pointed an accusing finger at the "gnomes of Zurich." The epithet, seized on by the British press with evident glee, had outraged bankers along the Limmatquai at the time. Many had been fuming ever since. Reuters itself had reason to be concerned about festering Swiss resentments. In 1967, the company had acquired Cosmographique, Switzerland's only financial news agency, which delivered a further blow to Swiss hubris, since, as a result, a foreign company—worse still, a British company—now controlled virtually all the financial information going into and out of Switzerland.

Suffused with a perspective of the world hardly less lofty than their own Alpine peaks, the leading Swiss financial institutions were always likely to be awkward customers. Supposed Swiss prejudice was contradicted by the fact that Reuters had actually done rather well in Switzerland. But that success was almost certainly less attributable to Swiss tolerance than to the absence of alternatives. (A few years later, the then head of foreign-exchange trading at Swiss Banking Corporation, Hubert Baschnagel, confirmed latent Swiss jealousies when he told me: "We felt then that the Baron, with his monopoly, was perhaps getting a little too big for his britches. And we still think so.")

Such animus might not have bothered Nelson in ordinary circumstances, but he had two specific reasons to be concerned. The first was that the Swiss banks, in a cooperative venture, had formed an information and computer services company called Telekurs—ostensibly to provide its owners with data processing and payment clearing facilities, but also, it was rumored, to offer information services in competition with Reuters. Around the same time, Bob Sinn of Ultronic reported that his sales executives were picking up rumors that Bunker Ramo, his chief competitor, was once again taking a close interest in Switzerland. What was especially worrying was that the initiative seemed to be taking shape as a joint venture with Telekurs. As if to confirm the Swiss banks' intentions, it also emerged that Telekurs had signed news distribution agreements with Dow Jones and the Commodity News Service, a newswire owned by the Knight-Ridder newspaper group. The immediate reaction at 85 Fleet Street to these developments verged on panic.

Panic is no exaggeration. Even Nelson, not a man susceptible to theatrics, recalled the period with a shudder. "It was the most terrifying time I had experienced since joining Reuters. Everything we had accomplished with Ultronic could have come undone very quickly. And we had nothing else."

Villeneuve was ordered to investigate pre-emptive measures. He was scarcely qualified for his mission. Most of his three years with the company had been spent in South America, an experience which, by all accounts, he had found neither professionally inspiring nor personally rewarding. As a confirmed Europhile and self-confessed gourmand, Villeneuve was personally glad to be back in London. Professionally, with Nelson's directive, he had landed in the catbird's seat. But he was no Renfrew, no charismatic trailblazer. His manner was diffident, and he tended to be didactic, which was odd since he knew next to nothing about markets and even less about technology. An uncanny ability to unearth little-known restaurants and undiscovered wines would be no more than marginally helpful in exploring the unfamiliar world of international finance. But he possessed a most practical skill: an ability to exploit the talents of others, as we shall see.

Villeneuve returned from a quick tour of Europe's leading banks with an unequivocal message. It was an echo of Fred Taylor's clarion call. Banks had all the stock-market information they needed, thanks to the proliferation of Videomaster; what was not readily available was information on the money markets, foreign exchange especially. Currency markets were becoming ever more volatile, access to current prices increasingly problematical. Even the Swiss banks had to admit as much.

"A good start," was Nelson's typical response. "Now let's follow it up."

Easier said than done.

Villeneuve had stumbled on the opportunity but he was ill equipped to grasp it. In fact, he now scanned the alien terrain before him much as an explorer might contemplate a primeval swamp known to be the habitat of venomous snakes and hostile tribes. What the expedition needed above all was a reliable guide, one who had already cut a trail through the swamp and back and, better still, made friendly contact with the natives. Fortunately, such a man was already on the payroll—a prickly old cove, by all accounts, but something of a legend. Villeneuve went in search of him.

He did not have far to look.

Fred Taylor needed no prompting to act as Villeneuve's jungle guide. In fact, he was already busy trying to convert the natives. His bully pulpit was a spot at the end of the bar in Bow Wine Vaults, a City lunchtime hangout popular with money traders. Nursing his half-pint of bitter and munching on his customary cheese and pickle sandwich, Fred had spent months flogging his dead horse. The poor creature was by now in an advanced state of decomposition. Fred had run through all the familiar arguments and the traders had responded with all the familiar refutations. The currency markets simply moved too fast, they said. By the time rates had been posted they could have changed several times over. Anyway, why should traders show their hands to competitors? And why should the banks pay Reuters rather than the other way round? And no sooner had Fred shot down those arguments than new objections were raised. Some of them drifted into such picayune realms as health hazards. Sitting in front of screens all day could expose traders to excessive doses of radiation. It would be harmful to the eyes. Ogling screens all day would be distracting, turn traders into zombies.

One of Fred's favorite lunchtime sounding boards was Geoff Bell, chief foreign-exchange trader at Banque Belge. Fred felt comfortable with Bell, who was a fellow Londoner from a working-class background and a man of infinite forbearance. He was also a straight-shooter, an attribute possibly acquired on the football field. In his day he had been an accomplished player, turning out several times for Romford, a team in one of England's top amateur leagues. A professional career might have beckoned, but Bell, as self-effacing as he was patient, did not have the necessary desire. "Tell you the truth, I was too lazy to be a really good footballer. Banking was a lot easier."

Bell's affection for Fred had developed in typical fashion. A pioneer in the Eurocurrency market, Bell had been one of the earliest subscribers to Reuters' International Financial Printer service. Fred, he recalled, had called him out of the blue. "He'd obviously found out that I was a new client and wanted to establish a relationship." Bell was recruited as a news source. "We talked a lot, mostly market chitchat. I passed my market rumors to Fred and he passed his on to me. It was actually quite a useful exchange. Fred was very bright, and a lovely bloke." They became fast friends.

As fond of Fred as Bell undoubtedly was, he had grown weary of the subject of quotes on screens. "We'd been kicking it around, on and off, for about three years. Fred and I often met in the Bow and I always listened to what he had to say. He usually had an interesting angle and I was always politely negative. But he kept coming back. I kept telling him, 'Fred, it's all rubbish. It'll never get off the ground.' But back he'd come again. There was simply no putting him off."

Like most traders, Bell felt that currency trading was too fast-moving for dealers to risk exposing their market positions on screens. Over drinks one day he told Fred to try a new tack: "Forget the banks. Why don't you get prices from the brokers?"

It was a plausible idea. The brokers acted strictly as intermediaries between banks, so neutrality made them a credible source of market quotes and they had no reason to worry about exposing market positions, since by definition they did not take any. The real question, it was thought at the time, was not whether the brokers would go along but whether the banks would allow them to. Brokers' quotes did, after all, originate with the banks, and it was the banks that called the shots in matters of trading practices, including the one most important to the brokers—their commission rates. Bell himself had no problems with brokers posting rates, but he continued to reaffirm his reservations about the practical and political aspects of such a service.

Villeneuve organized a couple of lunches. The brokers attended, but it was clear from the start that they were not really interested. Actually they were afraid. For as much as the brokers seemed cowed by the banks, they seemed to fear Reuters more. If the banks ever decided to use Reuters' service as a means of trading with each other electronically—admittedly a pretty far-fetched notion at the time—then the banks could conceivably bypass the brokers altogether. The possibility of a trade-matching system had, in fact, occurred to Reuters, but only as a passing fancy. The idea had certainly not been mentioned to the banks, which were still balking at merely posting prices.

Logic surely suggests that if the brokers were so concerned about being ignored they would have been better served getting actively involved in the project. And while the motto, "If you can't beat 'em, join 'em," was admittedly not a particularly attractive approach, neither was the chosen alternative, which one broker later summed up as, "If we close our eyes none of this will happen."

Spurned by the brokers, Villeneuve wearily turned once again to the banks. He and Fred had exhausted most of the obvious possibilities. They themselves were exhausted. The endless lunches and drinking sessions were taking their toll, particularly on Fred. They had become a source of worry to Fred's wife, Renee. "He's just not used to this sort of thing," she complained to one of his colleagues. Fred was as far from physically fit as it is possible to be, and at times he seemed to suffer from a severe shortage of breath. Although it was not recognized at the time, Fred was displaying early symptoms of the onset of emphysema.

The breakthrough came in the Bow Wine Vaults. Weary of Fred's constant entreaties, Bell suddenly agreed to cooperate.

"If only to shut him up," he admitted. "And frankly, I didn't have much to lose. As a small Belgian bank, my rates weren't likely to be very influential. But someone had to get the ball rolling."

The ball was actually rolling faster than Reuters suspected. Stimulated by Reuters' initiative, some banks had been quietly talking among themselves. They had even discussed creating an alternative system, to be owned and operated by the banks. It was never a serious proposition; such collaborations among rivals are notoriously difficult to manage. They recognized, too, that this one might even draw the attention of regulators, particularly the Bank of England, which, as the appointed guardian of sterling, took a close interest in foreign-exchange issues. They were also forced to admit that, if such a system were to prove viable, Reuters brought to the project two overwhelming advantages: market neutrality, and the proven ability to run a global network. Talk of a bank cooperative quickly evaporated.

As part of his conversion to the cause, Bell agreed to round up some of his pals in foreign exchange to form a discussion group. David Palmer of Hambros Bank was one, and probably the most important one, since he had personally arrived at the point where he could describe himself as a "genuine enthusiast." At the subsequent meeting, Palmer was impressed by Villeneuve's low-key tactics. "There was no hard sell. The conversation was very friendly and very casual."

The others around the table were Peter Day of Barclays Bank, the acknowledged "king" of the sterling market, and Bernie Furlonger of Bank of America. Palmer remembered them both as equivocal "but not in outright opposition. Day at first came out against, but later changed his mind. Furlonger was more or less friendly, though not entirely convinced that many banks, including his own, would pay much money for the service. However, we were all impressed by Reuters' approach. They seemed to be reasonable on all the sticky points."

Villeneuve, he noted, dispensed "charm and claret" while Fred brought a "disarming earthiness." Palmer also remembered that Fred "didn't always look well and had developed a persistent cough."

The group formed itself into an informal steering committee. All four men agreed, conditionally and with varying degrees of confidence, to contribute their quotes to the system. It was the breakthrough Reuters needed. Things had been touch and go, but an evangelical movement had attracted its first apostles.

While Villeneuve and Taylor were out sacrificing their waistlines, Reuters' technical groups preserved theirs by grappling with tricky issues of delivery and design. The biggest was the question of how to make the service what computer men like to call "user friendly." From the marketing perspective, the traders' fear of computers was potentially the biggest challenge. "I'm a trader, not a computer operator," was likely to be a common objection, along with, "I don't want my traders sitting around all day glued to a boob tube." Videomaster had paved the way, but that product had been sold to stockbrokers, a different breed in a market relatively accustomed to desktop automation.

One option was to go with an adaptation of Ultronic's technology, possibly by means of another joint venture. It was quickly ruled out by Nelson. By now, Reuters' relationship with Ultronic was winding down amid unmistakable signs that the romance had run its course. There had been murmured gripes from GTE, Ultronic's parent, not only that business was lousy but also that Reuters seemed to be inflating its expenses to avoid paying its share of the take from the venture. The countervailing attitude from Fleet Street was that the Americans had served their purpose. Ingratitude is a word that may come to mind, but Ultronic was plainly losing interest and, besides, Reuters was now determined in the electronic world to assert its independence and establish its own identity. In doing so, Reuters would have to tiptoe around an overriding legal issue: Ultronic might interpret the new service as an extension of its existing agreements with Reuters. Nelson quickly issued a decree that no Ultronic equipment or designs derived from Ultronic products were to be employed in the new system.

Reuters' engineers, like their marketing colleagues, were about to enter uncharted waters. The company had never built a computer system of its own, or operated a high-speed data network without American assistance. The first decision to be made, then, was which group in the company would be responsible for developing it. Two rival technology factions emerged. In simplistic terms, one was wedded to hardware, the other to software. The dichotomy was by no means unusual for the times. Hardware had held sway since the dawn of the computer age, but astonishing advances in microprocessors meant that software solutions were steadily gaining ascendance. Reuters now recognized that it had a problem: Nelson and his senior colleagues had scant expertise in deciding which form would be most beneficial.

Reuters had for many years relied on its engineering group, which was called Technical Services, representing the rump of Renfrew's original Computer Services Division. It was run by a Renfrew crony, David Russell, and considered itself the company's primary technology development resource. But with Renfrew preparing to decamp to New York, Nelson had created a second, rival department, Data Processing Services, and made it clear to Russell that the new entity would not only function independently from Computer Services but also with implied pre-eminence.

To run the new unit Nelson brought in Peter Benjamin, a senior data-processing executive at the London Stock Exchange. Benjamin was physically large, jovial and, for all his affected diffidence, highly opinionated. He did not suffer fools gladly. Perceived threats to his position would be fended off with threats of retirement to the country to pursue his extra-curricular interests in farming and restoring old houses. He looked the part of the country gentlemen. He was a curious choice. His interest and expertise in computers, by his own admission, had always been "ardent but frankly amateur." It was typical of the forthright Benjamin to say that he viewed his appointment as "one that could only have been made by a company that simply didn't understand technology." It was nonetheless true. At Benjamin's first interview, Nelson had called in a technical "consultant," Mike Warburg, managing director of Exchange Telegraph, to ask the right questions on Reuters' behalf.

Benjamin's real expertise was in nuclear physics, the subject in which he had graduated. His subsidiary interest in computers developed while he was working at the Aldermaston nuclear research facility, where Britain's atomic and hydrogen bombs were designed. It was a sign of the times that anti-nuclear demonstrators were stationed almost permanently outside the front gates. There they set up job stands to encourage Aldermaston employees to look for work more peaceable than bomb making. Benjamin, himself thinking about a change, would often stop by to see what jobs were on offer. "They were never very good—road-sweepers, that sort of thing." But he was inspired to move out of what he realized was a narrow as well as a controversial field. So he left Aldermaston to join British Overseas Airways Corporation (later British Airways) to help design an automated cargo routing system at Heathrow airport. The BOAC experience would later affect his decisions at Reuters.

"BOAC had decided to use Ferranti computers as intelligent terminals. In the late sixties the only VDUs [video display units] around were pure hardware boxes, no intelligence at all. BOAC made the rather innovative decision to use a computer-intelligent box to control half a dozen terminals. That was really what caused me to take the same decision for Reuters. I saw at BOAC the degree of flexibility it gave them, to actually have a computer driving the functionality at each screen."

There had been few opportunities to put his theories into practice at the London Stock Exchange, where he was involved in designing a stock settlement system. It never got off the ground. System design had to be determined, Benjamin remembered, by "committees of stockbrokers who patently preferred the old Victorian system of meeting every fortnight to swap bits of paper to determine who owed what money to whom." The project collapsed in chaos, the data-processing manager was fired, and Benjamin found himself a reluctant survivor of an experience he regarded as "a total farce, the biggest laugh of my life."

Disillusioned by "City old-boy incompetence," he was attracted one day by a Reuters advertisement. "After working for rigid and process-bound big companies, I saw an opportunity for getting into a little firm that might be interesting. Reuters, too, was set in its ways and suspicious of outsiders, but at least it was quite small."

Since Russell was Renfrew's man and Benjamin a perceived Nelson protégé, their contest to become the company's undisputed head of technology inevitably turned into a closely watched event. Russell moved quickly to pre-empt the Benjamin challenge by instructing one of his engineers, Peter Howse, to construct a general purpose data-and-news display system which, in Howse's phrase, "Reuters might want to use some day" for services yet to be identified. Howse set to work in the company's equipment warehouse in Saffron Hill, north of London, where, in his words, "I locked myself inside for a few weeks and cobbled together bits of Ultronic hardware, including a rotating data-storage drum."

The device he came up with, an impressive video presentation of text and price data, was unveiled at a demonstration for senior executives, including Long, Nelson, and Renfrew. Villeneuve, as the ultimate "customer," was there too. The stated purpose of the demo was to show what could be accomplished internally as an alternative to going outside the organization for expensive hardware systems. Or, perhaps more to the point, as Russell's preferred alternative to relying on untested internal data-processing departments.

Nelson's ban on using anything resembling Ultronic hardware made Howse's device unsuitable on legal if not practical grounds, but Villeneuve found it interesting enough to take Howse aside after the demo. "We could use something like that for a new money-market service we're working on. Tell me more about it."

Benjamin reacted with scorn. "It's not the answer," he told Nelson. "It'll work okay, but it's too inflexible."

He promised a paper setting out his own ideas for Villeneuve's project, naturally based on a software approach, or at any rate a viewing terminal with enough software for it to qualify as "intelligent."

Benjamin's paper—written, as he later described it, for the technologically challenged—was as patronizing as its title: "A Way of Using Computers." If nothing else, it contained plenty of practical advice. For customer sites, he recommended using one of the cheapest and smartest computers of the day, Digital Equipment Corporation's PDP-8, which would act as a "cluster" controller, driving three screen-display terminals. The central processing computer for the system would be a much larger DEC machine called the PDP-11.

In advancing his claims, Benjamin was typically uncompromising. Howse's hardware set-up, he believed, was "totally wrong, because I felt the age of the computer was here. However cleverly Peter had designed the system, and however high the performance, inevitably it was going to be less flexible than using the computer."

Nelson could not decide which way to turn, but the reason seemed perfectly clear to Benjamin: "Reuters didn't really know what it wanted. I remember going into meetings where Nelson would mutter, 'Well, you know, there are all sorts of possibilities…' without reaching any kind of decision." From New York, Renfrew was more forthcoming. Benjamin's plan, he thought, was inadequate—neither efficient nor cost-effective. He might have added, "And not invented here."

Having made his views known, Renfrew contributed nothing further to the debate. This was a Nelson project, and Renfrew was busy pursuing his own separate opportunities in the United States.

During this curious interregnum, Benjamin was often called into meetings of the executive committee to present simplified technical explanations. "How to understand computers in two easy lessons," is how he characterized them. "Funnily enough, it was Brian Stockwell, the staff manager, who was most in tune with new technology. He told me one day, 'Peter, we really need a technical man on this committee. The next vacancy that comes along I shall propose you.' It never happened, of course."

Nelson may have been hesitant, but in the end he surprised no one by ruling in favor of Benjamin's solution. The "defeated" Russell jetted off to New York in a huff to join his mentor, Renfrew.

Adapting Benjamin's idea to Villeneuve's money-market service posed fundamental and practical problems on several levels. For a start, Reuters employed no programmers. Moreover, programmers were suddenly in great demand in a tight marketplace. Moreover, having once hired them, Reuters would have to confront an issue with which it was long familiar but which it had given little thought: the attitude of Fleet Street's warring unions.

From the start of the Ultronic project, which had involved setting up a London computer center, Reuters had inevitably run into the problem of Fleet Street's traditional demarcation questions. Since there had been no way of defining functions by union without risking a strike, Stockwell had come up with an ingenious if clumsy formula: the computer room would be manned jointly—meaning double-manned—by NGA and NATSOPA members. Teleprinter operators and clerks would work in tandem. When critical moments arose, such as the pushing of a transmit button, the unions could take turns doing it. The computer room was declared a "union-free zone." Inside the company it was referred to as the "Joint Area."

Employing former operators and clerks was all well and good, but as Villeneuve's emerging money-market project entered a critical stage, it began to founder in the hands of employees with underdeveloped technology skills. For months Benjamin had watched with growing concern as they "struggled away without producing anything worthwhile."

When recognition finally dawned that the project would go nowhere fast without radical action, Reuters did what most troubled companies do in such circumstances: it brought in a consultant, in this case David Manns, from a computer services company called Logica. Manns found everything in a hopeless muddle. "He soon got fed up with it all," Benjamin said. "But one weekend he went home, worked day and night, and, bingo, came back with a working program."

By February 1972, Benjamin and Manns had finally come to grips with the project. At this point, Villeneuve and John Ransom, another of Nelson's bright young executives from the graduate trainee program, produced a detailed paper for the still-unnamed money-market service. It described a "fast video retrieval service on world money markets" designed to exploit "the lack of central dealing points, in the stock exchange sense, for money markets."[3]

The report described how the abandonment of Bretton Woods and fixed currency parities had forced banks and commercial firms to devote far greater attention to foreign-exchange and money-market operations. The service, it noted, was designed strictly for banks. Other market participants— corporations and private speculators, for example—were to be disqualified from subscribing. Although the report did not say so, corporations traditionally had never been permitted into the inner circle of bank dealers, and for good reason: the "inside" prices the banks quoted to each other were distinctly better than the "outside" ones they quoted to their commercial clients. The paper concluded by mentioning the proposed subscription fees. Receivers would pay about $500 a month, contributors $1500 per month as the "advertising" charge to which so many traders had strongly objected.

Passing the proposal up to Long, Nelson added comments of his own, citing some of the risks, including the potentially tricky problem of the relationship with Ultronic. His tone, though, in the words of Professor Read, Reuters' historian, was "carefully confident."

Long did not feel happy putting his recommendation to the board until June, to give the company time to secure adequate financial backing. Funding was required on a scale unprecedented at Reuters, and the man best equipped to find it was the finance director Nigel Judah. He came back from his last excursion to the City with a five-year, six-figure Eurodollar drawing facility.

Nelson's "carefully confident" tone underlined the first word rather than the second. Villeneuve and Ransom were projecting sales in the first four years of less than fifty subscribers using no more than 200 terminals. What they seemed to be saying was that the service would be successful but was unlikely to set the world on fire.

That may not be how it struck senior Reuters executives at the first internal demonstration, when the terminal started throwing off sparks and smoke, as Long, Nelson, and other dignitaries gawped in astonishment. Jack Wigan, a newly hired marketing manager, retrieved the situation, elbowing his way to the front to douse the fire with a pitcher of water.

The service was launched in June 1973. No customer terminals caught fire.

Meanwhile, the matter of a product name had been resolved. A competition had been launched and the winner, who graciously declined the token prize offered, was Gerry Long. The name he picked was Monitor. The title perfectly reflected the product's function, but Long, being Long, had found inspiration in more profound places. The name, he explained, was derived from a Roman goddess, Juno Moneta, whose temple had housed the city mint.

---

[3] J S Ransom/A F H Villeneuve, Reuters document, February 25, 1972

A mint was something Nelson and Villeneuve might have dreamed of making but did not anticipate making, unless circumstance changed. But then, as Bob Dylan reminded everyone in song, "the times they were a-changin'."

Sadly, they had already changed for Fred Taylor. Declining health forced him to retire less than a year after Monitor's launch. He died a few years later, at the age of fifty-five.

My last glimpse of him, at the new home his sons had bought him in a south London suburb, was of a gaunt, bedridden relic, with an oxygen tank at his bedside. Even so, he was as chipper as ever. His last words to me were unbearably poignant. "Funny old game it's been, cocker. But you keep on playin' it, just like I taught yer."

Nelson delivered the eulogy at Fred's funeral.

I could not bring myself to attend, and have regretted it ever since.

# Cable Vision

My marketing career at Reuters got off to a terrible start. It was inaugurated with an act of folly which in any other company would have been an act of suicide. My moment of lunacy was conceived in hasty collaboration with an equally unhinged colleague. Our jointly worked-out plan was to recommend that Reuters abandon in North America what has since been hailed as the most brilliant marketing campaign in the history of financial information. My comic partner-in-crime was John Hull, of whom more shortly. The product that went on to make history, it hardly needs mentioning, was Monitor.

Understandably, our advice was ignored. Inexplicably, it also went unpunished. Our survival stands as a tribute to a famously benign or, as some critics would insist, an absurdly tolerant, employer. One reason may have been that our boss at the time, Glen Renfrew, was busy committing his own ineffable blunder, one which, relative to our pipsqueak misdemeanor, qualified as a capital crime. It was committed in the cause of a revolution, which, like all revolutions, dealt only in absolutes and the overturning of the existing order. In this case, the grand objective was to vault Reuters into a dominant position as a provider of information to the American financial markets through the exciting new medium of cable television. CATV, as it was widely known, was then emerging as America's most dynamic industry. Not dynamic enough, as it turned out.

Both incidents, minor and major—the one a jaywalking offence, the other a case of aggravated assault—have long been forgotten, even within Reuters. So why bother to resurrect them now? The answer is that each in its own way epitomizes the angst-ridden purgatory into which Reuters had wandered in the 1970s, a period which, as we have seen, had reduced even the cool, calm and collected Mike Nelson to an abject state of terror.

Renfrew's great CATV miscalculation, impressive enough in its own right, was greatly amplified by the stature of the man behind it. That it greatly damaged Renfrew's hitherto stellar reputation was disturbing enough, but it was also a costly mistake in financial terms. Indeed, for a while it provoked genuine concern in the higher reaches of the company that the very future of Reuters had been placed in jeopardy by an initiative that its sterner critics suspected had been founded less on sound business principles than on unworthy motives of self-promotion.

When it became clear that the financial fears had been wildly exaggerated, the suspicion arose in "Renfrew's New York" that they had been whipped up in "Nelson's London" as part of a "dirty tricks" campaign designed to advance Nelson's claim to the succession. London predictably dismissed such charges as typical of New York paranoia. Actually, both perceptions contained grains of truth. For such was the climate of mutual mistrust between Reuters' capitals that if anyone on either side of the pond had ventured to declare that the world was round, someone on the other side would immediately have insisted, no doubt with supporting evidence, that it was flat.

Typical of this polarization was the plight of Scott Rumbold, who had arrived in New York after a three-year tour of duty in South America. Rumbold, a large, jolly Londoner with a snorting laugh, got on well with everyone. His job in the Wall Street sales office was to act as liaison between the big New York investment firms and their overseas offices. In this capacity he reported to John Albanie, Europe's marketing director. "Be careful what you tell our friend Scotty," Joe Daffin advised me one day. "And what you say in his presence. He's likely to report everything to his masters 'over there.' "

Reuters' tolerance, even encouragement, of such sophomoric infighting was reflective of a period largely defined by the inexhaustible flow of Watergate-related malefactions emerging from Nixon's White House, all committed in the vaguely analogous cause of re-electing the president. Watergate would first embarrass, then engulf, and finally destroy the Nixon administration. Reuters plainly did not self-destruct, but there were times when it seemed intent on doing so, and it may even have come close. The collective panic was induced by one of those nail-biting, transitional phases all too familiar to a company which, at regular intervals in its history, had felt compelled to seriously re-examine its role in the world.

In the 1970s it was a world in the process of being reshaped, at a bewildering pace, by changes in information technology.

Reuters was hardly unique in that respect: society at large was also nervously stumbling into the much-heralded and long-promised Information Age. Social pundits had already started to pontificate about "paradigm shifts," often invoking the almost forgotten name of Marshall McLuhan, master of the prophetic catchphrase in the 1950s. Paradigmitis was about to become contagious. Many a corporate management was succumbing to the uncontrollable urge to reinvent or re-brand itself. Nor was the movement confined to those companies directly involved in the business of communication, or "connectivity" as it came to be known. Applying the prefix "new" to brands was nothing new. Marketers of soap powers had been tossing the word about for years. So had politicians, going back to Franklin D. Roosevelt's "New Deal" of the 1930s, and probably before that. In that respect, Nixon offered the perfect paradigm, having been repackaged so many times as the "new" Nixon that some could scarcely remember who the original was until the Watergate revelations jogged their memories.

Even Reuters, as if anxious not be left out, began to ruminate that it ought to be regarded as something more complex and diverse than a cooperative news agency. But as what exactly? There was no question that a "new" Reuters was taking shape, but its business model was effectively unchanged. The company's chief source of revenue was still overwhelmingly news, and although company finances had improved remarkably, growth remained modest, operating margins too tight for comfort, and cash as scarce as ever. Data retrieval products such as Videomaster continued to contribute reliably to revenue and Monitor, it was hoped, would at least emulate its predecessor. But the new service had modest objectives and was, anyway, still unproven. Monitor also carried a high burden of risk, being more dependent on borrowed money than any project Reuters had undertaken in modern times. Great and sundry opportunities beckoned in the United States, the crucible of the impending technology revolution. But until they could be identified, Reuters' North American operating performance, derived exclusively from low-growth teleprinter services, would continue to stall, and perhaps deteriorate.

It was against this backdrop of tumultuous uncertainty that there occurred the executive cock-ups, major and minor, mentioned earlier. We were all at sea in a rowboat.

★

John Hull joined Reuters in the early part of 1974. He had been hired—much to my chagrin at the time—to introduce Monitor into the United States following its promising start in Europe. Since Hull, though something of a technologist, knew nothing about news or money markets, I was assigned to assist him as a supposed expert in both.

It so happened that we were virtual neighbors in Port Washington, a Long Island community fast emerging as a Reuters ghetto—with half a dozen senior Reuters executives in residence, including Renfrew—which meant that Hull and I saw a great deal of each other socially as well as professionally. We soon discovered that we shared a well-developed nose for controversy, a smart-ass attitude to authority, and an enthusiasm for an occasional evening out on the tiles. These mutual interests allowed us to convert what might have become a sour rivalry into a quirky but enduring friendship.

Hull ensured that his arrival would be noticed by sporting a beard, virtually an act of defiance in prim, upper-crust Reuters. "First one I've ever seen here," Renfrew saw fit to inform me. Hull's appendage gave him an appearance I hope he'll forgive me for describing as that of a hippie in his Sunday best. It was matched by the hair shirt he was given to wearing from time to time—occasions that usually signaled, as I would shortly discover, a mortifying public display of self-abnegation. He was also susceptible to what Winston Churchill referred to as "black dog" depressions, a susceptibility to which a fondness for marijuana may have contributed (though my own passing acquaintance with the stuff seemed to have just the opposite effect). Between these "black dogs" Hull was bright, enthusiastic, and innovative. He brought to Reuters a background in technology, which had greatly appealed to Renfrew, and a forceful personality well suited to pushing a brand-new concept such as Monitor. These attributes nullified my inexperience and complemented my market knowledge. We were considered "a good team." So were Laurel and Hardy.

Observant readers may have noticed that "launch" was not the word chosen to describe Monitor's American debut. "Launch" conjures up an image of a sleek ocean liner sliding majestically into the water; the exercise performed by Hull and me more resembled a rough-hewn bamboo raft being dragged to shore over a rock-strewn beach. Seasoned marketing executives would have disguised such ineptitude, perhaps with a few polished bromides about lights at the end of the tunnel, or corners about to be turned. Hull and I saw fit instead to bring our predicament directly to Renfrew's attention, like novices intent on confessing impure thoughts to Mother Superior. This was the "folly" I mentioned at the start of the chapter.

The cause of our frustration was the futility and frustration of the weeks we had just spent peddling Monitor to a resolutely hostile New York foreign-exchange market. Not a single bank had been signed up. Worse, none had shown the slightest interest in being signed up. Most chief dealers had told us, some in no uncertain terms, not to bother coming back.

Monitor had got off to a shaky start in Europe, too, but the project there finally seemed to be gathering momentum—a favorable precedent that Hull and I inexplicably chose to ignore. We chose instead to suffer death by a thousand cuts by reading the streams of glowing memoranda flooding in from London. British banks, it was reported, had started to sign up in decent numbers. German, Scandinavian, and French banks were clambering on the bandwagon with palpable enthusiasm. Even the leading Swiss banks, suppressing nationalistic envy, had been persuaded to subscribe.

For all Europe's progress, though, the fate of the project was still seen as hanging in the balance, reinforcing the view at 85 Fleet Street that active American participation in the project was critical. New York then was no more an important foreign-exchange center in its own right than it is now. But the leading New York banks were among the wealthiest and most aggressive on the planet, and by way of demonstrating the fact were busily opening branches all over it.

Wealthy and aggressive was not how the same banks were behaving at home. Hull and I had been ejected from every one of them. If I was bemused, Hull was deeply offended. Racked by feelings of unworthiness, he began to mutter threats of an "honorable" resignation. It may have been to avert such drastic action that we decided that the time had come to deliver a frank assessment of the situation to Renfrew. "Frank assessment" may be interpreted as "abject surrender." That was certainly how Renfrew might see it. In which case, I remarked, talk of resignation might be rendered unnecessary. "So be it," said Hull with a shrug. "Let's do it."

The fateful meeting with Renfrew was arranged for late on a Friday afternoon, always a good time to dispense bad news, as corporate public-relations men can testify. Hull had donned a particularly luxurious hair shirt that day. As a sensible preamble, we chose to indulge in a lunch hour of mutual flagellation at Michael One, a popular downtown restaurant and one of our regular hangouts. Lunch was more numbing than nourishing.

"We gotta come clean," Hull said, ordering the first bottle of house red. "It's pointless going on like this. The market's telling us it doesn't want Monitor. If we keep pushing it the banks will just get more and more pissed off. So, what do we do?"

What we needed, I ventured boldly, was a convincing story (for which, read excuse) and a plausible backup plan (for which, read escape route). These I proceeded to formulate over a second bottle of red. Because New York was not really a foreign-exchange town, I expounded, and since there was hardly any information on the system for American clients to look at (both observations being no less trite for being accurate) the project should be put on hold. It would give us some breathing space, a chance to reassess the situation. Far better, surely, to wait until the product was firmly established in Europe. Then we could go back into the market with a success story. And if Europe should for some reason falter, we could always claim that Monitor had been a misbegotten venture all along.

Hull nodded his approval, and threw in a hitherto unspoken justification. "I'm guessing that Renfrew won't be altogether unhappy with us. He hates Monitor. After all, it has Michael Nelson written all over it."

We took the plan to our boss, Joe Daffin, the North American sales director and our immediate supervisor, to gain his approval. Sensibly, he declined to endorse it. As an old Renfrew drinking crony from London, Daffin had an almost preternatural sense of his boss's moods and desires. Accordingly, he made a parting appeal for cancellation. "Meeting with Renfrew isn't merely a daft idea," I remember him saying, "it's madness. Asking him to agree to shelve Monitor is like asking Attila to order the Huns to stop pillaging."

We persisted. Daffin relented. "On your heads be it…" Appearing before

Attila was the mental image we took with us on what seemed a much longer than usual subway ride uptown to Renfrew's 47th Street office.

By the time we arrived, noonday sunshine had been replaced, figuratively as well as literally, by afternoon storm clouds. With the effects of lunch wearing off fast, what had seemed an hour earlier a perfectly plausible initiative now loomed as an irredeemable folly.

Renfrew's secretary, the imperturbable Charlotte Klotzman, offered hope of a last-minute reprieve. Mr. Renfrew, we were informed, was running a little late. How late? "Maybe half an hour." I clutched at the straw. "Um, tell Glen we're sorry we couldn't wait. Tell him we had to leave to meet a client."

The ping of an arriving elevator announced our escape, until the opening doors revealed the fearsome apparition of Attila himself. Renfrew had extricated himself from an earlier meeting. "Going somewhere?" he said breezily. "Come on in. I'll order some coffee. I must say you both look as if you could use it."

I recall the occasion now as it probably was at the time, as a kind of out-of-body experience. Renfrew endured our entire gloomy litany in stony silence, punctuated only by a rhythmic tapping of fingers on the desk, an ominous manifestation of Renfrew impatience—not a condition to trifle with. We awaited the response in a seat-squirming agony of dread. Amazingly, there was no wrathful outburst, just a lecture, avuncular in tone, though suffused with scorn and laced with menace. Here's the gist of it:

"I don't believe a single word of what you've just said. Not a single bloody word. Nor, I suspect, do either of you. What you seriously expect me to do, if I've understood you correctly, is to call Gerry Long and tell him that we're going to abandon an initiative vital to the company's survival, in the world's biggest financial market. Mike Nelson would relish that as yet another example of North American incompetence. [It was a relief that Renfrew had mentioned Nelson without any idiotic prompting from us.] Now, I realize that introducing a new product isn't easy, been there myself, took me weeks to sell my first Stockmaster. It's because selling isn't easy that we hire brilliant marketing executives like you. Now, I'm going to forget the gibberish I've just heard. You're going to start all over again, and you'll keep going until the banks come around, even if it takes until the Christmas after next. If Europe can sell the damned thing, so can we. I don't care a hoot if you insist on looking foolish, but I'll be damned if I'm going to. So, both of you get back downtown and go to work."

Then, looking from Hull to me, he added as an afterthought, "Well, Monday perhaps. I think you'd better take the rest of the day off."

Hull and I made a beeline for the nearest saloon.

On the Monday morning, Daffin greeted us with a knowing smirk, and an unnecessary question (Renfrew had almost certainly called him). "So how did it go?"

"We just keep plugging away," Hull said gloomily. "And if we survive Friday's little episode, it'll be a miracle."

"Yeah, miracle is the word I'd use," said Daffin.

We spent a day or two collecting our thoughts. Why were the New York banks so opposed to Monitor? What had we overlooked? And what next?

There may have been no more to American antipathy than the same early doubts and fears expressed about Monitor in Europe. There was, however, one negative market phenomenon peculiar to New York. In Sherlock Holmes's case file it would have been listed as "The Curious Affair of the Two Bobbies."

The Two Bobbies were Bobby Van Roten and Bobby LeClerc, respectively the chief foreign-exchange dealers of Morgan Guaranty Trust Company and the New York branch of Continental Illinois of Chicago, two of the most active trading banks in the New York foreign-exchange market. If the Bobbies sound like policemen, they often acted like policemen. Between them they dominated the market, not so much by exercising the power of the banks that employed them, as by exerting the force of their own personalities. To describe their authority as a reign of terror would be an exaggeration. But to say that their influence was pervasive and rarely challenged would not be. In short, nothing much happened in the way currency trading was conducted in New York without their joint endorsement. Monitor, the Bobbies made clear from the start, was not something they felt like endorsing. To be fair, most of their fellow traders seemed genuinely unenthusiastic, too—though to what extent they had been brainwashed it is hard to say.

Bobby Van Roten, a self-styled "pig-headed Dutchman," was a lifelong employee of the bank he reverentially referred to as "The House of Morgan." "They'll probably have to carry me out of here," he once told me, in a tone suggesting that it was something he actually looked forward to. It was a fate I sometimes silently wished on him myself. Van Roten had worked his way up through the trading ranks—not, I imagine, without hurting a few feelings along the way. A combative, abrupt, sometimes rough-tongued manner was his public persona, but it was plainly something of an act. Away from the bank, where he ran Morgan's currency-trading desk with the unbending autocracy of a Captain Bligh with hemorrhoids, he deployed a self-deprecating charm.

To one man, though, this Bligh was always deferential: his immediate boss, Dennis Weatherstone. It was a respect clearly rooted more in admiration than fear.

The trim, diminutive Weatherstone was British-born, the son of a railway worker. He had started at the bank as a sixteen-year-old errand boy, attached to the trading room. There, he quickly demonstrated an unusual aptitude for figures and, by attending evening classes after work, evinced a strong desire for self-improvement. Elevated to a junior trading position on the currency desk, he reinforced mathematical flair with fine judgment. In short, Weatherstone had started with even fewer advantages than Van Roten, and had advanced further in what was then regarded as the most venerable and aristocratic of the American banks, where he had to vie for recognition with Ivy League rivals, many with strings of Roman numerals behind their names. Within the decade he would become chairman of the board and chief executive, a position he occupied as *Sir* Dennis Weatherstone. Knighthood, success, and wealth did nothing to alter his modest lifestyle. When not traveling, he lived quietly in the suburban Connecticut town of Darien, where at weekends he struck a familiar figure pedaling around the local bicycle trails. Van Roten's kinship with his boss was genuine, and it was reciprocated. They were bonded as a couple of thoroughly blue-collar guys who had made good in America's most definitively blue-blooded financial institution.

Van Roten's Dutch origins apparently endowed him with a knack for holding back floodwaters. In the context of Monitor, he told me, "I don't say yes to anything the first time around, my young friend, or even several times after that. Nor do I give a fig what the rest of the market says or does." Since it was a market over which he held considerable sway, that was not saying a great deal. He had a favorite expression: "The House of Morgan is always a pioneer, but never a guinea pig." As far as Monitor was concerned, Van Roten would be a dauntingly tough pig to crack. It was a challenge I was prepared to take on—especially with Renfrew's recent admonitions ringing in my ears—and Van Roten made clear that he was prepared to enjoy the contest, too. We got along famously.

Bobby LeClerc of Continental Illinois was a different matter altogether. His public manner matched his friend's in every respect except for the occasional outbreaks of charm. I succeeded in getting an appointment to see him only after weeks of trying. Then, he kept me waiting for nearly an hour, obviously to make a point. From where I sat, waiting in a glass-walled anteroom, I could see him clearly, apparently mocking me by sipping coffee and leafing through the *Wall Street Journal*. The meeting took up considerably less time than the waiting. LeClerc assumed throughout an exaggerated expression of boredom, glancing with conspicuous regularity at his watch. His parting remark completed the impression of a man with a mind securely locked and bolted against new ideas, and very conscious of it: "Now, I've listened to your pitch, so don't you go around saying I didn't give you a fair hearing."

LeClerc, like Van Roten, came across as a man of curious contradictions. Although his manner was blunt and he habitually deployed the language of a truck driver, he was said to have come from a respectable middle-class family in Montreal. It meant, if nothing else, that he was organically fluent in French. He was also adept in Spanish. A gourmand and wine connoisseur, LeClerc and a male friend of the kind who would nowadays be described as a "partner" enjoyed entertaining selected colleagues over fancy home-cooked dinners. If he was gay, as was widely known in market circles, it represented an act of bravery for a man in his position during an age when exposure might have threatened his career. Keen as he was on fine wines, he was also fond of the harder stuff—inordinately so, according to some of his peers, who saw in his desire to drink them under the table a desperate need to command their affection, or at least their respect. All the more sad, then, that when his skill finally deserted him, it brought about a public humiliation that would cost him both job and career.

The occasion was a formal reception in London sponsored by the local branch of the Forex Club, formally and rather high-mindedly known as Association Cambiste Internationale, a global confederation of individual foreign-exchange traders. The venue was the City of London's ancient Guildhall, the event an ACI dinner given in honor of Roy Bridge, a revered market figure who was about to retire as head of the Bank of England's international trading desk. LeClerc, attending as head of the ACI, was a guest at the high table. The following account, which ignores some of the inevitable variations and embellishments, has been confirmed by several in attendance that evening, including John Christopherson, representing the New York Forex. LeClerc, it seems, expressed his appreciation for the laudatory speech by the governor of the Bank of England, Gordon Richardson, by falling asleep. Hardly an unusual phenomenon, you might say, except that LeClerc, observed by an audience frozen in disbelief, kept keeling over until his head came to rest on the shoulder of Mrs. Bridge, seated next to him. Her gracious response each time was to gently push him back to the perpendicular. Fatigue was understandable after an overnight flight from New York, but LeClerc had also spent the afternoon in the hotel bar, thereby relinquishing jet-lag as an excuse. And in light of what followed, he forfeited every other excuse as well. Dinner over, informal farewells were being exchanged when LeClerc, while in the act of giving Mrs. Bridge a friendly peck on the cheek, crowned his inglorious evening by vomiting into her cleavage. Stumbling and incoherent, he was escorted from the premises, by Christopherson and others. Before he had been returned to his hotel, a short taxi-ride away, the story was doing the rounds in New York.

And in the corridors of Continental Illinois.

On the question of Monitor, the two Bobbies could not be budged. Not, at any rate, by Hull and me. Nor even by André Villeneuve, who in Hull's phrase "honored the colonies" with a flurry of visits in the hope of breaking the impasse. Hull suspected that Renfrew had alerted "Villanoove" (as Hull insisted on mispronouncing it) to our infamous Friday meeting and that André had been summoned to "kick ass." Of course, Villeneuve was perfectly entitled, indeed obliged, to go wherever he saw fit, but Hull greeted him with open resentment. Nor, it must be said, did Villeneuve make any notable effort to placate his colleague by commandeering customer demonstrations and generally adopting the manner of a master instructing a particularly backward pupil. Left to fume on the sidelines, Hull found his contribution reduced to making restaurant reservations. A relationship that had not been endowed with warmth from the start, turned distinctly icy.

Hull felt increasingly threatened with every Villeneuve visit. "That's it for me," he would mumble into his vodka and tonic after Villeneuve had left for the airport. "I'm a dead man. Those fucking high-and-mighty Limeys hate us Americans. See how they look down their noses at us. Villeneuve probably has one of his friends lined up for my job." The thought occurred that Hull probably meant me.

"I doubt that," I responded in a barely concealed Limey accent. "But you can't expect him to sit back and do nothing. London needs the American banks, or thinks it does, and the fact is that we haven't delivered them."

"So waddya think we should do?"

The time had come to clutch at straws. I said, "There's someone at Salomon Brothers I should call. He seems to take every information service there is."

Salomon Brothers was not a bank but an institutional securities house, specializing in bonds. The firm had a reputation for innovation and, with several hundred traders populating an arena half the size of a football field, owned the biggest trading room in the business. Around Wall Street it was referred to, with unusual reverence, as The Room. Its more prominent residents would soon acquire a dubious and definitional fame as Big Swinging Dicks. As a reporter I had been a frequent visitor to The Room, had even enjoyed a passing acquaintance with William "Billy" Salomon, the firm's chief partner, who, in his last working years, used to sit, eagle-eyed, at a desk at the entrance to The Room, watching his pension grow. I also knew on a nodding basis the head of Salomon's institutional stock-trading desk, Jay Perry, and his assistant, a small abrasive fellow by the name of Michael Bloomberg. Two or three years earlier, when trading in giant blocks of shares was very much in vogue as a Wall Street status symbol, Bloomberg had enthusiastically agreed to my invitation to call the newsroom whenever Salomon executed a big trade.

My principal contact, though, and occasional drinking companion, was Mike Griffith, a young trader on the commercial-paper desk.

"Why would a commercial-paper trader want a foreign-exchange service?" Hull asked, reasonably.

"He probably won't, but let's find out what he does want. And you never know, he may just come up with some angle we've overlooked."

At five o'clock on a Monday evening Griffith was still busy on the telephone, flogging paper. Around him, The Room was winding down from the day's frenzy. While talking on the phone he peered at a video screen, checking quotes. Griffith noticed our interest. "You guys seen this thing? It's called Telerate. Great service. Gives me commercial paper, money markets, treasuries, all kinds of domestic stuff. Not been around long but it keeps getting better. So, what have you got to sell me?"

We told him about Monitor.

"Foreign exchange isn't really my thing. Got anything else on there?"

Not yet, we said, but adding wistfully that the possibilities were endless.

"Tell you what, I'll take one."

"What?"

"I'll take one. Look, here's how I see it. One day we're all gonna be trading in one big world-market: bonds, stocks, paper, FX—you name it. If this Minotaur, whatever, takes off internationally it might just become a real important product here in the States. Now, how about buying me that drink. And don't forget to send me a contract."

We called Renfrew in triumph the next morning. "Told ya," he said. "Now, go get the rest."

Triumphs, like tragedies, seem to come in threes. Within days, more or less out of the blue, two more clients signed up. We had sent a New York sales executive, Art Kasper, on a sales trip to the Midwest, or rather a speculative mission to find out whether the regional banks might be prepared to support the service their Big City colleagues had shunned. We did not seriously believe that they would. A wild goose chase, Kasper had called it. Damned if he didn't end up cooking a goose—and in Cleveland, of all places. Kasper had talked his way into a securing a contract, for a single terminal, from one of Cleveland's two main banks. Decorum demands that the name of his contact be withheld, as it was whispered that Kasper and the young lady in charge of the bank's foreign-exchange desk had formed a relationship that strayed beyond commercial bounds.

"Well, Art, now you know what you have to do," we chided him.

"You guys have dirty minds," Kasper responded sheepishly. "And, by the way, when you're a great salesman, as I am, you don't have to use your Johnson. Besides, how many female traders do you know in this market?"

There were none in Pittsburgh and Philadelphia, the final destinations on Kasper's grand tour, but he still came back with two more orders.

And so, at last, the penny dropped: the regional banks held the key to unlocking the American market. Bullied or ignored by the New York traders, they were institutional versions of Nixon's "forgotten Americans"—and we had made the mistake of forgetting them. "The Big Boys have been ripping us off for years," was their common complaint. It now became our theme. "Don't let the bastards grind you down; hit back with Monitor." (But please don't tell them we told you so.)

A new battle plan was hatched. It involved laying siege to Gotham. We would first take out the branches of foreign banks. Then we would hit the New York branches of regional American banks. Finally we would launch an assault on the lair of the two-headed, fire-eating monster represented by the Two Bobbies.

Orders now began to flow in regularly. "Suddenly, it's like taking candy from kids," Kasper chortled. I made a few speculative calls myself. One was to First National Bank of Atlanta, where the head trader, Paul Ellis, was an Englishman with whom I had formed a casual acquaintance on the telephone. He fell immediately. "I just saw Monitor in London and I've been meaning to call you. Count me in. And if I take one, you can bet my friendly rivals across the street will have to order one, too." And after a single telephone call, they did just that—actually going one better. "We'll take two."

From north of the border Hull called in with news of further conquests. He had persuaded John Christopherson, the head foreign-exchange trader at Bank of Montreal, to act as a reference site for the Canadian market. "You want to demo the produce, by all means use my office." The Canadians were, it seemed, as united in their resentment of New York as their American regional counterparts.

Between the United States and Canada we soon had a score of out-of-town subscribers.

Then a few branches of foreign banks in New York signed up. But we had still not managed to land the Big One—a Chase, or a First National City Bank, let alone a Morgan or a Continental Illinois.

"Betcha we get a visit from Lord Villeneuve pretty soon," Hull predicted. As if on cue, Villeneuve called to suggest it was time he dropped in. "I'll be there on Monday evening. I think we should have another go at Chase. And what about JJ's friends at Morgan? Perhaps a good lunch. Decent bottle of wine."

Hull was still scowling—"Maybe he wants me to fax him the fucking wine list!"—when the phone rang in my office next door. I ran in to pick it up. "Hello, old chap," said a voice affecting an English accent for my amusement but unmistakably Bobby Van Roten. What impeccable timing! Sensing something interesting was about to happen, I snapped my fingers at Hull to pick up the extension. It was not hard to guess what was coming. "We, that is Dennis and I, would like you to come down at your earliest convenience. Just for a chat. We've been talking things over and might, um, consider putting in one, maybe a couple, of your Monitor terminals. Strictly on a free trial basis, you understand—no commitments. Monday afternoon okay for you? Good. Say three o'clock?"

Hull and I exchanged high fives. He insisted on coming with me. "We could take Villeneuve along, too, impress the hell out of him."

"Not a fucking chance," I told him. "No offence to either of you, but this one is all mine."

★

Was Renfrew pleased that Monitor West was finally on its way? More relieved than delighted, I would say. Rising revenue from Monitor would make a handy contribution to his objective of making North America profitable and financially self-sufficient, but this was revenue based on a product carrying Nelson's imprimatur. And since Nelson's name was also on the label of every Stockmaster and Videomaster around the world as well, Renfrew sorely needed a triumph of his own making.

He had become increasingly preoccupied with just such a project. It contemplated the delivery of news and market quotes on a huge scale to a mass audience via the medium of cable television.

By 1972, cable television—formally known as Community Antenna Television, or CATV—was America's fastest-growing industry. CATV was first deployed as a means of delivering improved television reception by satellite to remote communities, which avoided the mountains and hills that impeded normal over-the-air signals. Topographical considerations aside, cable television soon acquired a broad appeal in its own right as a vehicle for extra channels of sports and entertainment on a subscription basis. Although capital-intensive in the early stages, CATV franchises promised enormous returns on investment, so long as subscribers signed up in large numbers. That seemed a pretty safe bet in a country populated by the world's most avid television viewers. By the late sixties, CATV stations were sprouting all over the United States.

Production companies, hurriedly created, scrambled to provide programming, a suddenly scarce commodity. One of the earliest and eventually most successful of the on-air organizations formed to gather content was Home Box Office, a subsidiary of Time Inc., the world's largest publisher of magazines, including *Time, Life,* and *Sports Illustrated.*

HBO made its debut in November 1972 on a cable system in Wilkes Barre, Pennsylvania. Nature intervened to make it an inauspicious event. The city had been devastated a few months earlier by Hurricane Agnes, leaving only half its 10,000 CATV subscribers still connected. Even at a modest subscription fee of $6 a month, HBO managed to sign up only 365 of them. The viewing menu that evening was more snack than banquet: a basketball game followed by a movie. As Time's official historian observed: "In retrospect, HBO's first night was historic. At the time, though, it hardly seemed worthy of notice and in fact was hardly noticed at all."

Through another subsidiary, Sterling Manhattan Television (later renamed Manhattan Cable Television), Time owned the most valuable CATV franchise in New York City, covering the lower half of Manhattan, embracing the commercial and affluent residential areas of midtown and the downtown financial district. New York needed cable television as much as any mountain community because of the canyon effect of Manhattan's skyscrapers.

Time Inc. spent heavily to get Sterling established in Manhattan. New York was a tough proposition. As Time's historian noted, Sterling "ate money voraciously. Compared with the Midwest localities in which Time-Life Broadcast was seeking out CATV franchises, and where wiring for cable was an above-ground operation, Sterling plunged the company into the catacombs under New York City streets. Cables had to be strung through underground ducts, then into the basements of office and apartment buildings, and finally, by means of a riser, up to the offices and apartments. And whereas suburban, overground cabling cost perhaps $10,000 per mile, in Manhattan the cost was more like $100,000 and sometimes as high as $300,000. By mid-1967, Sterling had spent $2 million to wire only thirty-four blocks, and it was serving only 400 subscribers."

Renfrew was undeterred by such problems. He was fascinated by cable television, some said obsessed by it. In truth, Reuters needed an obsession in a market in which the company had no real presence and, newswires apart, no products of substance. The printers happily chugged along, growing steadily. But a few hundred subscribers for the Reuter Financial Report and the Reuter Commodities Report, run out of Chicago, scarcely paid the office rents. Newswires spewed out paper, not profits. With Monitor still struggling to gain a foothold, Reuters North America continued to operate at a steadily worsening loss—not a situation calculated to advance the corporate ambitions of the region's new chief executive. Glen Renfrew had not come to New York to preside over a money-losing news bureau—or to act as Monitor's American sales agent.

Renfrew's vision in the world of cable dovetailed with that of the people in charge of Sterling Manhattan. His immediate objective, though, was to reach New York's financial community, represented by the thousands of financial institutions, great and small, that populated the downtown Wall Street area and the growing uptown banking community along Park Avenue. Sterling had already laid the trunk lines. The extensive bandwidth provided by cable television, as Renfrew saw it, offered a unique medium for blasting out information on an unprecedented scale and at little cost, and a means of leapfrogging over entrenched competitors still wedded to expensive leased telephone lines. There was just one potential snag: the new business would always depend on the pace of cable installation. But since cable television was catching on rapidly, and would surely soon blanket the entire country, the risk seemed acceptable. The idea of reaching every corner of the great Republic encouraged Renfrew to study another emerging communications phenomenon: satellite technologies.

Satellites had been spinning around the globe for a decade or more, mainly for specialized government purposes, notably espionage. Prohibitive cost at first put them beyond the reach of all but the biggest commercial users, such as the telephone companies, but as the number of "birds" orbiting the planet steadily grew, so the price of transponder space steadily retreated. By 1972 they were starting to come into their own as conveyances for routine international voice and data traffic.

All of which had been predicted in the 1940s by Arthur C. Clarke, a British writer of science fiction, a pioneering advocate of satellite communications and a self-styled visionary of the information age. Clarke's utterances have a McLuhanesque ring: "Radio waves have never respected frontiers and from an altitude of 36,000 kilometers, national boundaries are singularly inconspicuous. The world of the future will be an open world." Indeed, the McLuhan-Clarke concepts of an "open world" and a "global village" were fast becoming reality as ever-increasing numbers of satellites passed along a geo-synchronous spatial millrace designated the Clarke Ring, in honor of its prophet.

Simultaneously, ever-improving microchip technology encouraged a prolif-eration of receiver dishes sometimes called, in keeping with the popular affection for space-age nomenclature, earth stations. Dishes were rapidly shrinking in size and falling in cost.

The Nixon administration responded to all these developments, and specifically to lobbying from the business world for greater commercial exploitation of space, by promulgating an "open skies" policy governing domestic satellite use, paving the way for a switch to private from government ownership of the airwaves. Communicating by satellite was about to come within the economic reach of small, ambitious commercial enterprises such as Reuters.

Of course, Renfrew's space-age visions had to give way sooner or later to practical earthbound exigencies. There was, for a start, the design of the cable-head device that would process and transmit the information to client sites. There was also the question of the desktop terminal the clients would use to retrieve it. The terminal, Renfrew reckoned, was the least of his problems. It could be manufactured. The experience of producing homemade video-editing terminals for the Reuters newsrooms had given Renfrew a taste for building customized hardware. Besides, there were few, if any, inexpensive off-the-shelf alternatives around.

Then one day in 1973 there arrived in Renfrew's office a transmission device almost perfectly suited to his purpose, accompanied by its inventor, one Dr. Robert Nagel.

Dr. Bob, as he was known to his friends—who, unlike his enemies, failed to question the authenticity of his doctorate—combined the popular images of computer nerd and nutty professor. He was pale and unkempt, with a short-sighted squint that testified to years spent slumped in front of computer screens. He claimed a family connection with the world of news: two genera-tions of Nagels had owned a newspaper in Batavia, a small city in upper New York State. With neither the itch nor his father's aptitude for news, Nagel had taken up an early interest in computers. A permanently woebegone expression lit up whenever he was asked to expound on a favorite scientific theory. Nagel had many theories on many scientific subjects. He now added one more to the list: how Renfrew should develop his bold cable strategy.

Right from the start there were those at Reuters—and more than a few—who considered Nagel's febrile imagination a dangerous ingredient to stir into the boiling cauldron of Renfrew's ambition. Beware of geeks bearing gifts, should have been their advice. Nagel was aware of the whispered slights but remained contemptuously unmoved. Challenged on some of his more bizarre propositions, Nagel would furrow his brow into a puzzled expression, accompanied by a simpering smile. It seemed to say, "Okay, you got me that time," but also said, "I've not finished yet." Nagel was always hard to pin down. He could out-wriggle Marilyn Monroe and out-wheedle Uriah Heep.

Nagel's little evasions even had Renfrew chuckling: "Crafty little bugger, that Bob. Gotta watch him, that's for sure."

Des Maberley, Renfrew's deputy, and self-appointed, tough-talking chief of the Imperial Guard, failed to see the funny side. "Sneaky bastard. How Glen puts up with him I'll never know. I'll nail him one of these days, you wait and see." The pun—Nagel means nail in German—was unintended, as were most of Maberley's puns.

At the time he first appeared in Renfrew's office, Nagel was working at some obscure think tank in New York City called the Brain Research Laboratory, funded by the Massachusetts Institute of Technology. The work involved analyzing recordings of brain waves. "He should track his own," Maberley snorted derisively. The lab work occupied less than his full attention, leaving time to dabble in stock-market analysis for his own company, Computer Security Systems.

In that context, Nagel worked on a brilliant but little-known computer called the Linc, one of Digital Equipment Corporation's most complex but least successful models. Only a hundred Linc machines were ever sold. One of them, as it happened, was operated by LV Computer Systems, a company owned by Victor Vurpillat, a dapper, smooth-talking consultant and software developer and creator of a stock-market tracking system called Oracle, one of Wall Street's first computerized analytical products. One day, Vurpillat's Linc machine developed a fault that baffled even DEC's engineers. They gave him Nagel's name as a fellow user who might be able to help. Nagel duly came up with a fix. Vurpillat was impressed and saw an opportunity to return the favor. He had met Renfrew and was well aware of his search for a system to deliver data via cable. Nagel, he suggested, might be just the man to come up with a solution for that problem, too. Vurpillat brokered a meeting.

The more Renfrew explained his plans, the more Nagel became convinced he could help build a high-speed data-transmission system. He promised a prototype. Sure enough, a few weeks later, he offered a demonstration. It went better than either Nagel or Renfrew could have hoped.

"I just walked into Glen's office one day with this gadget, and by God it worked!" Nagel recalled twenty-five years later, still sounding astonished.

Nagel had designed a software package to run on a PDP-8 computer, another DEC machine, connected to a Hitachi disk loaded with a dozen screen "pages" of potted information. Sitting at a terminal, with Renfrew peering over his shoulder, Nagel proceeded to "capture" the pages, one by one, on the screen. Or, as he put it, "grabbed" them, frame by frame, as they sped through the disk in one continuous broadcast loop.

"Worked like a charm," was Nagel's verdict. "I said, 'Glen, this is really the world's simplest device.' He agreed. I'd say he was visibly excited."

The "world's simplest device," running at an analog speed of 60 frames a second, was dubbed a "frame-grabber." It was fast—but not quite fast enough for Renfrew's purposes.

"Can you speed it up?" he asked.

"No problem," said Nagel, promising a digital variation that would handle data by blocks of characters, or lines, rather than by the page, and send out 15,000 frames a second. Nagel called this version a "row-grabber."

Nagel's device had Renfrew spellbound. "Stick around after the demo, Bob, and we'll talk some more."

They talked for weeks. Renfrew took out a mortgage on a table at the Forum of the Twelve Caesars, a gaudy restaurant on 48th Street, directly across the street from Reuters' former office on Sixth Avenue, now the company's computer center. Occasionally they would eat. Mostly they talked, scribbling diagrams on table napkins as they went along. Years later, Nagel remembered the routine if not the particulars. "We'd have three-, sometimes four-hour lunches. Pretty liquid, too. Glen was used to it, of course, but I wasn't. Sometimes I could hardly walk back to the office."

The spellbinding became mutual. Nagel was soon an unabashed Renfrew admirer. Puffing up with pride, he recalled that Renfrew used to tell everyone, "Bob Nagel is the most brilliant technical person I've ever met."

Des Maberley could only fume at this blossoming infatuation. "This will all end in tears, you mark my words." Maberley's misgivings were ignored as those of a jilted lover.

To Maberley's horror, Renfrew decided that he wanted Dr. Bob and his row-grabber on board full-time. Nagel himself was no less keen, which may explain why he settled for a modest cash payment of $180,000 for his company and his invention, an amount that was promptly applied to the purchase of Nagel's 20 percent interest in a new venture. The other 80 percent went to Reuters, minus a few shares awarded to Vurpillat for making the introduction. (Vurpillat hung around for a year but moved on to become technical director of Telerate, a fledgling money-market system. Of Telerate, more later.)

Nagel was hired at a salary less reflective of brilliance than—as he put it— "commensurate with my modest needs." Even Nagel, for all his enthusiasm, at first balked at the deal, looking for more equity. But Phil Siegel, Reuters' in-house attorney, was adamant that Reuters needed 80 percent in order, he explained, to consolidate the figures on the parent company's books. When Nagel continued to hold out for more, Siegel, not among the more retiring practitioners in a profession not known for its reticence, became relentless in pursuit. Siegel, armed with mollifying reassurances and a wily affectation of charm, in Nagel's phrase, "worked me over good." In the end, Siegel's line of attack appealed to Nagel's vanity. "Let's not argue about trifles, Bob. Look, when this is a $100 million company, which it will be a year or two from now, you'll have $20 million in the bank." Nagel was no businessman, as Siegel recognized. Tired of the interminable meetings, he caved in. "To be honest, I barely remember signing the papers."

Before many years were over he would be serving them.

The company was formed in March 1973 and baptized with the title, aptly contrived on a bar-room napkin, Information Dissemination and Retrieval Inc.—an acronym for "I Drink." The name prompted much mirth in New York, but not in London. Benjamin, among others, considered it an ominous augury of impending disaster.

Renfrew's first cable initiative, a product called NewsView, had been launched a year earlier. A soufflé of news summaries, sports results, and horoscopes, it was designed with no greater ambition than to give CATV operators a schedule filler, and to stimulate appetites for the kind of sophisticated information Reuters might provide in the future. If nothing else, it gave employment to teletype operators displaced by video-editing.

At a monthly subscription of $250 per month, less than that of the teleprinter services, the revenue generated by NewsView was risible but enough to further the careers of Renfrew's favorite marketing executives, Peter Holland and Harvey Cooper. At a beanpole six-feet-three-inches and a stocky five-feet-six, respectively, they brought to mind the British comedy team of Peter Cook and Dudley Moore. Inseparable and indefatigable, they crisscrossed the continent in search of CATV deals like a pair of doorstep Bible salesmen. They managed to secure a score or more contracts—an achievement of sorts, but, as Joe Daffin acidly pointed out, it didn't even cover the Holland-Cooper expense claims. Holland-Cooper's most notable deal, or at any rate the most visible, was to supply Reuters news to the famous rotating news ticker in New York's Times Square. Tourists, tramps, and hookers no doubt enjoyed the show but, to borrow from the local vernacular, it hardly made the Reuters soup fat.

NewsView had merely been the appetizer. The time had come for the main course.

IDR opened a factory to produce Nagel's row-grabber terminals in Farmingdale, a dormitory community on Long Island, about fifty miles from New York City. Cyril Smith, who lived in a neighboring suburb, was placed in charge as office manager. The key job, that of production supervisor, was Dave Russell, who saw it as a chance to prove the superiority of Renfrew-inspired, American-based technology over Nelson-Benjamin's ill-conceived European Monitor.

Gerry Long and other dignitaries flew in from London for the Grand Opening. Some were openly determined to be unimpressed. As one visitor pointed out, IDR was located next to an amusement park, implying that the two functions might soon become indistinguishable. Gerry Long's chief complaint was about the food at a nearby restaurant. His enthusiasm for IDR and row-grabber seemed hardly more ardent. He later described his attitude as one of "resigned hopefulness." What that meant, if it meant anything, was that, "I'd put Renfrew in charge of the American operation. Nobody else had done anything with it. I was therefore prepared to go along with his decisions. I had every confidence that Glen could do the job." The truth is that Long simply lacked the knowledge or the intuition to question either the foray into cable television, or the venture into manufacturing.

One visitor, Peter Benjamin, displayed no such diffidence. In fact, his lack of confidence in IDR was palpable. Although he quietly admired Renfrew, and found Nelson's limited grasp of technology "disconcerting," in the combination of IDR, Nagel, and cable television he saw a triple risk to the company's hard-won success with Monitor, and rarely held back from saying so. The question that most preoccupied him was not whether the venture could possibly succeed—though he clearly had doubts on that score—but whether Renfrew, in pursuit of revolution, was capable of controlling his own daredevil impulses. Or those of Nagel, whom Benjamin, like many others, considered recklessly disengaged from reality. "Don't worry about Nagel," Maberley reassured Benjamin, and anyone else who would listen. "We may need him now, but once he's served his short-term purpose he'll be expendable. I'll personally see to that."

As far as London was concerned, American megalomania and conceit were busy doing the Devil's work. It was an attitude suffused with fear, too, at least among the Nelson crowd, particularly when Renfrew made it clear that row-grabbing was a technique he felt could and should be exported to the rest of the world.

Anxious to avoid accusations of technology envy, Nelson asked a young project executive, David Ure, to take a look at the potential for cable television in Europe. "Nothing doing now, or in the near future," was Ure's conclusion, about which he was precociously vocal. Ure's finding gave fresh impetus to London's protests that a huge bet—no less than Reuters' future—had been placed on technology that was not only untested in the United States but unusable everywhere else.

From London's perspective, IDR was not the only bad news. Some weeks before the company opened for business, Reuters' executive committee had convened in New York City. With an ostentatious pronouncement presumably designed as a local morale-booster, Long proclaimed that Reuters North America and Reuters Europe would henceforth be regarded as the twin—and equal—pillars of the corporate establishment.

Renfrew now had his seat at the top table, and the two-horse race for the succession was on in earnest, pitting Risky Technology, a formidable sprinter when the going was firm, against Outmoded Concept, a dogged "stayer" in heavy conditions.

My own role in IDR was relatively brief and insignificant. For a while—it seemed an eternity at the time—I was assigned to work with Nagel in creating what is known in the trade as a ticker plant, essentially an information-processing engine. Named "the Quote System," it was designed to take in, and pump out over Reuters' network, prices from every stock and commodity exchange in the world, alongside news and contributed data from Monitor. Nagel blithely promised "a ticker a week." A year into the project, we were still missing key exchanges. It was a grueling experience hardly worth recalling in any of its details, except perhaps one. After one particularly exasperating day— of which there were many—I threatened to throw Nagel out of the office window. In case there were repercussions, I mentioned the incident to Maberley.

"I wish you had," was his only comment.

Part of the problem was that Nagel presided over a band of programmers and developers who were even stranger and more volatile than he was. A number of them were Scientologists, which I found vaguely disquieting. Some, working the night shift, used to sleep in the office on soiled mattresses. Others worked through the night at Reuters before disappearing at sunrise to work in day jobs. Many were itinerants, who would drift in for a few days and then disappear. Some seemed to be on the verge of a nervous breakdown. Nagel and his dysfunctional acolytes were still struggling to complete the project when, mercifully, I was taken off the job and assigned to Monitor.

The Quote System had been my first intimate exposure to technology and its peculiar adherents. The experience had been invaluable, if only for instilling in me a profound skepticism about promises of delivery dates made by developers.

Equally frustrated by the delays, Maberley felt triumphantly vindicated. "I've been telling Glen all along this man is a charlatan. We'll be lucky if we have a service out in our working lifetime." In Maberley's favorite catchphrase, it all amounted to a case of "monumental complacency"—a refrain he rolled out randomly as the reason for anything that went wrong in any project, including those for which he himself had management responsibility. The buck, it seemed, never stopped at Maberley's uncluttered desk, or in an uncluttered mind. Complacency, monumental or otherwise, had nothing to do with it. The root of the problem was Renfrew's monumental ambition, which had placed onerous responsibilities on subordinates who, from naïve enthusiasm or overwhelming self-interest, had bitten off far more than they could chew.

Getting information into row-grabber was nothing compared to getting the product to market.

Nick Nicholas, Sterling's president (and a future chief executive of Time Inc.) had reserved an entire channel for delivering Renfrew's financial services and promised the full weight of his considerable organization to support it. Nicholas, like Renfrew, was a hard-driving visionary, equally intrigued by the possibilities in the convergence of coaxial cable and financial information. It was another dangerous liaison, replete with mutual admiration developed over many a Manhattan dinner, and much talk of the potential for joint ventures on a global scale, sponsored by two of the most famous names in the information industry. But first, there was the minor matter of conquering New York City.

In December 1974, the Reuters-Sterling initiative was launched at a press conference and reception in Time-Life's executive offices. Time Inc.'s president, James Shepley, and Gerry Long acted as joint masters of ceremonies. Nagel had proudly invited his father, the former newspaper editor, and introduced him to Shepley and other Time dignitaries. Even Long, no lover of New York or admirer of the American predilection for hooplah—and rarely at his best on such occasions—seemed to be swept up in the euphoria.

But even as the celebrations were taking place, the Renfrew-Nicholas vision of world hegemony through cable was already unraveling under the streets of Manhattan. The fact is that while many of New York City's streets were cabled, many of the buildings occupied by Reuters' prospective clients were not. Without wired buildings, Sterling's cable network was a subway system without stations. From the start, the presumption had been that cabling buildings would be a simple task—a simple matter of mechanics. So, in the strictly technical sense, it should have been. But the Devil lurked in the detail, and the Devil had manifold tricks to spring on the over-confident. His disciples included Manhattan building-managers and supervisors—not, some would argue, among the more imaginative or enlightened humans on the planet. Many proved reluctant to countenance the work involved, if for no other reason than that cabling meant disrupting their daily routines. Others professed a readiness to cooperate, but only in exchange for under-the-table compensation, something that should not have come as a shock to those acquainted with the mercenary instincts of their trade, especially as practiced in New York City.

The most serious problem was the prospect of having to negotiate with Local 6 of the electrical workers' union. Local 6 could be bypassed or ignored, but only at some peril. Disputes with Local 6 had been known to end with the mysterious severing of cables or, if the union's methods were anywhere near as unorthodox as they were reputed to be, even an occasional human limb.

The task of dealing with such bureaucratic impediments was assigned at Reuters to Harold Leblang, head of sales administration. A long-time Comtelburo employee, Leblang's sole but essential qualification for the task was that he was a street-smart New Yorker. His principal negotiating weapon was a secret stash of high-denomination bills, a "contingent reserve" to be used for the greasing of palms—for which the Yiddish term widely used locally was the "shmeer." The cash was kept in his office in a padlocked black box. A salesman once referred to it as "Harold's Special Assistant." A visiting London executive got to know of it. He shuddered at the thought. "This is most irregular. I shall pretend I've never seen it."

Back in Fleet Street he was less reticent. With the Watergate scandal unfolding to reveal the myriad financial shenanigans practiced by operatives of CREEP—the Campaign to Re-elect the President—he felt obliged to report to Nelson that Renfrew was running a secret slush fund.

Facilitated by Leblang's largesse, the row-grabber sales campaign brought a steady increase in the number of terminals installed, but the numbers fell short of spectacular. The project, it soon became clear, was not going to be anywhere near the transforming vehicle that Renfrew had promised. The cash demands of IDR continued unabated. By way of unwelcome contrast, Monitor's revenues were now climbing steadily. But not steadily enough.

Desperate for short-term relief, Renfrew ordered a 10 percent price increase for the printer services. "We'll get a rash of cancellations," Joe Daffin warned. The suspicion was that Renfrew secretly wanted a decline in printer revenue in order to make row-grabber's contribution to revenue look relatively healthy. If so, the result was disappointing. There were few defections and row-grabber remained North America's financial millstone.

Worse still, at a time when it could ill afford the slightest setback, row-grabber started to come under fire from clients because of poor response times. With ever-increasing volumes of data moving along Nagel's pipeline of supposedly limitless capacity, row-grabber was starting to suffer severe bouts of indigestion. Quotron and Bunker Ramo, using conventional technology, had no such problems, as perplexed clients who had switched to Reuters were at pains to point out. If competitors could deliver their services anywhere in the United States, and without all the paraphernalia involved in cabling buildings or installing receiving dishes, why couldn't Reuters?

Sales executives could only squirm with embarrassment. Disillusionment was widespread downtown. Morale was hardly buoyant out on the Island, either. Farmingdale's underworked assembly workers, many only recently hired, now faced layoffs. In short, the unthinkable was now common currency. Although Renfrew and Maberley could scarcely bring themselves to admit it, in every corner of the company the word was that, without a drastic improvement in business, row-grabber was approaching the beginning of its end rather than the end of its beginning.

There was trouble even in the ranks of Renfrew's once loyally unquestioning Praetorian Guard. Maberley, Smith, Nagel, Russell, Daffin, and Cooper-Holland had all had virtually taken an oath of fealty. (Hull and I had failed to swear allegiance because we'd never been invited to. And we had, in any case, become too closely identified with the hated Monitor.)

An unpleasant spectacle now unfolded. The Praetorians began to utter, at least in private, the once unutterable: that Renfrew, in his desire to succeed—and to succeed Long—might have overstepped the mark. What had never apparently occurred to any of them was that blind loyalty was not enough, that what Renfrew most needed to make the project succeed was something they were unqualified to offer: sound advice and an occasional restraining voice. Affection for Renfrew in New York now evaporated in an atmosphere poisoned by recrimination, including whispered complaints that Renfrew had somehow ungratefully let his team down.

Nagel was among the disaffected. Disillusioned and exhausted, he quit in a huff and promptly sued for breach of contract. (He would settle out of court for reclamation of the equity value he'd put in originally and, curiously, he remained an unreconstructed Renfrew admirer.) Holland-Cooper, the ultimate Renfrew acolytes, committed the ultimate betrayal by decamping to London to work for Nelson. Even Maberley ran out of platitudes to explain the disaster. He stuck around, even after Renfrew had moved on, but only to fester in his own embitterment, which increasingly found its focus in Renfrew's shortcomings. Daffin, close to retirement, meekly accepted a lateral "promotion" and the ignominy of being replaced by Alan Jackson, a Nelson disciple who had been "parked" in Chicago to await his triumphal entry into New York. Even the ever-loyal Dave Russell left in high dudgeon after Renfrew refused to sell him what was left of IDR, which, in order to stay afloat and in the ultimate irony, was reduced to assembling equipment for Monitor.

The cliché that Maberley perhaps should have trotted out more often was Paul Julius Reuter's old axiom: "Follow the cable." Renfrew, it can be argued, had been too busy trying to outrun it.

Meanwhile, Monitor was succeeding beyond Reuters' wildest expectations. Global revenue piled up to the extent that the original projections were made to look embarrassingly understated. Not that anybody felt in the least embarrassed.

Monitor had effectively changed the customs of the trading community and the landscape of the dealing room. Many traders were now prepared to acknowledge that Monitor, even if it had reduced trading margins, had more than compensated by increasing business volumes. Contributors of quotes admitted that the service had enhanced the reputations of their banks. Some lesser names had started to be known by their Monitor page codes.

European Banking Company in London, for example, dominated the trading market in the pound sterling for years through the simple expedient of keeping its Monitor page, EBCO, consistently updated with good "dealable" rates. David Mitchem, the chief dealer, boasted at a Forex meeting that, "We tripled our business within six months of going on Monitor."

Another beneficiary was Berliner Handelsbank in Frankfurt (Monitor page BHFX). A virtually unknown institution, once unable to compete with Germany's "Big Three" of Deutsche Bank, Dresdner Bank, and Commerzbank, BHF used Monitor to become the reference point for trading German marks. "We are the market in marks," BHF's chief trader, Richard Spanner, could plausibly claim.

What happened to the grave concerns about loss of transparency and

184

shrinking margins—and above all the feared market-domination by an alien institution? They simply dissolved in the foreign-exchange trading boom that followed the end of Bretton Woods. A growing number of traders could scarcely remember a market in which quotes were not derived from screens. All of which was curious because, in reality, all those early fears had been realized. The market had become Monitor, and Monitor had become the market. And Reuters could soon claim without blushing that it was richer than most of its customers.

Traders still wondered out loud about where Monitor might take the market next, but this time around with no dread of the consequences. They were still wedded to their telex machines for international dealing, but thoughts at Reuters turned increasingly to what would have been, a few years earlier, unthinkable: that Monitor, or some modified version of it, might be used to transact business as well as display prices.

In April 1975, André Villeneuve felt confident enough to produce a paper entitled "Reuter Monitor Dealing Feasibility Study." A canned dealing program involving a conversational routine that simulated a typical two-way telex communication was shown to a select group of Monitor customers, and with none of the grave shaking of heads that had accompanied the early Monitor demonstrations two years earlier.

Only one dealer voiced a serious objection. Pointing to a row of mini-skirted and well-proportioned young ladies employed to operate the telex machines along the back wall of his dealing room, he asked: "How can I possibly replace them?"

The principal objections came, oddly enough, from within Reuters, from executives who perceived danger in dragging the company away from its role as an information provider into a potentially dangerous involvement with the intimate functions of the marketplace. Nelson himself was known to have certain misgivings. But, just as he had once believed that Stockmaster and Videomaster might be threatened by more advanced products, he was now ready to believe that Monitor as purely an information vehicle might be usurped by a competitor offering execution capability.

Such a service had already emerged in the United States: Tafex, an auto-mated matching system for foreign exchange. Tafex was financed—hence the title—by Transamerica Corporation, an assertive California-based conglomerate with interests in the insurance and motion picture industries.

Tafex induced a momentary spasm of panic in London and New York. John Hull and I were among the concerned, perhaps the most concerned of all. We were both confirmed "matchers" and it occurred to us that Reuters, in order to retain its market position, had no choice but to get into the transaction business, either under its own steam or by entering into some kind of collaboration. Possibly even with Tafex. Most of our colleagues thought otherwise. The market wasn't quite ready for matching.

Or was it?

# Defection

All good things must come to an end.

Early in 1978, that consoling platitude—often trotted out after a busted romance—danced baleful attendance on my fading affair with Reuters. The estrangement was neither sudden nor acrimonious, more a slow and silent unraveling, which at some indefinable moment became irreversible.

Even so, it was wrenching to find myself at odds with the company to which I had gratefully donated a professional lifetime, and perhaps a vital organ or two in the process. Reuters' New York management contributed to my distress by adopting an attitude of stony indifference. I did not take it personally. Nor did I assume that it was personally intended. The fact is that, with every fresh manifestation of the collapse of IDR, Reuters North America descended a little further into despondency, and its management deeper into aphasia—an affliction exacerbated by Des Maberley's promiscuous recriminations and the sound of gloating laughter borne westward across the Atlantic.

To borrow Dean Acheson's wounding aphorism, RNA had started to resemble the country that had lost an empire but had yet to find a role.

Even a man of such prodigious intellectual vigor as Glen Renfrew seemed suddenly drained of inspiration. Without his commitment and drive, the division recently designated as one of the company's three global pillars was reduced once more to little more than a remote frontier outpost. To round off the imperial analogy, history seemed on the verge of repeating itself, the colonists once more managing to humble the invading redcoats, and the British again offering the impression that they would rather call it a day than impose themselves any further.

As one London cynic observed, RNA was now often translated at 85 Fleet Street as Rather Not America.

My own disaffection was not with Reuters itself but with its North American management. By neglecting to define its own purpose, RNA was also failing to define mine. Not once during our eighteen-year association had the company given me the slightest cause for ingratitude. That early promise of "a career in news with opportunities for overseas travel" had been satisfied in full as far as I was concerned. And if I had failed to scale the commanding heights of journalism—some would characterize reporting for a financial wire service as no greater elevation than base camp—I had managed to climb higher than had ever seemed possible, frankly much higher than I thought my editorial talents warranted.

Anyway, having emerged unscathed from the minor crisis described in the previous chapter, I was now embarked on a marketing career which, enhanced by Monitor's growing success in America, seemed poised to flourish. Some damned fool in 85 Fleet Street had even identified me as a marketing executive of promise. That, ironically, only served to contribute to my sense of disenfranchisement.

This transatlantic admirer was John Albanie. He telephoned one day to say that he had me in mind for a job in Europe. "We could use some American experience over here, and some Yankee aggression," was the way he put it. The position he had in mind for me was managing Europe's southern region, one of three territories he was creating as part of a European restructuring, a plan hatched by Albanie on his return from an advanced management course at Harvard.

Albanie was the first marketing executive at Reuters worthy of the term. It was hardly a pivotal role, management's attitude to marketing falling considerably short of wholehearted. Moreover, given the prevailing corporate custom of judging competence on the basis of company allegiances, Albanie was disadvantaged in London by being firmly identified as Renfrew's, as opposed to Nelson's, man. Albanie's understandable response was that he was his own man—and to hell with office politics. Although I cared nothing for his political stripe, whatever that might be, I also had no means of judging either his competence or his authority, both of which would be crucial elements in considering a move. I expressed a strong interest anyway. Albanie's response was to ask Nelson to approach Renfrew about my "availability."

Flattering as it was to be held in such warm esteem, I found it hard, in my winter of discontent, to discern the prospect of a glorious summer to come. I'm not sure why. The career dilemma—Europe or America—was hardly an agonizing one. A return to Europe in a brand-new post offered certain attractions, not only the prospect of tooling around the sun-drenched playgrounds of the Mediterranean but also an opportunity to parade my newly minted talents around head office, from which I had been absent for ten eventful years. But neither was it hard to imagine a few more years in New York, especially since John Hull and I were planning to use Monitor to launch a bold assault on the American bond market, the largest and most influential of its kind in the world.

My indecision was shortly resolved by Mike Nelson's note to Renfrew, a copy of which fell into my hands by complex and illicit means. It struck me as a masterpiece of calculated ambiguity, typical of its author. Nelson devalued the European opportunity, at least in my eyes, by his less-than-ardent endorsement of Albanie's proposed restructuring, and undermined it further by adopting a neutral stance on my prospective role in it. Even allowing for

Nelson's limpid prose style, the tone was disconcerting. The note concluded by invoking the company's unwritten edict against "poaching" and ceded the decision on my transfer entirely to Renfrew, the only person in a position to say whether RNA could afford to dispense with my services.

All of which left me rather uncomfortably wedged between a rock and a hard place—that is to say, between Nelson's frosty detachment and Renfrew's anger over what would be seen as my treacherous flirtation with the enemy. As a result, I found it hard to summon much enthusiasm for either job.

New York won the day, at least for the time being. Better Renfrew's wrath, I decided, than Nelson's disdain.

My quandary, I should mention, had a personal as well as a professional dimension, a failing second marriage adding personal complexity to professional ambivalence. I refer to the domestic matter only because it portended the dissipation of my net worth, such as it was. This in turn amplified a nagging anxiety to attain a greater degree of financial security than the "decent" salary Reuters paid me. I had already started to consider where and how I could earn "serious" moolah, in an environment in which the opportunities for wealth accumulation, especially in the field of information, seemed ever more dazzling. My conclusion was that such wealth could only be derived from equity ownership, or at the very least from some form of bonus or profit-sharing scheme.

At Reuters, neither seemed a realistic proposition. For all the attempts to re-brand itself, the company remained, both structurally and in the minds of its shareholders, a cooperative news agency. Although Monitor's accelerating income meant that profitability was no longer a chimera, consistently rising profits over a period of some years would be required if Reuters' owners were to be persuaded to cash-in by offering shares in the company.

Would such a flotation ever be possible? Who, in Reuters' complex ownership structure, was in a position to make that kind of recommendation? And how would the owners deal with the controversy that would certainly erupt over the protective 1941 Trust? Such questions were rarely asked in 1978. It was widely assumed that the company was forever "protected" by the Trust and, therefore, forever confined in its traditional role as a handmaiden of the British press.

What were the views of management? Whether the flotation issue was ever discussed informally in the executive suite at the time is unclear. Reuters' future structure had certainly exercised a few minds from time to time, Renfrew's for one. Although I never heard him mention the "F" word, he had occasionally mentioned, albeit in vague terms, the prospects for some kind of executive incentive scheme, possibly even one involving some kind of stake in the company's profits. Renfrew claimed that this was something he was "always working on"—though to be fair he also made clear that it was not something that should be regarded as anything but a long-term prospect. Nelson's viewpoint in such matters at the time is unknown. The man of caution would surely have been inclined to wait for some kind of cue from Long. As for Long himself, he had no recollection, years later, that the subject had been given any kind of airing. He added that, even if it had, he, too, would probably have adopted a passive stance on the arguable grounds that "such issues would have been for the owners, not management, to decide."

Deprived of the imminent prospect of commissions or bonuses, let alone stock options, my professional aspirations began to wander from a desire to merely continue clambering up Reuters' greasy pole to getting attached instead to some dynamic American enterprise more overtly committed to capitalist principles. In short, a thirst for wealth and a craving for adventure had led me to imagine what had once seemed unimaginable: a career outside Mother Reuters.

Two convergent developments brought me down off the fence on which I had been happily and comfortably seated. The first was the appearance of Tafex, the foreign-exchange transaction service briefly mentioned in the last chapter. The second was the internal plan to take Reuters into the American government-bond market. Our intention, Hull's and mine, was to turn Monitor into the same cathartic force in that market as it had become in foreign exchange, which meant confronting Telerate, the pesky newcomer he and I had first encountered at Salomon Brothers.

To my mind, Tafex had amply demonstrated the required functional attributes for a "matching" system—that is to say a system that matched bids and offers and, provided certain preconditions were met, converted the match into an electronic transaction. Hull and I, having seen the system in action, were convinced that Tafex, or something like it, had a very significant future. We had observed the fear in the eyes of traders who had seen it work. That told us that it worked only too well. As for Telerate, that product was now beginning to occupy by stealth and by default the very market on which we believed Reuters ought to be casting an avaricious eye.

This appetite for conquest was not something shared by our colleagues. There was no surprise there; isolation was a condition to which we were becoming disagreeably accustomed. Joe Daffin was prepared to go along with taking Reuters into what he called "the matching lark," though not to the extent of helping us sell the idea to Renfrew. It would have been a futile exercise anyway. For as Daffin never tired of pointing out, Renfrew had made it abundantly clear, in the interests of balancing RNA's budget, that he would be hostile to any post-cable initiative unless it was capable of producing instant, cost-free, and copious revenue. A tall, not to say impossible order.

In any event, the received wisdom around Reuters was that both Tafex and Telerate were doomed to failure. Both products had made too many enemies in their respective markets. In that case why not just let them fail? Why not indeed? But surely Reuters ought to have some constructive plan of its own. Doing nothing seemed a dismal option. Yet that, as far as Hull and I could see, was precisely what was contemplated. This negative view of the world begged the obvious and fundamental question: if Reuters had no interest in what its competitors were doing, or in the markets in which they were doing it, what exactly was the company's role in North America supposed to be? Answers came there none.

Undaunted, Hull and I spent a weekend putting together a strategic business document, if only for what we suspected would be our own amusement. Its focus, taking a long-term view, was almost entirely on the notion of introducing automated dealing products. The opening line went something like this: "Within ten years, most financial trading will be conducted on a 'black box.' " The term "black box," with its rather sinister resonance, was at the time a generic reference to trading by computer. The report was intended to be provocative. It succeeded to the extent of provoking incredulity. "Mmm, interesting," Maberley muttered with a thoughtful frown designed to convey the impression that he had actually read it. "Bit ambitious, don't you think? Why not something simpler, a product we can launch right now?"

"Abracadabra," I said ironically, waving a pencil as a simulated wand.

"What about this Monitor government-bond service you both keep going on about?" It was already underway, I replied, mentioning, however, that we had no budget for it.

"Now, you know very well how tight things are right now," Maberley retorted, "especially after all the recent foolishness. You'll just have to make do."

"Making do" was a phrase that evoked distant memories of my mother's frugal economic stewardship during the harsh post-war years of food rationing. At least she had an excuse. I suppose Maberely had an excuse too, RNA's make-do approach having been imposed by its parlous financial condition. Even so, the aversion to prudent risk-taking only served to feed my nagging doubts about Reuters' commitment to the world's largest capital market. It mocked Reuters' brave decision a decade earlier to go its own way in the United States. Renfrew's misfortunes in Cable Land had at least repre-sented a desire to do something venturesome, however foolhardy in hindsight. The "period of consolidation" that Maberley now proposed, drawing from his vast thesaurus of lugubrious clichés, was a perfect example of the "monumental complacency" he affected to despise. An affectation it was, too, for even monumentally complacent executives in Fleet Street were bestirring themselves to investigate some form of dealing system designed to protect Monitor's hard-won market position.

Hull's verdict after the Maberley meeting was succinct: "We're wasting our fucking breath here." We had, anyway, an alternative plan. We would take our proposal to Tafex.

Tafex, the first attempt at so-called "black box" trading, started to appear in foreign-exchange trading rooms in the United States late in 1975. With only forty users installed at the end of that year, mostly among regional banks, the company could hardly claim to have inspired a revolution. But the threat it posed to Monitor was not to be taken lightly—or so Hull and I believed. Our New York colleagues, though, dismissed the prospect of a Tafex breakthrough the moment its leading columns bumped into the Maginot Line erected by our old friends Van Roten and LeClerc. But hadn't Monitor's own campaign faltered in its early days? And hadn't the same New York banks now trying to repulse Tafex once tried to thwart Reuters? Yes, they had. Even Nelson, in a note endorsing Reuters' nascent dealing initiative, had warned of complacency. "We believe that if a successful dealing system were established by another organization it might make Reuters Monitor redundant."

By "another organization" he presumably meant one of substance. The category would certainly have included the organization behind Tafex, Transamerica Corporation, a financial services conglomerate with impressive resources.

Monitor's redundancy was, of course, Transamerica's primary objective. Taking a leaf from the Monitor marketing manual, Tafex had made a beeline for the regional banks and achieved some early successes. But the out-of-towners, though confronted with yet another opportunity to loosen New York's iron grip on the foreign-exchange market, this time responded disappointingly. Despite their contribution to Monitor's breakthrough, when Tafex came along, most meekly reverted to accepting their second-class status. It was a "pragmatic reality," Kathleen Zeider of Cleveland Central National Bank, told *Institutional Investor*, which in March 1976 had featured an article highlighting "the battle for supremacy in the foreign-exchange market." "If there is [a quote] in the market," Zeider was quoted as saying, "the obvious tendency if you're a broker is to show it to somebody like Morgan before you show it to an out-of-town bank that's one-tenth the size of Morgan. You're not going to be in business very long if you don't give better service to your higher-volume customers." Richard Stogdill, head trader at American National Bank of Chicago, wearily agreed. "If I go in with the best bid and a big bank comes along behind me with a bid for twice my amount, the chances are his trade will get done before mine. It's something you just have to live with."

There was no denying certain realities. The underlying appeal of Tafex was another leveler of the playing field and was therefore, like Monitor, bound to excite controversy. And as a trading system, Tafex had an entirely more difficult operating imperative from one that merely delivered information. To be effective, a matching product must provide deep and constant liquidity, displaying not just indicative prices, but quotes on which contributing banks are prepared to deal in large volumes, at all times. The regional banks alone simply could not generate sufficient volume to support such a system. What it boiled down to, then, was that Tafex had to break, as Monitor had once broken, the collective will of the Bobbies and their cronies.

Tafex executives, therefore, steeled themselves for a relentless campaign of subversion and sabotage compared with which the anti-Monitor campaign had been merely a warm-up. It was this potential for drama that *Institutional Investor* recognized in its story in March 1976 about a market the author described as "largely invisible and shrouded in mystery." Although short on revelations, the story shook the New York banks rigid. Particularly upset were the two Bobbies, who were depicted in an accompanying caricature with arms folded, wearing expressions of grim determination, evidently spoiling for a fight.

The article itself failed to raise many smiles, either. *Institutional Investor* got straight to the point: "Tafex threatens to shake the market to its foundations and revolutionize the way in which foreign exchange is traded, both in New York and eventually in other markets around the world. The immediate consequence could be a surge of competition and liquidity and a much more open market for out-of-town banks and the thousands of corporations that depend on the New York market to handle their foreign currency dealings."

Fred Meer, founder and chief executive of Tafex, was among the few who welcomed the story, which may have generated more interest in his product than could have been derived from a series of full-page advertisements in the *Wall Street Journal*. Meer was the driving force behind Tafex. He had formed the company after leaving his job as head of currency trading at American Express Bank, which counted Transamerica among its important corporate clients. Meer was not a man to suffer fools gladly, and he had made precious few friends during his trading years. He retained even fewer after the launch of Tafex. As one trader put it, Meer had never been "one of us." The inference was that a cultured, opera-loving, middle-aged, Jewish, intellectual, uptown Manhattanite didn't quite fit the bill in a community dominated stereotypically by raucous, beer-guzzling, pizza-lunching, Italian-American, New York Rangers fans from Brooklyn and Staten Island. "What kind of trader turns on his own kind like that?" wondered one affronted Rangers fan, probably speaking for the majority. "He's always looked down his nose at the rest of us, but I never figured the bastard would try to put us all out of business."

If it was from the ranks of such affronted mortals that Tafex was supposed to attract devotees, then the acerbic Fred Meer was decidedly not the man to do it. Sensibly, he decided to locate his company and its computer center in the leafy environs of Trumbull, Connecticut rather than downtown Manhattan where he would have risked daily encounters with his protagonists.

Meer may not have charmed his peers, but he had obviously done a number selling the Tafex idea to Transamerica's chairman, John Beckett, himself reputedly not a man overly endowed with patience. Meer's proposition was that Tafex could one day become the foreign-exchange equivalent of NASDAQ, the automated system for trading over-the-counter securities. Intrigued, Beckett accepted the challenge and placed the project under the supervision of Kent Colwell, an up-and-coming Transamerica executive with a pedigree in mortgage banking.

The crucial issue was whether the quiet-spoken Colwell, unacquainted with the rough-and-tumble world of currency trading, would have the resolve to weather the storm of abuse he could expect from the trading community. Only time would tell, and Colwell did not have a lot of it.

"You've got two years to make it work," Beckett told him.

Meer had no problem with that. "The market's just waiting for something like this," he assured Colwell.

Waiting in ambush, as it turned out.

Hull and I felt it only proper to warn André Villeneuve about the Tafex threat. He seemed unfazed. Although he and his colleagues had never displayed any great enthusiasm for computerized trading, neither had they ever evinced any deep-rooted philosophical objections. Indeed, Villeneuve and Ransom, in their original 1972 paper on Monitor, had alluded to the possibility of Reuters itself introducing automated trading. "It is possible," they had written, "that there will be scope in the medium term for a matching service to be introduced in the money market on the lines of the AutEx and BAS block share information services in the United States."

The paper described in general terms both the trading process and the marketing issues, and in enough detail to indicate that considerable thought had been given to it. "Potential buyers and sellers of money would insert messages into the central memory, which would then attempt to match. A potential match having been achieved, the lender would be advised of the borrower's name, and, if he wished, would then trade through the system. The additional advantages over the money retrieval service we are proposing are that users can not only obtain information but also deal, thus cutting extra costs. The objections are that the AutEx principle may not be fast enough for many types of foreign-exchange and money-market operations, that it would be a much more revolutionary step for the money market community to accept and therefore take longer to launch and have accepted, and would be more demanding in terms of equipment needed."

From the subsequent discussions between Villeneuve and his colleagues there emerged an idea for a dealing product, but not a matching device. The alternative favored was a system that would allow traders to conduct two-way conversations over what would essentially be an electronic replica of their beloved telex machines. Nelson, true to form, set up a Dealing Committee with a mandate to specify and implement the project. Presumably as a political sop to Renfrew, I was elected to the panel to represent the North American viewpoint. In the absence of firm instructions from local management, Hull and I brazenly used the position to advocate "black box" solutions, much to the annoyance of the other members of the team, and especially of David Ure, the committee's chairman, and Nelson's choice to manage the project. I was soon marginalized.

Ure was a tall, dour Scot with a permanent hangdog expression and a mordant sense of humor. His appointment marked him as a man destined for high office. The burden of expectation rested heavily on those permanently hunched shoulders. Of distinctly nervous disposition, brought about perhaps by a desperate desire to please his mentor, Ure deployed a career-conscious aversion to personal risk. This mania for caution was constantly undermined by a passion for calculated indiscretions. These, no sooner uttered, were vigorously denied. They became known affectionately as Ure-isms. "Let me tell you something in the strictest confidence," Ure would whisper, "but I shall deny it if you tell anyone you heard it from me." Such "confidences" were as often as not imparted to so many people that they soon became an open secret around the company. He was inordinately fond of political intrigue: "Privately I agree with you, but publicly I'm afraid I must take the opposite view. If you reveal this I shall, of course, disclaim it."

Protecting such indiscretions fostered in Ure considerable angst, which often verged on paranoia. It may have been one of the reasons why he suffered more or less permanently from severe stomach cramps. Ure's edgy depressions were palpable. When agitated he became a walking exposition of lisps, twitches, grimaces, and other peculiar mannerisms. Of the latter, the most persistent—at any rate the most disconcerting—was an incessant and vigorous massaging of what we shall politely refer to as the groin area. It earned him the nickname "Scratcher."

Ure's manifold eccentricities bestowed a fame of sorts: he became the most popular subject for the company's many consummate impressionists. He himself, incidentally, was no slouch in the other direction. Ure was mortified to learn of his dubious renown. "How can anyone possibly impersonate me?" he once asked me, hands kneading away industriously inside his pants. "I've got no obvious mannerisms. Have I? You would tell me, of course, wouldn't you?"

On the subject of matching, Ure's views were not eccentric. He was, in a word, skeptical—a view shared by the other two London-based members of the Dealing Committee. Of this unmatched pair, the more vocal was flame-haired Jack Wigan, elected to represent European opinion. Bluff Jack, as he was known to some, was a man of staunch opinions on every subject under the sun. In more than a few ways he was Ure's precise counterpoint: self-assured, in-your-face abrasive, openly ambitious, and rather lacking in humor. The quieter of the two was Steve Dawson, recently recruited from a well-known consulting firm, and seconded to the Dealing Committee to represent the technology aspects of the project. Non-confrontational and reserved, he came across as something of a cold fish, with opinions only on those topics susceptible to mathematical logic.

The collective verdict of the Ure-Wigan-Dawson axis was clear from the start. Tafex was at least a decade before its time and as a product it was poorly conceived. Furthermore, its marketing program was seriously flawed. On the first two counts I disagreed vehemently. On the third we were, all three, in complete agreement, the conclusion being indisputable. I readily conceded that Tafex might fail, given the clumsy way Tafex had gone about its task, but that failed to nullify my essential opinion, which was that Reuters' evaluation of its future ought to be founded on something more tangible and profound than some other company's cock-up. No doubt the Wright brothers' first crude attempts at defying gravity prompted some observers to conclude that flight was impossible. We were drawing the same conclusion about automated trading simply by watching in delight as Fred Meer crashed and burned.

Wigan jumped in with both feet. We were doing no such thing. The market was not ready for matching, and that was that. Such absolutism was positively Procrustean, Wigan being able to hear only what matched his preconceptions. He claimed to have taken "soundings" in the market. I did not doubt that he had. Nor did I doubt the results, even allowing for Jack's propensity for reaching conclusions before hearing the arguments. My quarrel with his findings was not that they were inaccurate, but that they were those of a poll-taker as opposed to those of a marketing man.

"Poll-taking is asking questions, marketing is interpreting the answers," I asserted in one meeting.

"In this case," insisted Wigan, "they're one and the same thing."

"Yeah, only because you've merged them arbitrarily," I said.

There were many such animated discussions. As a result, Bluff Jack increasingly regarded me with suspicion. A "cowboy" is how he described me to Ure, whose attitude to discretion naturally compelled him to repeat the comment to me. "Been out there with Renfrew too long," Jack had told him. "Sun's gone to his head. He's lost touch with reality." As one inevitably must, after years out on the prairie, herding cattle.

My position was far more complex than Wigan presumed. But then grappling with complexity was no more one of Jack's obvious skills than patient persuasion was one of mine. My advocacy was not for a stand-alone matching product. It made more sense to me to incorporate a matching application into Monitor with a view to offering the function as an optional service. Since Monitor had already commandeered the desk space in dealing rooms, we could thus avoid the difficult sell involved in installing a totally new piece of hardware in favor of the gentler approach of adding software to an existing one. Traders having access to a transactional facility on a familiar terminal might, over time, be encouraged to use it. Moreover, a matching product introduced discreetly by an established and trusted vendor was an entirely different proposition from one peddled insensitively by an organization with no previous stake in the business.

"Still far too risky," thought Ure.

"There are certain imponderables in the approach," opined Dawson enigmatically.

"The market doesn't want it, and that's all there is to it," pronounced Bluff Jack.

There remained little choice but to bow to the conservative consensus. It was reinforced by one of Nelson's beloved surveys. Conducted mainly in Europe, the results vindicated Wigan's findings emphatically. Predictably, it concluded that most traders would be reluctant to support a matching product. Ure and I followed up with a similar fact-finding mission in the United States, taking in New York, Chicago, Los Angeles, and San Francisco. To no one's surprise, least of all mine, the American results mirrored Europe's. Of course they did: in both surveys the crucial question was posed in a crude either/or manner, permitting no shadings in the responses. "Do you want a matching system?" we asked. "Yes or No?" The answer was, of course, invariably an emphatic "No."

With time to kill on airplanes, Ure and I argued the point interminably, but without falling out over it. My suspicion was that Ure, deep down, harbored closet revolutionary instincts. Far from falling out, we ended the trip by sleeping together. This, I hasten to add, had nothing to do with the satisfaction of lustful desires. I should explain.

Finding ourselves in San Francisco on a Friday evening, our fact-finding tour completed, we decided to take a side trip the next day. What I proposed was a drive down the famed California coast via Pebble Beach to Carmel, where we would stay overnight. Our intention was to rent a car, but that evening in a bar, Perry's on Union Street, we fell in with a couple of local ladies. No doubt in gratitude for being plied with drinks, dinner, and scintillating wit, they offered to accompany us on our jaunt. Better still, they had a car and would drive us themselves. The trip turned into the excursion to Hell.

Twice on the way down we pulled off the road to allow Ure to vomit. He repeated the function on the beach opposite Seal Rock, a famous tourist attraction, consequently becoming one himself. The seals were unimpressed. So were our female companions. The one I fancied, who had taken a shine to me, gently took my arm and guided me for a stroll down the beach. "We have a problem," she whispered.

"Oh, what's that?"

"My friend thinks your friend is very strange," she confided. "In fact, she thinks he's a bit scary."

"Oh, you mean the unscheduled stops. I'm afraid he's just not feeling well."

"He may be unwell, that's understandable, but he's also very odd. What she finds most disturbing is that he keeps fondling himself." To which I could think of no clever response, at least not one that I cared to utter.

From Seal Rock we proceeded in awkward silence to Carmel, stopping only to have Clint Eastwood's gated property pointed out to us. There, at the hotel, I checked the four of us into two rooms. Now arrived the critical moment. I handed one key to Ure and kept the other myself. "Where's our key?" demanded the ladies, looking thoroughly alarmed. There followed a painful hiatus. Wilting under their venomous glares I finally handed over a key. Ure looked as relieved as they did.

The rest is too predictable to be worth relating in detail. Dinner was an excruciating experience and what followed even more so. Ure and I spent the night together, in the same room—no others being available—but thankfully in separate beds. We discussed until the dawn hour the mysterious nature of life and love and happiness and probably the future of currency trading systems. I should add, just for the record, one thing more: nothing else happened on that balmy, moonlit night in Carmel.

The drive back to San Francisco the next morning was accomplished, mercifully without stopping for further bodily expulsions, in a brooding, jaw-clenched silence. Happily relieved of the ladies' company, Ure demanded from me a solemn promise. "Don't you ever tell a soul about this, and if you do, I shall simply deny it." (It is with a clear conscience that I break my oath of silence after learning that Ure spent the next couple of years dining out on the tale—or at any rate his version of it.)

The one thing on which every trader in Ure's survey seemed to agree was that they would welcome a service that would replace their telex printers with a device offering the same conversational functions at substantially reduced calling charges. Replacing the telex was an unexciting and uncontroversial soft option. The Dealing Committee accordingly delivered its verdict, by a vote of three votes to one, against matching in favor of a souped-up telex product. It presented Nelson with a tidy package and a pretty consensus to present to Reuters' executive committee for its seal of approval. The meeting was convened for some reason in Switzerland, in the Dolder Grand Hotel perched on a hill above Zurich. Ure, Wigan, Dawson, and I were invited to attend, presumably in case of questions. In the event, we spent three hours cooling our heels outside the room until Nelson emerged with instructions to prepare a press announcement.

Pondering defeat, I considered it less a tragic mistake than a lost opportunity. History would, of course, deliver its own verdict. It was one that, like so many such verdicts, encouraged further argument. The Dealing system proved to be a great success, but I remained unrepentant in the view that a matching product might well have succeeded, too. This view was eventually vindicated when Reuters, within the decade, introduced the matching service Hull and I had proposed all along. (By which time, various sectors of the financial community had happily accommodated computerized trading, some markets subsequently going almost exclusively online.)

The axis hardly needed evidence for its view that Tafex would quickly disintegrate. It was offered on a platter. Ground down by the relentless opposition of the New York banks, Tafex decided to change its marketing strategy from aggressive to suicidal. In an act born of desperation, Tafex threatened the banks with legal action. Its focus was not so much the banks as the local branch of the association of foreign-exchange dealers, formally called the Association Cambiste Internationale but informally known as Forex.

A global body, the ACI was then, as now, the collective sum of its many regional branches, of which New York, reflecting the power and influence of the city's banks, was one of the largest and liveliest. The ACI's ostensible purpose was to organize training and other improving professional schemes, and to regulate trading practices, though it had no legal authority in such matters. For all the good works, what the ACI always promoted most effec-tively and enthusiastically was its social calendar. Local branches would typically convene quarterly for a formal discussion of market issues—cutting brokerage commissions was always a favorite topic—followed by the far more important and enjoyable business of dinner. Drinks invariably preceded, accompanied, and followed any such function. But social activities organized locally paled in comparison with the ACI's main event of the year—an international jamboree rather portentously called the Congress. Held in a different city each year, the occasion at its peak attracted up to 2000 guests. The typical mix was two-thirds working delegates, one-third spouses or partners, the latter contingent turning out in substantial numbers whenever the Congress was convened in an exotic tropical location such as Hawaii or Singapore. For all the rousing Rotarian bonhomie and the endless rounds of cocktail parties and sightseeing excursions, the organizers strove mightily to promote the Congress as a serious business event, which allowed attendees to justify putting the trip on expenses. To validate the point, the ACI usually invited the finance minister or senior central banker of the host country to deliver the keynote address, and delegates were expected to attend various workshops and panel discussions.

As a digression, it should be mentioned that until the early eighties, information vendors and other perceived commercial riff-raff were barred from participation, for fear that delegates would be distracted from their primary mission of falling asleep during speeches. The vendors insisted on showing up anyway, our representatives mingling with the delegates in hotel lobbies, with the object of luring traders upstairs to hospitality suites for product demonstrations, at which liquor flowed freely, often served by female staff members apparently selected for attributes other than their sales figures. Before long this subtle infiltration was so complete as to create a role reversal, in which the delegates appeared to be mingling with the vendors. Affronted by the hijacking of their event, the ACI responded angrily by sending out letters warning vendors to stay away, but it was an unenforceable edict, safely ignored. Conflict was avoided when the ACI finally caved in, having realized belatedly that its beloved Congress, far from being tainted by crass commercialism, could actually be funded by it through exhibition fees and sponsored events. The vendors were only too happy to cough up and, as if to confirm the ACI's worst fears, it was soon hard to discern whether it was the ACI running the show or the vendors.

Even before the ACI's capitulation, more than a few Forex members, mainly from the old school, could be heard complaining that its authority, if not the market itself, was in danger of being changed irrevocably, and certainly not for the better, by encroaching commercialism and technology. As long as Reuters remained the only service provider, such outside influences were manageable. A successful Tafex would make them less so—and other incursions were bound to follow. Everyone, it seemed, was now interested in exploiting a market in which a few years earlier nobody outside it had shown the slightest interest.

It was perhaps in this spirit, the feeling that a line ought to be drawn in the sand, that the New York Forex committee reached the conclusion that Tafex was not in the market's best interests. The committee preferred not to advertise such matters because, as it always took pains to point out, Forex was an association of individual traders, not of the institutions that employed them.

This disclaimer served two purposes: it insulated the banks from any legal consequences of ACI actions and opinions, and allayed concerns that the banks might be operating some kind of cartel.

Even before the publication of the *Institutional Investor* article, the fifteen members of the New York Forex committee had started to twitch about possible legal scrutiny of the anti-Tafex campaign, especially when several committee members were questioned on the issue by senior bank executives and lawyers. "A lot of people are worried about the anti-trust laws," one anonymous committee member told the magazine, "so everything is done on an informal basis and we try to write down as little as possible."[1] One Forex committee member was reported to have resigned over the issue.

The Two Bobbies were asked by *Institutional Investor* to respond to allegations that Forex was running a coordinated campaign to destroy Tafex. Both declined to comment. LeClerc cited "legal reasons," which he refused to elaborate. His reticence was understandable; lawyers at Continental were said to be "running scared" that the Justice Department would soon start to take an interest.

Sent into a state of panic when Tafex first appeared, one of the Forex committee's earliest responses had been to commission Burroughs Corporation, a computer manufacturer, to conduct a feasibility study for an alternative matching system, to be owned and operated by the banks. The Burroughs report was supposedly circulated to Forex members, though few could remember years later having actually seen a copy. And few were astonished to learn that its principal recommendation was that Burroughs itself should be contracted to develop the competing service. Burroughs was perfectly capable of building such a product, but not of resolving the crucial anti-trust issue. Adopting a Forex-sponsored system would put the banks into the tricky position of having to formulate the operating rules, including the question of what kind of institutions would be allowed to participate. Would regional banks be invited to the party? If they were excluded would they thus be provoked into legal action? And would corporations, the banks' chief source of foreign-exchange profits, press for participation? To none of these questions were there obvious answers.

The Burroughs proposal was quietly shelved.

By then, however, the Forex committee had a much more compelling reason for inaction. Enraged by the apparently coordinated opposition to his product, Kent Colwell went to see Transamerica's white-shoe law firm, Patterson, Belknap & Webb. His complaint was that the New York banks had put unreasonable and thereby illegal pressure on the regional banks not to take Tafex. After a lengthy investigation, the lawyers agreed. PBW believed that it

---

[1] *Institutional Investor* magazine, March 1976

had sufficiently strong evidence with which to confront the banks, specifically an allegation that, through Forex, they had colluded to organize a boycott, an illegal act under United States anti-trust laws. A meeting was arranged between PBW and attorneys representing the ten New York clearing banks. It ended inconclusively. Colwell tried to play down the event as a little local difficulty. "It was a friendly thing," Colwell explained to *Institutional Investor*, an interpretation that may be considered resolutely naïve. "It was our lawyers talking to their lawyers, saying, 'Did you know that someone connected with your client was doing these kinds of things?' "[2]

Behind the legal process the gloves were coming off, too. John Beckett had been drafted in to flex Transamerica's corporate muscle by personally urging senior executives of the company's banks to try Tafex. Behind the tactic was an implied threat that those banks with a relationship with Transamerica might find themselves somehow "punished" if they failed to cooperate. It was an empty threat; especially as there was an unwritten rule in the financial community that the right to decide what was good or bad for the trading room rested with the trading-room managers rather than their masters in the executive branch. So, when several senior bank executives told Beckett they would have to consult their traders, they were doing no more than making a polite gesture.

The combined pressure from the *Institutional Investor* story, the legal maneuvers, and Beckett's blandishments had an impact. Bank attitudes appeared to soften. Even the House of Morgan took a Tafex terminal on a trial basis, Van Roten claiming with a straight face that he was "giving Tafex a chance." It could hardly be called a fighting chance, since the Tafex terminal was consigned to a remote corner of the trading room, unattended and ignored. Tafex terminals also suddenly appeared on the trading desks at Chemical Bank, Marine Midland, and Bankers Trust. Chemical's chief trader, Jan Gorski, echoed the Van Roten line: "All I'm committed to doing is giving it a fair trial."[3] Others were having no truck with such squalid concessions, LeClerc at Continental Illinois for one. To that fact, Colwell seemed resigned. "I'd say that LeClerc would be the last one to sign up," he conceded wearily.

One New York trader, alone among his more prominent peers, came out firmly in support of Tafex. Jimmy Wiseman of Bankers Trust placed a Tafex terminal in the middle of his trading desk and with every intention of generating trading activity by entering bids and offers. Wiseman was not the ideal stalking-horse. His support for Tafex was genuine, but it marked him as a maverick, as Meer had been identified, and he, too, did not command universal admiration in foreign-exchange circles. With few counter-parties on

---

[2] *Institutional Investor* magazine, March 1976
[3] Ibid.

the system, the opportunities to trade were rare. "Tafex sat in the middle of the desk and flashed our own market quotes back to us with blanks next to them," Wiseman complained.

One day, Wiseman managed to make a significant trade through Tafex. By coincidence, it happened just as Hull and I entered his trading room on a routine visit. He had entered a quote for one million British pounds. It had been sitting there for some time but finally a California bank hit the bid. "You see, it really does work," said Wiseman exultantly. "Deal's done. Paperwork's finished. No brokerage to pay, just a small transaction fee. Works just fine, but apparently nobody wants it. What more can I say?"

Very little, Hull and I agreed.

With some of its major opponents now committed to installing the system, the Tafex legal ploy had been pre-empted, but for Tafex the damage was already done. For most dealers, the legal threat had been the last straw. Even the company's few supporters felt affronted. And Beckett had finally run out of patience. Having given Colwell a final, make-or-break deadline of three months, he closed Tafex down.

The sighs of relief stirred the leaves in Battery Park.

Meanwhile, Hull and I had been busy working on the Americanization of Monitor. The rapid international expansion of Monitor in the second half of the seventies had occurred mainly in Europe, with Asia providing important support. The United States was relegated to playing third fiddle. Monitor had by no means failed in America, but foreign exchange remained at the margin of financial trading in New York, restricting Monitor's opportunities for growth.

Although foreign exchange then constituted the biggest global trading community, the single biggest national market anywhere, both in terms of volume and volatility, was the market in debt instruments issued by the United States government. When the huge markets in corporate and municipal bonds were added to treasuries, the volume in fixed-income securities dwarfed that of currencies, even surpassing the combined volumes in stocks and commodities. Only one vendor operated in this market: Telerate.

Telerate's name had cropped up quite often since Mike Griffith of Salomon Brothers had first pointed it out to us a couple of years earlier. He used the service principally for just two screen pages of commercial-paper rates posted by a couple of dozen direct corporate issuers such as General Motors Acceptance Corporation and Montgomery Ward Credit Corporation. Telerate had since diversified into information from other capital markets, notably US treasury securities.

"You guys ought to be able to knock Telerate out," Mike Griffith said one day. "It's a good service but it has no international presence and the company's short of cash. Instead of knocking 'em out, why don't you buy 'em out, before they get too big?"

It was something worth considering. Harvey Cooper had actually mentioned it to Renfrew, but Reuters, after the cable debacle, had neither the appetite nor the money for fresh adventures.

Hull and I decided to compete instead, by "stealing" Telerate's leading commercial-paper contributors. These were, typically, the finance arms of major industrial corporations. We cobbled together a mock page of commercial-paper rates, which I arranged to demonstrate to a group of CP issuers in Wilmington, Delaware, where several of the larger ones were headquartered for tax reasons. For the presentation I took with me a large black computer terminal the size of two suitcases, comprising a keyboard and screen attached to a device called an acoustic telephone coupler, through which I could dial into the Monitor computer. The trip turned into a farce from which the Marx Brothers might have drawn inspiration.

The presentation, held at the offices of Montgomery Ward, fell completely flat. Five minutes into it, the suspicion took root that the attendees were simply on a scouting mission for Telerate. After listening in stony silence, they asked a few perfunctory questions before ushering me out into the steamy July afternoon, with not so much as a hint of southern hospitality, like lunch.

Instead of heading straight back to New York, I decided to take the train in the opposite direction to Washington, where Bob Kearns, my former drinking companion from the New York newsroom, now worked as an editor. "A few beers" turned into a marathon session lasting well into the evening. The last New York train having departed, I took a hair-raising taxi drive out to National Airport, just failing to arrive in time for the last New York shuttle, and no option but to drive back to the capital and check into a hotel. There, I was taking a sobering cold shower when it dawned on me that I'd left the "computer" at the airport. Dressing hurriedly, I took another wild ride out to National to retrieve the infernal box—a rather forlorn hope, I feared. Miraculously, it was exactly where I'd left it, up against a pillar in the departure lounge. (No airport security concerns in those days.) The area was deserted except for a man pushing around a huge floor-cleaner. "Was wonderin' what that thing was," he said.

Back at the hotel, I found a small crowd had gathered outside my room.

"This your room?" a security man wanted to know.

"It is. What's the problem?"

"You left the shower running with a towel clogging up the drain. There's water pouring into the room below."

"You have another room?" was the exhausted response.

"We've already moved you two doors along, sir. And if you don't mind my asking, sir, are you aware that you're only wearing one shoe?"

The comedy spilled over into the following day. Telerate's lawyers had called Joe Daffin with a complaint. "You're representative has been down in Wilmington telling our clients Telerate is going out of business. You must cease and desist. You'll be getting a letter from us. One more incident of this kind and we'll file suit."

Looking back, I may well have alluded obliquely to Telerate's allegedly less than robust financial condition, though I'm sure I hadn't put it in such blunt terms. "Well, we'll just have to be careful," Daffin said. "Telerate obviously has some pretty aggressive lawyers and I sure don't fancy crossing swords with them."

"Fuck Telerate," I said to Daffin. "They're not worth all this trouble."

What an immaculately inapt remark that would turn out to be!

As it soon became plain, Telerate was not about to disappear. The company's financial concerns had been relieved by an infusion of cash, in return for a majority interest in the company, from a Beverly Hills bond brokerage firm called Cantor Fitzgerald Securities Corporation. Cantor's intention was to use Telerate to display brokerage markets in United States treasury securities—precisely the market Hull and I had in mind for Monitor.

Cantor Fitzgerald was a controversial iconoclast among the half-dozen inter-dealer brokers operating in the government market. The firm was widely resented for a number of reasons, some of them unclear, but most of all because of its use of Telerate as an electronic conveyance for tradable prices. Most of the thirty-odd officially recognized dealers in the market were appalled by the idea. Several, including the largest, Merrill Lynch Pierce Fenner & Smith, retaliated by refusing to deal with Cantor Fitzgerald, on or off the screen. Telerate terminals were likewise banned from Merrill's trading room. The powers that be at Merrill vilified B. Gerald (Bernie) Cantor, the firm's owner, as an unscrupulous opportunist. If the grapevine were to be believed, he was possibly something worse, a reference to vague rumors of a link with organized crime figures. (Such allegations swirled about Bernie Cantor, and by extension Telerate, for years. Was there a fire somewhere producing all this smoke? I never came across anything to substantiate the rumors, never for a moment believed them, and frankly never thought it worthwhile to investigate them.)

Villeneuve and his London colleagues had no objections to taking Monitor into the American treasury market, but showed no great enthusiasm either. Renfrew matched London's indifference. (This evident lack of interest in the American financial markets among senior Reuters executives was inexplicable then and continued to puzzle industry observers for many years afterwards.)

"Go for it, by all means," Renfrew told Daffin. "But make sure your boys understand that there's no money to spend."

Such a lukewarm endorsement left Hull more disappointed than shocked. "Biggest fucking market in the world and all they can say is, 'Who cares?' Why am I surprised?"

I mentioned that the Unmentionable Episode involving Monitor might have something to do with the attitude. "Yeah, you've got a point there. So now let's prove to the bastards that we can really shake things up."

We did. Our prospective contributors in the government market were the thirty-six so-called primary dealers, those "recognized" by the Federal Reserve Bank of New York, which supervised the market on behalf of the US Treasury Department. The dealers included most of Wall Street's leading banks and brokerage firms plus a smattering of smaller specialized bond houses. It was a huge market, the size of Treasury issues rising and falling in relation to the national debt, which, throughout the sixties and most of the seventies, soared without interruption, thanks mainly to the Government's heavy borrowing to finance the Vietnam War. For many years the Treasury market had been a quiet haven of stability and predictability, at least by Wall Street standards, one in which senior citizens could invest their savings without risk. But rising volume had made it an increasingly speculative arena, and from time to time the market experienced bouts of unprecedented and occasionally alarming volatility.

For as long as anyone could remember, the Primary Dealers had traded with each other by telephone through a half-dozen specialized brokers whose obedience to the trading rules and conventions imposed by the dealers was absolute. In that sense, the government market had come to resemble the foreign-exchange market: a cozy club-like association of self-regulating insiders, with the Fed keeping an eye on things as a benevolent club secretary.

And then, appearing from nowhere, and showing none of the polite reserve or eager-to-please manner expected of a relatively new club member, Cantor Fitzgerald started flashing Treasury bond prices across Telerate screens.

The reaction was predictably fierce, so much so that an informal boycott was organized against both Cantor and Telerate. But the dealers were far from unanimous in their condemnation. Some, for example, claimed to have more reason to resent Merrill Lynch, the boycott leader, than to fear Cantor Fitzgerald, and before long had broken ranks. Others followed, leaving Merrill Lynch and a handful of allies in a distinct minority. It is true that the majority lacked the collective power of the minority, but smaller firms were rewarded by gaining access to tradable two-way markets.

Hull and I had reason to believe that a number of dealers, whether in the pro- or anti-Cantor camps, would welcome a competitor to Cantor/Telerate. Merrill Lynch having announced its absolute opposition to screen trading of any kind, we gave the firm a wide berth. But John Tritz, the nonchalant,

Alsatian-born head of government-trading at Bankers Trust, and a staunch Merrill ally in matters relating to Cantor/Telerate, turned out to be warmly receptive. He had a profound suspicion of Cantor Fitzgerald and its works, which animated every discussion we had with him. "Anything you can do to kick Bernie's fat ass is fine with me." Tritz agreed to contribute his government market quotes to Monitor, provided we could persuade a few more dealers to join him.

Hull and I had designed a composite page that displayed four dealers on one screen "page." This was limiting, because the fifth contributor, and any subsequent contributors, would be "relegated" to a second page. The disadvantage of being in the reserve team was that traders, as creatures of habit, would remain glued to the primary page. It was regarded as one of the disadvantages of Monitor, in foreign exchange, that "shopping" for rates involved the constant chore of changing pages. Filling up the first page, we decided, could be turned into a kind of auction.

"Roll up! Roll up! First four dealers up get the best slots!" We soon had them.

Tritz was anxious about his prospective neighbors. "I want to be able to veto my compatriots on the page," he insisted.

"How about Harris Bank, Donaldson Lufkin & Jenrette, and Morgan?" we asked.

"They'll do," said Tritz.

Harris Bank was represented by Mel "Duke" Swanborn, a cowboy-booted, Stetson-wearing iconoclast from the Midwest. At DLJ he had a soul mate in William "Billy" Kidder, a South Carolinian with a florid turn of speech that brought to mind certain aging senators from the Old South. Myron Taylor of Morgan Bank provided a conservative counterweight. It was like picking a baseball line-up. Victor Chang of Goldman Sachs and Bob Hatcher of Chemical Bank were soon added to the squad.

They were, if nothing else, a richly diverse bunch, ethnically, culturally, and every otherwise. Some years later, Duke, Swanborn, Chang (who was of Chinese origin), and Taylor (who was black) talked about going into business together. Swanborn joked that they thought of calling the firm Dook, Spook and Gook.

It made a nice change to have such a rich embarrassment of contributors— six in no time at all! But despite having made it clear that the first four dealers up would get to occupy the first page, the other two, consigned to the second page, now voiced objections to their demeaned status. We were in danger of losing them when the ever-inventive Hull came up with a brainwave. Somewhere in his travels he'd come across a VDU containing six small screens— actually two boxes of three screens apiece. "If we put the service out on these six-packs we can display up to twenty-four dealers simultaneously, twelve if we just use a three-pack."

"Perfect," I agreed.

If nothing else, six-pack, like "I Drink," slotted nicely into the company's bibulous tradition. Three-packs it would be, to start with. All six contributors seemed happy. As the dealers practiced inserting quotes into the system, we planned a formal product launch.

It was about then that Hull, as ever full of surprises, made a startling announcement.

"I'm off," he declared one morning from my office doorway. He was wearing a raincoat. It was well before noon.

"Bit early for lunch, isn't it?"

"I'm not leaving for lunch. I'm leaving the company. Right now."

"Leaving? Right now? What the hell's going on?"

"I'm joining Telerate. Daffin wants me out of here immediately."

Joe loomed behind him. "Standard operating procedure, I'm afraid, old boy. Nothing personal."

Hull said, "I'll call you at home later and fill you in." And with that, he was gone.

Daffin instructed me to contact the Treasury market contributors immediately. Since Hull had been indelibly associated with the project, they were entitled to know right away. Swanborn was not entirely happy, nor were most of the others. But the ultimate response was a shrugging of shoulders. "What can you do?" said Swanborn. "It's a free country."

John Tritz was a different kettle of fish. He was livid. I was summoned to the bank, which was literally a few yards along Wall Street from Reuters' office. Somewhat appeased by my assurances that Reuters stood four-square behind the project (a fact of which I frankly needed some convincing myself) he ushered me out with a stern admonition: "I've supported this project from the start. I will continue to do so. But I don't want to find my—how do you call it?—Johnson on the chopping block." He made a guillotine motion with a hand.

"Nor I mine," I said.

A couple of months later I was obliged to pay Tritz a second visit. This time it was to report a second defection to Telerate: mine.

Tritz this time was apoplectic. After enduring an outpouring of Gallic abuse, and clutching my Johnson for dear life, I was virtually propelled out of his office. Tritz called Renfrew for an explanation. He wanted to know, from the horse's mouth, that the project was safe. Renfrew had hardly given it a second's thought but was smoothly reassuring. "The project will continue," he told Tritz. "We support it to the hilt, and it will receive whatever resources it may need." Finally!

It would be some years before I dared to set foot in Bankers Trust's dealing room again. By then, I noticed, it was teeming with Cantor Fitzgerald screens.

"I see we've both moved on," I remarked.

"*Oui, mais c'est la guerre*," said Tritz, smiling.

Before then, Hull had called one morning, completely out of the blue. It had been several weeks since he had left Reuters. "Neil Hirsch wants to buy you a drink."

Hirsch was president of Telerate. I had met him twice. The first occasion was a brief handshake at a trade show. The second was when Hull and I had dreamed up a madcap scheme involving Tafex. The idea was to get Bernie Cantor to buy Tafex and appoint us to run it. For that purpose we had formed a company called Cash Market Systems Inc.

Shortly after the fall of Tafex, we had met with Kent Colwell with a view to securing a finder's fee for selling the Tafex software. He readily agreed, on condition that we find a buyer within three months. We promptly contacted Bernie Cantor to arrange a meeting. This was held at Bernie's New York penthouse suite in the Dorset, a midtown residential hotel. Bernie, accompanied by Neil Hirsch, greeted us, resplendently attired in a red siren suit and bed-slippers.

Bernard Gerald Cantor was a curious figure in more than the sartorial sense. Born and raised in the Bronx, he was built like a longshoreman, had the rough tongue of the waterfront, and an explosive temper. He liked to tell the story that his first successful commercial venture, as a boy, was selling hot dogs at Yankee Stadium. "I only worked during Sunday doubleheaders," he recalled, because on those occasions "you could sell more things." After college he thought about entering law school but instead exploited a head for figures by drifting into Wall Street as a securities analyst. He made his fortune trading so-called flower bonds, one of Wall Street's passing fads in the 1960s, but later concentrated on building a business as a broker of US treasury securities. He contradicted the rough image of the Bronx-raised bond broker by presenting himself as a man of artistic sensitivities and a philanthropist. He was obsessed by the French sculptor Auguste Rodin and amassed over the years one of the world's largest collections of his works, with some 750 sculptures, sketches, and other artifacts. Most of them he donated to museums, such as the New York Metropolitan Museum of Art, the Brooklyn Museum of Art, the Los Angeles County Museum of Art, and Stanford University. Each of them gratefully named galleries or gardens after him and his wife, Iris, a glamorous but far-from-dumb blonde, originally from New York's other blue-collar borough, Brooklyn. Many in the financial markets saw behind the smiling host at fancy black-tie museum receptions a ruthless operator. Others perceived no more than a pompous buffoon and social climber, one who had succeeded on Wall Street more by luck and cunning than any innate genius. In short, Bernie Cantor was inexplicably a far-from-popular figure in market circles.

The proposition that Hull and I brought to the meeting was for Cantor to exploit Tafex by trading government bonds, possibly currencies as well. The meeting was not a success. Cantor said little and looked bored. Hirsch deployed a more vehement antipathy. No deal. Cash Market Systems Inc. was stillborn.

The Tafex idea may have fallen flat, but Hull and I had apparently given Hirsch and Cantor other notions. Hence Hirsch's call to Hull, now established as Hirsch's right-hand man, in March 1978, and now Hull's call to me. He was excited. "Telerate is doing some really interesting stuff. You'll really be surprised. Come take a look. And Hirsch wants to have a chat."

"I take it this is some kind of job interview."

"Call it what you like. Just come."

I went. The factors behind my interest mentioned earlier were now supplemented by a significant new one. Joe Daffin, it appeared, was about to be shoved aside in favor of a Chicago-based, Nelson-sponsored marketing hotshot, one Alan Jackson. Jackson evidently had been waiting in the wings, preparing for a grand entrance onto the New York stage. His cue had now come. Jackson was a small man with a goatee beard. He struck me, as he'd struck many others whose judgment I trusted, as a man of ruthless ambition, a man with a personal agenda against which all other professional matters took second place. Daffin loathed him. He had the more or less permanent conspiratorial expression of someone who loves to plot and scheme—Basil Rathbone as the Sheriff of Nottingham.

We met for a drink. I expressed my concerns. "I wonder, frankly, if we can possibly work together," I ventured at last.

"Probably not," was Jackson's encouraging response.

At that moment, my visit to Telerate loomed as a better idea, an infinitely better idea, than it had an hour earlier.

# Telerate

Nothing could be more insanely redolent of Telerate than the manner of my joining it.

The process, for want of a better word, involved two "interviews"—also a term used for courtesy—conducted on successive evenings by Neil Hirsch, Telerate's founder and chief executive. Both began routinely enough at the company's midtown office on Sixth Avenue, but on each occasion, after no more than half an hour, the venue was abruptly switched to Sybil's, a bar-cum-disco in the Hilton hotel directly across the street. Sybil's was one of Telerate's regular after-hours hangouts. "We can be a little more relaxed over there," Hirsch explained, just ten minutes into our first meeting.

I was slightly tense, as one tends to be on these occasions. Hirsch was perfectly at ease in his standard office uniform, an all-black ensemble of chinos, open-necked shirt, and moccasins. It contrasted starkly with the dreary formality of my gray business suit and conservative tie.

"Hey, good to see ya again," he gushed, barely rising from his chair and proffering a disappointingly limp handshake.

Already nursing a four-fingered glass of whisky, he refilled it twice during the course of our meeting with what I noticed was a slightly trembling hand. I accepted the offer of a Scotch but declined a cigarette, a habit I had recently kicked (but would soon feel compelled to take up again). John Hull sauntered in to join us, pouring a vodka and tonic before flopping into Hirsch's big leather sofa to enjoy the spectacle.

It was my first opportunity to observe Hirsch up close. At our only previous meeting—the brief and abortive Tafex presentation in Bernie Cantor's apartment—Hirsch had come across as a brooding and truculent presence. Now, in the familiarity of his own office, he was all affable charm. It was transmitted through a shy, toothy grin. He seemed younger and smaller than I remembered him. He was in fact twenty-nine, short, and verging on the chubby. His features, framed by black shoulder-length hair in a kind of Richard III style, were boyish but already starting to acquire a look suggesting a life lived on the edge. There was a louche, lounge-lizard look about him, but he exuded a quiet charisma. As he would tell a reporter years later, "I was an average kid; I was an average student. But when I was twenty-one, I realized I had always wanted to make something of myself. I doubted I could be a terrific lawyer or a doctor, but I realized I could make a lot of money."[1]

---

[1] *Time Magazine*, January 23, 1984

A mutual female acquaintance of mine had described him as darkly handsome and I could see why. He brought to mind the young Al Pacino, assuming at fleeting moments the haunted Michael Corleone look from *The Godfather*, the hit movie of the decade: shifty, slightly menacing and impenetrable, but with just a hint of vulnerability.

This latter quality was apparently what most impressed the young women who made up the greater part of Telerate's staff. "Ya know, that Neil needs a lot of mothering," one of them imparted indiscreetly later that evening in Sybil's. "So, we all just mother him to death. And boy, does he just love to be mothered."

Death, in the real sense, was one of Hirsch's curious and, for a man still in his twenties, startling preoccupations. The explanation was that both his parents had died of cancer at a relatively young age and the disease had also claimed the life of a sister. These family misfortunes convinced Hirsch that he himself faced an early demise (and if lifestyle has anything to do with longevity, it must be said that his premonition seemed more than likely to be fulfilled). "Dust in the wind," he would sometimes croon in melancholic moments, attracted to the lyrics of one of the hit songs of 1978. "All we are is dust in the wind."

Hirsch was then married to Caroline, his second wife—a strikingly pretty woman if judged by the framed photograph on his desk. Its sole desk-top companion was an autographed picture of Frank Sinatra. Caroline hailed from one of those Italian neighborhoods in Brooklyn that claim, by virtue of the *sub rosa* "connections" enjoyed by its residents, to have the safest streets in the city. His first wife, one Cindy Schwartz, was said to be the step-great-granddaughter of the mobster Meyer Lansky. Hirsch himself was the son of a gentile mother and a Jewish father who part-owned a well-known St. Louis department store. As Neil used to put it, "I'm only half a matzoh ball—and the wrong half at that."

Our meeting drifted into inconsequence and, for me, disappointment.

Hirsch asked me to present a brief oral résumé. He didn't ask for, nor had there been time to prepare, a written one. Given what I later learned of his aversion to the written form, it is doubtful whether he would have read it anyway. He listened, though, and with evident interest, occasionally grinning or nodding approvingly at my nervous puns. If I thought I had come off rather well, his response tended to disabuse the notion.

"Look, Hull has told me great things about you, but to be frank I'm not sure we can afford to take you on right now. We've spent all our spare cash hiring your friend here." He nodded at Hull, who grimaced. "We must stay in touch, though. Telerate is growing fast, gonna need good people. Maybe later in the year…"

And that, as far as I was concerned, appeared to be the end of the matter. If Telerate had no money, there was little more to be said. Hull thought otherwise. While Hirsch excused himself to take a telephone call, Hull delivered a reassuring nudge in the ribs. "Don't give up," he whispered, "You're in. He likes you, I can tell. You'll fit right in here, and that's his main concern. Look, this is a game. Now, and the rest of the evening, they're all a test."

A test of stamina, as it turned out.

At Sybil's, all attempts to steer the conversation to business matters were relentlessly undermined by the bone-jarring throb of rock music, not to mention the rising consumption of alcohol. If my intake that evening qualified as merely prodigious, Hirsch's was astonishing. Equally disruptive were the endless arrivals and departures of Telerate employees, apparently invited for the express purpose of giving me the once-over. Hirsch basked in the consensus of his staff. It indulged his cherished image of Telerate as "one big happy family." The family was one over which he presided, not so much as a patriarch—a status from which youth disqualified him—but in the manner of an older brother caring for an unruly brood of orphaned siblings.

Some time around eight o'clock Hull, after several vodkas, mumbled his apologies and left. I had neither the will nor the intelligence to leave with him. Common sense had been one of the evening's early victims. Hirsch and I were by then enjoying the company of a harem of Telerate ladies, reinforced by a gaggle of pretty stewardesses from some South American airline, all twenty-something and ready to party. It was, though, a tall brunette from the Telerate crowd who caught my eye. A decade older than the rest, and for my money more handsome, her name was Martha. All other things aside, the nature of her relationship with Hirsch intrigued me. Curiosity should have confined itself to conjecture—but of that, more anon.

My silent speculations about the Divine Miss M were interrupted as Hirsch draped an arm around my shoulder and hers. "Waddya think, JJ? Telerate's a fun company, huh?" He was yelling above a rampant Donna Summer tape.

"Sure is," I bellowed back. "By the way, is tonight some special occasion?"

"Nah, not even for you. Telerate's just a very social company. We go out most evenings. Listen, you're gonna have a great time working here."

I was digesting this apparently uncalculated throwaway line when several traders from Cantor Fitzgerald drifted in to join us. Cantor's offices, including its dealing room, were a few floors higher in the same building as Telerate's. Many of the names I managed to catch—Terranova, Desiderio, De Quattro, Avena—were awash in vowels, which I found mildly surprising. I had expected the ethnic flavor to be more Jewish than Italian. In more fertile imaginations than mine, all these accumulated "clues"—Lansky, Sinatra, Sicilian surnames—would no doubt have further stoked speculation about Cantor/Telerate's supposed Mafia connections. But then again, such rumors are often no more than speculative conversation-fillers in New York.

Hull had been wise to go home. By eleven I was flying at an altitude even our newfound airline companions might have found scary. Yet it was also becoming clear that Sybil's was merely a warm-up for what promised to be a long night on the town. There was no question of my backing out now, certainly not if the evening was, as Hull believed, some kind of initiation rite. And Hirsch was becoming friendlier by the minute.

Several more hours ticked by before I finally summoned the resolve to stagger out into the now near-deserted streets of Manhattan, head swimming. It was the preferred alternative to toppling off a barstool—or something even more humiliating. By now, I should mention, the whole riotous caravansary had moved a few blocks north to Studio 54, a legendary nightspot frequented by Manhattan's *beau monde*, of which Hirsch was a regular patron. It appealed to his vanity to mingle with such celebrities as Andy Warhol, Liza Minnelli, Cher, and Bianca Jagger (the latter destined to become, briefly, his intimate friend and muse). Hirsch tried to talk me into staying. There was no denying that Studio 54 offered greater attractions than Pennsylvania Station and a stiff-necked snooze on the Long Island Railroad, but my head was now an echo chamber and my conversation reduced, I suspected, to gibberish. Even so, before leaving I managed to snaffle Hirsch's parting words of endearment: "JJ, I think you and I are gonna be working together for a long time."

At least that's what I thought I heard. Three hours and a pot of black coffee later, it took a considerable effort to recall anything with clarity. "How did it go?" my wife naturally wanted to know from across the breakfast table. "Did you get a job offer?"

"I think so. I can't be sure. The fact is, I don't remember."

"Don't remember!" A job interview in a disco consigned to oblivion by dawn is a concept most wives would have found difficult to grasp.

Later that morning I called Hull for clarification. He found this hilarious. "You're asking me? I left early, remember? Anyway, Hirsch hasn't shown up yet. Sounds like you guys had a great evening."

Hull called back around midday. Hirsch had just arrived, he reported. And then the bad news. Actually, no news. "Guess what, he can't remember, either."

"What now?"

The response was a summons to a repeat performance.

It took place that same evening, and the script followed the same course as the previous one: drinks in Hirsch's office, more mumbled apologies that Telerate had no money to spend, and once again the inevitable proposal that we head across to Sybil's for further "discussions." This time I raised a traffic cop's restraining hand. "Look, Neil, at the risk of sounding rude, can we get business matters out of the way first? I have just one question: is there an interest here or not?"

Hirsch laughed. "Ah, what the hell, JJ, I guess you're in. Welcome aboard."

He mentioned a salary—hardly more than I was earning at Reuters. "Best I can do right now," he apologized.

"Okay," was the response, reprising an abject surrender twenty years earlier.

Sybil's provided once more the night's preliminary revelries and again we all drifted uptown, this time to some illicit gaming club to indulge Neil's passion for blackjack—and mine for sleeping on a pre-dawn train to Port Washington.

"You must be about to get married, or maybe divorced," said the same conductor who had punched my ticket the night before.

"I'm not sure which," I said. "Probably both."

And so it would prove.

When I showed up at Telerate the next morning, the reception desk was occupied by what appeared to be a large pink balloon. My discreet cough caused it to disintegrate in a minor explosion, revealing the lubricious, vigorously masticating face of the receptionist, Sherri Fleischer. A tongue darted out to gather in the dangling gobbets of bubble-gum.

"Sorry 'bout that. Hey, I hear you fellas were really living it up last night. Didn't waste much time, did ya? Way to go!" Telerate, if nothing else, operated an efficient grapevine. "Neil's out," she mentioned. "Hull, too. They said to tell ya sorry, but to show you to your desk."

Sherri led the way, not as I expected into Telerate's office but out through the glassed lobby and along a common-area corridor, lined by apparently deserted offices, that led to the lavatories. There, against a wall, stood a solitary table with a telephone on it.

"This is where I'm supposed to sit?"

"Have to do for now, Neil says, just for a few days. We're just wall-to-wall people inside."

"Well, I guess this way I'll get to know my colleagues in a hurry."

"Yeah," she laughed, "even if it's more than you really need to know."

Learning more than I needed to know took the form of suspicion that a fair number of the trips past my desk were undertaken for purposes other than calls of nature or ablutions. Hull chortled when I mentioned it. "Well, I can tell you one thing," he said. "It's unlikely most of these people are either incontinent or dirty, so you'll have to draw your own conclusions." When I looked a little baffled, Hull said, "Let me put it this way: not for nothing is it called the powder room."

Hirsch was all apologies for treating Telerate's newly appointed Marketing Vice President so shabbily. "We'll move you inside in a few days, just as soon as Nagel moves his stuff out."

"Nagel? Bob Nagel?"

"Yeah, Bob's been doing some work for us. You can have his office. He's hardly ever in it anyway."

Hirsch offered a guided tour with an apology. "There's really not much to see." He was right. Telerate had, as I recall, twenty-seven employees. That number also pretty much represented their median age. Some, still bleary-eyed from Sybil's, offered smiles of recognition. The offices were shabby and overcrowded. Nobody seemed to mind; being huddled together created intimacy and generated a buzz (in the meaning other than one I picked up from my lavatorial picket duty).

Our first specific port of call was Telerate's computer room. In the company brochure it had been referred to, with a certain license, as a "state-of-the-art data center." A walk-in closet filled with a spaghetti tangle of wires was certainly in a state and could have been exhibited as an example of modern art. Somewhere in the middle stood a pair of Perkin-Elmer computers, cooled by a cheap plastic fan of the kind sold in discount stores. A blanket on the floor behind a desk indicated that someone had been sleeping there.

"Yeah, that'll be Tony Sabatini, our resident technical genius," Hirsch explained. Sabatini, it seemed, had designed, and now operated, Telerate's network. "He mostly works nights," Hirsch mentioned. "Spends the day working on sound systems for rock groups. He's brilliant but a little crazy. You'll meet him one of these days."

"Didn't know Perkin-Elmer made computers," I remarked, attempting to sound knowledgeable.

"Yeah, great machines," Neil said. "Perfect for data distribution. Very durable." They needed to be, I thought.

Sabatini put in a rare diurnal appearance a few days later. Hirsch's eccentric genius turned out to be one of Professor Tolkien's lovable hobbits—short and rotund, with an expression simultaneously quizzical, distracted, and rather smug. A hobbit would have been more modest. "Hi, I'm Sabatini, the guy who makes this whole place tick," he proclaimed from my office doorway. "And, since nobody around here tells me anything, who are you?" I told him.

"Well, I suppose we can use all the help we can get," he retorted, with a look suggesting that he regarded me as another unnecessary overhead. "Can you write programs?"

More impressive than the mayhem of Sabatini's computer room was a nearby glass-fronted area Hirsch called the "newsroom," though it was plainly nothing of the kind. It was more a showroom than a newsroom, with one entire wall occupied by an expansive, illuminated display panel of multiple Telerate screens. The sole occupants were three clerks—"rates gatherers" in Telerate's awkward nomenclature—whose function was to update the Telerate system with market quotes, which they collected by continually telephoning market contacts. One of the three was the Divine Miss M, previously encountered at Sybil's. Another was one Elliott Fine, a lugubrious, nebbishy-looking young man with a Zapata mustache whose archetypically overbearing Jewish mother was given to calling him several times a day. The senior, and youngest, member of the trio was Jean Page, whose husband, it transpired, worked upstairs in Cantor Fitzgerald's "cage."

"This is where we create Telerate's Famous Page 5," she announced, as proudly as if it had been named after her, with Hirsch beaming paternalistically over her shoulder. "You've heard about our Famous Page 5, I'm sure."

Indeed I had. Telerate's Page 5 was a composite display of money-market rates and was the heart of the Telerate system. Clients found it essential. For many it was, unbelievably, the sole reason for subscribing to Telerate. Hirsch read my thoughts. "I guess it strikes you as funny that our single most important information page is nothing but a few quotes updated occasionally by these three dingbats. But don't knock it. That stupid page alone sells more fuckin' terminals than all the other pages on the system put together—including Cantor's."

Explaining to Jean Page my background in financial journalism, Hirsch took the moment to announce that I would henceforth be responsible for supervising the newsroom. "That okay with you, Jeannie?" It was. "How about you, M?"

"Sounds great," said M.

Hirsch gave me a sly wink. "Can't do nothing around here without M's approval." She and I exchanged smiles. "Now this could be trouble," was the thought that crossed my mind. Hull's, too. Some time later, he wagged an admonishing finger in my face. "You just watch your step, old chap, if you value your career here. And maybe your life." I didn't ask him to explain the somewhat dramatic afterthought.

The Telerate "newsroom" might benefit from my supposed expertise, but not in matters of United States treasury securities. These were provided exclusively by Telerate's owner, Cantor Fitzgerald, and inserted directly into the system from Cantor's trading room upstairs.

The only one of half a dozen brokers able, or to put it another way, permitted, to deliver treasury prices electronically, Cantor Fitzgerald had done so by overcoming a Street boycott and had emerged as the dominant force in the "long end" of the market, that is to say, those bonds with the most distant maturity. Cantor's prices were vital to Telerate, but access to its pages was strictly confined to primary dealers. "Outsiders"—meaning all other subscribers, defined as the retail, or institutional, sector of the market—had to be content with Page 5 plus Telerate's two pages of commercial-paper rates, the contributors of which I had vainly attempted to lure to Reuters a couple of years earlier. It was with those three "silly" pages alone that Telerate had contrived to become the dominant source of information in the American fixed-income market.

If that flimsy and improbable foundation made Telerate's success all the more astonishing, it also rendered it all the more impressive.

The one glaring omission in Telerate's coverage was foreign exchange. Glaring, but hardly crippling; Telerate had made such headway in the domestic market that Hirsch had been perfectly content to cede the international arena to Reuters. That was about to change. I now learned that Telerate, in partnership with AP-Dow Jones, had formed a jointly owned company to distribute Telerate everywhere outside North America. Foreign exchange, of marginal importance in the United States, would be crucial in overseas markets. Securing currency contributors would be one of my first marketing assignments, Hirsch said.

The AP-Dow Jones deal, concluded before I arrived, was the only disclosure at Telerate that I found disquieting. Our partners no doubt deserved the fine reputations they enjoyed in the field of news, but neither had any experience marketing online products—even if, as sworn enemies of Reuters, they had every incentive to succeed. The question in my mind was whether they would have the stomach. The AP was a notoriously, almost religiously, frugal organization in the finest penny-pinching traditions of the cooperative news agency. Dow Jones was a household name in the United States but had rarely seemed comfortable in the international arena, to the limited extent it had operated there.

As if to vindicate my concerns, the management of the joint venture promptly assigned Telerate distribution rights in the four key continental European marketing territories—Germany, Switzerland, France and Italy—to local agencies. Two of them had been given the boot by Reuters years earlier, for reasons not entirely unrelated to my own misgivings, and there was little evidence to suggest that the leopards had changed their spots. The other two were minor information vendors. This mass assignment in my view not only underlined AP-Dow Jones's lack of international sophistication but also devalued its commitment to the project. Worse still, the contracts had been hastily negotiated and carelessly drafted, specifying no meaningful performance criteria or minimum levels of investment in the project. Given the apparently dismal commercial record of the organizations concerned, such omissions might one day prove critical, or at the very least contentious. Hirsch, it became distressingly clear, had been perfectly happy to go along with this nonsense.

To add insult to injury, the Dow Jones executive responsible for Telerate's global initiative turned out to be my old newswire protagonist, Bill Clabby of Dow Jones. The AP representative, Claude Erbsen, I had never met, but all his credentials and, as it turned out, all his instincts were derived from the distinctly non-commercial world of agency news. Both men were pathologically suspicious of any and all activities connected with marketing, sales, or technology, righteously devoted instead to what they saw as the morally uplifting merits of operating on a shoestring. Clabby and Erbsen came as a matched pair. They were often referred to as Clerbsen. Their opinions differed only in the degree to which each could outscore the inbred prejudices of the other.

Hull was greatly amused by it all. "Funny game, isn't it, you and Buffalo Bill ending up on the same team. And now it looks like there are two of them to contend with."

What had prompted Hirsch to pick AP-Dow Jones for the deal? Why indeed pick anyone? Surely it would have been better to act alone, allowing Telerate to keep all the proceeds. These and other questions I put to Hirsch as delicately as possible. I have to say that his justifications were superficially plausible.

"They were really, really keen," he said, by way of explanation, which is precisely what it was not. "Telerate distributes AP-Dow Jones news here in the United States already, and they sell their newswires in all the markets we want to get into in Europe and Asia, so it makes sense. Besides, we were simply not in a position to do it ourselves. We're spread pretty thin even in our own backyard, as you can see."

As if reading my thoughts, Hirsch added. "Bill Clabby has been very helpful putting this deal together—and he really does understand the business in Europe."

"Mmm…" I muttered.

Hirsch's defense of AP-Dow Jones was the first indication of his curious indifference to Telerate's potential outside the United States. His lack of interest in the world outside the United States struck me as a mirror image of Reuters' attitude in the other direction. "If AP-DJ and associates sell a few terminals, fine. If they don't, then we've lost nothing," was the attitude. I countered it with the opinion that Telerate's international performance in an increasingly global marketplace might some day make or break the company. But with Hirsch responding to this new boy's reproaches with increasing signs of irritation, I backed off. In time, though, our differences over Telerate's global ambitions would become a source of friction between us.

After the little contretemps over international affairs, it was almost a relief when Hirsch suggested a pilgrimage upstairs to pay homage to Bernie Cantor. But no sooner had we been ushered into the Great Man's office than he angrily waved us away, having just launched into a violent diatribe on the telephone.

Our rapid exit brought us face to face instead with Bernie's right-hand man, John Terranova—and another diatribe, this one directed at us.

A number of people had warned me about Terranova. A small man with a big voice, he deployed an atrocious temper with all the aggressive reflexes of a spitting cobra. His conversation was so riddled with bilious profanities as to suggest to the uninitiated a virulent form of Tourette's syndrome. Delete the expletives and there was little much left. Someone once remarked that if the voice on the Watergate tapes had been that of John Terranova, President Nixon would have kept his job. But Terranova's abuse, as I quickly realized, was not to be taken personally, being applied universally and indiscriminately. One soon got used to it, even to the point of finding it endearing.

Terranova, an avid tennis fan, greeted us with an intimidating serve. "Another refugee from Reuters. So what the fuck do you think you can do for us?" I returned the attempted ace with a solid crosscourt forehand. "I expect to make Telerate a lot of fucking money—and me in the process."

Terranova greeted this remark with deliquescent delight. "I like this fucking guy already," he cried, turning to Hirsch. I liked him, too, even when we were rudely dismissed with some parting advice. "So, why don't you people get back downstairs, start kicking some ass, and sell some fucking terminals?"

Selling terminals, I found out, was literally a family business, the private preserve of Esther Zimet and Rod Fisher, an engagingly dysfunctional but highly effective pair of magpies who spent much of their time squabbling loudly over disputed commissions. They qualified as "family" by adoption rather than blood.

Esther was an attractive, well-turned-out widow in her forties. She had joined Telerate by virtue of her role as the long-time companion of Hirsch's late father, Harold, himself a widower early in life. Harold Hirsch had bankrolled the company in its early years, using the fortune he had made from the family business. Esther, it was said, had become a surrogate mother to Neil during his formative years, although she insisted on pointing out she had never actually moved in with his father, and had never considered marrying him. Rod Fisher arrived on the scene from the Cantor side of the business by marrying Suzie, the seventeen-year-old niece of Bernie's wife, Iris.

Zimet and Fisher were both acutely conscious of their duty to serve two masters, but both tended to gravitate to Bernie Cantor, as the controlling shareholder, much to Hirsch's frequent and ill-concealed irritation.

If some of Neil's social excesses involving broads, booze, and drugs were occasionally shocking to a traditional Jewish matriarch, Esther was always ready to leap to his defense. "He can be a little wild, but he'll grow out of it in time," was her stock defense. But woe betide anyone heard calling her a "matriarch"—or any other formulation that might denote advancing years. Esther possessed charm, style, and dignity aplenty, but to cross her was to confront a hellcat—and the fastest way to unleash the fierce feline was to refer, however obliquely, to her age. Having raised two sons of her own during a long and difficult widowhood she was, quite understandably, intent on appearing as youthful and sprightly as possible for as long as possible. In both aims she succeeded, dressing impeccably, with skirt lengths fashionably short and neckline contrived to reveal a generous, if slightly corrugated, décolletage. Her ensembles assumed a particular flamboyance on Fridays, traditionally Esther's day for lunching with clients.

More than Hirsch, or even Bernie Cantor, Esther Zimet was the public voice of Telerate, as much as Walter Cronkite was the public face of CBS television. Clients with problems were purred to seductively on the telephone. No requested favors were considered too small. At conventions and cocktail parties, clients succumbed fawningly to her coquettish charm. Anyone else attracting such accolades might have incurred Hirsch's resentment, but Esther transcended his jealousy.

Family connections aside, Esther had earned her spurs at Telerate. She had been with the company from its earliest days, when it was known by its original name of Telstock, and operating in a somewhat precarious financial condition from a poky office above Pennsylvania Station. There, for months, she and Hirsch were the company's sole employees. To convey the impression that Telstock was a more substantial organization than it really was, she used to answer the telephone with an affected secretarial voice before "transferring" the caller to the real Esther Zimet.

Telstock was conceived, as the name implies, as a stock-market service, but, at some point, one George Bakkerlow appeared on the scene with the idea of using the product to distribute commercial-paper rates. Hirsch embraced Bakkerlow's scheme, hired the man himself, and promptly changed the company name to Telerate.

The venture into commercial paper (a commonly used form of short-term lending and borrowing by industrial corporations) had two compelling advantages: it kept the company afloat and it brought Telerate to the attention of Henry Wattson, a bond trader at Cantor Fitzgerald. It was Wattson, a bearded giant of a man and not one to shy away from extravagant ideas of high ambition, who dreamed up the notion of using Telerate to "advertise" Cantor Fitzgerald's government-bond prices. He convinced Bernie Cantor that screen-based trading, though revolutionary and risky, was also potentially lucrative. Bernie bought in to the idea and followed up by acquiring 75 percent of the stock. Telerate had been saved from almost certain oblivion.

If Esther was largely absolved from Hirsch's resentment, Rod Fisher was often the target of it. Fisher had been foisted on Telerate by his uncle-in-law Bernie over Hirsch's strong objections.

"Give the kid a chance," Bernie had insisted. "He may be green but I promise you, he can sell."

Forced to relent, Hirsch had hired him on a commission-only basis in the hope that Fisher, having hitherto failed to make a decent living in any other field, would fall flat on his face.

In the event, Rod more than lived up to Bernie's promise. He sold Telerate terminals in substantial numbers with a line of patter worthy of a television evangelist. Fisher went on to make a great deal of money, most of which he managed to squirrel away by frugal living—"squirrel" being *le mot juste*. A miserly nature was augmented by a fanaticism for healthy eating. Thin to the point of emaciation, Fisher had a diet confined almost exclusively to fruit, nuts, and herbal potions. These he charged to the company—exploiting the company's policy of paying for lunch for employees, provided they ate in the office—much to Hirsh's disgust.

It was, therefore, an astonishing moment when Fisher, out of the blue one day, invited me to join him for lunch at a nearby Italian restaurant. The motivation became clear as soon as we entered the place: the establishment was celebrating its fiftieth anniversary and offering, just for that day, a menu at 1928 prices. The bill came to less than ten dollars. In observing such economies Fisher quickly accumulated enough cash to buy a substantial house in affluent Westchester County, without even the encumbrance of a mortgage.

Esther and Rod vied vigorously for primacy in a personal sales contest. For the most part it was a perfectly civil war, but at times, when commissions were up for grabs, tooth and claw was the order of the day. Daily skirmishing served as rehearsals for more serious end-of-week confrontations. Esther enjoyed the privilege, and potential advantage, of keeping all Telerate's sales and installation records. Each Thursday morning, by tradition, Telerate's two accountants were invited to sit at the big round table in Esther's office for a ritual totting-up of the week's business, leaving Fisher, excluded from the meeting, to hover anxiously nearby.

"I'm happy to leave 'em to get on with it," Hirsch chuckled, after a particularly acerbic session involving much yelling and slamming of doors. "The fact is, the sound of fighting over commissions is music to my ears."

As agreed, I wasted no time returning to my familiar old parish, the foreign-exchange market, in search of contributors.

As the first order of business, we set up a screen display unabashedly patterned on Hull's four-column government-securities page on Monitor. Taking advantage of Telerate's larger screen matrix, we extended it to six columns. (Telerate screens displayed twenty-four lines of eighty characters, whereas Reuters had designed Monitor for only twelve lines of sixty-four characters.) Each column would be devoted to a single contributor for each of the six main currencies: the British pound, Canadian dollar, German mark, Swiss franc, French franc, and Japanese yen. In a well-practiced routine, I once again invited the banks to get their names up in lights on the prestigious first page.

Much to my surprise, it was filled within a week. I can still recall the first six contributors. Corresponding to the currencies just mentioned, they were National Westminster Bank, Toronto Dominion Bank, DG Bank, Swiss Bank, Société Général, and Bank of Tokyo. Worthy names every one. In no time at all, three additional pages were filled. Hirsch was ecstatic. I found myself fêted as a hero of the revolution.

A minor triumph, then, in foreign exchange, but Telerate had not forgotten its roots in the domestic market. With Cantor Fitzgerald's treasury prices on the system, ignoring the domestic market could be viewed as an affordable luxury, but Hirsch was determined to forestall any attempt by Reuters to press its claims in the field. The threat was real only if Reuters could find a way to galvanize the primary dealers into a potent competitive force. As it happened, Hirsch needn't have worried.

Inexplicably, Reuters had made little progress with its domestic version of Monitor. Several of the contributors of treasury prices Hull and I had signed up months earlier were already disillusioned, doubting Reuters' commitment to the American market.

"Why don't we just put 'em out of their misery," Hirsch said one day. "Get them off Reuters and on to Telerate. After all, we're more their natural home."

That was true, given a satisfactory answer to one question: would Bernie Cantor want the dealers on his own network competing with his own brokerage firm? "Leave Bernie to me," Hirsch said. "My guess is he'll welcome it. The dealers can only make Cantor Fitzgerald's prices look even more tradable. And what better way to demonstrate an open, democratic attitude than to invite them to join us?"

Bernie surprisingly—some would say unaccountably—agreed. And so Hull and I went off on a new round of visits, and under new colors, to the thirty-six primary dealers, with more interesting consequences than we had bargained for.

The exercise precipitated the first corporate crisis of my nascent career at Telerate. Actually, I was more or less a bystander. At the center of it, this time standing alone, was my old controversialist-in-arms John Hull.

Of Reuters' original six contributors, Duke Swanborn at Harris Bank and Billy Kidder at Donaldson Lufkin & Jenrette had expressed themselves more than ready to bail out. So, with varying degrees of enthusiasm, were three of the others. The one predictable exception was John Tritz of Bankers Trust, who made it clear that there had been no softening in his antipathy for either Bernie Cantor or Telerate.

Pinching Reuters' contributors was all well and good, but new names were needed too. John Hull came back with a significant capture, Morgan Stanley, whose chief treasury dealer, Kerry Roche, had once been counted among Cantor's more vocal protagonists. Morgan Stanley was more than acceptable as a replacement for Bankers Trust.

But as we plowed through the list of dealers, one name kept asserting itself, and each time it did we deferred placing the call we knew we eventually could not avoid. Mighty Merrill Lynch—occasionally but not fondly known along Wall Street as the Thundering Herd—had remained steadfast in its refusal to recognize Cantor Fitzgerald, and staunch in its opposition to screen-based trading. Since Merrill had declined a perfect opportunity to hit back at both by rejecting advances from Reuters, Telerate could hardly expect a warm reception, or so we assumed. Yet Hull and I were well aware that we could hardly contact every single primary dealer except the biggest one, even if it seemed certain to be a complete waste of time. But what if it turned out not to be?

"Fat chance," said Hull, but conceded that once and for all we had to excise the name from our list.

That is pretty much all that I expected to accomplish when I telephoned Merrill's chief government trader, George Grimm, late one Monday afternoon. Grimm! The very name had a gloomy, gothic resonance. Having expected a secretarial automaton to recite one of the usual excuses, like "he's away from his desk," or "he's in a meeting," I was startled when a male voice said, "Grimm speaking." Grimm's tone was more than polite, it was friendly, almost unctuous. "Thanks for calling," he trilled. "To tell you the truth I've been half expecting you to. So why don't you come on downtown and tell us what you have in mind?"

The following evening, Hull and I, uncertain what to expect, were ushered by Grimm into a large, formal meeting room. Grimm had assembled half a dozen managers from the firm's various fixed-income departments. It was a sour-looking gathering. Hull and I exchanged glances that read, "Wish this had never happened."

Regretting having elected myself to make the presentation, I kept it brief, shorn of anything resembling sales spin. There seemed little point in expending more effort than was absolutely necessary. Half an hour at most, I reckoned, and surely we would be out of there, duty fulfilled. That seemed a reasonable bet when the group responded with no more than a few perfunctory questions, mainly of the kind asked more from courtesy than curiosity. I caught Hull sneaking a look at his watch.

Then, as the questions dried up, Grimm glanced at his own watch, the signal for a summing up. "You know the history of the relationship between Merrill and Cantor, so I won't bore you with repetition," he began before pausing, perhaps for dramatic effect. "But we're now prepared to open a new chapter." Another long pause followed. Hull and I exchanged glances again, this time anticipating some kind of bombshell. It was duly dropped.

Grimm said: "Forget history. Merrill is now prepared to contribute to Telerate. We'll give you governments, corporate and municipal bonds, money markets, research—you name it, the whole ball of wax. Merrill will also open up broker lines with Cantor Fitzgerald. We'll have to talk about how many Cantor and Telerate screens our trading room will need, and on what terms, but we'll give you some rough numbers so that you can come back to us with a proposal."

Grimm, smiling, added: "I imagine this is something you'll have to refer to your boss."

Hull and I nodded in silent shock. But there was yet another twist to the improbable tale now unfolding.

"There's something else," Grimm added. "We are prepared to do all this, and possibly more, but on one condition." He paused again—the man had the timing of a stand-up comic. "Merrill Lynch will proceed only if it is the only, and I mean only, dealer on the Telerate system."

Hull and I were then released to flee for a fortifying drink and a sanity check. It was hard to believe what we had just heard. Hull said, "There's no way Bernie can turn this deal down." If he was right—and I was sure he was— we would face the unpleasant task of dismissing the five dealers we had just persuaded to abandon Reuters for Telerate, not to mention Morgan Stanley. "That'll be the least of his concerns," Hull said ruefully. "You're about to see the biggest sell-out since Munich."

First there had to be a call to Hirsch. For a moment we pondered not making it. What if we said nothing, pretended we had never made the call? Perhaps Grimm had been indulging in a little leg-pulling. Perhaps Merrill would just go away. Not a chance; there had been too many Merrill executives present. Quickly coming to our senses, we made the call.

Hirsch's astonishment matched ours. "You're not fucking serious!" was all he could say. He soon recovered. "Bernie's gotta hear this."

"Shall we join you?" Hull asked.

"Nah," said Hirsch. "I'll handle it. You guys might as well go home. Good

225

work. And don't breathe a word of this. Not one fucking word to one single solitary soul, d'ya hear me? Don't even tell your mothers."

On the train home, Hull, smelling a rat, descended into gloom. "This is a disaster. The other dealers will be furious, that's for sure. I'm not sure I want to be around when the shit hits the fan." He was conscience-stricken, his distress aggravated by the imposed vow of silence.

Hirsch's insistence on keeping the affair under wraps was calculated to give Bernie Cantor time to conclude a deal with the firm Hull now disparaged as "Bernie's new friends." Looking directly at Hull, Hirsch said, "We'll make an announcement, whatever it turns out to be, when it's appropriate. Meanwhile, we'd better stay well away from the other dealers. Don't even think about taking their calls."

Hull managed to hold out for a few days before cracking under the strain. It happened on a day when I was out of town. Kerry Roche at Morgan Stanley, Telerate's newest and most enthusiastic recruit, had called for a progress report. His office was on Sixth Avenue, just a few blocks from Telerate's. "I'm coming over," Hull whispered down the line. "We gotta talk."

For "talk" read "spill the beans."

Hull, filled with remorse, promptly called Hirsch to tell him what he had done. And to resign. It was a short conversation. Hirsch was too angry to speak coherently and hung up. Bernie Cantor, equally enraged, had no such problem. He was intent on retribution. "I want that bastard fired, NOW." Hirsch pointed out the obvious, that Hull had already quit. "Then I want him sued. I want him ruined. Let's get the godammed lawyers in here right now."

Hirsch advised caution. "I don't think we want Hull loose out there. He could create havoc. Better to have him inside the tent pissing out than outside pissing in." Bernie saw the merit in that, but reserved the right to inflict future punishment. "I'll make sure that little rat never works in this town again—ever!"

All this *Sturm und Drang* I heard from Hirsch by telephone in Boston where I had spent the day looking for contributors. He was flattering in his concern. Just because Hull had resigned, that did not mean I would go too, did it?

"Let's discuss it tomorrow," I said, a guarded response dictated by the fact that I had been caught on the hop, but also because I was calling from a client's office.

Having avoided the temptation to call Hull that evening, I was surprised to find him in the office the next morning. He looked appropriately glum. Hirsch had called him at home and talked him out of quitting, but Hull knew perfectly well why he was being kept on. "It's a case of here today, gone tomorrow. Right now I'm confined to the reservation to keep me out of mischief. Pointless, really, since I've already done my straying. But I might as well stick around—take the money until they decide when I should go."

The Merrill crisis slowly abated, like receding floodwater. But for some weeks, with Hirsch and Hull barely on speaking terms, the atmosphere in Telerate's executive suite was toxic.

By contrast, between Cantor Fitzgerald and Merrill Lynch, until recently implacable enemies, all was suddenly sweetness and light. The opening of trading lines between Merrill and Cantor was quickly arranged. Merrill executives gaily swapped badinage with their opposite numbers, trooping in and out of the offices of the once-despised Cantor Fitzgerald as if there had never been so much as a tiff over a fumbled trade. Endless meetings and harmonizing dinners were arranged, and attended by hangers-on by the limousine-load. And Grimm's promise to provide Telerate with staggering amounts of market information proved no idle posture: 200 system pages were reserved for the purpose.

Hull watched from the sidelines with ill-disguised disdain and suspicion. He speculated that a deal might be cooking for Merrill to buy, or at least buy into, Telerate—and perhaps into Cantor, which would kill two birds with one stone. Given Merrill's startling and wholehearted conversion to screen-based markets, the notion was not so far-fetched. (No such deal was done, but Merrill must surely have given the matter some thought. Perhaps not, but a few years later the firm would get involved with another online information provider, Bloomberg, lending post-mortem plausibility to Hull's speculations.)

With or without a merger, the financial benefits of the Merrill deal were immeasurable to Cantor Fitzgerald. They were hardly less so for Telerate. Instructions were received to install Telerate terminals in most of Merrill's branch offices, of which there were more than one hundred. Hundreds of terminals were ordered for Merrill's head-office dealing room.

"Who gets the commissions?" Rod Fisher wanted to know. "Merrill was my account, you know."

"Get lost," Hirsch told him.

As for the six treasury dealers we had recently courted, and which we were now preparing to abandon, they reacted with benign resignation. How else should they have responded, and what else could they have done? Legal action was one option. There were rumors that Kerry Roche had considering filing suit, possibly in concert with the others. If so, nothing came of it. Reuters, its own treasury project staggering pitifully towards oblivion, seemed equally incapable of responding. A similar fate perhaps awaited our old colleague, Scott Rumbold. He himself had been wooing Merrill, he told us during a brief street-encounter. It had all been futile. Merrill must have been secretly planning this coup while he was talking to them. Anyway, he added, Reuters' management seemed forever occupied elsewhere, and was now left with nothing. Elsewhere was a place he did not define—not because he was being coy but because he couldn't. "Beats me what we're supposed to be doing," he sighed. "All I know is that you guys seem to be having all the fun."

One would never have guessed it looking at Hull.

Reuters and John Hull were the short-term casualties of the Merrill affair, but were there other, less obvious victims? Principles, Hull would say. But what principles exactly? The government dealers we had approached had every reason to feel disappointed, but no contracts had been signed. "Our word is supposed to mean something," Hull grumbled. He had a point. But in Telerate's favor, it could be said that its plans for a multiple-dealer service had simply been superseded by an event that was as extraordinary as it was unforeseeable. Hull curled his lip at that, too. This time my response was harsh. "Well, it's true that you resigned on a point of principle, but leaving the company in the evening and rejoining it in the morning hardly makes you Sir Thomas bloody More."

Our dispute was conducted less in anger than in regret. To a great extent I shared Hull's disquiet. But I could not help pondering that if Cantor and Telerate had behaved so badly, the dealers could have fought back, perhaps by rallying round the Reuters banner. They had not done so. Nor did they pursue any other course of action. On one thing Hull and I agreed: memories on Wall Street tend to be short, Merrill's conversion itself a case in point. It was a fair bet that Telerate's supposed treachery and Hull's indiscretion would soon be both forgotten and forgiven. So it turned out. Well, almost.

Meanwhile, I had contrived a personal crisis of my own, this time without the slightest assistance from Hull.

"M" and I had become, in the delicate jargon of the gossip column, an "item." Hirsch had been oblivious to it, but when, eventually, the penny dropped, he was in no mood for congratulations. That is to understate the case considerably. What most disconcerted him was the realization that when it finally dawned on him that something was afoot, his suspicions fell not on me but on Hull, putting their already soured relationship under even greater strain. As for the former relationship between my boss and what in the modern idiom would be called my new partner, there is no point in speculating on its nature, or its depth. Suffice to say that it was such as to send Hirsch into a week-long sulk. He emerged from it with an ultimatum: "One of you must go!" He made a point of not specifying which one.

I stayed. Further comment is unnecessary, except to say that Hirsch seemed palpably relieved by the outcome. "Now, for God's sake, let's all get back to work," he said, shaking my hand.

But the bond of trust had been broken, and things would never be quite the same between us.

As the Christmas holiday approached, Hull and I reflected that it had been an action-packed year. "Nobody can say we haven't made a mark on this company," he remarked over a seasonal lunch. That much was beyond dispute. My New Year's resolution, though, was that we should endeavor to put some distance between us and controversy. "Chance would be a fine thing," Hull said, with an ominously mischievous glint in his eye.

It was as well, perhaps, that Hirsch had meanwhile immersed himself in a major new project. Cantor Fitzgerald and Telerate had both outgrown their midtown premises, leaving neither with much choice but to look for new space, preferably in a building that could offer adjoining occupancies. The location selected was the World Trade Center. Completed a few years earlier in 1973, its twin towers—briefly the world's tallest building—had become an instant Manhattan landmark, a symbol of America's financial power and confidence. Ironically, the WTC's completion had coincided with a crisis in New York City's finances and a prolonged slump in the real-estate market. The WTC's landlord, the Port Authority of New York and New Jersey, a combined state agency, was still desperate for tenants. The rental terms were irresistible—barely into double digits a square foot.

Cantor signed a lease for the 105th floor in Tower 1, Telerate took the floor below. They were the highest floors in either tower designed for occupancy. The deal was something of a coup for the Port Authority.

Bernie Cantor assembled a collection of his beloved Rodin statues on the 105th floor, thereby creating the highest museum in the world. Not to be outdone, Hirsch wrote to the Guinness Book of Records to claim an entry for Telerate as the highest computer center in the world. Guinness had no interest.

In that crazy, eventful year of 1978, it may be counted as Telerate's one and only failure.

# Exco

Telerate's business prospects entering the eighties were no less impressive than the view from Neil Hirsch's office on the 104th floor of the World Trade Center. In both cases the horizon seemed to stretch to infinity.

But such unbridled optimism was far from rampant everywhere across the Republic. After a decade of unremitting international humiliations, the old America of unwavering certainty and swaggering confidence had given way, for the first time in 200 years, to a nation tortured by confusion and self-doubt. The seventies had embraced the joyous occasion of the American bicentennial, of course, but otherwise offered precious little for Americans to celebrate. The decade produced instead an endless cavalcade of degradations, each of which, taken in isolation, might have been dismissed as an aberration, but which in aggregate proved overwhelming. They included some dismally memorable firsts.

Abroad, a ragtag army of Vietnamese irregulars inflicted on America its first-ever military defeat. At home, a comic gang of burglars set in train a series of extraordinary and seemingly interminable revelations that would lead to America's first presidential resignation. American irresolution in Asia encouraged rising anti-American sentiment in the Middle East, leading to an unprecedented Arab oil embargo and a world energy crisis that threatened, among other things, America's gas-guzzling dependence on the automobile. Among its many strange and novel excrescences was the sight of American motorists, enraged or bewildered, waiting in line to buy gasoline at prices to which the rest of the world had become accustomed but which struck Americans as provocatively extortionate.

A ten-year pandemic of anti-war protest marches, along with the "hard-hat" counter-demonstrations they in turn provoked, had exposed divisions in American society as profound as hitherto they had been unsuspected. No less polarizing was the fall-out from the break-in, dismissed at the time as a "third-rate burglary," at the Democratic Party headquarters at Watergate. More significant than the fiercely partisan divisions it opened up between the main political parties, Watergate drove yet another contradictory wedge between Richard Nixon's downtrodden "silent majority" and their social "enemies" drawn from the affluent, country club elite. The contradiction was that the former had always been presumed solidly Democratic and the latter staunchly Republican. Suddenly, nothing seemed clear.

Once the Vietnam business and the oil crisis had been settled, and with the disgraced Nixon departed from the scene, Americans could dare to hope that quieter times would repair some of the damage inflicted on the national psyche. But there would be no miracle recovery, the healing process needing wiser and braver counseling than Nixon's successors seemed capable of giving. The half-term presidency of Gerald Ford—the first man to serve as president and vice president without being elected to either office—was dismissed by those on the political left as "illegitimate," and the single-term administration of his successor, Jimmy Carter, by those on the right as inept. It was the hapless Carter's ultimate misfortune to be the man in office when the decade signed itself off with yet another incident of national humiliation—and yet another manifestation of growing self-assertion in the Muslim world: the siege of the United States embassy in Iran. With sixty-six Americans held hostage, American impotence was once more exposed, this time compounded by American incompetence as a boldly conceived rescue mission ended ignominiously with the would-be rescuers stranded in the desert by the mechanical failure of their helicopters. (It was one of the decade's curiosities that some of its most dismally enduring images involved helicopters—from the panicked evacuation from the roof of the embassy in Saigon to the airlifting of Nixon from the White House lawn to the charred desert skeletons of Carter's rescue craft.)

These unremitting national disasters in themselves may not have been entirely responsible for undermining public faith in the financial markets, but neither was there anything to inspire it. Wall Street, meanwhile, grappled with worrying economic issues, like the triple threat of rising inflation, rising interest rates, and a soaring budget deficit. Market sentiment is a fragile vessel, and in October 1978 the investment community, baffled and frustrated by government inaction, finally cried enough—as it often does during that unruly month—and the stock market succumbed to the worst one-week fall ever recorded. The Dow Jones Industrial Average fell back 59 points to 838, a 7 percent retreat, which in later, more volatile times would scarcely be defined as dramatic but which was then considered pretty scary.

If matters were to improve, politically and economically, then clearly a change of regime and changes in thinking were in order. Accordingly, perhaps more from hope than conviction, American voters elected to the White House the affable Ronald Reagan, representing the forces of old-fashioned, uncompromising conservatism and, perhaps more importantly, an uncomplicated "can do" optimism. Many found Reagan's sunny, Hollywood-fashioned grin—and some the man himself—laughable, but at least it offered a welcome break from the permanently baffled mien of the well-meaning peanut farmer from Plains, Georgia.

There were similar political forces and social impulses at work in Britain, where an electorate exhausted by endless economic crises, culminating in the infamous "winter of discontent" that brought down James Callaghan's dispirited Labour government, turned for salvation to Margaret Thatcher, whose conservative instincts were more than a match for Reagan's. Liberals might cringe at the emphatic swing to the right, but even they had to concede that trying to manage despondency—an approach that had failed on both sides of the Atlantic—as opposed to fighting it, had never stood up as an election-winning, least of all a governing, formula.

American apostles of free-market economics would now have their day in the sun, a Californian sun that would shine brightly on deregulation, government minimalism, and an emerging phenomenon its advocates called trickle-down economics. And so, exasperated Americans and beleaguered Britons alike awaited, with a mixture of hope and trepidation, the liberating effects of Reaganomics and Thatcherism.

The investment community, no less than the voters (though perhaps with more hard-headed expectations), also appeared to like what it was hearing. Left-leaning social critics might round on Reagan and Thatcher for legitimizing avarice, but the financial community suffered no crisis of conscience. In *Wall Street*, one of the popular movies of the decade, a shady character, pointedly named Gordon Gecko, famously declared, "Greed is good, greed is right." The film was making a satirical point, of course, but, in the real Wall Street, stockbrokers stood and applauded enthusiastically.

So did investors. From early in the 1980s, taking heart from the tough, energizing talk from fresh political leaders, they returned to the market in droves, propelling the Dow Jones Industrial Average steadily higher on rapidly rising trading volume that could soon be described as soaring. At the start of the previous decade, daily turnover rarely went over 20 million shares; by 1983 100-million share days were pretty much the norm. Small investors wasted little time jumping on the bandwagon, usually a sign that the wagon is about to roll off the edge of a cliff. But this time the market had what traders sometimes refer to as the "legs" for a sustained advance. The bull market was back with a vengeance.

Other markets blossomed, too, treasury securities especially. Neither they nor other interest-sensitive instruments could fail to prosper—at least from a trader's perspective; not with interest rates fluctuating wildly and the Reagan administration forced to resort to ever-more profligate borrowing to cover the expanding federal shortfall.

All of which was undoubtedly good for information providers, Telerate in particular. But with the treasury market already unassailably under Telerate's dominion, our thoughts turned once again to the market for which Reuters could make a similar claim of pre-eminence: foreign exchange.

Telerate's tentative expedition into the market two years earlier—the one with which I had first earned my Telerate spurs—had long been stalled. It had taken, at the time, a pertinent question from Terranova to bring us down to terra firma: "So, you've got a bunch of fucking currency contributors. But let me ask you something: how much fucking revenue do they bring in?" The answer then had been "very little," and the answer three years on was no different.

Telerate could scarcely hope to match Reuters' depth or breadth of coverage in foreign exchange—perhaps not for years, if ever. Even drawing level in quantitative terms, apart from being an unrealistic objective, would have failed to give Telerate the distinct edge it needed to dislodge Monitor. To make our mark quickly and emphatically, we needed a radically superior product, one sufficiently compelling to win over a trading community still not entirely comfortable with desktop computers and, to a growing extent, not entirely comfortable with Reuters. That much we decided one day during a brainstorming session in Hirsch's office.

An unlikely white knight appeared in the livery of Robert Nagel. He rode into the lists armed with an idea that today would be regarded as absurdly simple but which, in the more incredulous age of the seventies, was positively bathed in brilliance.

Monitor's vulnerability was that Reuters had designed the system as a kind of advertising medium, with each contributing bank assigned its own page. This was not a conceptual flaw, but it did mean that users seeking a market consensus in a particular currency were obliged to refer to more than one page—an exercise which, in later times and other contexts, would be called channel-surfing. Changing pages was by no means a complex chore. It could, however, be time-consuming, especially when response times to page requests were slow, as they often were. The reason was that the networks operated by Reuters and Telerate were designed, for reasons of economy, at transmission speeds that by modern standards seem laughably slow. In 1981, and for several years to come, both networks ran at 1200 baud, which, to place it in a modern context, is several thousand times slower than the speed of the computer on which this sentence is being typed. To offer an alternative analogy, compare the performance of a First World War biplane with that of a modern jet fighter. The chief consequence of slow networks was that during peak market-trading hours, especially during times of heightened market activity, thousands of users would simultaneously attempt to call up the same popular pages. On such occasions, networks simply choked. Congestion was the source of most customer complaints and explained the popularity of composite pages, such as Page 5, which contained virtually everything a fixed-income trader needed to know. Most users left it on almost permanent display, leaving its ghostly imprint seared into thousands of Telerate cathode ray tubes.

What Telerate needed, we explained to Bob Nagel one day, was a composite foreign-exchange page, the equivalent of Page 5. Much to our surprise, he came up with an instant solution. He did so by calling our attention to a process called mapping, whereby currency quotes inserted into individual bank contributor pages could be automatically duplicated on a composite page. We knew all about mapping, Hull pointed out, but currency traders needed to see not only the quote but also the name of the bank behind it and, just as importantly, an update time. "No problem," said Bob breezily. "I can map both the rate and the name. We'll call it, for want of a better name, mapping-with-source. The time stamp will be added automatically."

"Perfect!" we chorused. But the critical question, bearing in mind Nagel's propensity—amply demonstrated in his days at Reuters—for promising the earth in two weeks and delivering Rhode Island in two years, was when could we have it.

"I'll have something for you to look at tomorrow," Nagel said, a promise that provoked gales of scornful laughter.

"Won't see him for a month," Hirsch predicted, after Nagel had left the room with a suggested page layout.

"Six months, more likely," interjected Sabatini, grateful for the opportunity to scoff at a perceived rival. "It is, however, a very simple procedure, and even Nagel should be able to deliver it fast. If he can't, I will."

But Nagel was as good as his word, reappearing the next day with a smug grin perfectly justified by a single night's work. What we had asked for, a page showing the latest four updates on the leading four currencies complete with name and time, was what we got. "Bloody brilliant!" was the collective verdict. "All I can say, Doctor," I added for good measure, "is that I'm glad I didn't throw you out of that window."

After a couple of days to allow for software debugging, we released three composite foreign-exchange pages: one for North America and another two to be held in reserve for Asia and Europe. Unable to give them easily remembered alphabetic titles such as those used by Monitor—Telerate pages being numeric—we had to settle for 260, 261 and 262. An immediate hit with users, they allowed us to sell Telerate terminals to currency traders in ever-increasing numbers. As a bonus we also attracted a great many new contributors. Telerate was now at last seriously in the foreign-exchange business.

Naturally the composite pages caught the admiring attention of Reuters, and we braced for the inevitable retaliation. But either the Monitor system lacked the flexibility to allow deviation from its original design, or Reuters was making so much money that responding to pipsqueak pretenders like Telerate was considered unworthy. Whatever the reason, the expected counter-attack never materialized.

"You buggers are always up to something," said an admiring Scott Rumbold at a trade show. "Can't seem to get anything like that done over here at Reuters."

"So why don't you come on over and get it done at Telerate?" I said.

"If you're serious, I may just do that," he responded.

I was, and he did.

How laughably primordial all this talk of composite pages and "mapping" must strike the reader, a generation later, in the gilded Internet age of word-processors and Windows and the World Wide Web. And primordial is exactly what it was, just as the sight of words on a screen had startled us a decade earlier, and figures on a screen a decade before that, and Quotron's tape-spewing stocks-on-demand device a decade earlier still.

The success of the 260-series led us to consider further ways in which to press home Telerate's foreign-exchange offensive. Hull bravely and predictably resurrected the idea of a matching service. "The market's now primed for it," he told Hirsch. "Let's go after the brokers. We can put 'em out of business. The banks hate the brokers. They'll thank us for doing it."

Hirsch winced. Times might have changed, but some things clearly had not—including Hirsch's resolute opposition to automated trading. "I say the market's still not ready. And I'm certainly not. Anyway, why all this talk about screwing the brokers? For God's sake, our own parent is a broker. Maybe we should go after them in a more friendly way. Why don't we sign them up as contributors?"

In the grand scheme of things, it was a relatively harmless notion, but it had considerable merit as a means to expand Telerate's foreign-exchange content, and in a unique way. Why hadn't we thought of it before? In the event it was a fateful decision, one that would set in motion a train of events that would transform Telerate's business in a way none of us anticipated.

If nothing else, "going after the brokers" in Hirsch's benign sense offered a shortcut to a long, hard slog trying to secure hundreds of bank contributors, many of which were in Europe and Asia under the aimless jurisdiction of AP-Dow Jones. Moreover, Hirsch argued plausibly, if we had the brokers we would by proxy also have the banks, since broker prices originated with the banks. "Broker quotes are much more reflective of the market," he pointed out. "We're talking here about aggregate prices that represent the best bids and the best offers in the market. No bank can offer that."

There were then half a dozen foreign-exchange brokers of consequence in New York, but the market was dominated by just two: Noonan Astley & Pearce and Lasser-Marshall. Like most currency brokers, they were both

British-owned. The potential benefit of that was that if we signed up their New York branches, there was every chance that their London parents, and possibly other overseas offices, would follow suit.

Neither firm was likely to be a pushover. As a breed, foreign-exchange brokers were notoriously hidebound, doggedly wedded to traditional methods of trading by telephone and telex and suspicious in the extreme of any form of automation, which they feared—not altogether unreasonably—had the potential to put them out of business. The brokers' dread of computers was exceeded only by their terror of their customers, a fear cynically exploited by many bank dealers through constantly baying for commission cuts. The response from the brokers was to cultivate personal relationships with traders through lavish—and frequently inappropriate—"business entertaining." As one banker bluntly put it, "I only have to mention that brokerage fees might be on the Forex discussion agenda and I can get myself laid, or be treated to dinner for two at La Côte Basque, with a fistful of Knicks tickets thrown in." As much as such practices were disparaged—and denied—in public, they were frequently indulged in secret.

If the electronic revolution seemed to have passed the brokers by, it was widely attributed not so much to their fear of automation as to Reuter's intransigence in excluding them from Monitor—a charge, it might be added, that conveniently ignored considerable evidence supporting similar allegations in the other direction. The brokers had a much better case in their resentment of Dealing, which, by encouraging direct bank-to-bank contact, constituted a much greater challenge to ancient rites and customs.

Telerate of course carried none of this baggage. But neither had we made any attempt to earn the brokers' trust. If Reuters had rebuffed them, we had ignored them. This we now resolved to change.

For insight into the state of mind sometimes referred to as "the broker mentality" we had a useful source in John Terranova, a veteran of the "boards" at Cantor Fitzgerald. The trick, as he enlightened us in his own inimitable earthy manner, was to appeal to fear, ego, stupidity, and logic, in that order. "Brokers don't make judgments and don't take risks. By making shitloads of money from commissions without risking capital by taking positions, they've got it into their fucking heads that they're brilliant. You gotta make 'em feel that this is their fucking project, not ours. Just plant a few seeds and let them do all the talking. Pretty soon they'll believe it was their fucking idea all along. Then all you gotta do is kiss someone's ass in Macy's window."

With that inviting prospect in mind, John Hull and I made an appointment to visit Phil D'Angelo, Noonan's chief executive. Separately, Rod Fisher offered to take on Tony Alloi, D'Angelo's counterpart at Lasser's, with whom he had a nodding acquaintance.

D'Angelo and Alloi were bookends: Italian by name and nature, short in stature, and equally matched in self-importance. "Jumped-up little egomaniacs in shiny suits," was how one bank dealer described them, before adding the warning. "And watch out. They have some very odd connections," referring to that old bugaboo about links with the Mob.

Predictably, the suggestion that they post their dealing rates on screens was greeted by both D'Angelo and Alloi with snorts of derision. For a start, they protested, the banks would almost certainly object. Second, they said, brokers were always far busier than the dealers and consequently would have little time to update quotes. Third—this point being framed as a question—where was the evidence to support the claim that Telerate would be far more broker-friendly than Reuters had been? In short, brokers being brokers, they smelled a rat.

Disappointed, but not deterred, we left our business cards in the hope of a follow-up visit. "Good," declared Terranova. "Let 'em stew for a while. And I betcha D'Angelo and Alloi were on the fucking phone with each other the minute you left their offices."

That indeed proved to be the case.

It was D'Angelo who came through a few days later with an invitation for a second meeting.

"Great," said Terranova. "Now it's his fucking meeting and, in his mind, his fucking project."

"You guys own this market," we cooed at D'Angelo the second time around. He seemed more susceptible to flattery than Alloi. "The banks can't touch you for accurate prices. Your quotes represent reality. Reality is tradable rates, which is exactly what our users want. No bank can give us that." We tried to come across less like a vendor looking for a sale than a victim of bullying in search of a savior. And we were, after all, fellow travelers: "Our parent company is a broker, too. We have mutual interests. You need to reach clients and we have the network to do it. If you want to service the banks, this is the most effective way to do it. And if you're so resentful of Reuters, then help us knock them off their pedestal."

Finally, there was the financial carrot: "If you'll update the major currencies, exclusively on Telerate, we'll supply the input terminals, and we'll put a screen in front of every single one of your traders, all at no charge."

That got D'Angelo's attention. "No charge?"

"None. We'll even pick up the line costs."

"How do you think the banks will react to this? They've had screen systems all to themselves up to now. They'll be really pissed off."

We had discreetly consulted a few banks. D'Angelo, we guessed, had done the same and was merely seeking a reinforcing opinion. The response in both cases had been positive, we confirmed, or at least not hostile. Even Bobby Van Roten felt that broker screens would be useful. And we cited Cantor Fitzgerald's experience. If it worked in treasuries there was no reason why it couldn't work in currencies.

D'Angelo was sold, but remained reluctant to stick his neck out. Actually, not his neck. As he colorfully phrased it, "It's not gonna be just my dick on the table." The obvious solution was for D'Angelo and Alloi to act together. "You know that old saying, Phil: two dicks are always better than one."

D'Angelo had in fact been working on Alloi. So had Rod Fisher. His latest bulletin was that Alloi would soon topple. D'Angelo asked us to deliver a message for his rival, presumably preferring that it should come from a neutral party. And as part of this coy maneuvering, Alloi had exactly the same message in reverse: "I will if he will. But if he says no, then I'm out, too."

The next step was a three-way meeting at Telerate's office. The jointly worked-out terms of the brokers were reasonable: both would go on the system at the same time, with exactly the same screen formats, and on exactly the same financial and contractual terms. Other brokers could sign up, but only as paying clients, and not for a year.

"Yours," we said, aping the jargon of the trading desk.

Noonan and Lasser went live, simultaneously, on a Monday morning. The broker pages proved an even bigger hit than the banks' 260 series. Their London parents were shortly persuaded to join them. They in turn recruited their European and Asian affiliates.

Telerate sales soared. Our lofty long-term objective had been parity with Reuters in foreign-exchange dealing rooms. In that we failed. But even by our own estimates—no doubt as inflated as the "kills" of enemy aircraft claimed by both sides during the Battle of Britain—we managed to grab a 30 percent market share. We were well satisfied.

Apart from the commercial consequences, the real significance for Telerate turned out to be the burgeoning social relationship between Hirsch and D'Angelo. (There was also a sad postscript: within weeks of the Telerate initiative, Tony Alloi fell seriously ill and died within months of his fortieth birthday.)

Physically, D'Angelo cut a curious and, to his detractors, an almost comical figure. His vanity projected a self-image as a businessman of unusual acumen. His critics found him more lucky than clever, pointing out that he had risen to the top job at Noonan's largely by virtue of his marriage to the daughter of Daniel E. Noonan, the firm's founder. So he might have, but D'Angelo had more than justified his elevation by running a tidy and profitable operation and by seeing off most of Noonan's competitors. And if he was no business genius, he was a much smarter and more thoughtful man than he was generally given credit for. Hirsch saw mainly the social D'Angelo, who was more than happy to be squired around the trendy Manhattan nightspots. For a while the two men became socially almost inseparable. But although D'Angelo undoubtedly enjoyed such diversions, what he really craved was to be regarded as something more substantial than his public image of the flash, fast-talking money broker. He was about to get an opportunity to show his worth.

Within weeks of the launch of the broker pages, D'Angelo invited Hull and me over for drinks. After a couple of rounds and some desultory small talk, he tossed out an interesting question. It was obviously the reason behind the invitation. "Think Bernie Cantor would ever consider selling Telerate?"

The question was more startling than strange. That D'Angelo had put it to us rather than to Hirsch aroused our curiosity. Perhaps he had some reason for not making a direct approach to his new pal. "Noonan got that kind of money?" asked Hull, impertinently.

"No, it doesn't," responded D'Angelo, ignoring the unintended insult. "But my parent company in London does."

Noonan's majority shareholder was Exco plc, a relatively new London money-brokerage firm. Exco, like Telerate, was an upstart. The firm, and its engaging chief executive, John Gunn, a former foreign-exchange broker at Barclays Bank, had become darlings of the City with a highly successful flotation followed by a string of diversifying acquisitions. Gunn, at five foot seven, was scarcely taller than D'Angelo but was different in virtually every other respect, from upbringing to personality to hobbies.

Gunn was a nice man, I thought, the kind people invariably describe as a gentleman of the old school. He came from a working-class background but spoke with an accent that only occasionally betrayed his North of England roots. Negating the popular perception of the money broker as a loud-mouthed New Age vulgarian, he was soft-spoken, charming, self-effacing, and by nature, as in appearance, rather academic. He avoided confrontation but, if required, could more than hold his own in oral fisticuffs. At Nottingham University he had read German, in which he became fluent after a year of teaching in Berlin. There he acquired a German wife, Renate, who had slipped over to the West—apparently with Gunn's help—just a few days before the Berlin Wall went up. Gunn's personal interests were diverse, running from German literature and classical music to cricket and stamp-collecting. If the latter two pursuits seemed quintessentially English, and somewhat out of sync with his avowed internationalism, they reflected an understated but heartfelt patriotism, which he allowed to surface now and then in defense of the realm.

Gunn's rise to prominence in the City was inevitably described in the cliché-ridden London press as meteoric.

It began when Gunn's employer, Astley & Pearce, a troubled money broker, was taken over by Gerrard and National, a London discount house, which in terms of old boy-ness boasted an impressive City pedigree and a suitably fusty management style to go with it. The view in the market was that the marriage was unlikely to last.

Nor did it last. Having been granted a 25 percent stake in the acquired business, which was operated independently from Gerrard's other activities, Gunn and eleven of his colleagues—inevitably dubbed the Dirty Dozen—had the foresight to pool their collective interest in a shelf company registered as Exco. (Unable to come up with something more imaginative, the partners simply stuck with the temporary acronym.) The plan was to use Exco, should the occasion arise, as a vehicle for a management buyout. Sure enough, Gunn, bristling with ideas, soon found Gerrard altogether too tradition-bound in the newly emancipated and fast-growing world of money and foreign-exchange brokering and a friendly separation was negotiated. It was financed by an investment management firm called Gartmore, whose ample provision of cash, combined with its relaxed, hands-off patronage, mentored Exco's brief and happy existence as a diversified financial conglomerate. Gunn proceeded to absorb several rival money brokers, including Noonan's in New York. He also took Exco into other financial activities, including stock brokerage, asset management and factoring. Gartmore happily allowed its initial controlling interest to be reversed, becoming itself one of Exco's acquired properties.

Having taken advantage of a bull market to float Exco as a public company, Gunn was regaled in the press as a paragon of the City's new breed of bright entrepreneurs, one of Thatcherite Britain's emblematic new tycoons. But having made his investors, his fellow directors, and himself a decent amount of money, Gunn started to attract criticism. He had started to believe his own press, it was said, to which Gunn's response was to keep acquiring aggressively. Increasingly, though, there were whispered reservations among his boardroom colleagues about the dangers of expanding too far, too fast. It was not apparent at the time, but Gunn and the Exco board were already on a collision course. It would eventually cost Gunn dearly.

The Exco board's misgivings would become even more openly and frankly expressed when Gunn, intrigued by D'Angelo's blossoming romance with Hirsch, announced to the board his interest in buying Telerate.

Information, Gunn believed, was fast becoming an addictive narcotic in the investment world. It was hardly a groundbreaking notion but one that Gunn felt Exco was in a unique position to exploit by combining the information generated by its varied brokerage operations with Telerate's data, using Telerate's fast-expanding network as a delivery vehicle. Gunn fancied—as had a few before him and many after him—that he could create a global information service more than capable of challenging Reuters' supremacy.

Although Gunn admired Reuters, it was with the money broker's inevitable chip on the shoulder. Like many brokers, Gunn had bristled at Reuters' rejection of brokers as participants in Monitor. "They wanted to develop it purely as an inter-bank system," he told a journalist later. "We were rebuffed by them time and time again in our attempts to become a contributor. Yet it was a natural fit for us. I always believed that money broking was really an information business. We were putting out hundreds of bits of information every day, and getting back the odd bit of commission."[1]

Most of Gunn's fellow directors, money brokers to a man, cringed at the disparagement of their collective contribution to earnings as "the odd bit of commission"—especially since such commissions then comprised the bulk of Exco's revenue and all of its earnings. They needed more than a little convincing that Telerate presented a better opportunity for profit than Exco's core activities. Undeterred, Gunn pressed on, until his boardroom critics fell reluctantly into line.

That Telerate was up for sale was not in question; Salomon Brothers was in the process of producing an investment document. Gunn read it and was impressed.

The next step was to ask D'Angelo to arrange a meeting in New York. They met with Hirsch and Terranova at the Knickerbocker Café, one of Hirsch's favored hangouts, just around the corner from his 10th Street apartment.

Hirsch was more than amenable to a deal with the London firm. So was Terranova, Bernie Cantor's right-hand man. On the Exco side, D'Angelo needed no convincing—making him Gunn's only supporter of the plan on the Exco board. Bernie, reluctant to let Telerate go, had been talked into approving a sale. How this was accomplished is worth describing.

It happened that both Hirsch and Terranova had been increasingly at odds with Bernie. They always felt greatly put out whenever they were summoned to the Great Man's presence, which was, they felt, more often than their dignity could stand. Hirsch in particular had been fretting for some time about how he could obtain a greater degree of management independence, not to mention a bigger slice of ownership, than he was ever likely to be granted by the autocratic Bernie Cantor. All else aside, Hirsch and Terranova secretly despised Bernie as a bombastic buffoon who had ridden his luck.

Telerate's financial condition at the time was robust. The annual growth rate, having moved rapidly into double digits, was now threatening to crack the triple-digit barrier. The profit margin was running close to 50 percent—impressive almost to a fault. In the preceding financial year, 1981, the company had posted spectacular results, with a pre-tax profit of $13 million on revenue of about $28 million. "Just as well we're a private company," was Hirsch's wry

---

[1] William Kay, *Tycoons*, Pan Books, 1985, p.93

comment. "If our customers ever saw these figures we'd be forced to cut our subscription rates."

Glowing financial results presented an obstacle to Hirsch's plan to persuade Bernie to sell. Another, though not insurmountable, was the fact that Telerate was the vehicle on which Bernie depended to distribute Cantor Fitzgerald's government prices.

So, the question was how Bernie could be talked into disposing of such a gold mine—to part with a business that, to most Wall Street observers, was rapidly becoming a white-hot property, in the hottest commercial sector of all.

The answer is that Hirsch and Terranova had hatched a plot.

Initially, Hirsch had been far from convinced that Bernie, a stubborn man with a considerable ego, could be manipulated. He could almost certainly not go it alone. The situation called for the discreet complicity of someone "on the inside," someone close enough to Bernie to command his respect. The name that popped into Hirsch's mind was John Terranova. Hirsch and Terranova had hitherto not been the closest of friends but, united in their scorn for Bernie, consequently found themselves drawn to each other as kindred spirits.

The timing for a move against Bernie, Telerate's glowing financial results aside, was not propitious. Terranova was beginning to fade in Bernie's esteem. Increasingly resentful of Cantor's dictatorial and egocentric management style, he was becoming less inhibited in saying so. Terranova held a poor opinion of Bernie's abilities. "If the man had twice the smarts, he'd still be pretty fucking stupid," he was once heard to say in an exasperated moment.

Bernie, for his part, had started to question Terranova's rough social manners and what he regarded as his cavalier approach to business. There had been, for example, a potentially embarrassing spat between Terranova and the Securities and Exchange Commission over alleged violations of securities trading laws. While Terranova was not found to have committed a criminal act, he received an SEC injunction—equal to a sharp slap on the wrist and probation—for failing to exercise "appropriate supervisory procedures." Bernie had never been one to shrink from public controversy, but this time he felt that Terranova had gone too far. In Bernie's mind Terranova was in danger of becoming a dangerous maverick, and something of a liability. Terranova accordingly proved to be a far from reluctant recruit to Hirsch's scheme.

The plot was simple: Terranova and Hirsch would work on Bernie in order to convince him that Telerate had seen its best days as an investment vehicle. They would claim that the company, though financially self-sufficient for the moment, would soon need significant injections of capital to maintain its momentum—capital on such a scale as to eat away at profit margins for years to come. In which case, selling Telerate offered a double advantage: not only could Bernie avoid spending all that money, but he could also rely on a continuing revenue stream by signing an exclusive contract with Telerate to distribute Cantor Fitzgerald's prices. It was a win-win situation, they told Bernie—in which case why not cash in the chips now?

Bernie Cantor rose to the bait. He would later deeply regret it, and resent having allowed himself to be talked into it so readily. But he had little cause to complain that he had been deceived. The grounds on which he was persuaded to part with Telerate may have been somewhat specious, coming as they did from colleagues with a concealed agenda, but he was less the victim of a conspiracy than of his own avaricious gullibility. And the arguments for Telerate's disposition were entirely plausible. The company actually would need investment on a much larger scale than he had ever been asked to commit to, or that he might be willing to commit to, and by selling now he would realize a substantial return on his modest original investment. Of course, he also had the option of turning down Exco's offer.

In Bernie's decision to accept the deal there lies a certain irony, because ultimately neither Hirsch nor Gunn would be prepared to make the substantial investment they had persuaded Bernie would be so crucial in ensuring Telerate's survival—Hirsch because he was not of a mind to, and Gunn because he would not be allowed to by his board. But that is getting ahead of the story.

What was Telerate's value in a private sale? A figure of $75 million, roughly three times Telerate's 1981 revenue, was the price that Gunn had been kicking about. It was in line with Salomon Brothers' thinking. An independent assessment would probably have pronounced it at least at the lower end of fair. Some at the time, and even more so later, described it as the giveaway of the decade.

Even so, the price represented a mighty impressive return on Bernie Cantor's original investment of little more than a couple of million dollars. The figure sounded good to Bernie, too, because it represented cash in the bank. For while Bernie's personal wealth was substantial, most of it was wrapped up in Cantor Fitzgerald and Telerate. The price was presumably also satisfactory to his wife Iris, who was said to exercise more than a passing influence on her husband's business decisions, particularly in matters involving his personal fortune.

And so the deal was done, and with unprecedented speed: a term sheet was signed before Gunn left New York. He was delighted with his trophy. "It took less than forty-eight hours to complete the thing," he remembered years later. "We didn't even bother with the normal due diligence. Telerate was a money machine. It was, frankly, a no-brainer."

Exco emerged from the transaction as the controlling Telerate shareholder. Guinness Peat, a London commodities trading house, came in as a co-investor in return for a substantial minority interest. John Gunn intended to become chairman, with Hirsch as president and chief executive. D'Angelo joined the board, as did Terranova, who, no doubt to Bernie's relief and possibly with his encouragement, quit Cantor Fitzgerald.

Gunn returned to London on a red-eye flight and went straight from Heathrow to an Exco board meeting. For Gunn it was a point of departure—literally—in his relations with his board.

The directors were stunned, appalled that Gunn had made such serious commitments without due consultation. They had a point, it must be said. At a stormy board meeting filled with angry recriminations, the Exco directors voted by a majority of one to dismiss its chief executive.

Gunn was unrepentant. Openly contemptuous of his colleagues, he was ready for a fight to the end. Years later he said, "My view then was clear and it hasn't changed since. I thought, to hell with the lot of them. They were all money brokers and not very good ones at that. They hadn't a backbone among them. They wanted to live in their own cozy little world of long lunches, reveling in the cachet of being City gents. It would have taken the company nowhere. I would happily have fired the whole bunch, taken Exco out of the money-broking business, and built an information business to be reckoned with. That, in fact, was my intention."

Gunn's response to his dismissal was to appeal to the shareholders over the heads of his directors. It was a clever move since the owners, almost to a man, were enthusiastic backers of Gunn. The board's decision was overturned. Gunn was back at his desk within hours. It was some time before he received visitors. Strangely, not one Exco director offered to resign, or was asked to resign. The tension was palpable then and simmered for years afterwards. The directors, all eighteen of them, mostly representing various money-market instruments, were inclined neither to forgive nor forget. They would wait for another opportunity to pounce—which duly presented itself, as will be seen later.

Within months, Telerate's ownership changed yet again when Guinness Peat—or rather its parent company, the investment bank Guinness Mahon—ran into financial difficulties. A large part of this block of Telerate stake was bought by Exco; the rest went to a private partnership formed by Hirsch, Terranova, D'Angelo, and a newcomer to the scene, Noonan's abrasively ambitious lawyer, Robert Fromer. Though a perfectly legitimate transaction, it was widely resented among Telerate's management—particularly because a significant share in the business had been offered to executives from Noonan and nothing to the managers who had helped to build Telerate's business. To some of them, myself included, it seemed that Hirsch had exhibited more regard for his new friends than for his old colleagues. Hull's disgust was palpable. "The man's now showing his true colors," he said.

But Hull was soon out of Telerate anyway.

For months, his relations with Hirsch had grown frostier, until the two were barely on speaking terms. The ultimate humiliation was when Hirsch, without warning to anyone, hired Dick Cowles, an executive with the Chicago Mercantile Exchange, as executive vice president—Hull's title. Cowles had been taken on, Hirsch made it known, to bring order and discipline to Telerate. It was a curious reason, to say the least, since order and discipline were precisely the qualities that Hirsch most abhorred, or at any rate ignored. Cowles's presence was bound to be troublesome, and so it would prove.

Cowles's bombastic approach to his job was that of a new headmaster taking over a school with a bad reputation. It guaranteed turmoil and conflict. He made clear from the start his view that Telerate needed to be "shaped up." He was a martinet, a stickler for project planning and flow charts and regulation and orderly procedure—in short, all the things that Telerate needed but also the things that would render him unpopular and ultimately ineffectual. Cowles opposed virtually every innovative proposal on the grounds that the sacred project list was already full. He was soon known as Doctor No, a nickname of which he was inordinately proud. "It means I'm doing my job," he pronounced. "I'll decide what his fucking job is," was Hirsch's retort.

All the signs were that Hull, resentful of Cowles and much else besides, was spoiling for a fight. Hirsch in turn gave the impression that he needed only an excuse to give him one. The perfect excuse arrived with the expiration of Hull's employment agreement. Hull approached Hirsch about renewing it. Hirsch's response was that he would be willing to sign a new contract, but only on drastically different, meaning less favorable, terms. And since Telerate might one day become a public company, Hirsch decreed any new package would have to be heavily weighted with stock options at the expense of salary, which accordingly would be reduced substantially. Hull was having none of it. The result was a brief, almighty row, audible from my desk two offices away.

Minutes later, Hull was stalking past my office, coat in hand, never to return.

Hull, by his own admission, had enjoyed "a good run." He'd often remarked, ever since the Merrill affair, that his days were numbered, that Hirsch would sooner or later exact his revenge. Hull's thwarted ambition to introduce a matching service had also contributed greatly to the decline in their relationship. Publicly, Hirsch claimed to have offered Hull a generous package, in which the loss of salary was more than balanced by the potential value of the stock options he would receive in lieu of it. Hirsch may have been acting coy, but the fact is that he was relieved to be free of someone he believed to be far too emotional and dangerously untrustworthy.

Within weeks, Hull showed up at Mercantile House, the holding company for a stable of money brokers (including Lasser-Marshall) that represented competition to Exco. His mandate was to generate revenue from market information. But he nursed a secret ambition: to persuade the firm to compete with Telerate by producing a matching service for foreign exchange. Once more he was doomed to frustration, this time by Mercantile's senior executives, who expressed the same fears and reservations that had been ringing in his ears for five years. Hull pushed on regardless, producing a business plan for a matching system, which, even if it had no appeal to Mercantile, could be offered to some other company. He had a company in mind, the name of which he foolishly inserted into the document. Even more unwisely, he asked his secretary to type it. She did so but promptly delivered it to Hull's superiors. Hull was even more promptly escorted from his office.

He wasted little time taking the paper to the company in question, one that had once rejected a similar proposal but which he felt might now listen more appreciatively. The company in question, almost needless to say, was Reuters. And the executive who heard Hull plead his cause, and far more appreciatively than Hull could ever have fondly imagined, was Glen Renfrew. It marked the renewal of their curious, and many at Reuters would later say inexplicable, love affair.

If the reports about the size of Hull's compensation were anywhere near the truth, I was envious. There was no need to be; my own was about to be unexpectedly elevated.

Shortly after Hull's departure, sometime late in 1982, while visiting a client in New Jersey with Rick Snape, I telephoned the office late in the day to say that I would be driving straight home. The client was a prospective contributor of information about oil and gas prices for a new energy service that I had launched a year earlier.

"Hirsch has been looking for you," my secretary informed me. "He needs to see you urgently. I think you'd better come in. There are lots of comings and goings. Something is definitely going on."

Some kind of crisis, was my first reaction—as it usually was when I was confronted with a long-distance summons from Hirsch. Rick Snape, whom I had hired to run the energy service, looked worried. Hirsch had not been at all keen on our foray into the energy market. Snape feared for his job. "Now, don't jump to conclusions," I told him. "If anyone's going to be on the carpet it'll be me."

A carpeting was what I anticipated when Hirsch greeted me in his office with a scowl and a grunted admonition about "going missing." Terranova, looking equally grim, was lounging on the sofa alongside him. "Waddya doing fucking around in New Jersey on this stupid energy stuff?" was Hirsch's opener. "We got more important things to think about."

They were winding me up. I was still trying to think of a suitable response

246

when he turned on a huge grin and held out a hand to shake.

"Congratulations," he said. "You've just become a millionaire."

John Gunn had wasted no time wondering how much his new property was worth. "There's only one way to put a tangible value on it," he had said, "and that's to test it in the public market." The process had been quietly under way for some time. Telerate was about to go public.

The plan was to sell about 10 percent of the equity. An application was being made to list the shares on the New York Stock Exchange rather than on NASDAQ, the over-the-counter market where companies of Telerate's modest capitalization were usually traded. "We're looking for a high profile right from the start," Gunn explained the next day. The decision had much to do with ego—his own, of course, and Hirsch's, but above all perhaps Bob Fromer's.

Fromer was Noonan's, meaning D'Angelo's, lawyer, a smooth talker and sharp dresser with a fierce drive to make money. It was said that his wife was financially privileged and that Fromer was desperate to at least match her personal fortune with one of his own. Fromer accordingly had high ambitions for Telerate and his part in it, and a short timetable for achieving them. "In ten years, maybe sooner, we can be the next IBM," he proclaimed passionately during one strategy session. "And that's what we should be aiming for. Starting right now." I saw Hirsch and Terranova wince in union at the "we." They tolerated Fromer's megalomaniacal outbursts but privately regarded him as a greedy interloper—by no means an exclusive view around the company—and something of a buffoon whose ignorance of Telerate's business should have disqualified his frequent assertions in matters of corporate strategy. I, too, found Fromer's opinions indigestible at times, but he was smart as well as aggressive and, agree with him or not, he often brought a refreshing outside perspective to Telerate's business.

The registration statement issued in March 1983 contemplated an offering of 4,400,000 shares at $20. Now, even I could calculate that if 10 percent of Telerate could fetch $90 million, then the whole company was worth nearly one billion dollars. It was a staggering valuation for a company with audited annual revenue for 1981 of less than $30 million and projected revenue for 1982 of less than $50 million. Little wonder, then, that Fromer was prone to delusions of grandeur. Fromer urged Gunn and the investment bankers to consider doubling the offer price.

"That arrogant sonofabitch has gotta be restrained," Terranova advised Hirsch after the meeting. "Above all, keep him away from the fucking investors, or we'll all find ourselves under SEC investigation." Terranova would know, of course.

Gunn was quietly confident. Hirsch's optimism was restrained only by the possible reaction among Telerate's subscribers to our newly exposed profit margin. As an additional public-relations concern, the prospectus made clear that the company did not actually need additional capital, a point underlined by the comment that "the company has not definitively allocated any portion of the proceeds of the offering to any specific purpose." It was a curious position to be in, the more so as many of Telerate's clients would also be its underwriters.

"The earnings are what they are," Hirsch noted. "But let's play them down, talk instead about other things, like competition and the need to invest to protect our future."

Fromer responded with, "Neil, this is America. Never apologize for being successful."

Both points of view were valid but irreconcilable.

It was Fromer's view of the world that prevailed in the management "road show"—a series of presentations for prospective institutional investors. Goldman Sachs, the chief underwriter, had prepared the script and it was about nothing but aggressively promoting the company and selling its shares. The normal custom would have been for Hirsch, as the company's founder and chief executive, to be the lead presenter, possibly backed up by Terranova, who had a better grasp of company finances than anyone else. Someone, Gunn perhaps, had other ideas. I was summoned one day to Hirsch's office. The underwriters were there. "We've decided you're the best man for this job," Hirsch said.

I have no idea who made the decision or why. I had no previous experience selling shares, or of answering tricky questions from potential investors. It seemed to make no sense to have a substitute from the bench on the field at the very start of the game. It was true that Hirsch did not particularly like public speaking, though he was not at all bad at it, and a reluctance to use Terranova was understandable, if only because of his recent problems with the SEC, and the ever-present danger of a lapse into expletives. But they were the executives the investors would most want to hear and talk to.

Pote Videt of Goldman Sachs, who would be my speaking coach, gave nothing away. "It was a collective decision," was all he would say.

My guess is that Gunn simply wanted someone who would come across as "conservative and respectable." These, I must say, would not have appeared at the top of my own list of personal qualities, but it is probably fair to say that they were characteristics even less associated with my two senior colleagues. As one sneering Exco director, not a known admirer of Telerate, put it, "The trouble is, old boy, that Hirsch looks as if he's permanently zonked and Terranova comes across as a small-time hoodlum."

Telerate's public image, as reflected in the behavior of the two senior executives, was something that exercised Gunn more than he cared to admit—even more so after the decision had been made to go public. He liked and respected both Hirsch and Terranova, but he also recognized the risk in having to place absolute reliance on colleagues who resolutely comported themselves in ways, as he once delicately expressed it, "considerably at variance with most of the accepted conventions of the day."

Gunn was well aware, of course, that Telerate had already attracted a certain reputation, not to say notoriety, in the financial community as a company that enjoyed itself to the limit, and possibly beyond. Such talk was inevitably subject to exaggeration. It was put about, for example, that Telerate threw wild client parties, supposedly adorned by battalions of gorgeous women, and where alcohol was dispensed with only slightly more abandon or discretion than the cocaine and other illicit substances said to be on offer.

Legends, once having taken root, invariably grow beyond plausible deniability. It is true that Telerate had a knack for employing ladies as handsome as they were competent. It would have been equally accurate to observe that party guests occasionally imbibed more than the recommended dosage, as party guests often do. Cocaine was no doubt consumed, too, and perhaps with less caution or shame than was wise, given the legal constraints on the practice. By and large, though, Telerate's events were probably no more palpably sinful than any of their kind, and were certainly a far cry from the orgiastic affairs of popular elaboration.

Hirsch himself was a large part of Gunn's worry. It was universal gossip that Telerate's chief executive had what is often commonly referred to as "a drinking problem." Hirsch, today if not then, would be the first to admit it. (Curiously, in all my years at Telerate, I can honestly say that I never saw him take a drink, in or out of the office, before five o'clock. That he was rarely separated from a glass after five o'clock is another matter entirely.) He would also, now, openly own up to the cocaine habit, though as addictions go, it was—and is—hardly unique on Wall Street, or for that matter among other high-profile, high-earning professions.

Hirsch, it must be said, took few pains to deflect all this attention, and sometimes gave the impression of actually courting it by indulging in a lifestyle of conspicuous consumption. He bought a luxury duplex apartment, complete with private elevator, overlooking the United Nations building. He also owned a country house in the Hamptons, the favorite weekend playground of wealthy New Yorkers. He was driven to work each day in a Rolls Royce. He was often seen about town and country in the company of Bianca Jagger and other celebrities from Manhattan's *beau monde*. Gunn's eyelids failed to bat even when Hirsch insisted on purchasing, in Telerate's name, a long-coveted corporate jet. The sleek, top-of-the-range Gulfsteam III came complete with flight crew of two pilots and a stewardess, and was registered to a Telerate subsidiary called YKK Inc., an acronym derived from Yom Kippur Klipper.

In accepting that Hirsch was entitled to celebrate Telerate's success in style, Gunn paid an unanticipated price. Certain senior figures at Exco were already privately voicing their alarm. They were entitled to be concerned about booze and drugs (though they could have taken a close look at their own company, which was far from cleaner than a hound's tooth in such matters). It is hard to avoid the suspicion that what really got up certain public-schooled British noses were what they saw as the egregious vulgarities: in material terms the Rolls and the Gulfstreams, in social terms the bad table manners and the preference for fast food. "Can't I get a fuckin' cheeseburger around here?" Terranova once barked at a waiter in a smart West End restaurant. Conspicuous consumption was simply not good form and the lack of social graces bespoke a poor upbringing. The attitude of some Exco directors was that, "These are simply not our kind of people." Hirsch did Gunn's policy of forbearance no favors by his occasional acts of contempt, or what was seen as contempt, for the corporate process. More than once he failed to show up for an executive meeting and once for an Exco board meeting in Hong Kong (allegedly for a dalliance with a lady he had met on the first leg of the flight).

As the months went by, the whispering campaign intensified, and though it was initially, or at least ostensibly, directed against the perceived excesses of Hirsch and Terranova, it soon became clear that the pot-shots were being aimed at Gunn as well. The inference was clear: if Gunn did not have the balls to control Telerate, how could he be strong enough to remain in charge of Exco?

The Telerate road show took in seven cities in four days—a coast-to-coast schedule only made possible by use of the Yom Kippur Klipper. Even so, it was a grueling trip—especially the intense audience-questioning that followed my 30-minute slide presentation. Curiously, the questions seemed to vary in focus from one city to the next. Boston seemed intent on probing the financials. Chicago worried about the marketability of the products. In Houston, for some reason, the audience seemed baffled by the whole concept. Perhaps it was because there were no oil wells involved—though it may have had something to do with the little joke I inserted into the presentation to relieve the evident boredom.

Part of the selling pitch was that, everywhere in the world, Telerate billed its customers in dollars, eliminating any risk associated with currency fluctuations. In Houston, instead of mentioning dollars I referred, on a whim, to Zambian kwachas. The would-be investors seemed not to notice. The joke was worthwhile anyway, if only for the startled look on Terranova's face. "I nearly fell off my fucking chair, you bastard."

On April 27, 1983 Telerate (stock symbol TLR) opened for trading at $20 a share. That same day, Telerate held its first board meeting as a public company around a vast mahogany table in the boardroom of the New York Stock Exchange. The eyes of past Exchange chairmen gazed down, watchful and intimidating, from the walls. It was my first board meeting of any kind. I was elected unanimously by a show of hands and a round of applause.

A butler served something from a silver tray. Sherry, I suppose; I don't actually remember. Whatever was served, it was not a mug of tea from Manzi's.

And how pleasing to reflect that I was not the one serving it.

# Frenzy

In the spring of 1982, the press barons of Fleet Street and their country cousins, the owners of Britain's provincial newspapers, received an unexpected treat: Reuters declared a dividend, the first for forty-one years.

At just under £2 million, the sum in question was hardly eye-popping, and by the time the cash was distributed among Reuters' principal shareholders— represented at the national level by the Newspaper Publishers Association and at the regional level by the Press Association—the figure on most individual checks would be whittled down to little more than a token payment. Even so, this was an event of far-reaching significance. It proclaimed the rejuvenation of a company that for nearly half a century had been regarded by its shareholders as no more than a necessary but money-losing encumbrance. Some owners had started to question "necessary." The dividend put a stop to that kind of talk.

Since Reuters had rarely approached them with anything in hand but a begging bowl, the shareholders' delight was understandable. Virtually overnight, the beggar had turned tycoon. Indeed, the word around Fleet Street was that the surge in revenue and profit laid out in the company's financial statement signaled the beginning of a remarkable business revival. If so, the owners, many of them now in the same financial straits that Reuters itself had always been in, could look forward to receiving regular and growing cash distributions. The prospect was about to send the Street into the kind of delirium that investment bankers have been known to call a feeding frenzy.

The spectacle of owners with a long history of calculated apathy towards Reuters being instantly converted to impassioned activists was less than edifying but perfectly justified. They had stakes to claim—big stakes—and given Reuters' almost incomprehensible ownership structure, many were sure to be disputed. Suddenly, then, it was important for the barons to stand up and be counted. For the unseemly scramble to establish who owned what in Reuters had one overriding purpose: it was to place a market value on the company about to shed its image as a news agency of faded and penurious respectability for that of one of the first hot investment properties of the Information Age.

Reuters continued to gather world news as it had always done and to sell it to the owners at knockdown subscription prices, as it always would. But the company was "hot" for reasons unrelated, or at least only distantly related, to news and of which the owners were complacently ignorant. Actually just one reason: the emerging market for electronically delivered financial information—represented at Reuters by a product called Monitor.

Collective chop-licking along Fleet Street was delayed only by a few last-minute questions. Were Reuters' 1982 figures an accounting aberration—say the proceeds of a one-time asset sale—or the beginning of an extended business cycle? What were the long-term prospects for this Monitor? And if the outlook was as good as management seemed to think it was, just how much could Reuters eventually be worth? All the answers seem to come out positive.

In which case, the only meaningful way to put a tangible value on the company was, as many owners immediately recognized, and the conclusion that John Gunn had recently reached about Telerate, to take it public. Such a notion in Reuters' case would have been unthinkable a few years earlier. To many, both inside and outside the company, it was barely conceivable now. But for certain prospective beneficiaries, floating Reuters was about to become not so much a desirable but vague long-term business objective as an evangelistic short-term mission to save Fleet Street from a fast-approaching Armageddon.

The ensuing campaign would offer an entertaining spectacle—or a degrading one, according to taste—bringing owners and management into the kind of intimate and abrasive contact that neither side had ever experienced. Inevitably it attracted the usual mercenary hangers-on, and Fleet Street was shortly invaded by brigades of lawyers, battalions of accountants, and platoons of investment bankers, some invited, others arriving merely in the hope of being summoned. Many would be called and almost as many would be chosen.

For additional color, there were innumerable minor skirmishes involving disputatious and missing shareholders, rebellious employees, and a rent-a-crowd alliance of outraged do-gooders and self-appointed conservationists—all dedicated to defending the perceived threat to Reuters' editorial integrity. At the end, even the British Government and Parliament would be ushered into the bloody arena, if only to recite the concluding *nunc dimitis*.

If nothing else, the event offered the struggling London papers a perfect opportunity for self-examination. The conclusions owed more to self-promotion than to introspection. By the time the great extravaganza had run its course, Reuters had provided more column inches of controversy, prurience, and misinformation than any previous Fleet Street *cause célèbre*.

For drama and tension, it surpassed Fleet Street's greatest sensation of recent times—Rupert Murdoch's "hijacking" a year earlier of *The Times* and *Sunday Times*. The subsequent very public battle with the editor, Harold

Evans, whose independence Murdoch had first solemnly pledged to support and then, according to his critics, cynically withdrawn, had kept the Street's taverns in gossip for months until Evans was finally forced to resign.

Murdoch would now play a leading, and perhaps pivotal, role in the Reuters flotation drama, once again assuming—at least in the minds of his many critics—the familiar role of villain. Already, early in 1981, he had brought his influence to bear on the story. Murdoch had been appointed to the Reuters board, and while he was acquiring *The Times* titles he approached Gerry Long about joining Times Newspapers Ltd. as managing director. Long, bored, restless, and looking for a new challenge, accepted. "After a full three-second pause I said, 'Yes', and I've still not discussed terms," Long had excitedly told Harold Evans, who was at the time under consideration for the editorship.

Long's departure—unfortunately timed from his personal financial perspective—paved the way for the resolution of the Nelson-Renfrew tussle for the succession. The nod went to Renfrew.

Against all expectations? Not really. Renfrew was by far the more popular and charismatic figure.

Against all the evidence? Absolutely. Virtually every triumph of Reuters' rejuvenation—Stockmaster, Videomaster, Monitor, Dealing—had Nelson's signature on it. The only product with Renfrew's imprint on it was row-grabber, which had failed and endangered the company. On the basis of tangible achievement, then, Nelson could rightly claim the accolade of the man who saved Reuters.

Long claimed to have influenced the succession by telling the board that he thought Nelson "had given everything he had to give." It seemed a somewhat specious reason, since Nelson was only a couple of years older than Renfrew, actually looked much younger, and showed no obvious signs of wear and tear.

Nelson, years later, and still smarting from Long's rebuff, offered a prosaic explanation. "Long had resented me all along," he told me once over drinks. "When Long took over from Cole he recognized that commercial services would save the company, but he knew nothing about them. I did, of course, and it frustrated him then and throughout our relationship. So when the time came to make a choice it was, frankly, more a case of 'anyone but Nelson' than a decision based on accomplishment." Many found it hard not to feel for him.

My own unconfirmed theory is that Long was exacting revenge for a past event: Nelson's victory over Brian Horton, Reuters' chief news editor and a Long favorite, after a bruising and personalized tussle for supremacy between

General News and Economic Services during the seventies, which led to Horton's resignation.

Anyway, Renfrew it was. Nelson, whom many expected to resign, elected to stay on as his deputy.

The story of Reuters' remarkable business turnaround makes for compelling reading. In 1981, after years of losses or lackluster results, revenues had leaped 50 percent above the previous year's figure. The operating profit had been even more eye-catching, quadrupling to £17 million. More of the same was promised. Earnings were expected to double in 1982. Such, at any rate, was the confident projection of Reuters' management, not previously known for its exuberance in such matters, admittedly having had precious few opportunities to exercise it.

Reuters' revenues, management explained, had been expanding steadily for several years on the back of a money-market information retrieval service called Monitor, soon to be supplemented by a transaction-facilitating service called Monitor Dealing. After a shaky start, Monitor had become firmly imbedded in the international money-trading community and was now producing robust revenue growth accompanied by rapidly expanding margins. Dealing augured equally favorable results.

For confirmation of management optimism, the owners had no need to look beyond the happy faces of Reuters' sales executives, who could be heard all over the City crowing loudly over their lunchtime grog to the effect that there had never been such times. They had every reason to crow: their expanding sales commissions offered the first tangible evidence of Reuters' turnaround. Monitor encouraged a revival of Lord Thomson's famous aphorism about commercial television: it had become a license to print money.

In short, only the dimmest of the City's compulsive eavesdroppers could fail to deduce that behind the Lutyens edifice at 85 Fleet Street something of great commercial significance had taken place.

Reuters' owners, among the last to pick up on all the sudden talk of hidden treasure, were now hot on the trail for more clues. Those NPA members who for years had treated Reuters as an inconvenient ward deposited on the doorstep by distant relatives now lavished on the company the kind of attention associated with doting parents of a precious only child. Few had more than the vaguest idea what kind of products Monitor and Dealing were, or how they could possibly have transformed Reuters' finances in less than a decade. A vigorous effort was soon underway to find out.

As Lord Hartwell, proprietor of the *Daily Telegraph*, and one of the

NPA's three Reuters directors, exclaimed: "It was as if we had all discovered oil at the bottom of the garden."[1]

Recognizing that Hartwell and his colleagues in the NPA, the beneficial owners of 41 percent of Reuters, had a great deal to learn about the company's business, Nelson and Judah arranged to brief them. To this end, on July 14, a dozen limousines glided up to Reuters' building, in some cases disgorging shareholders who had seldom, if ever, set foot inside the place. A separate presentation was planned for the Press Association, which also had a 41 percent stake in the business, though the PA visitors from the provinces were more likely to arrive by bus or taxi.

Inviting the two main shareholding bodies to separate meetings may have been dictated by logistics—attendance was expected to be high for both events—but may also have recognized the cultural and political distinctions that divided the two organizations. Although there was little love lost between them, they had one thing in common: each had a convoluted and informally administered structure, which in both cases would be exposed as inadequate when, for the first time, they were forced to confront dormant and complex issues of ownership.

The NPA's problem was that the Reuters shareholding resided not with its individual members but with the NPA itself in the form of a trust. Given Reuters' dismal financial performance over the years, there had been little reason to care which newspapers owned what. Now that there was every reason to care, the NPA was obliged to determine ownership on the basis of a curious and outdated points system under which shares had been allocated according to the type of newspaper represented. Daily papers, for example, had received six points, evening newspapers three points, and weeklies one.

That much seemed reasonably clear, except that the allocations, drawn up in 1941 when the NPA had first bought into Reuters, had not been updated since. In the intervening years, a number of papers had folded. Others had merged or become associated through joint ventures. Several new titles had been added. To complicate matters further, the NPA had failed to keep proper records of such transactions. Those share certificates and share-transfer documents that existed had been moldering for years in the basement of the NPA's shabby premises on Bouverie Street, a stone's throw from Reuters. When the NPA chairman, Lord Marsh, went down to look for them he found piles of cardboard files containing hundreds of scraps of paper. Some were unaltered from their original form, even though the newspapers concerned had changed hands. Others had handwritten notes scribbled on them, representing the sole record of ownership transfer. It was

[1] John Lawrenson/Lionel Barber, *The Price of Truth*, Mainstream Publishing, 1985, p.9

a perfect recipe for endless legal wrangling—and that was the inevitable result.

Indifference had long been the hallmark of the NPA. It was manifest on two levels: the indifference of the members to the organization itself and the indifference of the organization to Reuters. Ostensibly formed to provide a forum for discussing Fleet Street's internal—meaning union—problems, and to present a common industry position to outsiders, the NPA had never exerted much influence in either function. Newspaper barons were notorious for going their own way, propelled by Fleet Street rivalries that were as intense as they were often personal. Although meetings of the NPA's governing council were held regularly, they were often poorly attended, and then only by lesser functionaries. Most proprietors, reluctant to sit in the same room as hated rivals, stayed away. Lacking any other useful function, the NPA's chief remaining purpose, the only one behind which the owners had ever considered uniting, was to represent the newspapers in contract negotiations with the print unions. Even in that role it had not been notably successful, judging by the restrictive practices still rampant on Fleet Street. In short, the NPA was an organization in name only.

The Reuters ownership issue loomed as the most critical the NPA had confronted in decades. But if Marsh believed it might be the catalyst for a truce, he was probably the only one who thought so. It would have rather the opposite effect.

Though different in structure, the Press Association had similar problems. These, too, could be traced to administrative neglect. The PA did have a formal membership list, but it existed only in its original form, which meant that it had not been updated for half a century or more. During the intervening years the pattern of ownership of the regional press, even more than that of the nationals, had changed beyond recognition. The PA now faced the logistical and political nightmare of having to obtain documents identifying countless individual owners, or their heirs and descendants. In the case of "missing" owners there would be the additional chore of tracing them. It would prove to be a lengthy and complex process, often controversial and sometimes hilarious.

In any other circumstances, the NPA and the Press Association might have responded to questions of dominion with unconcerned bemusement. Such was not the case now though, as it became clearer by the day just how much money might be at stake for all concerned as owners of Reuters.

The summons to NPA members to the July 14 briefing came from Lord Marsh, who perhaps for the first time in his tenure as chairman found himself in a significant role. A former Labour Member of Parliament, cabinet minister and chairman of British Rail, Marsh had glided effortlessly from a political vocation in the service of socialism to a lucrative City career as an advocate of capitalism. Marsh was bright and urbane and a skilled mediator, but such talents were normally called upon only to round up enough members to make NPA gatherings worthwhile. These abilities were certainly not required on this occasion. Only a handful of Fleet Street's chieftains were missing from the procession of the great and the good striding eagerly through Reuters' front door for what promised to be a unique occasion and, for some, a potentially company-saving exercise.

It is not entirely clear who first raised the possibility of a public flotation of Reuters' stock, or when.

Gerry Long, for one, could claim the distinction. So could Sir Ian Fraser, a former Reuters correspondent and later a merchant banker, first with S.G. Warburg and later with Lazard, of which he became chairman. Long and Fraser had been close friends during overlapping postings by Reuters to Germany, where each had seen service with the British Army. They also had a common love of languages, Fraser's fluency in German being more than a match for Long's command of French—or perhaps vice versa.

On more than one occasion in the early 1970s, Long had occasionally called Fraser to discuss how Reuters could best financially support itself as its business became increasingly technology-dependent and capital-intensive. Among the various possibilities they reviewed was a scheme, apparently propounded by Long, to separate the commercial division from the general news operation, under a formula in which the former would somehow continue to subsidize the latter. The idea was apparently never discussed more than casually. In addition to the question of financing news, there were two critical issues to be resolved. First, how the owners, particularly the conservative members of the Press Association, could be persuaded to go along with any radical change in structure. Second, how such a plan might be effected without colliding head-on with the 1941 Trust guaranteeing Reuters' editorial independence and protection from unwanted outside interference.

Fraser remembered the conversations as vague and inconclusive. "I didn't bring the subject up, Gerry did," he recalled. "He said to me, 'we're on the verge of making big profits and we've got this stupid structure. What do we do?' The crazy capital structure had to be sorted out, of course, but Gerry didn't particularly want to do it. He didn't want to face the owners at that stage. Some were serious businessmen while others were not. On the Press Association side they simply wanted to keep the old cooperative. Gerry thought he'd leave it to others, later on, like Glen Renfrew. In other words, nothing was really under active consideration. In the end, he was too busy with his job and didn't really have the time, and I was busy getting on with mine."

Long, in avoiding aggressive action, seemed to fall back on his instincts, which were those of a journalist rather than a businessman (a conclusion he always disputed vehemently). In any event, he was excused from making a decision by joining Murdoch at *The Times*. Fraser, though, would still be in the picture when talk of a Reuters flotation first surfaced in a serious way. He wasn't directly involved, but as a director of Pearson Longman, Lazard's parent, which also owned the *Financial Times* and was thereby an NPA owner of Reuters, he was in an ideal position to donate his knowledge of Reuters to colleagues who were.

By then, ironically, the company's cash position had improved by leaps and bounds, substantially reducing the once critical need to raise external working capital. This fact provided further ammunition for those concerned citizens who considered the notion of Reuters as a public company at best unnecessary and at worst immoral. Their objections being of a philosophical rather than a financial nature, they clung to the belief that eventually the Trustees would intervene to save the day, if not by invoking the law, then by appealing to honor, so for now they kept their powder dry. But obscure issues of law and honor were already falling behind events. The July 14 management meeting had been a revelation to those who attended it and no sooner had they absorbed its implications—which in some cases may have taken no more than minutes—the flotation campaign may be said to have been launched. From that moment onwards, Reuters entered the curious twilight zone that investment bankers like to describe as being "in play."

Reuters might be said to have been in play for some time. Speculation about the company's future had appeared in print as far back as June 10—more than a month before the NPA briefing. Of all places, the article had appeared in *The Guardian*, a left-leaning newspaper not known for its original financial coverage and not widely read in the City. The reporter concerned, Maggie Brown, had suggested that Reuters' owners were just beginning to understand how much their shares in the agency might be worth. The timing of the piece was not entirely surprising, coming as it did soon after the dividend announcement. What was noteworthy was the reference to the difficulties the NPA owners would face in dividing up the spoils. It suggested inspiration from a source with intimate knowledge of NPA affairs. The finger of suspicion pointed to Brown's corporate boss, Peter Gibbings, chairman and chief executive of Guardian Newspapers.

Gibbings was a quiet-spoken barrister who, despite *The Guardian*'s relatively modest circulation, carried a big stick in press circles. He had wielded it very effectively in slashing *The Guardian*'s operating expenses. He had, in fact, brought the paper back from the brink of financial disaster and, even more remarkably, done so without upsetting the unions. That feat alone marked Gibbings as a very clever man. As head of a newspaper group with regional as well as national press interests, Gibbings enjoyed membership of both the

Press Association and the NPA—a convenient position from which to monitor gossip. Gibbings must have been among the first to discern the growing desire among his peers to gain an influential voice in Reuters' future.

*The Guardian*'s limited City readership notwithstanding, Brown's article generated considerable interest among investment managers, particularly those with significant holdings of newspaper shares, which had sustained considerable market losses and were thought to offer little prospect for recovery. A Reuters flotation might change that perception. Seen in that light, Reuters now became the talk of the City.

That the story had strayed into the public domain left Reuters executives feeling uncomfortable, not to say irritable. They feared the inevitable onslaught of inquiries, partly because nothing in their experience had prepared them for it, but also because few of the myriad complexities involved in flotation had been addressed, let alone resolved. The streams of exasperated "no comments" that began to emanate from 85 Fleet Street no doubt brought smiles to the faces of all those who had found themselves, at one time or another, on the receiving end of a Reuters news story.

In his sudden interest in Reuters, Gibbings was either a step immediately ahead of, or one just behind, Alan Hare, chairman and chief executive of the *Financial Times* and a Reuters director. If not the earliest proponent of a Reuters flotation, he was certainly among its earliest advocates, and one of the more vocal and energetic. A slight, mild-mannered aristocrat—the son of the Earl of Listowel—and somewhat rambling in speech, Hare had a daredevil past that belied his quiet public persona. It included service during the Second Word War with Britain's Special Operations Executive (a forerunner of the SAS regiment) in the service of which he was parachuted into Albania to help organize the local partisans. After the war, the talent for clandestine activities was allegedly placed at the disposal of the British secret service. Such a background, it might be said, equipped Hare remarkably well for spearheading the low-key, behind-the-scenes campaign to take Reuters public.

Right alongside him—or so it was generally believed—was the ubiquitous but equally slippery figure of Rupert Murdoch, no stranger himself to operations behind enemy lines, in his case in the cause of fighting Fleet Street unions. Murdoch's appointment to the Reuters board reflected his acquisition of the *News of the World* and *The Sun*, high-circulation Sunday and daily titles respectively, each based on potent editorial cocktails of sex, gossip, and sport. The following year, in another celebrated coup, Murdoch had acquired from the Thomson Organisation, in highly controversial circumstances, the more respectable though less lucrative titles of *The Times* and *Sunday Times*. This diverse stable of titles represented over 30 percent of Britain's national newspaper readership, potentially making Murdoch one of the principal beneficiaries of a Reuters flotation.

If Murdoch's early involvement in the campaign was active, as many claimed, it was far from obvious. In his younger days, Murdoch had been an avid poker player, and in this commercial version of the game he was as hard to read as he must once have been at the card table. To NPA colleagues who sounded him out about Reuters he seemed, early on, to offer quiet encouragement, but tended, once the flotation campaign was underway, to leave the impression that he had formed no definite opinion on the subject one way or the other. To some observers he even came across as an unlikely voice of circumspection.

Where Murdoch was concerned, few conspiracy theorists were plagued by doubts. He had always offered an inviting target, and their suspicion was that the "Dirty Digger," as he was fondly known in press circles, had been an enthusiast for flotation right from the start. And there were more sinister undertones, they argued. Murdoch wasn't merely interested in exploiting the borrowing power a public market valuation of Reuters would bring to his balance sheet but in taking over the agency, which he could accomplish more easily if it were a public company.

Among the accumulating list of "plots" this ranked among the more extreme. It was nonetheless taken seriously in some quarters, especially among Murdoch's compatriots in Australian press circles, where those who claimed to know him best were those who distrusted him most. Desmond Anderson of the *Melbourne Herald*, who sat on Reuters' board as the representative of the Australian Associated Press, a minority shareholder, was one. Early in the game, Anderson cabled his boss with a warning: "Murdoch stated that he is leaving his options open with Reuters, but the concern is that he has a master plan to take control of Reuters shortly after it is floated."[2]

Speculation about Murdoch's intentions had first flared up early in 1981, the year in which he lured Gerry Long away from Reuters to become managing director of Times Newspapers. The hiring of Long, which was no less a shock at Reuters than it was everywhere else, gave rise to the most popular conspiracy theory of the time. The belief was that Long was hired in order to facilitate the accession of Glen Renfrew to Reuters' top job. The reasoning, entirely circumstantial, was that Renfrew, as a fellow Australian, would be not only more sympathetic than Long to the idea of selling shares in the agency, but also to the idea of an eventual Murdoch takeover. Before and after board meetings, Murdoch and Renfrew forever seemed to be deep in conversation. And wasn't it Renfrew who had persuaded Reuters' board, soon after Long's departure early in 1981, to issue special "E" shares to himself, Nelson, and Judah? "E" shares were seen as the first phase of what Renfrew intended to expand into a much broader management incentive scheme and

[2] Donald Read, *The Power of News*, Oxford University Press, 1992, p.348

were regarded as the first overt move in preparing the company for flotation.

There is no supporting evidence for any of this—not that lack of evidence has ever deterred conspiracy theorists. And neither Murdoch nor Renfrew could be expected to own up to such skullduggery, if true, and sure enough neither deigned to comment. Still, it made for good bar-room gossip at the time, and contributed to the general penumbra of intrigue closing in around Reuters.

For the record, various figures close to both men dismissed the idea of a plot as not so much as unbelievable as unlikely. They include Gerry Long, even though his brief and miserable tenure at *The Times* left him bitterly resentful of Murdoch and his works. While conceding that scheming was by no means beyond the man, Long considered it altogether too incredible. There were too many unpredictable aspects of the situation at the time, not least the then unanswerable questions surrounding the 1941 Trust Agreement.

Other than the hiring of Long, what most helped to fan the Murdoch speculation was the close personal interest he took, before and after he became a Reuters director, in the company's increasingly influential role in the global information industry. That alone set him apart from his NPA colleagues. The company's revival, and the technology driving it, fascinated him. He had found much to learn from Reuters' exploitation of satellite communications, which also happened to be Renfrew's obsession. He took the trouble to visit Reuters' new communications center on Long Island. And while he was not the first visiting board-level dignitary, nor the last, he was by all accounts the one who lingered the longest and showed the most interest. "Reuters," Murdoch later commented to a biographer, "is a key story in the information revolution. A real key."[3]

That much reflected a view widely shared at the time, and falls well short of evidence of a desire to seize control of the company.

"Personally, I found Murdoch very straightforward," was Fraser's later verdict. But then, as conspiracy theorists might say, "Well, he would, wouldn't he?"

If Fraser would, it was because his own role in the flotation movement was discreetly active behind the scenes. Lazard would benefit indirectly from a Reuters share issue, since the bank's parent company, Pearson, owned an estimated 5 percent of the agency. Moreover, the Pearson connection put Fraser into close contact with Alan Hare, to whom he must have offered insights into Reuters both as an information vendor and a potential investment vehicle.

Fraser was later happy to admit that he was also in frequent contact with Murdoch. He found the Australian keen on a Reuters flotation, but with

---

[3] William Shawcross, *Murdoch*, Chatto & Windus, 1992, p.238

certain reservations. "Oh yes, he thought it should happen," Fraser recalled years afterwards. "The money was very attractive, you see." What about the reservations? These, Fraser guessed, had much to do with newspaper politics. "He also wanted to see the effect on his competitors. Some of the Fleet Street proprietors were really strapped for cash, including Rothermere [Lord Rothermere, proprietor of the *Daily Mail*]. Murdoch didn't want to help them out particularly."

Presumably with Fraser's help, Lazard was among the first City institutions to express its opinion about Reuters' prospects. In an internal memorandum dated July 19, just five days after the NPA meeting at 85 Fleet Street, the bank referred in glowing terms to the "exciting potential" of Reuters as a public company. Four days later, Hare came out openly and strongly in support of flotation in letters to Christopher Dicks, standing in as Reuters' chairman for Sir Denis Hamilton, who was ill with prostate cancer, and to Richard Winfrey, chairman of the Press Association. Winfrey was startled, not so much by the idea of floating Reuters as by the care with which the approach had been worked out. Hare underlined his position by circulating the Lazard study with a proposal that it form the basis of a discussion at the Reuters board meeting in September.

Glen Renfrew had said little publicly. The same held true for Murdoch. Hare claimed that neither was "averse to the idea" of flotation. However, in response to suggestions that Lazard be invited to take matters further, Renfrew expressed his opposition to any merchant bank "digging into Reuters" unless it was under the supervision of management. Until then, Renfrew had adopted a formally neutral stance on the reasonable grounds that Reuters' ownership structure was a question for the owners rather than for management. But his cautionary comment on Lazard's or any other outside involvement begged the question of exactly where he and his management colleagues stood.

Once the "E" shares had been issued it was inferred that they would be strongly in favor of a stock offering. If true, it was a view probably tinged with ambivalence, if not about the ends then at least the means. Flotation in Reuters' case was bound to be a long, unpredictable, and politically charged process, fraught with dangers for all concerned, particularly the chief executive. Neither Renfrew nor his two senior colleagues, Nelson and Judah, could claim any previous experience in such matters. Even if they could have, nothing would have adequately prepared them for the Byzantine maneuvering among the owners that now came into prospect.

"They [the management] were rather frightened," was Fraser's impression. "They didn't know what horses would be let loose. They were afraid of the unknown, of being projected out of a cooperative situation into Fleet Street politics, which can be pretty bloody." And so it would prove.

But even after the Hare letters had officially set things in motion, most of the probing and buttonholing going on among the owners was conducted for the most part with relative discretion. The wider constituency of interests—press, public, Reuters employees, even some of the less involved owners—although aware of the rising sentiment for flotation, remained only vaguely aware of the issues and personalities involved. And there was a common assumption at this stage that flotation was strictly a theoretical exercise, one that would be difficult if not impossible to convert to reality.

In October, however, all restraint was abandoned and perceptions changed by a single off-hand remark by Lord Matthews of Southgate. The former Victor Matthews was chairman of Fleet Holdings, corporate owner of the *Daily Express* and *Sunday Express* and half-owner, with Rothermere's Associated Newspapers, of the *Evening Standard*. Fleet was a big, and possibly the biggest, shareholder in Reuters.

His Lordship was a self-made business tycoon who had sharpened his tongue as a bricklayer and his commercial instincts, such as they were, as a top executive with Trafalgar House, a property, shipping, and entertainment conglomerate known for its acquisitive aggression. When Trafalgar's chairman, Nigel Broackes, decided to float off the faltering *Express* titles, he offered Matthews the challenge of turning them around. Matthews was new to the rough-and-rumble world of newspapers but confident that his confrontational style and blunt language would ensure success in dealing with the belligerent print unions. It was a false hope, as it turned out. "I don't think he had any idea what he was getting into," wrote William Davis, Matthews's former personal assistant, and a one-time City editor of the *Evening Standard*. "He thought he could handle the unions better than anyone else but he did not really know what to do with the papers themselves. He said that his chief reading material, up to now, had been the racing-form guide and he had little interest in politics."[4]

Although he was a leading shareholder in Reuters, Matthews was not a director. He was, however, a trustee, which in the opinion of many industry observers ought to have precluded his taking any active role in Reuters' affairs. Not a man to let some flimsy conflict-of-interest issue stand in the way of his involvement in what he saw as an epochal Fleet Street event, Matthews stood ready to assign himself a leadership role in the flotation campaign. For this he prepared by commissioning Fleet's chief financial officer, Ian Irvine, to find out exactly what the company's stake in Reuters might be worth. Irvine came up with a staggering figure: £100 million, perhaps more.

Fleet's financial picture at the time was less than rosy, its future far from secure. For years the *Daily Express* had been losing a fierce circulation battle

---

[4] William Davis, *The Rich*, Sidgwick & Jackson, 1982, p.161

with Murdoch's *Sun*. In retaliation, Fleet launched its own tabloid, *The Star*, but it had fared poorly, draining so much of its parent's capital that Fleet's share price had sunk to an all-time low of 20 pence from a high of nearly £4. Fleet's institutional investors were nervous, and many observers doubted that Fleet could survive as a credible investment. The perception would be changed overnight if Matthews and Irvine could put a tangible value for Reuters on Fleet's balance sheet.

On October 13, at Fleet's annual meeting, Matthews managed to address shareholders without once mentioning Reuters. He later told interviewers that he had not intended to discuss the matter under any circumstances. But in the question-and-answer period after his speech a shareholder brought it up. Matthews could have responded with a "no comment." He did no such thing.

"Their [Reuters'] profits are rising fairly dramatically," he told the meeting. "For many years we've been helping to prop them up. Now suddenly there's a new look about them. In the end it will mean a market quotation." Asked how likely this was, and how soon, he said Fleet had been "chivvying" Reuters in that direction. "I would imagine there would be two classes of shares. There would still have to be control." And then he added, "It could happen this year."[5]

The cat was now well and truly out of the bag. Matthews's indiscretion angered everyone involved in the Reuters situation—owners, directors, bankers, management, and Reuters' journalists—regardless of their viewpoint. As Sir Denis Hamilton wrote in his memoirs: "Matthews began a momentum that was hard to stop. It soon became obvious that a second gold rush had started."

The *Wall Street Journal* reported the next day that Matthews had apparently joined Murdoch in pressing for a flotation. A Murdoch spokesman denied it, expressing his boss's "irritation" at the suggestion. Mr. Murdoch, he added, felt that the whole affair should be allowed to "simmer down." That, of course, was the least likely outcome.

Mike Nelson tried to cool things off with a press statement. It emphasized that Reuters' management had "not authorized any action" in the matter, which was perfectly true, but then nobody had actually claimed that it had. Reuters' own journalists stirred the pot with a letter to *The Times*, expressing concern about threats to the agency's independence and demanding increased powers for the company's trustees. No ironic reference was made to the fact that one of them, Matthews, was playing defense for one team and offense for the other. *The Times* actually declined to publish the letter—naturally giving rise to the suspicion that Murdoch had censored it—but it was circulated widely anyway, bolstering the morale of the anti-flotation forces.

---

[5] Donald Read, *The Power of News*, Oxford University Press, 1992, p.350

Murdoch perked up a Reuters board meeting to ask management to consider changing its formal public position that no proposals for a change in ownership structure was contemplated. The curious reason given for the request was his concern about the conspiratorial atmosphere. Murdoch's opinion was that the subject ought to be brought into the open, giving Reuters control over the flow of uncontrolled news. He was heard but not heeded, and the flow of news continued unabated, naturally featuring prominently in the financial pages of Murdoch's own newspapers.

Throughout 1982, and well into the new year, Reuters' management continued to maintain, or at least publicly convey, a stance suggesting that it was unconvinced by the argument for flotation, and might even come out against it. When Ian Irvine in an interview with the *Financial Times* in March 1983 presumed to lecture Reuters, arguing that if the company intended to compete internationally it would have to "establish a much broader base for raising finance," he drew an acid response from Renfrew. Reuters had been competing internationally for 132 years, Renfrew pointed out, and continued to do so "entirely from its own resources—and still has surplus cash balances."

Weeks later, Murdoch's *Times* ran an article exposing the political arm-wrestling that had been going on behind the scenes at the NPA. What it revealed, among other things, was that the Reuters dividend for the previous year had still had not been distributed because squabbling members had failed to agree on who owned what. "When Fleet Holdings ... claimed it owned 10.18 percent of Reuters, other newspaper companies laughed. They laughed because the apportionment of Reuters shares among the companies is a complete unknown, ripe for deals and debate. Just who is really entitled to how much is going to prove a difficult if not impossible problem to resolve—to the intense frustration of the ailing Fleet Street companies." Solicitors' letters were flying, the article added.

"All this is very sensitive at the moment," conceded J. E. Lepage, a director of the NPA, and obviously a man of rare candor. "If I know the NPA, its members will not be able to sort this one out. When have they ever agreed on anything in the past? And anyway, there is still a strong voice which says that Reuters belongs to all its subscribers, not just the newspapers."

The sound and fury was titillating and deliciously indecorous but distinctly helpful. Because the barons themselves were reluctant to comment on it, they were losing the propaganda battle. Hoist with their own petard, they were powerless to intervene as even their own papers, sometimes with evident relish, depicted them as muddled, grasping, and irresponsible opportunists preparing to assault the freedom and dignity of a great British institution.

It was often mentioned that the owners' support for Reuters historically had been less than ardent. The owners could have argued in their defense that they had been saddled with a cooperative structure that had become increasingly unworkable; or pointed out that they had subsidized the company for so many years by readily coughing up for rising news subscriptions and were now entitled to some kind of payback. They could also have put the case that, while they recognized the genuine concern about Reuters' integrity as a news agency, there was no reason to believe it would inevitably be compromised merely by a change in corporate structure.

No paper bothered to mention that Reuters had been a public company on two previous occasions in its history. If they had, no doubt someone would have pointed out that it was during one of those periods that the company's purpose and reputation had been most seriously endangered. To which the owners could have responded with the truth—that the threat had come, not from sinister forces operating outside the company, but from a covert act of subversion inside it.

The owners might also have refuted the wooly notion that Reuters was a grand and uniquely British institution, and therefore untouchable. The view of Reuters as some kind of national monument to be listed for preservation, and by implication obliged editorially to represent the "British viewpoint" to the world, was out of kilter with the times. It harked back to the kind of jingoism Roderick Jones had once employed to secure secret government subvention. With government assistance out of the question—though there were a few who advocated it even in peacetime 1982, when it would have been even more obnoxious than in wartime 1941—why should Reuters be denied access to the capital market to fulfill its financial needs?

The press barons remained mute. As a result, the various interest groups purporting to represent Reuters' ethical interests plowed on, impervious to counter-arguments. Much to Renfrew's irritation, this diverse coalition included Reuters' own journalists. The company, in the jaundiced view from the editorial floors at 85 Fleet Street, had for too long invested too much energy, not to mention cash, in electronic data products, neglecting in the process its traditional news-gathering activities. There was resentment that management seemed to be constantly trying to ease the term "news agency" out of the corporate lexicon, in favor of the broader definition of "information services company."

Above all, the journalists objected to the profit motive being elevated above all other elements as the company's driving force. To prove their point, the journalists referred to a letter Renfrew had written to staff the previous year, soon after he had taken over from Long. The offending passage read as follows: "In the course of raising our sights for Reuters' business and deciding to aim not just for profitability but substantial profits, we have occasionally been asked how we justify the call for higher profits. Why, the question goes, when we look like beginning to make reasonable profits, do we try to make more? The question, I believe, typifies an attitude which is fortunately rare in Reuters but which, if allowed to take hold, could destroy any company. We cannot afford to stand still or go slowly. We are faced with strong and growing competition in the markets from which we earn most revenue. Companies with much greater resources than our own are preparing to enter these markets ... Substantial rising profits are the only guarantee that we shall be able to defend ourselves and prosper."[6]

This was ample justification for profitability, lucidly expressed, and inspired not by the avaricious impulses of the owners, who at the time had not yet "discovered" Reuters, but by the survival instincts of responsible management. When, shortly afterward, the "E" shares incentive scheme was introduced, many journalists saw in the combined events the end to the civilizing purpose of news-gathering, and perhaps of Reuters itself. It was a muddled view of the world and a distortion of the agency's history. It was colored by the knowledge that barely £5 of every £100 that Reuters earned could now be traced directly to news. Perhaps the one thing the journalists really wanted was to feel wanted.

Yet they were very much wanted, even if they didn't know it. News was a crucial and integral part of the Monitor and Dealing services, and management had repeatedly and emphatically said as much. If the journalists didn't understand that, then there was probably very little else that management could do or say to persuade them otherwise.

In May 1983 the beleaguered pro-flotation forces received a boost from New York, where Telerate's initial public offering was pronounced a great success. For several weeks, Reuters watchers in London became instead Telerate watchers in New York. Renfrew was impressed because it underlined his point that Reuters should be able to compete with well-financed competitors.

Telerate, in revenue terms, was less than a third the size of Reuters, but as Renfrew pointed out: "Telerate is now in a stronger surplus cash position and better placed to make strategic investments than we are."

But not for long.

---

[6] John Lawrenson/Lionel Barber, *The Price of Truth*, Mainstream Publishing, 1985, p.19

# Bonanza

After Telerate's successful share offering in New York the sound of pencils being sharpened could be heard all over the City of London.

The calculations homed in on a single question: if Telerate, just one-third the size of Reuters, was worth $900 million, what price might a flotation of Reuters command? A pretty rich one was the obvious answer. Sensible valuations came in at about three billion pounds. Sillier ones—of which there were many, and often from normally sensible sources—went breathtakingly higher.

On May 18, 1983, three weeks after the Telerate listing, Reuters held a board meeting in New York at the plush Helmsley Palace hotel behind St. Patrick's Cathedral. Needless to say, the agenda, and the extra-curricular conversations, were dominated by the subject of flotation. Sir Denis Hamilton, back in the chair after taking time off to treat his cancer, and visibly frail, opened up the meeting for discussion. It was the first occasion on which the board had engaged in a full-blown debate on the issue. Hamilton, who privately favored the status quo, remained meticulously neutral.

Renfrew was among the first to speak. He argued strongly in favor of flotation. If it was not the first time he had said so, it was the first time he had said it in a formal setting, and he came across more enthusiastically than he had on any previous occasion. Renfrew had obviously done considerable home-work. What he proposed was a multi-level share structure involving the sale to the public of a special class of non-voting shares. This would fulfill the purpose of raising capital without exposing Reuters to the risk of a hostile takeover and a clash over the Trust. What it would not accomplish, as Renfrew and others must have recognized, was the happiness of institutional shareholders. Investment managers do not take kindly to being excluded from the democratic process. But more on that prickly topic later.

To some directors, Renfrew's statement appeared to represent a conversion, but those close to him knew that it was not so much a matter of reaching an opinion as of picking an appropriate moment, and a suitable forum. Renfrew's presentation made an impression on at least two directors, both of whom had been slowly shedding, or at least submerging, their own doubts on the issue.

One was Richard Winfrey, the Press Association chairman who, it may be recalled, had been stunned a few months earlier by Alan Hare's infamous letter. Although constantly irritated by the public antics of some of the press barons, and deeply suspicious of their motives, Winfrey had remained steadfastly uncommitted on the flotation question. From both the ethical and commercial viewpoints he had reservations about flotation. But putting aside his own opinions, he now reported that Press Association members were gradually "coming around" to the idea. Most regional newspapers were losing money, some were in deep financial trouble. The Press Association itself had just recorded an annual deficit of £2 million. To keep its head above water the agency had been forced to sell off several profitable operations, including a popular and lucrative sports results service. Not surprisingly, some PA members were now beginning to see Reuters as the means of the agency's salvation, as well as their own.

Another apparent convert was Lyle Turnbull, representing the Australian Associated Press. He, too, had been a flotation skeptic, and also among those Australians wary of the motives of Rupert Murdoch. But the AAP was now ready to vote for a public offering, he said, so long as the structure was reasonable and was invested with all the appropriate safeguards.

These "conversions" had all the more impact coming from men who were regarded as rational, fair, and open-minded. But by all accounts it was Murdoch who made the most dramatic and influential contribution to the meeting, although typically what he said and what he meant were disputed even years later.

Here for example is an account by Donald Read, in *The Power of News*. "Discussion at the board had run on without much shape until Murdoch exclaimed 'equity is *for ever.*' He meant by this that if Reuters went public, the resulting equity would have to be serviced by a dividend, and that 'City considerations' would influence policy. He contrasted this unfavorably with the existing private company status of Reuters, under which it was possible to take decisions which might depress immediate profitability for the sake of long-term benefits."[1]

In other words, Read seemed to conclude, Murdoch was against a public offering.

Contrast Read with an alternative account by John Lawrenson and Lionel Barber in *The Price of Truth*, an excellent but, as may be inferred from the title, far from objective account of the flotation battle. "...the discussions on Reuters' future drifted back and forth until one shareholder made what Winfrey recalls as the decisive intervention. 'Equity is everything,' exclaimed Rupert Murdoch. The remark caught everyone off balance. Murdoch had been slouched in his chair, listening to the various contributions and waiting to pounce. After a pause and a mischievous grin, the Australian explained what he meant. Reuters could issue paper to expand its business. At present it relied on

---

[1] Donald Read, *The Power of News*, Oxford University Press, 1992, p.353

financing growth from its own resources. If it sold shares on the stock market, it could rapidly expand its capital base, which would give it an immediate cash injection. But above all, going public would help future expansion because it gave the agency the flexibility of either borrowing against shareholders' funds or making acquisitions through issuing its own shares. In short, equity was the springboard for Reuters' future growth and development."[2]

These differing reports of Murdoch's exclamation—equity being either negatively "for ever" or positively "everything"—are curious enough. The diverging conclusions are even stranger. Was this a case of Murdoch's often demonstrated knack of conveying whatever impression the listener wished to draw?

Neither version quoted Murdoch directly, which would have been helpful, but there is surely little doubt that the Lawrenson/Barber interpretation is the right one. Everything Murdoch represented in the business world, and everything that has been attributed to him in the Reuters affair, point to his being strongly in favor of a public offering. Read's account simply doesn't hold water and frankly suggests that in this, as in many of his conclusions, he simply failed to understand the issue he was writing about.

The conviction behind Renfrew's speech, coupled with the Winfrey/Turnbull "conversions," and capped by the Murdoch interjection, convinced Hamilton of the sense of the board: Reuters was now ready to investigate going public in some form or another.

And so it was proposed.

For public consumption, Hamilton continued to dampen expectations. After the next board meeting, this one in London, he denied to reporters that a decision on proceeding to go public had been made, which was literally true. It was realized, he conceded, that the owners had their own "reasonable aspirations" but he stressed that the board would be "taking its time to find the best way to retain its independence while financing expansion and channeling its new-found value to the newspaper groups." Winfrey was just as unforthcoming, telling an anxious annual meeting of the Press Association that "the realization is not going to happen for some time yet, if at all."[3]

"Reuters Still Undecided" ran a headline in Murdoch's *Times*, compounding the sudden epidemic of negative comments, and colliding, in tone if not in substance, with the "Reuters May Go Public" headline it had printed after the New York board meeting.

Binder Hamlyn, Reuters' accounting firm, was appointed to investigate the way forward. This was announced on July 14, 1983, which with uncanny precision was a year to the day after management's famous NPA briefing. With

[2] John Lawrenson/Lionel Barber, *The Price of Truth*, Mainstream Publishing, 1985, p.137
[3] Ibid, p.138

that formality, and regardless of the unending barrage of press speculation of every variety, the question increasingly asked on Fleet Street was not so much whether Reuters would go public as when.

Within Reuters itself, management activity was said to be feverish, as various executive bodies and their advisers reviewed the various flotation options. Murdoch had sensibly suggested, and the directors had authorized, a board-level working party to examine the choices. They essentially boiled down to four, of which two were quickly rejected.

The first to go was a revival of Gerry Long's idea of splitting Reuters into two entities, editorial and commercial. Murdoch himself seemed to favor it, possibly influenced by Long, who now worked for him at *The Times*. But Renfrew and Nelson were adamant—as they had been all along, but now with exaggerated conviction for the benefit of a public as well as a corporate audience—that news and the so-called "commercial services" were mutually dependent. Nelson in particular had bitter memories of the ill-fated attempt to separate them, which the reader may recall had resulted in Horton's resignation and may well have cost Nelson the top job. Also discarded was a proposal to issue non-voting shares to the public. This was turned down because none of the largest investment managers could reasonably be expected to buy shares without voting rights. In most institutions, holding non-voting shares was against the rules.

That left two not-dissimilar options. The first was to market shares with restricted voting rights, with existing owners retaining a 30 percent equity interest. The second was to market shares with those same restrictions but giving existing owners a "minimal" equity interest. In both instances one "master" or "golden" share would be created, to be held by the trustees, giving them the right to veto any changes in corporate structure they considered to be in conflict with the 1941 Trust, or which otherwise seemed incompatible with the company's ethical interests.

Meanwhile, as Reuters and its advisers reviewed the alternatives, the NPA became increasingly absorbed in its own curious machinations. NPA council meetings, which were now suddenly well attended, provided the arena for disentangling what Lord Marsh, the NPA chairman, described as a "mare's nest" of interlocking and disputed shareholdings. He was now called upon to preside over—actually, to referee—a series of bitterly fought bilateral contests between rival owners.

Lawrenson/Barber offered a visual insight into the proceedings. "The NPA council chamber is a daunting room. Around a huge oaken table are some twenty green leather chairs, to which each of the national newspaper proprietors can lay claim. If one of these so-called press barons is absent (which is all too often the case), then that chair must lie vacant. The seating arrangement is equally formal: each press proprietor must sit in alphabetical order according to the title or titles of his various newspapers. It is one of Fleet Street's great ironies that the owner of Express Newspapers, the heir of the [Lord] Beaverbrook tradition, had under this arrangement to sit next to his arch rival, Rothermere, the owner of Associated Newspapers, with the second Viscount Rothermere, his father, gazing down on the proceeding from a portrait on the wall."

Swarmed about by lawyers and accountants, the press barons went at it, hammer and tong, in an attritional war of words that continued without pause throughout the summer of 1983. Matthews and Rothermere in particular often engaged in a fascinating contest that pitted the stocky former bricklayer against a very large, aristocratic Old Etonian.

At one meeting in June, there emerged the first promising sign of cooperation between the two protagonists. Again according to Lawrenson/Barber, Lord Matthews, "to the astonishment of all seated around the NPA table, announced that he was close to agreement with Lord Rothermere on the two men's individual shareholding. There was a sigh of relief from those present, for Matthews and Rothermere had been slugging it out toe to toe over their shareholdings for weeks, with both men threatening to haul in their lawyers to settle their differences in court." It was, the account continued, "a brief respite, for two days later, at a second NPA meeting, yet another ferocious dispute broke out when Rupert Murdoch revealed with relish that Matthews had not paid his full Reuters subscription when he launched the *Daily Star*. The Reuters subscription was the one pre-condition of his share entitlement.

"Given that Matthews' stake in Reuters was worth almost £100 million on a valuation of £1 billion, *The Star* shareholding alone was worth between £20 million and £30 million. When the press barons heard the news they almost leapt across the table to strangle the hapless Matthews. And so what appeared to be a long-awaited truce collapsed and the trench warfare resumed."[4]

For all the sound and fury, it counts as a credit to the NPA owners that at no time had anyone suggested that creating a new Reuters meant ditching the 1941 Trust or ignoring its main principles. It was, of course, equally true that nobody at the table would have openly dared to suggest doing either. Yet it demonstrated the kind of moral sway exerted by the Trust, even on those who felt that it might well be from the legal perspective a less than rock-solid document. Those proprietors who were trustees as well as owners now faced underlying ethical dilemmas that went to the heart of their role. The issue came up at a June trustees meeting that was notable chiefly for another heated exchange between Matthews and Rothermere, with Lord Hartwell and other

---

[4] John Lawrenson/Lionel Barber, *The Price of Truth*, Mainstream Publishing, 1985, pp.140-141

trustees looking on, presumably with varying degrees of scorn at the attitude of Matthews.

It was Matthews who kicked off. "As trustees we would not be opposed to a public flotation in some formal manner provided the safeguards of the Trust were there, and you suggested obviously that proposals have to be put forward. But by who? Would it be improper for a trustee to put them forward, or would we look to management to initiate the proposals, or otherwise we remain silent on it? There is a distinct feeling that, while everyone else is rather shy of saying too much about it, I have a feeling that no one would be really opposed to it, because obviously there is substantial money involved..."

Rothermere countered: "I think the trustees only come into this at a considerable remove. Their fundamental duty is not to the shareholders and their profits but to uphold the objectives of the Trust, and I don't think in that connection that this Board of Trustees should take the initiative in anything. We should be fully informed, and we should contemplate and make our decision on whatever is put before us to ensure that it is in accord with the Reuters Trust..."

Matthews: "I would also suggest we have a responsibility not only for the Trust but for the shareholders as a whole. It is implied."

Rothermere: "I don't think so."

Matthews: "That is my view, that it is our duty to look after the Trust and the shareholders."

Rothermere: "I think that is the duty of the directors."[5]

No defense of the Trust, even one based on the highest ethical principles, could detract from the need for clarification of its precise nature. Was the Trust a grave and irrevocable legal obstacle, as its authors appear to have intended, or merely a minor corporate irritant, to be amended by shareholders if they chose to? If a legal interpretation should be required, the central point might settle on the original intentions of its authors. But given the vague language in which it was couched, these were hard to discern other than on the basis of anecdotal references and assumptions.

Focus came to rest on the phrase relating to ownership of Reuters—that it was "in the nature of a Trust rather than an investment." For some observers those words represented the Trust's guiding principle. For others it merely conveyed its most prominent ambiguity. Had the drafters specifically intended to rule out for all time any changes in Reuters' structure, regardless of circumstances? The Trust did not say as much—but then it left a great many things unsaid.

The fact is that the formulation "rather than" in itself did not categorically prohibit a broader investment than that undertaken by the original owners; it

---

[5] Donald Read, *The Power of News*, Oxford University Press, 1992, p.353

merely gave "Trust" a preferential emphasis. The author of the document, Sir William Haley, still hale and hearty in 1983 and living in the Channel Islands, was apparently not consulted. Nor was Sir Christopher Chancellor, Reuters' former chief executive, who had helped in the drafting, although he would at a later stage voice his uninvited opinion against flotation. If the views of the drafters were considered irrelevant, it may have been because the document they had produced was written at a time when circumstances were quite different and the present situation quite unforeseeable.

The newspapers had paid little attention to the Trust issue. It did not make for exciting copy and Fleet Street's finest could always find far more compelling angles in a story that was, after all, about their favorite subject: themselves. One publication, however, had been doing some legal digging and had unearthed some interesting facts.

*The Spectator*, Britain's oldest magazine, in its 155th year of uninterrupted publication, was a serious, bland-looking weekly magazine of opinion, largely of a conservative but not slavishly pro-establishment leaning. It had once enjoyed a certain influence in high places, but that had long since dwindled into insignificance along with its circulation, which had shrunk to 20,000 readers. Although *The Spectator* was regarded in much the same light as its remaining loyalists—aging Tories and fusty Whigs—once in a while it found some cause worthy of its cudgels. In that respect, its outrage was directed to the Reuters affair, in which it came out firmly, and with righteous indignation, against a public offering.

There were two good reasons why *The Spectator* should have a strong opinion on a complex subject, and to the extent of devoting three whole pages of the magazine to express it. The first was that the editor was Alexander Chancellor, a former Reuters correspondent. The second, and perhaps more significant, was that his father was Sir Christopher Chancellor, the former general manager of the agency. It was Alexander's byline that appeared at the head of the article, alongside that of Geoffrey Robertson, a former barrister. The tone of the piece was summed up in a succinct headline: "Reuters: The Price of Greed."[6]

The attack that followed, somewhat larded with emotive turns of phrase, was directed at owners and management alike. The press barons were depicted as "licking their lips" in anticipation of their windfall, while management was accused of being "shifty." As if to support the latter charge, the article mentioned that Renfrew's "E" shares alone were likely to be worth about £5 million (although it failed to point out that this would be true whether Reuters went public or not). The Chancellors—if it can be safely assumed that senior as well as junior was involved in the article—were particularly agitated about

---

[6] *The Spectator*, October 22, 1983

the fate of the Trust, of which Sir Christopher claimed partial authorship. Amid the propagandist sentiments, the article tossed around some interesting and potentially explosive legal questions, presumably the work of Robertson. Among them was the role the Lord Chief Justice, England's highest-ranking jurist, might be obliged to play in resolving any contentious issues involving the Trust. The chief issue was Clause 12 of the Trust document, which stipulated that any change in the status of the Trust be submitted to the Lord Chief Justice for approval. It gave flotation opponents a potential blocking device because it supported the contention that the Trust was a legally binding document, not just a statement of principles, or shareholders' agreement—in other words one that the owners could modify at will.

In the opinion of the authors "a properly constituted, valid trust imposed grave duties upon its trustees, and is subject to supervision by the courts." At the same time they admitted that questions of "when a trust is not a trust are among the most arcane and unpredictable in British law." The article's conclusion was that "in view of the uncertainty about the status of the Reuters Trust, it would be desirable for the company to seek a declaration in the courts as to its meaning and effect, and to clarify the role of the Chief Justice."

As for the financial aspects of flotation, the authors-cum-lawyers turned securities analysts as well. "In the meantime, investors should be warned. By conveniently ignoring all the legal, moral and political difficulties of exploiting the Reuters gold mine, Fleet Street newspapers may be substantially overvaluing it. And the flotation, which could leave Reuters both unloved and inadequately protected, may even now fail to take place."

"Fat chance!" was the popular reaction along Fleet Street.

But Renfrew and Nelson were incensed by what they read as a snide reference to management chicanery. Reuters' official response, through a spokesman, was significant. The official acknowledged that Clause 12 did indeed call for a referral to the Lord Chief Justice, but denied that this made the Trust legally binding. In the company's opinion the Trust was a shareholders' agreement. This was the view that Nelson and Judah robustly reinforced over lunch in a Covent Garden restaurant to which Alexander Chancellor had been "summoned." Management's position had by then already appeared in print in an interview Nigel Judah had given to the *Daily Telegraph*. The article was given prominence in the paper beyond its importance, a fact which some observers ascribed to the influence of Lord Hartwell, the *Telegraph*'s proprietor. Hartwell was known to be averse to a public offering and may have wanted to flush out management's hitherto guarded opinion on the subject of the Trust. Whatever the Machiavellian intrigues behind it, the article quoted Judah as asserting, as a counterpoint to Clause 12, that a public offering could be "perfectly justified" by Clause 5. This specified that "no effort should be spared to expand, develop and adapt the business of Reuters in order to maintain in every event its position as the world's leading news agency."

Alexander Chancellor, unmoved by Nelson's lunchtime entreaties, responded with another anti-flotation salvo in *The Spectator*, the first of many printed over the course of several weeks. "In the past, their attention has been focused on the Reuters news service and how to maintain its quality at the lowest cost to themselves; if Reuters goes public, their attention will be directed towards those aspects of the company which are likely to make them money—in other words everything but the news service."

By November, under constant artillery fire from *The Spectator*, management discussions had advanced far enough that a share capital plan had been agreed with S.G. Warburg, Reuters' investment bank.

The plan distributed to the owners was a complex document. A new company, Reuters Holdings plc, would be formed to replace Reuters Limited. There would be four classes of stock: "A" shares, representing 25 percent of the total equity, carrying four votes to preserve a voting majority for the existing newspaper owners; "B" shares, representing 75 percent of the equity, and worth only one vote, which would be the shares offered to the general public; one so-called Founder's share, known as the "golden share" because it had under certain circumstances veto power over all other shares and could be invoked if necessary to protect the Trust; and, finally, more "E" shares of the kind already created for the executive incentive plan, with no voting power.

No person or group would be allowed to own more than 15 percent of any class of shares. The principles of the Trust would be maintained, as would its essential language, but the wording would be modified to reflect Reuters' changed corporate circumstances. In other words, if the Trust had not been regarded as a shareholders' agreement before, it was now.

Everyone seemed happy with the structure expect Rupert Murdoch, who did not like weighted voting, including this particular version of it. At Reuters' November board meeting he is said to have dismissed it as "a typical piece of British hypocrisy."[7] His objection was that guaranteeing the existing owners control through the "A" shares was a case of wanting to have one's cake and eat it. Murdoch knew better than anyone else at the table how unacceptable it would have been to reorganize the company without some kind of protective multi-level equity structure. Still, the question had been raised and it was discussed at great length—and for several exasperating hours, according to some accounts. Alan Hare, an erstwhile Murdoch ally, dismissed the outburst as "pure theater," but in City circles many felt that Murdoch had made a valid point.

---

[7] John Lawrenson/Lionel Barber, *The Price of Truth*, Mainstream Publishing, 1985, p.160

There was more theater to come. The lingering *Spectator* controversy brought opponents of flotation an eleventh-hour offer of help from another unexpected source: former prime minister James Callaghan. The politician once popularly known as Sunny Jim had been following events through the magazine (to which, it was suspected, his attention had been directed by Sir Christopher Chancellor) and, no doubt with the best intentions, seemed to have developed an itch to get involved in Fleet Street affairs. Two years earlier he had offered his services in an elder statesman role during the period leading to Murdoch's controversial acquisition of Times Newspapers. Then, Callaghan had offered to intercede with the print unions in support of a potential bidding rival, *Sunday Times* editor Harold Evans. Now, he was apparently trying to thwart the newspaper owners once more.

"Jim'll Fix It" (taken from the title of a popular children's television show) had been a recurring headline when Callaghan was a beleaguered prime minister of curiously smiling disposition in the face of a crumbling British economy. Jim now offered to do just that on behalf of the anti-flotation forces. Obviously well briefed on the subject, Callaghan wrote to the Attorney General, Sir Michael Havers, asking him to offer his opinion on the proper role of the Lord Chief Justice in relation to the Reuters Trust. Havers admitted to knowing nothing about the Reuters situation but promised to give it his "urgent consideration."

The Lord Chief Justice was equally bemused, candidly confessing to *The Observer* that he was in "complete ignorance of his responsibilities in the matter."[8]

Sir Christopher Chancellor joined his son in print with a rather irrelevant reminder, in a newspaper interview, that the then Lord Chief Justice had been involved in drafting the original Trust document not only in 1941 but in subsequent amendments in 1946 and 1950. Sir Denis Hamilton privately lamented "the wanderings, in every sense" of his fellow knight.

Two days later, Havers settled the legal issue by telling the House of Commons that he had no responsibilities in the matter of Reuters going public. Management heaved a collective sigh of relief.

But then there arrived a countervailing warning from the chairman of the Trustees committee, Angus McLachlan of the AAP, a known skeptic of the merits of a public offering. In a press release issued in Sydney, he asserted that there would be no Australian "rubberstamping" of any Reuters flotation plan. Management heaved a sigh of exasperation.

And so, back and forth, the battle raged—or so it seemed, judging by the copious press coverage. In reality, though, the battle by now was all but over.

The Chancellors, deflated by the Havers ruling, their indignation

---

[8] *The Observer*, November 13, 1982

apparently spent, disappeared from the field with the same abruptness with which they had appeared on it. Callaghan, too, moved on, presumably to seek other matters worthy of the attention of a former prime minister. Anyway, the press had become bored with what seemed to have been little more than a storm in a teacup. Callaghan, in January 1984, could still summon enough energy to fire one last shot, by initiating a public debate in the House of Commons in which he and others invoked parliamentary privilege as a prerequisite to any decision on Reuters' future. But the occasion was less than riveting. Few members of parliament seemed particularly interested in the subject and the audience for his own speech comprised just a dozen MPs— half the number of reporters peering down distractedly from the press gallery. Hamilton complained in a letter to Callaghan that "someone is giving you the wrong story" on Reuters and expressed regret that Callaghan could think that he, Hamilton, would consider having any truck with any arrangement that compromised Reuters' integrity. Callaghan telephoned Hamilton to apologize. "I suddenly realized I'd been taken for a sucker on this," Hamilton quoted him as saying.[9]

Once the public furor over the Trust had receded, the trustees could meet on February 21 to consider, in an unleavened atmosphere, the proposed four-way shareholding structure. They liked what they saw. As for the Trust document, they agreed to modify it with a bromide to the effect that Reuters would show due regard to "the many interests which it serves in addition to those of the media"—namely "businesses, institutions and individuals and others with whom Reuters has or may have dealings."[10] The owners were required to enter into a binding deed of covenant with the company and the trustees to vouchsafe the company's independence and principles, a restraint with which no one had a problem.

Harmony seemed to be busting out all over. The NPA and Press Association, no doubt exhausted, finally agreed on the allocation of shares representing their combined ownership block. To get there had taken the better part of two punishing years. In the *Financial Times*, the influential Lex column, compulsory reading in the City, gave the deal its thumbs-up: "Even Chubb locks could not have designed a shareholding structure more burglar proof." And the previously antagonistic Alexander Chancellor was sufficiently impressed to print a gracious concession in *The Spectator*: "As an exercise in having one's cake and eating it, the restructuring of the company is to be admired."[11] Whether that also expressed the view of his father is not recorded.

There were a few last-minute chores, some of which introduced a diverting

---

[9] Denis Hamilton, *Editor-in-Chief*, Hamish Hamilton, 1989, pp.189-190
[10] John Lawrenson/Lionel Barber, *The Price of Truth*, Mainstream Publishing, 1985, p.157
[11] *The Spectator*, March 3, 1983

human element. The Press Association, still trying to track down some missing shareholders, the descendants of some of its original owners, launched a national advertising campaign. It worked only too well, causing Jack Purdham, the PA's financial controller, to complain that he was "besieged by everybody, every sort of person who thought they could trace a family tree. It was a constant battle, although we finally got them all."[12]

A Wiltshire housewife, one Diana Parsons, was among the last to be got. She was skiing in Switzerland when she received the news that she was the heir apparent to 1200 Reuters shares, once owned by her stepfather's grandfather. Their potential worth was £5 million. A phlegmatic Ms. Parsons told a reporter that she wasn't about to celebrate by "going out to buy ten yachts."[13] Which was just as well, as a long-lost stepbrother suddenly popped up, lawyers in tow, to claim the same shares.

Another family, from suburban Purley in Surrey, returned home from a holiday to be greeted at Gatwick airport by a reception committee of PA lawyers. Emerging from the baggage hall, they were flabbergasted to learn that they owned 600 shares worth about £2.5 million.

Another unexpected fortune was awarded to one Brian Bradley Croom-Johnson, whose grandfather, George Bradley, had been the editor of a long-defunct Welsh provincial newspaper, the *Wrexham Advertiser*. Someone had telephoned his wife with the news. "At first it didn't ring any bells," he commented appositely, "but my second name is Bradley so I dug out the family tree and it took off from there."[14]

Amid all this joy, however, there remained one distinctly unhappy community.

With all the owners identified, allocated, and foursquare behind the new structure, Reuters' bankers could at last devote all their attention to their true function: selling Reuters shares to the investors. And so to the final controversy in the Reuters affair, which involved not the sellers of shares but the prospective buyers.

The *Financial Times* might applaud "burglar-proof" voting structures but they tend to be scorned by investment institutions as no more than devices designed to protect owners or management. It was felt by many in the City that restricted voting undermined the principles of a free market. Echoing Murdoch's objection, two prominent investment groups, the British Insurance Association and the National Association of Pension Funds, told Warburg in February that the Founders share was alone sufficient to preserve Reuters' integrity. The rest of the structure, they felt, was nothing more than a ruse to

---

[12] Chris Moncrieff, *Living on a Deadline*, Virgin Books, 2001, p.248

[13] John Lawrenson/Lionel Barber, *The Price of Truth*, Mainstream Publishing, 1985, p. 159

[14] Chris Moncrieff, *Living on a Deadline*, Virgin Books, 2001, p.248

perpetuate the owners' control. Therefore, barring a change, the NAPF intended to recommend that its members, representing several billion pounds' worth of investment funds, should boycott the shares. Such a threat, while not likely to sabotage the float entirely, had the potential to inflict crippling damage on market liquidity. It also threatened to wreck Warburg's novel plan for a simultaneous sale of shares in New York, the first dual flotation of its kind.[15]

As late as May, Sir Ian Fraser, sounding more like a journalist than a banker, wrote to the *Financial Times* with a vigorous defense of management's decision to confront the issue of Reuters' integrity and independence with what he called "belt and braces protection." Acknowledging the City's antipathy towards differential voting, he claimed that the Reuters example was "quite different" from the normal. "The issue here is freedom of information and the temptation which a unique instrument such as Reuters would offer to those who would like to corrupt it."[16]

City men remained unconvinced.

Leaving the City boycott threat in the hands of the company's lawyers, Renfrew and Judah set off for America for a series of road show presentations. Even in that they contrived to provoke one final controversy. A *Financial Times* reporter, Clive Wolman, wrote a front-page article to the effect that the American reception to Reuters was disappointing. American fund managers, he wrote, seemed "mesmerized" by the uncertain stock-market conditions (the US was going through one of its regular banking crises, sparked by the government bail-out of Continental Illinois).

The FT story, appearing at a sensitive time, caused great consternation in London. Renfrew's response was to bar the reporter from all further presentations. (It would have been reasonable to ask what he was doing there in the first place.) Wolman countered by following up his first jibe with a couple more: first quoting negative comments from attending fund managers, then suggesting that the Securities and Exchange Commission was angered by all the pre-float publicity surrounding Reuters and might be considering legal action. Renfrew and Nelson complained to the FT that Wolman's second article, which they ascribed to motivations of revenge, was "the most disgraceful piece of reporting they had ever encountered."[17]

On June 5, 1984, Reuters shares were listed simultaneously in London and New York. The twin event, the first simultaneous dual listing in history, proved to be a classic anticlimax. The threat of an institutional boycott having been finally removed, British investors greeted the offering with enthusiasm, applying for almost three times as many shares as were offered. The striking

---

[15] John Lawrenson/Lionel Barber, *The Price of Truth*, Mainstream Publishing, 1985, p.158
[16] Ibid., p.160
[17] Ibid., p.162

price was a modest 196 pence, which Murdoch, Matthews, and others predictably attacked as overly cautious. In New York, the shares were only moderately over-subscribed, partly justifying Wolman's gloomy prognostications. If the initial result was disappointing, it could be explained by the fact that Reuters' name was much less famous in America than in Britain.

Those British newspaper proprietors who chose to sell their "A" shares netted some £200 million, which some rather ungratefully regarded as a somewhat scant reward for all the agonies of the previous two years. It was still enough to bail out many of the weaker sisters in the British newspaper industry. Murdoch was not among the ungrateful, nor was he among the sellers. Not selling would prove to be a shrewd decision: a few years later Murdoch used his Reuters shares in a complex refinancing of News International at a time when it was going through a rough patch of it own.

Reuters itself took £50 million in proceeds, which also seemed flimsy, being less than Telerate had realized from its own offering a year earlier. It was, though, more than enough for operating cash, especially since the company was generating cash in ever-rising amounts from Monitor and Dealing.

A year after the event, few on Fleet Street gave much thought to the violent controversies that had preceded it. A common conclusion, reached with all the advantages of hindsight, was that a very big fuss had been made over what ought to have been, and with more careful handling might have been, a straightforward transaction. It can be argued that it could never have been that, and that to say so was to ignore Reuters' history. But then, change is history, too.

The Trust at the center of the storm had endured intact—and probably better than intact. Even many erstwhile opponents of flotation agreed that it had emerged notably strengthened.

The "E" share scheme was extended, allowing a dozen Reuters executives to join Renfrew, Nelson, and Judah in the Instant Reuters Millionaire Club. More would follow, including senior editorial figures. Reuters' brooding journalists carried on working, not altogether happy, but with no more chips on the shoulder than they had started with.

Sadly, Sir Denis Hamilton finally succumbed to the prostate cancer he had been fighting valiantly throughout the entire Reuters affair.

Few tears were shed for Gerald Long, even among those who credited him with guiding Reuters to the commercial success that made flotation possible. By leaving Reuters when he did, it was often said, more frequently with a chuckle than with a sympathetic sigh, he had "missed out" on a fortune. Long claimed with some vehemence that he had never given it a second's thought.

He would have plenty of time to reflect on it. Within a year Murdoch had fired him. Long, bruised and affronted, retreated to his Normandy farmhouse, near Bayeaux.

Lord Matthews and Fleet Holdings had no better luck. The Reuters windfall kept Fleet afloat for a while, but before long His Lordship took what many regarded, one way or another, as a well-deserved retirement; and soon after that Fleet itself was on the block.

Murdoch of course remained at his post, as irrepressible as ever. Within two years he had stunned the newspaper world with a clandestine maneuver which, literally overnight, removed all four of his newspaper titles from Fleet Street to a fortress-like, razor-wire-enclosed plant in the rejuvenated Docklands, in the East End of London. To say that the Street was shocked is an epic of understatement. As one observer put it, "Fleet Street was scooped by its own funeral." In the process, the print unions were irrevocably destroyed. About that there were few expressions of regret, but the famous old street would never recover from the shock. In 1985, the Reuters newsroom was the only significant editorial operation left there, surrounded by invasive hordes of investment bankers and lawyers.

Telerate continued to thrive, though its brief but happy existence as a public company was about to end. John Gunn, unable to find common ground with Neil Hirsch and facing a revolt on the Exco board, decided to sell out. Neil Hirsch promptly talked Dow Jones into buying in.

# Markets 'R' Us

The resounding success of the Reuters and Telerate stock offerings opened a gilded age for both companies—and for the global trading community that each had done so much to create. The enthusiasm for the shares carried an explicit message: the financial markets of the future, as far as investors were concerned, would be increasingly, and in the end overwhelmingly, dependent on information technology, and Reuters and Telerate were visibly at the forefront of the approaching revolution.

Curiously, management at both companies seemed less at ease with the confidence being literally invested in them than might be imagined. Such doubts may strike the reader as idiotic, but from the perspective of a later generation thoroughly at ease with an astonishing array of electronic devices, it is easy to forget that the revolution in the technology of communication, though well underway as the decade of the eighties arrived, was still barely out of its infancy.

The communications utilities, entrenched at the time in remarkably few hands—government-owned monopolies in most parts of the world—still had not entirely completed the transition from the telegraphic to the electronic age. To say that this presented the market-data companies with a variety of frustrating logistical obstacles is to understate the case.

One such utility was the British Post Office, a creaking old state monolith on its last legs, staggering like an exhausted marathon runner towards the finishing line. (This turned out to be a privatized rebirth as British Telecom.) The BPO often took up to a year to install the local telephone lines that connected Reuters and Telerate terminals to their networks. Threatening, cajoling, pleading, and begging were widely deployed to get lines installed faster. The BPO was impervious to all of them. Bribery was no doubt considered as a last resort, if not actually tried, but even bribery would have been ineffectual in the face of systemic antiquity and management incompetence.

International circuits could be just as much a problem as local ones due to variances in reliability from one part of the world to the next. In some foreign parts, however, bribery *could* be an effective tool, and in certain Third World countries was often the *only* tool.

During heavy periods of traffic, users often experienced interrogation response times that left them tearing their hair out. As a complaining Telerate customer in America once commented, "What I've learned to do, whenever I call up a Telerate page, is to wander off for a cup of coffee, or perhaps go to the bathroom. That way, by the time I get back, the information I asked for might actually be up." The obvious solution for the vendors was to move to higher network speeds, but in those early years long-distance lines were prohibitively expensive, and replacing existing lines was a logistical nightmare because every user terminal had to be upgraded at the same time.

The result was that Reuters and Telerate, even as they started to rake in the profits that had so endeared them to investors, seemed slightly bemused, perhaps even overawed, by their new power—unsure how to wield it, even uncertain how long it would last. If the latter point needs illustrating, then consider Reuters' initial pathetic sales forecasts for Monitor, ostensibly a make-or-break project for a company still too close to its precarious financial past for comfort.

What the Reuters' less-than-intrepid business planners had come up with in the way of worldwide sales projections fell well short of three digits. That the enterprise was readily approved anyway suggests that the extent of management's ambition was not so much the opportunity to carve out a position of unassailable market dominance as much as a chance to establish some kind of bridgehead for future products yet to be defined. If Monitor, the thinking went, were to at least recover its costs and after that perhaps produce a modest flow of income, then it could be ticked off as a success.

I can almost hear the cries of "Nonsense!" from the ranks of distinguished former Reuters managers as they read this. To which all I can say is that they have short memories. Deny it they might, but "How long can this last?" was a question Reuters and Telerate managers often asked among themselves. Not in public, of course, with probing analysts and reporters constantly on the prowl, always ready to pick up on hints of management apprehension.

Reuters management could claim ample mitigation for caution. The company was breaking new ground internally as well as externally. The company had never built a dedicated computer-driven network of its own. As for those pathetic sales projections, John Ransom, one of Monitor's fallible forecasters, was prepared years later to put it much more succinctly and honestly than he or anyone else would have been prepared to do at the time. "The plain truth of the matter is that we were just guessing with the Monitor figures, completely in the dark. That we didn't know what we were talking about, events would later prove. And thank goodness we didn't."

When the number of Monitor clients installed soared into the thousands a year or so later, there were no blushes of embarrassment at 85 Fleet Street, just huge sighs of relief.

If Monitor had been hard work in the face of market suspicions, a second outbreak of market resistance broke out a couple of years into the new decade when Reuters introduced, again with more timidity than conviction, a conversational dealing facility. In all its essential functions, Dealing represented little more than a screen-based version of the old trading-room telex machines, but many banks objected to Dealing just as vigorously as they once had to Monitor. Even some prominent Monitor users cried "Enough!" The fear was that Reuters, by moving beyond merely providing news and quotes into intimate involvement in the transaction process, might be reaching beyond its preordained station.

In the event, history repeated itself almost precisely. Just as Reuters' management a few years earlier had dreaded a stillborn Monitor, it now found itself suffering similar anguish over the survival prospects for the new product. And just as Monitor had required a marketing relaunch to buck things up after poor initial sales, so, too, did Dealing. Both products, of course, eventually beat a path to success, but it is conveniently forgotten how badly both had stumbled during the early stages of the journey.

Reuters was not entirely alone in battling market prejudice against innovation. In New York, certain dealers in US government securities continued to fume over the "betrayal" by Cantor Fitzgerald in unilaterally introducing screen-based trading via Telerate. Right up to the start of the new decade, they were still plotting Bernie Cantor's downfall, though with rapidly diminishing prospects for success. I was frequently taken aback by the vitriol with which anti-Cantor sentiments were expressed. These were often laced with vicious personal invective, and abounded with references to the old, unproven accusations of Mafia connections. Even the Merrill Lynch "conversion" described previously, failed to end resistance entirely. Bernie was hardly an angel, but neither was he the devil incarnate often painted. His unforgivable offence had been to buck "the system."

Essentially the "system" was nothing more than a set of operating protocols imposed on the market by the larger firms to ensure their dominance over the smaller ones. It was ever thus in most financial markets—witness the power of the Two Bobbies, in the currency market, discussed earlier.

If there was one issue on which the entire trading community could unite—small firms as well as large—it was the concern that the new technologies now being introduced, and apparently destined to rule the trading rooms of the future, lay in the hands of outside interests like Reuters and Telerate, which might prove to be ruthlessly insensitive in their approach to market conventions long held in sacred esteem. At the extreme end of the opposition spectrum, many old lags convinced themselves that technology— any technology, regardless of ownership—heralded The End Of Civilization As We Know It. Their patriotic duty, as they saw it, was to protect and conserve the old ways. These self-appointed guardians of market traditions nursed a perverse pride in their endurance and their ability to resist external threats to their livelihood, whether real or imagined. Technology would be repelled, they boasted, just as all previous encroachments on time-honored customs had been rebuffed.

What they failed to recognize was that most of the incursions beaten off in times past had been contrived by politicians, central bankers, or other regulators—in other words, humans. Humans, even those representing officialdom, are usually reasonable and open to compromise, and their menace almost invariably proving to be more imagined than real, especially in the face of stubborn resistance. Technology was a different box of tricks altogether. Technology could not be lobbied or lunched. Technology also brought changes far broader in their implications than a few adjustments to daily routines. "Liberation" by networks that delivered instant prices to anywhere on the planet meant profound changes in market practices, altering the fundamental nature of international capital.

More thoughtful, modern-thinking members of the trading community recognized all this and more, but saw on the horizon blue skies of opportunity rather than threatening black thunderclouds. Above all, they recognized that technology was unstoppable, and the sooner the financial community recognized the fact, the easier it would be to cope with it—and control it.

But the questions lingered, and even the modernists were unable to answer some of them. Should traders position themselves as brave standard-bearers of a proven old model or bold pioneers of an unproven new one? Would using desktop terminals seriously diminish and demean the individual trader's role, or enhance it? Could technology eventually displace traders altogether, or at least require them to operate at some undefined higher level? And, if so, how soon? The questions were unanswerable, but events would finally demonstrate that they were valid.

I came across this telling quote in Volume IV of David Kynaston's mammoth and entertaining history *The City of London*, revealingly subtitled "A Club No More." It is attributed to one Paul Bazalgette, a senior partner of stockbrokers Phillips & Drew. "In common with a lot of my friends and contemporaries I have had at times grave fears about this computer era into which we are now well launched. Some of us have been, and will continue to be, supplanted by machines. We resent this for many reasons but two seem to predominate. Firstly, no machine can be as good as we are, with our fine education, our superb training, our delicate sensibilities, and our devotion to duty. Secondly, we would like to continue to eat."[1]

Hardly surprising, then, that the traders of an earlier generation

---

[1] David Kynaston, *The City of London, Vol. IV, A Club No More*, Chatto & Windus, 2001, p.422

occasionally broke into a cold sweat thinking about the uncertain future of their business and their careers.

Bazalgette's views may be considered all the more surprising because he was a stockbroker. Unlike other market people, stockbrokers were, in matters of technology, seasoned veterans. They had always pioneered the use of information retrieval devices, from technology's earliest Wall Street manifestation, the stock ticker, invented by the great Thomas Edison in the late 1880s, to Quotron, first introduced in the 1960s, and had done so without giving much more thought to them than they had to dialing a telephone.

Stockbrokers were different from traders in unregulated over-the-counter markets in one other crucial respect. The stock-market environment was created, regulated, governed, and entirely focused on a central exchange, a physical location, backed by national legislation, with strict rules, enforced by law, about everything from trading hours to public disclosure. Foreign-exchange treasuries, and certain other over-the-counter traders, operated with no such framework—very little framework of any kind, really—so it was natural that any technological device other than a telephone would be regarded with suspicion. Where Quotron and other machines of its kind had been merely processors of stock tickers representing information long decreed by law to be in the public domain, in the over-the-counter markets Reuters and Telerate/Cantor Fitzgerald were pushing traders long accustomed to transacting business in secrecy, through bilateral telephone conversations into unknown but clearly far more transparent methods.

If conflict between tradition and technology was therefore deemed inevitable, it became apparent very quickly that the war would be strictly of the phony variety. A few shots were fired, but they were hardly of the Sarajevo "shots heard round the world" variety. In the event, the putative Traders Revolt was as short-lived as it was powerless and therefore bloodless. Surviving the ravages of technology, it soon became clear, had not been the challenge after all. The challenge, rather, became how to exploit it.

John Christopherson, of Bank of Montreal, one of the more forward-thinking members of the currency market—and emphatically not a technologist—got the message from the start. "At first, it was a huge advantage being among the few with access to market prices though Monitor. But as soon as it started to become popular, the equation changed to one of huge disadvantage not having access to it. That was clearly the way it was going to be with any successful product. So we all moved on, to wonder or worry about the next development. And whatever it was going to be, I was wholly committed to being one of the first to sign on."

So it quickly came about that traders who had once talked defiantly about digging in for a long siege could be seen consorting, even cavorting gaily, with enemy patrols of the kind manned by foraging Reuters sales executives. Once regarded as dangerous buffoons, they were now welcomed as liberators rather than conquerors. Scales had fallen from eyes. Given a glimpse of an online future, traders saw that it not only worked, but could be made to work hugely to their benefit.

One overlooked aspect of what was now perceived as a perfect union between financial markets and technology was that it occurred without let or hindrance from governments. No one had ever seriously suggested that technology might result in disorderly markets, the principal concern of regulators and central banks, and many observers argued the contrary. Regulators could not have intervened if they had wanted to—and most by now did not want to. All had collectively recognized a harsh truth: in the post-Bretton Woods era of floating exchange rates, and a vast capital pool that had become more nomadic and volatile through access to global networks, they had been rendered largely powerless.

Or, as journalists would say, they had been scooped.

Even if they had not been, Walter Wriston, the then chairman of Citibank, would have pointed it out to them. He did so anyway, retrospectively, in his 1992 book, *The Twilight of Sovereignty*, which came to be regarded for a while as a seminal work on the subject.

Wriston's thesis, which, with the passage of time inevitably sounds more trite and platitudinous than ground-breaking and revolutionary, was that networks capable of conveying information to every remote corner of the planet at the speed of light were the pathways to an electronic global marketplace of enormous scale that could not be controlled or regulated. Foreign exchange in particular was a market blessed with virtually all the ideological qualities evangelized by Wriston and other weighty observers of the New Age: it was infinitely liquid, non-hierarchical, decentralized, and socially non-judgmental.

Canny old Walt saw it plain: "When a system of national currencies run by central banks is transformed into a global electronic marketplace driven by private currency traders, power changes hands. When a system of national economies linked by government-regulated trade is replaced ... by an increasingly integrated global economy beyond the reach of much national regulation, power changes hands. When an international telecommunications system, incorporating technologies from mobile phones to communications satellites, deprives governments of the ability to keep secrets from the world, or from their own people, power changes hands."[2] (For this, and all his other helpful contributions to the *zeitgeist*, Wriston was rewarded with a seat on the Reuters board.)

---

[2] Walter Wriston, *The Twilight of Sovereignty*, Charles Scribner's Sons 2001, p.4

If power, for good or ill, now lay in the hands of traders, they, in turn, found themselves at the mercy of an unseen, immeasurable market force beyond their control or ken. It was no passing phenomenon, but was a thing of permanence, to be respected and understood rather than exploited or feared. That force was represented by a massive new market constituency, to which we shall refer as We The People.

Thus dawned the age of market populism.

★

The distant trumpets of the *vox populi* announced the beginning of the end for markets as exclusive clubs designed for and run by its members, and the beginning of markets as the chosen medium for the expression of the democratic will, as represented by a rapidly expanding, ever more risk-tolerant investing public. Electors of America and Britain—assuming that the care and maintenance of free markets was at least among the reasons that they voted in elections the way they did, no doubt considered themselves fortunate to be represented by Ronald Reagan in the White House and Margaret Thatcher in Downing Street: ardent free-market advocates both.

The transition of the market to the vehicle for expressing popular democracy from the former secretive bastions of privilege was manifested in the first instance by changes that had been taking place in the demographic profile of the market traders.

Even as late as the 1960s, Wall Street, or at any rate its middle-to-upper reaches, was largely thought of as being (and by and large was) populated by White Anglo-Saxon Protestants. (The "White" prefix always struck me as redundant, but usage dictates its insertion in the popular acronym.) The popular image of the WASP was that of a male person (females were aliens on Wall Street) educated in a New England or Midwestern preparatory school, followed by an Ivy League or equivalent university. He voted Republican as if it were holy writ, tended to wear blazers, button-down collars and wing-tip loafers, spoke with a lazy drawl, and joined the kind of clubs from which Jews, and perhaps even Catholics, tended by discreet practice to be excluded. He might have the suffix of a monarchial roman numeric attached to his name. Author Tom Wolfe, in his novel *Bonfire of the Vanities*, derided the species as Masters of the Universe.

But even Wolfe, a "cool" and cynical interpreter of America's class-driven foibles, was somewhat behind the times. Archetypes die hard, especially fictional ones, but by the time *Bonfire* came out, Wolfe's blue-blooded MoUs were being overwhelmed by a stampede of "ethnic" newcomers. They were outsiders in the sense that they did not work in Manhattan, but also insiders inasmuch as they lived within the city's four other boroughs, or across the

Hudson River in the blue-collar sections of New Jersey. Few had experienced the gentle joys of a gothic, ivy-covered educational institution.

The writing had been on the wall for Anglo-Saxons for some time. Their once entrenched positions in the executive suites high above Manhattan's downtown canyons were being steadily overrun, foxhole by foxhole. Many defenders surrendered supposedly impregnable high ground without even firing a shot.

Not that the WASPs always had Wall Street entirely to themselves. An exception to the rule of Anglo-Saxon supremacy had long been provided by German Jews—the Seligmans, Goldmans, Kuhns, Loebs, and Warburgs—who had actively, successfully, and respectably achieved prominence as bankers in New York's financial district from as far back as its earliest days as a seaport. But Jews, it was always tacitly understood, kept to themselves by owning their own firms for which hiring was restricted to their own kind. They had survived, and thrived, by carefully falling in with the customs, including the exclusionary impulses, of their hosts.

As John Brooks put it, in *The Go-Go Years*, his splendid "exploration of Wall Street in the 1960s," "…the Jews of Wall Street had enjoyed recognition as equal to the Yankees in both prestige and power. But those Jews had tended to be sedulous apes, awed and inspired by the new nation in which they or their fathers were immigrants, inclined to put Old Europe behind them except in matters of business, they became more Yankee than the Yankees, more Protestant than the Protestants, and thus did little to change the atmosphere."[3]

Respected the Jews may have been, but they were expected, in keeping with unspoken conventions, to refrain from presenting themselves as candidates for visible roles of leadership in the financial community's ruling hierarchies. This was no less true of the New York Stock Exchange than of any other associative enterprise in the financial community; Jews and Catholics were welcomed to the Exchange as trading members, but somehow not to the extent that they could aspire to fill prominent positions on the Board of Governors.

Within a decade or so of the end of the Second World War, such ethnographic niceties had started to break down, and this time the atmosphere would certainly change. By the start of the seventies, the ethnographic niceties were simply looking absurdly redundant. For by then the whole place, especially the trading rooms, but also before long the boardrooms, suddenly swarmed about with people bearing all manner of distinctly "ethnic" names, with accents that could be traced to the mean streets of Brooklyn, the Bronx, and Staten Island. Given the need to fill the ever-expanding Wall Street vacancy list, it could hardly be otherwise. In an age of unprecedented affluence, stock-market investors, whether as high-net-worth individuals in

---

[3] John Brooks, *The Go-Go Years*, E. P. Dutton Inc., 1973, p.117

their own right or as contributors to the proliferating ranks of pension and other investment funds, were increasing in number at an unprecedented rate. As more and more money poured into Wall Street, accompanied by demands for higher and higher returns, more and more people were required to staff the firms charged with the responsibility of looking after it, and plainly many more people than the flow once generated by the exclusive old WASP pipeline could possibly provide. The influx from the boroughs was ethnically diverse, young, unburdened by seared memories of pre-war history, such as the crash of 1929 and the Great Depression, and eager to make the kind of money that their parents could scarcely have imagined making. By the start of the seventies, more than half of Wall Street's working population had arrived since the start of the previous decade, a ratio that would keep rising steadily.

So it was that Wall Street's blue-bloods simply melted into the crowd. In the end, natural attrition rather than combat had done for them, as elder statesmen retired or drifted away, accepting their fate with an air of relaxed resignation. There would be no valiant rearguard action, because in truth there was no war. The mass of invaders thus arrived to find that their advance guard had entered the city largely unopposed and was not solidly entrenched.

Whatever virtues (or vices) of aggression or innovation or changes in style were required for the rapidly building influx of liquidity, they tended to come from firms with names not associated with the Old Establishment. They were indeed often firms with Jewish names, though there was no suggestion that they were still "Jewish" firms in the original exclusionary sense. These firms, far more than their waspy-sounding counterparts, somehow seemed better equipped to represent the emerging approach to investing—which in overall terms may be described as adventurous, favoring rapid price-appreciation and massive portfolio diversity over steady dividend-based income from the shares of blue-chip companies.

And so it came about that for the next couple of decades the best-remembered headline-grabbing powerhouses of Wall Street turned out to be Salomon Brothers, Goldman Sachs, and Lehman Brothers (all thriving firms as this line is written) rather than Dean Witter, and E.F. Hutton, and Hornblower & Weeks (names that have long since disappeared). Merrill Lynch, a firm with a distinctly Irish brogue at the time, remained huge, but soon began to resemble not so much the Thundering Herd of popular conception as a field of contented cows.

If the once dominant WASP Establishment needed some form of representation in the new scheme of things, perhaps to show that the Old Guard could happily compete with the New, it emerged in the unlikely form of the once staid and unimpeachably respectable Drexel Burnham. That particular flag flew proudly until Drexel out-aggressed and crashed in the junk-bond collapse of the early 1990s (high-yielding bonds being a market masterminded by Drexel's very own Michael Milken, who was ironically neither an Anglo-Saxon nor a respecter of Wall Street traditions).

Across the pond, similar changes were being rung in the City of London—a town having literally no shortage of bells to ring. The refined accents of "jolly decent chaps" from the finest of the nation's private educational establishments steadily receded before a tide of "bleedin' good blokes" from the East End and south ("sarf") London, largely unfinished products of their local state schools. In no market sector was the shift more evident than in foreign exchange, a relatively new form of trading with none of the traditions of the stock and bond markets.

It may strike younger readers as a matter of small consequence, but the rising of the City proletariat was seen, even by liberals with little sympathy for the place, as a triumphant vindication of Britain's yearning for the venerated chimera of a Classless Society. (They were less sure about it later when they saw the scale of the year-end bonuses being handed out to greenhorns too young to have witnessed a prolonged market downturn.)

Practical men of the City, even those of the old school, saw it as nothing of the kind, but merely as a necessary step—as their colleagues in New York had experienced before them—in recruiting enough bodies for the talent pool that would be essential in maintaining London's role as a financial center. And to the surprise of even conservative diehards, it soon became evident that the working-class lads (and later lasses) manning the trading desks were often emphatically hungrier, cleverer, more intuitive, and infinitely more ruthless than their predecessors had ever been.

None of this is to say that old-fashioned ways of doing business disappeared overnight. Certain "City gents" insisted to the end on enjoying the tradition of extended and invariably liquid lunches in paneled dining rooms and low-beamed ale houses. Such charming old ways survived well past their natural time for one simple reason, one that the older generation simply couldn't bring itself to ignore. It was summed up in a single hackneyed phrase: "The system works, old boy, it works."

Little wonder, then, that its champions convinced themselves that their most useful remaining function in life lay in preserving traditional values. In such an environment, many of them could still think about going home at four in the afternoon, or even straight after lunch. After all, the decision whether to go back to the office, while sitting across from a congenial companion of many years standing, with a Havana in one hand and a third glass of port in the other, was calculated to tax any man's will.

There was, of course, the small matter of the New York market opening, which occurred immediately after London's normal lunch hour. But the City's lunchtime revelers believed, despite all evidence to the contrary, that Wall Streeters had only a passing interest in the international markets, being far more intent on devoting their energy and their capital to America's vast domestic markets. Perhaps if they had been less intent on the port bottle, the lunchers might have noticed that the old place was suddenly crawling with American, Japanese, and German bankers, and that most of them had arranged for accommodation, suggesting that they and their companies had come to stay, and that they had a very specific purpose in doing so.

Salomon Brothers, for one, had certainly come to stay.

We visited Salomon's Wall Street trading arena, "The Room," in an earlier chapter. The firm now appeared to be intent on creating something on a similar scale in London. Salomon's timing could scarcely have been less propitious.

While the City of London proudly reckoned that it was "doing its bit" for the national economy, Britain's industry seemed to be "doing its nut." The picture presented to the world in the mid-seventies was that of a country verging on anarchy, a sad image of a once great nation's loss of power, influence, and self-respect. The British Government, locked in a death struggle with the unions, notably the National Union of Miners (which for a while, it is sometimes forgotten, commanded great public sympathy), at some desperate point in the contest ordered millions of workers to go on a three-day working week. Domestic and industrial powercuts became an almost nightly occurrence. Uncollected trash piled up in the streets. The fourth or fifth largest economy in the world was starting to resemble that of a Third World country.

How all this would affect international markets was naturally something that troubled bankers and investment brokers as much as it did ordinary citizens. They were right to be concerned, as events were about to demonstrate—events that would give them no reason to feel superior to their industrial brethren. The City in particular, and global markets in general, were about to experience the worst crisis since the post-Bretton Woods era.

The 1974 stock-market crash in London was partly precipitated by the oil crisis, partly by the national economics downturn, and partly by a growing recognition on the part of the authorities that many British banks were seriously over-extended. The Bank of England had bailed out one peripheral banking firm, the London and County Bank, and quietly, behind the scenes, had organized the rescue of many others. Tremors ran through the City like seismic shock waves. By January 1975 the stock market had virtually collapsed, the *Financial Times Index* having fallen from a peak of 543 in May 1972 to 146 in January 1975. In the interval, the money markets were roiled by the collapse of Herstatt Bank in Frankfurt, the result of excessive foreign-exchange speculation. Herstatt was not a big player in the currency market, but its principal creditors were, most of them as it happened, blue-chip American banks.

The crisis abated and lessons were drawn. The event had provided an opportunity for the global markets to demonstrate their endurance in the face of potential calamity. They would be well prepared for the next test. New laws and restraints were introduced, some voluntary, some imposed. They were universally, that is globally, recognized, for the crisis had made abundantly clear that banks were interdependent on a scale that paid no attention to national boundaries or individual government policies.

So, as the British nation soldiered on dispiritedly, the London stock market regained its poise, reputation, and confidence, and, in isolation from the rest of the country, soon began to bask in its restored prosperity.

And its independence. Britain's industrial crisis and the concomitant banking upheaval represented a valuable lesson. From now on, the City would find its role in the global financial marketplace as an entity quite separate and distinct from the disunited kingdom of which it was a geographical part. If international capital was becoming more and more nomadic in its search for safety and a friendly environment, then the City of London, as opposed to Britain, represented relative certainty in a world of rampant uncertainty. Besides stability, London claimed significant other benefits: a universally used language, a long history of banking excellence, a perfect spot in the international time zone, and a ready-made labor force. Now for all intents and purposes an island within an island, a modern reincarnation of the city-state of Renaissance times, London's financial community marketed itself as such.

In short, to hell with governments and unions!

In spite of all the inconveniences of Britain's industrial breakdown and social upheavals, foreign banks and investment firms like Salomon Brothers continued to pour into the City in a steady stream that would soon become a lively torrent.

Salomon Brothers was already in place. The firm had opened a London office as early as 1968, but had kept a relatively low profile, mostly trading deposits, not among the most exciting markets. By the late 1970s, though, Salomon had staked out an aggressive position in the burgeoning Eurobond market largely by virtue of its willingness to trade huge amounts at tight spreads. In doing so, Salomon shook up London's financial community as no other American house had ever done.

Salomon's devil-take-the-hindmost approach to markets soon set the tone for the rest of the City—not altogether, it must be said, to the City's liking. Salomon's traders and salesmen were expected to work a twelve-hour day, from seven to seven. There would be no more long lunches, least of all of the liquid variety. Actually, no lunches at all, unless consumed at the desk or in one of the firm's executive dining rooms. London-based Americans, like their counterparts back home, just didn't "do" lunches, and rarely drank even in the evening; a visit to a health club was seen as more beneficial to one's physical and mental well-being—meaning more beneficial to profitable trading and salesmanship. Unlike their British rivals, who only occasionally popped across the Channel, and usually to Paris or Amsterdam, Salomon's salesmen readily jumped on airplanes to visit clients in dreary industrial cities with unpronounceable names.

This was all very irritating to traditionalists, but if Salomon people were in the office at seven, hitting the telephones to continental Europe, then there was little choice but for City gentlemen to follow suit. The City's club-like ambience—cozy, familiar, leather-bound, comfortable, unfazed—was about to be consigned to fond memory. Mourn it or welcome it, the City was about to become a very much more serious place—that is, it had to appear to be serious as well as being serious. Salomon's madcap trading room close by the magnificent pile of the Old Lady of Threadneedle Street became known among its rivals as the "London Zoo"—an offshore hangout for Masters of the Universe and Big Swinging Dicks.

The BSDs were the movers and shakers at Salomon Brothers, immortalized in *Liar's Poker*, a warts-and-all exposure of Salomon Brothers by Michael Lewis, who spent most of the eighties at the firm trading bonds, in New York and London. "Working beside traders at Salomon Brothers put me, I believe, at the epicenter of one of those events that help to define an age," he wrote in his preface, adding, "That was somewhere near the center of a modern gold rush. Never before have so many unskilled twenty-four-year-olds made so much money in so little time as we did in this decade in New York and London. There has never before been such a fantastic exception to the rule of the marketplace that one takes out no more than one puts in… What happened was a rare and amazing glitch in the fairly predictable history of getting and spending."[4]

Getting and spending was perhaps the social *zeitgeist* of the last third of the twentieth century.

Reinvention was the watchword, as change followed change upon change, in technology, lifestyle, social attitudes, sexual mores, and just about all other aspects of living for those swept along by the fast-growing economies of the industrial West. "New" has always been a handy word for re-branding products. Politicians had always embraced "New" to show electors that life was going to change permanently for the better. Roosevelt once promised a New Deal to take America, led by its workforce, out of the Great Depression. More

---

[4] Michael Lewis, *Liar's Poker*, W. W. Norton & Co. 1989, preface

recently, Tony Blair had gained several British election victories on the back of a party once known as Labour but now called New Labour. The habit caught on in other fields. Thus citizens were soon addressed in the New Media by New Age commentators, supposedly spouting a New Wisdom. There was also, of course, a New Economy, based on those same media, and new communications and entertainment technologies, as distinct from the Old Economy, one that had relied on the disconcertingly and sometimes destructively variable output of heavy-manufacturing industries. Along with New, Small became popular, Big having been too long identified with relics like Big Business and Big Government. The nickname "Big Blue" was once regarded at International Business Machines Corporation as evidence of its eminence and popularity. That was Old IBM. The New IBM would not wish to be Big Blue for fear of being regarded as unwieldy and unresponsive.

The New Economy, and particularly the role of the global market, might once have aroused the suspicions of the wider public as a threat to democracy, but many institutions of the democratic capitalist system, from Big Business to Big Government, were now suddenly out of favor, derided for having lost the plot. Big Business—including Big Blue—had laid off workers in the thousands, and still could not manage to turn in profits. Big Government just grew ever larger and in the process became addicted to taxing and spending. Neither business nor government had managed to bring about the desired improvement in the services provided. Far from it: those services appeared to be in precipitate decline.

In this climate of public cynicism and disillusionment with the former bastions of authority, it was The Market that emerged to replace them in the public imagination.

This apparent transference of faith from government to market, Thomas Frank observed in One Market Under God, was the central premise of a phenomenon he identified as "market populism." As interpreted by Frank, the New Wisdom was that "in addition to being media of exchange, markets were media of consent. Markets expressed the popular will more articulately and more meaningfully than did mere elections. Markets conferred democratic legitimacy; markets were a friend of the little guy; markets brought down the pompous and the snooty; markets gave us what we wanted; markets looked out for our interests."[5]

Or, as Newsweek columnist Robert Samuelson pungently expressed it: "Markets R Us."[6]

In the democratic revolution unleashed by lack of faith in older institutions, citadels of the Old Establishment fell with astonishing speed, toppled with

[5] Thomas Frank, One Market Under God, Doubleday, 2000, p.23
[6] Newsweek, April 27, 1998

scarcely a murmur of public concern. Among the earliest and most prominent of the overthrown were those finance ministers and central bankers of the advanced industrial nations, who, as late as the seventies, had been regulatory lords of all they surveyed in the world of finance. Now, all those architects of the post-war economic miracle, far from being able finally to bask in the gratitude of the masses, found themselves obliged to retire from the scene, humiliatingly reduced to observing the dismantling of the structure they had carefully erected in the righteous causes of market stability and consistent economic growth. Bretton Woods, it was now clear, had been just the first, heraldic casualty in the lost cause of interventionism. Ten years on, the battlefield was littered with the detritus of retreating regulatory army. By the end of the century, there were few signs that any conflict had ever taken place.

Amid all the carnage, one regulatory institution had somehow remained standing. Long resented by those private institutions responsible for running the financial markets in the United States, the Glass-Steagall Act had long separated the respective functions of commercial banks and investment banks on the grounds that, in terms of fiduciary responsibility, they were ethically incompatible. Stockbrokers were permitted, even encouraged, to put the common man's savings at risk. Bankers were supposed to safeguard them. Glass-Steagall was the last remaining regulatory edifice of the 1930s. Introduced in the aftermath of The Great Crash to protect a gullible investing public from exploitation by overzealous professional speculators, its repeal was perhaps overdue, as leaders of the financial community had argued strenuously for years. But in the end, the demise of Glass-Steagall was credited less to applied logic or changed circumstances than as a concession to Wall Street's sudden relish for building one-stop-shopping financial supermarkets.

Something similar had occurred in Britain, where, in 1985, a package of regulatory reforms, referred to somewhat mysteriously and inappropriately as Big Bang, resulted in a wave of mergers between banks and stockbrokers. America, for once, was following suit.

The sudden affection for *laissez faire* in matters of financial governance spread to the most unlikely political quarters. In many countries, parties of the left—notably the Labour party in Thatcherite Britain—had become tired of being dismissed as perennial election-losers and so blithely abandoned their socialist tenets to embrace those of the once despised proponents of free markets. In the case of New Labour the conversion would swing the party to a position most electors viewed as being, if anything, even more conservative than that of its Conservative opponents, paving the way for Labour's trium-phant return to power with a record parliamentary majority.

There had been a time, both in the United States and Britain, when the unions might have had something to say about such acts of "treachery," which they felt represented a cleverly camouflaged assault on the interests of the working man. But so rapidly had the decline of a largely industrial economy given way to a service-dominated model that organized labor no longer had much of a political voice in either country. It was a transition not so much lamented by the left, or even applauded by the right, as unnoticed by both. Whether union members or not, employees now apparently saw their economic interests as better safeguarded by their former nemesis, business, than by unions or "friendly" government.

Business was now acceptable as the worker's friend because it was no longer Big. New Business was as far removed from the ruthless, union-bashing, rust-belt titans of the Old Economy, such as U.S. Steel Corporation or the automotive giants of Detroit, as could be imagined. The satanic mills were closing down everywhere. In their place—most of the time in some other place—were clinically clean, classless, employee-friendly facilities operated by communications and technology companies, springing from an information revolution little more than a decade old, and untainted by the bloody history of industrial conflict. Their shares were floated with lashings of stock options for employees as well as for employers. Indeed, at many firms, workers and owners were considered one and the same—even at Microsoft, soon to become the corporate flagship of the Information Age, a company whose chief executive, Bill Gates, was compensated in billions of dollars. Where once the chairman of Big Steel would have been rebuked for earning just a few million dollars a year, nobody at Microsoft, or anywhere else, resented Bill's package as insane, even if it was bigger than the gross national product of most countries. The employees had all become rich on their boss's coat tails. Bill Gates was thus lauded as a New Age folk hero, a prophet of the age and a true man of the people, a geeky and lovable celebrity to be admired for his enterprise, not envied for his wealth. Overlooked was the fact that Microsoft was Big—Very Big.

But for all the startling changes in attitudes to establishment structures in the capitalist West, the most dramatic and unexpected fall in the established order occurred in the Soviet-dominated East. That the eastern revolution was as bloodless as its western counterpart was remarkable, given the region's legacy of violent suppression. As late as the 1980s, communism was depicted by President Reagan as an "Evil Empire," an insidious menace to the entire civilized world. Staying with the Star Wars nomenclature, Reagan called on Congress to fund development of a space-borne defensive shield to protect itself against a Soviet missile attack, to be built at a cost as astronomical as its concept.

In the event, America would need not so much as a picket fence. Mikhail Gorbachev's liberalized but exhausted and divided Soviet regime could not have summoned the will or the energy to lob a few grenades, let alone launch a barrage of intercontinental missiles. The long-subjugated people of Eastern Europe sensed that the game was up. Soon, determined processions of German and other would-be émigrés from behind the once unassailable Iron Curtain were defying border guards to shoot them as they attempted to cross over to the West. When it was clear that they could get across without so much as being detained, let alone shot—the guards obviously acting under orders from on high—the procession turned into a flood. The great Marxist edifice, undermined by decades of inept economic mismanagement, its will sapped by corruption and intrigue, imploded like a building demolished by a controlled explosion.

So ended more than half a century of Cold War, and almost apologetically, as if half a century of neurotic and perilous confrontation, with its underlying threat of a nuclear holocaust, had been, all along, no more than a silly misunderstanding between friends across a shared fence.

However great the rejoicing that the cause of freedom had finally prevailed, to the financial community it meant, as much as anything else, that several billion citizens had just been admitted to membership of the world's largest and least exclusive investment club.

As Mr. Samuelson might have put it, "Markets R Them, too."

At this point, London experienced a seismic upheaval that validated the democratization of markets. It became known as Big Bang.

# Big Bang

What exactly was this Big Bang, and what were its implications for London's financial community?

One possible misconception should be eliminated immediately: London's Big Bang described an event entirely different from the one depicted by its metaphorical namesake, New York's Great Crash. The Crash of 1929 depicted a stock market in peril, the Bang of 1986 a stock market about to be reborn. The rebirth was the transformation of the London Stock Exchange from a gentlemen's club with its cozy, parochial, self-serving traditions, into a newly minted, global, electronic marketplace, open to all who might wish to compete in it.

The reforms were initially sponsored by the Government by way of the Office of Fair Trading, a government watchdog agency. In 1979, during the final days of a Labour government, the OFT horrified the City by filing a legal action against the Exchange's time-honored system of fixed brokerage commissions. The betting among gambling men, including many in the City, was that the OFT would probably win its case. If that happened, City men calculated with a shudder, it wouldn't be too long before just about all other aspects of the Stock Exchange's often eccentric way of doing business would come under scrutiny.

To be fair, the need for reform, on commissions and sundry other matters, had already been accepted by more modern-thinking members of the financial community. The modernizers included—surprisingly, one might suppose—the chairman of the London Stock Exchange itself, Sir Nicholas Goodison. Was he poacher-turned-gamekeeper, or the other way around? Lanky and gaunt-faced, Goodison's physical appearance marked him as a tub-thumping evangelist, which is what some felt he seemed on the verge of becoming. He had long been an advocate for change in some of the Exchange's more anachronistic rules, but always in the face of implacable opposition from the more hidebound elements of his membership. Evangelist or not, Goodison was above all a realist. If the Exchange didn't reform itself voluntarily, he recognized, the Government would force it to.

Finally, in exasperation, Goodison was forced to enter into a pact with the Devil. He and the Conservative Minister for Trade and Industry, Cecil Parkinson, a close associate of Prime Minister Margaret Thatcher, came to an understanding. It was notable for its simple audacity. Its essence was that if the

OFT could be persuaded to drop its court case on the commission issue, Goodison would champion a broader package of reforms, one that would go much further than anything the Government had insisted upon to date, and almost certainly beyond anything that Exchange members would have volunteered.

Goodison and Parkinson worked together in secret for many months before coming up with a comprehensive package of reforms. It had four principal components. Fixed stock-brokerage commissions would be abolished; the distinction between stock brokers, who dealt with the public, and stock jobbers (the equivalent of New York Stock Exchange floor specialists), who acted as wholesale price-makers, would end; the Exchange trading floor would be abandoned in favor of computerized, screen-based trading (later to be known as SEAQ, for Stock Exchange Automated Quotations); finally, and perhaps most radically, long-standing restrictions on foreign ownership of Exchange member firms would be lifted completely.

The "deal," presented as virtually a *fait accompli*, came as a severe shock to older City hands. Many felt betrayed. Margaret Thatcher's Conservative victory at the 1979 election had been greeted in the City much as Mafeking must have celebrated as the relief column arrived. Surely a Conservative administration, in keeping with a perceived *laissez faire* tradition in matters concerning the City and its works, would take a more benign view of that community's quaint little collection of restrictive practices than that of a Labour administration. Why didn't Parkinson simply respond to demands to call off the OFT? Something had clearly gone wrong. James Callaghan's Labour government had pretty much left the financial community to its own devices. Now, here was a Conservative government sticking the knife in with evident relish.

The financial men ought to have done their homework. Thatcher's free-market credentials were unimpeachable, but she had never been an admirer of the City. Nor had Parkinson, who would later comment that he viewed the Stock Exchange at the time as a "self-perpetuating oligarchy."[1] The real point, though, was that Thatcher was upholding free-market principles, resolutely against restrictive practices of any kind, whatever their origin. It was holy writ. Breaking the closed shops operated by the unions was a cornerstone of her administration's legislative program. How, then, could she justify letting the Stock Exchange off the hook? Pinstriped gentlemen of the Square Mile would simply have to fall in line with their dungaree-clad counterparts on the factory floors. And, kicking and screaming, so they did.

The launch date for Big Bang was set for October 27, 1986—some seven

---

[1] *The Times*, October 21, 2006

years after some of the reforms had first been proposed. The event more resembled Big Bust than Big Bang. The great day began inauspiciously. About half an hour before the start of trading, the SEAQ computers went down, apparently overwhelmed by the sheer volume of electronic orders and "page" requests from the Exchange's by then rather creaky old Topic information system, which was connected to SEAQ. The computers stayed down for an hour.

Goodison explained the glitch in picturesque terms: "If you want to put a monkey or a dodo in a zoo, everyone will want to look at it on the first day."[2] Meanwhile, many brokers gleefully rushed back to the empty trading floor where, for the rest of the morning, they conducted business as they always had done, face to face, sweating, shouting at each other like playground schoolboys. For refugees from the *ancien regime* it made for a poignant, if fleeting, reunion.

Big Bang has been depicted as the event that "saved" the City of London from terminal decline. That is not strictly true. The reforms of 1986 were applied only to the securities market, which represented a very small portion of London's trading activity. The biggest trading volumes by far, and the fastest growth, belonged to the global Eurodollar market, which London had fostered since the 1960s and dominated almost to the exclusion of other financial centers. Getting rid of a few claret-swilling oligarchs was hardly relevant to the exercise.

While a free and competitive market in securities was undoubtedly essential to London's surge to the top of the league table of finance capitals, the most significant impact of Big Bang had nothing to do with the disposal of the London Stock Exchange's rulebook. It was, rather, the opening of the City gates to foreign, mainly American, banks. The American houses had global ambitions and deep pockets. Even before the new rules took effect, they developed a sudden and, in some cases, almost irrational desire to own a British financial institution. After October 27, scores of celebrated London financial houses—merchant banks and stockbrokers alike, some with histories dating back before Victorian times—disappeared in a buying frenzy that defied belief, especially in the "perfect" operating synergies claimed by the acquirers, and above all in the prices paid.

Thus did the City, now largely in the hands of American institutions, become a more serious, businesslike, sober, impersonal, ruthless, and infinitely less sociable place to work. The shock was relieved for a while by the sound of merriment floating up from the streets. Its source was those partners and shareholders who had sold the venerated institutions of yore laughing all the way to the bank.

---

[2] *The Times*, October 28, 1986

# Useful Hooligans

For market-data companies the eighties were halcyon, carefree days, a time that most of us involved in the business would remember nostalgically, in some cases sheepishly, as one prolonged and exuberant coming-out party.

And much there was to celebrate. By the mid-eighties, both Reuters and Telerate were generating growth and returns on a scale that startled their managers no less than it delighted their shareholders.

Ostensibly the companies were bitter rivals, but the contest was largely a fiction, Reuters and Telerate offering complementary rather than competing products. Reuters maintained its dominance in the international arena, where it might be challenged but could not easily be usurped. Telerate pretty much ruled the roost with similar near-impregnability in the domestic American market. Reuters, because it was well established in scores of countries, grew much faster. Telerate, unburdened by expensive international communications lines, enjoyed higher margins. Both became darlings of their respective investment communities in London and New York. Reuters, attracting rave reviews from analysts for the brilliant foresightedness of its management, saw its shares rise steadily. At Telerate, a secondary stock offering was a sell-out, and the board voted rather mystifyingly for a two-for-one stock split. The mystery lay in the fact that the shares were trading at little more than $40 at the time.

Each company occasionally probed the other's defenses, but these half-hearted forays provoked nothing but a few local skirmishes. Despite attempts to diversify beyond traditional areas of expertise, Reuters remained solidly identified with the international markets, notably foreign exchange, Telerate with United States government bonds. Since traders needed information on both markets, many were perfectly willing to subscribe to both services. Clients welcomed the supposed rivalry on the grounds that it would keep their subscription fees low. Information services would have sold like hot cakes on a cold night regardless of price. Markets everywhere were booming, beneficiaries of an enormous infusion of capital as investors, renouncing such old-fashioned and discredited notions as prudence or safety, restlessly roamed the world into the high-risk so-called emerging nations, as well as the supposedly stable, established ones, in search of the most spectacular returns.

In the summer of 1984, the growing public enthusiasm for global trading proved to be as catching as an outbreak of measles at a school. This rendered even more implausible the lack of enthusiasm at AP-Dow Jones, the company responsible for marketing Telerate outside North America. Such complacency could be explained only by incomprehension. Claude Erbsen of the AP, having spent a lifetime as a correspondent and editor in general news, during which he had little exposure to financial markets, might be excused for not grasping the significance of market behavior and the forces behind it. His partner, Bill Clabby, as a former editor of a financial newswire and a correspondent of the *Wall Street Journal*, ought to have known better.

If all my banging on about poor old Buffalo Bill strikes the reader as unfair, his failure to grasp certain inalienable phenomena, such as the biggest financial market boom in history, was perplexing. Clabby's lifetime achievement award would have been for perfecting the role of devil's advocate. Whenever business opportunities presented themselves, Clabby was to be found lying in wait, like a troll under a bridge, to ambush them. His talent for sabotaging positive ideas was unerring and all the more galling because it was invariably deployed from an executive position invested with considerable influence. Clabby's self-appointed role at Dow Jones was to act as a gatekeeper who had been given no mandate other than to prevent anyone remotely suspicious gaining entry. Since Clabby suspected anyone with an idea that might cost money, few got past him.

To observe that, by largely leaving Europe and Asia to the hapless devices of its international partners, Telerate was in danger of missing out on a huge opportunity to establish a huge global presence, is to understate the glaringly obvious.

The chance to say so arrived soon enough. I was summoned one day to a meeting in Neil Hirsch's office attended by Erbsen, Clabby, and Terranova. The subject was a review of our progress in Europe. Terranova lounged on a sofa, chain-smoking, occasionally offering facetious responses to Clabby's more extreme fatuities. I was invited to express my views. I did so with a volley of musket fire directed at what was for me an easy target—the lack of marketing vigor outside the United States. It was an awkward occasion, made the more so by my ill-disguised impatience.

Hirsch's response was a scowl of disapproval. He remained staunch in defense of "my friend Bill," a reward for past favors, presumably Clabby's early advocacy of the Telerate international franchise, which now seemed to me to be a wasted opportunity. Hirsch proceeded to undermine my position by venting his resolute insularity. "Bill says we're doing okay over there," he insisted feebly. "Why rock a boat that doesn't need rocking?"

Comments like that were open to criticism on two counts. "Okay" implied a limited expectation, one to which minimal resources should be committed. "Over there" struck me as a curiously antique phrase, confirming the suspicion that Hirsch's view of Europe was that of a distant, shadowy land of marginal business potential, inhabited by people who couldn't speak American, didn't spend dollars, or eat hamburgers. Obviously this was a place best left to the local tribes to fight over. (Hirsch would make precisely four business trips to Europe stretched over twelve years.)

"I couldn't disagree more," I ventured. "We should be going all-out to grow the European business. The international markets are exploding. With Big Bang approaching in London, what have we got there on the front line? Three aging printer salesmen, not one of whom could demonstrate Telerate if his life depended on it."

I was on a roll now. "In the four key countries of continental Europe we rely on distributors that plainly don't know what they're doing, and give the impression that they'd much rather be doing something else. Meanwhile, we seem to be fixated on keeping the stationery costs down. What we should be doing is planning a big marketing campaign, putting sales people on the ground. To hell with counting the fucking pencil sharpeners, let's grow the revenues."

Blank looks from Clabby and Erbsen at the mention of Big Bang suggested that they were only vaguely aware of it, if they had heard of it at all.

Clabby snorted derisively, and launched an energetic riposte. Cost cutting, the holiest of all his many sacred management cows, was the theme.

"This project's still losing money and you want to go on a spending spree." He looked across at Hirsch for approval. "Neil, this is typical—" (presumably typical of me) "—and it's dangerous. Godammit. Let's learn to walk before we run."

Walking was evidently something that doubtless appealed to Clabby, if for no other reason than it saved on transportation costs. On an early visit to London, he and Erbsen had provoked much merriment by questioning why sales executives often felt the need to take taxis to appointments. "London is a great walking city," he gushed, as his audience stifled their giggles. "Our clients are concentrated in one square mile. That's walkable."

"What if it's raining?" someone had the temerity to ask. "Take the bus or the Tube," Clabby replied.

Titters all around.

"Goddammit!" cried Clabby. "This is no laughing matter."

If I paint this as typical of AP-Dow Jones marketing meetings, it won't be believed. So I won't say it.

Further bad-tempered debate in Hirsch's office was fruitless. I left the meeting, skipping the in-house lunch, for which Neil, as a humorous concession to frugality, had pretended to order peanut-and-jelly sandwiches. "Sounds good to me," said Erbsen.

Later, Terranova wandered into my office. "For what it's worth I agree with you," he said. "So does John Gunn. Maybe you should talk to him. You'll get nothing out of these fucking idiots."

I was reluctant to go over Neil's head, but an alternative tactic had come to mind. I ran it past Terranova. I would go on a fact-finding mission to Europe, and write a paper on my findings. I reckoned to be gone for a month. Hirsch would almost certainly approve the trip, I figured, if only to see the back of me for a while. "I'll keep an open mind. Maybe I'll even find a favorable situation," I said. "If so, there's nothing more to be said or done. But if Europe is the mess that I think it is, then we'll need to put together a business plan and install a strong local management to execute it."

As an idea it was less than breathtaking. AP-Dow Jones should have done something years earlier.

Terranova bought into the plan immediately and then prodded Hirsch into going along.

The defining business report was written on the flight out to London, rather than on the flight back to New York. Delivering the verdict before the evidence had been heard was hardly testament to an open mind, but as far as I was concerned this was an open-and-shut case. My principal recommendation was the creation of a European management team, based in London, to be led by a managing director of substance. The MD would report formally to Erbsen, but with the implicit understanding that the position would enjoy considerable independence.

In London I dropped in for a chat with Gunn. He was an enthusiast for anything that expanded Telerate's global reach. He also candidly admitted being "more than a little concerned" about Exco's investment in Telerate. He may have been speaking for his board, which was far from unanimous that Telerate represented a wise use of shareholders' money. He was particularly put out by Hirsch's apparent lack of interest in the world outside New York.

As for AP-Dow Jones, Gunn's primary observation was succinct: "Those guys wouldn't know how to get rich if they fell into a diamond mine." Gunn promised intervention if the plan should run into trouble. I doubted that it would be necessary.

Nor was it.

Hirsch, much to my surprise, not only approved my recommendations in full but volunteered to recruit Erbsen and Clabby to the cause. This he duly accomplished, presumably with certain strings attached. That left one remaining chore: to find a managing director.

No London-based candidates sprang immediately to mind. Telerate had nobody suitable to spare in New York. Scott Rumbold would have been a contestant, but he was heavily involved in local projects, and in any case evinced no personal enthusiasm for a move to London.

Talent was obviously a rare commodity at the time. A London-based executive recruitment firm came up with a list of prospects, none remotely qualified. A New York headhunter had no better luck. The problem, they both explained, was that information companies were making so much money that senior managers were reluctant to switch jobs.

Several weeks went by. Time was pressing. My fear was that if I didn't come up with a candidate, the European initiative would sink without trace. But then, after several weeks of fruitless telephone calls and tiresome interviews, I came up with the name of a person uniquely qualified for the job. It was one who was already working for Telerate.

The candidate was me.

I was also less than passionate about a move to London after sixteen years in New York. Still, I ran the idea past Terranova and he liked it. The crucial question was whether Hirsch would. Terranova smiled enigmatically. "Why don't you talk to him? I think you might be surprised."

I did talk to Hirsch, and I was surprised.

His reaction was expressed with droll amusement. "I reached that conclusion weeks ago, old chap. So, have a good flight. And y'all come back and see us some time, ya hear now?" He added: "By the way, I've already squared things with our friends at AP-Dow Jones."

How had they responded?

"Let's just say they weren't ecstatic," Hirsch said. "But let's also say that they'll go along because I asked them to."

Why, I asked Terranova afterwards, hadn't Hirsch made his view known from the start? Why the silly subterfuge?

"That's easy," Terranova said. "Don't you get it? He didn't offer you the job because he wanted you to ask for it."

Telerate's first London office, with apologies to the Bard, had been a place of flat spirits, infirm of purpose, and definitely in need of a little touch of Harry in the night.

For five years it had been located in the warren-like headquarters of the Associated Press at 83 Farringdon Street, 200 yards from Reuters' office on Fleet Street. No Lutyens masterpiece this. A typical 1960s eyesore, the building was a dereliction of concrete and glass that must have been a candidate for the wrecker's ball as soon as it was completed. Par for the course, the place had been trashed by the resident journalists. The lobby was permanently piled high with packing cases. Bicycles were often parked in the halls.

It was not the kind of office to which we enjoyed inviting customers. It was not the kind of office to which one would consider inviting one's mother-in-law. For client meetings and demonstrations, Telerate had access to a large, shabby, windowless room on the ground floor. Actually, there were windows, but these were blocked out by a large cardboard display panel that served as the backing for a street-side exhibition of contemporary AP news photographs. It was suggested that the board be removed to brighten up the room, but the AP's office manager declined indignantly on the grounds that he had a thriving business selling the photographs to passers-by for a few pounds apiece.

The very first Telerate presentation we put on there, sometime in 1979, was interrupted by the Queen Mother.

Our guests were envoys from the House of Morgan, which had assigned to the meeting a team of half a dozen typically buttoned-down transatlantic bankers. They attended only because Bobby Van Roten in New York had put in a good word for us. The presentation was in full swing when it was disrupted by the appearance of a spectral figure. Desmond was the AP's resident handyman, a pale, diminutive, disheveled Irishman in a dirty brown work-coat, an unlit cigarette permanently soldered to his lower lip. Desmond had slipped into the room unannounced and was gliding furtively towards the window.

"Excuse me, sorr," said Desmond, feigning surprise that he'd been noticed, "but oi've got to get a photo out of that display case there."

"Surely it can wait. For God's sake, can't you see we're busy?"

"Sorry, sorr, but I've got a fellow outside who wants to buy a picture of the Queen Mum. There's one in the window there, and it's our last one."

He retrieved the photograph and left. Five minutes later he was back.

"What now, for the love of God?"

"He doesn't seem to want it after all, sorr, so oi'll be after putting Her Majesty back in her rightful place."

The expressions on the Morgan faces were as one, betraying the unspoken words: "Just what kind of show are you running here?"

Claude Erbsen listened patiently to my telephone rant. "We're looking at an order from Morgan worth hundreds of thousands of dollars, and suddenly there's this silly little man bursting in for a bloody £5 photograph."

The response was perfectly serious and impeccably priceless. "Well, you know that the AP is a non-profit organization. We have to find revenue wherever we can."

Morgan was never likely to be our first London customer. That honor instead fell to Banque Belge—kind of. I have mentioned the inefficiencies of the British Post Office. The Banque Belge order was a prime example of how the vagaries of the BPO could wreck a deal.

The bank had ordered two terminals and we duly ordered the lines. "It might take ten months to get 'em in," was the word from someone at the

BPO. There was nothing to be done, he added. When, finally, after a nine-month wait, a Telerate technician finally showed up at the bank to install the terminals, he was turned away. A bemused trader explained that no one had ordered any Telerate machines and moreover no one had any intention of doing so. In fact, he claimed he had never heard of Telerate.

"But we have a signed contract from the bank," our sales representative, Alan Wickett, protested.

"Whose signature is on it?" the trader wanted to know.

Wickett mentioned the name.

"I'm sorry," said the trader, "but I'm afraid he left the bank six months ago."

After some reflection, the trader reluctantly allowed the installation to go ahead. "Well, if the bank has signed a contract then I suppose we ought to honor it. So, tell me, what does this thing actually do?"

Although we could not bribe the BPO in such matters, nothing stood in the way of the BPO bribing us. Some senior manager from the BPO called one day to offer a shortcut to installations through a scheme known as "overlay." In return for paying £50,000 we could reserve twenty "priority" circuits, which would always be available on a rolling basis for installation within thirty days.

"That's out-and-out blackmail," was Erbsen's outraged view. I agreed with him. But with our business in irons, we had little option but to fork out.

Getting clients installed on the Continent was usually less hazardous, but there were blessed moments of comic relief. My favorite involved those renowned Gnomes of Zurich and America's very own gnome, Dr. Robert Nagel.

Nagel's monumental achievement, one that may never again be equaled, was to get himself locked inside a Swiss bank.

Two of Switzerland's then Big Three banks had signed on as Telerate contributors. This was regarded as something of a coup, deserving of special attention. Accordingly, Nagel was dispatched from New York to Zurich to install Telerate's equipment in the fortress-like headquarters of the Swiss Bank Corporation and the Union Bank of Switzerland. The first installation at SBC went off smoothly enough, but at UBS Nagel ran into some kind of problem.

So it came about that, late one Friday afternoon, Nagel found himself rummaging around in a communications closet in some remote part of the bank. Poor old Bob's eyesight, poor at the best of times, deteriorated even further in the Stygian gloom. As a result, he took longer to finish the job than he had intended. He finally emerged a couple of hours later to find the bank deserted, most of the lights switched off. He tried several possible exit doors and found them all locked. His calls for help went unheeded. Everyone, it seemed, had left for the weekend. Bob found a telephone. Frank Hawkins, in charge of AP-Dow Jones marketing in London, was himself about to leave the office when Nagel's call came through.

"Frank, I've got a problem. I'm locked inside UBS. They must have forgotten I'm here. Everyone's gone. I don't know what to do."

To this there was only one response, and Hawkins gleefully seized the moment. "Congratulations Bob, I always knew you were a fucking genius. Master criminals have been trying for a century to figure out a way of breaking into a Swiss bank. You've managed to pull it off by accident. Found any gold bars lying around?"

Several calls to UBS failed to raise the alarm. An hour later, however, Nagel called back, this time from a police station. After bumping into an understandably startled security guard, he was escorted from the premises and placed in custody by an equally incredulous policeman. Now, after enduring an hour of interrogation, his explanations accepted, he was free to go.

"Well done, Bob," said Hawkins. "Now get your ass out to the airport before you get into any more trouble."

"I would, Frank," said Nagel, "except that I seem to have lost my passport. I may have left it in the bank."

Years later, Nagel boasted: "That UBS situation was one of my proudest accomplishments."

"You mean getting locked inside a Swiss bank?"

"No, in completing a very difficult installation," Nagel protested. "Let me tell you what the problem was and how I solved it…"

History fails to record whether UBS subsequently reviewed its security procedures.

Amid all this hilarious fumbling, so typical of the early days of AP-Dow Jones/Telerate, it would have been hard to believe that Reuters had not experienced similar trials and tribulations. Reuters had.

In the early days of Monitor, Reuters had been unable, or unwilling, to hire seasoned sales executives from outside the company. Whether this was a consequence of the company's poor financial condition, or an inbred suspicion of the breed rooted in the company's editorial tradition, it is hard to say. Salesmen were instead recruited internally, sometimes to the bewilderment of the candidates. One of the bewildered was John Roberts, one of my old NATSOPA colleagues from Comtelburo days.

Roberts was "lured" into sales by that tireless and mischievous rascal, Fred Taylor, who had been engaged in the Monitor project to secure new contributors. Not that Roberts needed much luring. "Fred called me one day and said, 'Look, cocker, you're wasting your time. You don't want to be playin' around with price lists for the rest of yer life. Come down 'ere and work with me on this Monitor lark. It's going to be huge, I'm tellin' yer.' "

Roberts was, as Taylor suspected, thoroughly bored with his job. "So I just thought I'd give it a go. There was no title, no defined function, and no pay increase. I asked Fred on my first day, 'What am I supposed to do?' He said, 'Just pick up that phone, cocker, and start calling the banks. Get the buggers round here for a demo if you can.' Frankly, we didn't have a lot to show them at the time, but a few showed up."

A few showed up! It sounds like the after-action report of a Boy Scout hike on a wet Monday.

In marketing terms, Reuters seemed to have regressed since Renfrew had established the Computer Services Division to sell Stockmaster and Videomaster. Back then, he had brought about a radical change in the company's fusty, news-dominated culture by introducing aggressive selling plans, entertaining clients, and holding team-building sessions in the pubs after-hours. Now, with Renfrew in America, and most of his old cronies scattered around the world, the group had to all intents and purposes disintegrated.

Nelson was still in London running the whole shop, but presumably with far loftier preoccupations than mere sales. Villeneuve, the project manager, was around only when he was not traveling. Anyway, his particular flair was better suited to presiding over client lunches than to masterminding sales campaigns. Sales of the product representing the company's most ambitious project ever had thus fallen, literally, into the hands of Fred.

"After all the excitement of actually getting the system to work," Roberts recounted, "it was some time before it occurred to anyone in the executive office that organized selling was the project's critical component, and that we ought to have somewhere decent to bring clients for demonstrations."

The second half of the complaint was entirely justified. A demonstration room of sorts had been set up in the basement at 85 Fleet Street. It was not the kind of facility normally associated with a company intent on conveying a dynamic, high-tech image. Roberts remembered it with a grimace. "The basement, for God's sake! It was barely habitable, an airless, windowless room, poorly lit. The concrete floor was covered with faded olive linoleum, worn through in parts and curling at the edges."

Roberts complained to Villeneuve about its dilapidated state. "The response was: 'It's not perfect, of course, but for the time being it will have to do.' "

Frustrating employees was one thing; terrifying visitors another.

Midway through one of Roberts's early subterranean presentations, the chief dealer of a London merchant bank unexpectedly leapt to his feet, plainly horrified. "I just saw a rat," he exclaimed. Roberts had spotted it, too. "The damn thing crossed the room with studied nonchalance."

Only after much vainly chasing around in search of the creature could the demo continue. The rat had disappeared, but then it was hard to hold the visitor's attention. "He kept glancing fearfully around the room, making sure his feet were propped up on his chair. He kept muttering, 'I'm sorry, but if there's one thing I can't stand, it is rats.' I must say I wasn't too keen on them myself."

Within months, Reuters moved the Monitor sales team, by now expanded to half a dozen, to the International Press Centre, a modern building a short walk from Fleet Street. By then, Reuters felt confident enough to hire several new, experienced sales executives from outside the company. Roberts was involved in the recruiting drive. "They were a motley crew. We interviewed most of them in pubs." It was a questionable practice with predictable consequences, as Roberts admitted. "Candidates tended to get the job if they could keep up with the alcoholic consumption of the interviewers. We always seemed to show up in threes, including me. It was in its own way a pretty formidable test—as much for the interviewers as for the candidates. After a while, the process got to be more formal, but only when we discovered that some of the people we had taken on had a serious drinking problem. How could we have spotted them?"

One sales applicant, John Lowe, was offered a job for the singular accomplishment of being the only one present at a five-hour lunchtime interview at El Vino who could remember the details the following morning. "We were very impressed with that," Roberts said. "All the more so since two from our side couldn't even remember being there." (For the record, the others were Roger Hawkins and David Mulhall.)

A senior Reuters executive, hired in similar circumstances, later loftily condemned such methods as "downright irresponsible." He would know. "We were not a public company in those days, thank God, but things hadn't changed a whole lot even in the eighties, by which time we were. The analysts didn't do much poking around, and it was just as well. If they'd bothered to ask for sales projections, nobody would have known what to tell them. It was seat-of-the-pants stuff from the very start and frankly it continued that way."

In between taking telephone orders, many sales executives spent their working days in a state of stunned disbelief about how effortless the job was, and how easily the commissions rolled in. The evenings tended to be devoted to wreaking havoc in saloons, restaurants, hotels, and clubs and, in one or two instances, police stations. "You're just a bunch of hooligans," David Ure of Reuters once remarked to his London sales manager, John Lowe, after receiving reports of yet another riotously destructive evening in some posh West End restaurant. "But I have to say you're useful hooligans."

"David was completely schizophrenic about salesmen," Lowe remembered of his former boss. "Socially, he thought of them as very inferior examples of humanity, the kind of vulgarians he'd rather have nothing to do with. He wasn't alone; it was a common view in management. Then again, they all loved the money we were bringing to the business, and to the value of their "E" shares."

Most of Ure's Useful Hooligans had joined an industry of which they were profoundly ignorant. As one former Reuters sales executive put it, speaking for many, "I knew nothing about the financial markets, nothing about technology and, if the truth be told, very little about selling. I was directed to a desk and told to answer the telephone. Half the time, thank God, the callers were placing orders."

The hiring criteria were as informal as the hiring process, with the inevitable result that the performance of those hired was decidedly inevitably mixed. Prior experience in selling technology was considered, at best, only marginally desirable, at worst a distinct disadvantage on economic grounds, as the salary demands of candidates would rise in direct proportion to their past success in selling online information. Economic factors aside, there were precious few people at Reuters with enough technical knowledge to ask the appropriate questions. The second best practice, therefore, was to hire people who knew next to nothing.

Jonathan (Jonny) Fitzgerald became part of the resulting infusion of ignorance, joining on a whim in 1979 from a firm that sold industrial catering equipment. He was a tall, handsome, and outgoing fellow, with the stage presence befitting the son of an actor. His father, Walter Fitzgerald, had made regular appearances in post-war British films, being perhaps best known for his role of Squire Trelawney in Walt Disney's version of *Treasure Island*.

A week or two into the job, Jonny Fitzgerald could hardly believe his good fortune. In a state of great excitement, he called a former colleague and drinking partner, Bob Etherington. Bob's first love, as it happened, was acting, at which he had occasionally dabbled in amateur theatrical circles. Professionally, he had been trained as a salesman by Xerox, which at the time was widely considered the nearest thing Britain had to a national sales academy. After Xerox, Etherington "somehow ended up"—as he put it—trading currencies at M.W. Marshall, one of the City's leading money-market brokers.

Fitzgerald reached him at Marshall's. "I've just joined Reuters. They've got this thing called Monitor for currency traders like you. It's easy to sell and I think it's going to take off. They want people from the markets. You're perfect for the job."

Etherington was only vaguely aware of Monitor largely because his colleagues constantly rubbished the service. "They were always telling the bank dealers, 'Your quotes are crap, mate,' and I'm sure they probably were."

Such comments made Etherington skeptical of both Monitor and Reuters, but Fitzgerald persisted. "Ignore the flak from the traders. You'll make a fortune here, believe me. It's not difficult. You don't have to do much. The telephones ring all day and you take orders. Otherwise, you do a few demos and rush around having lunches and drinks."

Etherington caved in. He went on to become one of Reuters' top sales executives. A consummate raconteur, he also used his stage training to become the company's most celebrated and feared mimic. Ure was his favorite target.

"You should be on television," someone told him one day. "You could be a star."

"I'm already a star," was the response, "and I'll probably make a damned sight more money at Reuters than I would on the telly."

Fitzgerald, too, went on to achieve legendary sales success and to peripheral fame as one of Reuters' most enthusiastic party animals. This proud status was acquired in part by a story that he had once hijacked a London bus after missing his last train home. Years later he denied doing any such thing. "Of course I didn't—but I wish I had."

I rather wish he had, too, but I'll follow the advice attributed to the Hollywood director John Ford: "When the legend clashes with the truth, print the legend."

Curiously, Etherington, like many of his contemporaries, expected a short career at Reuters. "What else was I supposed to think, given the company's limited expectations for Monitor? John Roberts had told me that the original London sales target was forty-nine locations. Forty-nine! For God's sake! I remember the number distinctly because I'd given a presentation to a bunch of graduates coming into Reuters and John gave me his notes. And there was the figure. Forty-nine!"

In the event, Etherington lasted twenty years, as did Fitzgerald. By then Reuters probably had 49,000 users.

One newcomer, his name long forgotten, failed to last a week. The problem was his disconcerting habit of nodding off during demonstrations in which he was supposed to be participating. As Roberts remembered, "He used to excuse himself by claiming to be on medication that made him drowsy. After several incidents he was given a final warning and told not to attend demos unless he could offer some assurance that he could stay awake." In his frequent absences, demos had to be assigned to other salesmen. One meeting recalled by Roberts was important enough to be attended by several senior company managers. "Halfway through the demo there was this odd growling noise, loud, and persistent. It seemed to be coming from a broom cupboard. We opened the doors and there was the sleeping salesman, curled up in a ball like a dormouse, snoring loudly. Needless to say, he left the company that afternoon."

Recruits naturally expected to benefit from some form of ritual training in sales and product, but no such program existed then. "It was strictly on-the-job immersion," Roberts remembered. "There was no time for anything organized. Anyway, there was no one around who knew how to do it."

The lack of training became a perverse source of pride. One veteran boasted: "I knew fuck all when I got there, I knew fuck all when I left, but in the five years in between I managed to make a small fortune."

New sales executives would be handed a list of sales prospects. They were expected to cold-call these leads by telephone, using a script of sorts. Alistair Todd, an early Reuters recruit, remembered giving a rookie an extensive list that had taken several weeks to compile. The salesman whistled through it in a couple of days before walking into Todd's office with an announcement: "I've called everyone on the list. None of them want the service. Got something else for me to do?"

Todd was aghast. "That man simply eats leads!"

"Eating leads" became an enduring office catchphrase, directed to anyone who could not be bothered to follow up initial calls.

Eating leads was perfectly acceptable, of course, if they were successfully converted to contracts. This happened occasionally. Mike Driver, hired specifically to sell Monitor to industrial corporations (something that Reuters had once promised the banks it would never do, on pain of a bank boycott) decided to send out a mail-shot to a list of prospects he considered marginal at best. To Driver's astonishment, BICC, a big international telephone company, ordered a terminal by return post, sight unseen, without even questioning the cost. BICC may have been a rare event, but it was an augury. By the eighties, unsolicited orders—"bluebirds" as they are often called in the trade—had become commonplace.

There came a time when Reuters felt able to encourage its sales executives to take prospective customers to lunch, a privilege previously confined to André Villeneuve and senior managers. Such invitations were approved by sales managers, usually with the accompanying health warning, "Just remember, Villeneuve himself might decide to tag along."

On one occasion Villeneuve decided to attend such a lunch. The venue was a French steak-house called Baron de Boeuf on Gutter Lane, behind St. Paul's Cathedral. The restaurant had long been a favorite lunchtime haunt for Reuters salesmen. Renfrew had been a frequent visitor, usually with a band of cronies in tow. The rookie salesman on this occasion—we'll call him John Smith—was unnerved to find himself in a taxi chatting with his boss's boss.

"Been to this place before?" asked Villeneuve.

"Just the once," Smith lied. A silly mistake.

"Decent wine list?" enquired Villeneuve, a renowned oenophile.

"Don't really know," said the salesman, "More a beer drinker myself."

No sooner had they been seated than the waiter approached Smith and asked, "Your usual Montrachet, sir?"

Villeneuve said nothing, presumably in keeping with an unspoken maxim steadily acquiring currency at Reuters and implicitly adopted by every sales executive: "Spend what you like, but bring in the business."

Etherington had the odd experience of being scolded for turning in low expense claims, surely a unique event in the annals of Fleet Street. "It was a complaint to which I responded with excessive enthusiasm," he recalled with a chuckle. "Reuters alone probably kept a number of eating and drinking establishments in business. I certainly did more than my bit for the economic welfare of the City catering trade."

Work hard, play hard!

The cliché, much bandied about at Reuters at the time, pretty much summed up Telerate's approach to business as well. And if there were times when the second part tended to overwhelm the first, no one was prepared to quibble with the results.

I arrived in London to take over Telerate's European operations late in November 1983. It was the start of a three-year period of extraordinary growth, for which the Big Bang provided only part of the explanation. The remainder derived from the fact that, everywhere across Europe, there was an eruption of spending by financial trading firms on information and communications products. London, New York, and Tokyo might have all the market advantages of size and liquidity, but smaller continental financial centers such as Milan, Madrid, Stockholm, Oslo, and Amsterdam had no intention of missing the party. One of my first acts, accordingly, was to open offices in these cities.

The first question asked of me at the first full-scale London sales meeting was how I defined the company's marketing strategy.

"Sell fucking terminals," was my flip initial response. The motto stuck. The next day I found "SFT" painted in large letters on a poster on the wall of the sales department.

The sales manager hired for the SFT campaign in London was Christopher Hume, an Australian-born money broker by trade and a director of Exco. Hume was not so much hired by Telerate as donated by Exco. John Gunn's motives were almost certainly more political than practical. Gunn admired Hume's breezy personality and his prodigious energy, but his loyalty, as a member of an Exco board almost pathologically consumed by intrigue, was suspect. Besides, as Gunn told me much later, Hume was between assignments at the time and no one had come up with anything more useful for him to do. I suspect that a subsidiary, and perfectly understandable, reason was that Gunn wanted someone to keep an eye on the European portion of Exco's investment.

"I don't need Hume to tell me how to run the business," I protested.

Gunn said, "He's not there to do that. Just put him to work in sales. You won't be disappointed."

Nor was I.

Hume more than lived up to his billing as a live wire. He was short, dapper, and somewhat birdlike in appearance. An acquired English home-counties accent had buried all traces of the Australian original, and he happily adopted the life of a country squire at a small farm in Sussex, where he raised wallabies. He also owned a sheep farm in Wagga Wagga, New South Wales.

Hume was intensely ambitious, anxious to show Gunn what he could do. When I was elected to the Telerate board, largely at Gunn's insistence, Hume was furious, claiming that Gunn had promised him the seat. After that, he vowed to "take no prisoners" in selling Telerate terminals, demonstrating the point by hanging a noose and an axe on his office door *pour encourager les autres.*

"We're a democratic company," Hume assured recruits. "Miss your numbers and you're dead, but at least you get to choose between hanging and beheading."

"Why not just fire us?" someone was brave enough to ask. Hume fired back, "Because, my friend, that would deprive us of the pleasure of topping you."

The motivation proved to be highly effective.

A year later, I was again asked about marketing strategy. My earlier response was modified. The new motto became SMFT: "Sell More Fucking Terminals."

Hardly an approach of which McKinsey & Company and the Harvard Business School would have approved, but it possessed the great advantage of simplicity.

By then, sales were advancing in leaps and bounds, not just in Big Bang-inspired London, but in most of the European capitals. Except, that is, in France, Germany, and Switzerland, the countries in which Telerate was represented by agencies appointed by AP-Dow Jones. I resolved to fire them all at the earliest opportunity.

In the face of soaring revenues and profits, Erbsen and Clabby could afford to feel more relaxed. To be fair they had proved to be less destructively intrusive than I had expected them to be. But old habits die hard, and investigations were launched at the merest hint that we might be thinking of spending more money than budgeted. Moreover, as far as they were concerned

I was still on probation. This peculiar status did not bother me in the least, especially in light of Europe's stellar performance, but it was one that I violated in two incidents early in my tenure, either of which might have scuppered my career, if not the entire operation. Just for the record, I was guilty as charged.

The most serious contretemps was one that involved the ever-smoldering issue of resources. Why it should have been a constant source of friction was beyond me, given the fast-rising sales numbers. But Claude Erbsen, powerfully abetted by Clabby, objected to every single head we proposed adding to the payroll. If the heads are successful sales heads, I would explain in exasperation, they don't cost a penny. And in this market, I added, even the family retriever could sell terminals.

Eventually, I managed to sweet-talk Erbsen into approving a modest hiring program. Hume, typically, had insisted on twenty heads, putting the case to me with some vehemence, with a broad hint that he had the backing of John Gunn—a ploy to which he often resorted to get his own way. Eventually, I compromised, reluctantly, at twelve. I decided to keep this decision from our New York partners for the time being for understandable if not commendable reasons. I did, however, call Hirsch to enlist his support, confident in the belief that it would be forthcoming. Erbsen and Clabby, I calculated, would listen to him.

Much to my consternation, Hirsch was not supportive. He was livid. "We don't fuckin' cheat on our friends," he thundered, and ordered me on a plane to New York to explain myself. I realized immediately that he had every right to be peeved; I had let Hume, as persistent as he was persuasive, push me into a corner. Still, the decision was mine alone, and at the next AP-Dow Jones board meeting a few days later, I expressed contrition in suitably abject terms. I then put forward a formal proposal of the kind that should have been submitted in the first place. After much animated discussion, the twelve heads were agreed.

Terranova, I must say, was stalwart in support in the face of Hirsch's wrath, which I understood had been activated to the extent of having me fired.

"Don't worry," Terranova reassured me. "With your numbers, no fucker around here is gonna do any firing, believe me."

The supposedly thin ice on which I'd skated during the hiring issue had been even thinner a few weeks earlier as the result of an incident of a quite different kind. It was destined to be enshrined in legend as The Sack of Rome.

I had organized a European sales conference in the Eternal City as a goodwill gesture to our Italian distributor, Agenzia Giornalistica Italia. AGI returned the compliment by offering to host a dinner at a well-known Trastevere restaurant. This turned out to be a curious, not to say bizarre establishment, decorated in the manner of a gypsy encampment, with waiters flouncing around in bandanas to the accompaniment of a trio of wandering minstrels and a troupe of highly energetic dancers. It was an ambience that tended to stimulate exuberance—not that any Telerate gathering ever needed much encouragement to attain such a condition. Sure enough, bread rolls were soon flying in all directions, and, inspired by the insanely twirling gypsies, our delegates were soon dancing on the tables. All this to the skirl of bagpipes, thoughtfully provided and played with awful incompetence by Hume.

Before long, there was an argument, which the protagonists decided to settle physically. The fight was quickly broken up, but in the pacification process several bottles and glasses crashed to the floor. The sound of shattered glass always contributes disproportionately to drama.

None of this would have been remarkable, except that the president of AGI, one Signore Nobili, had decided to grace us with his presence, accompanied by his wife, a Fellini-proportioned matron who, we were informed, spoke not a word of English. Nobili, it seemed, intended to make a speech of welcome, which he vainly tried to rehearse during dinner. Finally, as the tables were cleared, this time by the waiters amid a rising crescendo of sound, Nobili rose to his feet. But not, it instantly became clear, to make a speech. He and Mrs Nobili were leaving.

Their cue to leave came when Mrs. Nobili, suddenly possessed of at least a rudimentary knowledge of English, took fright as one of our salesmen, little Stanley West, normally the mildest and most inoffensive of men, inexplicably announced that he intended, for the purpose of demonstrating his prowess as a ballet dancer, to remove his trousers.

The timing of the insult could hardly have been worse: the Nobilis were traveling to New York the very next morning, and would be paying a courtesy call on Claude Erbsen. Later that night, I called Erbsen at home to warn him that the evening had been "enlivened" by a few high jinks.

"Thanks for the warning," Claude said. "How bad was it?"

"On the Telerate scale, I'd say no more than five out of ten."

"And on the normal scale?"

"Mmmm."

Erbsen called back the next day. Signore Nobili had indeed stopped by and had given a harrowing account of the previous evening.

"I would say 'enlivened' inadequately conveys the evening just described to me," Erbsen reported.

A memorandum followed: "These sophomoric outrages must cease. You, as senior man present, should have stopped this one before it started. I must have your assurance that nothing like this will ever happen again."

There was simply no answer to that. I was guilty as charged. The punishment was to write abject letters of apology to the Nobilis and to Erbsen,

Clabby, Hirsch, and Gunn. Only the Vatican failed to make the list.

Gunn responded to my letter with mystified amusement. "If you can't have an orgy in Rome, for goodness sake, where can you have one?"

How about Amsterdam, Zurich, Hamburg, and Stockholm…?

Telerate, I should mention, had meanwhile moved from the grubby AP office on Farringdon Street to a slightly less grubby AP office on Norwich Street. This, too, proved inadequate to our needs and we soon moved yet again, this time to a modern glass-fronted building on Fetter Lane. Away from the fetid air of the AP tenements, we all felt more comfortable, more like a real company than an unwanted tenant.

I felt more and more inclined to exercise independence from New York. Erbsen, for his part, obviously felt less and less inclined to curtail it, comfortable to play the role of figurehead. First, though, there would be one final row, one so ineffably petty that it hardly deserves to be called a watershed, but that is what it became.

The incident was the Great Coffee-Machine Scandal of 1984.

The item in question was a rented, push-button device that dispensed coffee according to the type selected, of the kind commonly used in offices. At my direction it was installed in the sales department's kitchen. Its practical purpose was to discourage staff members from constantly popping out to the coffee shop around the corner. Somehow, word of this outrage reached Erbsen, who reacted much as Kennedy had reacted to news that Soviet missiles had been installed in Cuba.

I was at home when he called.

"Who gave you permission for this?" he fumed.

"I made the decision," I responded calmly, somewhat lost for words suited to the occasion. "And not for one second did it occur to me that it required approval from New York."

Erbsen clearly thought otherwise.

"Before we spend money on stuff like that, I want to be in the loop. Do I make myself clear?"

I suddenly found the words. They were appended to an ultimatum.

"Claude, with the greatest respect, if you think that what you need in Europe is a managing director who has to go to New York for approval to install a coffee dispenser, you'd better get yourself a new man. As a director of Telerate, a public company, and AP-Dow Jones/Telerate, I will continue to refer major strategic and policy decision to the boards. In all other respects, and always within the confines of the budget—which before I arrived no one had ever bothered to prepare—I intend to run the business here as I see fit. Take it or leave it. If that doesn't suit you, then call Hirsch and have me impeached. In which event, I expect to hear from you by close of business tonight."

As I slammed down the phone, my wife Martha appeared with a calming Irish whiskey.

"We going back to New York?"

"Not a chance," I told her.

Years later, Erbsen and I could laugh about the incident. I laughed more than he did, especially when he explained what the problem had been. At the AP's London office, the custom was for each department to make its own tea and coffee, for which there was a whip-round every Friday to buy the ingredients. One of the AP unions had complained that, by having access to free coffee, Telerate employees were receiving a hidden employment benefit.

Yeek!

It was about this time that someone at Telerate discovered Vagabonds.

Vagabonds was a private drinking club, which meant that it was not required to observe London's then restrictive opening hours. It was owned and run by a garrulous Irishman (County Fermanagh), John Mullally, who had been a decorated detective with Scotland Yard's Fraud Squad before retiring from the force with a degenerative heart problem. (It can only be assumed that his decision to open a bar was taken contrary to medical advice, running a late-night drinking club being less than ideal therapy for someone with Mullally's condition.)

Vagabonds was conveniently located just a few hundred yards from Telerate's new office on Fetter Lane and, in observance of a long-standing Fleet Street tradition, soon became the company's official "watering hole." As an office annex, it served both Telerate and the *Daily Mirror*, which had offices just around the corner. The *Mirror* crowd welcomed it as an alternative haven to their traditional watering hole, officially called the White Swan, but more generally—and more appropriately—known as the Stab in the Back.

Vagabonds was a narrow, dingy place with a bar that ran almost the entire length of the ground floor. From a post at the far end of it, Mullally held permanent court, drinking steadily and shouting orders to the two or three pretty barmaids on duty. The orders were often about identifying those customers who could be served as opposed to those whom Mullally could remember having banned for causing some fracas the evening before. Bans were a common occurrence, issued randomly. I received one myself after objecting vigorously to Mullally referring to a black AP-Dow Jones technician as "his type"—as in "We don't want his type in here." The ban was lifted after three months when the customer, in a curious reversal of roles, extracted an apology from the landlord.

Vagabonds was that kind of joint.

Mullally permitted, perhaps encouraged, his patrons to run bar tabs. These were settled by the end of the week, or whenever Mullally decided to issue a receipt, a pink chit with a solitary number on it. How the figure was calculated no one knew or cared. Customers paid up without complaint, even when the amount seemed inordinately high. Most of them were destined for expense claims. After a while, I was obliged to instruct Telerate managers not to honor non-itemized expenses in pink, ostensibly on the (valid) grounds that they would not be recognized by the tax authorities, but more pertinently because the figures were insanely high, even by Telerate standards.

Mullally once told me, "I've got the best business in London here. Most people spend eight hours in the office with a one-hour break for lunch. Most of *my* customers spend eight hours here and one at the office. And none of them spend their own money."

Vagabonds hosted exploits that may be counted as extraordinary even by Fleet Street's demanding standards. Most will not be recounted here in deference to reputations and marriages long since repaired. Fistfights were not uncommon, though they were usually harmless affairs, the contestants being usually too inebriated to inflict damage either on each other or on the premises. One contest, vividly remembered, involved two patrons who insisted on remaining on their barstools, the loser being designated as the one who fell off first. It went on for ten minutes, with hardly a blow landed, before they were both pushed off their stools.

Newcomers by tradition donated their neck ties. Several dozen severed ties were pinned in rows to the bar canopy, along with a few shirt sleeves and one or two brassieres.

Claude Erbsen would have been proud of us.

On Friday nights Vagabonds degenerated into a heaving, shouting, shoving, swearing, wall-to-wall melee, with the *Daily Mirror* people jammed into the rear of the bar and the Telerate crowd packed in the front. Friday nights at Vagabonds ruined many a weekend and probably threatened a marriage or two. A few tales can be told, with the courageous permission of certain individuals who always seemed to be in the thick of things.

One of these was Andrew Brodie, a Telerate sales manager, a diminutive Old Harrovian, and a man for whom the phrase hen-pecked might have been coined. Wee Andrew was once physically removed from Vagabonds by his wife, who showed up after several telephone assurances from Andrew that he was "on his way home." She marched in, and to a rousing chorus of boos and jeers, dragged him outside by his ear.

My secretary, Sheila Nicholls, a formidable female herself, occasionally tried the same methodology to extract me from extended lunches. I quickly discovered a disarming counter-measure. "Fancy a gin and tonic, Sheila?" "Well," she would invariably respond, "since I'm here, I don't mind if I do."

Some time earlier, just five days into the job, Brodie had made the finest possible start to his Telerate career by vomiting on Christopher Hume's shoes. The occasion was his first Friday outing to Vagabonds. He had left the place distinctly the worse for wear, and was subsequently found lying supine in the doorway of a nearby bank, mumbling incoherently and dribbling vomit. His driving license revealed that he lived in Islington, a couple of miles away. Hume and I took pity on him and escorted him home in a taxi. It was raining hard. We were greeted on his doorstep by his formidable wife. Taking one disdainful look at his condition, she refused delivery. "Just take him back to wherever you found him." With that, the door was slammed in our faces. Standing there in the rain, still supporting the wretched Brodie, we devised a plan. We would ring the bell again, and as soon as the door opened, heave our semi-comatose comrade through the opening. This ploy we executed perfectly, and swiftly departed.

On the Monday morning, I found Brodie waiting for me outside my office, wearing a morose expression on his face and a large sticking plaster on his head. He was clutching a letter of resignation.

"What's all this about?" I asked.

"Well, my behavior on Friday night was disgraceful. So I wanted first to apologize, and second to resign, to save you the embarrassment of dismissing me."

"Don't be daft, man," I told him. "Disgraceful behavior at Vagabonds is *de rigueur*. This was your first appearance there. I dare say it won't be the last. So get back to work."

As he turned to leave, I said, "By the way, I can't help noticing that you've been wounded. Is that a result of our pitching you through your own front door? If so, then perhaps I'm the one who owes you an apology."

"No, it wasn't you," he said. "After you left, my wife and I had a bit of a row. She threw a lamp at me. I forgot to duck."

Brodie stayed with Telerate for fifteen years. More surprisingly, perhaps, Mrs. Brodie stayed with him.

Brodie was a veritable saint compared with Peter Lomax, another Telerate sales manager of nefarious renown. A tall, handsome, public-school chap of the "bounder" type, Lomax had an uncanny knack for getting into scrapes in the most benign circumstances. He is best remembered for his favorite party piece, an astonishing feat of athleticism that involved performing one-handed headstands on restaurant tables, while reciting Shakespeare. (Curiously, but obviously not coincidentally, his sister Louise was equally adept at the same trick, though without the Shakespeare.)

Of his more devilish exploits, discretion demands silence. One "event" in particular might have had serious personal consequences. It occurred on a flight to New York, in the course of which he "accidentally" elbowed a fellow passenger in the face. Much blood flowed and Lomax, along with two traveling colleagues, Stephen Butcher and Rodney Jones, were detained by Federal agents on arrival at John F. Kennedy, the pilot having radioed ahead for assistance. Given the sensitivity of the authorities in such matters—then thankfully less extreme than now—the boys were fortunate to be released without charge after a two-hour interrogation and a warning. The "victim" later attempted to sue the company. We sent his lawyer packing with $10,000 in pre-emptive compensation.

"Don't ever get the company involved in anything like that ever again," I told him. Lomax promised to be good. Two evenings later he was questioned by police after an incident in a bar in Harlem.

Butcher and Jones were perfect companions in notoriety.

A crowd of us once watched in amused horror as Butcher, a six-foot-six beanpole, returned home from a bar clinging to the back of a New York City garbage truck. His particular party trick was to place a condom over his head and then blow it up to heights of up to two feet. This bizarre achievement he often performed for charity.

The third musketeer was the diminutive, combative, and perpetually chirpy cockney, Jones. Always looking for a life-changing deal, Jones found Telerate too small an arena for his money-making aspirations, his commissions insufficient to finance a lifestyle that included a mansion in the Surrey countryside and, Jones himself admitted, a high-spending spouse of questionable sanity. It was often said of him, "That boy will either end up a multi-millionaire or in jail." Sadly, years later, it was the latter. Jones, pushing the boat out one-time-too-many in his quest for financial glory, served six months at Her Majesty's pleasure—as the British like to say—for fraud.

Another prominent figure among Telerate's resident oddballs was Peter Taylor, a marketing executive. He was a Yorkshireman, which many regarded as sufficient explanation for his decidedly eccentric behavior. He once resorted, or so I am told, to hiding under a desk to escape my wrath. Taylor, like Brodie, suffered marital troubles. His, too, were sometimes played out on a public stage, much to the amusement of an enthusiastic and ever-expanding audience. At one time he was widely known to be involved in a liaison with a female colleague.

The affair became universally known when Taylor, for reasons as unclear as they were bizarre, decided to declare his undying love for the woman in question by means of a public announcement to a packed Friday-night crowd in Vagabonds. He was not just howling at the moon, for even as he spoke his arms were around the waist of the woman herself and hers around his—plainly a couple in love. They would be leaving their respective spouses that very evening, they proclaimed, to live together in everlasting bliss. (Her identity may have been an ill-kept secret at the time, but will now become a well-guarded one, since the advertised event was postponed, never to take place.)

Not surprisingly, word of the affair reached Taylor's wife Rebecca, herself of Yorkshire stock, and a redoubtable woman of robust physique and stern mien. Her retribution was terrible and swift. She marched into her husband's office one day, intent on confrontation. By chance, she was barely ten paces behind her rival. The resulting violent showdown caused sufficient damage to the premises to lead to her ejection by security guards. Still not satisfied that honor had been done, she marched back to the building the following morning to dump her husband's entire wardrobe, packed in black bin-liners, in the lobby.

"Bloody unreasonable woman," complained her husband. "She could at least have packed 'em in suitcases." Makes it difficult not to side with the wife, doesn't it?

In reacting so vigorously to her husband's infidelity, the woman scorned attracted much sympathy. She elicited even more sympathy in a later incident, this one the cause of physical rather than mental damage. During one of the tiresomely regular reconciliations with her husband, Rebecca attended a company outing, for which Telerate had hired an open-topped, double-decker bus. Rebecca was seated towards the front of the bus on the top deck. Behind her, the party became steadily more boisterous, inspiring Rebecca to stand up, facing the rear of the bus, for the purpose of expressing her displeasure. At that precise moment the bas passed under a tree, an overhanging branch of which came into violent contact with Rebecca's head. The bus, complete with its entire riotous complement of passengers, was promptly diverted to the nearest hospital.

Both stories have happy endings. Rebecca, suffering nothing worse than a bad cut and a mild concussion, survived. So, much to everyone's surprise, did the Taylors' marriage (still intact at time of writing).

Perhaps my favorite bad-boy story involves yet another Telerate executive of pugilistic tendencies, Dan Casey. Casey was Martin Church's deputy managing director in Europe. Though highly intelligent and competent, he was moody by nature and notoriously ill-tempered, especially when under the influence of the devil rum. Casey decided one day to soften the company's hard-driving image, and perhaps his own, by inaugurating an employee of the month award. The glittering prize was lunch in the company dining room with Casey himself. The lucky winner, a senior field technician, duly arrived to be fêted. Dan apologized that he was on the wagon, but invited his guest to feel free to drink whatever and as much as he pleased. After a bottle of wine all to himself, the fellow became bold in his criticism of management, and into a second bottle, bolder still. Provoked and incensed, Casey decided to break his pledge. Another bottle of wine was ordered. And then another.

The punchline (there's a clue) is easily predicted. Before long, blows were exchanged. The din of crashing furniture brought the intervention of colleagues and security guards. The boys were sent home to cool off.

By the following Monday, the news having spread all over the company and beyond, some wag published a pamphlet, celebrating the event. The cover took the form of a cartoon depicting Casey slugging his cowering employee-of-the-month, accompanied by the caption: "And a smashing time was had by all."

Casey was not amused then, nor will he be when he reads this. To which there may be only one response: "C'mon, Danny Boy, put 'em up; let's see what you've got."

Restaurants were inevitably among the victims of Telerate's bacchanalia. They fell like Roman outposts overrun by pillaging Visigoths. Even Rome itself wasn't safe, as we have seen. One café—again in Trasteverde, and no farther than the toss of a spaghetti bowl from the site of the infamous Sack of Rome—was flooded after several Telerate salesmen engaged in a brawl in the men's lavatory. This was apparently the result of an attempt, on the occasion of his birthday, to remove Alan Wickett's trousers. What was removed instead was an entire sink unit. Water from the broken pipe cascaded through the packed restaurant, inducing panic among staff and patrons. Had there been a sudden torrential downpour? Had the normally placid Tiber overflowed its banks? Only after many apologies and the compensatory payment of countless billions of lire, was the Telerate party allowed to leave. My abiding recollection is of Martin Church doling out the billions until his fingers ached.

The denouement is priceless. Just a year later, Church and I happened to be wandering through Trasteverde late one evening, when we found ourselves passing the same restaurant (the name of which, for some reason, I've remembered to this day: Arco di San Calisto). The owner, leaning against the door, spotted us. Just as we were preparing to bolt, a friendly voice beseeched us to stop.

"Aha," he cried, "the lovely people from Telerate [pronounced "Teleratti"]. You have returned. Come on in, my friends, and share a bottle of brandy with me. I want to show you my brand new *toilettas*. Thanks to you they are like, 'ow you say, Buckin'am Palazza."

We all laughed heartily, none more so than the proprietor. "You come back to see us anytime," he roared. "Break whatever you like."

"How much did you give the man last year?" I asked Church.

"Obviously far, far too much," he replied sheepishly.

Countless stories come to mind, but it is images rather than events that remain in the memory. Mine, picked at random, include:

—a gaggle of Telerate sales executives emerging from a bus with plastic seat head-rests on their heads, marching up the Reeperbahn in Hamburg like a crocodile of chattering nuns on their way to St. Peter's. They had just been to a "live sex" club;

—a Telerate gang gaily tumbling out of an elevator into a Zurich hotel lobby, shouldering pillow-cases filled with the contents of their mini-bars after being told that the hotel bar had closed;

—Reuters' German salesmen, talked into a "war game" by their British counterparts at a sales conference in Switzerland, being locked in a barn as prisoners after losing the battle, and missing half that evening's dinner until someone realized they were absent;

—a senior Telerate executive, having forgotten what hotel he was staying in, being driven by an infuriated taxi driver to every hotel in Park Lane, London, before finally arriving at the right one;

—buttoned-down Japanese executives from Kyodo, Telerate's distributor in Japan, gyrating with the girls on a pole-dancing counter at a night club in Manila, and naturally denying the following morning that they were ever there;

—Telerate's German manager, naked, hiding behind a palm tree in a hotel lobby, vainly trying to attract the night clerk's attention, having locked himself out of his room by mistaking his room door for the bathroom door.

The city has a million stories, an American television series used to tell us. You have just read a select few of them.

"A thousand stories, yeah, but you've left out all the ones with the sex," I hear someone complain. I shall respond briefly.

Sexual relations of the kind sometimes referred to as illicit certainly abounded in the market-data industry. They abound in every other industry, I am reliably informed. I myself married a former office colleague, as did several other executives featured in these pages, including Renfrew, Villeneuve, Rumbold, and Snape. These little beans will be the only ones spilled.

My reticence on the subject is based on two considerations: the gentleman's code of conduct and self-preservation. Apart from observing the rule that authors in glass houses should not cast the first stone—or something like that—I fear that many of my friends would hardly remain so if it were revealed that they succumbed, one night long ago, to the temptations of the flesh at a sales meeting in Amsterdam. And, frankly, who cares?

It is, however, reasonable to consider, these many years on, whether the shenanigans—sexual and otherwise—perpetrated by senior industry figures, overwhelmingly male, offended more vulnerable employees lower down the order, especially women. Were they shocked, afraid, offended? Not in the slightest apparently, on all three counts. On the contrary, those who sensibly elected not to join the hedonistic thrill-seekers seemed to have been perfectly content to enjoy the entertainment as spectators.

As one former Telerate female employee, preferring anonymity, pointed out, "Most of us, whether single or married like me, just went home at night to Queens or Brooklyn, made dinner, and watched a little television. We knew we were missing out on the fun, but we made our own choices. Were we ever shocked by some of the stories that did the rounds on Monday mornings? Not that I can recall. Some of them were hilarious, and great material for water-cooler gossip. Yes, Telerate was a crazy company in many ways, but even if you weren't the life and soul of the party, it was still a great place to work."

Has passing time changed the moral perspective of those who were the life and soul of the party? I asked the question of several former Telerate women, now approaching their fifties. In response, I was regaled with anecdotes, many of them unprintable.

Eveyln Aguilera (Cordisco) joined as a receptionist straight from college. "I expected, as the company's most junior employee, to be largely ignored, other than being smiled at by people passing the front desk. Boy, did I get that wrong. Within days, I was spending evenings out on the town with the company's most senior executives, sometimes at restaurants and clubs I'd read about in the papers. At first it was a little scary. I was twenty-three and pretty naïve. But I soon got into the swing of things. Nobody ever tried to force me to do anything I didn't want to do, like drugs, or even bother to ask me."

Fran Schreiber worked in the newsroom, her first real job. Her father had once worked for Bernie Cantor. "I'd no sooner got there than I found myself swept up in the regular Friday evening outings. 'Expeditions' they were called. I was up for it, that's for sure, at least after the first time. That was when some executive came up to me and said, 'Are you buying tonight?' I was petrified. I thought he meant I would have to pick up the bar tab, as some form of initiation. I hid in the ladies room."

Mary Ivaliotis, a sales assistant at the time, remembers small things. "Like the little notes, folded in two, being handed to her boss, Charles (Chuck) Palmer. For a while I thought they must contain some deep company secret. One day, though, while Chuck was out, I found one lying on his desk. Curiosity got the better of me and I opened it. The 'note' was a drawing of a wine glass, with an arrow pointing downward and a question mark. The mystery deepened. Was this some kind of code? It was nothing of the kind, as Chuck explained, just a summons to the Market Bar, a regular Telerate hangout on the ground floor of the World Trade Center. Some secret!" Ivaliotis herself was soon a member of the Friday Club.

Ann Rostow, head of the newsroom, more Venus Flytrap than shrinking violet, wasted little time becoming one of the expedition's leaders. She was the daughter of Walt W. Rostow, an economics professor at the University of Texas, but more famous as a foreign-affairs advisor to Presidents Kennedy and Johnson (one of the most prominent advocates of America's escalation of the Vietnam War). In the Market Bar one evening, Rostow noticed two executives poring intently over something they had written on a napkin. A confession was wrung from them. They had been compiling a list of names of the Telerate women they had slept with. "Not very impressive," Rostow sneered. "I've slept with most of them myself, and more besides."

No apologies required to these ladies, then.

The halcyon days of the market-data business were marked by behavior that may be decried as silly, irresponsible, irrational, boorish and, in some cases, potentially self-destructive (Neil Hirsch being a well-documented example of the latter), but they were far from heinous. Adolescence was ever thus. And if even those modest souls who declined to nourish the legends by contributing to them could look back on the period with nostalgia, then to hell with apologies.

Of one thing we can be reasonably sure: such times will never return. That may be just as well. Let the reader be the judge.

# Bloomberg

"Fired!" shrieks Michael Bloomberg indignantly from the first page of his 1997 memoir.[1]

Clearly the shock of being dismissed from Salomon Brothers—"Wall Street's hottest firm" at the time, he points out—still rankled sixteen years after the event. "So there I was, thirty-nine years old and essentially hearing, 'Here's $10 million; you're history.' "

But surely the shock was ameliorated by that eight-digit golden handshake? Apparently not. Bloomberg's anguish, if the man is to be believed, transcended such base motives as greed. "On Saturday, August 1, 1981," he laments, "I was terminated from the only full-time job I'd ever known and from the high-pressure life I loved. This, after fifteen years of twelve-hour days and six-day weeks."

It is vintage Bloomberg, at once outraged, sad, and boastful—and, of course, very good copy.

"Bless you!" is what he ought to have yelled. For although Bloomberg became history at Salomon Brothers that day, he was about to make history elsewhere as a media mogul, attaining a celebrity that may not have been of the Hollywood hands-in-the-cement variety but one that was recognized in the highest reaches of Wall Street and in media circles everywhere. On the way up he would humiliate Reuters and virtually destroy Telerate. For those achievements Salomon Brothers, his beloved corporate mentor, had trained him perfectly.

Bloomberg would no doubt insist that he had trained himself. Michael and modesty were no more meant to fit than an ugly sister and Cinderella's slipper. He made no bones about it; he loved publicity and courted it relentlessly. Not that courting ever became necessary. Journalists beat a well-trodden path to his office, there to feed off the ego of the first genuine uber-celebrity to emerge from the market-data industry. The resulting articles were always accompanied by mugshots of the subject looking in turns angry, smug, sly, and threatening. The clippings were framed and prominently displayed in the reception area of every Bloomberg office, where waiting visitors could scarcely fail to spot them and where employees were constantly reminded of them.

In every Bloomberg office I ever went to there was always above all a sense

---

[1] Michael Bloomberg, *Bloomberg by Bloomberg*, John Wiley & Sons, 1997

of purpose, an almost manic activity. Access would first have to be gained by going through a high-tech check-in procedure, at which a photo-identity card would be produced for first-time visitors. Visitation details were recorded in a database. The security guards in New York who showed you to the elevators were always militarily erect, smartly turned out, and politely crisp in manner. Once upstairs, an inner lobby resembled a market square, a meeting point thronged with employees swapping experiences while helping themselves to the fruits, nuts, and juices (only healthy foods) all offered free of charge. Open-plan spiral staircases struggled to accommodate a constant two-way flow of traffic. All this purposefulness was of course ergonomically contrived but nonetheless real. The contrast with the languid informality of a Reuters or Telerate office lobby was stark. The Bloomberg message, in short, was delivered the moment you walked into the joint: "This outfit means business."

Bloomberg employees were even more evangelical than their counterparts at Reuters or Telerate, often ridiculed as Bloomies, a play on the Moonies, the followers of the religious cult led by the Reverend Sun Myung Moon.

Perusing the magazine clippings on the wall for a random list of personal attributes revealed a colorful adjectival grab-bag: "smart," "innovative," "tough," "demanding," "aggressive," "brash," "blunt," "arrogant," "egotistical," "ambitious," "dynamic," "charming," "scary," "dangerous," "fast-talking," "flashy," and "profane." There could be no doubting the kind of image Michael Bloomberg wished to project. Not that he had to try very hard; the talent for self-promotion was to the manner born. But it was also cleverly harnessed to provide the theme for a relentless and calculated branding campaign designed to promote his business. Selling Bloomberg-the-personality, Michael decided from the start, was the most effective way of selling Bloomberg-the-company and Bloomberg-the-product. The ethnic name would do no harm either, especially in New York City where the Nice-Jewish-Boy-Makes-Good theme is always calculated to strike a chord.

The image was not drawn from film-star looks or physique. Michael Bloomberg was below average height and of unremarkable build. A toothy smile was exercised sparingly and he peered through eyes narrowed by hoods above and pouches below. The voice, a nasal drawl, is unmistakably blue-collar in origin. He liked to think of himself as a man-about-town, and after a friendly divorce from his English-born wife—they remained friends—was sometimes described as one of America's most eligible bachelors, an image he liked to promote by being seen in the company of attractive women from the worlds of media and show business. He flew his own plane, which he admitted he once nearly crashed with his son on board, and boasted of artistic prowess on the ski slopes. He sometimes leaped to the piste from helicopters, he mentioned in his book.

Michael Bloomberg was born to middle-class parents in Medford, Massachusetts, a suburb of Boston. Precocity was a mantle worn from an early age. In his memoirs—entitled, naturally, *Bloomberg by Bloomberg*—his enthusiasms and ambitions are earnest, blatant, and cliché ridden, offered without the slightest trace of self-consciousness. Time and again he refers to absorbing life's lessons, and how he applied them to his business career. One of his schoolteachers made "current events come alive." Another "opened my eyes to a whole new world." Having read *Johnny Tremain*, a novel about a teenage patriot in the Revolutionary War, more than one hundred times, Bloomberg was encouraged to assume "a maverick role I still try to emulate." And being a Boy Scout brought together "my sense of community with my ambitions of personal accomplishment." He seemed inordinately proud of an award as an eagle scout. At college he became president of the Inter-Fraternity Campus and "all-around Big Man on Campus" where he learned "how to campaign for office while seeking elected school positions."

With an engineering degree from Johns Hopkins University and a post-graduate business degree from Harvard, Bloomberg took his life-enriching mantras to Salomon Brothers. How could Wall Street resist? Salomon Brothers fell at the first fence, although he was first obliged to spend a probationary spell in the "cage," the firm's internal paperwork clearing-house. It was, he remembered, a hellhole located physically as well as metaphorically in the basement. On hot days he was reduced to slaving in his underwear. There, counting securities certificates by hand, Bloomberg learned the rudiments of Salomon's business. His "big opportunity" arrived with a promotion to clerical duties on the Utilities Desk, located on Salomon's famous trading floor, which the reader has already encountered as The Room.

His primary function was to keep the trading position book updated. The job also entailed, he recalled, the "grave responsibility" of keeping the pencils sharpened for two of the partners. One partner insisted on having six sharp No. 2 pencils in front of him first thing every morning, the other, six No. 3 pencils. In that and other aspects of the job, Bloomberg was well regarded as a diligent worker and fast learner—until one defining act of rebellion. One day, to relieve the tedium of the job, or perhaps to test his status, he switched the pencils between partners and broke off all the lead tips. One of the partners, enraged out of all proportion to the crime, demanded Bloomberg's head on a platter. But John Gutfreund, Salomon's managing partner, had obviously seen something he liked in the young smart-ass. Ignoring advice, Gutfreund switched Bloomberg to another desk, out of harm's way. He was not there long, moving a month or so later to the Equities Desk—and as Bloomberg recalls with typical lack of coyness, "the rest is history."

In a firm largely known for its expertise in bonds, trading stocks was not necessarily a career step in the right direction. But Salomon was keen to jump on a passing Wall Street bandwagon, of large blocks of stock for institutions. Bloomberg's promotion put him alongside Jay Perry, a volatile character who had been brought in from Salomon's St. Louis office to head the operation. Bloomberg described Perry as a "glib, fast-talking salesperson." That made two of them. "Actually, Perry and I were a dynamite team," Bloomberg boasted. "We could sell anything to anybody. If you wanted to dispose of a block of stock, we probably could even have convinced your spouse to buy it." Bloomberg reveled in the job and the business milieu. But he "didn't love Wall Street for the money, I also loved it for the lifestyle it provided." Early in his career, he "gawked at the opulent surroundings" of a fancy French restaurant, La Côte Basque, and was impressed when his fellow passenger in a "big black limousine" tipped the driver fifty dollars for what would have been a two-dollar ride in a cab. "Sometimes I thought I'd gone through the looking glass into another world."

In 1979, Bloomberg's career, in his words, "reversed its magical upward climb." By then, after a "skyrocketing" career, he had made general partner, a distinction that put him in the ranks of Salomon's Big Swinging Dicks. But the glory days were over. Negotiated commission rates and increased competition had made block trading unprofitable. Worse, the highly emotional Jay Perry had got involved in a fistfight with Dick Rosenthal, head of the arbitrage department and his chief rival on the trading floor. Perry was exiled in disgrace to the Dallas office. Rosenthal, receiving a lesser sentence, was banished to some remote corner of the floor to "do deals." For Bloomberg the consequences were mixed. The good news was that he was promoted to run Salomon's entire equities program. The bad news was that it ensured that the feud with Rosenthal would continue. Given Rosenthal's seniority in the firm, it was an unfair fight that could end only one way. As Bloomberg put it in his memoirs, "Determined, and armed with that great advantage lack of knowledge gives one, Rosenthal was a winner. Our rivalry was preordained to end in my divorce from the company."

Bloomberg's fate was sealed with a surprise announcement that Rosenthal had been promoted to the executive committee, and would henceforth manage the firm's equity business, which was essentially Bloomberg's existing job. Michael marched into Gutfreund's office with a declaration: "I'm not going to work for Rosenthal, and he won't want me anyway."

"We know that," Gutfreund replied. "We want you to go upstairs and run the computer area."

If managing Salomon's Information Services division was a demotion it was, in retrospect, an entirely fortuitous one. Bloomberg was no technologist but his engineering degree came in handy. So, too, in a department in which purveying mystification was often considered evidence of competence, did his natural aggression. The desire to get things done provided him with a bully pulpit from which to preach to the partners about how Salomon Brothers should really be managed. Such presumptions were no doubt forcefully expressed. For that reason, the role would be his last role at Salomon.

Bloomberg's personal date of infamy arrived on the day Gutfreund announced to the partners at a weekend hotel gathering that Salomon was to merge with Phibro Corporation, a publicly traded commodities firm specializing in metals. Although it was clear that Salomon rather than Phibro would be running the combined company, Gutfreund revealed that sixty-three of its senior managers would be leaving. Bloomberg was on the list.

And so, across the table from his boss and mentor, Bloomberg heard the words he had never expected to hear: "Time for you to leave," said Gutfreund quietly. Bloomberg had paid the ultimate price for having, as he put it, "stirred the pot, lost the battle."

Licking his wounds, Bloomberg briefly considered spiting his former employer by joining another investment firm. He decided instead to exploit his newly acquired expertise and technology by building an information business. As he reflected modestly in his memoirs, "Nobody had more knowledge of the securities and investment industries and of how technology could help them." He was probably as right then as he would prove to be later.

The rise of the Bloomberg "media empire," as journalists insist on calling it, was rapid but executed more by stealth than assault: a moonlit commando raid rather than a full-blooded daylight attack. Curbing his flamboyant impulses, he was content to stalk the information market-leaders, Reuters and Telerate, intent on catching them napping. That would prove less difficult than he could possibly have imagined. His rivals were not merely dozing but in a deep slumber. Such complacency may charitably be considered, in light of their shared market-dominance, understandable if not excusable. At any rate, while Reuters and Telerate slept, or counted their money, or basked in their prestige, Bloomberg quietly began to build a service that combined enough market data, real-time and historical, with clever user-functions to make their products appear primitive by comparison.

Michael Bloomberg was dangerous not just because he was smart but because he was smart and focused, a zealot who was prepared to pursue his objectives with a single-mindedness that sometimes shocked his friends as much as it would later frighten his enemies. Starting from scratch, Bloomberg and three former Salomon "protégés," buckled down to the unglamorous task of planning and building what he intended would be a "different" system. Different in Michael's mind meant "a business built around a collection of securities data, giving people the ability to select what each individually thought the most useful parts, and then providing computer software that would let non-mathematicians do analysis on that information. This kind of capability was sorely lacking in the marketplace. A few large underwriting firms had internal systems that tried to fill this need, but each required a PhD to use and weren't available off the shelf to the little guy."

For two years, Bloomberg virtually disappeared from sight.

"Michael who?" Neil Hirsch asked in 1985. He was responding to intelligence reports of a new online market-data service called Market Master. It was offered by a start-up firm called Innovative Market Systems and had begun to appear on Merrill Lynch's bond-trading desk in New York. Merrill's fixed-income department had long been recognized as Telerate country. The Thundering Herd's flirtation with Bloomberg was the first clear indication that Telerate's territory was about to be invaded.

If Hirsch was worried about the possible loss of Merrill's business he did not show it. Privately as well as publicly he professed not to be concerned at all. On the face of it, he had no reason to be. His own enterprise, a successful and well-regarded public company, was growing rapidly and profitably around the world. Business was brisk in the United States, on a spectacular roll in Europe, and growing rapidly in Asia. Though not yet in a position to topple Reuters internationally, Telerate did not need to, being content to carve out a significant slice of the global pie. Telerate aside, Hirsch had a great deal to be happy about in his personal domain. He basked in the status of a thirty-something multimillionaire, with all the accoutrements of the Manhattan man-about-town—the fancy East-side duplex, the chauffeured Rolls Royce, unrestricted access to a private jet, and memberships in all the *beau monde* clubs. He himself was the proud owner of a small but popular establishment on 28th Street, Caroline's Comedy Club, named after his wife (though clearly not in homage to her sense of humor).

If wealth and social standing tend to go to a man's head and warp his judgment, Hirsch, it may be argued, proved no exception to the rule. He ran Telerate—"his" company, as he still considered it, Exco's majority interest being regarded as a minor irritant—much as Michael would later run Bloomberg; that is, as if by divine right. "Love it or leave it," Hirsch used to say to complainers at Telerate, of which there were very few. In short, Hirsch's cup ran over. "Don't worry, be happy" he was fond of saying, echoing a popular song lyric.

But there was a dark side to Hirsch's triumph. As conservative or complacent as he was in his professional role, he was destructively immoderate in his private life. What one does outside the office may normally be regarded as one's own affair, but Neil's social excesses, which allegedly included a serious cocaine habit, binge drinking, and intemperate womanizing, were not only common knowledge within Telerate but also starting to attract attention in the investment community. Investors worried about the impact of these excesses on his business judgment. As one analyst confided to me, "I like everything I see about Telerate except the management. All this talk of drugs and booze worries me no end. And to be perfectly frank, Neil and his pals don't seem to give a damn what we think." He was far from alone in his concern.

Unfortunately, there were few moderating influences around Hirsch. Terranova, his closest professional friend, was hardly a model of executive probity, sharing most of Hirsch's vices. Bill Miller, another refugee from Cantor Fitzgerald, hired as an investment advisor with the title of executive vice president, seemed unconcerned. Most of Hirsch's close personal friends enjoyed the same toxic lifestyle, and those who did not were sycophantically tolerant of it.

It was inevitable that Hirsch, in walking his public-relations high wire, would experience the occasional brush with disaster. One such incident involved Hirsch and a senior colleague (who shall remain nameless) in a wrongful dismissal action threatened by two female former employees. They claimed to have been involved in long-running affairs with the two executives. The allegation was that they had been fired for no other reason than that Hirsch and his colleague wished to end the entanglements. After protracted negotiations, the ladies were paid off, or so they told as many people who would listen. Another female employee, a sales executive, also threatened legal action, this one for unpaid commissions, which would not in itself have been remarkable except that she, too, claimed to have been involved in an affair with a senior executive and that she was being punished for calling it off.

Telerate's corporate owner, Exco, had every reason to be concerned about Telerate, on several levels. But London was hardly the ideal place to pick up early warning signals from New York, whether in business or extra-curricular matters. John Gunn may or may not have been aware of the looming Bloomberg threat, but he was well aware of the whispers about Hirsch. More to the point, so were other Exco directors, some of whom seemed considerably more alarmed about the situation than their boss. Gunn was a clever but in certain ways unworldly man and seemed perfectly content to accept at face value his chief executive's glowing reports on the state of Telerate's business, curiously reluctant to confront what was fast becoming known in Exco circles as his "Neil problem."

Gunn's colleagues had none of their boss's tolerance. "Hirsch makes it plain that he doesn't want to be here," was the reaction of Bill Matthews, Gunn's deputy. "I mean, we all like a drink and a bit of fun once in a while, and we can all curse like troopers, but business is something else." Matthews would become one of Hirsch's many implacable adversaries on the Exco board.

"Bunch of toffee-nosed pricks," was Hirsch's verdict.

Hirsch always showed up for Telerate board meetings—they were "his" meetings—but these were usually brief, routine affairs, uncontroversial and self-congratulatory. The minutes may contradict me, but I do not recall the name Bloomberg ever being mentioned. Nor, of course, was the "Neil Problem," which was something that Gunn, a man of discretion, would have to tackle privately, if he had a mind to.

Like Gunn, I often felt isolated from events in New York. As managing director of Europe I was largely left to my own devices. Communication between Hirsch and me was minimal, not because we were not on speaking terms but because Hirsch did not seem interested in talking. He was not, I have to say, a great conversationalist at the best of times, except on topics in which he had suddenly developed a devout interest. Curiously, his curiosity did not seem to include Telerate's European progress. Our rare telephone conversations tended to be brief, curt, and, from my perspective, uninformative. "What's happening on the western front?" I might ask. "Nothing for you to worry about," he would reply. "You're doing a great job over there. Just keep that money rolling in." Terranova was usually more instructive. I occasionally asked him about Bloomberg. "Forgeddabout it," he'd say. "Our friend's got a long way to go to catch us. And even if, God forbid, he eventually makes it over here, there'll be nothing for you to worry about for some time." Since neither Hirsch nor Terranova seemed to be troubled by the emergence of Bloomberg, there seemed little point in my losing sleep over it. Ouch!

As for the Neil Problem, which so exercised the Exco crowd, all I can say is that on occasional visits to New York I failed to detect any marked deterioration either in his physical appearance or his behavior. I should perhaps add, however, that neither had been entirely reassuring to start with.

It was late in 1984 when I first heard the name Bloomberg mentioned in a European context. Steve West, Telerate's client-support manager in London, handing in his resignation, disclosed that he had been hired by Merrill Lynch for a new market-data service. As I understood it, Merrill either owned the product or was somehow sponsoring the product—even West seemed unclear. I tried to hold on to him by offering a decent salary increase but it was a case of too little, too late. West had made up his mind to go. His new employer had offered about 50 percent more than my raised figure, with a company car thrown in for good measure—a BMW. Only later, perhaps a few weeks, did the true identity of his employer emerge. Alarm bells should have started ringing then, I suppose. All I can say is that they did not, which represented my personal contribution to a multiple lapse by Telerate's management. My only excuse is that Telerate in Europe was then happily wrapped up in its glorious present, busy reaping the very favorable whirlwind of Big Bang. Before long the company would be more preoccupied with an uncertain future.

Reuters' management seemed no less complacent about Bloomberg than Telerate's. But with its own order-book bulging, the appearance of a new product in the United States fixed-income market, which anyway had effectively been ceded to Telerate, Reuters had much less reason to feel threatened.

Anyway, information start-ups were two-a-penny in the 1980s, coming and going like chorus girls at a Broadway audition, so why should either company worry about yet another anonymous contender, least of all one with a single customer, very little money, and no credibility?

If Telerate's lack of concern was a fault, then it was a grievous one. And grievously would we answer it. The advent of Bloomberg was disguised and unanticipated, like an ambush staged by those clever Apaches in Western movies, lurking in canyons ready to descend on the unsuspecting, and plainly stupid, cavalrymen.

And so, like those pesky Apaches, Michael Bloomberg succeeded where he had no business succeeding. It had been foolhardy to enter a business field already dominated by two seasoned and global competitors, each with a more than ten-year head start, and each one a public company with access to sufficient cash to fight back. But in challenging Reuters and Telerate, Michael Bloomberg claimed two distinct advantages: he had been a successful trader and had an intuitive grasp of trading-room technology. More important, he had the brass to believe that he knew instinctively better than either of his rivals how to bring these two elements together to create a user-friendly product.

He set out with certain other advantages, personal financial independence for one. It is not given to most men to be fired with a payoff of $10 million before the age of forty. Bloomberg was lucky, too, in the way that fortune so often favors the brave. His landing of a Merrill Lynch order early on was a typical slice of luck. We should not have been surprised, since Telerate itself once profited mightily and unexpectedly from Merrill's mischievous penchant for breaking its own rules. History was about to be repeated.

Michael Bloomberg's initial connection with Merrill was the result of a minor consulting contract, which he secured shortly after his departure from Salomon. Merrill asked him to produce a study of the brokerage firm's relationships with its institutional customers. It was not much of an assignment, as he himself admitted, "but they seemed pleased with the report we wrote. We received $100,000 plus expenses for our six-month effort. That paid some real bills."[2]

At the time, Innovative Market Systems was a penurious vehicle occupied

---

[2] Michael Bloomberg, *Bloomberg by Bloomberg*, John Wiley & Sons, 1997

by a Gang of Four: Michael himself and the three Bloomberg "protégés" from Salomon—Duncan MacMillan, Chuck Zegar, and Tom Secunda. MacMillan's role was to assess what potential customers might want. Zegar created the software infrastructure. Secunda wrote many of the first analytics, and would later manage the programming staff. Michael, in his memoirs, takes a rather cruel delight in referring to a fifth, unnamed colleague who dropped out after a few days. The man complained that he could not take the risk of starting with a brand-new company without being paid more money. The excuse was that he had "kids to think about." Michael, playing therapist, said, "This isn't about your children: it's you who has the problem." The man left.

The remark chimes with Bloomberg's enduring, and for some insufferable, credo in matters of loyalty: unconditional devotion. As Michael himself put it, "Either they believe in me, trust me, and are willing to take the risk that I will deliver success, or they don't. It's that simple. I don't negotiate."

Bloomberg's product was still unhatched when Michael took advantage of the successful consulting project to arrange a meeting with Ed Moriarty, head of Merrill's Capital Markets Division.

By way of background, at the time of Bloomberg's meeting, Merrill Lynch had been planning a market-data venture of its own in partnership with IBM and a software house called Monchik-Weber. Monchik had approached Merrill in 1982 with a "conceptual proposal" to build a branch-office network that would link Merrill's 450 branch offices and 10,000 account executives with an office automation system, supplemented by news and market quotes. IBM would provide the desktop hardware. The system was code-named Hermes. At the time of Bloomberg's visit, it was still a live project—but only just. (It would expire within a few months.)

Moriarty, in typical Merrill style, gathered together a very large, diverse group to listen to the presentation. They included accountants, lawyers, computer programmers, sales executives, traders, and administrators (shades of George Grimm, of fond memory) all arrayed, many no doubt wondering why they were there, around a 40-foot mahogany table in an enormous boardroom. Michael made his pitch with all the brash confidence of a man who knew exactly what he was talking about. "'We can give you a yield-curve analysis updated throughout the day as the market moves…We can show you the futures market versus cash and graph it for you as it's changing…For your traders, we'll keep track of every transaction as it's made and mark their positions to market instantly without any fussing…' No one else had done any of these things; and neither had we—yet."[3]

Moriarty turned to his technical man, Hank Alexander. "Well, Hank, what do you think?"

---

[3] Michael Bloomberg, *Bloomberg by Bloomberg*, John Wiley & Sons, 1997

"I think we should do it internally," Hank replied. "Build it ourselves."

How long would that take? Moriarty wanted to know. Alexander's response, while admirable in its frankness, struck Bloomberg as a "fatal mistake."

"Well, if you don't give us anything new to do," Alexander said, "we'll be able to start in six months."

Bloomberg pounced. "'I'll get it done in six months, and if you don't like it you don't have to pay for it!' I practically shouted…Moriarty got up. 'Well, that sounds fair enough,' he said, and he left the room."

Innovative Market Systems, the Gang of Four now supplemented by a team of programmers, came up with the goods within the self-imposed deadline. As Bloomberg explained, "We took the problem and broke it down into little, manageable, digestible pieces…Then each of us took responsibility for the ones we were best suited to…It wasn't elegant. It was laughably simplistic by today's standards. But we did it, and it worked."[4]

Michael Bloomberg was not in the least bit surprised by Merrill's conversion. "From the very beginning, I was convinced we were doing something nobody else could do. Nor was anyone else trying. Our product would be the first in the investment business where normal people without specialized training could sit down, hit a key, and get an answer to financial questions, some of which they didn't even know they should ask."

The rest, as Michael would say, is history.

The job done, a deal was struck. Merrill would pay Bloomberg a one-time fee of $600,000 for developing the product and $1000 a month per terminal for two years. A year or so later, Merrill followed up with an order for 1000 terminals, in the process taking a 30 percent interest in Bloomberg's company for thirty million dollars.

Bloomberg had started to put together a service that its users quickly came to appreciate as something that went beyond the merely novel. From the start, it was audaciously special, a terminal that far surpassed in breadth of data and functionality anything offered by other market-data vendors. By the time Telerate and Reuters recognized the threat, they lacked the expertise, or the will, to mount an effective counter-offensive. They fell instead to picking holes in the product.

Bloomberg was vulnerable, they said, in one crucial respect: it was a closed system. Its stand-alone terminals could not be hooked up to a client's network to allow a flow of data from Bloomberg's database into a client's computer— the kind of connectivity that financial firms were starting to request. But the closed nature of the Bloomberg system was really no disadvantage at all, for the simple reason that neither Reuters nor Telerate readily allowed such links

---

[4] Michael Bloomberg, *Bloomberg by Bloomberg*, John Wiley & Sons, 1997

either, and indeed were intent on resisting the rising tide of demand for them. Nor was it a problem for Bloomberg, even in later years, when resistance had crumbled at Reuters and Telerate; for Bloomberg by then had so proved the superiority of its service that many institutions, especially those on the buy side of the market, considered it, closed or otherwise, almost indispensable.

Bloomberg suffered early on another perceived disability, potentially a fatal one. This, too, it managed to surmount. As a condition of its 30 percent stake, Merrill had insisted that Bloomberg agree, for a period of five years, not to sell its terminals to Merrill's fourteen major competitors. The list included most of the blue chip Wall Street houses of the day: Bankers Trust; Bear Stearns; Citicorp; Daiwa Securities; Drexel Burnham Lambert; E.F. Hutton; First Boston; Goldman Sachs; JP Morgan; Kidder Peabody; Lehman Brothers; Morgan Stanley; Nomura; and Salomon Brothers. Reuters and Telerate saw this as a severely debilitating restriction.

Hirsch was exultant. "Bloomberg can't get away with that. The others will all gang up and retaliate." Hirsch apparently had forgotten that Telerate had made a similar pact with the very same devil a few years earlier and got clean away with it.

Hirsch was right in predicting rebellion. Six of the fourteen formed a consortium, somewhat unimaginatively named Electronic Joint Venture, to block Bloomberg by producing its own information service. But like most ventures of its kind, it foundered on the shoals of internecine squabbling.

Still, even Michael Bloomberg was sufficiently concerned by the EJV threat to visit Merrill's president, Dan Tully, to ask him to drop the exclusivity clause. At first, Tully turned him down. He saw great merit in pushing Merrill's name out to the buy-side institutions that formed the bulk of Bloomberg's client base. But there was another dimension, as Michael Bloomberg argued forcefully. By restricting Bloomberg's ability to service the sell side, Merrill was also devaluing its investment in the company. It took a year of lobbying by Bloomberg before Tully finally waived the restriction.

By then Merrill had milked its privilege. As Michael pointed out, "Merrill had such a significant edge in experience with the Bloomberg terminal, it would take these other firms years to appreciate the benefits Bloomberg provided in cost reduction and improved controls, to order the terminals and have them installed, and to train their employees in their use."

Was there no soft underbelly in the Bloomberg offering? Arguably, there was. The vital missing element, at least in the early years, was news. Reuters and Dow Jones had long been the only companies capable of offering comprehensive and global financial news. Given the high cost of running a news service, they seemed likely to retain their duopoly. At least for the foreseeable future. Reuters had always taken a resolutely proprietary view of its news, never allowing its services to be distributed on alien networks. Dow Jones was far less possessive. In addition to the arrangements with Telerate and AP-Dow Jones/Telerate, distribution contracts had been signed with a number of other market-data vendors, including Bloomberg itself. (That was not Dow Jones's only link with Bloomberg; a subsidiary had a lucrative field service contract to install Bloomberg terminals.)

Dow Jones reserved the right to review its distributors from time to time, and, because of its close links with Telerate, had from the start been ambivalent about its deal with Bloomberg. The subject was discussed endlessly and inconclusively, with and without Telerate's participation. The talks were animated as much by internal politics as commercial considerations. Dow Jones marketing executives suffered pangs of conscience about undermining Telerate by providing news to an emerging competitor, but not *Wall Street Journal* editors. The *Journal* had no hesitation in 1987 in signing a contract with Bloomberg to provide the paper with a daily list of government-securities quotes. Bloomberg's advantage in replacing the paper price-sheets provided each afternoon by the Federal Reserve Bank of New York was that its list was delivered electronically. It was unclear whether the *Journal* had failed to consider Telerate as a source or had and for whatever reason rejected the idea. Nobody from the *Journal* had called Telerate to ask for a proposal; nor did Telerate, oblivious to the *Journal's* overtures to Bloomberg, volunteer one. It was a relatively small matter but symptomatic of the lack of coordination within the Dow Jones extended family. Hirsch was livid. "Bloomberg now gets a free advertisement, every day, in the newspaper owned by our partner," he yelled at Bill Dunn, an executive vice president at Dow Jones, and then widely tipped as a future chief executive. "Does that make sense? And while we're at it, why are you still selling your fucking news on Bloomberg?"

Hirsch's anger was justified, but given his dismissive comments about Bloomberg's prospects, he was short on credibility. Dunn, an ardent Telerate advocate, was sympathetic but hamstrung by politics. "We'll review the news situation again, Neil. But opinion over here is very mixed. Maybe it makes sense to blacklist Bloomberg, but you know, for us there's a big revenue consideration involved here, too. As for the *Wall Street Journal*, those guys have always made their own editorial decisions. Church and State, and all that…"

And so the pointless skirmishing continued. The Bloomberg contract expired twice and each time, amid further outbreaks of Dow Jones soul-searching and Telerate protestations, it was renewed—or, as Dunn preferred to express it, extended. Meanwhile, Michael Bloomberg grew tired of having the Damoclean sword of a Dow Jones withdrawal hanging over his head, and resolved to settle the issue once and for all. He did so with a stroke of typical boldness. In 1989 he announced that he would create his own news service from scratch, and, in a further insult to Dow Jones, hired a senior *Wall Street Journal* reporter, Matt Winkler, to help him do it.

Bill Clabby and I were deputed to talk Winkler out of leaving. We were an unlikely pair, but Clabby had some kind of counter-offer to make and I was to convince Winkler that Telerate's plans were every bit as ambitious as Bloomberg's. We failed. By the time we got to Winkler the genie was already out of the bottle. Our meeting was no more than a debriefing. Winkler, who in the past had affectionately claimed that his "blood ran Dow Jones red," made it chillingly clear that he was disillusioned with Dow Jones's lack of direction and drive. He was equally unimpressed by Telerate's prospects. Conversely, he had a very high regard for Michael Bloomberg and his product. He had researched the matter thoroughly, he told us. Bloomberg was becoming popular with bond traders because of its extensive analytical capabilities, and Bloomberg kept adding data and functions. Bloomberg's clients were not just satisfied—they were ecstatic. Telerate, Winkler thought, was maintaining its market share by complacent reliance on customer inertia. Its declining popularity in the United States, he pointed out, was merely masked by overseas growth. Clabby put up a spirited defense, but I found myself uncomfortably in agreement with a great deal of what Winkler had to say.

As for news, Winkler believed that Bloomberg had every chance of winning a newswire contest with Reuters and Dow Jones. "This man Michael Bloomberg has vision and determination and the balls to go with them," he warned. "Watch him!"

The clear inference was that Dow Jones/Telerate was lacking in all three categories.

As if to prove the point, the attitude of the Dow Jones newsrooms was sanguine. Start a newswire from scratch? It could not be done, was the prevailing opinion—at least not quickly or profitably.

It was not the universal view. Three Dow Jones journalists from the Capital Markets Report paid a clandestine visit to Hirsch around this time. They wanted Telerate to start its own fixed-income newswire, a product that would tie in with Telerate's market data. The service would have its own unique character, they said, and it would compete head-to-head with the CMR. Jim Feeney, Phil Hawkins, and Lindley Richert were experienced reporters; there was no question that they could have produced a good service. I was all in favor of the idea from the marketing point of view, but I shared Hirsch's opinion that for Telerate to compete with Dow Jones would have constituted a grave act of betrayal.

Bloomberg had no such constraint. Nor, with financial resources a plenty, was he limited by caution. If Reuters and Dow Jones could operate news services there was no reason why he could not. "History shows that any gutsy entrepreneur (Joseph Pulitzer, William Randolph Hearst, Henry Luce, B.C. Forbes, Ted Turner) can enter the news business any time he wants. And, Bloomberg being Bloomberg, we had some advantages those guys didn't. When we started, there were lots of very competent reporters looking for jobs. In the face of the 1990–1991 recession, the news industry was cutting back exactly when we were expanding. We had a reputation as an exciting, innovative place to work. In the Bloomberg terminal, we had a distribution device par excellence. Best of all, we had revenue from terminal rentals, which meant we didn't have to worry about a news service paying for itself as a stand-alone product—one heck of an advantage."[5]

Dow Jones finally retaliated by cutting Bloomberg off from Dow Jones news as well as rescinding the service contract, thereby slamming the stable door shut on an empty stable.

All of these events, I should now mention, had taken place during a time of great upheaval for Telerate. These included a change of ownership. In the summer of 1985, Exco decided to sell its Telerate interest. Hirsch immediately persuaded Warren Phillips, Dow Jones's chairman and chief executive, to buy it.

If Exco's decision to sell Telerate was something of a surprise to Exco's shareholders, it came as a profound shock to Telerate's management, though not necessarily, as far as Hirsch was concerned, an unpleasant one. Exco's shareholders were delighted with the windfall. The company had owned Telerate for less than five years and an $80-million investment had been converted to £360 million, more than $400 million at the prevailing exchange rate—a handsome return by any standards. Neil Hirsch was equally pleased for different reasons. Just as John Gunn was happy to be relieved of his intractable Neil Problem, Hirsch was released from what he regarded as onerous obligations to a parent company that did not appreciate him. He had found being in the spotlight as the chief executive of a public company less and less rewarding over the years, and whatever personal affinity had once existed between him and Gunn had long since dissolved. The sale to Dow Jones meant a welcome return to ownership in "friendly hands."

Gunn naturally painted the sale as a sensible business decision. The information business, he told investors, could only get tougher. Exco was at heart a money broker, run by money brokers, and would never be able to devote the care and attention, not to mention the investment, to keep Telerate competitive. Gunn's colleagues hardly needed convincing. They had fretted for years over Telerate, and particularly over Gunn's inability to bring Hirsch to heel. In the end, it was difficult to discern who was more convinced of the need to dispose of Telerate: Gunn, or his boardroom colleagues. It is hard to

---

[5] Michael Bloomberg, *Bloomberg by Bloomberg*, John Wiley & Sons, 1997, p.77

avoid the conclusion that Gunn, had he elected to fight the decision, would have faced a palace revolt and found himself discarded along with Telerate.

The capital gain notwithstanding, Gunn deep down must have been disappointed that Exco's Telerate venture had failed. He had justified the purchase by drawing attention to the synergies between money brokering and information, and that much had not changed in five years. But Hirsch's behavior had changed and for the worse, at least in the opinion of Gunn's colleagues. They made constant references to two alleged episodes. Hirsch had failed to show up for an important board meeting in Hong Kong, allegedly after meeting a woman during a stopover in Los Angeles. The second incident involved a non-executive Exco director, Richard Davy. Gunn had stationed him in New York, supposedly to keep an eye on Exco's American investments. The intention was that Davy would work out of an office at Telerate. Hirsch naturally saw this as an intrusion. Davy was by profession a banker, and came across to some Americans as a despised British archetype—the lofty, condescending, colonial-bashing, City gent. He was none of those things, but nor was he the warmest or most diplomatic of souls. But whatever Davy was, or was not, he was fated by virtue of his mission to be branded a John Gunn spy. One day, after a particularly heated argument, an enraged Hirsch had Davy ejected from Telerate's office by a security guard, with instructions never to let him back in.

Gunn's despair over Hirsch was a disappointment, but not the only one in Exco's North American strategy. Another, not directly related to Telerate but involving the same unfortunate Richard Davy, was Exco's failure to capitalize on an opportunity to acquire Cantor Fitzgerald, Telerate's former owner. For weeks Davy had been engaged in secret and predictably difficult negotiations with Bernie Cantor. They had, by all accounts, taken various twists and turns, sometimes verging on complete collapse, but terms and conditions had finally been agreed. Gunn was keen on the deal for obvious strategic reasons: a combination of Exco's international money-market operations with Cantor Fitzgerald's in US treasury securities, allied to Telerate's distribution capacity, would create a potent force both in brokerage and information terms. Gunn was buoyant when documents were prepared for signature, and the deal seemed assured when Bernie invited Davy out to his Beverly Hills mansion for the ceremony.

Bernie's pen was actually in hand, poised over the documents, when he hesitated. He would like, he told Davy, just one more, very minor condition. Although he intended to withdraw from the business completely, as agreed, he wished to have access to an office on the premises of his old company, somewhere to go in the mornings, a place where he could spend his day tending to his private business affairs. Davy, presumably under general instructions from London not to offer any further concessions, however small, balked. "Sorry, Bernie, no more changes. We sign the contract as it is or there's no deal."

Cantor, according to Davy, put the pen back in his pocket in a ceremonial flourish, rose from his seat, and snapped, "In that case there's no deal."

Bernie's request seems harmless enough at face value. If so, was Davy's intransigence, or Gunn's, misplaced? Not at all, insisted Davy. It was a red herring. Bernie had made the request, knowing that it would be refused, and for one simple and very personal reason: he could not bring himself to relinquish power over the company he had founded and which bore his name, and which he had ruled as an absolute monarch for over forty years.

It was Hirsch, in a rare call from New York, who broke the news of Exco's decision to sell Telerate. It came as a shock to me. I had not heard so much as a whisper locally. It was also disappointing. I felt a personal regard for John Gunn. He had been supportive in a thousand small ways in the struggle to take Telerate into the global arena. He had done me several personal favors. He had always been ready to accept an invitation to lunch knowing that he was letting himself in for an earful. Above all, perhaps, he was a serious cricket fan.

"Yeah, but those Exco guys were really tough to work with," Hirsch said, without irony, surprised to hear me say that Exco had been such a positive benefit. He was also aggrieved by my cool reaction to Dow Jones as a partner. "Having the world's biggest financial news organization behind us is great for Telerate," he said. "Now we can get done some of the things we've always wanted to do."

I agreed in principle with the first part, but getting things done did not strike me as one of Dow Jones's demonstrated virtues (except in those cases in which the *Wall Street Journal* was the beneficiary). Nor was it clear to me exactly what it was that we had always wanted to do but could never have done without Dow Jones.

Yet the more I thought about Telerate's situation, the more I came around to Hirsch's view that throwing in with Dow Jones made sense. It was, admittedly, a virtue manufactured from necessity, but the fact is that few appealing alternatives sprang to mind.

The only natural buyers of Telerate—"natural" meaning companies in the same line of business—were ruled out for one reason of another. A Reuters-Telerate combination would almost certainly encounter anti-trust difficulties in the United States, and perhaps even in Europe. Michael Bloomberg had an incentive to buy us, if only to steal a dramatic march on Reuters, but spending a billion dollars or more just to poke a stick in a rival's eye made little sense. Anyway, acquiring Telerate would have flouted Bloomberg's loudly trumpeted make-not-buy policy. Thomson had the money and was aggressively acquisitive, but was more interested in buying content than distribution. Knight-Ridder did not have the money.

Other perceived candidates had been bandied about, including such august names as IBM, ATT, General Electric, Citicorp, Time Inc., Pearson (owner of the *Financial Times*), and British Telecom. Each at some time had expressed a desire for a more conspicuous presence in the financial community. A couple on the list had ventured into the field already (IBM in the ill-fated venture with Merrill Lynch, ATT in an alliance with Quotron). Others would follow (see the next chapter). But in the context of Telerate, they represented in aggregate no more than an exercise in "rounding up the usual suspects."

Hirsch's call to Phillips may have been reflexive and self-serving in that a Dow Jones deal was the most convenient option for him personally, but it was also the one that made business sense as the most predictable and therefore the least dangerous scenario for Telerate. Without Dow Jones, Telerate would find itself in an uncomfortable state of limbo, until either a suitor had appeared or Hirsch had made arrangements to purchase the Exco shares.

Dow Jones it was, then. Only time would tell if it was the right decision as opposed to the easy one.

# Dow Jones

Time did tell—and a tortuous tale of woe it turned out to be.

If the twelve-year marriage of Dow Jones and Telerate was supposed to be a fairy story, it failed by reversing the convention of a genre that demands a sad beginning and a happy ending.

Whatever its classification, the story began on a cheery note when Dow Jones, having passed up similar opportunities on at least two occasions, finally took the plunge in 1985 and picked up a controlling interest in Telerate. The response on Wall Street was almost universally positive. To most analysts the synergies between the companies made them a perfect match. Dow Jones was anxious to enter the real-time information field in which Telerate had already made its mark. Telerate, moreover, was a primary distributor of Dow Jones's international news, and the two companies were partners, along with the Associated Press, in the company that marketed Telerate everywhere outside the United States.

Reuters, some industry observers were moved to observe, ought to be trembling at the prospect of having to compete with such a powerful combination.

The joy was restrained by just one note of criticism. It concerned not the idea of the purchase but the manner in which it was to be accomplished. Rather than acquiring Telerate outright, Warren Phillips, Dow Jones's chairman and chief executive, chose to buy it in installments, a method known in investment banking circles as a "creeping tender." The creeping tender is considered a legitimate form for acquiring a company, but is usually employed only in hostile bids in which the target company takes measures to defend itself. In the Telerate case, the opposite was true. In the world of finance no less than in the world of consumers, anything bought under an installment plan invariably costs more, much more, than if paid for up-front. Phillips knew this, of course, but defended his decision to eat Telerate in small bites rather than swallow it whole by citing Dow Jones's traditional aversion to taking on debt. If the decision was hard to justify at the start of the process, it would become even harder at the end, when the final reckoning had ballooned to a staggering $1.6 billion.

The immutable law of physics, and a common facet of corporate life, is that like poles repel. The stormy relationship between Dow Jones and Telerate was proof positive of this. Far from being a marriage made in heaven, it seemed to have been contrived in the other place. The parties somehow managed to endure it for twelve years, which must at times have seemed more like ten times as long. During the period, relations unraveled in a cavalcade of misses: misjudgments, misconceptions, miscalculations, and mishaps. The greatest miss of all, everyone agreed, was missed opportunity.

If the story has an underlying theme it is one of mutual incomprehension. Forget all the supposed synergies. Dow Jones never forced itself to grasp the nature of Telerate's business. Telerate, in turn, came to feel neglected by the parent company's preoccupation with the *Wall Street Journal*, the world of print emphasized at the expense of electronic delivery. The facile explanation bandied about was that hoary old chestnut often trotted out to excuse bad management: cultural differences. In this case, bad management was compounded by an almost complete absence of trust between the partners. In both aspects, blame could be assigned equally, but, as senior and controlling partner, Dow Jones must accept the greater share.

Dow Jones's reputation was badly tarnished by the Telerate affair, but at least most of its assets remained intact at the end of it. Telerate was less fortunate. By treating Telerate as a difficult stepchild to be left by and large to its own devices, Dow Jones failed to exercise proper parental control. In the absence of much-needed investment, the charge virtually starved to death. The money had in fact flowed in the other direction. At a time when the *Wall Street Journal* was suffering a severe downturn in advertising income, Dow Jones was only too grateful to haul in Telerate's operating surpluses to bolster the company's financial statements. When the surpluses dried up, Dow Jones came under attack on Wall Street for hanging on to what many investors by then felt was a wasting asset and a corporate albatross. The first response from Dow Jones management was panic, in the form of a belated plan to rescue Telerate by injecting massive amounts of capital. The second was capitulation.

By then, Dow Jones had broken Telerate's back as well as its heart. It was in that deplorable state that the company once considered the potential jewel in the Dow Jones crown was delivered into the arms of a new and, as it turned out, equally unworthy suitor.

The failure to nurture Telerate had troubled analysts and investors long before it finally disturbed the sleep of Dow Jones's management. For this narcoleptic lapse, Dow Jones could offer no plausible explanation. If Telerate's deficiencies had been apparent from the start, the obvious question is why Dow Jones saw fit to shell out so much money to buy the business and why it failed to address the problems right away. And if they were not apparent at the time, then the problems must have developed later, when Dow Jones had complete control of the company and unrestricted power with which to correct them.

Dow Jones would later claim that it *had* recognized the problems at an early stage and dealt with them by dismissing Telerate's entire management team, which Phillips—or someone—had identified as the root cause of the company's troubles. Blaming the previous management was a classic response, but it would have been more convincing if it had squared with the comment in the 1991 annual report that Telerate had "proved to be the strongest component in Dow Jones with an operating gain of more than 20%."

In ridding himself of Telerate's *ancien régime* Phillips assumed responsibility for rescuing Telerate. If that is what he felt was needed, he must have given the matter considerable thought. But what were the conclusions? An obvious move would have been to commission some individual or group to work out a business plan designed to exploit the strengths of both companies. It never happened, perhaps because Phillips, having disposed of Telerate's key executives, realized that he had nobody to replace them. Not that he would ever admit as much.

But then Dow Jones management rarely admitted anything. Nor did it have to. With the voting shares controlled by a loyal and unquestioning family trust owned by the descendants of one of the company's earliest and most successful proprietors, the legendary Clarence Barron, Dow Jones's hierarchy felt itself impervious to criticism from shareholders. The Bancroft family always backed management.

But even that fact contributes little to understanding of Dow Jones's inept stewardship of Telerate.

What follows may shed some light.

Before 1985 Dow Jones had pondered long and hard how it might exploit the online information market in which Telerate had carved out a significant global share. Senior Dow Jones executives had at various times considered building a system from scratch, only to recoil every time from the prohibitive cost. Telerate offered a ready-made if not perfect alternative, one that could readily be adapted to Dow Jones's requirements. One obstacle was Telerate's slow network, which at 1200 baud might prove incapable of handling the volume of traffic that Dow Jones, and particularly the *Wall Street Journal*, might produce. But the network would also prove too slow for Telerate's own purposes, in which case a new network would have to be designed anyway. The network was an issue that would require attention, but it was not a critical issue requiring immediate resolution. The fact is that it was good enough in 1985 to support thousands of users around the world, was growing fast, and offered a perfect outlet for time-critical information.

The acquisition brought instant financial benefits. The most significant was that Telerate's income would substantially reduce Dow Jones's reliance on revenue from print sources. The *Wall Street Journal*'s advertising and circulation income had always been vulnerable to cuts in discretionary corporate spending during economic downturns. Real-time services were far less exposed. At the time of the Telerate acquisition, the combined income from Telerate and Dow Jones's Information Services Group, which included the newswires, was already more than half the revenue from print sources and was likely to overhaul it within a few years.

From Telerate's perspective, the arguments in favor of the merger were, on the face of it, even more compelling. To be associated with two of the world's most recognizable news brands was the foremost benefit. Exclusive access to Dow Jones news—and perhaps *Wall Street Journal* copy—would nullify the advantages of integration that Reuters exploited by operating homegrown newswires. Telerate employees also took on board the reassuring news that a prestigious magazine survey had listed Dow Jones as one of America's most admired companies.

What, then, could possibly go wrong?

The answer was just about everything. Right from the start, relations between Dow Jones and Telerate were dominated not by cozy notions of shared objectives but by rancorous arguments about operating procedures. Telerate acted on intuition. Decisions were made with a minimum of discussion and bureaucratic process. Dow Jones favored caution and planning. Decision making emerged from interminable meetings, endless research, and upward delegation. These contrasting approaches spanned the entire operating spectrum: from budgeting methods to accounting practices; from technology management to product development; from sales policies to the management of human resources. Even Christmas parties intruded as an early and needless source of friction.

Dow Jones did not have a Christmas party. Given the size of the company, it was a sensible policy. It was not motivated by economics; Dow Jones's custom was to set sufficient funds aside for a party but to deliver the cash to charity. Telerate, a much smaller company, had always enjoyed a lavish seasonal bash, usually held at some trendy nightspot frequented by Hirsch. For many employees the company party was one of the highlights of the calendar.

"Not this year," Phillips decreed in 1986. If Dow Jones could survive without a party, so could Telerate. The same rule had to apply to all parts of the organization. It was a reasonable position to take, but it masked Phillips's unspoken fear of bad publicity. Telerate parties were notoriously wild, and potential revelations of drug-use posed a particular threat. "Sure, like we're gonna invite the fucking press," was Hirsch's ironic response.

Hirsch prevailed that year. The Telerate Christmas party went ahead, and without embarrassing incident. But there would be no Telerate parties in future, Phillips insisted. The edict was a minor irritant. More significantly, the clash over a peripheral issue had drawn attention to the "cultural differences" separating the companies.

If buying Telerate made all the business sense in the world, Dow Jones's chosen method of buying it seemed to make no sense at all. Phillips's decision to go with the installment-plan approach was based on the recommendation of Ken Burenga, his chief financial officer. Burenga, a former circulation manager at the *Wall Street Journal*, had occupied the financial post less than a year. It provoked speculation about why Phillips had allowed himself to be influenced by someone so inexperienced. Or, it was reasonable to ask, had the influence been exercised in reverse? Later, Burenga would attribute the decision to company tradition. "It was Dow Jones's way not to incur debt," he told an interviewer.

Critics of Phillips's largesse added insult to injury by pointing out that Dow Jones had previously passed up two opportunities to buy Telerate for laughably minute fractions of the amount eventually paid. Hirsch claimed that as far back as 1974 he had invited Ray Shaw, then the head of Dow Jones's newly formed Information Services Group, to buy the business for a paltry $1 million. Shaw, having failed to convince his superiors to do the deal, countered by inviting Telerate to join the joint international venture that Dow Jones was about to form with the Associated Press. In 1981, Hirsch made a second approach, again to Shaw, now Dow Jones's president and chief operating officer. He was again rebuffed, paving the way for Exco to pick up Telerate at the bargain price of $80 million. Even in 1985, an outright tender for Telerate, by then a public company with a known market value, would have cost no more than $880 million, half the price Dow Jones would eventually pay.

Dow Jones opened its creeping tender for Telerate—launched would be too strong a word—by paying $285 million for a 32 percent stake. In order to secure a controlling interest, Dow Jones simultaneously brought in a co-investor, Oklahoma Publishing Company, to take up a further 20 percent. OPC's chief executive, Edward L. Gaylord, was an old friend of Ray Shaw, a fellow Oklahoman. An inscrutably dour character, Gaylord was reviled or extolled, according to taste, for his extreme right-wing views. These were peddled in the company's most prominent publication, *The Daily Oklahoman*, a paper once described by the *Columbia Journalism Review* as the worst big-city newspaper in America. Gaylord's positions on social issues were said to make the *Wall Street Journal*'s famously conservative editorials sound positively Marxist. Gaylord's empire was a curious pot pourri of media and entertainment interests. They included the Grand Ole Opry country music theater and Opryland Hotel in Nashville, Tennessee, and a share of the Texas Rangers major league baseball franchise. Just the kind of connections Telerate needed.

Gaylord and two fellow directors were appointed to the Telerate board. They had no interest in Telerate as a business. The understanding was that Gaylord's Telerate stake would be held as if in escrow until Dow Jones was in a position to acquire it, naturally with a little profit for OPC into the bargain. As for the rest of Telerate's equity, Phillips let it be known that Dow Jones would take up the balance through open market and other purchases, as and when opportunities arose.

The first of these transactions was completed eighteen months later in February 1987, Dow Jones taking up half of OPC's interest for $133 million or $15 a share, a price close to the level of the public shares. A month later, Dow Jones sold its 25 percent interest in the international venture to Telerate for $65 million, equal to $12.50 a share. These deals aroused little controversy but the next one raised a few eyebrows. In September, Dow Jones laid out $300 million for the 10,543,200 Telerate shares owned by Forstmann-Leff Associates, a fund management firm, at $28.75 a share, a hefty premium on the market price. Analysts angrily questioned Phillips's generosity in paying an inflated price for shares in a company in which he already held a majority interest. Surely, with all the time in the world to pick up additional shares, he could have afforded to wait for a market downturn? The response from Dow Jones's spokesman was that Telerate's business was doing very well and that its shares were regarded as substantially undervalued. Reasonable assertions at the time, they would be less so a month later when the stock market suffered the biggest crash in its history, the Dow Jones Industrial Average plunging more than 500 points in one day, stirring dark memories of 1929.

One Dow Jones executive who was particularly exasperated by Phillips's timid approach to acquiring Telerate was Bill Dunn, who had taken over from Shaw as head of the Information Services Group. Dunn had waged a long campaign to convince Phillips to buy Telerate as part of his ambition to "take Dow Jones into the twenty-first century." He was a maverick at Dow Jones, the kind of man sometimes described as an unguided missile. Dunn propagated the image by expressing himself in the earthy vernacular, expletives undeleted, of his native Iowa, where by his own account he had spent a deprived and unhappy childhood. He openly admired Neil Hirsch, in whom he recognized a kindred entrepreneurial spirit and a fellow carouser. Dunn was widely acknowledged to be Dow Jones's cleverest technologist. He also boasted a degree in economics. He deployed both talents to promote his image as a consummate corporate visionary and a man to be reckoned with. Around the company he was worshipped or loathed in more or less equal measure. While few disputed that he was very bright, few regarded him as stable. Phillips was no exception. Dow Jones's courtly, soft-spoken chairman appreciated Dunn's talents and his advice but not the blunt, hectoring manner in which the opinions were often delivered. He was distinctly uncomfortable with Dunn's well-deserved reputation as a profane, hard-drinking and sometimes emotionally volatile rabble-rouser. He rarely conveyed his concerns to Dunn, who consequently fancied his chances of eventually filling Phillips's shoes.

If many in the company hoped that Dunn would achieve his ambition, few of them were to be found in the newsroom. Actually, the journalists had every reason to be grateful to Dunn. It was Dunn in the 1970s who had supervised the plan to transmit the *Wall Street Journal* to eighteen regional printing plants by satellite, a monumentally successful project that saved the company a fortune in production costs and established the *Journal* as America's first truly national newspaper. In doing so, Dunn had fulfilled the dream of Bernard (Barney) Kilgore, a lionized former managing editor, and later chief executive, who had rescued the *Journal* from financial disaster in the years following the Second World War by transforming it from an insular trade publication into a national business newspaper. In the process he created his own memorial in the form of the *Journal*'s distinctive and defining front-page format, in which feature articles, not always about business or finance, and often of a whimsical nature, appeared alongside hard news. Kilgore was a newsman to his fingertips. Dunn's "problem" was that he was not a newsman at all.

The *Journal* regarded itself as a self-governing principality within the Dow Jones kingdom and by virtue of tradition claimed the exclusive right to groom the future monarch. Pretenders to the throne outside the newsroom were treated accordingly with hostility or suspicion according to the level of perceived threat, and always with the kind of condescension reserved for useful servants. Not that there had been too many pretenders to worry about. Dunn was the first to appear in many years.

Dunn's only rival from the news side of the business—his only rival anywhere—was Peter Kann, then associate publisher of the *Wall Street Journal*.

Kann, a Harvard history graduate, could claim none of Dunn's broad professional qualifications, least of all in technology, but in editorial circles he enjoyed heroic fame. He had made his name reporting from Asia, including some famously heretical dispatches from the Vietnam War. Later he won a Pulitzer Prize for his vivid reports from the India-Pakistan War of 1971. In contrast to Dunn's "white trash" upbringing in Iowa, Kann came from a privileged academic background. His Austrian-born parents, refugees from Nazi Germany, had both been lawyers. His father went on to become a professor of history at Columbia. Kann disguised assertiveness with a shy and self-deprecating charm. He wrote beautifully, of course, and spoke persuasively, if sometimes interminably. There was an "aw, gee" goofiness about him that disarmed his adversaries in face-to-face arguments. In short, he possessed all the social graces that Dunn lacked. He was, to boot, everyone's idea of a nice guy. "Gee, that's awfully nice of you to say so," he would have responded with a trademark crooked grin. Dunn would have bellowed, "Just cut the fuckin' crap, will ya."

As Kann steadily emerged as a Phillips favorite, Dunn seemed to be the only senior Dow Jones executive not to notice. Rarely mincing words, as Kann would have done, Dunn continued almost unfailingly to irk his chairman. He upset Phillips one day in 1985 by storming into his boss's office to insist for the umpteenth time that Dow Jones make up its mind once and for all to buy Telerate. "Enough is enough," Dunn is said to have told Phillips, concluding a lengthy harangue. "We've just got to do this deal. It's our future, for chrissake. Print's dying. Electronic data is the future."

Phillips, as it happened, had already been talked into buying Telerate, but Dunn, when he found out how it would be done, was still not satisfied. He was at a loss to understand why Phillips was sticking to Burenga's plan to pick it up piece by piece. As he complained later, "It baffled me why Phillips kept doling out the money this way. It was a fuckin' expensive way to do business."

In March 1987, as Dow Jones embarked on its program to acquire the balance of Telerate's shares, I received a telephone call from New York from another blunt fellow. It was John Terranova, ringing to let me know that he would be paying a rare visit to London. He would be arriving the next morning, if convenient, accompanied by his wife Susan, but not by Neil Hirsch. "Susan wants to do a little shopping," he explained, "and you and I need to have a little chat."

Since Terranova seldom traveled without Hirsch, and even less frequently with his wife, it was a reasonable guess that he had something significant on his mind and that it involved me. I was right.

We met the following afternoon at the bar of his Park Lane hotel. Typically, Terranova skipped the pleasantries and got straight to the point. "We need you back in New York," he said. "We gotta put in some fucking management over there. Business is okay, but Neil's frankly out of it, and we need to get organized. Dow Jones doesn't trust him to do it, or me for that matter. There's nobody else here who can do the job."

Terranova added a few disturbing details. Hirsch was bored and distracted. More to the point, he had suffered two severe angina attacks, of which few people, least of all the public shareholders, were aware. He had undergone a medical procedure called an angioplasty to open up a clogged artery. His doctors had advised him to take things easy for a while. They had also told him in no uncertain terms to lay off drugs, alcohol, cigarettes, and fried foods—Hirsch's staple diet for twenty years. Hirsch was not feeling well, Terranova said, and his appearances at the office had become occasional rather than regular. "At least he's off the cocaine and the booze," he added. "That's a good start. If he goes back on, it'll be the finish."

Several of Hirsch's night-clubbing cronies, alarmed by the medical prognosis, had finally rallied around to offer constructive advice. They included Bianca Jagger, Neil's girlfriend at the time, who presumably knew a thing or two about over-indulgence. "I have to say she's been a helpful influence," Terranova conceded. Hirsch himself later acknowledged Jagger's role. She had once told him, he said with a chuckle, "Hey, I want to be your lover, not your mother."

Hirsch's own strange presentiment of an early demise had come perilously close to self-fulfillment. Longevity was now in his own hands, no longer a matter of chance but of abstinence. He was still two years away from forty.

There was no question that I would return to New York, as I am sure Terranova had anticipated. The terms were generous enough, but my acceptance was motivated less by greed than a sense of duty. Terranova had painted a picture of Telerate adrift. I could hardly fail to rally to the flag.

There was the question of succession in London. I felt that Europe could safely be left in the hands of my deputy, Martin Church, who, if far from an adventurous spirit, would be a competent caretaker. Terranova was less sure and Hirsch, he said, would be vehemently opposed. We agreed on a compromise: to appoint Church on an interim basis, to be confirmed or otherwise at some future time.

On that mildly contentious note, the Park Lane business meeting was concluded. "Great," said Terranova. "Now let's have a few drinks and then we'll take our ladies to dinner." He left for New York the next morning.

I was left in London to puzzle over Terranova's visit, particularly his sudden concern about Telerate's management, in which he had not always been so proactive. For years, acting as chief "buddy" in a system of management-by-buddies, he had loyally followed Hirsch's lead in pretty much everything. Flying to London was not something he would have undertaken on his own initiative. Obviously he had discussed it with Hirsch, but it was certain that Dow Jones had been involved as well. The inescapable conclusion was that Terranova was reflecting the views of Warren Phillips as much he was representing Neil Hirsch.

It was clear from the start that Dow Jones had inherited Exco's concerns about Telerate's wild and wicked ways, and that they focused on the chief executive. The difference was that the new owner was considerably more straitlaced than its predecessor. As the publisher of a newspaper with a proud tradition of muck-raking in high places, including those on Wall Street, Dow Jones was understandably sensitive to the slightest threat of internal scandal. The high living enjoyed by Telerate's two senior managers being the stuff of legend, Dow Jones had placed Hirsch and Terranova in the high-risk category.

For that reason alone, Phillips was intent on changing the Telerate guard, and evidently I was regarded as someone less likely to grace the gossip columns than my two senior colleagues were. That notion, given my own far-from-monastic social life, struck me as slightly odd.

The plan that emerged was that Telerate would be run jointly by two executive vice presidents. I would be responsible for the "front office" functions of sales, marketing, and product development. Steven Rappaport, a former Bob Fromer sidekick at Hartman & Craven, Telerate's law firm, and who had acted as company secretary for several years, would handle the "back office" duties of finance and administration. Rappaport had no previous corporate management experience but he was formidably intelligent and well acquainted with Telerate's business issues. He also brought to Telerate the hitherto unknown quality of a quiet and non-confrontational manner. An additional virtue, in light of Dow Jones's preoccupation with image, was that his affinity with alcohol was virtually non-existent, rarely extending beyond the occasional glass of wine or beer. Night clubs? Rappaport would far rather be tucked up in bed by ten with a good book.

Hirsch's fate, then, was to be kicked upstairs. He already held the title of president. He was now given the additional, rather pointless position of chairman. He had presumably been eased out of his executive role, with the eventual intention of removing him altogether. In other words, he had been fired Dow Jones-style. Phillips softened the impact by inviting Hirsch to join the Dow Jones board. Terranova remained in place as Telerate's chief operating officer. Rappaport and I would ostensibly report to him.

As a management structure, it sounded as good as any. None of us had any doubt that, for all our inexperience, we could make it work. Phillips seemed happy. My one concern was that placing Hirsch in his curious limbo might create a somewhat strained atmosphere—not only within Telerate but also between Telerate and Dow Jones. Hirsch himself seemed unconcerned. "We just carry on as before," he said, though in the short term, with Dow Jones taking an active interest in its new charge, there seemed little chance of that.

With Phillips now steadily building up the Telerate stake with a combination of private and open-market purchases, the company had for all intents and purposes become an operating division of Dow Jones. The most obvious change at Telerate board meetings was audible, as clipped British accents were replaced by the Midwestern drawls of the Dow Jones members and their Oklahoman allies.

"Reckon there's anything Telerate can do together with the Grand Ole Opry?" Terranova inquired of the taciturn Ed Gaylord, mugging for the benefit of his new all-American audience.

"Well, y'all need to think on that some," was the quiet response. "But you're surely welcome to join us in Nashville anytime to hear some good ole country music." Terranova's tortured expression made it clear that country-and-western music was not to his taste, unless, as he delicately put it, this would afford him the opportunity to "get a close-up view of Dolly Parton's hooters."

The Oklahomans had little to say for themselves in the boardroom. Even the most senior of the Dow Jones board members—Phillips, Shaw, Dunn, and Clabby—seemed content to confine themselves to routine questions about operational matters. The atmosphere was oddly serene. I found it curious that there still appeared to be little desire on Dow Jones's part to more actively integrate the two companies. Phillips seemed perfectly content. I was happy, for the time being, to settle into the job. Fortunately, Telerate was still performing reassuringly in North America, and splendidly in Europe and Asia.

Turbulent times, though, lay immediately ahead. For these the stock-market crash and the economic recession that caused it were partly to blame. However, I was equally responsible in recommending two major corporate initiatives, both of which marked a departure from Hirsch's relaxed approach to Telerate's development. Both entailed considerable expenditure of the kind Hirsch would never have contemplated. One involved considerable risk.

The timing could hardly have been worse, both projects being adopted in the same month that the stock market fell into its spectacular swoon. The crash itself had no direct impact on Telerate's business, other than on the share price. There was, however, collateral damage. Although stocks staged a remarkably rapid recovery, Wall Street remained edgy, less confident that the bulls would keep running. As investment institutions resorted in typical fashion by reducing trading activities, Telerate cancellations began to rise. For the first time in its history, Telerate's growth faltered. As yet it was only a hiccup, but there were unprecedented frowns of concern in the sales department.

Clearly this was not the most propitious moment to persuade the company to embark on new corporate adventures. But what choice does any management have but to run its business for long-term gain regardless of short-term market fluctuations? That, at any rate, is my story, and I am sticking to it.

The first, and less controversial, of the two initiatives in question was the acquisition of Telerate's exclusive Canadian distributor, a local stock-quote vendor called CMQ Communications, at a cost of $80 million. In normal circumstances CMQ would not have presented itself as a priority target for acquisition, especially since Telerate already collected a cost-free part of its revenue in the form of royalty payments. However, CMQ's general manager,

Henry Becher, tipped me off one day that the company's principal owner, David Campbell, had agreed in principle to sell the business to Thomson International, a Toronto-based media group. Many industry observers, and most of my colleagues, viewed Thomson as a potential Telerate competitor. Concerned, I called Campbell to ask why he had not seen fit to offer the deal to Telerate. He had done just that, he told me with some bemusement. "But frankly, Neil didn't seem particularly interested. And as Thomson definitely was, I went with the flow."

I took my preoccupations about Thomson to Hirsch. He seemed indifferent, as always reluctant to spend Telerate's money. "Anyway," he added, "it's too late to do anything now. Campbell's already agreed terms." My response, worked out with Becher, was that we might be able to block the deal if Telerate objected to Thomson acting as Telerate's distributor in Canada. We had every right to, in the event of a sale, under the terms of the CMQ contract with Telerate. Hirsch grudgingly agreed that I should approach both Campbell and Thomson. As it happened, Hirsch got along well with the Thomson executive concerned, Peter Shipman. I called him for an appointment.

Shipman was startled and somewhat miffed, but gracious. "Look, if you guys have problems with Thomson representing you in Canada, then frankly I have a problem with the deal." He wanted to proceed, he said, but given our objections, Thomson would be prepared to step aside. I informed Campbell. He seemed unruffled. "Hey, if it makes sense for Telerate, as I always thought it did, then go ahead. I'm happy either way so long as I get my money." With Campbell's approval, Shipman agreed to give Telerate an option to pick up the deal on the terms and conditions already negotiated with CMQ. We had thirty days to take it up.

We signed the contract to acquire CMQ against a disconcerting clatter of cascading share prices. The crash was front-page, banner-headline news. "Sure you want to do this?" Hirsch asked. My response was that it was a worthwhile transaction. Telerate would pick up 100 percent of its Canadian revenue, which was running at $25 million a year and growing fast, instead of the 25 percent royalty. At that rate the cost would be paid off within two to three years. "You'd better be right on this one," Hirsch growled. I am amazed to this day that he let the deal go through.

The other initiative with my prints all over it was more problematical. It involved taking Telerate into the business of foreign-exchange transactions, a bone of contention between Hirsch and me from my very first day at Telerate—actually even before that. Now was the time to act, I argued. Reuters Dealing, a conversational facility for currency traders, had turned into a money-spinner, and Reuters had since introduced a matching system, masterminded by our old friend John Hull. Foreign exchange was still the world's largest capital market and growing fast. Without some kind of transactional capability, Telerate was in danger of being frozen out of it.

My first choice, to be honest, had been to attack the treasury-securities market, in which Telerate was still dominant, but the exclusive with Cantor Fitzgerald precluded that. An approach to Bernie Cantor was out of the question. He was still in a funk over the loss of Telerate and could be expected to extract the most punitive terms in any renegotiated contract. Since no other over-the-counter market sectors seemed ready to embrace a matching product, foreign exchange it had to be.

Hirsch remained as unconvinced as ever, but even he finally conceded that Telerate had to do something bold to protect its business from erosion. The overseas markets were especially vulnerable. Europe and Asia were already fretting that we lacked a transaction product, and without any prompting from me. Julian Childs, Asia's managing director, mentioned with helpful timing that a group of Japanese banks were rumored to be planning a trading system.

The whole issue would have to be discussed at board level, Hirsch said. I had no quarrel with that. We reached an informal arrangement: I would argue the case for the prosecution. Hirsch would remain more or less neutral, leaving the case for the defense to be argued, if at all, by the Dow Jones directors. The boardroom discussion was disappointing, being neither animated nor enlightening. Phillips, on unfamiliar ground, deferred to Hirsch. "I think this one's your call, Neil." Hirsch had anticipated the moment. Setting aside his personal doubts in favor of the enthusiasms of his marketing group, he said, "Let's do it." But he had more to say. "Let's not do it alone, though. We need a partner, a big-name partner, one that will lend credibility and share the risk."

This was, at face value, a reasonable approach, but all my misgivings about joint ventures were aroused when Phillips weighed in with a suggestion of his own. "How about ATT? They're sure credible enough, and certainly rich enough. I know Charles Allen [the then ATT chairman] very well. Why don't I give him a call?"

Phillips's offer was born of good intentions, but ATT would have been my last choice, not the first. Nor, apparently, was it appealing to others around the table. I noticed Bill Dunn rolling his eyes in disbelief. But he said nothing. Ma Bell, as the company was still known even after a government-mandated break-up, was famously bureaucratic, a club-footed behemoth, and justly renowned for being a difficult partner—hardly an ideal choice for a venture likely to demand improvisational agility.

Phillips reported back that Allen was enthusiastic. The next step was to form an operating company, to be owned equally by ATT and Telerate. We settled on the name Global Transaction Services Company. The product itself would be called the Telerate Trading Service. All this was negotiated over a period of weeks at ATT's great marble edifice in midtown Manhattan. The first thing Rappaport and I noticed was that the vast executive floor where the early meetings were held was virtually deserted. The reason, someone explained, was that the chairman at the time it was built lived in New Jersey and hated commuting to Manhattan. The building was a mausoleum with no body.

Allen plucked a trio of anonymous executives from Ma Bell's extensive range of idle talent to join a management committee of six. Telerate contributed Steve Rappaport and me, plus Brian O'Heron, Telerate's technical director, a gruff man of few words, or so we had thought. Our mandate was straightforward: we would jointly design a dealing product, which ATT would build and Telerate would sell.

Scott Rumbold, quoted in the joint press release, noted that "a number of decentralized global markets are potential users of the service," and that "the rate of growth and change in these markets is outpacing the abilities of existing transaction systems."

O'Heron, unimpressed to distraction by the choice of partner, gloomily confided that he doubted that any of us would live long enough to see ATT produce anything, let alone something good enough to replace existing systems. He added a grim warning. "Just wait, this is going to be like wrestling in mud with a fuckin' elephant." He was wrong; it was like wrestling in mud with a herd of elephants.

ATT offered, and we approved, the project's chief executive, one Peter Yunich. His father had been some kind of noise at Radio Corporation of America and had been, for reasons obscured by time, a pioneering legend in the electronics industry. It was soon apparent that Peter the Younger, a large, overbearing man of strong opinions, had inherited none of his father's talent for project management—or, some thought, for anything else.

The first meeting of the GTS management committee was convened somewhere deep in the heart of ATT country in New Jersey, probably Morristown; I do not remember. It gave us a foretaste of the grim battles that lay ahead. ATT wanted to develop the product in, of all places, Cincinnati, Ohio, where the company had some kind of advanced research facility. "Not on your life," said Rappaport. "We'll spend half our time on airplanes. What's wrong with right here in New Jersey?" This objection incensed ATT's key man on the committee, Alexander C. Stark Jr., a former naval officer we were told, and who regularly barked at us as if we were junior officers on the bridge. "Hey, who's supposed to be building the product anyway?" he yelled. "I say we build the godammed thing wherever we see fit. This is our call, not Telerate's."

The tiff was eventually resolved in our favor, but it took three hours to achieve, leaving no time to discuss other more pressing issues. It was a bad start on several levels. "Told ya," O'Heron muttered smugly as we left the building accompanied by a violent thunderstorm that only added to the sense of foreboding.

Nor was the general mood lightened when news broke that Reuters had written to the Justice Department asking for a review of the venture for possible anti-trust violations. Reuters' attorneys claimed that the venture breached the 1984 consent decree that broke up the Bell system and which barred ATT from entering the electronic publishing market until 1989. ATT responded that it believed the venture to be in compliance with all aspects of the decree. My response in the trade press was more aggressive. Reuters "obviously doesn't like the idea of a competitive service. My own preference is to get on with my business, and I think they should do the same." It would become a moot issue, as it soon became clear that O'Heron was right: ATT was incapable of building anything, or at least of building anything quickly. Part of the problem, to be fair, was that we ourselves had yet to define what it was. In that context, Rumbold put forward a clever idea. It involved a familiar figure from Telerate's past—Jimmy Wiseman, the former chief foreign-exchange dealer at Bankers Trust, and more recently of Citibank, who readers may recall had been an avid fan of the now forgotten Tafex system. Wiseman had recently retired from trading. He was unrepentant about his affection for "black box" trading and anxious to help. We hired him, promptly sending him off on a world tour with a mandate to find out what currency traders really wanted. Neither the appointment nor the trip met with Yunich's unqualified approval, but he reluctantly and sullenly went along with both. Even at that early stage of the project, ATT's role was being consigned to that of back-seat observer.

This odd situation prompted O'Heron to explode after yet another pointlessly acrimonious meeting, "Will somebody tell me just what the hell we need ATT for? Why don't we just send them on their way? We can do everything ourselves. We're already doing it, for Chrissakes."

It was a valid point, but as Rappaport pointed out, the two companies, like it or not, were harnessed together. ATT was unlikely, he said, to relinquish its position without a fuss or, perhaps more to the point, considerable compensation. That much would soon become horribly apparent.

Wiseman came back from his travels with findings that displeased me but which seemed incontrovertible. The market would welcome an alternative to Reuters Dealing but did not yet have the appetite for a full-blown matching product. It was a disappointing result. A matching system was in many ways easier to design and the time seemed right, whatever opinion polls might conclude. "See, they're still not ready out there," Hirsch said with a told-you-so look. Wiseman now offered a middle way. He had in mind a system that resembled Reuters Dealing in function but without the free-format conversational element. Traders would be able to contact each other on the system—with four distinct quadrants at their disposal, as Reuters allowed—but would have to follow more rigid procedures in order to agree a trade. It meant eliminating the "chat" facility that had made Dealing so popular, but the theory was that doing so would make the product more attractive by speeding up the trading process.

Wiseman came up with a product blueprint. What we needed now, and quickly, was the system to make it work, one that would give the product a distinct identity. Much to O'Heron's disgust, ATT promised a solution. The device, from memory, seemed perfectly suitable, but no sooner had we expressed our surprised gratitude than ATT suddenly withdrew the promise. The solution, it now became clear, would have to come from Telerate, as O'Heron had long predicted.

Someone in Asia had come across a device that we could use. O'Heron put on a demonstration, using a keyboard he called the "slate," apparently because it produced a display that resembled an electronic scribbling pad. It seemed to work well enough, but there was a catch. Where ATT's device had been in full color, this one was disappointingly monochromatic. It seemed to me retro-gressive to offer a product with the kind of display panel not seen since the earliest days of desktop computers, but by now we were on the rack to produce something.

Though few of us were happy with the aesthetics of the system, rigorous testing confirmed that at least it worked reliably. A decision now loomed: to launch or not to launch. A vote was taken. It went, unanimously, in favor of going ahead. Wiseman was enthusiastic. Rumbold seemed happy. So, too, was David Barnes, a former Reuters salesman hired to coordinate the project. Barnes, who boasted experience with Dealing, thought we stood an excellent chance of succeeding. "Traders won't be worrying too much about the aesthetics," he asserted, "so we shouldn't either. Let's just focus on the functionality."

It was ultimately my call. I felt distinctly uneasy. As efficiently as the product worked to its specifications, the "slate" was as unattractive a device as I had ever seen on a trading desk. Nor did the screen display make too many concessions to presentation. Hirsch was equally unimpressed. He was secretly horrified, I suspected, but he said nothing for or against a launch. There was no product alternative. The choice was the slate or nothing. Or to delay the whole project. It was left to me to make the fateful decision.

"We go," I said, to which I silently added, "And may the gods have mercy on us."

To make sure that enough bids and offers were entered into the system to achieve critical mass, we deployed a number of sales executives, mainly in London and New York, to perch on the shoulders of early subscribers. Most prospective TTS users already had Reuters' trading products in front of them and we were in for a fight to gain their attention. Some of our trading-room "persuaders" took the battle to excessive lengths. A trader called me one day with a typical complaint.

"Look, I want TTS to succeed, I really do. Nothing would please me more to shove that Dealing terminal up Reuters' ass. But I can't have your people swarming all over my trading room telling my traders what to trade and when to trade. I've already thrown them out of here. They can come back, but only after you've told them to ease off."

Other complaints followed. Several were focused on the TTS sales manager in London, Peter Harrison, who was bent on reducing his image as a no-nonsense Yorkshireman to a grotesque caricature. He was banned from two dealing rooms. "Don't let that ridiculous man near me or my bank ever again," was the blunt message from one head trader.

Trading activity increased slowly, but without the kind of spectacular breakthrough all such projects must have. Still, the first revenue had been booked. As the transaction count inched higher, Barnes provided morale-boosting daily summaries. We pored over them anxiously, desperate to detect signs of significance. "It's getting there," was Barnes's message. "The curve is rising." There was no outbreak of applause—just a few sighs of relief.

All this ATT watched with growing resentment from the sidelines.

If the CMQ and TTS initiatives did nothing else, they seemed to have marked me down, in the eyes of Warren Phillips, as a bold innovator. Within months of my return to New York, Phillips took me under his wing. He called regularly, usually with a few quick questions, but sometimes with lunch invitations. "I know how much you like to go out to lunch," he said slyly on the first such occasion.

Of all the Dow Jones executives with whom I had come into regular contact, I got along with Phillips the best. As Phillips was a New Yorker of Jewish extraction (he later converted to his wife's Protestant faith) his appointment broke a sequence of predecessors of Midwestern or Irish extraction. He was tall, dark, and slightly stooped. His manner was impeccably polite. He wore a more or less permanently lugubrious expression underscored by a black walrus mustache. He had been chief executive at Dow Jones for ten years, a hugely successful decade from which he derived great personal credit. It rode largely on the back of the phenomenal rise in the circulation and advertising lineage of the *Wall Street Journal*. Phillips's accession to the top post did observe a couple of apparently immutable Dow Jones traditions: he had risen through the editorial ranks and he had been mentored by his predecessor.

Such traditions went all the way back to 1902, when Clarence Barron, the owner of a Boston-based financial news agency, had been "selected" to buy the company by one of its three founders, Charles Dow, originator of the Dow Jones Industrial Average. Before retiring, Barron had handpicked and trained his own successor, Kenneth "Casey" Hogate, a Detroit newspaper reporter. Hogate in turn cultivated Barney Kilgore, another journalist from the Midwest, and the man who conceived the *Wall Street Journal*'s front-page format. Kilgore followed the rule of succession by entrusting the job to his good newsroom friend William Kerby, who passed the baton to his young protégé (and Brooklyn Heights neighbor) Warren Phillips. If the pattern was solidly institutionalized, as it seemed to be, it could only be good news for Peter Kann and bad news for Bill Dunn.

For all the triumphal progress of the *Wall Street Journal* on his watch, Phillips found no shortage of detractors, inside and outside the company. Inside, the criticism focused on matters of style—his serene temperament and even-handedness, the one being interpreted as a lack of dynamism, the other as indecisiveness. The more virulent attacks, however, came from the outside, and on the evidence seemed far more justified. Most concerned his choice of acquisitions (although it must be said that, if these were the follies his critics claimed they were, they paled in comparison with the unfolding Telerate debacle). I was aware of them only anecdotally.

There had been his curious decision in 1978 to buy a publication called *Book Digest*, positioned as a kind of intellectual antidote to that icon of middle-of-the-road, semi-literate *Reader's Digest*. The company had no strategic affinity with Dow Jones—nor, as it turned out, with its own target market. *Book Digest*'s circulation figures never seemed to match what its previous owners had claimed they were, and under Dow Jones they plunged relentlessly. On all the evidence, Phillips had been sold a pup. After four years of declining readership—partly caused by restrictions on promotional mailings imposed by a much-publicized lawsuit brought by the state of California for transgressions against the state's strict sweepstakes laws—Phillips was forced to shut the magazine down. At a purchase price of $10 million, *Book Digest* had not been a catastrophic mistake, but it was immediately followed by another curious decision. In 1981, Phillips had approved a passive and ultimately pointless investment in Continental Cablevision, buying 25 percent of its stock for $79 million. It was the deal Phillips had picked in preference to buying Telerate at more or less the same price. Continental was not a financial disaster—in fact the stake was sold for $140 million, a return close to 50 percent—but it demonstrated to many that Dow Jones seemed to have no clear strategy guiding the expansion of its business base.

After those two transactions, Phillips's cautious approach to Telerate was perhaps understandable, but it branded him as a timid man. Al Neuharth, chairman of Gannett Newspapers and founder of *USA Today*, was one of the branders. Quoted by Francis X. Dealy, a former Dow Jones employee, in *The Power and the Money*, marketed as an insider's exposé of his former company, Neuharth said: "Warren does not seem to have the guts to do a deal, to hang in there. He always has to have a partner, a back door, some avenue of escape, someone to share the blame with if the deal goes wrong."[1] He spoke with the authority of experience. Several years earlier, Neuharth had outbid Dow Jones to buy the *Des Moines Register*.

Phillips survived these setbacks not just because the *Wall Street Journal* continued to sail on majestically—though even the flagship became becalmed for a while after the 1987 market crash—but because Dow Jones's board was as compliant and unquestioning a corporate body as had ever been convened. Most of the outside directors were big-name corporate executives, presumably selected for their wider influence and contacts in commercial and government circles. They contributed little to boardroom debates about company strategy, least of all when the discussion came around to something as obscure as Telerate. Two of the directors had companies of their own to run; a couple of others served on so many boards it would have been something of an achievement if they had known whose board meeting they were attending.

Three of the external directors were not so busy. They were defined as "family" directors, which meant that they represented the interests of various trusts held in the names of the nine great-grandchildren of Clarence Barron. The heirs divided into three distinct family branches, each one derived from the marriage of Jane Barron, one of Clarence Barron's two adopted daughters, and Hugh Bancroft. (His other daughter, Martha, predeceased her parents and her widower was excluded from Barron's will.) The three family board seats represented a complex web of trusts with a collective ownership of about 80 percent of Dow Jones's voting shares and they always voted as a bloc. For those who enjoy historical ironies, Hugh Bancroft offers a delicious example. Clarence Barron—a stern and tempestuous taskmaster whose refusal to suffer fools gladly was legendary—twice hired his hapless son-in-law and twice fired him on the grounds of incompetence. There was no question of anyone firing his later heirs.

The sole male scion at the boardroom table was William C. Cox Jr., the son of Jessie Bancroft and William C. Cox. An amiable man of few obvious business talents, Cox was listed as an executive director. His role as a Dow Jones employee fell into the field of client relations, meaning that he was

---

[1] Francis X. Dealy, Jr., *The Power and the Money*, Birch Lane Press, 1993, p.328

retained less for his business acumen than for his skill in entertaining Dow Jones customers on the golf course.

A more formidable physical presence in the boardroom was that of his second cousin, Bettina Bancroft Klink, the daughter of Hugh Bancroft Jr. and his first wife Bettina Gray. Klink represented the trust with the second largest bloc of Dow Jones shares. A charming and vivacious woman with a haughty, aristocratic manner, she often dressed in the flamboyant style of the flapper era. She enjoyed a legendary reputation for entertaining in grand style at her Hollywood Hills mansion and indulged a passion for horses by breeding Morgan horses at a farm in Rancho Santa Fe, California. She rarely said anything of consequence at board meetings but was unwaveringly devoted to the management line, the cue for her cousins to follow suit during a vote. Afterwards, at lunch, she liked to regale her table guests with tales from California's country-club society, smiling regally at their delighted responses.

The third family board member was Martha Robes, a daughter of the four-times-married Jane Bancroft Cook. A pleasant and pretty woman, whose husband earned an unnecessary living making Shaker furniture in New England, Robes had nothing to say in the boardroom either, but she, too, contributed to the cozy lunchtime ambience in her own way with engaging small talk accompanied by a coquettish smile.

The Bancroft heirs had every reason to smile, with dividend checks aggregating $50 million a year or more. And they could rest easy that the dividend was in the safest possible hands. Dow Jones always paid a dividend. Not to pay one, or even to attempt to reduce it, would have been to risk disturbing a long-standing arrangement under which management could do pretty much as it pleased except touch the sacred dividend, in return for the unquestioning loyalty of the family trustees.

Dow Jones's voting structure was unusual, to say the least, for a public company. Investors are inclined to shy away from such undemocratic artifices. It was tolerated in Dow Jones's case because the *Wall Street Journal* and the newswires had always been such profitable performers that the dividend was almost invariably well covered by earnings. Telerate, with an equally solid history of growth and high margins, was not expected to upset the applecart.

My first invitation to lunch from Phillips took us to a downtown restaurant, Bankers and Brokers. It was a "dry" occasion. As Phillips explained with a friendly jibe, "I hope you don't mind if I try to break Telerate of some of its ingrained habits." Even so, we managed to stretch it to almost three hours. Phillips was intent on understanding Telerate's business better, and summoned all his journalistic instincts to ask all the right questions. He seemed generally satisfied with the answers, which naturally stressed the need for continuing and rising investment in new products, backed by the adoption of sound management principles, especially financial discipline. Our extended session made Phillips very late for an internal meeting. He told me later, with a smile: "I apologized profusely, but when I told them I'd been to lunch with you they seemed to understand perfectly."

A short time later, Phillips was ready for a follow-up lunch, but I was planning to be in Europe for the rest of that week. "Good," he said. "I'll come with you. We'll take Concorde together. It'll give us a chance to chat on the way over." We went at it again for three airborne hours. My message was consistent. "If Dow Jones supplies the discipline, Telerate will provide the flair. Above all, we must be bold in taking Telerate global, out of its confined space as a domestic distributor of treasury prices."

All this sudden attention seemed to have an underlying purpose, and within a few months it became clear.

Towards the end of 1998, Dow Jones resumed building up its Telerate stake. The balance of Oklahoma Publishing's interest was acquired, representing 9 percent of Telerate's equity. On top of that, one million shares, worth about $16 million, were purchased from Hirsch, who needed the cash to finalize his divorce from Caroline. There were also, from time to time, open market purchases, and by the end of the year Dow Jones owned 67 percent of Telerate. It seemed only a matter of time before a formal tender was launched for the balance.

It was duly announced on September 21, 1989. Phillips paid a visit to Hirsch to alert him to the impending announcement. It was a pleasant late-summer afternoon and the office was quiet. Hirsch was whiling away the day in Terranova's office playing Nintendo. It was not a visit that Phillips would have dreaded. Or Hirsch. The decision to acquire the balance of Telerate was unlikely to surprise anyone, least of all Hirsch. Phillips probably considered it a formality. If so, he was in for a rude shock.

Dow Jones's bid would be announced at $18 a share, he told Hirsch. This was just under three dollars above the previous day's market price. An awkward silence followed. Hirsch, absorbing the news, was clearly not pleased. "It's way too low," he told Phillips.

"The announcement is going out this afternoon," Phillips said, plainly flustered by Hirsch's reaction. "We think it's a fair offer. I don't intend to call it off."

Hirsch disagreed but could only shrug. "So be it. But I'm not happy."

Phillips left, looking grim.

Hirsch called a war council of his three Telerate-employed directors, Terranova, Rappaport, and me. "The bastards are trying to low-ball us," he said. "Can you believe that? No fucking way am I going to vote my shares at eighteen bucks. What about the rest of you? It's your business, too, you know."

We all agreed. Hirsch, as owner of 7 percent of Telerate's equity had more, much more, at stake than the rest of us, but we all agreed with his assessment.

"Good," he said. "So let's go to war."

Phillips's formal letter of notification to Hirsch referred with unintended irony to "an exciting opportunity for Telerate's management." What it failed to mention were several interesting facts that came to light soon after the lawyers started getting involved. For example, it emerged from certain documents connected with possible litigation on behalf of a group of minority shareholders that Phillips and his management colleagues had actually recommended a bid of $19 a share. This had been presented to the Dow Jones board, which rejected it on the advice of the company's investment advisors, Dillon Read and Goldman Sachs, who considered it too high. Yet those same two firms, eighteen months earlier, in an analysis presented to Dow Jones in anticipation of the bid, had both put an even higher valuation on Telerate. They had disagreed on the figure: Dillon Read had proposed a bid of $20 a share; Goldman Sachs had thought that nothing less than $25 would do. The logical conclusion, from a plaintiff's point of view, was that the bid of $18 implied that Telerate's value had fallen significantly during the intervening period. Dow Jones in its defense noted that it was because the earlier valuations were too high that management had declined to act on them. That was a fair point, and Dow Jones had other reasonable things to say to justify the $18 bid. The trouble was that whatever the company said to question whether Telerate was worth a high price tended to raise doubts about the company's future, and about why so much had been paid for it already.

Much of the haggling over an appropriate price was related to the thorny matter of Telerate's projected growth rate. Over this there were yet more seeds of conflict between the two companies. Dow Jones's bankers, presumably with input from their client, were projecting Telerate's annual growth at 12 percent. Telerate's management was anticipating a rate of 20 percent, a figure that had been explained to and accepted by its own advisors. It was a significant gap. It would be a critical one in the event a court was asked to rule on the fairness of the bid. The difference partly hinged on what might or might not have occurred at a Telerate strategic planning meeting that had taken place earlier in the year.

The event, which I myself had organized, was held at Arrowwood, a golfing resort in Westchester County, north of Manhattan. It was supervised by management consultants, Kepner-Tregoe, and was attended by a score of senior managers from Telerate. Bill Dunn, Carl Valenti, and Bill Clabby were present as participating "guests" from Dow Jones. By the end of the meeting the walls were festooned with flip charts, as is normal for such occasions. The message on one of them, purporting to represent a consensus around the table, was that Telerate should aim for, with every confidence of achieving, a 20 percent growth rate over five years. That much everyone who attended seemed to remember. But was it a projected rate or merely a desired rate?

Bill Clabby recalled it as nothing more than a wish, pointing out that it was made at a marketing meeting, not at a financial seminar. This view he affirmed in an affidavit related to a shareholder suit being prepared against Dow Jones. "To the extent that a 20% aggregate growth rate for the business of Telerate was discussed," he wrote, "it was referred to as a goal or target for which Telerate should strive and not in any sense an attempt to forecast or project actual results in the near future." He went on: "I did not believe then, and I do not believe now, that an average growth rate of 20% for Telerate over the next five years is realistic in the business and competitive environment as it exists now and in the foreseeable future."[2]

I have to say, as much as it pains me to, that Clabby was right on both counts: Telerate at Arrowwood did not formally adopt a 20 percent growth rate, and it would have been hard to attain. I cite the incident here to illustrate the lack of affinity in all matters, great and small, real and imagined, that divided Telerate and its controlling shareholder, soon to be its sole owner.

While charges and counter-charges flew back and forth between lawyers and investment bankers representing the two sides, Telerate's management prepared to hit back in a very public way. A public relations firm, Kekst and Company, was called in to prepare a campaign on behalf of the minority shareholders. The first shot would be fired in an advertisement strongly expressing Telerate management's opposition to the bid. We planned to take a full page for it in both the *Wall Street Journal* and the *New York Times*. We particularly relished its appearance in Dow Jones's own newspaper. We spent the best part of a day working on it with inappropriate glee. After racking our brains for a catchy headline, Hirsch came up with one inspired by the title of an old Broadway musical called *How Now, Dow Jones*. Our version was "What Now, Dow Jones?"

The text was equally forceful and couched in emotive language: "How can a company of Dow Jones's reputation persist in a coercive attempt to squeeze out the minority shareholders of Telerate at the low-ball price of $18 a share?" Dow Jones was accused of refusing "to engage in anything resembling good faith negotiations." The ad called for a bid of not less than $25 a share. "We are forced to consider Dow Jones's actions as hostile—to Telerate's shareholders, management, and employees. The executive directors of Telerate will not tender any shares. In addition, we recommend that all other Telerate shareholders not tender their shares. So what now,

---

[2] Affidavit of William R. Clabby, October 27, 1929 (Court of Chancery, New Castle County, Delaware)

Dow Jones? Does Dow Jones's name still stand for integrity and fairness?"

The advertisement carried the signatures of the four executive directors and of two independent directors, Frederick Frank of Shearson Lehman Hutton, and Timothy Neher, president of Continental Cablevision. (Continental, as the reader will recall, was a former Dow Jones investment vehicle, and by way of further irony, Neher had been elected to Telerate's board after being introduced to Hirsch by Warren Phillips.)

"The ad should get Phillips's attention," Terranova chortled.

It did, and it was for that reason that the advertisement never made it into print. The *Wall Street Journal*, in common with most newspapers, operated some kind of fail-safe procedure to screen advertisements of a controversial nature, especially those involving Dow Jones itself. The mechanism, though seldom invoked, gave Phillips the opportunity to pull any offensive advertisements at the last minute. Fail-safe worked; Phillips was tipped off about the Telerate bombshell just before the print run. Thoroughly alarmed at the embarrassing prospect of being attacked in his own newspaper by a prospective subsidiary, he put a call through to Hirsch.

"You can't run this, Neil," Phillips said. "Just think of the terrible publicity for both companies."

"Terrible for Dow Jones," Hirsch told him, "but not for Telerate."

Phillips was reduced to pleading. "Let's do this. Let's hold the ad for twenty-four hours. That'll give us a chance to talk. Maybe we can work something out."

"Okay," Hirsch agreed. "Just twenty-four hours. But if we can't reach a deal, the ad goes ahead."

Meanwhile, Hirsch had formed a special committee of the two independent directors to determine the fairness of the bid. Frank and Neher duly announced on October 10 that they had "unanimously determined ... that [the] Dow Jones tender offer is inadequate and not in the best interests of Telerate and its stockholders..."

As it happened, their press release went out the day after Telerate reported rather disappointing third-quarter results. At $128 million, revenue was only £1 million higher than the previous quarter and net income was actually down $2 million, which Hirsch attributed to the cost of developing TTS. He added that the joint venture with ATT would "continue to affect results for the remainder of the year." He also disclosed that Telerate was negotiating to buy out ATT's half-share in the business, which would result in a further short-term drag on earnings. The news did nothing to help Telerate's cause.

Phillips was advised to seize on these negative developments to justify the $18 bid price. He confirmed as much later. "The economic downturn of '89–'90 was severe. We were laying off people right and left. It was a tough time.

And in this environment, some of Telerate's costs and other problems started to surface. Telerate's customer service, for example, was less than perfect. That's why we offered the price we did for the last of the Telerate shares."

But rather than brandish a stick, Phillips offered an olive branch. He needed a settlement more than he wanted an argument. Sensing as much, Hirsch asked Neher to arrange a private meeting with Phillips. Neher booked the appointment, with an admonition from Hirsch that Telerate was in no mood to compromise. "Anything less than $21 a share and we fight on," Hirsch told him. Some investors were still baying for $25 or more, but that went too far, and even Hirsch was starting to tire of conflict.

Neher called back elated. Phillips had surrendered at $21 a share without much of a fight. Hirsch, having just added several million dollars to his already considerable fortune, was delighted, too. "My only regret is that we never got to run the ad," he said, rather peevishly. It was not a matter for regret, as the text leaked out to the press anyway.

Phillips, though publicly relieved, was privately furious. He had suffered a personal humiliation. It must have been hard to bear, especially as Wall Street now calculated the final cost of the creeping tender. Analysts had found the dispute, and particularly the manner of settling it, perplexing. It raised all kinds of awkward questions. If Telerate really was worth $1.6 billion, why had Dow Jones quibbled over a few hundred million dollars? Was it because Telerate's business was starting to falter? If so, why the abject capitulation? And why provoke a public squabble that was bound to damage both companies? Phillips could only smile through gritted teeth and dismiss the incident as a minor family tiff, now resolved and best forgotten.

Phillips organized a celebratory, let's-get-to-know-each-other-better party for key Telerate and Dow Jones managers. It was held at the Whitney Museum of Modern Art, where one of his daughters worked. The gathering exuded an atmosphere of forced bonhomie, but the tensions were palpable.

Phillips took to the podium and in the emollient language reserved for such occasions declared how pleased he was to welcome the Telerate family into the Dow Jones family.

Bill Clabby found it necessary to add a few reminisces about the "good old days," when he and Claude Erbsen and Neil Hirsch had toured Europe to establish Telerate there. Then he made a tactical mistake: he offered the microphone to Hirsch to share the memory. Hirsch's response was short and to the point, and given the occasion, rather unfortunate. "To be honest, Bill, I hardly remember a fucking thing about it."

There were guffaws from the Telerate attendees, embarrassed titters from the Dow Jones people, unaccustomed to hearing the F-word used in front of royalty. Phillips could only smile wanly. The smile remained in place even when Hirsch presented him with a framed copy of the "What Now, Dow Jones" ad.

Phillips wasted no time exacting his revenge, and I would be cast in the role of an unwitting accomplice.

Soon after the Whitney Museum party, yet another invitation arrived from Dow Jones's chief executive. Would I care to come over right away—for coffee and a chat? Flattery was the first order of business. "I've been very impressed with how you've handled yourself," Phillips said, and proceeded to illustrate the point with a few examples. I could sense that he was holding back the punchline.

"So, what I'd like to say is that we want you to take charge of Telerate's operations, effective immediately." Answering my question before I had asked it, he added, "Neil and John will be staying, but with no executive responsibilities. We'll still be able to call on them for the benefit of their experience, of course, but they'll act strictly as advisors." There was another shoe to drop. "You'll report to Carl Valenti, who's being appointed president of Telerate. Any problems with that?"

Valenti's promotion explained why Valenti himself had asked me to lunch two days earlier, ostensibly for "a casual exchange of views." Valenti was pleasant enough but I found him a cipher. His reputation was that of a man of no specific talent except in the art of political survival, which usually involves giving away nothing. Nothing was what he had given away to me; there had been no hint of Phillips's impending surprise. As for Valenti, the little that I had known about him before lunch was precisely what I knew after it.

Valenti's elevation to the Telerate post was his second promotion in the space of a few weeks. Earlier, he had been named head of the Information Services Group, Bill Dunn's old job. Dunn, his friend and mentor, had left the company in a huff after being told by Phillips that Peter Kann would replace the retiring Ray Shaw as president and chief operating officer. It was the job Dunn had long coveted, felt he deserved, and had confidently expected to get. He felt that he had been thwarted by the tradition of appointing only journalists to the executive office. Nor was he alone in thinking so. But he had done himself no favors by exhibiting some odd traits, including a few unaccountable emotional outbursts widely attributed to heavy drinking. As Phillips later explained, "Bill Dunn was smart, brilliant, a visionary. But in the last year or so his behavior was off the charts. There was an instability about him, as if he were reacting to some inner tension, which made me fear he could not do the job."[3]

Valenti shed no tears over his friend's self-destruction. He confided to me

---

[3] Francis X. Dealy, Jr., *The Power and the Money*, Birch Lane Press, 1993, p.332

over lunch, "Bill wasn't the architect of all his achievements, he just took all the credit for them. Bill was very big into self-promotion." Later, Valenti told an interviewer that Dunn had called him for advice immediately after the Kann announcement. "I didn't try to persuade him [from quitting]. Bill was not an operator. He was no longer needed at Dow Jones."

With friends like that…

Dunn's departure may not have bothered Valenti but it was a cruel blow to Telerate. For years Dunn and Ray Shaw had been the only senior executives prepared to promote Telerate's interests at Dow Jones. Now that both of them had gone, Telerate stood alone in a corporate world of strangers, most of them indifferent to its fate. (Shaw was still around. After retirement, he stayed on as a consultant, and remained for a time on the Telerate board, though without the power or influence that would have made him useful.)

It was the sense of Telerate's vulnerability that as much as anything influenced my decision to accept Phillips's offer. I added a further rationalization for agreeing to report to Valenti. He was, I told myself, the choice of Telerate's owner, which meant apparently that he was admired by Phillips and Kann. Even Dunn had spoken well of him. Telerate desperately needed to be represented by a sympathetic senior figure in the Dow Jones organization, someone familiar with its personalities and its politics.

With Dunn gone, there was nobody who could do it except perhaps Clabby, whose star seemed to be waning and who, frankly, seemed to be lacking his old fizz.

And so Phillips and I shook hands. He seemed very pleased with himself. "Dow Jones and Telerate are going to achieve great things together," he bubbled, rolling out the standard platitudes. "I'm really looking forward to working with you and your team." Kann popped in, beaming as usual, to add his congratulations.

Hirsch was visibly shocked when I gave him the news, shaking his head sadly. He despised Valenti. He told me then what he told an interviewer later: "We all knew Valenti was a lightweight, Bill Dunn's bag carrier. I said so [to Phillips] but I didn't beat on the desk. I figured Jessop would never take the job."

"Why the hell did you?" he asked at the time. "Carl Valenti knows shit about our business and everyone knows he's a fuckin' snake in the grass. You two will never get along. All this is typical Dow Jones bullshit."

He was right. Phillips, it seemed, had arranged to meet me separately, and only minutes after meeting with Hirsch, depriving us of the chance to confer. He had pulled a fast one on both of us. It left a sour taste. If Hirsch and I *had* conferred, would it have made a difference? Perhaps, but to this day I am not entirely sure.

"You can still change your mind," Hirsch said in a hopeful tone. I felt, however, that the die had been cast. Anyway, I told Hirsch, a policy of passive resistance, or non-cooperation, or whatever it was, made little sense. I put my case to him in the form of questions. What should I have done? Refused the job? Resigned on the spot? Taken the job but insisted on nominating my boss? The last, on reflection, might have been the best option, though it was hardly a practical one. Phillips, I pointed out, was bound to put his own man in to oversee Telerate, especially with earnings under pressure and TTS struggling for market acceptance. Now more than ever, Telerate needed a champion at Dow Jones, even if it had to be Valenti. If Telerate's management refused to cooperate, as Hirsch seemed to be proposing, then Phillips would be obliged to install his own managers—a foolproof recipe, we both agreed, for running the company into the ground.

Hirsch shook his head, plainly not convinced by my line of argument. But he recognized that he did not have an effective one of his own. "I think we can agree on one thing," he said. "We've both been had and Telerate's been had. And the sad thing is that it can only end in tears."

Truer words were never spoken.

# *Casualties*

January can be a trying month. For Telerate, the 1990 version was particularly testing. The merger with Dow Jones, formally completed two days into the year, was an occasion to consider the prospects of life under yet another new owner, Telerate's third in a decade.

A study of the habits of new owners pointed to the probability of changes both in method and style. Telerate employees evinced their usual cheery optimism, which dovetailed nicely with their other residual qualities of pragmatism and resilience. They were a proud group, with much to be proud of. There were, of course, underlying anxieties. The most prominent was that Dow Jones would impose changes that would extinguish the company's unique spirit. Since that spirit was embodied to a large extent in the recently demoted figure of Neil Hirsch, it had all the potential to become a divisive issue. I mentioned it as an aside to Warren Phillips at one of our now routine lunches. He offered soothing words of reassurance. "Don't worry. That spirit is part of what we've bought. We're anxious to preserve it." I was sure he meant it, too.

Some of his senior colleagues appeared to have different ideas. Kevin Roche, Dow Jones's deputy chief financial officer, a combative Boston-Irish sourpuss, seemed to relish the prospect of implementing draconian reforms. "We're gonna shake this company up," he told me one day, rather in the tone of a Marine drill instructor about to get his hands on a squad of raw recruits. "We'll have to straighten out the financial side especially. Some of your people are just out of control. This whole damned thing is a mess." The tone was hostile, and that "we" sounded like the royal pronoun. It was hard to tell whether he actually believed what he was saying or was merely intent on asserting his new authority to impress. Either way, they were rich remarks coming from someone who knew, as he uttered them, that Dow Jones was about to come out with poor financial results that would contrast sharply with Telerate's still relatively buoyant figures. He was clearly a man intent on cleansing the temple whether it needed cleansing or not. I bit my lip and made a mental note to myself: Roche was a man to be treated with caution.

Roche was right in one respect, even if he hadn't mentioned it specifically: the faltering TTS project was giving rise to real concern. It was leeching cash and diverting resources, and sales were disappointing. It was already apparent that TTS was no sprinter; the question was whether it would prove a long-distance runner. Even the ever-optimistic David Barnes admitted that progress was painfully slow, but he continued to make encouraging noises. Rumbold and Wiseman reminded me that I had warned the board that critical mass would not be achieved overnight. We all agreed, however, that as soon as TTS was established and producing healthy revenue, a number of radical design changes would become necessary.

There had been one TTS development that some construed as positive. We had disposed of ATT by purchasing its half-share in the venture. I found it positive only in the sense that we were relieved of the burden of attending pointless meetings and enduring endless backbiting. It was, in fact, an admission of failure and the consequence of a bad original decision. Our partner had contributed nothing of value to the project and could be said to have held it back. But ATT's lawyers had no intention of riding into the sunset without a final shoot-out. They were masters of simulated outrage, which they reinforced with far-fetched calculations of the financial losses incurred and the corporate anxiety suffered. After weeks of painful negotiation, we reluctantly agreed to cough up close to $40 million for ATT's share. Critics of the deal offered the opinion that a fairer deal would have had ATT paying us. It was hard to disagree with them but that was never likely to happen and we needed to move on. It was, for me, an occasion to renew a pledge: no more joint ventures.

Meanwhile, Carl Valenti and I had settled into an uneasy working relationship. For "relationship" I almost wrote "truce," but so far there had been no real hostilities. To be honest, there had not been much of anything. Valenti was evidently held in high esteem at Dow Jones. At Telerate he was an enigma. The rarity of his visits to Telerate offered nothing in the way of clarification.

Valenti obviously felt he could be more effective working out of his own office at Dow Jones. But more effective at what? Courting the approbation of his senior management was one explanation, which was usually expressed in less delicate language. Terranova had another. "The bastard's avoiding us so he won't have to make any decisions." Whatever the reason, the general's prolonged absences from the front struck many of his troops as a curious way to discharge his duties. We were left to fret anxiously about the character, judgment and management style of the new chief executive.

In appearance Valenti was unremarkable. He was fifty-something, slightly built and of medium height. A well-lived-in face conveyed a vaguely decadent look. It was topped by crinkly iron-gray hair, which in some men might have lent distinction. He dressed conservatively in the uniform of a pinstriped suit. It was invariably worn with a vest that was usually unbuttoned. The other jarring touch came from ever-present, high-heeled, pointed-toe, alligator boots. Shit-kickers, they call them in Texas. He walked with a jaunty, shoulder-rolling gait and smoked as if it were an Olympic event, the cigarette always held Bogie-style between thumb and forefinger. The general impression was that of a B-movie actor typecast as a mobster's sidekick.

In our personal backgrounds, Valenti and I had much in common. We both came from inner-city backgrounds, mine in London's East End, his on New York's Lower East Side. Our accents betrayed their respective origins. Each of us had worked our way through life without the advantages of higher education. We had both spent a working lifetime in the information business, in my case virtually straight from school, in his after two years of service with the Air Force. There was even the shared experience of living with a Telerate employee, in my case former, in his, current. In the social context, comparisons were harder to draw. We both enjoyed a drink after work, but I cannot recall us ever having one together. Valenti appeared to have few interests outside the office. My impression was that his marital history might be as complex as my own, but he never talked about it, or about any other aspects of his private life. I resolved not to talk about mine, either, though he seemed to know more about it already than I would have volunteered.

It was hardly a state secret that our management styles differed. They sprang from two distinct personalities. To point out the differences is to risk self-justification, but I do so because they affected a working relationship that was crucial to Telerate's future.

My approach to business, as to life, tended to be open, breezy, and somewhat diffident—perhaps to a fault in all three respects. Valenti operated by stealth and calculation. Both were deployed, as far as I could see, to ensure his survival in the snake-infested swamp of Dow Jones politics. Of course, we were both influenced by the contrasting cultures of our respective companies. Telerate was driven by confident intuition. Decisions were validated by feet-on-the-coffee-table, brainstorming sessions in Neil Hirsch's office. Dow Jones deplored intuition. Its decisions emerged from endless deliberation, always guided by an aversion to risk. Meetings were formal, over-populated, and designed, it seemed to me, more for grandstanding than decision making. The company's most democratic forum was a management committee of about twenty department heads. Convened irregularly, it functioned more as a parliament than a committee, a venue for interminable talkathons dominated by windy oratory from *Wall Street Journal* editors.

Valenti brought to Telerate the public reticence he had practiced to perfection at Dow Jones; he asked questions occasionally but offered opinions rarely. An abhorrence of politics, or naïveté, often left my flanks as exposed as those of Foch's army at Verdun. Valenti extended coverage of his flanks to his front and rear. If these defensive maneuvers left little scope for advance or retreat, they also rendered him impregnable to attack. He played corporate politics with impressive skill but always, I felt, with the instincts of someone more determined to survive than to achieve.

In exchanging informal banter with Telerate people, Valenti often seemed ill at ease, but he was a clever picker of brains and the wheels of calculation were forever turning. His impulse was to manage by fiat, but only to implement the decisions of others. He himself seldom made decisions without a broad consensus offering plenty of scope for deniability. There was one overriding professional distinction between us. I tended to concentrate on managing downward, Valenti on managing upward. While I could claim a certain skill in my direction, he was undoubtedly brilliant in his.

Years later, I was quoted somewhere as saying that we argued endlessly. That is not my recollection. It is, rather, that we found little to say to each other. What little time we did have together was spent dancing around each other in a kind of lobster quadrille. The result was that we never got around to the essential business of setting out a business agenda. I certainly had one in my mind and there is no reason to doubt that Valenti had one in his, but at no time were we in danger of putting the two together.

Our combined failure was negligence of a high order. I doubt that he would make the same confession.

The effect was to raise my level of frustration, which increased steadily during the weeks following our appointments. It was manifested in minor tremors rather than in major eruptions, but a Vesuvian explosion always threatened. One occurred during a trip to Los Angeles, where I was due to speak as part of a Dow Jones management presentation to newspaper analysts.

The evening before flying out, I took a call at home from Valenti. "How are you getting out there?" he wanted to know. I told him I was booked on an early-morning commercial flight. "Cancel it," he instructed. "Some of us are going out on the company plane. You should join us. It'll save time."

That was fine with me, except for a serious logistical problem. The Dow Jones plane, a well-traveled Hawker Siddeley (which Dow Jones had inexplicably chosen to keep in preference to Telerate's spanking new Gulfstream) was parked in Princeton, New Jersey, a two-to-three-hour drive in rush-hour traffic from my home in Connecticut. "Don't worry about that," Valenti said, "I'll send the company helicopter to pick you up. You'll be down here in half an hour." As indeed I was.

On arrival at Princeton I expected to find a full complement of Dow Jones executives but, other than Valenti and me, the only passenger on the plane was Kevin Roche. As glumly irascible as ever, he told me he intended to take advantage of five hours in the air—extended in the event by a two-hour delay in taking off and a one-hour refueling stop in Des Moines, Iowa—to give a lecture on Telerate's profligate attitude to expenses. It was started somewhere over Pennsylvania and ended over Illinois. As it happened, I found myself in reluctant agreement with much of what he had to say, but his approach was all belligerence and sarcasm, delivered with a fixed leer. One of his contentions was so absurd that I was tempted to deck him. Telerate, he complained, was "constantly flying people all over the fucking world with no real purpose. It has to stop." My response, under the circumstances, was a model of restraint. "All I can say, Kevin, is that your comments are breathtakingly stupid, coming from someone sitting on a corporate jet designed for eight passengers and carrying only three." The take-off and landing fees alone, I pointed out, would have dwarfed the regular commercial fares. Add the cost of fuel, and the helicopter shuttle, and the bill must be preposterous. I invited him to calculate it. "And when you've done that, if your calculator can accommodate all the fucking zeroes, you'll figure out that your comments are hypocritical bullshit."

Roche had no intention of engaging in mathematics. He was too busy working himself into a rage. "This is typical of Telerate. Here we are trying to bring some semblance of order and common sense to the business, and you're fighting us all the way."

We spent the rest of the flight in stony silence. Valenti had said nothing throughout this spat. Hunched over papers near the front of the plane, he had either studiously ignored the row or quietly enjoyed it. I suspected the latter. The cipher playing the enigma. Of one thing I could be certain: my disrespectful outburst would be reported to Phillips or Kann at the earliest possible opportunity.

Though hardly a major incident in itself, the row typified a condescending attitude to Telerate that was all too prevalent at Dow Jones. It represented an imperialistic view of Telerate as a troublesome colony riddled with troublemakers intent on insurrection. The next episode in the colonial uprising—of which I was now presumably marked as a ringleader—was far more serious.

One evening early in May, three Telerate managers appeared in succession at my office door to demand an explanation. I had just returned from a client visit. In my absence there had been a TTS meeting. Each of them had attended it. I had not been invited, for reasons that were unclear then but make sense now. The first visitor was Brian O'Heron, in his customary state of high dudgeon, joined minutes later by Scott Rumbold and David Barnes, both in barely less a state of agitation. What I was invited to explain was why a decision had been made to abandon TTS. "No such decision has been taken," was my response—to which I felt obliged to add, "at least not to my knowledge."

How had this rumor started?

"It's no rumor," said O'Heron. "We've just been in a TTS meeting with Carl Valenti and he says we're killing the project. If it's true, how come you weren't there to tell us yourself? If it's not, then just what the hell is going on?" I called Valenti to find out.

"It's complete crap," he responded. "I said no such thing."

"Then how do you explain the fact that I've just had three managers in my office saying that's exactly what you said?"

"Well, they're not telling the truth," Valenti said.

"So, you're saying all three of them are lying. Or maybe that they're just plain mixed up? If that's the case, how do you explain the shared confusion?"

Valenti adopted a patronizing tone. "Look, you of all people should be able to figure it out. This is just Telerate political bullshit. Just remember, they've all got axes to grind."

"Politics my ass. I know these guys. They wouldn't lie."

"Then you're as good as calling me a liar. I resent that."

"I haven't called anyone a liar," I exploded, "But I've got three senior executives here giving me one account, and you a different one, of a meeting I knew nothing about. And all you can tell me is that they're playing political games. I'd call that the real bullshit."

There was no response. I broke the silence with a proposition, in hindsight a foolish one. "Look, I think we need to talk about this face-to-face, clear the air. Maybe Warren Phillips should be involved. How about tomorrow morning?"

Valenti promised to call me back. He did, with an invitation to meet with Peter Kann at eleven o'clock. Phillips was out of town.

In every life there occurs at least one of those dark metaphorical journeys on which the unwary traveler, fascinated as if bewitched, is taken to a place where dangerous beasts are known to lurk. My meeting with Kann was such a journey.

Kann kept us waiting a few minutes while he escorted an advertising representative from *Playboy* magazine, a tall willowy blonde, to the elevator. "Well, there's one good reason to take out an ad," he quipped as he returned. He settled into an armchair and lit a small cheroot. He had on his crooked grin, but he seemed nervous. I had no doubt, not a scintilla of a doubt, that Valenti had already briefed him. "So what do we have to talk about today?" he asked perkily.

I spent the next ten minutes telling him. To say that I lost my cool would be an exaggeration; to say that I spoke with a blunt abandon not normally advisable in a meeting with the head of one's company is probably undeniable. I say "probably" because much of what I said is beyond recollection, memory loss being the first casualty of anger. What I do remember distinctly is that during Kann's long and rather limpid response, I heard myself repeating, over and over again, a single dogmatic mantra: "Peter, this is just not going to work out."

How many times I said it is beyond my recall, but it was often enough to goad Kann into an angry response. "Okay, if it's not going to work out, then you'd better do what you have to do." Without hesitation I replied, "You'll have my resignation on your desk this afternoon."

And that was that. Kann looked thunderous. Valenti, who had not said a word, studied the yellow legal pad balanced on his knee. It was blank I noticed, as I rose to leave.

Kann and Valenti may have more precise, perhaps differing, recollections of the event, but I think I've captured the gist of it.

I hurried back to Telerate to brief Hirsch and Terranova. "Resign?" exclaimed Hirsch, genuinely taken aback. "Don't be so fucking stupid. I'm going over to see Kann right now, get this whole thing straightened out."

"My guess is that it's too late for that," I warned him. "I really pushed him into a corner. I honestly don't think he can find a way out of it."

That proved to be the case.

For months afterward, I pondered a few alternative consequences. What if Warren Phillips had not been away? Would a meeting with him have taken a different turn? Would I have been less angry? Almost certainly, I would say—and I'm sure that Phillips would have handled the situation more adroitly than Kann had. Could Valenti and I have patched things up over a drink? Perhaps, but I doubt it. We were on different wavelengths. What wavelengths are ciphers on? Anyway, the man had more than a few reasons to rejoice at my departure. Frankly, I was glad to see the back of him, too.

Packing up my office that afternoon, I received a parting gift from Dow Jones. Peter Skinner, an executive vice president and house counsel, faxed over a press release for my approval. I had no hesitation giving it, but asked that the statement be delayed until I had reached my wife in case she heard the news from someone else. Skinner's response was unyielding. "We want it out right now, before the market closes. That's our policy. If you want to tell your wife, you'd better find a way to reach her right now, but I'm afraid that's your problem."

I had been in the job just four months. That, I suppose, counts as a meteoric career—but then shooting stars always have short lives. My wife's wistful comment was that the only shooting involved came from me taking aim at my foot.

With three of Telerate's four senior executives now out of the way, Valenti was free to assume unfettered control of the company. Rappaport, no admirer of Valenti or Dow Jones, stayed on. "I don't know why I don't just get out, too," he told me with a sad look as we shook hands. "My guess is that I won't be here much longer, anyway. Or TTS."

My guess, too, was that TTS would be gone in a matter of weeks. In the event, the patient lingered well into 1991 before Dow Jones finally unplugged the life-support system. The company took a $30 million write-off. That figure, when added to the $40 million paid to ATT and the project's operating expenses, made TTS a $100 million cock-up. But what kind of cock-up, exactly?

David Barnes, though plainly not the most objective source, was in a better position than most to deliver an opinion. Barnes thought TTS had "come close to making it." How close? "Well, the service was working well. We had $7 million in signed contracts and were doing more in certain currencies after three months than Reuters. The product was not perfect, but at every show we attended traders took to it with ease. We had the fastest and most reliable network, four-conversation capability, profit and loss in real times, and order entry for trades done. In short, it was superior to anything else." Well, I did say he was not the most objective source.

If TTS had all those qualities, why did it not succeed? Barnes believed that, given another year or two, it would have succeeded. "It needed three things: more marketing talent, especially in the regions, fewer internal agendas, and above all time more to succeed. It had taken Reuters five years to get anywhere with Dealing. TTS was killed within two years of launch. In eighteen months we built the software, hardware, sales teams, and a global network reaching thirty-five centers. No one has ever come close to this effort."

"Internal agendas" is a phrase that catches the eye. Throughout the latter stages of the TTS project it seemed to be constantly dragged down by political undertows. There remained the unsolved mystery of what Valenti did or did not say to O'Heron, Rumbold, and Barnes immediately preceding my departure. Then there was what struck me as the unhelpful attitudes of two of Telerate's regional managers, Becher and Childs. Neither was brave enough to express open hostility to TTS but both found it difficult to camouflage their doubts that it would prevail. They seemed to resent that precious resources were being diverted to it. It goes without saying that Valenti agreed with them.

All of which became even more curious when, during what were destined to be the dying days of TTS, Valenti and Becher paired up to champion an alternative foreign-exchange transaction product, while Childs and Clabby combined forces to push for another.

Three weeks after I left Telerate, Valenti, attending the annual Forex convention in Madrid, was openly declaring to TTS sales executives that the project was all but dead, thereby ensuring that it soon would be. The general assumption was that Valenti was opposed in principle to Telerate offering a transaction service. This was not entirely true, and Valenti proved it in Madrid, where he had been given a demonstration there of a product called FXNET, a foreign-exchange netting and trade-tracking system developed jointly by

Quotron and its owner, Citicorp. Thoroughly impressed, Valenti approached Quotron to suggest some kind of working relationship. Quotron seemed equally interested and several follow-up meetings were held in New York. But Valenti had put the cart before the horse. Burenga intervened, to order a due-diligence report on the system. A comprehensive review produced by David Barnes and Dennis Warner, a Telerate technical manager, was predictably cool to the idea. The Quotron product, they said, was similar to TTS in many respects, but inferior in most of them. The negotiations with Quotron died a natural death.

But all was not lost! A second possible alternative to TTS had appeared in far-off Japan. Minex, a foreign-exchange trading system developed and jointly owned by a consortium of Japanese banks and KDD, the Japanese state-owned telephone utility, had caught the fancy of Julian Childs. He in turn found a sponsor in Bill Clabby, who was highly suspicious of Quotron and, it may be presumed in light of their adversarial history, of Valenti. The campaign was joined, indeed may have been inspired, by Fumio Matsuo, a general manager of Kyodo, Telerate's Japanese distributor. Matsuo's interest in Minex was excited less by his view of its business potential than by his lifelong patriotic compulsion to promote the interests of Japan in an industry dominated by Western enterprises. Matsuo was a curious mixture of Eastern and Western tastes. A modernist, he was also passionate about Japanese traditions. An admirer of all things American, he was also a proud member of Japan's dormant samurai class. His grandfather, a retired army officer, had sacrificed his life trying, unsuccessfully, to protect Prime Minister Keisuke Okada, his brother-in-law, from assassins during the failed coup of 1936. A former Washington correspondent for Kyodo, Matsuo saw in Dow Jones an exemplar of American journalistic excellence. He had always respected Bill Clabby but secretly scorned Carl Valenti as a vulgarian with poor manners.

An investment in Minex was quickly negotiated, Telerate paying $10 million for an equity interest of 4 percent, acquiring in return exclusive distribution rights to the product outside Japan. Once this was accomplished, TTS could be shut down for good and the project team folded into Minex.

All this provided a fascinating glimpse of Dow Jones's bewildering approach to management, to marketing, and to Telerate. The view of Valenti and Clabby, neither of whom knew the first thing about foreign exchange, was apparently that TTS, a transaction product already up and running, and—if Barnes and other project managers were to be believed—making progress, ought to be abandoned in favor of an unproven competitor. If Clabby and Valenti had put their heads together, done a minimal amount of homework, and picked one alternative, their antagonism towards TTS might have made sense. Instead, flying by the seats of their pants, they seemed intent to compete not only with TTS but also between themselves. It left TTS executives, even as they battled to keep the project afloat, watching in astonishment as two senior management figures openly flirted with two of its potential rivals.

What both men should have recognized was that both FXNET and Minex were fatally flawed, if only because of ownership issues—Quotron because it was tied to a single bank, Minex because it was effectively tied to a particular country. Other considerations were ignored. Quotron, assuming its interest in a joint venture had ever been real, was never likely to give Telerate more than a junior partnership. Equally, Telerate's equity stake in Minex could only become interesting if Minex first succeeded in Japan. In the event, both companies failed. Even more curiously, both met the same fate. They were subsumed into yet another foreign-exchange trading initiative called the Electronic Brokerage Service, this one owned by a coalition of twelve major European and American banks.

This sudden epidemic of transaction services suggested that banks everywhere were looking for an alternative to Reuters. From this fact, any company other than Dow Jones might reasonably have concluded that electronic foreign-exchange trading might just be the right business to be in. But Dow Jones was not looking ahead. In closing TTS, Dow Jones had no more motive than reducing Telerate's operating expenses and, in pursuing partnerships with others, had reverted once again to its ingrained habit of avoiding risk. Dow Jones painted TTS as a fiasco. Well, having closed it down, they would. Whether it was a fiasco, or a project that, given enough time and money, might have succeeded, will forever remain an open question. I remain an unrepentant advocate.

In the end, Dow Jones—that is, Telerate—came up with nothing; the worst of all possible results.

Mine was not the only senior departure from Dow Jones in 1990. Towards the end of the year, Warren Phillips announced his retirement after sixteen years as chief executive. He was invited to remain on the board. He left a company grappling with more than a few problems, of which Telerate was among the most intractable. His performance during his final years in the top job had attracted more than a few critics. I had become one of them. His handling of the Telerate acquisition had been expensive and clumsy. In the matter of my appointment he had proved devious. In all my other dealings with him, however, I had found him to be fair and considerate. Returning a compliment, I wrote him a note saying so.

Phillips was duly succeeded as chairman and chief executive by his protégé Peter Kann, who in turn replaced himself with Ken Burenga as president and chief operating officer. There was a nice irony in this: the man blamed for spending an unwarranted fortune to buy Telerate would now be responsible for preserving the investment. For added piquancy, Burenga was known to have a very poor opinion of Valenti's management talents, and vice versa.

"This should be fun to watch," Terranova chortled.

Immediate management changes at Telerate were inevitable, too.

Julian Childs was announced as my successor. A former money broker, Childs had been "donated" to Telerate by Exco's Hong Kong office soon after the Telerate purchase. The son of a retired British diplomat and a French mother, he was raised in Istanbul. He boasted a Cambridge education and spoke fluent French and passable Turkish. From a height of six feet three inches he dispensed an enigmatic charm that seemed to turn people on or off in equal measure. As a dashing bachelor with a face some might call handsome, he had acquired a pin-up celebrity that attracted the curiosity of the opposite sex inside and outside Telerate. His management in Asia had been competent but, in my view, was open to criticism for too often placing regional above corporate interests. In that regard, he had been poorly served with partisan advice from management colleagues largely made up of expatriate misfits. He had little grasp of technology or strategy and was as uncurious as he was uncontroversial. I liked him personally, but thought of him as someone who would ride rather than create waves. In that respect he was tailormade for Dow Jones.

Opportunity knocked, too, for Henry Becher, one of the malcontents who stepped boldly from the shadows as soon as I had left. A year or so earlier, I had persuaded him to leave Canada to manage Telerate's North American Division, created by me as a third profit center to stand alongside Europe and Asia. Soon after that, I persuaded Rick Snape to return to New York after a three-year posting in London to take up a position as his deputy. Becher immediately voiced an objection to Snape on the grounds that he, Becher, ought to have the right to name his own deputy. There was some merit in the argument, but not much. I thought I had done Becher a favor; Snape knew considerably more about Telerate's business than Becher did and had international experience. Becher, in response to my question, denied holding any personal grudge against Snape. "In which case," I told him, "I'm sure you two can work out a way to work together."

But Becher continued to fret—about Snape and about various other matters. Twice he tendered his resignation, each time by means of an obtuse, scribbled note left in my in-tray overnight. Each one had all the hallmarks of having been composed in a bar. My response was to ignore them, a policy justified by the fact that on both occasions Becher failed to say anything the morning after he had written them. Becher was one of the few Telerate managers who enjoyed Valenti's company. It encouraged the widespread belief that he was a Dow Jones mole.

But even moles surface occasionally.

Whatever other interests Valenti and Becher might have had in common, it was soon clear that they shared a distaste for Snape. It came as no surprise, then, when, a few weeks after my departure, Snape was ceremoniously frog-marched out of the office by a security guard. The stated reasons, as related to me by Snape, seemed trivial. The real reason, we both suspected, was that he had been expunged as "one of Jessop's boys."

"I think Telerate is about to be rebuilt in Valenti's image," was Snape's interpretation of his fate.

Hirsch and Terranova remained under house arrest for two more years before being consigned to permanent exile. Rappaport left with them. "One step ahead of the axe," as he put it. Scott Rumbold, by now friendless and neglected, soon joined Market Data Corporation, an information offshoot of Cantor Fitzgerald run by Rod Fisher, Bernie Cantor's nephew-in-law, who had left Telerate several years earlier. Brian O'Heron went back to the telephone industry from which he had sprung, taking most of his technical group with him.

A changing of the guard was hardly unexpected. What left me puzzled, as it did others peering into the palace forecourt through the railings, was that at no time during the ceremony did Dow Jones show the slightest inclination to fill senior Telerate vacancies with Telerate managers, or to strengthen the company's governance in other ways. Roche claimed, of course, that he had purged the company of financial mismanagement. Burenga put in a few appearances at Telerate. Kann hardly seemed interested.

Surely, critics asked, a $1.6 billion-dollar investment was worthy of the attention of the chief executive. Even worthier, they argued, than the *Wall Street Journal*, which, although feeling the effects of the recession in the form of sharply reduced advertising and circulation, was hardly under threat, at least not in the short term.

Telerate, on the other hand, was imminently endangered by fundamental factors such as heightened competition and product deficiencies, squeezed from above by Reuters and from below by Bloomberg. A newcomer, Knight-Ridder, added to the discomfort by picking off Telerate's weaker clients.

Canceling TTS had temporarily boosted Telerate's bottom line, but without a transaction product what other arrows did Telerate have in its quiver? A stand-alone bond analysis service called Teletrac found a few takers. So did Giltnet, a rudimentary bond analytical product developed in Australia by a South African entrepreneur named David Vanrenen, who, as soon as Telerate had demonstrated that it was incapable of selling the product in large numbers, took Giltnet and himself off to Reuters, which sold even fewer.

Third-party service providers, contributing analysis and other subjective material, produced income that generated more than 20 percent of Telerate's revenue, but Telerate had to share much of this. Telerate was otherwise reliant on the income from its basic service, still represented by the old green-screen, page-based terminal. That product had served Telerate well since the early 1970s and it still worked well enough. But it was like an antique car: it could not travel at speed, guzzled fuel, and needed constant maintenance. In short, it was starting to acquire the unmistakable aura of obsolescence.

If distant alarm bells were tolling, Kann seemed deaf to them, continuing to express his satisfaction both with Valenti's management and Telerate's progress. The 1991 annual report noted with satisfaction that Telerate had "proved to be the strongest component of Dow Jones." The company had indeed reported strong results that year, posting a rise in earnings of 25 percent. Analysts noted, however, that the increase was largely a rebound from a 1990 figure depressed by TTS expenses. Revenue, a more reliable guide to underlying business health, had actually fallen 3 percent. Telerate, along with Dow Jones Information Services, looked strong in relative terms because the *Journal* had suffered such a steep decline in revenue, which had fallen almost 10 percent from its 1983 peak.

A year later, Kann was still extolling Telerate's virtues, this time to *Forbes* magazine in an article that was highly critical of Dow Jones's risk averse management. "We are in no way unhappy with the price we paid for it [Telerate]. We are in no way unhappy with the results, and I think we bought it at strategically the right time."[1]

But the concern in investment circles contradicted the assertions that Dow Jones did not seem to have a coherent business strategy for Telerate, and Valenti seemed disinclined to produce one, presumably because Burenga had failed to insist that he did. The most glaring omission was the absence of an integrated strategy designed to exploit the supposed synergies between Telerate and its parent company. It had been glaring since 1985, the year in which Dow Jones first acquired its controlling interest. Admittedly Valenti and I, and others before us, had contributed little to the cause. Shame on us. But to observe that a thing has not been done is not the same as saying that it does not need doing.

Kann may have taken his eye off Telerate in favor of another medium—television. An opportunity to take Dow Jones into broadcasting, dramatically and on a large scale, presented itself late in 1990, shortly after he had been installed as chief executive. Financial News Network, a cable television network connected to thirty-five million American households but in a constant financial bind, was put up for sale. FNN by common consent was a natural fit for Dow Jones, a perfect outlet for copy from the *Wall Street Journal*,

---

[1] *Forbes* magazine, February 3, 1992

breaking stories from the Dow Jones newswires and prices from Telerate. Kann was keen to do a deal. FNN managers were even keener, anticipating that Dow Jones would need them all to keep the network running.

But old habits die hard. Kann hesitated, reverting to the familiar Dow Jones custom of refusing to act until all the familiar risk-avoidance contingencies had been assembled. These inevitably included taking on a co-investor. The partner of choice was Paramount, a cable television operator with a stake in USA Network, an all-news channel. At first, Paramount sounded enthusiastic but then pulled out of the deal before a bid could be prepared, ostensibly on the grounds that USA Network competed with FNN. Since Paramount had been aware of the fact from the start, it struck many as a lame excuse, and not the real one.

Disappointed but apparently undaunted, Kann turned to Westinghouse Broadcasting, with better luck. Westinghouse agreed to join Dow Jones as an equal partner. The purchase price they worked out was $90 million. Despite FNN's financial problems, many analysts considered it a steal at that price.

But then bad luck again intervened. With the Dow Jones-Westinghouse bid pending and virtually assured of success, FNN was forced to file for court protection under Chapter 11 of the bankruptcy code. That changed the rules of engagement, of course, and almost immediately a new suitor appeared in the formidable form of General Electric, owner of the CNBC cable network. GE, which had shown no previous interest in FNN, now put in a bid of $105 million. The presiding bankruptcy judge rejected it, but GE expressed its determination with a revised bid of $115 million. Dow Jones, having had plenty of time to think about its next move, responded with what many observers thought of as an extraordinarily foolish act. Kann countered with exactly the same bid but simultaneously filed a complaint with the Federal Trade Commission that a combination of CNBC and FNN would violate anti-trust laws. Dow Jones had miscalculated badly. The FTC ruled that GE would be an acceptable owner and deferred the decision on FNN's future owner to the court.

Dow Jones then, with yet more misplaced confidence, raised its bid to $167 million, of which $125 million was to be in cash, the balance in payments contingent on FNN's future earnings. GE hit back with a lower bid of $154 million, but which had the advantage of being all but $9 million in cash.

Bankruptcy proceedings are designed to secure maximum compensation for creditors, and cash always rules. In ignoring that obvious fact, Dow Jones had got it wrong again. The presiding judge had little choice but to award the winning bid to GE.

All this Michael Bloomberg, not yet embarked on his own ventures into broadcasting, had watched from the sidelines with apparent disinterest. He was, by his own admission, a late and reluctant convert to broadcasting as a medium for distributing business news. He turned down the chance to buy FNN on the basis of his long-standing build-rather-than-buy principle. "I was glad to leave them [Dow Jones and GE] fighting over it," he would say later, when he could afford to be smug. But if Michael Bloomberg had somehow missed a trick not looking at FNN, Dow Jones had missed a far bigger one by failing to land it. And Bloomberg had learned from the experience.

Michael Bloomberg made his first move into broadcasting, not into television but into radio. WNEW, a popular New York City music station, came on the market and Bloomberg snapped it up for $13.5 million. The call sign was immediately turned into WBBR, a twenty-four-hour business-news station. Television was a logical follow-up. Bloomberg Information Television was formed as a twenty-four-hour, seven-days-a-week service offering "business" and lifestyle programming. The initial offerings were limited and crude, but the packed, multi-screen format provided a perfect advertising vehicle for BIT's corporate cousin, the professional Bloomberg terminal. After that, Bloomberg-produced business and lifestyle programming began to infiltrate television and radio stations around the world.

Bloomberg was hardly modest or clandestine about any of this. Huge Bloomberg billboards suddenly dominated every highway into and out of New York City. The man was every bit the publicity-hound his rivals said he was, but the snipers were missing the point. The interdependence of Bloomberg's products, from print to desktop to broadcasting, was a source of strength. Michael Bloomberg had no problem grappling with the concept of synergies. Each product line, feeding off a common pool of information, helped to sell the others. As for Michael's self-promotion, while naming his company and all its products after himself may have satisfied his ego, it also reinforced the brand, exploiting America's fondness for Horatio Alger stories, especially those with an ethnic flavor.

The new decade had opened with enough omens and portents to suggest that business conditions would be far more challenging than in the previous one. Although few recognized it at the time, the early 1990s were replete with signals pointing to a general decline in the fortunes of the market-data industry.

Bloomberg, of course, was the one spectacular and instructive exception. The Evil Empire, as envious rivals were given to calling it, advanced relentlessly, knocking out Reuters, Telerate, and Knight-Ridder terminals indiscriminately. Bloomberg's annual growth rate stayed in double digits and kept rising, while those of its rivals slipped towards single digits and kept falling. Michael Bloomberg's eponymous enterprise and its founder were becoming conspicuously and, for his rivals, insufferably ubiquitous. And not just in the professional trading arena. Early in the decade Bloomberg launched an attack on the expanding consumer market, where business information aimed at private investors—day traders and assorted high-net-worth speculators—was becoming educational entertainment through the media of radio and television. Neither Reuters nor Telerate seemed terribly interested in broadcasting, except as a sideline, despite the obvious fact that while there were hundreds of thousands of professional customers for market data there were hundreds of millions of private investors looking for the same thing in diluted form.

# Losers

With Bloomberg rampant and competition heating up in worsening market conditions, it was inevitable that, sooner or later, there would be casualties among the market-data companies.

Among the earliest and most prominent of these, as we have seen, was Quotron. An industry pioneer and not so many years past its prime as the dominant information provider in the equities sector, over the course of the roaring bull market that ran throughout the 1980s, Quotron had steadily lost market share to assorted rivals, some new and others familiar. Some offered better "mousetraps," others more open systems. All seemed to be able to offer better pricing. Quotron still offered a product as reliable as any of those offered by competitors, but it was inflexible, used dated technology, and in a market forever demanding new functions was regarded increasingly as old hat. Clients who had once spoken in admiration of "good old reliable Quotron" now uttered the phrase as a pejorative.

The company had done little to help itself. Management made few attempts to diversify out of equities, a market in which the sources of stock quotes were multiplying rapidly, evidently not convinced that the effort was worthwhile. George Levine, Quotron's sales and marketing director, a grizzled but charming veteran of the early market-information wars, seemed almost alone in his concern about the company's fast-fading glory. From time to time he would pop into Telerate, ostensibly for a chat with Esther Zimet, but in fact to see if Hirsch might be interested in some form of co-operation, such as exchanging data or joint marketing or sharing networks. The two companies did come up with one joint initiative. It was called Cash Market Profile, and represented a diluted form of Telerate. It was aimed at those equities clients who wanted a snapshot from other markets. There were few buyers. Egos stood in the way of more radical ventures. Hirsch had little interest in equities and regarded Levine as nothing more than a lovable old rascal singing a sad song on a broken record. Levine saw Hirsch as a pipsqueak *arriviste* presiding over a company with its own limited shelf life. They met regularly, but once the exchange of gossip was out of the way, they soon became bored with each other.

To his credit, George Levine had over the years almost single-handedly kept Quotron alive. Clients loved him. Some even trusted him to save the day for them. Good old George—he was well into his sixties by now—was a silver-tongued charmer. He could talk the monkeys out of the trees, it was said, a skill he was frequently called upon to deploy, and he could talk them back up again if necessary. But charm alone was not enough to hold together a company in dire need of a savior with deep pockets, and perhaps an even deeper belief in Quotron's future.

In 1986, belatedly and unavoidably, the company offered itself for sale.

Rescue—or such it seemed at the time—came from an unlikely quarter: Citicorp. The bank's pockets were certainly deep and its belief seemed genuine enough. Citicorp was the world's largest bank, and certainly one of the most aggressively innovative. Its chief executive, John Reed, not yet forty, basked in a reputation as the *wunderkind* of banking, a self-proclaimed New Age prophet in an updated image of his mentor, Walt Wriston. Citicorp could hardly grow much bigger as a bank, but Reed had grand ideas about turning the company into a multifaceted financial conglomerate worthy of the Information Age. Quotron seemed to suit Reed's purposes perfectly. And so Jack Scantlin's old shop disappeared into the maw of Citicorp's vast bureaucracy for a consideration of $650 million. Given Quotron's severely reduced circumstances and questionable prospects, the figure was regarded as generous beyond reason.

A disastrous outcome was widely predicted by people familiar with Citicorp's eccentric approach to managing its non-banking properties. But even Citicorp needed a little time to kill Quotron. After admitting that it knew nothing about the information business, Citicorp proceeded to fill Quotron's senior management positions with bankers who knew nothing about the information business. Some of them, as a few critics liked to point out, seemed to know little about banking, either. Clients continued to desert Quotron in droves. The exodus was led by some of the leading investment banks, fearful that Citicorp—which had made no secret of the fact that it wished to be known as a stockbroker as well as bank—would have access to any proprietary information they transmitted through Quotron's network.

Within four years Citicorp had written down its Quotron investment by $500 million. Even that seemed too little. By 1992, the company was fighting a desperate rearguard to retain business at unprofitable price points dictated by its two principal rivals. These were ADP, the market-data arm of Automatic Data Processing, and ILX. Originally developed for E.F. Hutton, an investment bank, by a nutty, self-aggrandizing genius named Bernie Weinstein, ILX was now owned by Thomson Financial.

It was a year of reckoning for Quotron. Its biggest customer, Merrill Lynch, was already all but lost. Other prominent clients defected, notably Dean Witter, an old-line New York retail house, and A.G. Edwards, a St. Louis-based firm, with 10,000 and 7500 users respectively. The winner in each case was Weinstein's ILX.

After two years of unstoppable decline, bowing to the inevitable, Citicorp put Quotron up for sale. It was a fire sale. Prospective buyers were told that the price was any figure they cared to mention, which Citicorp let it be known included zero. (It was even offered to me during one of my visits to the bank in connection with the sale of another property.) Even at zero there were no bites. Due diligence revealed a company with a huge pension liability, losing market share, and burning cash at a rate of $10 million a month. Citicorp's salvage experts turned in desperation to Reuters. Just take it off our hands, they pleaded. As an additional incentive, Citicorp offered to indemnify Reuters against operating losses for one year, amounting to some $200 million. It was an offer Reuters could scarcely refuse. The indestructible George Levine went with the deal. (He was still at Reuters at the time of writing.)

The second prominent casualty was no pioneer of the industry but a relative latecomer. Knight-Ridder Financial, a division of the Knight-Ridder newspaper group, had long been known for its commodity newswire, but commodity trading was a cyclical business and KRF was soon sniffing the air for opportunities to diversify into the financial markets. The conclusion was that the low end of the market—savings institutions, regional banks, and mortgage bankers—offered the best prospects for success. Telerate had a lock on this space but was considered vulnerable, especially in light of the scandal-racked troubles of the savings-and-loan industry. KRF produced a good-looking desktop device, with some neat functions, called MoneyCenter. A shameless facsimile of Telerate's popular Page 5 was produced, complemented by mortgage-securities information that Telerate lacked. KRF sales executives were invited to undercut Telerate pricing, even to the point of offering to pay subscribers the amount remaining on their Telerate contracts. It was a plan of sorts; no marketing genius was needed to work out the fundamental flaw. A strategy of paying money to knock off the weakest clients of the weakest information vendor in an industry on its knees was never a likely candidate for the marketing Hall of Fame.

Telerate naturally hit back, or at least withstood the assault, which left KRF nowhere else to go. Nowhere, that is, except Europe, which is where the company went, hoping to pick off a few more Telerate stragglers. The parent company realized, finally, that the venture was unlikely to be profitable in the lifetimes of any of its internal sponsors, notably a K-R executive named David Ray. With its pathetic market share rapidly crumbling on the eastern as well as the western side of the Atlantic, Knight-Ridder started to scan the horizon for rescuers.

It had almost despaired of finding one when out of the blue swooped Bridge Information Systems, a brand-new financial information enterprise. Bridge was generously funded by venture capitalists, who seemed so desperate to join an already packed field that the cost of doing so seemed almost irrelevant. Bridge snapped up Knight-Ridder for $278 million, a figure that bemused observers agreed was by any standard of value at least twice the true worth of the business. Knight-Ridder would not be the last of Bridge's acquisitions—or even the most foolish—but that extraordinary sequence will feature later in the narrative.

Two of the biggest losers in the financial data business belonged, ironically and perhaps predictably, to some of Wall Street's biggest names.

Among these, the first of note was Imnet, or International Marketnet, a joint venture of Merrill Lynch and International Business Machines Corporation. It was announced, amid great fanfare, in 1985, somewhere near the height of the boom in market data. The idea was beguiling: a business owned by Wall Street's largest stockbroker and America's leading technology company. Joseph P. Castellano, the head of the venture, declared: "In five or six years we think the market for Marketnet could be as big as $1 billion."

Alas, Castellano's dream rapidly descended into nightmare. On New Year's Eve 1987, just two and a half years after the launch, the 270 remaining employees were called to a meeting to be told that the venture would be terminated. Imnet had paid the price for hubris. Few clients could be found for its expensive satellite-delivered analytical software. "The market just evaporated," a mid-level executive was quoted as saying. "Starting about the middle of this year, it became clear the whole idea was a disaster."[1]

No sooner had the ashes of Imnet been interred than along came EJV Partners, or Electronic Joint Venture, an initiative financed by six of Wall Street's investment houses: Citicorp, First Boston, Goldman Sachs, Lehman Brothers, Morgan Stanley, and Salomon Brothers. They were all fierce competitors in the government-securities market on which EJV had set its sights. The business was conceived as the market-makers taking up common cause against the struggling Telerate and the up-and-coming Bloomberg. Ill conceived, as it turned out.

EJV never managed to formulate a clear strategy. Was it supposed to be primarily an execution system, or an analytics product? Or both? At what specific audience was it aimed? Was it supposed to be a low-cost alternative to Telerate and Bloomberg, or a high-priced advance on existing technology? Few answers were forthcoming from a management group with which the partners became progressively disillusioned. EJV changed owners a couple of times before eventually ending up as part of an agglomeration of market-data companies snapped up by an acquisitive newcomer: Bridge Information Systems.

---

[1] The *New York Times*, January 1, 1987

To the established market-data vendors, the moral of the story was clear. Joint ventures, especially those in which buyers of systems try to become sellers, don't work.

Not all disasters were fatal. Some were merely major errors of judgment committed by managers at well-heeled companies, eager to prove that Michael Bloomberg was not the only market-data executive capable of trail-blazing deeds of derring-do.

Meanwhile, Bloomberg marched on, a growing influence in all market sectors, particularly in Telerate's. Bloomberg was following a strategy, of which the core premise was almost grotesquely simple. It was the one that Bloomberg had enunciated from the start, namely to keep all the information and functions on one box and to add to them at no additional charge to the basic subscription fee. And Bloomberg kept on adding—news, analytics, calculators, third-party services—all of which were used to convince customers that everything they could ever possibly need was either available on their Bloomberg terminal already, or very soon would be. The sales message was compelling: buy a Bloomberg terminal and watch the service expand before your eyes.

Reuters and Telerate seemed unable to find very little extra information to add to their systems, other than the occasional contributor. When something was added that they considered significant, they insisted on charging extra for it. The unintended effect on Reuters and Telerate, which only became apparent over time and was even then not fully understood, was the erosion of the price differential between their supposedly "cheap" volume-discounted terminals and Bloomberg's "expensive" closed-off device.

Reuters continued to rely on its apparently unassailable position in the international markets. It did from time to time convey the impression it had a major strategy, but only by executing minor stratagems, such as renaming products, upgrading networks, and effecting complex changes in pricing.

Bloomberg was running rampant, gobbling up market share like a flesh-eating virus as rivals desperately sought to find an antidote.

# Rolling Thunder

The only contribution Dow Jones made to the greatest bull market in history was to record it.

While the *Wall Street Journal* provided a daily chronicle of the mighty advance, and the Dow Jones Industrial Average measured its progress, the shares of the company that owned both properties headed in the opposite direction, a consequence of shrinking profits and allegations of management incompetence.

Reduced to the role of spectators, the company's senior managers could do little but mope around their mahogany-paneled executive suite on Liberty Street, a mere stone's throw from the New York Stock Exchange, epicenter of the unfolding spectacle. The Dow Jones executive suite began to resemble a fortress under siege. Gathering outside the metaphorical gates was an assault force of angry investors and incredulous analysts. Investors were furious because, at a time when just about every publishing and media stock was riding the crest of a buying wave, Dow Jones's share price had tumbled from its 1987 high of about fifty-six to the mid-thirties. Analysts were more perplexed than angry. What they could not fathom was why the management of America's most valuable and coveted publishing franchise no longer seemed able to extract a decent profit from it—or, for that matter, from some of its other supposedly valuable properties, Telerate included.

Reporters tagged along, expecting a firefight. They would not be disappointed. They had long been sniffing around for a hint of scandal and had now caught a whiff of cordite. The Bancrofts were stirring. There was rebellion in the air. Sabers were being rattled. As objective as they tried to be, journalists left few readers in doubt about which side they were on. Their endlessly entertaining accounts of the looming battle spurred the rebels on and drove Peter Kann and his fellow defenders ever deeper into their isolated redoubt.

Such was the strength of the dissident cause that it even attracted two of the younger members of the Bancroft clan, Dow Jones's very own silent majority. Their protest marked the first time since Dow Jones had become a public company in 1963 that representatives of the owners had been provoked into questioning the safety of the family inheritance.

Dow Jones's shares had fallen in response to some truly awful investment fundamentals. In ten years from 1987 to 1997 the return on equity had been

398

virtually halved. Earnings had virtually stood still. Operating margins had receded to insignificance. What struck many critics as worse than the terrible figures was the fact that management appeared to have fallen into a paralyzed funk. "We're afraid to fail," Kann confessed to *Forbes* magazine in 1992.[1]

But the company *had* failed, and in just about every accepted measurement of corporate performance. Like Phillips before him, Kann seemed capable only of offering bland assurances that things would soon get better, without actually going so far as to describe how. More disconcerting still was his habit of telling anyone who would listen that the company's condition was not nearly as bad as people seemed to think it was.

Many thought it was a great deal worse.

Critics may exaggerate but statistics rarely do. Dow Jones's financial results were consistently terrible, which meant, the critics reasoned, that the company's underlying condition had to be terrible. To support their case, they could have seized on any number of statistics, absolute or comparative. Among the most compelling in the latter category was the difference in market value between Dow Jones and Reuters, the company's closest competitor in electronic information. In 1987, the companies had stood almost shoulder to shoulder with a market capitalization of about $3.5 billion. Since then Dow Jones's market value had remained virtually unchanged, while Reuters' had shot up to $20 billion. (A publicly owned Bloomberg would almost certainly have overhauled Dow Jones, too, but as a private company it could not be included in the exercise.)

The company's most valuable asset, the *Wall Street Journal*, was foremost among its most pressing problems. All newspapers must occasionally weather the vicissitudes of economic downturns, of course, and the recession that led to the 1987 crash, and which lingered for some time after it, had been one of them. Three years later, advertising was hit again by the impact of a banking crisis and the Gulf War. But these events only served to disguise internal operating difficulties. Rather than admit to such problems, Dow Jones preferred to take comfort from the fact that it was adrift in the same leaky boat as every other publisher. An unwillingness to admit to problems meant that little time was spent seeking solutions. The excuses offered for the prolonged slump in the *Journal*'s advertising revenue were accompanied by the nostrum that all would be well when the economy and the market turned around. But even when both the economy and the market did just that, and in grand style, the *Journal*'s revenues were slow to recover and profitability remained elusive.

Phillips and Kann had pointed out in their defense that they had not been sitting around idly dreaming of better times to come. They had expressed their confidence in the *Journal*'s future by spending a fortune expanding the paper

---

[1] *Forbes* magazine, February 3, 1992

from one to three sections. They had launched European and Asian editions. They had ventured into the field of glossy, up-market business magazines with *SmartMoney* (another joint venture, incidentally). The critical response was tart. All these initiatives were well and good but none of them had made money.

For some the prospects for doing so seemed remote.

By the mid-nineties the recession had receded into distant memory, along with the excuses. So where now was the promised recovery in the company's fortunes? An expanded paper presented opportunities for expanded advertising, especially during a rampant bull market such as the one now underway. Sure enough, the *Journal*'s advertising and circulation revenues did pick up. Revenue finally seemed to be getting back on track. But still the company's operating margins refused to expand. And still the share price failed to recover. Why?

Peter Kann and Ken Burenga came up with a freshly minted excuse. The company's biggest headache was no longer the *Journal*, they explained, but the struggling Telerate division.

In December 1996, at a gathering of media analysts in New York sponsored by the investment firm Paine Webber, Kann allowed that Telerate's recent results had been poor. It meant that Dow Jones's overall results would be "mildly disappointing." He went on to describe in vague terms some of the measures under discussion for turning Telerate around. Most of the attending analysts, according to contemporary press accounts, reacted with extreme skepticism. "Underwhelmed" was one of the milder responses. One analyst professed to be shocked: "Telerate is losing market share to new companies like Bloomberg and they didn't seem to have a plan for stopping that." According to another, Kann seemed not so much disappointed by Telerate's poor performance as surprised.

Few analysts were. Wall Street had been worrying about Telerate for some time. As far back as September 1990, *Business Week* had expressed the headline view that "Dow Jones's $1.6 Billion Baby is Hardly a Bundle of Joy"—and that was only because Telerate's revenue had fallen short of the inflated forecasts invoked during the row over the bidding price the previous year. After that, Dow Jones was a regular topic of negative press coverage. Two other widely read business glossies, *Forbes* and *Fortune*, subsequently weighed in with attacks on management. Even when reporters wrote articles about the stunning rise of Michael Bloomberg, Dow Jones was invariably mentioned as one of the primary reasons for his success. Over the course of the decade, Kann and his colleagues may have been worked over by the press more often than a Hollywood stunt man gets worked over in a Sylvester Stallone movie.

Inevitably speculation arose that, unless results improved, either Kann or

Burenga, or both, might face the chop. And so they might have in any other company—but not at Dow Jones. Who, for a start, could be counted on to do the deed? Not the corporate fat cats on the board. Surely not the ever-faithful Bancrofts. In troubled times, the directors, far from questioning company policies, always rallied around management, rubber-stamps poised. Such misplaced loyalty created a damaging paradox: the worse Dow Jones performed, the more secure its management seemed to become.

Burenga let it be known in an interview that he thought Telerate had been in less than perfect shape when Dow Jones bought it. It was an absurd comment to make six years after the event and its effect was to expose Burenga to ridicule. Evidently it did not occur to him that Dow Jones should have acted to solve Telerate's problems, whatever they might have been, at the time. And if the problems had developed since then, obviously they had developed under his watch. To some extent, Kann and Burenga were hoist with their own petard: only in recent times had they stopped expressing their satisfaction with Telerate's performance.

To his credit, Kann had already taken steps to repair the damage he and Burenga had so often denied was anything of the kind. Midway through 1996, the hapless Carl Valenti was removed from his post as Telerate's chief executive. Kann replaced him, in an acting capacity, with Burenga.

Astonishingly—or so it seemed to most observers—Valenti was not fired. He simply returned to what one journalist called the Dow Jones "mothership," retaining his corporate title of senior vice president and his seat on the board.

Burenga at least looked the part. Before long he was appearing in full-page Telerate ads in the *Wall Street Journal*, projecting an image of a dynamic, hands-on executive with a no-nonsense look and rolled-up sleeves. Things are going to change around here, was the message.

There was one immediate change: Telerate would henceforth be known as Dow Jones Markets, a name selected to underline the parent company's commitment to the business. Telerate employees suffered the "outrage" in silence. (I shall continue to refer to the business as Telerate, not out of shared indignation but for reasons of clarity.)

"Dow Jones' fondest hope," wrote Dennis Waters in *Waters*, his eponymous magazine devoted to the financial information industry, "is that Burenga will do for Telerate what Barney Kilgore, one of the company's great folk heroes, did for the *Wall Street Journal*."[2] Fondest hope seemed a poor substitute for great expectations.

Kann, interviewed by Waters for the same article, was asked about his priority for Telerate. "I put content at the top," he said. "I'm not saying other things aren't important—the packaging of information, the delivery of

---

[2] *Waters* magazine, July 1997

401

information, the relationship with customers—all of these are very important, and I think in some of those areas we can make major strides. But again, which of them is more important? Content."

As a rallying cry for a rejuvenated Telerate, the words fell short of inspiring.

Nor did Burenga, in discussing an emerging rescue plan, quite come across as Henry V before Agincourt. "Where the high value is, is in the proprietary content," he said, explaining for the benefit of those who might not know what proprietary meant, that it was "the content that no one else has."[3]

What else? Waters wanted to know, as if waiting for a big shoe to drop.

"We think there's an opportunity to leapfrog the competition and take a leadership position in the delivery of information using the latest technology which our competition have not shown an inclination to do in a fully integrated way. I think in this time frame we are going to create a leadership position in—I'll use an Internet word—electronic commerce directed at the financial services industry."

What Dow Jones planned to do right from the start, Burenga said, was to build a brand-new Telerate network. But that did not mean, he warned, that it would be a significant source of value. "The delivery system has to be there. It has to be fast. It has to be reliable. It has to be easy to use. But in these days of open systems it's hard to build proprietary value into that. You can take a leadership position and get out ahead of the competitors, but I'm not sure there's any magic technology that provides value."[4]

So, there it was, finally, the grand blueprint for a New Telerate: proprietary data—meaning, the astute reader will recall, what nobody else had—and a new network based on Internet technology.

If the concept was bold, it was hard to tell from the language used to describe it. Any chief executive might have used pretty much the same terminology to describe any routine corporate initiative. Peter Job, Reuters' new chief executive, had often used the same words. They were standard issue for the kind of speeches he frequently had to make to a broad, unquestioning audiences—say, the Press Institute of Liechtenstein.

What Burenga failed to clarify was what the investment plan would cost. Figures of $650 million and $700 million had emerged from somewhere—exactly where was not clear. The *Waters* article referred to the $650 million, without attributing it to Burenga. Various other publications mentioned the higher figure. Whichever was the real one—and the difference between the two was hardly significant—the question was whether the Dow Jones board had approved it. If it had, what were the conditions, if any, and what was the timetable? Kann had not bothered to deny either of the published figures, but

---

[3] *Waters* magazine, July 1997
[4] Ibid.

he also seemed strangely reluctant to confirm anything. He would admit to *Fortune* only that he had "discussed with the board various levels of investments. This is still in the discussion stage. We've been talking about a wide range of figures at this stage."[5]

Another missing element in the plan was where the money was to come from. Was it to be raised by borrowing? By issuing stock? By tapping into internal cash resources? Given Dow Jones's record of financial management and its lagging share price, none of these options sounded remotely feasible in the short term. The company was throwing off cash, but it was still saddled with $40 million a year in amortization for Telerate. Burenga, on the evidence of history, presumably would be opposed to any scheme involving debt. There was no telling. The proposed method of financing was never disclosed to the public, nor was it discussed in the press.

Discussion would have been pointless anyway, since Kann had not yet confirmed how much would be needed or when it would be needed.

In masterminding Telerate's regeneration, Burenga was assisted by Jon Robson, a Telerate marketing executive who had been Julian Childs's marketing director in Hong Kong. A gangly, personable Englishman with an unruly mane of hair, which he was constantly tossing back from his forehead in a trademark gesture, Robson had caught Burenga's attention as a man brimful of grand ideas—a thinker, a visionary, and a master business strategist. Robson may have been all those things, or at least some of them, but what he was not renowned for was seeing something through to execution. Or even as far as the planning stage. In the parlance of the day, Robson talked the talk, but could he walk the walk?

In the likely event that the answer was no, at least not on his own, Robson would need help. Consultants were duly called in. One group, Stanford Research Institute, was charged with planning and implementing the new campaign. A second firm was brought in to evaluate the staff requirements, which involved interviewing Telerate's operating managers.

Already, and before a single shot had been fired, millions of dollars were going out the door in the cause of what *Waters* magazine depicted as "Telerate's Last Stand."

Inside Telerate, no less than on Wall Street, cynicism abounded. Most observers considered it well founded. Even the name of Burenga's Grand Plan gave ammunition to the cynics. Its internal designation was "Rolling Thunder." Whether this title had appeared on any formal documents was not clear, but inevitably it leaked out—much to the delight of the press. What possessed someone to name a rescue plan after a failed military offensive undertaken in the lost cause of the Vietnam War can only be imagined.

---

[5] *Fortune* magazine, February 3, 1997

Telerate insiders were soon openly calling it Strolling Blunder.

Enter the Bancrofts. But first an exit.

In May 1996, about the time that Valenti was ousted, and presumably while Rolling Thunder was still a mere twinkle in Burenga's eye, a death was reported in the obituary columns that would cancel all bets, opening up all kinds of alternative and unpredictable scenarios. The death, from lung cancer at the age of fifty-five, was that of Bettina Bancroft (her married name, Klink, had been dropped after her divorce) the Grand Dame of the Bancroft heirs and a former occupant of one of the then three family seats—later expanded to four—on the Dow Jones board.

The news was hardly noticed on Wall Street. But it was about to open an extraordinary sequence of events at Dow Jones, with far-reaching consequences for Telerate. As with a stone dropped into a pond, the ripples took some time to reach the shore.

*Fortune*, in February 1997, was the first to detect the disturbance on the usually calm waters. "Disgruntled Heiress Leads Revolt at Dow Jones," ran the headline. Below it the author, Joseph Nocera, produced a story that offered a fascinating glimpse into the privileged world of the Bancrofts and would split the family along a generational divide. More importantly, it shook the company they controlled to its foundations by calling attention once again to the deficiencies of management and to their cozy relationship with Clarence Barron's assorted heirs.

*Fortune*'s apparent good fortune in stumbling on the story was no accident. The magazine was well acquainted with the affairs of Dow Jones. The editor-in-chief of Time Inc., *Fortune*'s owner, was Norman Pearlstine, a former executive editor of the *Wall Street Journal*. And the magazine's managing editor was John Huey, a former editor on the European edition of the *Journal*. Before leaving Dow Jones, Pearlstine and Kann, who had once been close friends, had fallen out. Obviously Kann was not amused by the *Fortune* revelations. It would be surprising if he had not also been afraid.

Bettina Bancroft's death marked a transition in her family from the fourth generation of Clarence Barron's heirs to the fifth. The torch in her case passed to her thirty-two-year-old daughter, Elisabeth "Lizzie" Goth. *Fortune* reported that Goth, after her mother's death, received outright about 700,000 shares of Dow Jones stock worth $23 million at the prevailing market price. Additional shares worth hundreds of millions of dollars were tied up in various other trusts until all the fourth generation heirs had died.

Lizzie's first act was to call her investment advisor for an assessment of the potential value of her inheritance. As reported by Nocera, "His report was grim. At that point, according to a confidant, she woke up and said 'I care. This is my fortune. This is my asset. Now what do I do?' "

What she did was to set out on a personal crusade to find the answer. In the course of it she visited some of the stellar names in the investment world. They included Warren Buffet, America's foremost investment sage. From him the trail led to Nancy Peretsman, an investment banker at Allen & Co., to Tom Murphy, former chief executive office of Capital Cities/ABC, and to Ira Millstein, a Wall Street lawyer and a renowned expert in matters of corporate governance.

Lizzie Goth took after her mother in at least two obvious ways: she was a strikingly attractive blonde and a champion horsewoman. Like Bettina, Lizzie loved the high life. She was said to have once had a "drug problem," evidenced by an arrest in 1995 for cocaine use, resulting in a prolonged stay in a Minnesota clinic. In the alien ways of the investment world she was naïve and disarmingly candid in admitting it. But she was no pushover. Recently divorced and "cleaned up," she was now on her own in the world and by all accounts determined to prove herself by standing on her principles.

After listening to accounts of Dow Jones's business decline, she was appalled. So was one other member of the family, her cousin William "Billy" Cox III, sometimes known as Billy Three-Sticks, whose father, William Cox Jr., sat on the board. Billy, like his dad, worked full-time for Dow Jones but he parted company with his father both in his negative view of his employer and in his readiness to speak his mind about its management. He told *Fortune*: "The last ten years speak for themselves. In all honesty, if I were a portfolio manager, I would have to have been a fool to have this stock in my portfolio over that period."[6]

His father was shocked by this display of familial disloyalty. "How could you?" he asked Billy. But Billy plowed on regardless. Lizzie, he insisted, was right in her reforming campaign and his father was wrong to oppose it. It was Billy who arranged, through a friend, the meeting with Buffet. Buffet had no specific remedies to advance, but he told Lizzie and Billy that, as owners, they had significant standing in the company and should start to wield their influence to effect change. Millstein had the same message, and unlike Buffet was prepared to help. For a start he arranged to meet Roy Hammer, a Boston attorney and the trustee responsible for managing several of the family trusts. "I'm not here to cause trouble," he is said to have told Hammer, though if that were not the intention it would be hard to say what was. Through Hammer, Millstein arranged to lecture the family on what he thought needed to be done to bring about positive change at Dow Jones.[7]

The Bancrofts were unimpressed. By now the family divisions were palpable. Some of the senior members were said to be outraged, the younger

---

[6] *Fortune* magazine, February 3, 1997
[7] Ibid.

ones disturbed and curious. Martha Robes, the most gentle of women, tried to paper over the cracks. "I think Lizzie is very much behind the company," she told Nocera, which was true. "But she's listening to a lot of outsiders ... who are getting her all wound up."[8] That was not true. It was Lizzie Goth who had done all the winding up and the "outsiders" who had responded.

The day after the *Fortune* story appeared, Dow Jones's stock briefly rallied—an indication of Wall Street's sympathy for Lizzie's campaign. New York always admires a fighter, even one with hundreds of millions in the bank. Gutsy Goth, one smitten stockbroker, called her. Some Dow Jones's employees, it was reported, stood and applauded after someone in the office read the article out loud. One *Wall Street Journal* reporter commented that it was "the most faxed article in history. It was the talk of the town."

A week after the story appeared, Kann confirmed that Dow Jones indeed planned to spend $650 million on Telerate, spread over three years. On this news the Dow Jones share price promptly fell back again.

The conservative wing of the family took the row public—not that it had ever been very private. In a co-signed letter to *Fortune*, Martha Robes, William Cox Jr., his sister Jane Cox MacElree, and Christopher Bancroft, Lizzie's half-brother, reported that at a recent meeting "all parts of our family unanimously reaffirmed their commitment to Dow Jones's remaining an independent public company ... The family has absolutely no interest in relinquishing control of this important and unique enterprise." More revealing than this refutation of something that had not actually been proposed was the paragraph that followed. "A sound system of corporate oversight is critical to the success of the company. Dow Jones has a long history of strong and capable independent directors. We all believe that this tradition should be continued."[9]

In short, most of the family was perfectly happy with the status quo—happy with management, happy with outside directors who could be relied on not to rock any boats and, above all, one has to suppose, happy with their dividends.

Lizzie's response was immediate and spirited. Her views had been misrepresented, she claimed. "As those of you present at our weekend meeting will recall, I said I could support a statement of unanimity only regarding our commitment to the company remaining independent. I said quite clearly that I would not support a statement of satisfaction with the governance or direction of the company ... My position has not changed. I am still convinced that we do not have adequate assurance that the interests of all shareholders are being well served."

Lizzie was prepared to be more pointed in her observations. "In fact, I am growing more concerned by the day about the governance and direction of the

---

[8] *Fortune* magazine, February 3, 1997
[9] *Fortune* magazine, March 3, 1997

company as the vast majority of informed experts express serious reservations about the plan for Telerate. As major shareholders we need more input into the board's decision-making process and composition. Again, we need to be sure that the board is composed of individuals with a proven commitment to building the long-term value we all want, and the independence to question and guide management's decisions in that regard." Telerate was the problem.

"Their [Dow Jones's] plan to go head to head with Bloomberg and Reuters is a bust," said Peter Appert, an analyst at BT Alex Brown. "They're going to have to have a different strategy. The original plan of throwing bucks at it is not going to work."[10]

Another critic was Michael Ellmann, an analyst with investment bankers Schroder Wertheim & Co. Noting that some people were saying that even God couldn't fix Telerate, he said, ironically, "I would bet God could fix it."

Michael Bloomberg, whose revenue had already overtaken Telerate's, was also unimpressed. "We will increase our R&D [research and development] spending by more than six hundred and fifty million dollars in the next three years. That's just the increase!"[11]

Other influential, louder, and more insistent agitators had begun to appear. They included fund manager Michael Price, of Price Associates, who had accumulated a position of four million Dow Jones shares, or close to 6 percent of the company's equity. Price was the man said to have prodded Chase Manhattan Bank into a merger with Chemical Bank, for which act of daring he had once graced the cover of *Fortune* as "The Scariest S.O.B. on Wall Street." Another activist was James J. Cramer of Cramer Berkowitz, a hedge fund manager. A former journalist, he had once written a column for *SmartMoney*, and was said to know more about what went on inside Dow Jones than its own management did. Like Price, Cramer enjoyed and milked his tough-guy reputation. He had bought one million shares of Dow Jones as a value investment. After a meeting with Kann, he sold most of them.

Price and Cramer were in no doubt about what Kann should do with Telerate and not shy about saying so: sell it or close it down.

Price thought it should be spun off. Cramer was not sure that it could be. "There's nothing there to sell," he told a reporter.[12] Either way, both were adamant that Dow Jones should not invest any further money in it. Cramer had earlier written to Kann to tell him so. "Telerate clearly is a losing venture and does not warrant additional foolhardy funding."

He told *Fortune*: "The Bancroft trusts were set up to protect the journalistic integrity of the *Wall Street Journal*, not some third-rate bond quote provider like

---

[10] Reuters newswire article, November 19, 1996
[11] *The New Yorker*, March 10, 1997, "The Bloomberg Threat," Ken Auletta
[12] *Fortune* magazine, February 17, 1997

Telerate. They've been pouring money into Telerate and milking the *Journal* to support an investment decision that isn't working. I'm trying to save the *Journal* from the Bancroft family."[13]

So, too, if press reports were to be believed, was General Electric Company, owner of the CNBC business news channel. GE's name cropped up as a potential buyer of Dow Jones in an article on Bloomberg in the *New Yorker*, written by Ken Auletta, a respected business writer. Auletta's source was someone he called "an important GE executive." "There is an opportunity for GE," the source told him, "if we could be a white knight for the company with the family. But it would work for GE only if Dow Jones should become a more profit-driven company." The executive speculated that GE could buy a 20–25 percent stake and then link the Dow Jones news operations with NBC and CNBC. But GE would want to see Dow Jones sell Telerate, he added.[14]

A Dow Jones official quoted in the same article had Kann proposing that the companies "weave together the resources" of Dow Jones's New York television station and CNBC's national business-news channel. GE, however, was more interested in joining forces overseas, where NBC was weaker. In the end, according to Auletta, "with neither side wanting to dilute its strength, they parted amicably."

Still the Lizzie Goth ripples continued to flow. The next "white knight" to enter the lists, if hearsay could be believed, was Reuters. Reuters was mentioned variously as a prospective buyer of Telerate, or the *Wall Street Journal*, or perhaps even Dow Jones itself. "Nonsense," said a Dow Jones spokesman, bravely departing from the usual "we don't comment on rumors" line. It probably was nonsense, if only for the reason that a Reuters move would almost certainly have attracted the attention of the anti-trust division of the Justice Department.

Lizzie Goth's crusade had provided, if nothing else, much entertaining grist to the Wall Street gossip mill. Much of it had been nonsense, of course, but much of it was instructive nonsense. Lizzie had seen something that she thought badly needed fixing. In this view she was hardly in the minority— certainly not outside the Bancroft family—but she had given influential voice to opinions perhaps shared secretly by many, even among the Bancrofts. She had sought good advice and taken it. She had spoken her mind, which was more than any of her relatives had ever done. She had a single, simple motive: she wanted Dow Jones's management to add value to a lagging share price and to be held accountable by the board if it failed. She apparently rejected an invitation to sit on the board herself with a response that says much for her

---

[13] *Fortune* magazine, February 17, 1997
[14] *The New Yorker*, March 10, 1997, "The Bloomberg Threat," Ken Auletta

common sense. "Why would you want me? I don't know anything about business. What we need is people who do."

Lizzie Goth was right. She did not belong in the boardroom. She belonged in Peter Kann's office.

But common sense and straight talking were not enough in the end to inspire a general uprising. Lizzie lacked this power. She owned less than one percent of the voting stock and, having failed to win over other members of the family with logic, she had no other resources to call upon. Her relatives had, in fact, formed a protective circle around Kann and his management team.

So, for the time being, Kann was safe, though not completely safe. A suddenly proactive board slashed his bonus on the back of a report card that might have said "...not completely satisfactory." There were even rumors that the Bancrofts had delivered an ultimatum to Kann to get the stock price up to a certain level by a certain date, or start looking for a new job. The rumor was denied, and it is hard to believe that there was much truth to it. Still, many observers thought they perceived from afar signs of writing being applied to walls.

Kann could fall back on his charm to carry him through. He was personally well liked by the family. Even his critics—Michael Price for one—considered him "a nice guy." Which allowed Kann to dismiss the whole Lizzie Goth episode as a storm in a teacup. "The two family members who are critical, together have substantially less than one percent of the stock, which is not a fact I see very often mentioned. They're entitled to their views, but I guess context would probably say how much do those views matter?"

He was right, of course, but it was the voice of a man who may have been in touch with the world of the Bancrofts but who seemed completely out of touch with the rest of the planet.

By the end of the year 1997, it was clear that Lizzie Goth's crusade, reinforced by others, had succeeded in one crucial respect. On November 19, Dow Jones announced that it no longer ruled out the possibility of selling Telerate. The $650-million investment plan would be "substantially scaled back," Dow Jones announced, which meant in essence that it was being abandoned. Dow Jones elected instead to take a $900 million write-off. Telerate was now carried on the books at about £550 million but additional write-offs were likely, the company said in a filing with the SEC. Meanwhile Telerate's workforce of 4000 would be cut by 300–400 people, through layoffs and attrition. The result would be a "very sizable" charge against earnings, resulting in a loss for the year, the first annual loss since the company went public thirty-four years earlier.

"My gut is it's on the block," said Michael Price.

Another analyst, Michael Kupinski of A.G. Edwards, agreed. "It's obvious they have to do something. I think they're dressing it up for sale. They're trying to improve the operating line and cut costs to make it more attractive for sale."

The potential buyers were listed in another of those round-up-the-usual-suspects exercises of which Wall Street is so fond. For one reason or another—including those mentioned earlier—Reuters and Bloomberg were ruled out. At the head of the list appeared three names: Thomson, Bridge Information Systems, and Cantor Fitzgerald.

Thomson was on it because the company had acquired an impressive collection of content companies and so it was assumed that the parent would benefit from access to a global network—although many of the services were distributed via Telerate already. Bridge was a candidate because it was well known that it was in the market for distressed information-vendors. Bridge had acquired Knight-Ridder Financial in similar circumstances two years earlier. Cantor's dependence on Telerate as a distributor made the broker a natural candidate.

Thomson gave every impression of being interested before performing its usual disappearing act. Cantor Fitzgerald stayed in the hunt by forming an alliance with Texas Pacific Group, an investment company, and with Greg Smith, a former Telerate employee from the time, a few years earlier, when Telerate had bought his company, In-Depth Data. The greatest hurdle faced by Cantor Fitzgerald's Howard Lutnick was antagonism at Liberty Street. Dow Jones had no desire to do any more business with Cantor Fitzgerald or Lutnick than it was obligated to under Cantor's long-standing agreement with Telerate.

That appeared to leave the field open to an ambitious, cash-laden latecomer: Bridge.

# Bridge Raised

In the summer of 1997 I was among the many outside observers idly watching the Dow Jones-Telerate saga stagger towards its dismal denouement when I received a call out of the blue from Tom Wendel, chief executive of the suddenly ubiquitous Bridge Information Systems. We had never met. Would I be interested, he wanted to know, in talking about managing Bridge's operations in Europe?

Other than a few morsels of intelligence gleaned from the trade newsletters, and crumbs from occasional lunches with Rick Snape, now a senior executive at the firm, I knew very little about Bridge or Wendel.

What I had heard was positive. Bridge's products enjoyed an excellent reputation, which, after some investigation of my own, I was pleased to endorse. They were represented by a suite of clever desktop applications, fed by an impressively comprehensive database, and were delivered over a state-of-the-art, TCP-IP (Internet-compatible) network. Some Bridge users told me they considered its products the best in the market. So did some non-Bridge users, locked into contracts with other vendors. As for Bridge's chief executive, he was considered in some quarters to be an emerging challenger to Michael Bloomberg. Wendel was far from a reluctant candidate for the role.

It was not my former comrade-in-arms Snape who had mentioned my name to Wendel, but Ken Marlin, a Bridge marketing executive with whom I had a passing acquaintance. "You'll probably be getting a call from my boss. He's looking for someone to run Europe. It's a bit of a mess, needs a radical restructuring. Right up your street, I'd have thought."

Marlin, like Wendel, had spent some time in the US Marine Corps. He closed with a useful military tip: "Talk tough with him. Go on the offensive right away. He likes that."

Wendel soon called to suggest a meeting. "How about right now?" I suggested, following Marlin's advice. "Sure, come on over," he said. "I'll stand you lunch."

The attraction of the job, frankly, was the promise of stock options. Bridge, Snape had told me, was generous in that regard, naturally at the expense of salary. Getting back into the information business with Bridge represented a last opportunity to top up my dwindling personal wealth. Of course, options in a private company only acquire value when a public market is established for them, a point I made over lunch to Wendel. He assured me that an initial public offering of Bridge shares would probably occur within a year, certainly no more than two.

Whenever my attention wandered to my lunch plate I sensed I was being weighed up. Wendel's persona was as intriguing as it was impressive. He spoke directly and to the point, wasting no time on the conventions of conversational politesse. It was on the subject of Bridge's business plans that he was most articulate and most convincing. The connection with Welsh Carson, Anderson & Stowe, Bridge's financial backer, he told me, gave the company access to deep wells of funding. "There's nothing they won't do for us." The owners expected in return nothing less than Bridge's rapid rise to domination of the data business market. This Wendel confidently expected to accomplish within two or three years. "Telerate has had its day in the sun. Dow Jones has blown it. Reuters is too fat and complacent to move quickly. It's going to be Bridge and Bloomberg from now on. And we will win through superior technology."

Something about Wendel reminded me of Glen Renfrew. They had the same restless energy, the same confidence, the same sharp intellect, but also, at times, the same rather distant manner. In Wendel it was manifested by a beetle-browed glare, which I found slightly disconcerting. My overall impression, however, was favorable.

Whether the same was true in reverse is another matter. The man of decision after our meeting, and a second one, seemed unable to make up his mind about hiring me. He may have had personal matters on his mind.

Between the initial phone call and our second meeting, he had married Debbie Butterfield, a scion of the Bermuda banking dynasty. The event exposed a softer side to Wendel. He and his wife, who was considerably younger but seriously handicapped by the effects of diabetes, had met when they were both by chance doing business with the same institution in Toronto, he as an investment banker, she as a public-relations executive. Wendel had mentioned to her that he was not looking forward to returning to New York, where the weather was bad, so Debbie invited him to spend the weekend in Bermuda. While on a motor scooter tour of the island, Wendel crashed into a wall. He was badly hurt, requiring hospital treatment and several days of convalescence. Debbie stayed on to take care of him. "I fell in love with my nurse," he told me, eyes moistening at the memory. It was my first, and last, sighting of the human Wendel.

Wendel boasted an interesting professional pedigree. He had spent most of his early working life with Lockheed Corporation, a defense contractor and builder of airplanes. He had been the chief financial officer of Pan American World Airways at the time it went out of business. For a change of pace he hawked his talents around Wall Street, where he occupied senior positions at two respected financial firms, Paine Webber, a leading investment bank, and

Liberty Brokerage, a money broker owned by a consortium of banks, where he became the chief executive.

With his background in defense systems, a degree in electrical engineering, and authorship of a book on COBOL, the computer language, his grasp of technology was broad and comprehensive. The personal attributes were more compelling than the professional ones. He was a stocky six-footer, ruggedly handsome with distinguished silver-gray hair. He had the rasping voice of someone used to barking orders, every inch the Marine officer he had once been. He had, I learned later, lost a lung as a result of heavy smoking. Even in his calmer moments, a baleful stare emerged like a laser from a visor of strikingly animated black eyebrows that called to mind a pair of hairy caterpillars performing a mating ritual. He brought to the task the virtues of vision, intelligence, eloquence, and charisma.

There was also a debit column. He was vain and egotistical and the owner of an explosive and unpredictable temper. The rages which I was to witness on several occasions demeaned him as much as they terrified their victims. In his late fifties by the time he joined Bridge, Wendel carried a dossier of residual health problems. Besides the badly damaged lung, there were the discomforts left over from a couple of serious road accidents, including the Bermuda mishap; one eye had been damaged in some mishap. None of these afflictions undermined the prodigious enthusiasm he brought to his role. The question in my mind was not his health or his energy but whether he had the ability to manage a complex organization made even more so by the diverse business components from which it had been created. They included, at that time, EJV, Knight-Ridder, and Telesphere—shortly to be supplemented by ADP's brokerage services division.

Our discussions continued inconclusively for a month, mainly by telephone, until one afternoon I decided to impose an end-of-week deadline, claiming that other suitors were knocking at my door.

By six o'clock that Friday evening, having received no communication from Wendel, I had pretty much written off the whole enterprise when the telephone rang. It was Wendel. "We're on," he said abruptly. We agreed terms in precisely four minutes, or so my wife tells me.

It took me that figure in weeks to recognize that I had made a bad mistake. For Wendel, I suspect, it may only have taken as many days. In the event I stayed for four years.

One usually needs a little time to work out how a company operates and how its guiding personalities shape the corporate culture and ethos (two words which, in the context of Bridge, verged on the oxymoronic). There was nothing remotely complicated about the Bridge management style (another contradiction in terms). Its dominant feature was motivation through intimidation, backed up by character assassination, excommunication, and an occasional public flogging. Bridge, I soon learned, was a ship terrorized by a gang of bullies, rule imposed by a network of eager enforcers and informers acting on behalf of a latter-day Bligh. New midshipmen were well advised to watch their step.

"This company is evil," a just-dismissed New York sales executive hissed at me melodramatically during my first week of orientation in New York as she tearfully cleared out her desk. "It uses people and then tosses them aside. Take care you don't become one of them."

The warning struck me as overwrought; she was, after all, leaving under circumstances that often cause temporary distress. But there could be no denying, even on the basis of fleeting first impressions, that Bridge was an organization wound up tight, the result of what the departing sales executive had spoken about: a careless brutality inflicted on employees who fell short of Wendel's unreasonably exacting standards or fell victim to his unexpected whims.

Despite his fearsome reputation, Wendel somehow managed to retain a vestige of trust and respect among employees. The same could not be said of the other two members of his inner management circle. They were Rob McCormick, the chief technology officer, and Dick MacWilliams, the sales and marketing man.

McCormick, barely into his thirties, was a Wendel protégé and, according to the company grapevine, his most likely successor as chief executive. He was also said to enjoy the uncritical admiration of certain partners at Welsh Carson, Anderson & Stowe. Scarcely tall enough to glower over his bully pulpit, his strutting personality was such that he attracted the charge, often leveled against those of short stature, of being Napoleonic. Wendel's rough manner could be softened when the owner allowed, by a patrician gravitas, which he used to good effect to charm owners and clients. McCormick, blessed with no such gift, relied on blunter instruments. He affected a cocky air at all times, deployed a relentless belligerence, and carried a quiverful of apparently random antagonisms. Tolerance and humility were disdained as symptoms of a weak character.

McCormick's closest colleagues kept their jobs by emulation; those working under him labored under no illusion that the one immutable condition of their employment was that they become McCormick clones. Two brothers on the payroll had obvious genetic advantages over everyone else.

McCormick was undoubtedly very bright and he basked in Wendel's patronage. The body language was instructive. At management meetings he contrived to sit in a position facing his boss, allowing him to respond to every

Wendel pronouncement with visible signs of adoration. His own utterances were punctuated with endless glances across the table in hope of a return nod of approbation.

Wendel reciprocated by relying inordinately on McCormick's judgments, and not just on technology issues. His views on a wide range of subjects were often accepted at the expense of those expressed by more qualified executives, who were left to simmer in frustration and resentment. McCormick's declarations were disputed at some peril, as they were presumed to be those of his master. The Wendel-McCormick act was that of a ventriloquist projecting his voice through a loquacious dummy. Or was it the other way around? Sometimes it was hard to tell.

MacWilliams failed to command either the boss's respect or affection to anywhere near the same extent as McCormick enjoyed. MacWilliams's severe disadvantage was that, in his particular fields of expertise, markets and marketing, Wendel probably felt that he himself possessed equal or perhaps greater talents.

MacWilliams in some ways had the toughest job of all. He suffered the singular burden of being responsible for the management function most critical to Welsh Carson's business ambitions and to Wendel's reputation: sales. MacWilliams's abiding problem was that his sales figures rarely came anywhere close to the optimistic projections he had given to Wendel, and which Wendel presumably had in turn presented to the board. MacWilliams's visits to Wendel's corner office were frequently a summons for explanations. He often emerged with the crestfallen expression of an errant student leaving the principal's office after a dressing down.

"I wouldn't go anywhere near Tom, at least for a few hours," he once warned a waiting line outside Wendel's office. "I've just given him this month's sales figures."

Wendel tended to regard marketing, MacWilliams's other area of supposed expertise, as a needless overhead. "There's too much fucking marketing around here, and not enough selling," was a favorite Wendel aphorism. One of his rare concessions to marketing, exercised through a raw but smooth-talking young acolyte called Tim Kelly, was his desire for personal publicity. Wendel loved to give interviews, and his statesmanlike poses began to grace the pages of financial magazines, much as Michael Bloomberg's once had. Employees often pinned the clippings to cubicle walls. Before long they would be using them for darts practice.

Almost as irritating to Wendel as the constantly disappointing sales figures was MacWilliams's fancy, which he freely and frequently expressed to people he thought he could trust, that he was locked in fierce competition with McCormick for the succession. It was a contest that MacWilliams was virtually alone in thinking he had any chance of winning. If talking the hide off an elephant had been the principal requisite, he would have won hands down, even against a rival not renowned for his reticence. MacWilliams could talk, mellifluously and effortlessly, for hours on end. It might have been an impressive talent except listeners rarely came away certain of what they had heard, or indeed whether they had actually heard anything at all. A philippic from MacWilliams was the conversational equivalent of Chinese food, satisfying only for an hour or so.

Wendel seemed genuinely fond of one other close associate, Jim Miceli. Miceli was a sidekick of Wendel's from way back. He could be relied on not only for strategic and financial advice (a reliance exercised either all too seldom or all too often: it is not clear which), but also for structuring clever business deals. Socially, he was very good company. A small, gnomish figure with a florid complexion, he possessed a puckish wit and he alone among Bridge executives seemed to enjoy a wide range of creative pursuits outside business, including a fondness for good food and fine wines. Miceli may have been a member of Wendel's inner circle, but he was seldom seen in the office, preferring to work from his Philadelphia home or on the road. His absences derived less from compelling logistical reasons than from an apparent desire to be isolated from the incessant corporate infighting, and perhaps from Wendel's temper tantrums, which, though rarely directed at him, Miceli secretly found distasteful.

This, then, was the executive team charged with converting Welsh Carson's risky business-investment into one of the stellar triumphs of the information industry.

Welsh Carson, Anderson & Stowe was a well-regarded venture capital firm with interests mainly in the health-care industry. The grand scheme to dominate the financial information business was launched in 1995 with the acquisition of Bridge Trading Company, a St. Louis-based institutional stock-brokerage firm with a modest sideline in market data. (The sideline had been around since the mid-seventies. Telerate had offered Bridge stock-market quotes through a dial-up facility in 1978, the year I joined the company.)

The brokerage made decent profits, but Welsh Carson's main purpose was to turn this information pygmy, which it temporarily renamed Global Finance Information Corporation, into a media giant. The endgame was a public stock-offering—perhaps multiple public offerings. The plan was intriguing because it was backed by big money, but in a market dominated by Reuters and Bloomberg it clearly carried a high degree of risk.

The man chosen to effect the transformation was at the time the chief executive of Liberty Brokerage Company (in which Welsh Carson had briefly owned a financial interest). Wendel's GFIC mandate, backed by the promise of virtually unlimited financial resources, was to supplement organic growth with expansion through opportunistic acquisitions of companies in financial distress.

Over the next three years, several such "opportunities" came to market. Each of the companies concerned had the desired ingredients: good products, a decent market share, and troubled finances. Bridge Information Systems, as the company was renamed, gobbled them up with relish.

The first on the table was MarketVision, a dealing-room data platform in which Liberty had owned a stake. It was followed by EJV, the long-troubled partnership formed by several leading Wall Street investment firms to compete with Bloomberg in the fixed-income market. These relatively modest operations bought at modest prices were just the beginning.

The stakes were raised substantially with the acquisition of Knight-Ridder Financial, the struggling market-data offshoot of the eponymous newspaper group, for $275 million in cash. KRF was followed, at about $30 million, largely in Bridge stock, by Telesphere, which operated a securities database (and was owned by Ken Marlin). The program was capped by ADP for about $150 million in cash.

The London operation I inherited seemed to be going nowhere in a hurry, except backwards. It was divided physically, as in most other respects, with the administrative staff located in Knight-Ridder's old office at 78 Fleet Street, and the sales group in the cobbled precinct of what had once been the Royal Mint, near the Tower of London. Both departments were the "mess" that Marlin had pictured—over-manned, disorganized, and demoralized. The finances, such as they were, presented a shambles. Revenue appeared to be in steady decline. Morale had been undermined by a recent purge of the former Knight-Ridder managers who had formed the bulk of the executive group.

Most of the remainder had to go, too, I decided. Some were competent, but they appeared to resent Bridge for taking over "their" company. It was a sentiment shared by others from acquired companies, but one with no justification other than nostalgia. Besides, it played right into the hands of certain "indigenous" Bridge executives, who harbored an irrational bias against the "immigrants."

The second task was to clean up the books. These would not have been out of place on the shelves of Foyle's cookery department. For that purpose I replaced a hapless finance director with Tony Smith, a former colleague of mine at Reuters, a man with a booming voice and sufficient physical bulk to ensure order in any department. Bridge's finance department in St. Louis donated Greg Vance, presumably to keep an eye on us.

What Smith and Vance uncovered, within weeks of my arrival, brought about my first, and probably fatal, conflict with Wendel. Bridge, they found, had been knowingly recording as revenue, subscription fees from "clients" that no longer existed as commercial entities, let alone as Bridge customers. Even many real clients were receiving bills for services they had formally canceled months, in some cases years, earlier. The initial clean-up revealed a revenue overstatement of over one million dollars. Vance thought at least a further million might be in jeopardy. Against a total income of about $45 million, the shortfall was significant but not, as far as I was concerned, a disaster. To Wendel, though, it was a catastrophe, and one that he did not wish to hear about. There was an explosion when Vance and I called with the bad news.

"I didn't send you over there to fiddle around with the fucking accounts," Wendel roared. "I can hire someone off the street to do that. Get out and sell something, for Christ's sake."

I had been warned about Wendel's enthusiasm for the ancient custom of flogging messengers bearing bad tidings.

Snape, who sported a few Wendel-imposed scars himself, had invented a word for it: "Flendeling," meaning a flogging by Wendel.

Snape told me that it once almost came to that, literally. He and Wendel had been engaged in some kind of contretemps in the office when Wendel suddenly put up his fists and challenged Snape to "duke it out." Snape sensibly declined the offer. For the record, my money would have gone on Snape.

The one enduring consequence of my own "flendeling" was that Wendel and I, from that day on, never again had a serious business conversation.

His anger was reignited a few weeks later when we had another run-in at the annual European sales conference, for which Bournemouth, a seaside resort on the south coast of England, had been selected as the venue. There was no serious business issue involved. In fact, the matter could hardly have been more trivial. Buses had been laid on to take delegates from the Bridge office to the hotel. A last-minute schedule change by MacWilliams meant that everyone had to be notified of a new departure time, an exercise successfully accomplished with one exception: Rob McCormick—of all people. He alone among 200 delegates had somehow failed to receive notice of the change. A bus stopped to pick him up at the Ritz Hotel on Piccadilly. It was hardly a diversion from the designated route, and no delay was involved, but McCormick made clear to Wendel that he was far from happy about having been overlooked.

"How could you so cruelly abandon poor Rob all alone in London's swankiest hotel?" one passenger was moved to observe, icily.

I had made my own way to Bournemouth independently by car, an arrangement made necessary by an overnight bout with gastroenteritis. Wendel's contribution to my delicate recovery was to greet me in a rage. "If you can't even organize a fucking bus trip, how the hell can I trust you to run Europe?"

There was no accounting for such vehemence, nor coping with it. Wendel stayed in a funk, at least with me, for two days. The conference seemed to last for two years.

If Wendel's persona was merely perplexing, that of Dick MacWilliams was confounding. There was no collision between us. There is no colliding with a phantom. He was a clone of Carl Valenti, as was our relationship. Three months after joining the company, I had barely conversed at length with him on any issue of substance. Even before I had joined the company, when Wendel invited his senior colleagues to interview me, MacWilliams had struggled to donate just fifteen minutes of his time. He had done most of the talking, while changing for a black-tie dinner. I had never before been interviewed by a man with no trousers. What was plain to me then—plainer still now—was that Dick regarded me neither as a companionable colleague nor as a useful addition to the management team. For all the effusive personal greetings—"Hey, JJ, how's it all goin', buddy?"—he always contrived to give me a wide berth, even on the telephone.

One afternoon, after making unsuccessful attempts to reach him in New York, I took my frustrations to George Yepes, the London sales manager, an import from the New York office recommended by MacWilliams. "Have you talked to Dick lately?" I wanted to know. With his hand over the receiver, Yepes whispered that he was talking to him at that very moment, indicating that he might be some time. He looked grave. I retreated back to my own office. Two hours later Yepes stopped by, eyes rolling. "Dick's just given me an earful about our lousy sales. Wants to know what the hell we're doing over here. Says Wendel's been on his case for a week. I'd say we're in more than a spot of trouble, old boy."

"You're the sales manager, George; what did you tell him you're going to do about it?"

I knew the answer even as I asked the question: blame me.

Someone, if not Yepes, had apparently accomplished that quite effectively. While my own calls to MacWilliams continued to go unanswered, George regularly got through to him without any trouble. It did not take clairvoyant powers to assign meaning to that, or to the other proliferating signs of estrangement.

Wendel felt neglected if not called regularly. Peter Coker, my opposite number in Asia—and Wendel's favorite manager—telephoned almost daily. He may have had a lot to talk about; I did not. There was certainly nothing to crow about. Sales were not merely poor but non-existent. The reason was, as every sales executive claimed, that the network was unreliable. Wendel refused to recognize the fact: McCormick himself had told him it was not so. Breaking into the European market was feasible, but for a company virtually unknown to most of its prospective clients, delivery problems were potentially fatal. Clearly we were in for a long, hard slog—and patience was a virtue for which Wendel was not renowned. With the benefit of hindsight, I realize that I should have called Wendel more often, if only to "talk the talk." And I have to say that this was the advice I received at the time.

I called Snape one day with a blunt question. "Seems I'm not doing so well in this company. Nobody wants to talk to me. Am I in trouble?"

"Doesn't look good," he said with disarming frankness. "Doesn't look good at all, I'm afraid."

I had been with the company less than six months. Six months too long, as far as I was concerned.

On that point, at least, Wendel and I seemed to be in agreement.

In the last few months of 1997 rumors flew thick and fast that Bridge was considering yet another major acquisition. It was one that for me had special poignancy. The target, by no means a reluctant one, was Dow Jones Markets (which for the sake of clarity I shall continue to call Telerate).

In hindsight, the Telerate acquisition was a mistake—not for fundamental business reasons but because Bridge had great difficulty integrating Telerate's products, which catered to markets with which Bridge was not familiar. Bridge also failed to embrace Telerate's employees, whose remarkable tenacity and *esprit de corps* had somehow survived the seven disastrous years under Dow Jones. Actually, acquiring Telerate did not appear to be a bad move at the time. My impression was that most of Bridge's senior executives were also in favor of it, some admittedly with certain reservations, which I shared. MacWilliams may have been an exception. I do not remember him vocally opposing the deal, though in light of his later attitude it must be assumed that he had been against it all along.

Wendel received the benefit of my unsolicited opinion. It was nothing more than the prevailing wisdom: "I don't think you've got much choice, Tom. If Bridge doesn't buy it, someone else will—maybe Thomson—and use it to compete against us. In any event, our coverage of equities and Telerate's position in fixed-income markets does make for a strategic fit." Wendel nodded without conviction, apparently harboring unexpressed doubts.

At one meeting between executives from the two companies, a sullen Greg Smith showed up as a member of the Dow Jones negotiating team. Smith was said to be interested in buying Telerate himself. His attitude was truculent and he seemed reluctant to answer questions put to him by Bridge executives. Wendel promptly demanded his ejection, on the reasonable grounds that, as a potential buyer himself, Smith could hardly represent the seller in a meeting with a competing bidder. Dow Jones agreed and Smith stomped angrily from the room. The only reason to mention this minor incident is that Wendel appeared to derive great pleasure from relating it, suggesting that he was finally warming to the deal.

Wendel's earlier wavering had been based more on financial than strategic grounds. Telerate clearly offered product and other operating synergies, but the asking price of $510 million was no bargain for a company suffering serious declines in revenue and profit. In that year, 1997, Telerate's revenue had fallen from $827 million to $760 million, operating earnings from $223 million to $46 million. Operating expenses had soared by $120 million.

Further declines in revenue and earnings were projected for the coming year. Dow Jones had clearly reached the outer limits of Peter Kann's patience and would soon be testing that of his already disgruntled shareholders. The land of Rolling Thunder, he had decided, would have to be evacuated.

Raising the loan necessary to purchase Telerate would put Bridge's indebtedness above one billion dollars. That would result, as Wendel was well aware, in the kind of leverage investment advisors usually warn against. Balancing that was the comforting knowledge that Welsh Carson had deep pockets, at any rate access to someone else's deep pockets. When Dow Jones agreed to take $350 million in cash and the balance in Bridge stock in return for a 10 percent equity stake, the transaction was all but assured.

And with it, though few suspected it at the time, Bridge's fate.

Shortly before the closing, Harris Bank of Chicago, leading the lending syndicate, sent several representatives to Palm Springs, California to attend Bridge's annual President's Club event, a junket for top sales executives. It offered the bankers an opportunity to mingle with key employees and to sit in at meetings to observe Bridge management in action. A similar invitation was extended to several Telerate executives. Members of the management committee tagged along, many of them, including me, with spouses in tow. After a gloomy London winter, we found the dry desert heat bracing. The political climate was less invigorating.

Already in the doghouse, I was soon consigned to the pound. The reason was a droll aside I slipped into my remarks to the assembly, to the effect that with some "gentle manipulation" of the accounts, Europe might soon achieve profitability. It would have been a harmless jibe in most circumstances, but I had forgotten that Wendel had invited the bankers to sit in on the meeting. Dozing at the back of the hall, they did not seem to notice the remark. But Wendel was livid. Or so I was told. He said nothing to me, which I took as another telltale sign that I was about to be busted. The desert air turned distinctly chilly, and not just in the evenings.

Shortly after Palm Springs, the Telerate acquisition all but closed, Wendel organized a European road show of motivational presentations to Telerate staff. As Europe's managing director, I was obliged to join the caravan, though strictly for display purposes, since my fate was by then already sealed, if not yet signed. In London, Frankfurt, and Zurich I stoically suffered the humiliation of sitting on the executive platform alongside Wendel, McCormick, and MacWilliams as they set out to charm Telerate's employees with grandiloquent talk of a brave new Bridge world of enlightened technology, exaltation of excellence, and humane management.

I was approached by a number of my former Telerate colleagues. "Glad to have you back," was the congratulatory message. "Don't count on it," I cautioned.

One former colleague became a conspicuous member of Wendel's ever-expanding entourage during that trip. I had not seen the lean, elegant figure of Julian Childs for several years. He had become Telerate's chief operating officer, my old job, and was now part of the road show himself, ostensibly representing Dow Jones's management. What he was really there to represent, it dawned on me, was the job that I was about to relinquish.

Sure enough, word began to circulate that Childs had been pegged as my replacement—"You seem to be following me around," I told him—which naturally inspired the assumption that I had been fired. The uncertainty made for an unpleasant working environment. A few days after the road show I decided to call Wendel in New York for "clarification" of my position. A senior executive having to make a transatlantic phone call to confirm rumors of his dismissal must be an unusual experience. It struck me as odd that Wendel had not seen fit to bring the axe down while he was in London—but then odd things happened at Bridge all the time.

I got straight to the point. "It appears you've decided to make a change over here. If so, let's make it sooner rather than later. The place is full of rumors. I'm sure you'll agree we need to get this thing resolved."

Wendel, with MacWilliams on the speaker, confirmed my fate with the usual pro forma regrets. He naturally expressed the hope that we could arrange an orderly separation, which was the usual code for "We expect you to go quietly." I had no intention of making any unnecessary fuss. Frankly it was something of a relief to be removed from duty. Anyway, I had the financial cushion of a six-month notice period, which I had no reason to suppose Wendel would dispute. MacWilliams, assigned the task of disposing of me, flew to London with other ideas.

He revealed them to me over lunch in a restaurant located a few hundred yards from the Tower of London where, I reflected, a number of other irksome figures had been given the chop. Would I consider taking severance (how appropriate!) in Bridge stock options rather than cash? "Not bloody likely," was the unspoken response. The spoken one was that I would have to think about it, in consultation with my solicitor.

Whether the offer reflected Bridge's shaky liquidity or a spiteful desire to prevent me profiting from our brief association, there was no telling. A few days after I had been honored at London's most expensive leaving party of the year, further speculation was superfluous. The matter was resolved in a most curious and unexpected fashion.

I was enjoying the spring weather in my garden a few evenings later when MacWilliams telephoned. What I expected to hear was a new severance offer. What I heard was exactly the opposite.

"Are you sitting down?" he wanted to know, giggling childishly. "And I hope you've got a drink in hand?"

The answer to both was affirmative.

"Good, because you're not gonna believe this. Obviously we can't use Dow Jones Markets as a product brand, so the Telerate name is being revived. In fact, we're going to run Telerate as a separate company. Now, here's the cool part ["cool" along with "neat" and "awesome" being among MacWilliams's favorite sophomoric epithets]. We'd like you to come back—not as Bridge's European MD, but as president of Telerate. Same terms and conditions as you had before."

I was flabbergasted, but curiosity beckoned. "I can't wait to hear more."

Telerate, MacWilliams explained, had to be maintained as a separate entity from Bridge because royalty payments to Cantor Fitzgerald, amounting to over $50 million a year, and based on the number of Telerate workstations, would otherwise be applied to Bridge terminals as well. Since Bridge users were mainly equities traders who had no interest in Cantor's government-securities prices, paying royalties on them would mean incurring a huge and unnecessary expense. My principal duty would be to maintain the legal and operating distinction between the two companies and their product lines. Telerate would outsource most of its operating functions to Bridge under an inter-company service agreement. Telerate information would be made available only to Telerate terminals and Telerate customers would receive Telerate contracts and invoices. I would join Bridge's management committee to give the position status and credibility. A real emperor with a phantom empire.

A host of questions came to mind, but one above all. How did Bridge expect Howard Lutnick—a man acquainted with lawsuits the way most of us are acquainted with buying groceries—to react other than to sue, on the grounds that the whole scheme was a thinly veiled subterfuge to avoid paying royalties? We were confronting a man who had allegedly wrested control of Cantor Fitzgerald from Bernie Cantor, the firm's founder—and Lutnick's muse and mentor—by having Bernie, then on his hospital deathbed and attached to a life support system, declared mentally incompetent. An unseemly and very public row with Bernie's widow, Iris, had been followed by protracted court proceedings, most ending to Lutnick's advantage. Clearly Howard Lutnick was not a man easily cowed or embarrassed.

"We think we've got him covered from the legal perspective," was MacWilliams's considered opinion. "Anyway, that's for the lawyers to fight over."

"Bugger off," was my instinctive response. Six months of Bridge had been more than enough for one working lifetime. Divine intervention came from my wife, to whom I'd whispered a summary of the call. Mindful of the need to maintain the household income, Martha counseled caution: delay a response until after the weekend. What she really meant was, "Do it."

"Hey, JJ, I truly hope you'll see your way clear to coming back on board," MacWilliams trilled. "We'd love to have you back, and this could be a hoot."

Cool, too, no doubt.

Economic considerations prevailed over the desire for a moment of vengeful triumph. Two days later I called back to say yes. "Great news," gushed Dick, still affecting unbridled joy and enthusiasm. "We're gonna have a lot of fun and make a lot of money. I'm looking forward to working with you again." Dick seemed to have developed a sudden penchant for irony.

"Speaking of working," I said, fishing, "who's going to be running Europe?"

"Your friend Julian Childs," was the response. "But we're still talking about it."

Childs was apparently keen to take the job but was balking at the financial terms. Unwilling to match the salary he had enjoyed at Dow Jones, Bridge had loaded up its offer with stock options. The appointment had already been announced inside the company and been widely reported in the trade press. Childs suddenly refused to budge on terms. As someone familiar with the negotiations put it: "What he's looking for is embossed green paper inscribed 'In God We Trust.' What Wendel is offering is blank white paper that says 'In Tom We Trust.'"

Amid charges and counter-charges of broken promises, Wendel called off the chase. The boxes of personal effects Childs had already moved into the Telerate office were quietly shipped out a week later. "We need revolving doors to handle all this executive traffic," quipped one bewildered secretary. "Whoever next?" "Whoever" was named shortly in a surprise announcement: Dick MacWilliams.

Cool!

A few months later, I ran into Lutnick at a charity cocktail party given by Wendel's wife on a yacht on the Hudson River. He could not resist a dig at the Bridge-Telerate segregation. "I see the great Telerate Corporation is represented in force here tonight," he said to me with a knowing wink. "And where are your other two employees?"

I mentioned the encounter to Wendel the next day. "He's preparing to sue," I said.

"Let him come," Wendel said. "We're ready for him. And you'd better be ready, too."

I was ready. But Lutnick never came.

Few Bridge employees knew or cared about the overhanging threat of a Cantor Fitzgerald lawsuit. The acquisition of Telerate gave rise to an interlude of euphoric optimism. Particularly happy were the exasperated Telerate sales executives, not to mention their long-suffering clients, who had spent years clamoring for a replacement for the tottering old Telerate page-based data feed. They were now promised delivery, within weeks, of a digital, or itemized, feed driven by brilliant new Bridge technology.

What McCormick failed to tell them—because he did not believe he had to—was whether Bridge's network, with its history of breakdowns, was up to the job. More than a few customers expressed reservations on that score. They were dismissed, sometimes to their faces, as cynical mischief-makers. "You either believe in us or you don't," McCormick declared to one important London client, in the manner of a football coach addressing players of a losing team at half time. "If you don't believe in us, then frankly we don't want your business." No one, least of all a few recalcitrant customers, would be allowed to spoil McCormick's great Telerate coming-out party. The client was too astonished to respond.

And so began a time of great rejoicing, not just in New York and London but also in every other hitherto forlorn outpost of the revived Telerate empire. As with every instance of good news at Bridge, the rejoicing was short-lived.

McCormick did come through with the promised new data feed, but in every critical respect except the crucial one: the timetable. The McCormick calendar, obviously at variance with the widely accepted Julian version, converted weeks to months and months to years. An enervating, disillusioning, and damaging two years, as it turned out. In the meantime, the persistent vagaries of Bridge's network began to lay waste to Telerate's European customer base.

Multiple reasons could be offered for the chronic unreliability of McCormick's celebrated, state-of-the-art, cutting edge, best-of-breed paradigm-altering data-delivery system. Multiple reasons *were* offered. But as the various diagnoses were debated at length across the Atlantic and the Pacific, Europe and Asia continued to suffer through a daily routine of network "incidents," many of them of extended duration. Clients were being pushed well beyond exasperation. "Love the product but it never works," was a lyric that could have been set to music.

The irony was that network durability had always been touted as one of

Bridge's Unique Selling Propositions. Wendel and McCormick harped on and on about scalability, meaning the capacity to handle whatever vast quantities of data the world's stock exchanges might generate as stock prices moved irreversibly higher. Wendel's boast was that Bridge alone among market-data vendors would be able to withstand the expected onslaught as trading volumes exploded. Reuters and Bloomberg, he confidently predicted, would be driven to desperate resorts such as "throttling back" data, which in plain English means discarding updates in order to keep up with trading. There was evidence that they were doing it already, McCormick chimed in.

If Reuters and Bloomberg had indeed been reduced to desperate measures, then their clients seemed happily oblivious to them. McCormick was missing a vital point: "Scalable may be good but reliable is better."

McCormick's response to international network problems tended to assume one of three forms: denial, blame, or a combination of both. Paraphrased, it usually went something like this: "Nonsense. The network performs perfectly well in the United States. You're asking me to believe that it doesn't work anywhere else. That's crap. I'll tell you why it doesn't function properly over there. It's because you people have hired stupid technicians who simply don't understand how it works."

If there is such a thing as an ideal communications environment, then America represents it, which is why within the United States McCormick's network seemed to perform pretty much as it was designed to. Outside America, where the environment tends to become more complex as the potential points of failure multiply, it plainly did not.

One reason was the persistent failure of sensitive network devices called replicators, which were crucial to Bridge's international network. As the word implies, they acted as transmission relay stations designed to replicate the data flow as if they were the source itself. Whenever a replicator fell out of sync with the rest of the network, however, those clients attached to it lost their service. The reason why Bridge's replicators were forever "falling over" in overseas locations but never in the United States had nothing to do with foreign incompetence; they were not used on the American network.

Replicator and other problems were compounded routinely by McCormick's St. Louis network-management group, which had fallen into the dangerous habit of adding or changing system software, usually on weekends, without informing overseas offices. It did not occur to anyone in St. Louis that Europe and Asia operated in different time-zones. It was one of many examples of American insularity, magnified perhaps by Bridge's headquarters being located slap-bang in the middle of the Middle West. "Those guys think the world ends at the Verrazano Bridge," summed up Europe's view. Where it actually ended, as far as St. Louis was concerned, was on the western bank of the Mississippi.

Monday mornings in London, Hong Kong, and Tokyo were occasions for trepidation. For clients there was the irritation of disrupted service, for Bridge employees the unpleasant prospect of a McCormick tongue-lashing.

Not until March 2000, when a new transmission protocol was introduced, would the network issue finally be resolved. By then, many of Telerate's surviving European and Asian users, battle-weary and suspicious, refused to convert to the new feed. "I've been patient up to now but I've had enough and I'm moving on," sums up the common response. McCormick disciples were disappearing as fast as the customers.

If the revenue losses alarmed London sales executives, whose commissions depended in large part on stemming them, they appeared not to disturb unduly the sleep of Dick MacWilliams. He dismissed the rising cancellations with a pet formulation. They would soon dry up, he liked to say, for one very good reason: Telerate was "rapidly running out of victims."

If there were no restless nights in London, there ought to have been in New York, but even there the company's managers seemed to be sleeping soundly. And the owners. Whatever Welsh Carson was being told about the state of Bridge's business, it did not seem to include the growing sense of foreboding in Europe and Asia. One reason may have been that business in the United States was robust, as sales piggybacked a buoyant stock market (although such halcyon days, a more or less permanent feature of the 1990s, were about to change abruptly and drastically). The overriding attitude inside Bridge, apparently, was that Europe and Asia were just sideshows, populated by culturally and linguistically challenged bands of cynics, idlers, and complainers.

At management committee meetings Wendel continued to exude confidence, almost invariably reporting that the board was "very pleased" with Bridge's overall progress. If so, the owners had developed a remarkable immunity to disappointing profit statements—assuming that was what they were receiving, as opposed to some heavily doctored version, as some of us believed—or a curious tolerance for endless flights of metaphorical mitigation. At Bridge, metaphors were bountiful: corners were forever about to be turned, lights glowed alluringly at the end of tunnels.

The reality of course was that the board was not pleased at all. Poor financial results could not be gussied up or explained away indefinitely, not even by Bridge's remarkably adroit chief financial officer, Daryl Rhodes. It was not obvious that Rhodes was cooking the books, though many suspected he was doing exactly that. Judging by Rhodes's increasingly haggard look, it was more likely that the books were cooking him. Either way, the smell from the kitchen was of something not altogether pleasant. And since no one had spotted the ingredients arriving, no one could possibly guess what dish was being prepared. Whatever it was, the most damaging consequence was that customers were not being billed or were receiving invoices they could not understand and refusing to pay them. Bridge had a cash-flow problem of frightening and expanding dimensions.

Extracting management accounts from Rhodes or his budget director, Kevin Schott, would have defied the American School of Dentistry. Tony Smith and I, conscious of our fiduciary responsibilities as Telerate directors, were constantly after St. Louis for Telerate numbers. These were always promised but rarely delivered. The excuses were so remarkable in their diversity that Smith's initial anger always subsided into chuckles. "It's perfectly obvious they've got what we want but for some reason can't, or won't, give it to us." After a while we gave up trying, content with sending routine requests that were routinely ignored.

If the jig was not up yet, the feeling was growing that without a turnaround in the company's financial performance—that is, a genuine as opposed to a contrived turnaround—it soon would be. The cash crunch loomed ever closer.

Speculation about strained relations between board and management became publicly apparent in the late summer of 1999 when a new figure slipped into place in Bridge's executive office. David Roscoe, a thirty-year veteran of JP Morgan Bank, and a golfing buddy of Pat Welsh (founding partner of Welsh Carson and a Bridge director) had been enlisted, ostensibly, to clean up the administrative mess. It was generally supposed that the real motive was to groom him as Wendel's eventual successor. On the company grapevine "eventual" steadily lost ground to "imminent."

Enigmatic rather than charismatic, Roscoe was a man of pleasant manners who spoke in articulate riddles. These were presumed to be manifestations of a superior mind until it became evident that Roscoe was often as bewildered by his own oratorical conundrums as everyone else. None of which prevented him from throwing himself into the fray with gusto. But his ignorance of the company's business rendered him as an operating executive at first ineffectual and in time obstructive. Roscoe's talents might have been an asset in a bank but were of little use at Bridge.

Wendel introduced Roscoe to the company at the international sales conference in Las Vegas, inviting him to present his thoughts on administrative and financial restructuring. It was hardly the customary occasion for airing matters of such complexity and Roscoe suffered the additional disadvantage of appearing in the last slot of the last day. An audience numbed by the excesses of the night before was duly baffled—especially by Roscoe's hastily prepared organization chart, which might have been, for all anyone knew or cared, a map of the Tokyo subway system.

Still, the delegates went home, if somewhat bemused, at least in one respect happy. Someone at last seemed to be doing something about a problem that had driven them and their customers to distraction for years—namely, getting the invoices out on time and in a form that was comprehensible, and collecting the cash.

The most interesting aspect of the Las Vegas event was the somewhat subdued nature of the social scene. Late-night preoccupations on such occasions and in such places usually boil down to two things: satisfying various carnal desires or getting sufficiently inebriated to eliminate them. But in Las Vegas, the bar-room conversations were unusually reflective, impervious to the vulgar distractions all around. I had the startling experience of observing a group of salesmen in a striptease club discussing the company's problems and the potential impact on their stock options, apparently oblivious to the leggy pole-dancers gyrating energetically a few feet away.

When even sales executives, not usually the most reflective of people, are sufficiently concerned to question whether their employer can really afford to fly 500 people from all points of the globe to a remote desert resort to celebrate what by common consent had been a dreadful year, the conclusion must be that it cannot.

# Bridge Lowered

The first quarter of the new millennium brought a few fleeting moments of relief from growing concerns over Bridge's financial condition. After that, however, the year marched on in an atmosphere of unrelieved gloom and crisis.

The year began on a positive note, dead on the stroke of midnight. Like Sherlock Holmes's curious incident of the dog that failed to bark in the night, it was an event that did not happen. In this case, what was not heard, despite the many cataclysmic prognostications to the contrary, was the sound of millions of computers crashing. In the event, wherever in the world clocks struck the witching hour on January 1, 2000, Bridge's computers continued to suck in and spew out data just as they had one second earlier. The gloomier pundits had got it wrong. Bridge, along with just about every other company on the planet, had passed the so-called Y2K test with flying colors.

Of greater positive consequence, at the end of the first quarter, was the "fix" of the overseas network problem with the introduction of a new transmission protocol. It was called multi-casting, and its singular benefit was that it relieved the replicators of the burden that had broken their backs too often and for too long. From then on the network behaved as good as gold. London celebrated as if Mafeking had been relieved.

But neither the Y2K matriculation nor the newfound reliability was in itself a triumph, as neither presented Bridge with any competitive advantage.

More tangibly encouraging was the announcement in February of an initial public offering of shares in Savvis Corporation. Savvis, a small Virginia-based network-services company, had been acquired the previous year to serve as a publicly owned vehicle into which Bridge would spin off its client network, at the same time opening it up to third-party traffic. The acquisition was celebrated on two counts. First, it marked the opening of Welsh Carson's promised flotation program; if the Savvis initial public offering proved successful, then a large portion of Bridge's debt could be paid off and a Bridge IPO accelerated. Second, Rob McCormick was named as Savvis's chief executive, which removed him from the Bridge management group (though not far enough for many of his former colleagues).

Joy gave way to envy as McCormick received enough Savvis stock options to make him, at the initial public-offering price of $24 a share, a multi-millionaire. Joy and envy were both short-lived. The Savvis flotation was an unmitigated disaster. After an initial and brief surge, which took the price to $28 a share, the shares tumbled within months to less than a dollar.

There was no wondering why.

The timing of the issue could not have been worse. The market's infatuation with communications and technology companies—all of them plagued by excess capacity, faltering demand, and Himalayan debt—was about to end in tears, as most infatuations do. Savvis was not singled out for rough treatment; stellar stock-market performers representing household-name products, such as Lucent, Dell, Intel, and Compaq, all fell out of bed, too. Deteriorating market sentiment might alone have wrecked the Savvis offering, but even on a fundamental evaluation it was given little chance of success—especially after the publication of the Savvis prospectus.

It is the essential nature of such documents—indeed part of their purpose—to be peppered with pro forma warnings about potential investment risks. But the Savvis prospectus contained an unusual health warning from the auditors about the parent's financial condition. Referring to Bridge's debt burden, the auditors' report raised doubts about the company's ability to continue as a "going concern." As Savvis derived 90 percent of its revenue from Bridge, the warning assumed a sinister significance. The auditors' comments were not so much a health warning as a death certificate.

If the timing was bad, the handling of the Savvis offering was even worse. Merrill Lynch, the lead underwriter, with a confidence that ignored bearish market sentiment, decided to raise the number of shares issued from 10.5 million to 17 million. Welsh Carson purchased six million of them, which was just as well since there were virtually no other institutional buyers.

In fact, the only overtly enthusiastic investors were Bridge's employees who, in a collective act of misplaced loyalty, bought Savvis shares in great quantities under a company-sponsored "family and friends" concession. Many of us had joined the company in the expectation of cashing in stock options. Now we seemed to be funding it instead. The fact that I lost a little money on the Savvis float was of no great consequence, but I felt sorry for the many secretaries and other junior employees who took out loans to finance their share purchases.

For many industry-watchers, the failure of the Savvis offering marked the beginning of the end of the Bridge adventure.

A few observers still believed that the company might yet save itself, but as the year unfolded—unraveled might be a better word—Bridge experienced the strange sensation of being the subject of a post-mortem examination conducted while it was still alive. Industry analysts tended to ask "What went wrong?" rather than "What is going wrong?"

What had gone wrong was naturally a matter for debate. The business plan, some critics claimed, had been far too ambitious, and Wendel's timetable far too aggressive. Perhaps they were, but arguably not more so than those of many a successful grand design before it. The frenzied acquisition program, others said, burdened the company with too much debt. The loan repayments were indeed onerous, but many companies had carried greater debt-to-equity ratios and thrived. The process of integrating the products of acquired companies had been painfully slow, some observed. So it may have been, though for every opinion of that ilk there could be found a countervailing view that it was actually too fast.

While none of these, nor other contributing factors, could be dismissed, Bridge's problem was at root its inability to manage the household economy. To the obvious prerequisites of maintaining income and controlling expenses—disciplines that shopkeepers, small-business owners and indeed domestic householders are obliged to observe the world over—Bridge seemed institutionally blind.

Sharply rising costs were ignored even as they converged with, and then exceeded, sharply declining revenues. A festering cash-collection problem was inexplicably neglected at a time when the business desperately needed cash to service its debt. The runaway receivables were the direct consequence of yet another unattended problem. Bridge's chaotic billing system was actually several diverse billing systems cobbled together, those of its acquired companies. It produced incomprehensible invoices that clients were understandably reluctant to pay. The aggregate amount they had failed to pay was said to be north of $100 million. It proved to be understated.

An absence of detailed management accounts left line managers operating in the dark. There were occasional sightings of financials but only those covering overall corporate performance.

The irony was that the day-to-day management of financial affairs represented one of the few instances in which authority had been delegated to mid-level executives. It might better be described as dereliction than delegation. Most of Bridge's financial executives were neither professionally nor temperamentally qualified for their jobs. The latter deficiency was fatal, for when circumstances demanded difficult decisions or blunt advice, these managers tended to cravenly defer to their mentors, perhaps out of gratitude, but in any event in blatant disregard of their fiduciary obligations. No alarm bells ever went off in Bridge's finance department, not even when the place started filling up with smoke.

Prominent among the sundry manifestations of Wendel's maladroit financial supervision was his inability, or unwillingness, to tackle an inflated headcount, which after a four-year acquisition spree had ballooned from 500 employees to 5000. To accommodate most of the American contingent,

Wendel spent millions of dollars building a sprawling campus in the St. Louis suburb of Creve Coeur (aptly translated as broken heart). It smacked of a memorial, a place destined one day to be renamed Tom Wendel Plaza. The one thing of which it did not smack was financial prudence.

To be fair, Wendel did from time to time publicly, even vehemently, call for what he considered draconian cuts in staff, but tough talk was never converted to tough action. One management meeting I recall—early in 2000 I would guess—was devoted entirely to the subject of headcount. In grave tones, Wendel called for an across-the-board staff reduction of 10 percent. It was not, in my view, nearly enough, but it was at least a start. What soon became apparent was that the specific figure was academic, since the appeal for cuts went largely unheeded. Department managers paid public lip service to it but privately finagled their numbers with an imaginative variety of ruses, such as eliminating open positions and counting them as real cuts. If as much creativity had been channeled into job elimination as into job preservation, the company might have survived.

During a follow-up meeting two weeks later, when managers were supposed to present their "downsizing" plans, the only sound heard around the table was that of mumbled dissembling. Instead of provoking an angry outburst from Wendel, it drew merely an expression of resigned disappointment. Somehow, the fight seemed to have gone out of him. Amid audible sighs of relief, the meeting moved on to other matters. It struck me as a defining moment.

Whether Wendel's apparent collapse reflected a failure of will or a disorganized mind there is no telling. My suspicion is that the explanation could be found in Wendel's belief that the company's true path to salvation lay in selling its way out of trouble—in simply overwhelming rising costs with massive sales. In Bridge's unstoppable drive to market domination, what could a few heads matter one way or another?

This and other multiple failures of oversight were symptomatic of a management that in virtually every aspect of the company's affairs had scorned due process and hard-nosed realism in favor of anarchy and an almost surreal optimism.

If Wendel lived in a fool's paradise, as a growing number of people around the table silently believed, then he and the company were about to experience a slippery descent into a living hell.

In January, Roscoe was joined in the executive suite by Steve Wilson, a financial executive with high-level experience in the pharmaceutical industry, brought in to replace Daryl Rhodes as group finance director. In contrast to Roscoe, Wilson came across as disarmingly frank. "Financially, this company's in a bloody mess," were his first words to me. "The cash position isn't good at all. We've got our work cut out, I can tell you. And we're in a race against time." Daryl Rhodes had never uttered such blasphemies.

"Wilson won't be around long talking like that," was the reaction in bars. But there was no retribution. How could there be? The "bloody mess" was now apparent to everyone. And Wilson soon endeared himself to skeptics by announcing a series of senior appointments purging the old guard in the St. Louis finance group. Rhodes was subjected to the ignominy of three successive demotions, for which he appeared to be more grateful than aggrieved.

Wilson turned over rocks that had lain undisturbed for years. Under most of them he found a scorpion. The biggest scorpion of all was under the rock marked receivables. The elusive Miceli now found a cause worth being elusive for. Hastily assembling a swat team, he locked himself and his press-ganged crew into an unused office suite and set about collecting cash in what was taking on the appearance of an eleventh-hour rescue mission. The numbers involved were said to be enormous. The exercise was successful in bringing in short-term cash, but it also resulted in huge write-offs, which, by the time Miceli had completed the project, were said to be closing in on $200 million. The extraordinary irony in that extraordinary figure was that it was attributable to some of the most trusted and credit-worthy institutions in the land.

His immediate task completed, Miceli did not hang about to ponder the issue. No sooner had he emerged from the "War Room" than he announced his retirement. Wendel was losing friends fast. The question on everyone's mind was: "What does he know that we don't?"

Collecting cash had been a vital task, but it had been applied to symptoms rather than causes. The underlying reason for the receivables problem, Bridge's billing system, had to be addressed or "bad debts" would simply start accumulating all over again. Wilson brought in Deloitte Touche, Bridge's accounting firm, to examine the company's entire order-to-cash process. The consulting fee was reported to be over one million dollars a month. "Nice work if you can get it," was the cynical response but tempered by recognition that if Deloitte could come up with a solution then it might be worth ten times that. Deloitte issued a report, but it was not widely circulated and almost needless to say no solutions materialized. In the event, there would not have been enough time to implement them anyway.

Just as Bridge began to confront its internal problems in earnest, external events started to conspire against the company. Talk of an economic recession surfaced in the press. The equities market, spooked by the burst technology bubble, fell into a prolonged swoon across the board. Trading volumes receded amid talk of a severe market correction—a Wall Street formulation meaning market crash—to which financial institutions responded, as they always do, by drastically scaling back trading operations. And, of course, their information services.

Of the three leading data vendors, struggling Bridge, with a long list of black marks against its name, offered cost-cutters the easiest mark.

My own mood at the time was far from ebullient, reflecting the inexorable decline in Telerate's European business. Frustration was a constant companion. The company clearly needed all the help it could muster in staunching the revenue outflow and it seemed to me—you may think immodestly—that with nearly forty years in the business I might have had something, perhaps a great deal, to contribute to the cause. Months earlier I had greeted MacWilliams's arrival in London with an offer to assist in any way he saw fit, short of sweeping the floor. The response was cool in the literal as opposed to the "groovy" sense. It was an offer I repeated at regular intervals. I was used to dealing with clients at a high level, I told MacWilliams over a rare lunch. "Use me as a glad-handing elder statesman, if nothing else. If not that, then there must be something else I can do to help you turn the business around." Apparently there was not.

"It's turning around already," was the response, accompanied by the goofy grin MacWilliams always adopted to camouflage insincerity. "You're doing a great job doing just what you're doing. Just keep doing it."

What I was mainly doing was signing legal documents. In that respect I was indeed doing a great job, perhaps a brilliant one, though not one that justified what Bridge was paying me. Telerate's little ghetto on the fifth floor of Fetter Lane—a corner of some foreign field that is forever Telerate—was just fifty paces from the Telerate office I'd occupied in the 1980s. It might as well have been in Ulan Bator.

Pretty much ostracized by Bridge's management (though not by the staff), Tony Smith and I spent a good part of our working day attempting to analyze the state of the business. In truth, we did it to fill the hours, but it needed doing anyway, and no one else seemed to be doing it.

MacWilliams, in keeping with the Bridge business ethos, harbored a deep suspicion of facts and a particular aversion to numbers. Unlike Daryl Rhodes in St. Louis, Greg Vance in London published monthly financial statements, but MacWilliams never invited him, or anyone else, to discuss them. "I doubt whether Dick and I have had more than a dozen meetings in two years," Vance told me one day. "He seems to despise bean-counters." He might have added, "Except when they process Dick's remarkable expense accounts."

Every month, Smith and I used Vance's figures to produce charts showing the direction of sales, installations, and cancellations. The results were far from reassuring. In the first two instances the trend-lines declined, without serious interruption, from the top left corner to the bottom right, and in the third it traveled steadily from bottom right to top left. We did not need Deloitte to point out the implications.

One day I showed the charts to MacWilliams. After a cursory glance his reaction was as predictable as it was mystifying: "You can't rely on numbers to tell the true story."

On another occasion, I mentioned that we had produced a chart projecting net sales and operating expenses twelve months ahead that showed European business heading towards a state of virtual insolvency. As before, he was uninterested: "Look, I'm really too busy to look at pretty pictures right now." As I left his office, he theatrically tossed the chart into the waste-paper bin, making sure I had noticed.

"Haven't you figured it out yet?" someone said to me when I mentioned the incident. "Disregarding any personal antipathy between you and Dick, what this is really about is something else: MacWilliams hates Telerate. To him, Telerate is a discredited company with a lousy product, a shrinking market and no future. His agenda is to build up the Bridge business and in the process kill off Telerate completely."

Numerous incidents lent support to the theory. "I don't want to hear that word Telerate around here ever again," MacWilliams had once snarled at a sales meeting.

The irrational animus against Telerate was not confined to MacWilliams: it flowed like an underground stream through the entire Bridge organization. It was starkly apparent in St. Louis, where every single employee was proud to be considered above all a Bridge employee, culturally and operationally devoted to the American equity business. A similar attitude pervaded New York, too, although there it was less obvious because the office had surviving pockets of former Telerate employees. Several senior executives thought of Telerate as the company's ball and chain, the principal reason why Bridge seemed to be losing what was now perceived as a life-or-death struggle for survival.

They were right. Measured by all the standard measurements of success—growth, profitability, and market share—Telerate *was* a ball and chain. But it was only one of many. None of Bridge's product lines seemed to be doing particularly well, the performances ranging from adequate to atrocious. The truth was that Bridge was encumbered with more restraining irons than poor old Jacob Marley.

I was among the first to concede that Telerate's old business model required a radical overhaul, but was left at a loss to understand why measures were not taken to that end. And if the equity markets appeared to offer greater opportunities than the capital markets traditionally served by Telerate, which appeared to be the case at the time, then certainly that is where Bridge's business emphasis should have been placed. But was that the case?

If MacWilliams was right in thinking that Telerate had little chance of survival, or at any rate few immediate prospects for growth, then Bridge had three options: reduce Telerate's operations to a manageable size, sell the business, or shut it down. Presumably none of them was considered because that would beg the uncomfortable question of why Bridge had spent half a billion dollars buying the business in the first place, just eighteen months earlier.

Instead of applying business solutions to Telerate's problems, Bridge simply succumbed to blind prejudice. It was an extraordinary attitude towards a product that represented 50 percent of Bridge's revenue in the United States and 90 percent of it in Europe and Asia. Inaction was as dangerous as it was inexplicable. If MacWilliams had it in mind to virtually abandon 90 percent of Europe's revenue while struggling to develop the 10 percent—and in a hostile market environment—then he must surely have had a plan. Otherwise, he was performing a high-wire act without a net.

Of course there was no plan. There may have been some kind of scheme lodged in MacWilliams's head, but from that unfathomable place it was never likely to emerge. MacWilliams no more believed in producing formal business plans than most other senior Bridge executives. To Wendel, they smacked of "marketing."

I confided my concerns about Europe's lack of direction to Snape, the only senior executive in New York remotely sympathetic to Telerate. He sounded resigned to chaos.

"Sure it's crazy," he admitted, "but trying to figure out the strange mind of MacWilliams is a futile occupation. Just go about your business and leave him to his."

I finished the call with a gratuitous observation designed to wind him up—not the most difficult of tasks: "Let me put it this way: if Bridge were not Telerate's parent company, I'd be obliged as a director to file suit against Bridge for breach of contract, gross negligence, financial mismanagement, and probably a few other things besides. Telerate's lawyer tells me that you're in blatant conflict with the service agreement."

"Yeah, you've got a point there," Snape snapped. "So why don't you go ahead and sue?"

No strains or distractions diverted Wendel from hosting in June the market-data industry's biggest social bash of the season. For the second successive year, Bridge's cocktail party provided the grand finale to the Securities Industry Association's annual exhibition at the New York Hilton. Two thousand attendees—comprising, in addition to exhibition delegates, Bridge employees, competitors, assorted hotel guests, hotel staff, and even a bevy of enterprising hookers—enjoyed a munificent event, memorable if only for an ice floe bearing the world's biggest display of shrimp. The bars were free and the dance floor shook visibly as three rock groups thumped, twanged, and wailed deafeningly, well into the night.

"All I can say," said one of many uninvited attendees from Reuters, "is that if Bridge can afford all this, it must be doing a damn sight better than we read about in the press."

The press, I refrained from pointing out, did not know the half of it.

Soon after the SIA show, Wendel became sufficiently concerned about Europe to pay London a rare visit. It occurred to me that Snape had mentioned our conversation, although Europe's results were reason enough to demand Wendel's attention without any prompting from me.

London and regional sales managers were asked to prepare sales forecasts, which they would be invited to present to Wendel in person.

"Be upbeat," they were admonished by MacWilliams.

Needless to say, my participation in the event was not required. Nor, I was told, would Wendel have enough time to fit me into his schedule. It was probably just as well, since I would have been hard pressed to come up with conversation topics other than telling tales out of school. Anyway, those tales had been told already, through various channels, always to deaf ears.

The European sales managers trooped disconsolately into London for the great event. The dread was palpable. For days they had sweated over business plans for which the reward was two days of interrogation on which they were convinced their jobs depended. The rest of the company, from receptionists to accountants, awaited Wendel's arrival with hardly less trepidation.

The presentations had just finished when I happened to run into Wendel in the lobby. He was leaving for the airport in thigh-slapping high spirits, almost euphoric. "How did the meetings go, Tom?"

"Great," said Wendel jauntily. "Sorry we didn't get a chance to chat."

"Me, too," I fibbed.

He had been "impressed, overwhelmed almost," by everything that he had seen and heard. "This has been a real good trip. I'm very glad I came. Europe really seems to be finally turning the corner. Everyone has a positive attitude, raring to go. The business projections are pretty damned good. They're a great bunch of guys. I'm really pleased and, to be honest, mightily reassured."

In search of my own reassurance, I joined some of the presenters in the pub that evening. Dread had given way to relief. They were in high spirits, raucously toasting Wendel's departure.

"Tom seemed pretty pumped up," I reported. "Congratulations. You guys really seem to have put on a good show. I just hope you can make your figures."

The grog-fueled response was cynically unanimous: "Not a fucking chance." "What do you mean?"

One spokesman represented all of them: "I mean, to be perfectly honest, what we told him was what he wanted to hear, and what he wanted to hear was good news. Tom's gone home smiling, Dick's off the hook, and we're just relieved we got through the week without fucking up. So everyone's happy. Cheers."

There had been one dissenting voice. Nick Slater, responsible for Belgium, Holland, and Luxembourg, alone had given a conservative appraisal of the business outlook. It had not been well received by Wendel. To borrow MacWilliams's elegant phrase, "Tom reamed that little sucker a new asshole."

Slater was distraught. "I've just called my wife," he sighed. "I told her I'm a dead man."

I amended the remark. "If Europe doesn't make its numbers—and you're all telling me that it won't—then we're all dead men."

I left them to their "celebration" in an angry mood and with a profound sense of impending doom.

From April onwards, Bridge was assailed by rumors and speculation about its financial condition. Most of it focused on Bridge's ability to meet its debt repayments. In an interview with *Inside Market Data*, Wendel took the extraordinary step of confirming, in response to rumors, that Bridge would meet its June loan payment of $75 million. Welsh Carson made sure of it with an investment commitment of $305 million.

Wendel mentioned that Bridge was looking for additional investors, hinting that one could be a well-known technical firm. Rumors abounded that it was Microsoft. AOL was another name mentioned. (The company in question was, in fact, Global Crossing, a network-services company. Nothing came of the negotiations, especially when it emerged that Global Crossing was experiencing financial difficulties of its own.)

The reduction of debt brought about by Welsh Carson's capital infusion meant that Bridge would have no further debt repayments to make until September 30. Reporters and nervous Bridge employees marked the date on their calendars.

August marks the height of the silly season in the media world, a time when half the working population takes its summer break while the offer half sits around exercising idle speculations and enjoying daft newspaper stories that most people assume have been invented to fill excess editorial space. For that reason, I paid little attention to a call I received one day from an executive at one of Telerate's third-party information providers. "Tom Wendel is out," he said flatly, quoting what he called "reliable sources." "He'll be gone by Christmas, is what I'm hearing."

"There is no such thing as reliable sources in August," I told him.

A week or so later Welsh Carson announced that Wendel would be retiring early in the New Year.

The circumstances were murky but hardly inscrutable, the news more startling than surprising. At any rate, few felt the need to ask the customary question, "Did he jump or was he pushed?" The immediate effect was to bring into dramatic focus, as nothing else had, Bridge's increasingly desperate predicament.

Wendel did not wait for January. One reason may have been a brief and unpleasant corridor exchange between him and Tom McInerney, a Welsh Carson partner, in Bridge's office.

"Good luck, Tom, it's all yours now," Wendel told him in a derisory tone, which sufficiently incensed McInerney that he insisted on finishing the conversation behind closed doors. "Don't you ever speak to me like that again in public," McInerney was heard to shout, before the voices rose in such an angry crescendo that even the secretaries sitting outside, gape-mouthed, could not make out what was being said.

Wendel fled New York for St. Louis. There, to the amazement of many, he and his wife were given an office on the Bridge campus from which to operate a website for her diabetes charity, the Insulin-Free World Foundation. Some employees felt moved to express their opinion of Wendel by slipping poisonous anonymous letters under his office door. He arrived one morning to find two dead rats in a desk drawer.

"The guy should count himself lucky," one local manger volunteered. "The way a lot of people feel around here, it could have been a fucking bomb."

With Wendel out of the way, McInerney took up residence in Bridge's New York office and proclaimed himself interim chief executive. He expected to fill the post only until a permanent replacement had been found—someone from outside the company. Roscoe, once (and perhaps still) the heir apparent, was named chief operating officer of Bridge Information Services, the principal operating division.

The serious, quiet-spoken McInerney made an impressive first appearance at a management meeting. The message was somber, delivered in somber tones. The company was in trouble but fundamentally sound. Things would be changing, both in method and style. Formal business plans would be prepared and the managers responsible for them held to account. Profitability and cash generation would be the new watchwords. Layoffs were unavoidable, but the atmosphere of fear would be replaced by one of tolerance. The cleansing of the company's finances initiated by Steve Wilson would be vigorously expanded. A budget would be prepared to reflect realities, however unpalatable.

He failed to say that he had nothing to offer but blood, toil, tears, and sweat, but then he did not have to. He did, however, borrow from another Churchillian theme. "Consider this not as the beginning of the end for Bridge," he said, "but as the end of the beginning."

McInerney's manner was quietly reassuring. "At long fucking last we've got some sanity here," muttered Snape as we trooped out of the meeting.

Sanity alone would not be enough. Midas might have saved the company; McInerney could not. Until then, everything Bridge had touched had crumbled to dust, and for all McInerney's skill and motivational diplomacy, the process of disintegration continued. It was more insidious than instantaneous, and for a while it proceeded almost imperceptibly, with occasional fleeting glimpses of salvation.

The September repayment was made, but October brought a big chunk of the Bridge edifice crashing down with confirmation of what the grapevine and the trade press had been anticipating for weeks: the company had violated a key covenant of its bank credit agreement. Bridge's loan repayments were no longer in immediate danger, thanks to the June capital infusion, but the company had failed to achieve in the third quarter a certain level of operating profit as required by the banks. The disclosure came via Savvis in a routine filing with the Securities and Exchange Commission. The free-fall in Savvis shares accelerated and Bridge was subjected to renewed and constant public and press scrutiny.

"It's a troubled investment, Bridge is a troubled company, but we've had them before and been able to turn them around," Pat Welsh told the *Wall Street Journal* in December, "We're working hard on this."

A Bridge spokesman, quoted in the same article, put a brave face on things. "We're meeting all our payment obligations and we're fine with our bankers," he said—omitting to mention whether he had actually spoken to them. It can be safely assumed that they were far from happy.

Dow Jones was none too pleased either, announcing in the new year that it was writing off $84 million, about half its investment in Bridge, and shareholders were warned that the balance might have to be written off as well. Then there was the more substantial matter of the indemnity that the company had given to Cantor Fitzgerald at the time of the Telerate sale in the event that Bridge failed to make its royalty payments. At $50 million a year over the remaining six years of the contract, these royalties amounted to another potential write-off of $250–$300 million.

For diehards like me who would stay to the bitter end—we shall always wonder why—Bridge's final slide into bankruptcy was painful and interminable, but in the end it came as a blessed relief from endless misery and muddle.

The process began in earnest on February 1, 2001, when a disgruntled and relatively minor creditor, Highland Capital Management of Dallas, Texas, filed against Bridge under Chapter 7 of the US Bankruptcy Code. If accepted, the petition meant putting Bridge into involuntary liquidation. At the time, Bridge had been negotiating with creditors for a debt restructuring, which would have included a further investment from Welsh Carson of $150 million. Highland was owed a mere $26 million, but James Dondero, the company's president, complained that "good-faith negotiations have broken down, and we felt that creditors' interests were best served by an immediate filing."

Welsh Carson responded angrily that it was "truly unfortunate that the unilateral action of a single creditor, representing less than 8 percent of the senior debt, has disrupted this process" of reorganization.[1]

Highland had indeed placed Bridge in an invidious position. The company now had just twenty days in which to have the petition dismissed or, alternatively, to file its own petition for a voluntary reorganization under Chapter 11 of the Bankruptcy Code. Why Highland had acted as it did, when it did, became the subject of much lurid speculation, including a rumor that Dondero had been put up to it by Michael Bloomberg. That seemed far-fetched, but Bloomberg's mysterious response was to announce that he stood by to help the company in its hour of need.

Lurid speculation would be Bridge's unit of currency from that point forward.

In London, the unfolding drama was observed with sad bewilderment. Soon after Wendel's departure, MacWilliams had been recalled to New York, not, it can be assumed, as a returning hero. Before leaving, he had introduced as his replacement one Chip Steinmetz, another expatriate American, and with a background in banking technology.

The choice, and the manner of it, was vintage MacWilliams. As odd as Dick had been regarded, Chip was odder. A genuine eccentric, he had many peccadilloes, including a habit of working with his office lights off, earning him nicknames such as Dracula and Prince of Darkness. He seemed to be in the dark about a great many things, including his precise role in the company. What he told me, and others, was that he thought he had been hired by MacWilliams, not as Europe's managing director based in London, but as Bridge's chief technology officer based in St. Louis—McCormick's former job.

"What happened?" I asked him. "Did you get on the wrong plane or get off at the wrong airport?"

"I'm not quite sure," he replied with a grim smile, "But this is not what I expected to be doing."

"Perhaps you'd better re-read your appointment letter," I added helpfully.

---

[1] *Wall Street Journal*, February 2, 2001

The bemused Steinmetz had little time to bemuse the staff. Within three months, he was hired away to run the Walt Disney website, inviting the inevitable response: "From one Mickey Mouse outfit to another."

Apparently hell-bent on sabotage, MacWilliams wasted little time in appointing yet another incongruous successor, Malcolm Stewart-Smith, a journeyman systems consultant from the banking industry, who had written in looking for a job. "Mad Malcolm," as he was known to many of his former associates, was a project manager of some skill but with no experience in the market-data industry. He knew little about Bridge's products or its markets. It also emerged, in keeping with what was fast becoming a Bridge tradition, that he was another loner, trusting no one. The lugubrious Stewart-Smith could conjure up a conspiracy from any statement that failed to chime with his own opinion. His remedy was to construct around his office a defensive redoubt of reliable former acquaintances, reliable being defined as having absolutely no desire to disagree with him on any subject. In a matter of weeks, the managing director's office was swarmed about with worshipful acolytes, some of whom were paid more than the managers they had replaced.

Bridge's struggle to survive had now descended to the level of a soap opera. This one was bound to have a final installment, and did, as Bridge countered Highland's petition with the long-dreaded but now unavoidable Chapter 11 filing.

The rest is merely postscript.

McInerney, saddled with a conflict of interest between his role as Bridge's senior executive and that of a creditor, disappeared from the Bridge office as summarily as he had arrived.

Roscoe, Wilson, Snape, and Zachary Snow, Bridge's attorney, formed a management group charged with selling off the assets in a court-supervised auction that quickly acquired the characteristics of a post-Christmas department-store sale. Welsh Carson announced that it would be among the bidders but soon faded from the scene to the sounds of scornful laughter.

The ineffable Roscoe found himself in charge of a management team soon known as the Four Horsemen of the Apocalypse. Among its first actions was to award each member a seven-digit "retention bonus."

SunGard Corporation appeared as a credible buyer of most of Bridge's North American assets, excluding Telerate. But on the verge of completing a deal said to be worth about $250 million, SunGard lost interest in the face of a dramatic last-minute bid from Reuters.

Telerate was predictably left at the altar. Reuters had been ruled out as a buyer for anti-trust reasons—its purchase of Bridge alone was the subject of Justice Department scrutiny—and other prospective bridegrooms were conspicuous by their absence. There was talk of a bank consortium comprising some of Telerate's leading clients. That initiative lasted a week or so, after which the Four Horsemen published an extensive list of allegedly interested parties in a re-enactment of Inspector Renault's instruction to the Casablanca police force to "round up the usual suspects."

Moneyline, a minor vendor with financial backing as shaky as its management's credibility—the team was led by Jon Robson, of Rolling Thunder fame—finally convinced a skeptical Bridge management team (now known, according to taste, as the Three Blind Mice or the Three Stooges, Wilson having moved on) that it had enough cash lined up to do a deal. Thomson had turned the trick in convincing Bridge that Moneyline was viable, having made a "strategic" investment in the company with an option to acquire the entire company within three years. It was typical of the whole benighted transaction that only days before Moneyline had to come up with the cash to close the deal, Thomson dropped out, leaving Moneyline to scramble about for a substitute investor. This turned out to be Bank One, a subsidiary of JP Morgan.

The price paid for Telerate was staggeringly small: $10 million, plus some cash for cure costs. Ten million! For a company which, a little over a decade earlier, had commanded a price of $1.6 billion. And the revenue had been much lower then than now. Even at $10 million, some observers felt that Moneyline might be overpaying.

It was an ignominious end for Bridge and, particularly, for Telerate. But was it to be Telerate's denouement? Telerate had survived—just about—under its fifth owner, and industry observers were left to speculate whether the company could perform yet another Lazarene rising from the deathbed.

# Dry Rot

While Bridge was paying the ultimate price for management incompetence, an erstwhile, much larger rival across the Atlantic was forced to confront its own demons and frailties. The company in question was Reuters, which, in the indiscreetly frank assessment of one of its senior executives, was itself suffering from "a severe case of dry rot."

The analogy indicates an invisible degenerative process, one that develops slowly and insidiously over time, flourishing quietly under floors and behind walls, the householder often oblivious to its presence until significant damage has been done. Just when the "rot" set in at 85 Fleet Street it is impossible to say, but, as the final decade of the century wound down, it became increasingly clear that the House of Reuters had suffered some kind of dilapidation.

Once a bold, pioneering, market leader, Reuters, in the eyes of many observers, had lost its confidence and become consumed by organizational turmoil and philosophical doubt. If senior executives were privately aware of the problems, they were publicly obliged to deny them, and did so. The question is, were they aware? Or had they lapsed into a Micawber-like trance, hoping that something would eventually "turn up" to save the situation. The "something" could only mean an unexpected success for one of Reuters' many hitherto abortive product initiatives, or some fortifying external event. When, as time went by, it became apparent that neither of these events would occur, Reuters was finally obliged to face the consequences.

Certainly many of the company's mid-level managers professed to be aware of the company's difficulties and were far from discreet in airing their opinions outside the office. (It is reasonable to wonder whether they were equally frank inside the office, though naturally they all claim to have been.) A common complaint—the one most often voiced to me, and presumably to others—was that the company was stuck with a senior executive group (and board) that was well past its prime, deficient in energy, creativity, even knowledge, and determinedly averse to risk. The executive group, they said, appeared to have divided into two distinct camps: those still groping bravely but blindly for salvation and those contentedly awaiting their retirement date.

If these were harsh judgments, they were vindicated by cruel numbers. In 2003, after a string of half-yearly profit declines, Reuters reported its first annual operating loss since flotation. The City was shocked, and Reuters' share price tumbled.

That same year, with exquisite timing, a pair of disgruntled former Reuters journalists, Brian Mooney and Barry Simpson, plainly angered by what they saw as the sad and disgraceful plight of their *alma mater*, poured gasoline on the fires of discontent by publishing a rather polemical book called *Breaking News*, subtitled *How the Wheels Came off at Reuters*. The flyleaf referred to "the sorry tale of Reuters' precipitous fall from grace."[1]

The book's principal thesis was that the company had been taken over by "a bunch of journalists who thought they had become bankers." This and other barbs were somewhat blunted by the fact that both authors had been laid off. Even so, most of the book's conclusions were inescapable.

Unhappy executives and resentful authors were not alone in taunting the wounded beast. By the time the Mooney-Simpson book came out, Reuters shareholders had registered their own verdict by baling out in huge numbers, knocking down the share price from a peak of over £17 to less than £1. The free-fall in the shares enabled Reuters to join an exclusive corporate club. It was not one for which there was a waiting list. The only membership qualification was to have recorded a loss of 90 percent of the company's capital value. Superfluous it may be to say so, but any company that deprives its shareholders of that much equity has been either a victim of uniquely negative circumstances or has been doing something terribly wrong. In Reuters' case, unique circumstances could be eliminated, since every other company in the market-data business faced similar challenges to those confronting Reuters. Bloomberg, to pick the most obvious example, had not faltered. Far from it. If the claims of a privately held company are to be believed—and most industry observers had sufficient anecdotal evidence to believe them—Bloomberg had quietly and consistently surpassed Reuters' growth, not just by a whisker but by an embarrassing country mile. In terms of market share, Bloomberg had pulled within striking distance of its rival.

Two other market-data vendors, it is true, had fallen by the wayside, as we have seen, but the demise of Telerate and Bridge presented such prime examples of gross mismanagement that they can be said to have disqualified themselves from the race. Surely Reuters could not be in danger of scratching as well. Few believed that, but few were able to avoid the conclusion that Reuters' problems were very serious indeed, and fewer still concluded other than that the problems were largely of the company's own making.

The City was by now thoroughly disillusioned. Healthy growth and robust profits had been delivered for so long that an excellent semi-annual report card from Reuters had become a date on the London calendar as predictable as Trooping the Colour, Henley, and Wimbledon. Of equal concern alongside

---

[1] Brian Mooney/Barry Simpson, *Breaking News: How the Wheels Came off at Reuters*, Capstone Press, 2003, flyleaf

poor financial results was the deepening impression that Reuters' management had run out of perspiration as well as inspiration. Why had the company allowed itself to be caught napping by Bloomberg? And now that it had happened, what were Reuters' plans for some kind of counter-attack? Was there a turnaround strategy?

The lack of a plausible response bemused analysts, and Reuters' share price remained in the doldrums. Talk at City lunch counters began to embrace a notion once regarded as unthinkable—that mighty Reuters had fallen so far as to become a potential takeover target, irrevocable Trust and "golden share" be damned.

Any account of Reuters' distress must, this author recognizes, strive for balance—always a delicate high-wire act for armchair critics with axes to grind. Opinion is free, but facts are sacred, a renowned British newspaper editor once said. In Reuters' case, opinions might vary, but certain facts seemed inalienable. To most interested observers—allowing for the resentments of a growing army of embittered sacked employees—the Reuters of the late 1990s appeared to be guilty as charged on three counts: complacency, short-sightedness, and arrogance.

The prosecution produced an array of damning evidence. First, management had failed to successfully integrate a string of strategic acquisitions, some of which had turned out to be strategic only in theory. Latent managerial and technical talent entering the company through these acquisitions had been wasted. Several important acquisition opportunities had been missed. Second, products had not been delivered to market when they were supposed to be, and were deemed inadequate when they finally were delivered. Part of the problem was that the Internet revolution had failed to fire management's imagination and so passed the company by. Finally, the recommendations of outside advisors, who had advocated management and product restructuring, were ignored. All these faults, prosecutors concluded, stemmed from one overarching defect: certain senior executives and directors had been allowed to overstay their welcome, either because no one in high authority recognized that the place needed shaking up, or they had recognized as much and did nothing.

The case for the defense rested largely on mitigating external factors beyond the company's control. There could be no denying that there had occurred in the last years of the nineties a marked deterioration in the company's trading environment. A prolonged stock-market swoon at the millennium meant an unprecedented tightening of spending budgets by banks and securities houses. Falling share prices encouraged an outbreak of institutional consolidation. Mega-mergers among the banks, of which the JP Morgan Chase-Chemical amalgamation was among the more spectacular, led to the elimination of thousands of dealing-room positions, and the consequent elimination of thousands of Reuters' terminals. Finally, in the cruelest blow of all, the terrorist attack on the World Trade Center in New York City in September 2001 delivered a savage blow to public morale and market confidence. The three years following 9/11 (as it became universally known) were referred to in the financial community as the "Arctic Winter" or "The Time the Earth Stood Still." During this prolonged chill, markets fell or slumbered, buying decisions were postponed, budgets were slashed. Reuters' results, management argued, reflected this degraded environment.

In the midst of all this, Reuters went through a change of chief executives, as Peter Job opted for retirement in 2001, leaving the shop in the care of the company's former New York attorney, Tom Glocer. The event was either timely or untimely, depending on your point of view. Switching a seasoned Reuters campaigner for an American mergers-and-acquisitions lawyer with limited operational experience was at least bold—the first bold move Reuters had made in many years. Whether it was also sensible remained to be seen.

Two key questions must be asked of any jury considering a verdict on Reuters' performance during the five-year period leading up to the millennium. First, to what extent should management have anticipated Reuters' difficulties (market slump and the impact of 9/11 aside, of course) and taken precautionary measures to avoid or at least alleviate them? Second, given its collective skills and experience ("journalists pretending to be businessmen," as some critics alleged), was management actually qualified to recognize that radical measures were necessary?

These are the recurring themes that invest the account that follows.

One year into the 1990s, Glen Renfrew decided to call it a day.

His retirement was hardly a bombshell, though the timing was something of a surprise. He was almost certainly nudged into his decision by Reuters' chairman, Sir Christopher Hogg, who felt that Renfrew, after ten years in the job, had given his best, and much more besides. Renfrew did not put up much of a fight; in truth he probably welcomed the chance to go. A decade at the top is more than enough for most corporate chieftains, a point that Hogg would almost certainly have emphasized (though he himself would ignore his own edict by allowing Renfrew's successor to serve a similar term, and by staying in his own job for almost twice as long).

Even Renfrew's many admirers thought he had begun to show his age. He often appeared to be worn out, not so much physically tired as emotionally drained. Renfrew had found it hard to get over the death of a daughter in a hiking accident in Scotland, and colleagues said he had not been quite the same man since. Whatever the reason, the once dynamic, restless, devil-may-care

Renfrew had begun to present a frail, ageing figure, far from the dynamic harbinger of the future he had once been.

Renfrew's announcement sent the company into its customary paroxysms of speculation. Many pundits inside and outside the company, apparently so little impressed by the qualities and personalities of the three front-runners, believed—or at least regarded as possible—that the company might for the first time in its history consider an outsider. But no names were offered up, and in the end it was hardly a shock that Reuters reverted to habit, of sticking with insiders—and journalists to boot—for board-level executive positions.

There were ostensibly three contenders: Peter Job, David Ure, and André Villeneuve. Each had been apprenticed by his regional stewardship of Asia, Europe, and North America respectively. Job was thought to be Renfrew's choice. More importantly, Job had also earned the confidence of Hogg. One of the other two contenders would have been Mike Nelson's preference—probably Ure—but Nelson himself had retired two years earlier to write books and to reflect ruefully on what might have been.

All three candidates had joined the company in the 1960s as management trainees from Oxford University. That may have been all they had in common.

Job was of medium height and stocky build. He came across as a driven, self-confident man. He would no doubt have interviewed well. By contrast, Villeneuve and Ure had, as we have seen, accumulated a variety of disconcerting tics and peccadilloes. Even Ure's most ardent advocates had trouble imagining their man standing before the annual meeting of shareholders with his hands thrust down his trousers. Ure's personality was, anyway, more that of a Rasputin than a Tsar—a figure of influence rather than authority, better suited to hovering around the throne than sitting on it. Villeneuve was hard to imagine as either Tsar or Rasputin, more plausible perhaps as a faithful old retainer. Of the three he came across as the least colorful or inspirational figure. Ure and Villeneuve were both essentially shy, never entirely at ease with colleagues or customers. Neither had ever demonstrated more than a rudimentary grasp of trading markets. Ure could claim with some justification that he understood technology. Villeneuve gave an impression of being baffled by it. Ure was desperate for the job. Villeneuve was said to be ambivalent; he had seen the strains of office etched into Renfrew's face. Besides, he seemed more comfortable operating at a less frantic pace—quiet lunches and dinners, picking over menus and wine lists—than tangling publicly with clamorous shareholders, analysts, and reporters. As Tom Glocer once put it, "I'll never have to buy a *Good Food Guide* to London; all I have to do is go through André's expenses."

Personality quirks aside, neither Ure nor Villeneuve was thought to possess the strategic vision to take Reuters to new heights of achievement. Such peaks would not easily be scaled after a long period of growth that could probably be maintained only if underpinned by new products with the explosive potential of Monitor or Dealing.

If business performance were the main criterion, Job was bound to win hands down. Reuters Europe had thrived during Ure's regime, but it was hard to argue that he had himself had transformed it. For that, Reuters' man in Switzerland, Jean-Claude Marchand, could claim much of the credit. As for Villeneuve, the feeling around the company was that he had not made much of a fist of the perennially problematic North American operation. That alone may have been enough to put him out of the running. Job, by contrast, had ridden to glory on the great economic boom in Japan and the so-called Tiger economies of Southeast Asia.

Job had never been described as shy. He could be diffident and stand-offish, but also, when the mood seized him, boorish and argumentative. As much as his rivals, he possessed all the qualifications traditionally favored by Reuters; he was an Oxbridge man and spoke at least two languages fluently. He had demonstrated in Hong Kong that he was a man of drive and commitment. Though not universally admired or liked, he came to be respected by his superiors as a man who got things done, and by subordinates as someone who motivated them by knowing as much about their jobs as they did. His ambition was rarely camouflaged, but his passion for the company was plain to see. From Hong Kong he rode his regional managers hard. They were expected to be available at any time, day or night, to provide instant briefings on whatever topic had taken his fancy. There was never a shortage of topics.

John Lowe, Job's sales manager in Japan, was among the victims of the nocturnally inconvenienced. "Peter called often and habitually at the most inconvenient times. Dinnertime and bedtime were strongly favored. He'd want to chew the fat over this burning issue or that. I'd say, 'Peter, this isn't a good time,' and he'd say 'Well maybe you could get up here first thing in the morning. I'd really like to talk this over.' " Lowe often went, and by the time he arrived a new burning issue had replaced that of the previous day.

Job's microscopic attention to detail was legendary. At presentations, whether internal or external, he was usually better briefed than any of his subordinates, a constant source of irritation to them, as he invariably ended up stealing the show. He could be brusque and dogmatic on such occasions. Fools were not suffered gladly, and dissenting views could be dismissed with a sharp tongue, often in public.

So, all the signs pointed to Job—and Job it was who received the summons from the chairman.

"Told you so!" cried the doubters in unison.

As energetic and dedicated as Reuters' eighth chief executive undoubtedly was, a question hovered over him like a dark cloud: could he adequately fill Renfrew's seven-league boots?

During the first few years of Job's tenure, the answer appeared to be a definite if not resounding yes.

The act he had to follow had been impressive, at least in headline-grabbing terms. Under Renfrew's watch Reuters had indulged in a spending spree on what were regarded at the time, if not later, as important strategic acquisitions.

Few of the deals qualified as mega-mergers, but, relative to Reuters' capital base, some were substantial. With one exception, they neatly augmented Reuters' core business—or, as the Americans like to say, provided great synergies.

The ancillary benefits, at least in theory, was that they introduced Reuters to fresh talent, though the practice seldom matched the theory, as we shall see.

The first of such acquisitions, and for its defining impact arguably the most significant, was Rich Inc., a Chicago-based producer of analog video-switching systems, bought in 1985 for $60 million. Video-switches represented a platform capable of distributing around trading rooms video pages from Reuters and other content-providers. The Rich system replaced tens of thousands of stand-alone, page-defined terminals of the kind that traders had been using since the early days of Monitor. Rich lived up to its name by becoming a significant source of revenue. And because the Rich system, unlike single terminals, was embedded in the dealing-room infrastructure, it generated the kind of revenue that sticks.

Successful as it was, Rich enjoyed a relatively short shelf-life. Emerging digital technology soon made analog systems seem by comparison inflexibly old-fashioned. The digital replacement that evolved from the Rich system was a product called Triarch. The Triarch advantage was that it allowed clients to assemble customized displays of individual items of data, rather than their having to rely on off-the-shelf pages of data.

The days of stand-alone terminals that forced users to scroll through page after page of green characters on black screens were clearly winding down fast.

The following year, 1986, Reuters further flaunted its expansionist ambitions by picking up an American institutional off-the-market share block-trading system called Instinet. The deal, while supported enthusiastically by Renfrew, was inspired and masterminded by the peripatetic John Hull. "We should have done the deal at Telerate," Hull told me gleefully. "Now I've finally landed the fucker."

(Hull was referring to the occasion when Neil Hirsch and I had looked at a struggling, loss-making Instinet as far back as 1979. Back then it was largely owned by the Weeden family, who ran an eponymous institutional brokerage firm. Frank Weeden it was who gave us a demonstration, with son Alan in attendance. The price, I seem to remember, was barely into six figures. I wanted to do a deal, but Hirsch decided that Telerate was too small to handle it, having enough on its plate already. Anyway, Bernie Cantor, always reluctant to spend money, would almost certainly have declined.)

At $100 million, Instinet was Reuters' boldest and biggest acquisition to date.

The man Hull later selected to take Instinet to hitherto unscaled heights was Michael Sanderson, formerly the manager of the Merrill Lynch office in Toronto—a case of poacher turned gamekeeper. The gamekeeper at first found it difficult to dodge the poachers. Instinet's progress was checked by market politics. While electronic trading of stocks and bonds away from the exchanges was hardly a novel idea—Instinet itself had been around since the late 1970s—it was still far from being universally accepted by the stock market's more conservative elements, which also happened to be the biggest.

In the world of Instinet the political adversaries facing each other were, in the blue corner, the big banks and investment houses, collectively known as the sell side, and in the red corner their institutional clients, typically mutual and pension funds, usually referred to as the buy side. Sell-side firms guarded their traditions jealousy, erecting all kinds of Chinese walls designed to beat off raids by predatory "retail" institutions. By the 1980s the raids had turned into a siege, and by now the besiegers were loaded with cash from a long-running stock-market boom. The investing institutions made very clear their intention to wield their new economic power to get what they wanted, which was access to the wholesale market. Electronic systems had started to break down Wall Street's Chinese walls. Instinet was a big part of that process. The sell side had little choice but to fall into line.

Within a few years, Instinet was turning over several billions of dollars daily in equity transactions and contributing hundreds of millions of dollars annually to Reuters' bottom line. Sanderson found himself lauded as the hero who had finally "cracked" the American market for Reuters and was soon being touted as a future chief executive.

Other, smaller, acquisitions followed in quick succession. There would be about twenty-five in all, most notably Schwartzatron, a stock-options analytics product, I.P. Sharp Associates, a Canadian-based content management company, and Finsbury Data, a London corporate-news database.

All these additions were chalked up on Renfrew's watch. Investors applauded the company's empire-building acumen and rejoiced in the healthy growth in shareholder value.

"Never mind bloody Bloomberg," a Reuters manager crowed to a reporter. "Just watch this space."

Job's elevation interrupted the acquisition program, but once he had settled into his position, normal service was resumed. By now Reuters was sitting on a cash pile that Long and Nelson could only have dreamed about and which even Renfrew might have envied.

In 1994, three years into Job's regime, Reuters purchased Teknekron, a California-based producer of trading-room software, for $125 million. Teknekron either dovetailed nicely with Triarch, or clashed pointlessly with it, depending on one's point of view. Either way, it gave Reuters absolute control of the dealing-room systems market. The Teknekron purchase was largely championed and negotiated by David Ure. It represented his first important strategic contribution to Reuters since Dealing. Ure's triumph was tarnished when it was put about in the trade press that the deal was a pre-emptive strike against Bloomberg, which had also supposedly shown a keen interest in the company. Ure, miffed by the suggestion, denied it. He was supported by Mike Bloomberg himself, who asserted that he had never had the slightest interest in Teknekron. The denials rang true: Bloomberg had always been wedded to home-grown rather than acquired products. All of which suggested to those of a more cynical nature that Teknekron itself planted the Bloomberg rumor to boost the price.

Also on the shopping list appeared poor old pioneering, once-mighty Quotron, now a pale facsimile of its former self. Having paid $700 million for Quotron, Citibank recognized, as the business decline continued apace, that it had made a hash of it, both in strategic and operational terms, and was happy to unload it for a fraction of the purchase price, which by now was nothing. Actually, less than nothing. Reuters agreed to pick up the pieces, which included taking on the obligation of Quotron's staff-pension scheme. The compensating balance was that Reuters would receive payments from Citibank covering the company's losses in the first eighteen months. With Quotron's demise, another former industry giant had been felled.

Of Reuters' various other acquisitions, many simply disappeared, like plankton into the whale's mouth. Years later few could recall, for example, why Reuters had acquired Liberty SA, an order-routing business purchased from Cedel, a Luxembourg-based electronic clearing system, for a price said to be about $50 million. Nor were there lasting benefits from a substantial investment, for a one-third equity interest, in GL Trade, a French company that offered clients access to electronic trading exchanges. The original theory was that Liberty would make a logical fit with GL Trade, and readers of tea-leaves thought they had spotted a significant strategic initiative—a plan to build up Reuters' capacity in electronic trading and its aftermath, a process known these days as straight-through-processing.

For Reuters the integration of acquired companies and their employees would always prove to be a vexing problem, one that management never

453

seemed capable of solving. The acquired were not to blame. No doubt there were pockets of resentment among the staff of absorbed companies, but most of the recruits were glad to be associated with a famous name and its unequalled global distribution facilities. But Reuters, consciously or otherwise, seemed intent on stamping its imprint on the acquired companies, which meant stamping out theirs. It sent out a clear message of negative import: there could be only one culture and only one technology, and both were copyrighted by Reuters.

Much of the imported talent, disappointed, and recognizing the immutability of their inferior status, drifted away.

Lib Gibson, who was exposed to Reuters' management ethos as an I.P. Sharp employee, bluntly summed up the feelings of many of her fellow "immigrants." "Reuters had a militaristic, top-down, don't-argue-back, we'll-tell-you-what-to-do policy. Most of us from I.P. Sharp left within a year of Reuters taking over."

Rosemarie Corscadden, who arrived with Liberty SA, offered a similar view. "We were never made to feel wanted, part of a team. Constant changes in managers meant constant changes in methods and policies. We never knew where we were. Most of us just drifted away, including me."

Justifying Reuters' hearty appetite for takeovers, Job referred in an interview to "planting acorns"—adding, perhaps more wistfully than he intended, "We'll have to see if they turn into oaks."

Some critics scorned the analogy. Their complaint was not that Reuters was actually barking up the wrong tree acquiring smaller companies, even those that reinforced or diversified its business model, but rather that management should have skipped through the acorns to get to the full-grown oaks; in other words, "go for the big one"—create a combined company that would form an instant, giant information-conglomerate. Several such candidates were considered at various times, including, it has been reported, Dun & Bradstreet, a huge corporate database company, and AOL, a global Internet service provider (later acquired, disastrously, by Time-Warner).

To be fair, such lofty aspirations were more easily fantasized than executed, and for a variety of reasons, most notably the fact that most acquisition target companies in the blockbuster category were based in the United States, where industry consolidations invariably fell under the scrutiny of anti-trust regulators. Telerate, for example, dominant in the treasury market, which Reuters had long coveted, would have been an obvious target, but such a deal would almost certainly have been ruled out by the US Department of Justice.

As if to reinforce Job's acorn analogy, in 1995 Reuters formed a venture capital enterprise called the Greenhouse Fund, to act as an incubator for fledgling companies with the kind of state-of-the-art technologies that Reuters itself might eventually exploit. The Fund was initially financed from Reuters' substantial cash flow, but the intention was that it would quickly stand on its own feet as investments paid off, either in the form of dividends, sales, or public offerings.

The Greenhouse Fund emerged from an earlier initiative called NewMedia, which had been formed in New York to act as a kind of self-financing "skunk works," with a focus on the Internet. NewMedia was the brainchild of Buford Smith, a soft-spoken Kentuckian, who had been hired by John Hull to bolster the transaction products program. Smith had risen rapidly through the ranks to an exalted position as one of Glen Renfrew's global technology gurus. He bristled with ideas as a porcupine bristles with quills, and the focus of most of these ideas was the Internet, on which subject Smith had become an expert. Ure, perhaps alone of Reuters' senior managers, was a Smith admirer. Smith in turn took on Andy Nibley, an affable and popular former reporter and senior editor who, bored with his editorial assignments, had migrated to marketing.

Nibley had joined Reuters in 1980 from United Press International, a once aggressive and innovative American news agency, since fallen on hard times. As UPI teetered on the brink of bankruptcy, Reuters pounced. Nibley arrived with a posse of UPI colleagues after a raid by Reuters, one of a series of incursions known in the UPI newsroom as the Invasion of the Body Snatchers.

Like Buford Smith, Nibley had become something of an Internet freak. His vision was to sell Reuters content to the web sites that were springing up all over America, thereby gaining a foothold in the vast American consumer market. In this, Nibley was spectacularly successful. NewMedia's annual revenue at its peak ran at $40 million and, as Nibley never tired of pointing out, "most of it fell directly to the bottom line." Nibley's problem was that the Internet was not yet a recognized unit of currency at Reuters, being commonly referred to as the "I" word. Consumers were represented as the "C" word.

This odd, inexplicable prejudice sprang from Job himself, an avowed Internet skeptic—which meant *ipso facto* that most of his senior colleagues were, too. Further down in the executive pecking order, the Internet actually inspired fear. New technology carries risk, and taking risks can cost a manager his job. It soon became clear to Smith and Nibley that they were on their own, and way out on a rather flimsy limb.

Reuters was not entirely unique in its ambivalence in Internet matters. Throughout the 1980s, the Internet was exploited by few and understood by fewer still. That would remain true for most of the following decade, too, though by the middle of it, scales were being lifted from incredulous eyes after Tim Berners-Lee, a professional geek working at CERN (the European

Organization for Nuclear Research) in Geneva, came up with a protocol to facilitate widespread access to the Internet, a scheme that quickly evolved into something known as the World Wide Web. Even then, universal bafflement was by no means eradicated—and understandably so. A limitless global network, conceived by American scientists and academicians for national political purposes but now freely available to everyone on the planet and owned by no one, was a difficult concept to grasp.

It is probably fair to say that even information providers—not least the market-data companies—initially found the Internet as hard to grasp in its commercial implications as everyone else. It was clearly a resource to be admired—much as, say, democracy is admired—but sociological issues aside, was it a potential boon or a looming threat, a passing fad or a permanent fact of life? The answer, this author would assert, is that company technologists found it as fascinating and promising as their business colleagues found it perplexing and intimidating. By the millennium, stock-market investors seemed to be providing the response that many corporate managers had been avoiding. The Internet was the "Coming Thing," it was proclaimed on Wall Street and in the City. Any company in the information or communications business failing to recognize the fact was not itself worth investing in. The so-called dot-com boom, named after the web-address convention, was soon underway.

The advent of the Internet caused Reuters all kinds of philosophical problems. It was a brand-new phenomenon and Job was right to take a cautious view of how it could be exploited, but surely wrong to be as dismissive as he was for so many years.

So long as NewMedia made money, no one in Reuters' management seemed terribly bothered to find out exactly how it was done. And so, without management sponsors, and with only the vaguest process of management consent, Smith and Nibley started to invest in Internet start-ups. These investments largely paid for themselves. Among the most promising of them was an interesting start-up in Palo Alto, California, the intellectual capital of Silicon Valley.

The discovery was made by John Taysom, a London-based product executive and fellow Internet traveler, who found himself sucked, quite enthusiastically, into the NewMedia slipstream.

As a technologist, Taysom was an autodidact. As a business analyst he had been formally trained by the accounting and consulting firm, Price Waterhouse, where he was an auditor. He had originally been interviewed twelve years earlier for a position as a journalist. Job talked him out of that but, impressed by Taysom's obvious business sense, hired him anyway to become a commercial manager. Taysom then virtually disappeared from sight, spending the next dozen years in various foreign postings. If nothing else, the wilderness years gave him time to bring together his accumulated technical savvy with an instinctive eye for a business opportunity.

When Taysom eventually returned to London, where no suitable job was immediately available, Ure dispatched him to Palo Alto, with instructions to see what he could dig up from Silicon Valley's fertile soil.

Soon after arriving, Taysom was idly flipping through a Stanford University newspaper when he came across an article about an Internet start-up trying to create an online directory. It was run by a couple of youthful entrepreneurs, Jerry Yang and David Filo, both fresh out of college and brimful of ideas about how to exploit the Internet's lack of navigability.

Taysom called them. "Hey, if you guys put Reuters news up on your index, people won't skate through, but will come back regularly and search for stuff."

The tyros took up the idea with enthusiasm, and Taysom was rewarded with an invitation to invest in the company's second funding round. Reuters put in $1 million. It was to have been $4 million but, according to Taysom, by the time Reuters had staggered through its convoluted approval process the other $3 million on offer had been snapped up by other investors.

The name of the company, I nearly forgot to mention, was Yahoo!

The time inevitably arrived when Job was asked the "I" question in public: was Reuters an Internet company or not? The financial communities in London and New York were desperate to know. The City had latched on to the Internet with a passion it had not expended so single-mindedly since North Sea Oil two or three decades earlier. Headline writers dubbed it the dot-com boom. Internet companies sprouted like weeds in a neglected garden. The Internet *was* a neglected garden. A few of these dot-coms became instantly, if briefly, profitable. Most, though, not only lost money but never for an instant looked like making any. Many never even approached the point of generating revenue. No matter, said City pundits who should have known better, if it was a dot-com then it was worth a punt.

Job's early responses to the "I" question clearly and unequivocally indicated that Reuters was *not* an Internet company. In one interview he dismissed Internet users as "geeks."

If they were, the world was rapidly becoming a geek-infested planet.

Reuters' share price reacted to Job's evident lack of enthusiasm for the Internet with a sharp fall. The City's response produced scenes of controlled panic at 85 Fleet Street, as analysts and reporters persisted in demanding to know where Reuters stood. Strategy meetings were hurriedly arranged. Discussion flowed from the boardroom down to the pub and back again. Once virtually proscribed, the "I" word was now the only word being talked about.

Job, a stubborn man, initially stood firm, but as pressure mounted for a clarification of Reuters' position he reluctantly changed his mind—or at least his tune, which, if nothing else, fulfilled the need for a positive public-relations exercise.

Yes, of course Reuters was an Internet company, he announced one day, with more or less the same lack of equivocation with which he had once denied it. What else could Reuters be in this day and age? The share price rose sharply in response.

When, in the waning days of Job's term, the dot-com bubble finally burst, it left bloodied casualties stumbling all over the City. And along Wall Street, too, where it was revealed that one renowned stock-market analyst, supposedly a dot-com specialist, had been telling her clients to buy Internet stocks of which she later admitted she had no more than a superficial knowledge.

Reuters' management, perhaps understandably, once more went to ground on matters concerning the Internet. The first casualty was NewMedia, its revenue dependent on hundreds of companies now going bust. Reuters' finance director Rob Rowley, among others, heaved a sigh of relief. He had spent years fretting over the money spent by the Smith-Buford-Taysom investment bank and was sick of hearing the defiant response: "You gotta spend money to make money."

"We tried very hard to change attitudes," Nibley recalled years later, "and at every level." At some point he and Smith even collared Sir Christopher Hogg on one of his infrequent visits to New York. "Do something," they implored. "The Internet is really, really important, but no one at Reuters is listening." Hogg, as Nibley recalled later, "was charming, listening carefully and nodding politely. Then he picked up his briefcase and left. We never heard from him."

Smith did not last long. After undiplomatically and, it has to be said, uncharacteristically telling several directors to their faces that they were "technically illiterate," he was fired.

Soon afterwards, the Greenhouse Fund, which at its peak had accumulated nearly $500 million in investments, was spun off to its executive team, led by the tireless Internet evangelist, John Taysom.

Reuters' on-and-off aversion to the Internet was in some measure one of perception. On paper at least, Reuters, far from ignoring the Internet, had endorsed it thoroughly. NewMedia must have received some kind of management patronage or it would not have lasted as long as it did. And the company had sponsored a number of Internet projects through the Greenhouse Fund.

The trouble was that none of the Fund's Internet properties, though often profitable as investments in their own right, had failed to yield any obvious strategic benefits to Reuters. Nor, at the end of the day, could it be denied that Job had never really bought in and few of his senior strategists in London had summoned the courage to tell him that he might be wrong. As in all matters under what was perceived as an increasingly autocratic regime, Job's views were not merely the last word, they were The Only Word.

But Nibley, unlike Smith, was not quite done yet. After a period in the wilderness—"twiddling my thumbs in some remote corner in one of Reuters' many New York offices"—Nibley was rewarded with a curious assignment, a return engagement as head of NewMedia International, a more management-friendly reincarnation of its NewMedia predecessor. Nibley was astonished and pleased in equal measure, but his relief was to be short-lived. NMI generated little revenue and received no more high-level patronage than its forerunner had done. And so, inevitably, it suffered the same fate. The decision to abandon NMI was taken in London. Nibley found out by reading it in the *Wall Street Journal*. "Nobody had bothered to call me," he recalled with wry amusement. "They probably didn't know where to find me."

Some time afterwards, Nibley, still dutifully but pointlessly showing up for work each day, received a curious call from Peter Job. "The boss wanted to apologize for having called the Internet 'an American fad.' I remember him adding, 'You were right and I was wrong.' It was bizarre." Then, even more bizarrely, Job told Nibley that Reuters intended to replace NewMedia International with a new project called ReuterSpace.

But the man designated to run ReuterSpace was not Nibley—an obvious choice, one might have thought—but Rob Rowley, the finance director. Many thought Rowley, who had no previous front-line operating experience, an odd choice. So he was. But he had apparently been identified as a potential chief executive by Job and Hogg, who felt he needed exposure to broader horizons than those offered by the finance department. To help Rowley pass this examination, Job drafted in Jeremy Penn from Reuters' spanking-new Asia headquarters in Singapore to assist him. The unspoken consensus in the management ranks was that Penn had not done a particularly good job out East—nor earlier on Project Armstrong—but Job had faith in him, if nobody else did. Penn retained his status as a rising star with royal patronage.

Nibley was uncertain whether to be angered, flabbergasted, or merely disappointed. He resolved the dilemma by quitting.

"I loved working at Reuters," he reflected ruefully years later. "I loved it more than any company I'd ever worked for. But by then I'd simply had enough. I'm a likeable guy, I think, but I was very outspoken, and often with a humorous or sarcastic tone. I think management regarded me as someone not to be taken too seriously, perhaps even dangerous."

ReuterSpace lived up to its name to the extent of achieving lift-off, though none could say a few years later where it had landed or indeed whether it had managed to land at all. Adrift in space was pretty much its eventual fate, as was that of Rowley and Penn.

For all Reuters' apparent ambivalence to the Internet and its works, some analysts seemed reasonably satisfied with Reuters' performance during the waning years of the Job decade. Reuters' revenue rose steadily and profits held firm. The company had weathered the dot-com storm. The impression had been successfully conveyed that management knew what it was doing and where it wanted to take the company. The ten-year acquisition spree had greatly expanded Reuters' revenue base and earnings potential. That most of the acquired companies had not been properly integrated, either in terms of technology or culture, and may have actually hindered Reuters' progress as much as advanced it, was not readily apparent to outsiders.

And so the City applauded in the only way that it knows how: Reuters' share price rose steadily, returning once more to the realm of double digits.

But not for long.

# Under Fire

The expansionist impulses of the late-Renfrew and early-Job years had unexpectedly negative consequences externally as well as internally. Concerns began to surface among the company's biggest clients that Reuters was getting far too big for its breeches. It was by no means a novel sentiment, Reuters' rise always having generated as much resentment as admiration, but for the first time Reuters faced a revolt.

Its focus, perhaps not surprisingly, given Reuters' dominance of the sector, was the foreign-exchange market. The science of currency trading, if not the art, was to all intents and purposes a miracle of Reuters' invention. Reuters held sway over every one of the market's essential mechanisms. Monitor was the accepted medium for disseminating prices and news. Dealing had sole domain over electronic transactions, which were rapidly becoming more the rule than the exception. Reuters owned the global network on which these and all other applications depended.

Citibank was a prominent malcontent. "Pretty soon I won't be able to take a crap without Reuters' permission," was how one senior Citibank trader colorfully expressed it. If the language was not to everyone's taste, the sentiment was.

Seeking to avoid a head-on conflict, a group representing the banks approached Reuters with a view to forming a joint venture for trading currencies. Reuters had always shied away from intimate collaborations with clients, and Reuters' management could find no grounds for making an exception now. It is understandable that the company looked askance at inviting others to take a stake in a gold mine which Reuters alone had excavated, and in which Reuters had taken all the financial risks. Indeed, the banks were reminded that the investment had been committed at a time when Reuters could ill afford it and in the face of considerable opposition from some of the banks. How serious this approach by the banks really was is open to doubt, but Reuters' negative response, while intellectually reasonable, was commercially risky. Monopoly can bring substantial economic benefits, but can also court resentment and reaction. For Reuters, the consequences of scorning the banks were soon apparent.

A dozen leading foreign-exchange market-makers—known these days as liquidity providers—responded to rejection by forming a consortium called Electronic Brokerage Services. Its mandate was to develop an electronic matching system as an alternative to Dealing. By extension it would also compete with Monitor. The stated objective was to bring brokerage fees down, but there was an underlying one of greater significance. As expressed by one bank it was to "put the Baron in his place."

Naturally EBS had little difficulty obtaining the required investment. The sources were twelve of the thirteen leading foreign-exchange market-makers. Collectively they represented a global "Who's Who" of global banking: ABN AMRO, Bank of America, Barclays, Citibank, Commerzbank, Credit Suisse, HSBC, JP Morgan Chase, Lehman Brothers, Royal Bank of Scotland, and Union Bank of Switzerland. A Japanese electronic foreign-exchange broker called Minex, owned partly by the leading Japanese banks and purchased by EBS soon after the group's formation, joined the club. The only non-participant of note was Deutsche Bank, which decided, for reasons unclear, to plow its own furrow.

In terms of system design EBS was an outgrowth of a foreign-exchange netting system designed, almost as a sideline, by Peter Bartko, a credit analyst at Chemical Bank. Bartko was American by birth but a long-time resident of London. He was something of an enigma; with people he did not know or trust he could be taciturn to the point of catatonia. Lunch with Bartko could be an hour of long, awkward silences. He was a reluctant hero, a devoted family man more at home in the comforting warmth of his own kitchen preparing complex meals than in the heat of the political caldron that the EBS boardroom was bound to become. Bartko would have been happy to hand over the product and disappear back into the oblivion from which he had emerged. The banks had other ideas. The product at the root of EBS had been his, and he had impressed the owners with his organizational and diplomatic skills. Both would be crucial in keeping a dozen quarrelsome shareholders in line. He found himself reluctantly talked into signing on as chief executive.

"Just for an interim period," Bartko told his masters, beginning what was to become a twelve-year term.

EBS had an immediate and—for Reuters—troubling impact. A large share of the business in spot foreign exchange, especially in the four major currencies—German mark, Swiss franc, Canadian dollar, and Japanese yen—moved from Reuters to EBS. Reuters held on to the sterling market and the so-called Empire currencies and remained dominant in forward contracts. Even this advantage would dissipate with the introduction of the Euro, which eliminated dozens of currency "pairs." Within a few years EBS, taking the lion's share of big-ticket transactions, had overhauled Reuters in dollar trading volume.

Reuters showed little appetite for fighting back. Instead its spokesman tended to resort to bombast. "We welcome competition," was the party line.

To be fair, what else was there to say? It is hard to suggest what else Reuters might have done differently, other than collaborate, to combat a competitor owned by its own customers.

Bombast only went so far. Reuters still owned the dominant market-share in providing information to the financial community, but was now challenged by three well-funded rivals in the three most important market sectors: Bloomberg in fixed income, Dow Jones-Telerate (later Bridge-Telerate) in US treasuries, and EBS in currencies. Bloomberg represented a clear and present danger. Bridge threatened for a while and then, as we have seen, imploded. The sudden appearance of EBS, and in Reuters' backyard, must have hurt the most. And then there was Thomson, the perennial bridesmaid among market-data vendors, but always anxious to become a bride.

The acquisition program is evidence that Reuters' management had started to take competition seriously. The company was plainly far too reliant on foreign exchange. Only aggressive expansion into other markets would ensure Reuters' survival, maintained a consulting firm, Oliver Wyman, commissioned by Villeneuve to examine all aspects of Reuters' strategy. The Wyman report should have created waves; at most it caused a few ripples. Later, another consulting firm, the Hawthorne Group, made the same point and went further. Reuters' management structure, consultants told the board at a weekend working retreat at Cliveden, a resort hotel in the Berkshire countryside and formerly the family seat of the Astors, was inadequate in a changing world. Management itself might be inadequate, too, they added.

The board could hardly claim that it had not been warned.

Acquiring successful companies had been a mixed blessing, but another way forward presented itself. It was one in which Reuters would occasionally dabble but never wholeheartedly endorse. The second option was to acquire successful people.

Over the course of the decade, Reuters made various attempts to attract pedigree names from the markets that it served. The objective, often discussed but never bestowed with a coherent plan, was to bring into the company much-needed market knowledge, marketing nous, and fresh perspectives on the world.

Reuters should have stuck with companies.

The first of these market "stars" to appear on stage was Dr. Steven Levkoff, a former senior executive at Smith Barney, a New York securities firm, and a serial developer of financial databases. Levkoff joined Reuters in 1989 as a consultant with an ambitious mission: to develop a "Bloomberg Killer." (To be fair, the tag was the invention of a journalist in the trade press, not by Reuters, but it stuck regardless.)

The "BK" would be focused on the fixed-income market, in which Bloomberg had become the dominant vendor, largely on the basis of its extensive database and advanced analytical tools. The project was designated Decision 2000.

It would be run from Levkoff's office in Stamford, Connecticut, an hour's train ride out of New York, from which he ran his own company, Capital Markets Decisions. The deal was that CMD would receive royalties on every terminal installed. I.P. Sharp, acquired by Reuters earlier, was expected to provide the raw data, supplementing his own. Levkoff would then organize it into a comprehensive and customer-friendly database, adding all the necessary analytical applications.

Things went wrong pretty much from the start. Reuters executives found Levkoff dogmatic and prickly, as he undoubtedly was—as entrepreneurs almost invariably are. Levkoff in turn found Reuters ignorant, hidebound, and riddled with politics. His first bone of contention was Reuters' insistence on using I.P. Sharp data. Levkoff considered the data unreliable. Sharp, he claimed, had a 50 percent error rate. His own prices were much better, he maintained. Reuters disagreed.

Levkoff was also asked to integrate a bond analysis software product from Australia called ESL, which had a good-looking graphical presentation. Reuters had invested in the business largely at the instigation of Job's Asia management, which patriotically regarded it almost by definition as a superior product to anything that the Americans might devise. ESL's Giltnet bond analytics package had been distributed on Telerate with some success; luring the company away from Telerate presented an additional reason to support it.

ESL was the brainchild of David Vanrenen, a burly, pugnacious South African, whose appearance suggested that he might once have played as a front-row forward for his country's rugby team. Vanrenen had no particular loyalty to Telerate and was deeply impressed by Reuters' superior market share and global reach. He had also, as it happened, fallen out with his fellow directors and wished to make a fresh start.

Levkoff and Vanrenen made for very strange bedfellows. Predictably, sparks flew from the very start of their relationship, the South African's arrival merely compounding Levkoff's growing disenchantment with Reuters. It turned what had been a bilateral contest for supremacy into a three-way fight.

The then newly appointed Peter Job sent Hubert Holmes, an Asia-based American executive, to sort out the mess. Holmes was a boyish-faced beanpole with a soft Floridian voice and the charming manner of the good-ole-boy from the South. He was no pushover in any argument, but by his own admission he knew next to nothing about bonds. So what exactly was he supposed to accomplish? Keep the peace, presumably, in which skill he was well qualified. But peacekeeping was a thankless task, and it was one for which he duly received few thanks.

Holmes reported to a London marketing executive, Krishna Biltoo, a man of intelligence and independent thought, so now there was a four-way permutation in the ever more convoluted management structure behind Decision 2000. To add to this volatile mix, Ure, representing the official management line, was forever pulling strings through Biltoo.

Decision 2000 did reach the market, the first customer terminals being installed in 1991, but it never really caught on. Some clients bravely supported it on the grounds that, although it fell far short of fulfilling their long-term requirements, it could only improve. It never did.

Amid mutual recriminations, Levkoff and Reuters were soon at legal loggerheads over the terms of their contract. These went on for some months until Levkoff and Ure renegotiated it, largely through the legally rather dubious device of handwritten amendments. According to the *New York Times*,[1] Levkoff claimed in an affidavit filed with the court to have asked for a formal version of the agreement, further alleging that Holmes refused to give him one.

By 1993, the partners were barely on speaking terms. Reuters accused CMD of breaching the contract, citing various failures and omissions on Levkoff's part. Levkoff retorted that Reuters' accusations were designed to "break us down into selling the business" to Reuters, thus eliminating the obligation to make royalty payments.

Levkoff also alleged that Reuters had also mounted a campaign to undermine CMD by secretly poaching its employees.

According to Levkoff's affidavit, a "showdown" was arranged with Holmes at a dinner at the Homestead Inn, a popular waterside restaurant, decorated in the colonial style, in Greenwich, Connecticut. Over dinner, according to Levkoff, Holmes told him that Reuters would be terminating the contract with immediate effect. Holmes admitted that a number of CMD employees were now working for Reuters. Levkoff believed that Reuters had hired them to produce a clone of Decision 2000. Holmes then allegedly produced a document representing an offer from Reuters to buy CMD.[2]

"Every day that goes by, Decision 2000 is worth less to Reuters," Holmes was quoted as saying.

Levkoff turned down the bid, as well as a second one delivered a few weeks later, instead suing Reuters for $30 million in compensation. After weeks of collecting depositions, the two sides reached an out-of-court settlement. The details have never been disclosed. Whatever they were, it left Levkoff an aggrieved and bitter man. CMD was renamed Reuters Analytics.

Vanrenen, equally disappointed, likewise disappeared from the scene.

---

[1] *New York Times*, February 2, 1998, article by Kurt Eichenwald
[2] Ibid.

Informal estimates were that Reuters had invested $15–$20 million in ESL alone.

The time and money spent on the Levkoff and Vanrenen projects would not have been quite so significant if Reuters had come out with a decent product. There was a product of sorts, but its shelf life was doomed to be short. Within a few years, few people inside the company remembered that it had ever existed. Clients had soon forgotten it as well.

The vaunted "Bloomberg Killer," far from being the marauding tiger it was supposed to be, had turned out to be a toothless tabby with a severe migraine and a missing leg.

Levkoff's severance, incidentally, had been negotiated by one of Reuters' New York attorneys, one Tom Glocer. Glocer's hiring was largely the work of Reuters' legal supremo, Simon Yencken, who was said to be in grace and favor after rescuing Job from a couple of legal scrapes in Hong Kong. Yencken proceeded to build up Reuters' legal department to nearly one hundred attorneys, turning it into a corporate power to be reckoned with. Which was just as well, since its services would be called on far more frequently than Reuters could possibly have predicted. Reuters Analytics, apparently fated from the start to be attended by legal controversy, became one of its major internal "clients."

The second guest artiste to grace the stage at Reuters, straight from a sensational appearance as a senior broker with the soon-to-be-defunct New York securities trading firm, Drexel Burnham Lambert, was Rosalyn Wilton.

Her credentials, like Levkoff's, looked impressive enough on paper. They included a senior role at GNI, a London money-brokerage firm, and a non-executive seat on the board of the London International Financial Futures Exchange. John Hull it was who hired her, to oversee the Globex partnership with the Chicago Mercantile Exchange, and to rescue the floundering Decision 2000 product. Hull was sufficiently impressed to offer a remuneration package that was said to be commensurate with her status as a major star. Whatever the offer, it could hardly fail to attract intense resentful speculation in the taverns of Fleet Street.

Measured by the market knowledge she brought to the company, Wilton may or may not have been worth whatever it was that Reuters paid to secure her services. Based on her relations with many senior colleagues she represented negative worth. Imperious and acerbic, Wilton betrayed little but contempt for most of her management peers. They reciprocated in kind, and then some.

One former associate found her company "at times dispiriting and never inspiring." Another went further. "When she strutted into your office the atmosphere immediately turned bleak, as one prepared to listen to a major harangue. It wasn't just a case of longing for the end of the meeting. One tended to lose the will to live."

Her problems with the lower ranks notwithstanding, Wilton evidently managed to endear herself to senior company executives. Job was said to be "tickled" by the idea of a dynamic, aggressive woman in a high-level position, the first in Reuters' history. Hogg emerged as another admirer, going so far—and doubtless conscious of the favorable publicity it would generate—as to nominate her for the Veuve Clicquot Business Woman of the Year Award. (For the record, she was shortlisted.)

Still, whether by skill or sheer good fortune, Wilton arrived in time to preside over the belated success of Decision 2000. She had a less positive impact on Globex, but then the project partners had never really hit it off. Under Wilton, relations, if anything, worsened. Reuters and the CME eventually fell out and parted company.

Years later Wilton would recall her days at Reuters as "happy and successful." Why, then, did she decide to leave after eight such glorious years? Wilton's explanation is that she simply felt it was time to move on. Company sources say, rather, that she resented a sideways move to a new role under a new boss, John Parcell.

Her legacy remained unclear—which can be construed as another way of saying that she did not leave one.

An award of a very different kind might have been bestowed on another aspiring star. Barry Drayson, a former top executive with a London-based money broker, MKI Securities, was recruited in 1990 for the specific purpose of spearheading Reuters' drive into Telerate's domain, the government-bond market. As only a money broker can be, Drayson was bright-eyed, brash, opinionated, supremely confident, and convinced that he and he alone could make a difference to whatever he was paid to do. In the event he *would* make a difference by enhancing Reuters' growing reputation for getting involved in expensive, time-consuming, and ultimately pointless lawsuits.

Reuters, Ure in particular, had long yearned to wage battle with Telerate in the US treasury market. Telerate still carried, courtesy of Cantor Fitzgerald, what had long been regarded as the best tradable prices in the market. Reuters had approached alternative brokerage sources without success. The company's efforts had fallen far short of irresistible. Two of those brokers described the offers they received from Reuters as risible. To be fair, there may have been a perfectly sound economic explanation for this; perhaps Reuters was afraid to offer too much money for treasury quotes in case it caused other paid market-data providers to raise their rates. Whatever the reason, Reuters remained out in the cold, fuming over its inability to break into what had become a hugely influential global market.

The Ure/Drayson proposition was to approach Cantor Fitzgerald, not for quotes on US government securities, which Cantor was unable to provide under the terms of its Telerate agreement, but for equivalent treasury data from other countries, which lay outside the scope of the contract. Howard Lutnick, Cantor's chief executive, intent on turning his company into a truly international business and no friend of Dow Jones or Telerate, was happy to go along with the plan.

So began what Reuters hoped would be its own long-running love affair with Telerate's long-standing bride.

Amid much fanfare, a ten-year deal was signed, involving a third party, Market Data Corporation, Cantor's licensed distributor of market data, run by Bernie Cantor's nephew, Rod Fisher. Drayson and Lutnick soon appeared to be having some kind of love-in, reveling in each other's company at social events around Europe. As Ure's Cantor "coup" was made flesh, he beamed approvingly in the background. The smile was that of the Cheshire cat; privately, Ure found Lutnick and his American sidekicks "loathsome." They were about to improve on that.

Enter a familiar figure. Scott Rumbold—an old market-data hand, endowed with experience at Reuters, where he still had many friends, and Telerate, where very few remained from its glory days—had been lured away by Rod Fisher, MDC's chief executive, to manage the project. Rumbold's easygoing nature was perfect for the role.

Some observers regarded Reuters' courtship of Cantor Fitzgerald as a highway pile-up waiting to happen. Rumbold was well aware of the gossip. "Yeah, I know," he sighed. "But Reuters really wants this to work. Lutnick, too. We'll just have to see." The ever affable and diplomatic Scotty was unique in being able to get along well with Lutnick, Fisher, and Drayson. For that alone he deserved a Victoria Cross for valor beyond the call of duty.

The Cantor price feed was rolled out in 1993.

But scarcely had the sound of trumpets faded than more rancorous noises could be heard.

As proud of its new service and "coup" as Reuters may have been, the market reception was palpably disappointing. Beyond disappointing; dealers pointed out to Drayson that there appeared to be serious gaps in market coverage in terms of both breadth and depth. Drayson and Ure were taken aback. At first the complaints were dismissed, but there were soon too many to ignore. Drayson subjected the Cantor price feed to a thorough examination. The results were alarming: Cantor Fitzgerald was not providing nearly the kind of comprehensive service promised, or so it seemed to Reuters. There were glaring omissions in the coverage, Drayson told Lutnick. How could he explain it?

Lutnick insisted that Cantor, to the best of its ability—market-price feeds being notoriously difficult to qualify in specific terms—was living up to its side of the bargain. Reuters, he said, simply did not understand how markets worked. There was an explanation. Cantor conducted certain transactions off-the-market, but these were confidential, private-treaty deals and Reuters was not entitled to receive such data. What Lutnick was reluctant to admit was that some of his influential customers had threatened not to do business with Cantor if their transactions were going to be blasted out to Reuters screens all over the world.

History, as it so often does, had repeated itself. In earlier times, readers will recall, many of the primary dealers in US Treasury securities had boycotted Cantor Fitzgerald for the same reason, at that time for putting market quotes on (Telerate) screens. Several years were to pass before the rebels, led by turncoat-in-chief Merrill Lynch, eventually surrendered.

Lutnick also made the point that Cantor, being relatively new to the international business market, would need time to establish itself in certain sectors of the market. Reuters would just have to be patient while Cantor worked on increasing its market share. Reuters was unimpressed with these arguments. The contract was quite specific on Cantor's obligations and Reuters was paying good money—as much as $40 million a year, some people estimated—for good data. Reuters had delivered the money, but Cantor had not delivered the data.

Neither side felt able to reach an accommodation. Their respective positions were too rigid for that. Lutnick insisted that Cantor was giving Reuters everything the contract called for. Reuters argued, in effect, that it had been sold a pup. And so the battle lines were drawn, between a once relatively easygoing company, no longer bashful about rattling legal sabers, and one of the financial world's most vigorously litigious enterprises.

"Into the valley of death, into the jaws of Hell…"

Looking down from seats in the dress circle, as many of us were, one could only marvel from afar at Drayson's bravura performance on stage. Equally impressive were Ure's gallant attempts to paint the contract as a masterpiece of drafting. A lawyer involved in the negotiations described the document as "monstrous, at least an inch thick, and without doubt the longest, most detailed, complex, baffling, and indigestible contract of its kind I'd ever seen." Old Telerate hands like me could only chuckle at the grim familiarity of it all.

Reuters eventually won the day. The arguments were settled by an arbitration tribunal. Such panels traditionally come up with rather arbitrary solutions. But not this time.

The company's legal department took enormous pride in the result. "We slew the evil dragon," one Reuters lawyer was heard to gloat over celebratory drinks.

Drayson took hubris to new heights. As quoted by Mooney/Simpson, he boasted, "The fact is that we negotiated one hell of a deal and I can't think of any other company that beat Lutnick over fifteen rounds."[3]

Reuters may have won the decision, but Drayson's "fifteen rounds" had been stretched over five years. The battle with Cantor Fitzgerald, with its endless depositions, briefings, preparation of court papers, and other legal procedures, had consumed thousands of hours of management time and presumably millions of dollars. And in the end Reuters emerged with no product or revenue to show for it.

Drayson dabbled in a couple of projects before quietly leaving the company—perhaps the only quiet thing he had ever done. Ure survived the experience exhausted and disgusted in equal measure. "I've never dealt with such awful people," he told colleagues, "and never want to again."

The next star turn bounded on stage in 1998 in the bespangled form of Carolyn Chin. She was "snapped up" from International Business Machines, at considerable cost, which allegedly included a signing-on fee said to be worth $1 million. Chin was taken on by Sanderson to be chief marketing officer for Reuters North America. Chin was fifty-something, short, voluble, and so fast-talking that many colleagues had problems understanding her. She otherwise had all the theoretical attributes for the job. She had technical knowledge and marketing savvy. She was evidently well connected in government circles. She owned a forceful personality. Her résumé on paper was even more eye-catching than Ros Wilton's. Prior to her corporate strategy role at Big Blue, she had spent time at Citibank—including a management position at Quotron—American Telephone & Telegraph, and Macy's, the American department store chain. She had also worked for several government departments in Washington.

Chin's financial package became, like Wilton's, the subject of much corridor gossip. No doubt Reuters' intelligence service would sooner or later have worked it out, but Chin was out of the door before she had served a year.

The final, top-of-the bill performer, or at least the most senior, was Philip Green. Recruited in 1990 from DHL, a parcel delivery firm, Green was hired to head Reuters' Trading Solutions group. Green was small, silver-haired, and dapper, with an unusually high forehead. Behind his back he was known as the Mekon, after an egg-headed extra-terrestrial character in a defunct British comic. He professed to be a devout Christian and, it was rumored, occasionally liked to invite a colleague to join him in a prayer in the office. Many found this, like certain other traits of Green's character, nauseating. Green, like Wilton, quickly became a rather isolated figure on the executive floor.

---

[3] Brian Mooney/Barry Simpson, *Breaking News: How the Wheels Came off at Reuters*, Capstone Press, 2003, p.60-61

For all his public piety, Green's corporate record was not unblemished. Before working at DHL he had been a director of Coloroll, a decorative appliances company, which had gone bust at the start of the decade. In his capacity as a trustee of the company's retirement plan, he had fallen foul of his fellow directors over the purchase of the chief executive's apartment, which was allegedly bought at an unusually high figure and sold at a considerable loss. Hauled in front of a pension tribunal, he was charged with breach of trust and warned as to his future conduct.

Green convinced himself that the move from DHL had been a short and logical step, since, as he explained to an interviewer, both companies were in the business of "moving things from one place to another."[4]

Peter Job, apparently inspired by this insight, gave Green a seat on the board. Green had been with the company less than six months. Two years later, Job's successor, Tom Glocer, also finding in Green something positive that everyone else seemed to have missed, appointed him to the newly created post of chief operating officer.

Glocer at least recognized his mistake: two years later Green was sacked. The reason given was that in a review of management structure aimed at expunging excessive management layers, his post had been eliminated. Enough said.

All these high-level comings and goings over the years left many senior and middle company managers bemused. The message that Reuters seemed to be sending out was that internal candidates for top jobs were either unqualified, incompetent, or not to be trusted. Yet virtually every attempt to bring in super-qualified, high-profile outsiders had failed. Whether this was a question of poor selection or evidence of defective organization is debatable. Either way, Reuters emerged looking foolish.

It left a bad taste at every level of the company's executive branch. Morale sagged. The gossip mill turned ever more scurrilous and cynical. Soon the company began to experience the first voluntary departures among disillusioned middle managers.

The company would soon be helping many of the remainder on their way.

Though bruised and bewildered by the Decision 2000 debacle, Reuters was not about to give up on its lingering obsession with producing a Bloomberg Killer. The new attempt would prove to be infinitely more complex than its predecessor—this fusing of real-time data with historical data, all gathered into a vast mass, and overlaid with clever analytics—and ten times more expensive.

The project was conceived in great secrecy. It received the blessing of Job and was awarded a budget in keeping with its ambition. Responsibility for

---

[4] Brian Mooney/Barry Simpson, *Breaking News: How the Wheels Came off at Reuters*, Capstone Press, 2003, p.182

masterminding the project—which Reuters, seeking to invest the thing with appropriate grandeur, liked to call "program"—was handed to the ubiquitous, ever-willing David Ure.

It was code-named Project Armstrong, apparently after Neil Armstrong, the American astronaut who had walked on the moon in a triumphant vindication of the ten-year development program set in train for that very purpose. The analogy was clear.

Unlike Decision 2000, Armstrong would be planned, designed and built using entirely internal resources. This was fine as a concept, but less commendable in practical terms. Reuters still had little experience of building a database, especially one that would have to interact with real-time delivery systems. Spewing out real-time market prices was familiar ground to Reuters, but once those prices had been overtaken by updates they were tossed away, no longer of any use to traders. By contrast, constructing a coherent historical archive to help users analyze, evaluate, and price portfolios represented relatively virgin territory.

The expedition embarked in 1993. Hubert Holmes, apparently fully recovered from his bruising encounter with Levkoff—and armed with a reasonable amount of residual and usable raw data—was put in charge of Armstrong's fixed-income element; Jeremy Penn oversaw the equities side. Both reported to Ure, Holmes from Stamford, Penn from London. Also involved was a Reuters-owned software development company, Equisoft, based in Colchester, a commuter dormitory thirty miles northeast of London.

Some readers, even now, are doubtless muttering, "Mmmm."

The massive warehousing machine selected to store the data was an NCR Teradata 3600. Three were purchased at $15 million a piece. This decision was attributed to Buford Smith—not one of his better decisions for the company. Teradata was the kind of device used by supermarket chains—Walmart for one—for inventory control. Whether it could do as effective a job for bonds and stocks remained to be seen.

Dean Ratcliffe, a young database expert hired to work on Armstrong, did not think it could do the job. As quoted by Mooney/Simpson, Ratcliffe thought Teradata "was hopeless for two reasons. Firstly when you interrogated it you never knew how long it would take to come back with the answer, and secondly it could not do joins, so none of the relational properties ever functioned. It was the wrong tool for the task. Teradata is fine for a data warehouse, but totally unsuitable for a production system with lots of updates."[5]

Outside firms were brought in to help move the project forward. Equisoft

---

[5] Brian Mooney/Barry Simpson, *Breaking News: How the Wheels Came off at Reuters*, Capstone Press, 2003, p.77

came up with Equation, a piece of software for calculating options in real time. Armstrong programmers found it slow and too difficult to program. An Iowa firm, the incongruously named Human Factors, contributed a user display interface called the Tablet. This was widely regarded in the Armstrong team as aesthetically inadequate.

It was then decreed, apparently by Ure, that Tablet would have to run on Reuters terminals as a separate application, obliging users to have two distinct programs running on the same desktops, one for real-time prices, the other for historical data. Such an arrangement did not invite favorable comparisons with Bloomberg's all-singing, all-dancing, seamlessly integrated terminal.

Finally, and in hindsight prematurely, a demonstration was arranged for management in 1995. Taped data was used because real data could not be processed in time. It was not a success. Management representatives present may not have recognized the fact, but senior technical managers and sales executives knew in their hearts (and minds) that Armstrong was a botched job, with only a marginally greater chance of success than its unlamented Levkoff-inspired predecessor.

Nonetheless, the following year a product was released under the name Securities 3000. It was soon followed by Treasury 3000 and Money 3000. The reception in the market would have been disappointing if it had not been almost perfectly indifferent. Trumpeted as a new generation of Reuters desktop terminals, the so-called 3000 Series was perceived by clients as expensive, complicated to install, just as difficult to maintain, and far from easy to use.

All of which stood in stark contrast with Bloomberg's supposedly clunky stand-alone system, which carried data that users found perfectly adequate, and which they found easy to navigate. Bloomberg also compared favorably on price, being not much more expensive than the collective elements of the new Reuters product. Even if Bloomberg had cost much, much more, clients would have preferred it for reasons of convenience and low maintenance.

Reaching for the sky, Reuters had once more plunged to the ground. In trying to rush through a project in two years that probably should have taken several more, ambition had again overwhelmed common sense. Recriminations filled the air. Among those who worked on Armstrong there were sundry disagreements on what had gone wrong, especially on questions of hardware and software choices. Most, though, agreed on two basic deficiencies: first, the project all along lacked a coherent management structure; second, the insistence on producing a complete version, rather than focusing on a Mark I version, to which missing bells and whistles could have been added to later releases.

One of these managers, to illustrate the lessons not learned, circulated a passage from Mike Bloomberg's autobiography, *Bloomberg by Bloomberg*, setting out his approach to product development. "We made mistakes, of course. Most of them were omissions we didn't think of when we initially wrote the software. We fixed them by doing it over and over, again and again. We do the same today. While our competitors are still sucking their thumbs trying to make the design perfect, we're already on prototype No. 5. By the time our rivals are ready with wires and screws, we are on version No. 10. It gets back to planning versus acting. We *act* from day one; others plan how to plan—for months."[6] If there were lessons to be learned from Bloomberg, there were ways to go about it. Reuters was soon to be reminded that there were wrong ways.

Early in 1998 there came out of the clear blue sky a legal thunderbolt that would shake Reuters to its ancient and proud foundations. The point of impact was Reuters Analytics in Stamford, rapidly acquiring a reputation within Reuters as the epicenter of company disasters. Its implications were potentially profound and they reduced the battles with Levkoff and Cantor Fitzgerald to minor spats over a parking space.

Inevitably, the incident acquired the epithet "Reutergate."

This metaphorical lightning strike took the form of a newspaper article by Kurt Eichenwald, an investigative reporter for the *New York Times*. "Federal prosecutors," he wrote in *The Times* on Monday, February 2, 1998, "have obtained more than 100 written communications between a US subsidiary of Reuters Holdings plc and a consulting company that investigators believe was hired to steal information from the computers of a competitor, Bloomberg LP, people in touch with the investigation said Sunday."

Robert Crooke, the spokesman for Reuters America, declined to comment on *The Times* report, but Reuters had already acted following Eichenwald's call by putting three executives from the Stamford office on paid leave. One was Hubert Holmes, a legal veteran of the Levkoff wars, the others Jeff Walker, a former CMD employee, and a James Feingold. Clearly, this was not of those "little local difficulties" that British politicians used to talk about. Corporate headquarters was not beyond the reach of collateral damage: Holmes reported directly to John Parcell, a senior executive in London, who in turn reported to David Ure, a member of Reuters' board.

"According to people briefed on the investigation," Eichenwald reported, "prosecutors have obtained evidence that Reuters was stealing information from Bloomberg's operating code, the underlying software that governs the functioning of Bloomberg's data terminals."

Clearly this was no parking-space spat. The sources of Eichenwald's infor-

---

[6] Michael Bloomberg, *Bloomberg by Bloomberg*, John Wiley & Sons, 1997, p.52

mation were not revealed, but his report was sufficiently detailed to convince Reuters' senior management that the situation was serious, and that something fishy might indeed have been going on in normally sleepy Stamford.

Job wasted no time launching a damage limitation exercise. Peter Thomas, Reuters' press relations director in London, put out instructions that nobody, but nobody, under absolutely no circumstances, was to discuss the case with the press, or with anyone else for that matter. The penalty for doing so was indicated by a throat-slashing gesture. This monastic vow of silence would remain in place for many months and, remarkably, given Reuters' sieve-like history, prove to be highly effective.

Job was distraught but determined to fight if necessary. He told Thomas: "I'm damned if I'm going to be the chief executive who presides over the destruction of Reuters' 150-year-old reputation for integrity and honesty."

On advice from counsel, Job issued a deliberately innocuous statement. "We, like our competitors, try to compare the performance of our products and services to those of our competition. We have not viewed these kinds of assessments to be illegal or improper… If in the course of doing comparative analyses, and trying to improve our products and services, we have improperly used certain Bloomberg proprietary information, then we, as an ethical company, will take appropriate steps to fix the problem."

As if the legal ramifications alone were not serious enough, there was a wider political dimension to the case. In 1996, the American Congress had passed the US Economic Espionage Act, which made stealing company secrets a criminal offence under federal law. The Act stemmed from a seven-year-old case in which a General Motors executive had left the company to join Volkswagen, allegedly taking piles of sensitive papers with him. There was more than a suggestion of nationalism in the new act. It was easy to paint General Motors as an American victim, Volkswagen as a foreign predator. The echo from the earlier case was obvious: Bloomberg was an American company, Reuters a British one.

Americans can be supremely nationalistic when their commercial interests are thought to be under assault, and American prosecutors, armed with brand-new laws and propelled by a fierce tailwind of patriotism, were unlikely to give quarter. The Federal prosecutor in New York's southern district, Mary Jo White, felt she had a case under the 1996 Act. The core of it was that unusually high downloads from a Bloomberg terminal had been made at the office of a New York consulting firm, Cyberspace Research Associates, run by one David Schwartz, a former Bloomberg employee. FBI agents had been on the case for some months when it leached into the public domain via the *New York Times*. They had traced shipments of material from the CRA office to Reuters' office in Stamford. They had bugged Reuters' office. They had accumulated lots of circumstantial but potentially damaging background material, mainly from the Levkoff case.

Steve Levkoff had obviously been singing his head off to investigators.

Reuters' New York lawyers urged caution and patience. The Feds, they believed, had less than a copper-bottomed case. The firm was Wachtell, Lipton, Rosen & Katz, whose lawyers enjoyed a reputation for being "brilliant and arrogant." The attorney assigned to Reuters, Lawrence Pedowitz, may well have been brilliant, but he exhibited not a hint of arrogance. He was, according to those who dealt with him, a quiet and thoughtful man, measured in his approach, careful with his words, and altogether far more low-key than his firm's reputation warranted.

Low-key was how he thought Reuters should act. In that respect, Job and colleagues needed little prompting. It was heads-down time in London as much as in Stamford. Job stayed out of the United States during this period, afraid that he might be grabbed at the airport and whisked off to the slammer to await indictment. This was probably an unfounded concern. Actually, Pedowitz believed the prosecutors' evidence to be flimsy and ill-prepared, the FBI agents having demonstrated a lack of understanding of computers or the business of financial information. The most important fact was that no charges had been made. "Hold tight and shut up," was Pedowitz's advice. "This thing may just blow over."

Pedowitz's opinion was prescient. Two years later—perhaps the longest two years any of Reuters' top executives had ever experienced—the investigation was dropped.

Bloomberg publicly shrugged his shoulders but, according to his associates, privately seethed. A Bloomberg source told me at the time: "We, and especially Mike, honestly believe Reuters was up to no good. It should all have come out through the legal system. The commercial repercussions alone would have been devastating—and obviously good for us."

Reuters' management, which must be presumed innocent, had by then been punished enough. Job and his team felt deeply chastened. No senior Reuters executive that I ever spoke to, then or later, could come to terms with the idea that any senior executive of the company might have sanctioned, let alone encouraged, such behavior. The truth may never be known, but as one senior executive later put it: "I just felt somehow a little grubbier after the Bloomberg episode. We had all been on tenterhooks for two years and we all felt mighty relieved when it was over. But for a long time I couldn't help thinking, 'What the hell really went on in that Stamford office…?' "

Over the course of the 1990s, it became increasingly clear that Reuters' dominance as vendor of choice in the financial markets was under genuine, as opposed to perceived, assault. A number of incompetently managed rivals had fallen by the wayside, but Bloomberg marched on relentlessly, and Bridge, having swallowed up many of the casualties, ostensibly loomed as a threat. In niche markets, new, smaller, and more nimble competitors were mopping up business with specialized products of the kind that Reuters plainly ought to have been accumulating in its own portfolio. Reuters' own clients were looking for alternative mousetraps and were increasingly prepared to engage in cooperative ventures to produce them.

Following in EBS's footprints, FXall, a foreign-exchange trading platform funded and developed by many of the same banks that had collaborated on EBS, appeared on the scene. Reuters threw in its lot with a rival bank-owned product, Atriax. The wrong horse had been backed. Atriax failed to catch on and died a quick death.

Reuters failed to exploit other market opportunities resulting from the rapidly developing taste for electronic trading platforms.

TradeWeb, designed as a trading platform for US treasury securities, was launched in 1998 after two years of development. It was founded by Jim Toffey, a former bond trader at Credit Suisse First Boston, the firm in which his father had been head of bond trading. With seed money of $12 million from CSFB and three other banks, Toffey set up shop with eight programmers in a downtown loft. In these respects—his emergence from a trading firm, the modest beginning with a small group of "techies"—Toffey's career had faint echoes of Michael Bloomberg's.

Their attitudes were not dissimilar either. "My business plan didn't even use the word e-commerce," Toffey told the *New York Times* in 2004. "We just put our heads down and focused on execution. Our mantra was under-promise and over-deliver."

TradeWeb's trading volume that year approached $20 billion.

The company was quickly put up for sale, partly to repay the original investors. Reuters announced itself an interested party. So did Thomson Financial, increasingly keen to secure a major stake in the market-data industry, smarting over its reputation as a gallant also-ran. The auction produced a winning bid of $500 million—$385 million in cash, with contingent payments of a further $150 million based on achieving growth targets. None of these figures went beyond Reuters' means. But the winner, much to everyone's surprise, was not Reuters but the plodding old tortoise, Thomson. The bridesmaid had finally become a bride. Reuters, according to unconfirmed reports, had dropped out of the bidding when the price exceeded its limit of eight times earnings.

BrokerTec, another platform business, appeared a year after TradeWeb, financed by fourteen Wall Street firms. BrokerTec's plan was to execute trades in any and all fixed-income securities. Starting later and at first growing less quickly than its rival, BrokerTec might have presented Reuters with an ideal alternative investment to TradeWeb, but Reuters showed little interest. The acquirer this time was Icap, a London money-broking conglomerate owned by one of the City's most aggressive entrepreneurs, Michael Spencer. There was no telling what Spencer was up to, but whatever it was it was unlikely to be in Reuters' long-term interests. Icap was a major Reuters client and a paid provider of content. These factors no doubt preyed on Reuters' mind, especially as Tom Glocer, by then Reuters' chief executive, was thought to be close to Spencer.

Had Reuters missed two boats? Many industry observers thought so.

Reuters' management maintained that the asking price for TradeWeb had been far too indigestible. Critics countered with the argument that long-term strategic value nearly always carries a short-term premium. Reuters had not been reluctant to spend money in the previous decade, even if the money had not always been spent wisely. What had changed in the early years of the new century? There was at least one off-the-shelf answer: Reuters financial power, derived from earnings, was on the wane.

It was inadequate as an explanation for management inertia, or whatever it was that made the company stick to its knitting. Reuters, through Dealing, had been a pioneer of trading platforms. Instinet in its day had been one of the most successful trading platforms in market history. For Reuters, surely commanding the execution and post-execution capability in the markets to which it supplied data and network was the most natural extension of its business model? Apparently not.

What price a swap of investments in GL Trade, Instinet, and Liberty for TradeWeb, Yahoo!, and FXall?

If Reuters had not missed these three boats, then what was its alternative strategy? Put another way, as many did put it, what exactly was Reuters for?

The growing criticism of management focused on that question, one to which Reuters seemed unable or unwilling to articulate a satisfactory answer.

Job had shown, if nothing else, that he was a fully paid-up pragmatist. Fair enough, but it was still reasonable to ask whether the chief executive nursed some underlying strategic vision. When, for example, an analyst asked about the content-versus-technology issue, Job had no hesitation in saying, "Technology."

It had the virtue of qualifying as a straight answer, if nothing else. What it actually meant was less clear. Nor was it clearer after Job had tried to explain matters. "The problem is that if you formulate a vision, conditions change, and your statement becomes outdated. That confuses everybody. You shouldn't have a strategy unless you're not going to change it for ten or twelve years. That's how long it will take to realize it."[7]

---

[7] Brian Mooney/Barry Simpson, *Breaking News: How the Wheels Came off at Reuters*, Capstone Press, 2003, p.127

With remarks like that, Job's avowed policy of not confusing people managed to achieve precisely the opposite.

If discarding the idea of a strategy in favor of tactical opportunism meant anything, it could only suggest that Job wanted Reuters to be a lean, innovative, aggressive company capable of reacting quickly to events or sudden changes in market conditions. It was a reasonable stance. Unfortunately, Reuters was none of those things. With 18,000 employees around the world in hundreds of offices, many of them operated as tribal fiefdoms; Reuters had become increasingly bureaucratic, procedure-bound, and political. If Job's vision for Reuters was that of an opportunity-driven, fast-acting innovator, he might have considered creating the corporate equivalent of a military rapid response unit, like the SAS or the Navy Seals. What he presided over instead was a vast, globally dispersed, administratively top-heavy, risk-averse organization open to the charge that it was functionally incapable of recognizing, let alone exploiting, opportunity. The market added another grievous fault: arrogance.

None of this was specifically of Job's making. Job's fault, his critics contended, lay in not taking responsibility for the unmaking.

Job would not have to worry about it much longer. In 2001, he announced his retirement at the age of sixty. Before leaving, he followed in Sir Christopher Hogg's footsteps to Buckingham Palace to be pronounced a Knight Commander of the British Empire, for services to news and the media. (As an interesting aside, it was revealed in a newspaper at the time that Job's two predecessors, Gerald Long and Glen Renfrew, had declined the same honor, in both cases because such gratifications were seen as a nonsensical relic of Britain's past and were, in any event, inappropriate for journalists of supposedly scrupulous independence.)

So what did Peter Job—that is, Sir Peter Job—have to say to his critics, four years into his retirement; a reasonable time for reflection? In a word: nothing. At least, not to me.

Job freely admitted to being an interviewer's nightmare. He seemed proud of it. For understandable, though unhelpful, reasons he was reluctant to talk about himself, or his time as Reuters' chief executive. He was plainly an unrepentant and contented man. A wealthy one, too, the owner of a home in Oxfordshire, where he liked to tend his rose garden, a house in Spain, to which he repaired occasionally, and a flat in London for convenience. He was still serving on two boards, Shell and Deutsche Bank. He made little effort to see his former colleagues. An exception was David Ure, whom Job stoutly defended as "a man of wisdom."

"Look," he explained, "I had a wonderful career at Reuters. Frankly I didn't care much what people said about me then, and I care even less now. No, I haven't read the Mooney-Simpson book, or anything else. I have no desire to defend myself, nor do I wish to attack anyone. It's all in the past. I've moved on. Some things we did right, some wrong. If you ask me 'Which things would I change?' I'd have to think about it very hard—and then say 'Probably nothing.' "

The closest Job came to being drawn into a discussion about Reuters' decline was to admit that the company was "a hard place to reform. My predecessor [Renfrew] found it difficult. My successor has no doubt had the same experience. Expense reductions were necessary, I'll admit, and I'm glad I wasn't the one to have to let people go." Reuters, he ventures, "is still a fine global brand, for all its ups and downs." But as for the future, Job was just as noncommittal as he was about the past. "We shall have to see," was the best he could manage. The impression he conveyed—or, more accurately, the one that I received—was that the company had seen its best days.

It is reasonable to ask, finally, where Reuters' board of directors stood as the company declined in the fading years of the century. Sir Christopher Hogg's effectiveness as chairman only belatedly fell under the microscope. Either he had failed to recognize Reuters' faults, or he *had* recognized them and failed to take corrective measures. A third, rather feeble explanation is that he and his fellow directors were lulled into a false sense of well-being by the reports it received from management. Bridge's board had made the same mistake, with fatal consequences.

To stretch the quality of charity, it can be said that Reuters' latent difficulties were camouflaged for many years by a roaring bull stock-market, but the purpose of any board is to dispense wisdom in easy as well as difficult times. A few discreet but firm warnings against complacency, delivered over lunch, sincerely would not have gone amiss. Perhaps they *were* delivered. If so, why were they not heeded?

Market downturns can be painful but are not inevitably disastrous. Chief executives (and board chairmen), like sailors, must expect storms and be prepared for them. The company often boasted that it did not mind in which direction markets moved, so long as they moved. But bear markets invariably lead clients to take a less benign view of spending on information services. When, in the early years of the new century, stock markets around the world fell into one of their periodic swoons, belt-tightening resumed with a vengeance. In the Internet age, the cost-effectiveness of complex dealing-room infrastructure, much of it hard-wired in outmoded technology, became the subject of intense review by financial institutions. Many turned to Reuters for solutions and were disappointed, even shocked, when few were forthcoming. This failure to respond exposed Reuters' hitherto hidden problems. Under Admiral Hogg and Captain Job, the ship found itself seriously unprepared for foul weather.

In 2003, as the financial storm raged at its fiercest, Hogg had been a Reuters director for nineteen years, eighteen of them as chairman.

Hogg qualified, at least on paper, as *un homme trés serieux*. He was a grandee in the worlds of finance and politics, and his regal presence also honored London's artistic institutions. He collected directorships and committee seats the way some people collect Toby jugs. In the City, Hogg served at various times as chief executive, chairman, and director of several major corporations, notably Courtaulds Textiles plc, GlaxoSmithKline, the pharmaceuticals giant, and Allied Domecq, a diversified drinks company. He was a member of the International Council of JP Morgan. Across town in Westminster, he was a familiar figure in government circles, notably as a member of the Department of Industry's Industrial Development Advisory Board. He served as non-executive chairman of the Royal National Theatre. Whatever his role, Hogg invariably attracted controversy. As chairman of Glaxo he was forced to scrap a £20 million remuneration package for the chief executive. At Reuters, he came under fire for a "golden parachute" clause in Tom Glocer's package that equaled three years' worth of salary. His own £1.8 million pension was questioned as excessive for a part-time chairman. Domestically, he acquired a trophy wife by marrying Miriam Stoppard, the former wife of playwright Sir Tom Stoppard, a celebrity in her own right as the author of books on pregnancy and childcare. Great was the demand for the Hogg-Stoppards at social events and dinner parties.

It is not unreasonable to ask, as many did, whether Hogg, given his many responsibilities, actually had enough time in the day to fully grasp what Reuters was doing, or should have been doing, to protect its franchise. (The same point might be made of Peter Job, who also made a point of collecting board seats, including one alongside Hogg at GlaxoSmithKline.)

On the occasion of Hogg's retirement that year, Job's successor, Tom Glocer, was unstinting in his praise for the chairman's "wise counsel and guidance"—which may or may not have been heartfelt, such accolades often being made merely in observance of a polite custom.

The essential and unremitting complaint of a growing army of critics was that the good ship *Reuters*, on the Job-Hogg watch, seemed to have lost its way, perhaps irretrievably.

It was a charge that acquired resonance in 2003, when Reuters, for the first time since flotation twenty years earlier, reported an operating loss for the previous year, accompanied by a decline in revenue. After that, the losses abated as the headcount overhead was ruthlessly cut, but revenue growth remained elusive for several quarters. The City was far from pleased with all this, even after signs appeared that the worst might be over. Reuters was still regarded as a growth company, and growth companies are supposed to grow, not shrink.

Early in 2004, Tom Glocer, in the top post for three years, would feel able to issue an upbeat statement about the company's prospects with a phrase he would probably regret. "I am confident that we have now passed the inflection point in our recurring revenue decline." Talk of inflection points attracted a great deal of ribald comment, especially among the ranks of recently departed managers.

These embittered souls, now consigned to the chattering classes, had left the company during and after a cull of 3500 employees, representing about one-fifth of Reuters' workforce. Many of the dismissed executives took to the Internet to vent their spleen on the company's message boards. Very entertaining they were, too, if a little intemperate. The infamous cull was the first and largest of a series of what some Reuters' journalists, themselves no longer immune to layoffs, would describe as Stalinist purges. Most analysts agreed that a headcount reduction was necessary and overdue. That it tended to accentuate Reuters' misfortunes was regarded as an unavoidable consequence. Peter Thomas faced the press bravely with every piece of bad news.

Naturally the layoffs put a dent in company morale. Of particular concern was the perception that the exercise had been poorly conceived, with quantity rather than quality the order of the day, resulting in a great many babies disappearing down the drain with the bathwater. It was a fact that a number of senior managers of undoubted talent, with the collective wisdom of generations, were discarded, making it hard to avoid the conclusion that Reuters ought to have executed a less wanton cull; firing, just as much as hiring, ought to be subject to some kind of selective process. But it was almost as hard to argue with the proposition that the new chief executive, facing a financial crisis, and armed with a new broom, was almost obliged to indulge in a sweep.

The epithet most often applied to the man wielding the broom—almost inevitably, given his previous occupation—was ruthless. To ruthless could be added cold and opportunistic. Glocer faced other charges: that he was disdainful of Reuters' traditions, fixated on achieving instant results, and much too concerned with his personal financial arrangements—which duly became the subject of much public debate. Given his inheritance, one might well ask what he was supposed to be if not ruthless.

In terms of company history, Glocer had a couple of things going for him. Like Reuters' legendary founder, he was a foreigner and a Jew. Socially, he had some of Julius Reuter's graces. Refusing to measure up to the shark-eyed legal stereotype beloved of his critics, Glocer came across as charming, affable, and gregarious. He also came equipped with the priceless accoutrement of a rather dishy Finnish wife (who, it was said, wanted nothing more than to return to New York, with or without Reuters in tow). His most interesting facet was that he was the first Reuters chief executive who had not been a journalist.

"A wolf in sheep's clothing," would no doubt be the riposte from his detractors, but there was clearly more to Glocer than the prototypical hard-nosed Wall Street attorney.

There would have to be.

For Glocer, the burden of nursing a badly damaged patient back to health loomed as a formidable assignment. If he was not ideally equipped for the job, that was hardly his fault. If blame was to be assigned for the company's "failure" to pick a suitable candidate, then many observers thought it should fall upon Sir Christopher Hogg and the Reuters board for not insisting on a long-term succession strategy.

But there, frustratingly, the story must end. There is no neatly packaged denouement. The rest of the plot will unfold in its own good time.

Time, though, for just one late, ironic twist.

In 2004, Reuters purchased most of the assets of Bridge for just under $400 million, plus $30 million in interim funding and $38 million in debt financing for struggling Savvis, Bridge's network provider and former subsidiary. Telerate was left out of the transaction, having been sold for a nominal fee to Moneyline, a company founded by former Telerate marketing executive Jon Robson. But Telerate's agony of embarrassment was not over yet.

A year later, Reuters, with the approval of the US Justice Department, acquired the sad remnants of Telerate for $145 million, plus Reuters' interest in Savvis, acquired as part of the Bridge deal, representing another $70 million. Telerate had long since receded into insignificance as a global competitor. Its disposal, in what was essentially a fire sale, took place a mere fifteen years after Dow Jones completed its purchase of the company for a total consideration of $1.6 billion.

Based on those figures, Telerate had declined in value by about $100 million a year. Dow Jones and Bridge between them had achieved the improbable: they had made Reuters look like a model of exemplary management.

The sole consolation was that Telerate's prolonged suffering as the object of a commercial version of pass-the-parcel was finally over.

Neil Hirsch would once have been inconsolable. Now, drug-free and sober, he was too busy enjoying his wealth to care. "The company was shafted," he said, "but life goes on. We had ourselves a great time while it lasted—and nothing lasts forever."

Telerate's former employees in London and New York held simultaneous wakes. They were attended by hundreds.

For those few of us—we happy few—who had bridged the divide between Reuters and Telerate, as much as we grieved the passing of the one we were also saddened by the decline of the other. My twelve happy years at Telerate were made possible by the eighteen equally happy years I'd spent at Reuters. The old news-agency-turned-media-powerhouse had been for me a life-enhancing experience. I joined as a boy and left as a man. At Telerate I had scaled the heights of my chosen profession.

Who could be less than eternally grateful for the experience? Not this writer.

# Afterword

Wrapping up a constantly evolving story like this one can be hazardous. To explain why, let me quote a British prime minister. Asked what he most feared as a threat to his government, he replied, "Events, dear boy, events."

And sure enough, events have intervened in this tale. No sooner had I finished writing this book than two of its most prominent corporate subjects, Dow Jones and Reuters, grabbed the kind of headlines they had so often generated for others by becoming takeover targets themselves.

Curiously, but as far as is known coincidentally, the two stories broke within two weeks of each other. The first, on May 1, 2007, revealed that Dow Jones had received a distinctly unwelcome bid from News Corporation, representing the Bancroft family's declared nemesis, Rupert Murdoch. As if not to be outdone, Reuters followed with an announcement that it had agreed, as a result of entirely friendly negotiations, to be merged into Thomson, the Canadian publishing group and owner of a rival market-data vendor, Thomson Financial.

Both announcements took the stock market by surprise, though for different reasons. Dow Jones had long been perceived as a potential takeover candidate and Murdoch's desire to own the *Wall Street Journal* had long been an open secret in media circles. Given those facts, the market was surprised less by the identity of the bidder than by the timing of the bid—and the price.

The Reuters Thomson news by contrast hit the newswires as a genuine bolt from the blue. There was additional cause for astonishment in the ingenious structure of the deal: Reuters, apparently the instigator of the negotiations, would be reversed into Thomson and operate as an independent entity as Thomson Reuters, but under Reuters management, with Tom Glocer in the top job. In other words, Reuters appeared to be buying Thomson Financial using Thomson money, at the cost of forfeiting Reuters' corporate independence. Thomson would own 53 percent of the combined business. The deal was well received by analysts and journalists, who almost fell over each other in their haste to pronounce the companies an almost perfect commercial fit.

Murdoch's offer for Dow Jones was $5 billion in cash—generous to a fault in the considered opinion of most Wall Street analysts. Especially so for a company that had spent many years fighting a relentless industry-wide decline in print advertising, and by general consent with a management palpably not up to the task. At $60 per share the offer represented a premium of 70 percent over the previous day's closing price of $35, which was more or less the level at which the shares had languished for the best part of a decade. With no concession to irony, News Corporation depicted its approach as "friendly." Friendly was the last thing it could be, of course, since it pitted the Bancrofts, whose various trusts owned the majority of the voting stock, against an opponent they had publicly despised in what could only be a fight to the death.

For many members of the Bancroft clan, especially those representing the older generation, a bid from Murdoch was their worst nightmare, whatever the price. To these self-ordained guardians of their beloved *Wall Street Journal*, Murdoch was a pariah, a peddler of vulgar tabloids, a man who unashamedly tailored his editorial policies to suit his business interests—the print industry's equivalent of Hollywood's "Creature from the Black Lagoon."

They were far from shy in airing their opinions on the matter. James Ottaway, a Dow Jones director and a stalwart family retainer, was among the first to man the ramparts. A sale to Murdoch, he told reporters, "would lead to loss of the unique news quality and integrity of the *Wall Street Journal* and other Dow Jones publications and Internet services, and loss of independence and integrity of a leading national editorial voice." Christopher Bancroft, also a director, and the clan's unelected chieftain, took a similar tack on editorial independence. "Why would I risk that? I'm open to any situation that benefits the *Wall Street Journal* and Dow Jones and its shareholders. At the moment, I don't see anything that would do that."

For three months Murdoch was made to wait for a response while the Bancrofts defiantly, and to most observers mystifyingly, hurled personal insults at him. "Why they're doing this baffles me," one analyst commented with a bemused shake of the head. "For sixty bucks a share they should be kissing his ass." That pretty much summed up the Wall Street consensus, but the Bancrofts had rarely heeded the views of the Street, and they were not about to break the habit. This time, however, there was no retreating behind the walls of the family compound, especially as the walls were already crumbling.

When they were not hurling invective at the besiegers, the Bancrofts battled among themselves—trust pitted against trust, generation against generation— all the while desperately casting about for salvation from some "white knight." Several potential saviors briefly emerged, including the *Washington Post*, the *New York Times* and, more credibly, the General Electric Company, owner of television interests that might benefit from owning America's most highly regarded source of business news. None stayed around for long, none being bold enough to face the prospect of a bidding war with Murdoch, especially at an opening price already above what most of them felt could be justified by normal commercial considerations.

In the end, a Bancroft delegation, led by Christopher himself, agreed to turn up for a face-to-face meeting with That Man. They must have made the trip with all the enthusiasm of royal passengers in a Parisian tumbrel. Journalists wished out loud that they could attend the event as flies on the wall. Once at the negotiating table they had little choice but to accept grudgingly what the rest of the industry had for some time regarded as inevitable: they did a deal. They accepted Murdoch's original price, which all along he had made clear was not negotiable. They also bowed to Murdoch's assurances of editorial independence, which would be "guaranteed" by an independent editorial watchdog committee. (Shades here, cynics pointed out, of similar assurances Murdoch had made some years earlier when buying the *The Times* of London, only to ride roughshod over the paper's committee of independent directors once the deal had been done.)

Thomson's $17 billion bid for Reuters raised fewer eyebrows, least of all on the price, which at 705 pence a share represented a 40 per cent premium on the previous day's close. If the price was considered reasonable, as most shareholders seemed to accept (many having forgotten that Reuters shares had once been worth twice as much), the deal structure was regarded as masterful. Credit for this was duly assigned to Tom Glocer, who had proved that, whatever critics might have thought about his virtues as a corporate manager, it could not be said that he had lost the skills he had polished in his former profession as a mergers-and-acquisitions lawyer. Most industry observers applauded in admiration, perhaps none more loudly than *Market Data Insight*, a trade newsletter. "In short," wrote the editor, Andrew Delaney, "Glocer has managed to engineer a reverse of Reuters into Thomson, while maintaining the Reuters brand and leadership of the combined financial information and technology businesses, which ostensibly would have the scale, clout and content to take on Bloomberg, supported by the kinds of delivery technologies that are required as the trading industry moves from being human-led to server-led. It's clever stuff."

The combined revenue of the new entity would be in the order of $12 billion, which, according to another trade newsletter, *Inside Market Data*, would give Thomson Reuters a 34 percent market share, a short nose in front of Bloomberg's 33 percent. The anti-trust authorities in America and Europe were bound to take more than a passing interest. Lawyers for Thomson Reuters would no doubt respond by claiming that Bloomberg, as the dominant market force, was merely facing stronger competition. Even so, a couple of duplicated business operations would probably have to be discarded, if only for the sake of appearances, but otherwise few serious regulatory objections were anticipated.

Nor were there squabbling family trusts to hold up the deal. The trustees of

Reuters' Founder Share had been consulted, of course, and well briefed by Glocer. Their blessing of the deal, representing a marriage of news organizations of universally recognized respectability, was duly delivered as almost a formality.

Even Reuters' journalists seemed, for once, lost for words. Equally stunned, apparently, were the many former Reuters executives whose vitriolic attacks on the Glocer regime had constituted an underground resistance movement. The deafening silence on the Internet message boards reflected not so much an endorsement of the company's fate as an admission of defeat, a collective sigh of regret that yet another treasured old British franchise was about to be relegated forever to no more than a hyphenated appendage to a foreign enterprise.

It was not just the corporate landscape that was radically altered in the early years of the new century. On September 11, 2001, a date destined to become one of the most famous in history, a physical landscape of endearing familiarity to me and countless thousands associated with the financial markets was brutally obliterated when the Twin Towers of the World Trade Center collapsed after a suicide attack by terrorists using passenger aircraft as weapons. Markets reopened after a respectful hiatus and the Life-Must-Go-On attitude as an affirmation of defiance assumed an epic quality. But downtown Manhattan had changed palpably and perhaps irrevocably. The change was obvious physically, but the collective psyche of Wall Street's community of residents and commuters, as to a lesser degree that of America, was profoundly affected, its swaggering confidence replaced by a sense of insecurity, dread, and perhaps worst of all a simmering American resentment against the world, an attitude unforgivably exploited for political reasons by an unpopular American administration from base political motives.

Tragedies, after the initial shock and grief, affect people in diverse and often insubstantial ways. For Telerate people—for this one anyway—there was the slow-dawning realization that the violent implosion of One World Trade Center had eliminated every trace of the company's former elevated campus on the 104th floor. Also atomized were the familiar ground-level environs: bars, coffee shops, restaurants, hotels, stores, and subway stations—all those prosaic, everyday places where we had eaten, drunk, argued, fought, reconciled, met new friends, said final goodbyes, started affairs, ended affairs, hired and fired, and laid out many a futile business plan on many a wine-stained table napkin.

It is reasonable to suppose that I was not alone in developing a palpable dread of looking into that awful hole, forever fated to be known, in the revived nomenclature first applied in the 1950s to nuclear bomb test sites, as Ground Zero. The hole would eventually be filled in, of course, providing the foundation for some soaring tower block created by some prominent architect. But while it might erase the hated void, and perhaps even stand as a place of work for thousands, it would surely stand first and foremost and forever as a monument to the violence once perpetrated there.

As far as this author knows, only one Telerate figure, a former employee, lost his life that morning. Stephen Tompsett, a mild-mannered Australian, married to Dorry, one of the company's earliest employees, shared his unwarranted doom with dozens of others attending a market-data conference at Windows on the World, the landmark restaurant at the top of Tower One. Cantor Fitzgerald, occupants of the 105th floor, as well as Telerate's former quarters on the 104th, suffered far worse, losing hundreds, virtually its entire staff. Some Cantor people were fortunate beyond imagination, among them chief executive Howard Lutnick, who was running late that morning, having taken his son to his first day at kindergarten school. His brother Mark died. Some Cantor people were half-lucky. Lauren Butler Manning, wife of Greg Manning, a former Telerate executive, was one. Waiting for an elevator in the lobby of Tower One and oblivious to the attack that had taken place moments earlier, she and others were engulfed by a fireball that exploded from an arriving elevator. She survived, but spent years undergoing surgery to repair tissue damage that extended to 80 percent of her body.

Inevitably, several Telerate alumni had been either on their way to or from the place. Jack McConville, a former Telerate business analyst, had intended to go to the Windows conference, but changed his mind at the last moment. "I'd just taken my car to be repaired and decided–while actually entering the building, that I wasn't dressed smartly enough, so I went to the office instead." My old colleague Scott Rumbold emerged from a nearby subway station after the first air-strike and, having briefly glimpsed the horror from two blocks away, wisely hurried back down again. They, and many others, must still be thanking their various gods for such whimsical deliverance.

Sadness usually arrives in less savage circumstances. For many old Reuters hands, a poignant moment arrived in 2005 when the company announced that it would be leaving 85 Fleet Street, its home for sixty-five years, for a site close to the same Docklands location to which Rupert Murdoch had infamously decamped some twenty years earlier. A few felt—somewhat irrationally it must be said—that Reuters' defection constituted a similar betrayal. Reuters had for some years stood proudly as the Street's last remaining news organization, unless one counted the token editorial office of a Scottish publisher best known as the proprietor of the *Beano*, one of Britain's oldest children's comics. To mark the end of the era a "Service of Thanksgiving" was held at St. Bride's, Fleet Street, the so-called "Journalist's Church." Murdoch was among the invited speakers.

Perhaps the most dispiriting aspects of Reuters' defection was the knowledge that a stroll along Fleet Street, even one taking in a visit to one of its famous old watering holes (a few survived), would never again offer the prospect of a chance meeting with an old acquaintance. No more corners foul, then, except, inevitably, El Vino, its seedy numen resolutely preserved for the sake of old times, one likes to imagine, rather than for reasons of economy. But the place was now patronized largely by unappreciative lawyers, often to be seen sitting alone with an egg-and-cress sandwich and, perhaps, a single glass of house white, dully committed to the heresy of the Lunch Hour as a term to be taken literally. But, as Ronald Reagan might have remarked, there I go again…

Just a couple of minor tasks remain before ending this narrative. One, I decided, should be to nominate an unsung hero of the market-data industry. Readers may make their own choices. My vote, for what it is worth, goes to one for whom my admiration is substantial. If it falls short of unbounded it is only because I feel obliged to confess, as many others have before me, that I did not personally warm to him. That, I suppose, makes the award all the more genuine. In presenting it, I invoke the words of some anonymous sage at Reuters, whose name I have forgotten. He once said of the nominee: "When the modern history of this company is written, one name above all will be associated with its emergence from the obscurity to which it once seemed consigned, and that name is Michael Nelson." I have to agree.

There were other candidates, some arguably boasting greater accomplishments, most armed with infinitely greater charisma: Jack Scantlin, Gerry Long, Glen Renfrew, Neil Hirsch, Mike Bloomberg. They all qualify in their own right for the market-data industry's Hall of Fame. I am sticking with Nelson, though, and for one overriding reason: he invariably picked winners. In doing so he took a series of brave leaps into the unknown. Stockmaster, Videomaster, Monitor, and Dealing were all his, and each in its time proved to be a commercial coup, the first three qualifying as triumphs that rescued the company. In the ensuing decades, Reuters failed to come up with anything remotely like a transforming product, and so paid the price in growth, profitability, shareholder loyalty and, ultimately, independence.

Nelson's latter-day successors, Tom Glocer and Devin Wenig, would probably care little for his, or even their own, places in history. In engineering the Thomson coup, Glocer conceivably earned his inflated compensation by ensuring Reuters' future, even if in doing so he also guaranteed his own. His talent and his motives may always be open to question; neither will be resolved on these pages. My own impression of the man, derived from just a few face-to-face meetings, was that of a pleasant and thoughtful chap, though not necessarily one troubled by the inconveniences of sentimentality and doubt.

Here at any rate was a man with both feet firmly on the ground—or so one might have believed until reading his Internet blog site. Here in Tom's very own chat pages—"Hi. This is my blog site"—the former lawyer regaled readers with his tastes in music and literature (both very eclectic, from lowbrow to highbrow, but above all "cool") and explained why media companies ought to become "seeders of clouds" and how denizens of the blogosphere would become empowered as "citizen journalists." To which I feel obliged to observe in response that while every single soul on the planet may have something to say, very few have something interesting to say.

Wenig, his deputy, was soon spouting the same funky, ethereal blather. In one online interview he gave to a group of fellow bloggers, Wenig discussed "data concordance" and "vertical pillars"—blogs apparently—and a Brave New World in which Reuters workstations would offer not just news and quotes but a "multi-media experience … fully social-network-enabled and collaborative."

Go for it, Devin, by all means, but heed this author's admonition not to overlook that first immutable law of the market-data industry: "Sell fucking terminals."

Let the last word on the subject be reserved by gentlemanly tradition for a member of what some of us old-fashioned things still call the fairer sex. Julie Holland, a senior manager of Reuters, at her retirement party to celebrate a career spanning three decades, was invited by an earnest Tom Glocer, microphone in hand, to answer a question. Her response, no doubt emboldened by imminent departure, must serve as some kind of literary epitaph.

Glocer: "So, Julie, what makes Reuters today different from Reuters back then?"

Holland: "We used to make money, Tom."

And that, ladies and gentlemen, really does conclude today's entertainment from the South Pier.

# Where Are They Now?

The following is a partial list of principal characters, based on the author's knowledge immediately prior to publication.

John Albanie (Reuters): Retired, living in Grenada

David Barnes (Telerate): Retired, living in New Jersey

Peter Bartko (CEO EBS): Working for BGC (formerly Cantor Fitzgerald), New York City

Geoff Bell (Banque Belge): Retired, living in Essex, England

Peter Benjamin (Reuters): Retired, living in Devon, England

Krishna Biltoo (Reuters): CEO, Standard & Poor's, Europe

Mike Bloomberg (Bloomberg): Mayor of New York City, serving second term. Rumored to be considering presidential campaign

Andrew Brodie (Telerate): Retired, living in France

Iris Cantor (widow of B. Gerald Cantor): Active in charities. Homes in Bel Air, California, and New York City

Dan Casey (Reuters/Telerate): Retired, living in Croydon, London

Alexander Chancellor (editor, *The Spectator*): Occasional journalist, London

Julian Childs (Telerate): Retired, living in London and France

Carolyn Chin (Reuters): Business consultant, New York City

Martin Church (Telerate): Retired, living in Sussex, England

John Christopherson (FX manager): Retired, living in Greenwich, Connecticut

Barry Clark (Reuters/Telerate): Retired, living in Tucson, Arizona

Harvey Cooper (Reuters): Retired, sailing in Asia and Australia

Dick Cowles (Telerate): Retired, living in Santa Fe, New Mexico

William C. Cox III (Dow Jones/Bancroft heir): Retired, living in New York City

Phil D'Angelo (Exco): Retired, living in Florida

Richard Davy (Exco): Banker, London

Bill Dunn (Dow Jones): Retired, living in New Jersey

Claude Erbsen (Associated Press): Retired, living in Westchester County, New York

Bob Etherington (Reuters): Business consultant, London

Rod Fisher (Telerate): Retired, living in Beverly Hills, California

Jonathan (Jonny) Fitzgerald (Reuters): Retired, living in Isle of Wight, England

Robert Fromer (Telerate director): Practicing law, New York City

Tom Glocer (Reuters): Chief executive Thomson Reuters, London/New York City

Elisabeth Goth (Bancroft heir): Living in California, successful equestrian

Philip Green (Reuters): CEO of a utility company, London

John Gunn (Exco): Occasional investment banker, City of London

Hubert Holmes (Reuters): Executive, financial software firm, New York City

Neil Hirsch (CEO Telerate): Retired, living on Long Island, New York, and in Florida (where he owns a restaurant and occasionally sings to patrons)

Sir Christopher Hogg (Reuters chairman): Active in public affairs, London

Peter Holland (Reuters): Retired, active in British police affairs

John Hull (Reuters/Telerate): Retired, living in New Hampshire. Makes and sells decorative walking sticks

Christopher Hume (Exco/Telerate): Retired, living in Sussex, England, and Australia

Sir Peter Job (CEO Reuters): Retired, living in Oxfordshire, London, and Italy

John Jessop (Reuters/Telerate/Bridge): Businessman, part-time author, living in Esher, Surrey, England

Martha Jessop (Telerate): Still (amazingly) married to author

Peter Kann (CEO Dow Jones): Retired, living in Princeton, New Jersey

Harold Leblang (Reuters): Retired, living on Long Island, New York

Steven Levkoff (Reuters): Technology consultant, eastern United States

George Levine (Quotron/Reuters): Sales Manager Reuters, New York City

Gerald Long (CEO Reuters): Died in Paris in 2006

John Lowe (Reuters): Retired, living in Essex, England

Howard Lutnick (Cantor Fitzgerald): CEO of BGC, New York City

Fumio Matsuo (Kyodo Press/Telerate): Retired, living in Tokyo, Japan

Rob McCormick (Bridge/Savvis): Living in St. Louis, Missouri. Resigned as CEO of Savvis after much-publicized New York City nightclub scandal involving $240,000 credit card bill

Tom McInerney (Welsh Carson, Anderson & Stowe): Partner WCAS, New York City

Dick MacWilliams (Bridge): Working for software firm, New York City

Rupert Murdoch (Reuters director): CEO News International, New York City

Michael Nelson (Reuters): Retired, living in London/South of France. Lectures and writes books

Bob Nagel (Reuters/Telerate): Retired, living in New York City

Andy Nibley (Reuters): President of BBDO advertising agency, New York City

Warren Phillips (CEO Dow Jones): Retired, living in New York City

John Ransom (Reuters): Retired, living in Surrey, England

Steve Rappaport (Telerate): Retired, living in New York City

Glen Renfrew (CEO Reuters): Died in 2006, in St. Alban's, England, after long illness

John Roberts (Reuters): Retired in 1986, living in Essex, England

Jon Robson (Telerate/Reuters): Senior executive Reuters, London/New York City

David Roscoe (Bridge): Retired, living in New Jersey

Ann Rostow (Telerate): Reporter and columnist, Austin, Texas

Scott Rumbold (Reuters/Telerate): Consultant, vintage car trade, living in Danbury, Connecticut

Tony Sabatini (Telerate): Technology consultant, New York City

Tom Secunda (Bloomberg): Executive, Bloomberg, New York City

Phil Siegel (Reuters): Investment banker, New York City

Herbie Skeete (Reuters): Owns specialized publishing firm, London

Buford Smith (Reuters): Retired, living in Seattle, Washington

Tony Smith (Reuters/Telerate): Retired, living in Pennsylvania and England

Rick Snape (Telerate/Bridge): Died in 2006 in New Jersey, aged fifty-six, from Lou Gehrig's Disease

John Taysom (Reuters): Retired, living in Putney, London

John Terranova (Cantor Fitzgerald/Telerate): Retired, living in Westchester, New York. Received suspended sentence after conviction for money-laundering related to sale of Long Island horse farm

Peter V. Thomas (Reuters): Retired, living in Barnes, London

David Ure (Reuters): Chairman of London-based software company

Carl Valenti (Dow Jones/Telerate/Bridge): Retired, living in Penang, Malaysia

André Villeneuve (Reuters): Chairman, London Financial Futures Exchange

David Vanrenen (Reuters): Business consultant, London

Victor Vurpillat (Reuters/Telerate): Business consultant, Los Angeles, California

Sir Dennis Weatherstone (CEO Morgan Guaranty): Died in June 2008, Darien, Connecticut

Tom Wendel (CEO Bridge): Retired, living in St. Louis, Missouri. Helps wife run a diabetes website

Jack Wigan (Reuters): Retired, living in Sussex, England

Matt Winkler (Dow Jones/Bloomberg): Chief News Editor, Bloomberg, New York City

Rosalyn Wilton (Reuters): CEO Hemscott, London financial publishing firm

Jimmy Wiseman (Bankers Trust/Telerate): Personal financial advisor, New Jersey

George Yepes (Bridge): Living and working in Boston, Massachusetts

Esther Zimet (Telerate): Died in 2006 in Fort Lee, New Jersey

# Select Bibliography

Bloomberg, Michael, *Bloomberg by Bloomberg*, John Wiley & Sons, 1997

Brooks, John, *The Go-Go Years*, E. P. Dutton Inc., 1973

Cooper, Kent, *Barriers Down*, Farrar & Rinehart, 1942

Davis, William, *The Rich*, Sidgwick & Jackson, 1982

Dealy, Jr., Francis X., *The Power and the Money*, Birch Lane Press, 1993

Emery, Edwin, *The Press and America*, Prentice-Hall Inc., 1962

Evans, Harold, *Good Times, Bad Times*, Weidenfeld & Nicholson

Fenby, Jonathan, *The International News Services*, Schocken Books, 1986

Frank, Thomas, *One Market Under God*, Doubleday, 2000

Hamilton, Denis, *Editor-in-Chief*, Hamish Hamilton, 1989

Jameson, Derek, *Touched by Angels*, Ebury Press, 1988

Johnson, Paul, *A History of the Jews*, Harper and Row, 1987

Jones, Sir Roderick, *A Life in Reuters*, Hodder & Stoughton, 1951

Kay, William, *Tycoons*, Pan Books, 1985

Kynaston, David, *The City of London, Vol. IV, A Club No More*, Chatto & Windus, 2001

Lawrenson, John/Barber, Lionel, *The Price of Truth*, Mainstream Publishing 1985

Lees-Milne, James, *Another Self*, Hamish Hamilton, 1970

Lewis, Michael, *Liar's Poker*, W. W. Norton & Co. 1989

Mabee, Carleton, *The American Leonardo*, Alfred A. Knopf Inc., 1943

Moncrieff, Chris, *Living on a Deadline*, Virgin Books, 2001

Mooney, Brian/Simpson, Barry, *Breaking News: How the Wheels Came off at Reuters*, Capstone Press, 2003

Read, Donald, *The Power of News*, Oxford University Press, 1992

Scharff, Edward E., *Worldly Power: The Making of the Wall Street Journal*, Beaufort Books, 1986

Shawcross, William, *Murdoch*, Chatto & Windus, 1992

Storey, Graham, *Reuters' Century*, Max Parrish & Co. 1951

Wicker, Tom, *One of Us*, Random House, 1991

Wilson, Derek, *Rothschild: A Story of Wealth and Power*, Mandarin Press, 1988
Wolfe, Thomas, *Bonfire of the Vanities*, Farrar Straus & Giroux, 1987
Wright, Dennis, *The English Among the Persians*, William Heinemann, 1977
Wriston, Walter, *The Twilight of Sovereignty*, Charles Scribner's Sons 2001

# Index

# C

383–91, 398–412, 420–24, 441, 463,
468, 483, 485–86
Dow Jones Industrial Average · 107, 114,
231–32, 354, 366, 398
Dow Jones Information Services Group ·
352
Dow Jones Markets (Telerate) · 401
Dow Jones News Service · 103–10, 112–15,
121
Dow Jones Newswire (Broad Tape) · *See*
Dow Jones News Service
Dow Jones Ticker (Broad Tape) · *See* Dow
Jones News Service
Dow, Charles · 366
Drayson, Barry · 467–70
Dresdner Bank · 184
Drexel Burnham Lambert · 342, 466
Driver, Mike · 316
Drogheda, Lord · 104–5
Dromfield, John · 133
Dun & Bradstreet · 454
Dunn, Bill · 343–44, 354–56, 359, 361, 366,
370, 374–75, 493

# E

E.F. Hutton and Company · 292, 342, 394
*Economic X-Ray* · *See* Reuters
*Economist, The* · 71
Edison, Thomas · 117, 288
Eichenwald, Kurt · 474–75
Eisenhower, Dwight D. · 27
El Vino Wine Bar · 12, 43, 100, 313, 490
Electronic Brokerage Service (EBS) · 386,
461–63, 477
Electronic Joint Venture (EJV) · 342, 396,
413, 417
Ellis, Paul · 172
Ellmann, Michael · 407
Equisoft · 472
Erbsen, Claude · 219, 305–7, 309, 319–20,
322–23, 373, 493
ESL Giltnet · 464, 466
*Esquire* · 114
Etherington, Bob · 314–15, 317, 493
European Banking Company · 184
Evans, Harold · 132, 254, 278
Evans, Peter · 72
*Evening Standard* · 74, 264
Ewing, Mclean · 95

Exco plc · 230–51, 283, 307, 317, 337–38,
345–48, 353, 387
Express Newspapers · 273
Extel (Exchange Telegraph Company) · 57,
71, 155

# F

Faraday, Michael · 23
Farouk, King of Egypt · 123
Fasciocco, Leo · 114
Federal Reserve Bank of New York · 144,
206, 343
Feeney, Jim · 344
Feingold, James · 474
Ferguson, Don · 119
Fields, W.C. · 37
Filo, David · 457
Financial News Network · 389–91
*Financial Times Index* · 68–69, 294
Fine, Elliott · 217
Finsbury Data · 452
First National Bank of Atlanta · 172
First National City Bank · 172
First World War · 59, 93, 233
Fisher, Rod · 220–22, 227, 236, 238, 388,
468, 493
Fitzgerald, Jonathan (Jonny) · 314, 494
Fitzgerald, Walter · 314
Fleet Holdings · 264, 266, 283
Fleet Street · 12, 28–33, 35–39, 60–62, 64–
67, 78, 90, 96, 99, 104, 106, 116, 124,
126, 128–30, 132, 141, 150, 154, 158,
252–53, 255, 257, 260, 263–67, 272,
276, 278, 282–83, 285, 308, 312–13,
317, 322, 417, 445, 457, 466, 489–90
Fleischer, Sherri · 215
Fleming, Alexander · 38
*Forbes* magazine · 389, 399, 400
Forbes, B.C. · 345
Ford, John · 315
Ford, President Gerald B. · 231
Forex · *See* ACI
Forex Club · *See* ACI
Forstmann-Leff Associates · 354
*Fortune* · 400, 403–8
Forum of the Twelve Caesars · 177
Founder share · *See* Reuters
Foyle's Bookshop · 417
Frank, Frederick · 372
Frank, Thomas · 297

Marconi's Wireless Telegraph Company · 86, 87–88
Marine Midland Bank · 202
Market Bar · 329–30
Market Data Corporation · 388, 468
*Market Data Insight* · 487
Market Master · *See* Bloomberg
MarketVision · 417
Marley, Jacob · 132, 436
Marlin, Ken · 411, 417
Marsh, Lord · 256–58, 272
Marshall, M. W. · 314
Massachusetts Institute of Technology (MIT) · 176
Matsuo, Fumio · 385, 494
Matthews, Bill · 337
Matthews, Victor · 264–65, 273–74, 282–83
McCallum, Alex · 106–7, 110–11, 116, 121, 133
McCann's bar · 106
McConville, Jack · 489
McCormick, Rob · 414–15, 418–20, 422, 425–27, 430, 442, 494
McInerney, Tom · 440–43, 494
McKinsey & Company · 318
McLachlan, Angus · 278
McLuhan, Marshall · 135, 162, 175
Meer, Fred · 193–96, 202
Mercantile House · 245
Merrill Lynch Capital Markets (CMD) · 340, 464–65, 474
Merrill Lynch Pierce Fenner & Smith · 206, 224–25, 227, 286, 292, 338–40, 348, 394, 396, 431, 452, 469
Miceli, Jim · 416, 434
Michael One Restaurant · 165
Microsoft · 299, 439
Milken, Michael · 293
Miller, Bill · 337
Millstein, Ira · 405
Minex · 385–86, 462
Mitchem, David · 184
MKI Securities · 467
Monchik-Weber · 340
Monckton, Sir Walter · 96
Moneta, Juno · 159–60
Moneyline · 444, 483
Monitor · *See* Reuters
Monitor Dealing · *See* Reuters
Montgomery Ward Credit Corporation · 203–4
Montgomery, Field Marshal Bernard Law · 104

Mooney, Brian · 446, 470–72, 480
Moore, Dudley · 179
Morgan Guaranty Trust Company · 111, 167
Morgan Stanley · 224, 225–26, 342, 396
Moriarty, Ed · 340–41
*Morning Advertiser* · 53
Morris, Mowbray · 53
Morse Code · *See* Morse, Samuel Finley Breese
Morse, Samuel Finley Breese · 13, 15–20
Mulhall, David · 313
Mullally, John · 322–23
Murdoch, Rupert · 31, 34, 140, 253–54, 258–66, 270–73, 277, 280–83, 485–89, 494
Murphy, Tom · 405
Murray, Albert · 36–38, 60

# N

Nagel, Dr. Robert · 176–84, 216, 233–34, 310–11, 495
Napier, Mark · 81, 83–84, 87–89
Napoleon, Emperor Louis III · 50, 53
NASDAQ (National Association of Securities Dealers Automated Quotations) · 194, 247
Nasir ed-Din, Shah · 55
National Association of Pension Funds (NAPF) · 280–81
National Graphical Association (NGA) · 36
National Society of Operative Printers and Assistants (NATSOPA) · 36, 62, 69, 158, 311
National Union of Journalists (NUJ) · 35, 72, 74, 76–77
National Union of Miners · 294
National Westminster Bank · 223
Neher, Timothy · 372, 373
Nelson, Michael · 67, 70, 103–4, 106, 118–20, 122, 125–26, 132–41, 148–51, 154–66, 173, 179–80, 182, 184–85, 185, 188–90, 192, 195, 199, 210, 254–56, 261, 263, 265, 272, 276, 281–82, 312, 449, 453, 490, 494
Neuharth, Al · 367
New Deal · 162, 296
New York Forex (ACI) · 169, 200
*New York Herald Tribune* · 16

# S

Sabatini, Tony · 216, 495
Safire, William · 142
Salomon Brothers · 170, 190, 203, 241, 243,
    292, 294–96, 331, 333–35, 339–40, 342,
    396
Salomon, William "Billy" · 170
Sam's Cordial Bar · 140
Samuelson, Robert · 297, 300
Sanderson, Michael · 452, 470
Savvis Corporation · 430–31, 441, 483
Saxe-Coburg-Gotha, Duke of · 56
Scantlin Electronics · 117, 118
Scantlin, Jack · 117, 119, 394, 490
Schott, Kevin · 428
Schreiber, Fran · 329
Schroder Wertheim & Co · 407
Schwartz, Cindy · 212
Schwartz, David · 475
Schwartzatron · 452
Second World War · 41, 93, 105, 291, 355
Secunda, Tom · 340, 495
Securities and Exchange Commission
    (SEC) · 111, 242, 247–48, 281, 409, 441
Securities Industry Association (SIA) · 437–
    38
Shaw, Ray · 353–54, 359, 374–75
Shearson Lehman Hutton · 372
Shell Oil Company · 479
Shepley, James · 182
Shipman, Peter · 360
Siebenmann, Max · 139
Siegel, Phil · 178, 495
Siemens, Werner · 52
Simpson, Barry · 446, 470–72, 480
Sinn, Robert · 119–20, 136, 150
Skeete, Herbie · 12, 495
Skinner, Peter · 383
Slater, Nick · 439
SmartMoney · 400, 407
Smith Barney · 463
Smith, Buford · 455, 472, 495
Smith, Cyril · 106, 116, 118–19, 179
Smith, Greg · 410, 420
Smith, Senator F.O.J. · 20
Smith, Tony · 417, 428, 435, 495
Smithfield meat market · 42
Smithsonian II Conference · 145
Smithsonian Institute · 145
Smuts, Jan · 82

Snape, Rick · 246, 328, 387–88, 411, 418,
    420, 437–38, 441, 443, 495
Snow, Zachary · 443
Spanner, Richard · 184
Spectator, The · 275, 277, 279
Spencer, Michael · 478
Stanford Research Institute · 403
Star, The · 265, 273
Stargardt, Joseph · 49–50
Stark, Alexander C. · 362
Stein, Herb · 142
Steinmetz, Chip · 442–43
Sterling Manhattan Television · 174
Stewart-Smith, Malcolm · 443
Stock Exchange Automated Quotations
    System (SEAQ) · 302–3
Stockmaster · See Reuters
Stockwell, Brian · 158
Stogdill, Richard · 192
Stoppard, Miriam · 481
Stoppard, Sir Tom · 481
Storey, Samuel · 96
Strauss Turnbull · 148
Studio 54 Nightclub · 214
Sturgeon, William · 17
Sun, The · 260, 265
Sunday Express · 264
Sunday Times · 253, 260, 278
SunGard Corporation · 443
Swanborn, Mel "Duke" · 207, 208, 224
Swinton, Stan · 103, 105
Swiss Bank Corporation · 310
Sybil's Discotheque · 211–17
Sylvania Corporation · See General
    Telephone and Electronics Corporation

# T

Tafex Systems · 185–86, 190–96, 199, 200–
    203, 209–11, 363
Taylor, Frank · 60–61, 67
Taylor, Fred · 67, 69, 74, 76, 148, 151, 154,
    160, 311–12
Taylor, Myron · 207
Taylor, Peter · 325
Taylor, Rebecca · 326
Taylor, Renee · 153
Taysom, John · 456, 458, 495
Teknekron · 453
Telekurs · 118, 150

# *X*

# *Y*

# *Z*